THE NORTH

(AND ALMOST EVERYTHING IN IT)

PAUL MORLEY

BLOOMSBURY

LONDON · NEW DELHI · NEW YORK · SYDNEY

Bloomsbury Publishing Plc
50 Bedford Square
London
WC1B 3DP

www.bloomsbury.com

Bloomsbury Publishing, London, New Delhi, New York and Sydney

A CIP catalogue record for this book is available from the British Library

ISBN 978 1 4088 3401 5

10 9 8 7 6 5 4 3 2 1

Typeset by Hewer Text UK Ltd, Edinburgh
Printed and bound in Great Britain by CPI Group (UK) Ltd, Croydon CR0 4YY

To Elizabeth
And the Morleys
And the Youngs
And the Hydes of Hyde

Contents

PART ONE

'A something in the air'

In the middle of these cogitations, apprehensions and reflections, it came into my thought one day that all this might be a chimera of my own, and that this foot might be a print of my own foot.

> Robinson Crusoe in the novel of the same name
> by Daniel Defoe, 1719

I

This is the first step, the first brick, the first drop of rain. There is the mountain to climb, the breathtaking viaduct to cross, the enterprise to explain. Look at the vast nineteenth-century mill, still standing, scrubbed nude, exposed to a time and economy it wasn't built for, free of smoke and noise and cloggy clattering gothic commotion, remade, remaindered, dolled up as a museum, a titanic souvenir, a loft dwelling, its soul long gone. It stands a few postered knocked-about miles from the shiny money-mad modern mall, which never really had a soul, and there is much to marvel at in how one structure led to the other.

Here is the north, up here, where all things start – stories, fights and journeys, crimes, games, plans and ventures, proposals and accidents, public lives and private schemes, mysteries, changes of heart and false starts, rivers and obsessions, apologies and murders, words and spells

– the north, at the top of the page, black marks on a white void, distant and remote, not quite sure what will happen next.

Here is the north, this is where it lies, where it belongs, full of itself, high up above everything else, surrounded by everything that isn't the north – which is off the page, somewhere else. This is the story of how I found the north, as a young boy, born in 1957 – the same year that L. S. Lowry painted *Man Lying On a Wall*, that the riotous comedian Frank Randle died, that the 250-foot radio telescope was finished at Jodrell Bank, Cheshire, that Richard Hoggart's *The Use of Literacy* was published, that Harold Pinter mentioned an Eccles cake in *The Dumb Waiter*, that Lennon met McCartney, one hundred years after Prince Albert disembarked at Cheadle Hulme station and travelled via Stockport Road (now Albert Road) to Cheadle and Abney Hall to visit the Great Exhibition in Manchester. And then, as a man, over forty years later, remembering when I was a young boy who spent a lot of time walking around, from one centre of attention to another, because the streets were irresistible. This is where I find what I am looking for: the north, and where it begins.

This is the next step, and the rain starts to fall like it means it.

2

1976

A jumped-up seventeen-year-old pop music fan writes a letter to the *New Musical Express* in June, 1976:

> I pen this epistle after witnessing the infamous Sex Pistols in concert at the Manchester Lesser Free Trade Hall. The bumptious Pistols in jumble sale attire had those few that attended dancing in the aisles despite their discordant music and barely audible lyrics. The Pistols boast having no inspiration from the New York/Manhattan rock scene, yet their set includes 'I'm Not Your Stepping Stone', a number believed to be done almost to perfection by the Heartbreakers on any sleazy New York night, and the Pistols' vocalist/

exhibitionist Johnny Rotten's attitude and self-asserted 'love us or leave us' approach can be compared to both Iggy Pop and David Johansen in their heyday. The Sex Pistols are very New York and it's nice to see that the British have produced a band capable of producing atmosphere created by the New York Dolls and their many imitators, even though it may be too late. I'd love to see the Pistols make it. Maybe they will be able to afford some clothes which don't look as though they've been slept in.

Steven Morrissey, Kings Road, Stretford.

One day Morrissey, as he becomes known, will say in an interview, 'You're southern – you wouldn't understand. When you're northern, you're northern for ever, and you're instilled with a certain feel for life that you can't get rid of. You just can't.' And he will write a song called 'Cemetery Gates' about meeting the artist Linder Sterling in 1976:

> So we go inside and we gravely read the stones
> all those people all those lives
> where are they now?
> with the loves and hates
> and passions just like mine

L. S. Lowry died of pneumonia and a stroke on 23 February 1976, aged eighty-eight, at Woods Hospital, Glossop. The vast majority of Lowry's paintings share themes relating to scenes in the industrial north of England. Almost always outdoors, they often feature a backdrop of chimneys and dark rectangular buildings with some sort of event or incident going on in the foreground. Lowry used only five basic paints, mixing these together to form other colours as necessary. 'When I was young I did not see the beauty of the Manchester streets. I used to go into the country painting landscapes and the like. Then one day I saw it . . . suddenly I saw the beauty of the streets and the crowds.'

Eight years before he died, the Crane Kalman Gallery, which championed Lowry from the late 1940s until his death in 1976, mounted an exhibition called the Loneliness of L. S. Lowry, with the idea of countering the stereotypes that had become attached to him through being known almost exclusively for his smoky, simplified, romantic northern factory views, around which pipe-cleaner people scurried like worker ants. The intention was to promote Lowry as the most distinctive and comprehensive artist recording pre- and post-Second World War northern industrial towns. The effort was not entirely successful, and the myths have lingered around Lowry – that he was a naive eccentric, a talented but limited weekend painter of tea-towel art.

3

The north of England, with England being north-west of Europe, and Europe being in the northern hemisphere, and north being a word that says so much and leaves plenty to the imagination. A certain territory, this English north, this island of islands, coldly exotic, mysteriously ordinary, this gathering of fields and brick, trees and chimneys, lakes and clouds, mud and memory, boundaries and boroughs, washing lines and shop signs, lies and byways, rust and revolution, stadiums and stones, kids and schools, puddles and puddings, public houses and corner shops, pets and churches, men and women – with their ways, which are something else altogether, surrounded on two sides by land, on two by sea, existing below Scotland, which is another north altogether, and above the rest of England, above where the south has become the amorphous midlands, which itself, in fits and starts, over rivers, in buildings, in the mind, across fences, becomes the north. This north geographically, bluntly speaking, is where England itself is at its narrowest, at times a mere tens of miles across, the shortest distance between sea and churning sea, between the sea that there is between England and Ireland, which meets up with the northern Atlantic Ocean, which meets up with the rest of the world, and the sea there is between England and Norway, Denmark, Holland, Belgium and Germany, between England and a vast east, which eventually turns back on itself and ends where it starts.

All that it once was leading to all that it now is, representing everyone that ever lived there, everyone that now does, and everything that ever happened, accidentally, deliberately, gradually, suddenly, historically, geographically, politically, tragically, comically, to produce this north, which is still on the way to becoming the north, as if the final decision about what the north is, this English north, will not be taken until a few thousand years of preparation has been resolved, which may yet take a few thousand more years. The north is what it now is after a few grinding, transformative centuries that were a mix of excitement, decline, patience, persistence, pain, pleasure, acceptance, defiance, invention, obedience, nothing much, an awful lot, a mix of those that came from elsewhere, invading or visiting, passing through or sticking around, those that were born there and left, and those that stayed rooted to the spot.

No other north but this north, inside and outside England, which consists of this fluid, static piece of land, this tangle of internal borders, these lengths of coast, this number of hills, this collection of voices, these boundless acres of heath and forest, this cluttered, stratified arrangement of cities, towns and villages, with names that are definitely, irrefutably northern, this list of events, records and discoveries, this collection of minds, attitudes and certainties, this change in circumstances, this passing-on of attitude and atmosphere, this sharing of a place and of places next door to each other across time, these multiple ghost images. A north however built up, closed in and fiercely urban, however paved and derelict, smoked and stained, charged and noisy, always close to sea, river, meadow, dale, scrub, cliff or moorland, to more natural noise, and lavish, ageless calm. A north packed with intrepid people handing on the north, as they see it, all that history, and nature, and difference. A north, all on its own.

4

1976

On 16 March 1976 Harold Wilson announced his sudden resignation as prime minister and his intention to retire from politics altogether. Although he claimed at the time he had always intended to retire at sixty, it may well be that he was aware of the early signs of Alzheimer's disease.

1974

Oldham has lost much of its industrial prowess and former civic glory. During the 1960s and 70s it was pitilessly redeveloped and lost not only much poor-quality housing, but many good, substantial, public and commercial buildings. The final indignity might have come in 1974, when there was a proposal to give the newly created metropolitan borough a different name. Newham, Milltown or even New Oldham were suggested. The idea was rejected.

1973

Last of the Summer Wine, an amiable sitcom featuring an eccentric trio of rural west Yorkshire pensioners at home, or not, airs for the first time on BBC 1 as a pilot entitled *Of Funerals and Fish* in a Comedy Playhouse series of one-off comedies. Based on a slightly darker novel by Roy Clarke, it was set in the eternally pretty surroundings of a small isolated market town to the north of the Peak District, a few miles south of Huddersfield. Clarke wasn't sure about making it into a series until he decided to write about the elderly characters as though they were small children. It would eventually become the world's longest-running situation comedy. Peter Sallis, an actor born in Middlesex, faked a Yorkshire accent for his character which was so convincing that Preston-born Wallace and Gromit creator Nick Park, when calling him to ask him to voice Wallace, refused to believe that Sallis's natural accent was his own.

5

Where does the north begin? This is often the first question asked when the idea of the north of England comes up – as the subject of a book, as the place you come from, or visit, or move to, or live in. The north, a definite territory, a certain reality, an assorted spread of times and spaces pulled together, charged with feeling, a famous base for outsiders and strivers, beggars and visionaries, zealots and loafers, jokers and poets, somewhere solid, authentic, which you can think about, and feel you understand. The north begins over the border where one thing, specified by a collection of statistics, truisms, anecdotes, landmarks, accents, addictions, events, buildings, beliefs, occupations, boasts, gates, resolutions, timetables and signposts, becomes another thing.

The north begins over half a million years ago. Some enterprising explorers were there in 500,000 BC: a large Lower Palaeolithic stone axe was found in Knutsford, Cheshire, a rare find in northern England as the area has been covered with ice several times and the mountains and hills profoundly eroded. This book of the north can begin with this crude, magnificent roughly chipped axe, found in a place that first appeared in the 1086 Domesday Book as Knut's Ford, nothing to do with King Canute no matter how much romantics would like it to be. This axe will be used to clear the path ahead, clear the way through the north, from the beginning of time to the end of this book.

The north begins 18,000 years ago, when much of Britain was covered in a thick blanket of snow and ice and the north-east of England, as we know it now, was an uninhabitable freezing wasteland. The north begins with the ice nonchalantly sculpting the geological mass of what is now known as the Lake District into the distinctive, imposing mountains and valleys that we take for granted and/or marvel at today. It begins in this nowhere, this not yet somewhere, rocky cold land stark under dismal moiling skies, this desolate zone that would surely never become anything or be occupied by such pushy, determined life and language. How did that implacably frozen void heat up so much that eventually it would contain all that wild, nutty, self-reliant human character and variety? Is it the result of centuries of endeavour based on an ancient tenacious need to escape the cold, to outwit the circumstances, to find a home, but without moving away, because where else would you go, and how would you get there? How could you be sure that there was anything else to find? Where you found yourself was all there was, and you stayed, despite it all.

The north begins about 10,000 BC, as the Ice Age was finally coming to an end. The islands of Britain appeared slowly from under the receding ice, mysterious landscapes, small and large, taking shape as the melting glaciers caused the seas to rise, covering some areas, leaving others alone. Ireland was cut off. The land bridge between Britain and mainland Europe disappeared. By about 6000 BC Britain was an island, and naturally there was a northern part, closer to the North Pole, and a southern part, closer to the now separated European land mass. As the climate warmed and forests developed, people began to migrate into the area that would eventually become the British Isles.

The north begins with the glaciers melting away around 5000 BC, with early hunter-gatherers edging into what is now Cheshire and finding dense, damp oak forests nursed on rich clays and loams. These new inhabitants lived in caves and holes dug into the ground and prospered by hunting down and eating red deer, wild boar and the wildfowl hugging the meres. Mammoth, wild ox and packs of wolves and hyenas roamed Cheshire in those days. The rivers cutting and shaping the landscape into hills and hollows, producing bogs, mosses and peat, were teeming with trout, and fishing was a quick way to satisfy hunger. Oak trees dominated the land, supported by alders, willows and birch, with ash and elm on the higher slopes. Few English counties owe more of their history to their geographical position and surroundings, and to the character of their natural features, than Cheshire.

The north begins in the Cheshire Plain, a flat area of land covering thousands of square miles bounded by the hills of north Wales to the west, the Derbyshire Peak District to the east and the Pennines to the north-east. It was once under the ocean, but emerged from the water, dried out, leaving vast salt deposits, and remained remote from the early maritime influences affecting the English south. It begins with the mossy, peaty, fast-flowing or lazily drifting and nameless rivers cutting through the plain, which would eventually, once there was a need, a way, a variety of ways, to name things, be called Dee, Weaver, Gowy, Dane, Wheelock, Bollin, Goyt, Etherow, Tame and Mersey. The rivers flowed west and north into the Irish Sea, changing the landscape as they went, as if from the very beginning they knew that they were heading for greater things, that they would cause more than just geographical change.

From around 4000 BC there were slow changes in life in what would be the far north-east of England. As well as hunting and gathering, it appears that people began to plant crops and domesticate animals. It took a long time for these early farming techniques to become the main source of food, and the sea in particular remained a vital source of nourishment. The slow growth of farming led to forests being cleared more methodically, and although the environment is harsher in northern England than other parts of the country, people successfully farmed animals and crops. They lived in relatively varied types of settlements: hill forts, open settlements and square or circular enclosed settlements. In some places evidence of settlement is sparse, and quite large areas of land would have been used to support small communities.

6

1972

Alan Bennett's first small-screen play, *A Day Out*, was filmed for the BBC by Stephen Frears, who would direct and/or produce the majority of Bennett's television work over the next decade. Both this and 1975's *Sunset Across the Bay* were wistful, elegiac pieces, with Bennett drawing on his Yorkshire roots for the first time in his portraits of, respectively, a Halifax cycling club in 1911 and an elderly couple (based on his parents) retiring to Morecambe but feeling desperately homesick for Leeds.

A word about what I always consider rather a dubious role, namely 'a northern writer'. Northern writers like to have it both ways; they set their achievements against the squalor or the imagined squalor of their origins, and gain points for transcendence, while at the same time asserting that somehow northern life is truer, and in some undefined way, more honest than a life of southern comfort. 'Look, we have come through,' is the message, but I can't quite see why a childhood in the industrial north is less conducive to writing or whatever, than a childhood in Peterborough or Wimbledon or wherever. I mean it's quite true if you're born in Barnsley and you set your sights on becoming Virginia Woolf, it's not going to be roses all the way.

On 10 June Michael Parkinson's guests on his chat show include both Bernard Manning and A. J. P. Taylor.

The brooding, perfectionist actor James Mason teamed up with Yorkshire Television to make a fifty-minute feature called *Home James*. He was filmed revisiting and rediscovering Huddersfield, where he was born in 1909, the son of an affluent wool merchant. 'I was born in Huddersfield. When I was young I had very little affection for this part of the country. In fact when I finished my schooling I couldn't wait to get away from the place and try my luck in London, but recently for family reasons I've been returning here more and more frequently and in the process being more and more won over by it. My growing enthusiasm has made me as bad as any other sort of convert.' He observed in the film how his mother's attitude to Huddersfield had rubbed off on him: 'She was always reaching for a grander way of life that was more than could be expected of Huddersfield.'

1971

Bernard Manning was forty-one when he made his television debut in 1971 in Granada producer Johnnie Hamp's *The Comedians*, alongside Mike Reid, Charlie Williams, Frank Carson, Colin Crompton and thirty or so others. The briskly edited show, which featured quick-fire gags from hard-working no-nonsense club comics mostly new to television, was a huge success, and Manning swiftly became one of its biggest stars. With the national fame came the notoriety – with Manning cheerfully praising Enoch Powell, even Hitler, in various newspapers. 'I am an admirer of Adolf Hitler,' he told the *Sunday People*. 'Not everything about him, of course. I deplore his gas chambers and Gestapo as much as anyone, but I admire him for the things he got right, which I reckon was about 50 per cent.'

1970

A bronze bust of William Wordsworth is unveiled opposite Wordsworth House in Cockermouth on 7 April, the bicentenary of William's birth, by his great-great-grandson. As part of the same celebrations, 27,000 daffodils were planted on open spaces and approaches to the town.

7

The north begins with my own search for the north, as a particular place, written into history because of one thing leading to another across helter-skelter centuries that tumble on one after the other, across the minds, struggles and achievements of millions of people, who keep overcoming obstacles, replacing each other and starting all over again, because they have no choice. The north begins with a few stray bloody-minded humans and hardy small communities fighting for survival through fog, damp and supernatural-seeming dangers. The north begins, becomes all it becomes, because these diffuse obscure individuals find ways to resist the oblivion that threatens to wipe them away. They develop techniques and strategies that enable them to defeat or control the elements, and they set up the momentum that ultimately leads to the very changes that inexorably lead to more changes which affect the whole world. They protect themselves, against all the odds, against all manner of enemies and perils, and progress from there. They do battle with the speaking of language itself, which leads to greater understanding and a certain amount of cultural and psychological difficulty.

A north, a source of northern spirit, an analysis of how the north was formed geographically and then psychologically, a survey of its origins, could develop through a description of the Roman occupation of the area for the first few hundred years of the first millennium. The Roman pacification and colonisation of Britain was a massive violent upheaval for the pre-existing small-scale Iron Age cultures and societies, which had been developing for 500 years since the arrival of the Celts from mainland Europe. The Celts – not known as that for centuries – were the first in a long line of invaders, the first to influence a shadowy indigenous population but not completely overwhelm and assimilate it.

Once the drilled, disciplined and self-important Romans arrived, and events were written down, key dates, events, battles, skirmishes, decisions, social structures and eventual failures help explain how the territory itself and the attitude of the people who, by luck good or bad, accident or intention, happened to live there was created – and how a layer of northern character based on the attacks, force, discipline and civilising innovations of these committed visitors from the distant south developed, a character based on resistance, objection, contempt, but also on a certain level of acceptance and agreement, perhaps a reluctant sort of understanding and admiration.

How those who found themselves in this part of the world adapted, advanced or retreated, faced with all of the real and unreal threats specific to such a location, surrounded by sea, land, distance, internal threats, external enemies, specious, petulant gods, trapped by terrain and compromised by climate, hindered or liberated by a succession of competing superstitions, bullied or inspired by a series of intolerant tongues and despotic, vicious regimes, would ensure the character and personality of the northerner.

I found it, my north, smoking and babbling, battling and loving, scattered and glittering, lush and brisk, nattering and trusting, plain and fancy, high up and low down, forgotten and fantastic, rickety and plush, conspiring and cracking, rich and poor, poorer and poorer, mean and generous right where you'd expect, but also in less obvious places. I found everything I found by walking in what turned out to be the right direction, and seeing what happened. I found the north by looking. Sometimes out of the window of a train or of a car, at some point on a short journey from, say, Macclesfield to Manchester, via Poynton and Cheadle Heath, past freshly scattered leaves, curtained rooms and all those dense connected bricks, all those hills and all those chimneys, all those kerbs, pylons and sudden turnings. Past some stubborn, colossal buildings that seem to have been around for centuries, and others, glassier and slighter, which seem to have impetuously popped up and might burst at any moment. Sometimes I found the north as I looked at a picture of something that happened before I was born, or a few years after. Sometimes it was at the side of the road that I was walking along, wondering where it would lead, or the stream, or the field, or the hill, or the pub, or the playground inside the park, which was surrounded by houses, which were surrounded by the north.

I found it by looking at a piece of text written by someone with the finest of minds who was also looking for the north, or who had found it, and they were trying to explain what they had found – something, perhaps, not yet formed, or buried in the past, hard-edged, not sun-spoiled southern soft, generous, grander, better, deeper, realer, sootier, poorer, harsher, brighter, stranger, slushier, something that came with a tremendous amount of baggage that you had to get rid of or felt proud of. Sometimes I was walking in the footsteps of others, opening up their own meanings and directions. They found a north, a defamiliar-ised England, which was an essential part of the classic endlessly discussed north–south divide – deprived, ugly, industrial north; prosperous, lovely, arrogant south – which has become a more or less permanent feature of the standardised national story.

The Merseyway shopping centre, Stockport, 1972

Sometimes, in how the north was recalled and defined, it was merely if magnificently grim – for some this formidable grimness was a form of unique exotica that suggested the north was out of this world, and for others it was how the north had become a cliché of its own sentimental self-pity, making a way for non-northerners to keep it in its place, condescend to it, even dismiss it. The north was truly grim, stuck in the mud, stuck where it was, permanently pinned to this planet with no real chance of achieving lift-off. All its attempts to change that situation, its regular outbursts of activity and bravura, of defiance and ambition, of adventure and hilarity, the time when it was the future created by shrewd, forceful and radical self-made men and women, and the south was the quaint, uninspired and deeply conservative past, were always destined to come to nothing.

I found the north through what I was hearing, or remembering, or checking, or exaggerating. By waiting on a platform, catching a bus, walking into a shop, talking to a stranger, arguing a point, researching a technical invention, hearing a pop song, watching a television programme, by seeing a northern football team formed in the nineteenth century win international tournaments like a continental conquering force, or tumble down into bleak non-League status as though the very town it represented had shrunk in size and lost its dignity. It turns out the north is quite an easy place to find: it's there on the map, comprehensively drawn, full of gutsy towns and unyielding rivers that connect to each other, one by one, marked by railway lines that criss-cross themselves and turn the north into an intricate patchwork of straight lines that somehow go round in circles. It's there on the television in some form, fact or fantasy, gag or verse, curse or smirk, every day.

So much about the north, the people and places, the names of those people and places, their position on the planet, the connection to those that came before them, remains the same, even after the last 200 years or so of tumultuous change. So much about the north could be summed up quickly and simply, and the results of such an assessment would be generally acceptable to those looking for a glib description, a hasty dismissal, a tidy list of northern attributes, stereotypes and presumptions. This north, though, would be too quick, too tidy, too obvious, and a north that covers up, with a pale, complacent version of accuracy, the north, a better, other north, which is always on the move, never fixed, always redefining itself, even as it seems to have been fixed in place, because of how it sounds, and the uniform it's been given.

8

1969

Dominating the entire length of Piccadilly station approach, Gateway House is a visitor's first view of Manchester once off the train. Replacing a row of nineteenth-century railway warehouses, it was built as part of the 1960s refurbishment of the station and completed in 1969. Nicknamed the Lazy S, designed by the Swiss architect responsible for slamming the inscrutable Centre Point into central London, Richard Seifert, and reputedly based on a doodle on a menu, it sends people down a hill into the heart of Manchester following definite, gentle and proudly modern curves. If you wanted, you could use this ramp to make a show-business entrance into a city set up by a clamouring succession of mouthy, passionate showmen and -women. The curving slope instantly mocked the notion that this was a city stalled in a strait-laced Victorian past, even as at the bottom, suddenly amid the multifarious city itself, you were faced with lingering evidence of that past. Some of this evidence was solid, some of it was in ruins, some of it was just around the corner, and some of it was submerged under the flat diminished surface of occasionally sighted stretches of sunken inky canal that had been left to rot. A short distance from Piccadilly, deeper inside the city centre, there is the smaller Oxford Road station, the 'little sister', connecting Manchester with places to the north-west. The entrance to the station is also up a hill, more modest in length but steeper than Piccadilly, which means leaving the station also encourages a dramatic entrance into town – this one ending with the sight over the road of Alfred Waterhouse's ebulliently baroque late-nineteenth-century Refuge Assurance building, a solid,definitive example of late-Victorian, Manchester-style commercial pride, extended with a conspicuous 210-foot tower in 1910 by his son Paul. By the sixties, the multi-tiered, richly ornamented, granite-and-terracotta-loaded building seemed ghostly and adrift, an ugly, enormous and ultimately tasteless sign of decline.

'W. H. Auden does not fit. Auden is no gentleman. Auden does not write, or exist, by any of the codes, by the Bloomsbury rules, by the Hampstead rules, by the Oxford, the Cambridge, or the Russell Square rules.' Geoffrey Grigson (1969)

Both BBC1 and ITV started colour transmissions on Saturday 15 November. The first colour episode of *Coronation Street* – number 928 – was transmitted on 17 November. The colour title sequence, used until June 1975, featured a shot of a modern tower block to represent changing times.

1968

Robert Harper (Bobby Ball) and Thomas Derbyshire (Tommy Cannon) were both born in Oldham. They met in the early 1960s while working as welders in the same factory. Becoming friends, they formed a club act known as Bobby and Stevie Rhythm, which became the Sherrell Brothers then the Harper Brothers. Initially they were a vocal duo, but over time started to introduce more comedy into their act. They turned professional in the late 1960s, and eventually changed their name to Cannon and Ball. Their first TV appearance was on *Opportunity Knocks* in 1968, when they came last.

1967

Opened in 1967 St Peter's shopping precinct was to become Oldham's main retail destination attracting the major chain shops. Influenced by the popular newfangled Merseyway centre in Stockport, opened two years previously alongside the Mersey Square bus terminus, it was hoped that the winning formula would work in Oldham. Given the cold Oldham weather, its windswept location won few friends with shoppers and retailers. The subway link from the precinct to C&A acted as a wind tunnel, which was exacerbated by the precinct being mostly open to the skies. For most of its time, empty units plagued the precinct. The precinct's anchor store was a Tesco supermarket, opened by Ken Dodd in 1968. The Post Office was moved to the precinct from Union Street, to a unit overlooking George Street near the Tesco store. A NORWEB electricity showroom took up a unit under the office block. The rest of the precinct included a handful of chainstore retailers and independently owned shops, and a café.

Together with his wife, John Ravenscroft returned to Britain in 1967 and because of his experience in the USA was hired by the pirate radio station Radio London. There managers decided that John Ravenscroft, or indeed Ravencroft without the 's', as he had become known in America, was too much of a mouthful and requested something shorter. John Peel, apparently the suggestion of one of the secretaries at the station, was duly adopted as his new radio name. The new Peel made his first appearance on Radio 1 on 1 October 1967 when he presented *Top Gear*. Initially he was only one of a rota of presenters assigned to the show but by 4 February 1968 he had become the sole presenter.

By mid-1967 the BBC's Manchester Dickinson Road studio had become too small for the increasingly complex *Top of the Pops* production, and the show was moved to Lime Grove studios in London. It was also becoming more difficult to get bands up north to perform due to the fact that most of them were now based in London.

Philip Larkin reflected: 'Sometimes I think I shall never leave Hull – I am growing defeatist . . . I am not even turning into a regional poet, with his clay pipe and acknowledged corner in the snug of the Cat and Fuddle. Just an anonymous figure, whom people will dimly remember seeing when the evening paper says "Hull Man Dies".' The same year he wrote 'Annus Mirabilis'.

> Sexual intercourse began
> In nineteen sixty-three
> (Which was rather late for me) . . .
> Between the end of the *Chatterley* ban
> And the Beatles' first LP.

The jaundiced middle-aged narrator simultaneously romanticises and ridicules Britain's 'swinging sixties'. While he laments that he is too old to indulge in the free love of the sexual revolution, he also mocks the notion that it will provide the young with any more happiness than traditional marriage. Anthony Burgess would talk of how Larkin had given Hull (officially Kingston upon Hull) a voice, and 'that voice is larger than the city'.

James Corrigan, who came from a Yorkshire fairground family, built what came to be seen as the biggest variety club in Europe. James had married a Batley girl, Betty, and together they opened a bingo hall in the town, but James's dream was for something much bigger. They found a derelict site in Bradford Road, Batley which had once been the site of a municipal sewage works. On Easter Sunday 1967 the Batley Variety Club opened its doors. It had taken just fourteen weeks to build after the Bachelors had laid the foundation stone. Corrigan was impressed by the supermarkets springing up in every northern town. He thought pile it high and sell it cheap could be applied to showbiz, and he engaged stars who were at that time the biggest names in the business. The A653 Bradford Road soon took on the glamour of Broadway, as Jimmy Corrigan drove stars like Shirley Bassey, Louis Armstrong, Jayne Mansfield and Roy Orbison to his new club in the gold Rolls-Royce he owned.

Prime Minister Harold Wilson officially opened the Mancunian Way on 5 May 1967, the second time a section of motorway in the region had been opened by the PM. It travelled across the southern edge of the city centre, to ease congestion, and modernised the look of the city along with Piccadilly Plaza, featuring the thirty-storey Sunley – later City – Tower, completed in 1965, the narrow side of the block decorated with a relief pattern inspired by the circuit boards of a computer. While the cranes and concrete mixers were at work on the new road, a local schoolboy won an *Evening News* competition to name the road. The *Manchester Evening News* ran article after article on what they called the 'highway in the sky', which was seen as a major engineering feat and a very positive modern development for Manchester. Despite the publicity, the road wasn't quite as impressive as intended when it opened. The A34 junction included a famous mistake: there is an unfinished slip road leaving the eastbound carriageway which ends in mid-air because during construction the contractors realised that it would direct traffic the wrong way on to a one-way street.

9

Everyone knows, up to a point, what you are referring to when you say 'the north', especially when it's clear that what you are talking about is the north of England. The north of England is a very real thing, separated from the very real south for all manner of solid and imagined reasons, and it's easy to list a few objects, people, sights, disputes, scandals, reports, buildings, clichés, poets, comedians and references and come up with an image of the north that does the job. The north all wrapped up and firmly in its place as a combination of nostalgia and obedience to the notion that the north is summed up by a cloth cap, an Eccles cake, a bangin' tune, a witty catchphrase, a no-nonsense hard man, a once-vital political struggle, a stick of rock, a vast ocean of coal under the ground, a stagnant canal, meandering backstreets clinging on to a narrow layout first established in mediaeval times, the careful brick detailing on an everyday railway tunnel, a comedy double act, an outside toilet, a deep gorge, a rags-to-riches story, a situation comedy, ghosts forever rehearsing the same futile rigmarole, a smoking chimney in a pre-clean-air-act sky.

But the north is also not so easy to find. There is an invisible, a less stable north co-existing with the flat tempered same old north that we think we know from that book, that song, punchline, landmark, anniversary or accent. There is the north that is the result of a series of communal decisions, collected wisdom and general understandings that we can be very comfortable with even if it annoys us with its simplicity or predictability. Then there is another north, still made up of the usual names, achievements and history, but one that might perhaps be a little truer – to a certain something, to a sense of how the north actually came to be so fixed even as it was resisting being fixed and controlled and organised by indifferent, or all too attentive, outside forces. A north that routinely emerges from the geography, the weather, the landscape, the humour and the settled patterns of behaviour. But a north that also emerges from the shadows, from its own mysterious position as something that contains such tradition and militancy, brilliance and persistence, acceptance and slyness, dirt and glamour, and from the fact that in the end the north is made up of lots of norths, all of them containing their own invisible north.

These different norths, these norths within the north – clear, obscure, competing and overlapping with each other inside such a short cramped enclosed space – are all very different, to the extent that the only thing they have in common is that they happen to be a few miles apart, just across the river, over the hills, down the road, the other side of the island. Perhaps all that submerged, simmering tension between one coast and the other, between one county and another, between this city and that city, that valley and this gorge, village versus village, neighbour against neighbour, has compressed into a tart, brittle togetherness connected only to their shared position of not being in the south. The beauty of the north is that it is all about difference and a refusal to sacrifice a pungent hard-won sense of difference. This difference, from the south, from those close by, explicitly represents an independence that has been difficult to officially, formally achieve, and this difference, this abstract independence of thought, is loudly, boldly, brazenly, excessively, romantically and sometimes subtly represented through the walk and talk that the classic northerner uses even when it appears to confirm and clarify the cold, simple and undermining stereotyping that the northerner traditionally – and yet radically – despises.

10

1966

While training as a teacher, Abdur was interviewed by the BBC for a television series called *Minorities in Britain*, transmitted on 27 June 1966. 'I became one of the first Asian teachers in Bradford. To children, I was a novelty. To teachers, there was a mixed reaction. I was invading their territory in some ways but I got on with people very well. Pakistan means "land of pure" and people started to call Pakistanis Pakis as if it was a swear word, so that sort of thing started coming on. The streets were littered with graffiti, Paki go home, and all that business. Some people even criticised the smell of curry.'

German-born writer W. G. Sebald, a concerned perceptive analyst of the emotional dissipated post-war aftermath, moved to Manchester in 1966 to take up an assistant lectureship at the University of Manchester. In his book *The Emigrants*, published in 1981, Sebald's narrator arrived in the city by plane.

Looping round in one more curve, the roar of the engines steadily increasing, the plane set a course across open country. By now, we should have been able to make out the sprawling mass of Manchester, yet one could see nothing but a faint glimmer, as if from a fire almost suffocated in ash. A blanket of fog that had risen out of the marshy plains that reached as far as the Irish Sea had covered the city, a city spread across a thousand square kilometres, built of countless bricks and inhabited by millions of souls, dead and alive.

Driving in from the airport, Sebald's narrator, no doubt mirroring the author's own experience, notes the almost graceful suburbs of Gatley, Northenden and Didsbury, before he encounters the soiled inner-city areas of Hulme and Moss Side, 'whole blocks where the doors and windows were boarded up' and then a city centre that was 'hollow to the core'.

I never ceased to be amazed by the completeness with which anthracite-coloured Manchester, the city from which industrialisation had spread across the entire world, displayed the clearly chronic process of its impoverishment and degradation to anyone who cared to see. As we drove in among the dark ravines between the brick buildings, most of which were six or eight storeys high and sometimes adorned with glazed ceramic tiles, it turned out that even there, in the heart of the city, not a soul was to be seen, though by now it was almost a quarter to six. One might have supposed that the city had long been deserted, and was left now as a necropolis or mausoleum.

In 1966 Julie Goodyear's successful modelling career – she had been named Miss Britvic and also Miss Astral Cream – led to a part in one of the four *Coronation Street* spin-off comedy series that emerged in the sixties, *Pardon the Expression*. She also made a six-week appearance as Bet Lynch in *Coronation Street*, then joined the Oldham Repertory Company. After roles in *Family at War*, *The Dustbinmen*, *Nearest and Dearest* and *City 68*, she rejoined *Coronation Street* in 1970 as the feisty, definitively busty and defiantly down-to-earth barmaid in the Rovers' Return. Her earrings, sharp tongue, animal prints and piled-high rough blonde hair would become legendary, but as dramatic as her role was in the soap, her chaotic private life driven by a host of lusts was often even more intense and far-fetched.

1965

Forton Services on the M6 near Lancaster opened. It was operated by Top Rank Motor Inns, part of the giant media and entertainment combine J. Arthur Rank. It was Top Rank's second 'motor port' as they called them. The centrepiece of Forton was a hexagonal tower, which resembled an aircraft control tower. The Tower Restaurant, which it contained, was the most upmarket dining experience offered at Forton. Diners had views over Morecambe Bay and to the Lakeland fells beyond. In spite of the ambitions of Top Rank, when *Motoring Which?* visited Forton during a survey of motorway service areas, they found the quality of the food 'only fair'.

1964

In February, at their first American press conference, when the Beatles were asked, 'Can you explain your strange English accents?' George Harrison replied, 'It's not English. It's Liverpudlian.'

The Rolling Stones concert at Rochdale's Cubi Klub in April 1964 was cancelled after trouble broke out among nearly 1,500 youngsters trying to get in. Queues had formed outside the Slack Street club hours before the show, and over 800 people eventually packed inside waiting for the pop stars to appear. Two of the Stones arrived on time but the other three were delayed coming from Knutsford after their car had a puncture.

Riffat Akram arrived in Bradford with the rest of her family. She was only eleven years old.

> The journey was long and dreary. My father tried to teach us some English on the way. I hadn't come across English before so he taught us a few words on the train. When we arrived in Bradford it was an extremely cold November evening. Foggy, smog, drizzle – horrible. And I remember my mum's face when we got off. Some of my father's friends were there to meet us. Dad said, 'We're here.' And Mum looked around and she looked at the horrible, cold, dull, dark place and said, 'THIS is England?!' I'll never forget that expression for as long as I live. She was just horrified!

Bob Dylan played his first show in Britain on 14 May 1964 at ABC Television's Didsbury studios in Manchester on the corner of School Lane and Parrs Wood Lane. The studios were a former 'super cinema' opened in 1931. ABC broadcast in the north at weekends until 1968, while Granada took care of the weekdays. Dylan sang 'Chimes of Freedom' and 'Don't Think Twice'. The studios first went on air on 5 May 1956, opening with the FA Cup Final of that year between Manchester City and Birmingham.

Ray Allen opened the UK's first Kentucky Fried Chicken restaurant in Fishergate, Preston. Ray had met Colonel Harland Sanders in 1963, securing the UK rights to the famous 'secret recipe' American fried chicken.

Top of the Pops is first transmitted from a converted church in Dickinson Road, Manchester, which had been acquired by the BBC and fitted out as a studio some years earlier. It was used because other studios were busy. The first show was broadcast live at 6.35 on BBC 1, New Year's Day 1964. It was presented by Jimmy Savile, who opened the show with the immortal line: 'It's Number 1, it's *Top of the Pops*.'

'We are living in the jet age but we are governed by an Edwardian establishment mentality. Over the British people lies the chill frost of Tory leadership. They freeze initiative and petrify imagination. They cling to privilege and power for the few, shutting the gates on the many. Tory society is a *closed* society, in which birth and wealth have priority, in which the master and servant, landlord and tenant mentality is predominant. The Tories have proven that they are incapable of mobilising Britain to take full advantage of the scientific breakthrough. Their approach and methods are fifty years out of date.' Harold Wilson

In summer 1964 Barbara Hepworth travelled to New York for the unveiling of her monumental sculpture *Single Form*, a towering shield-like block of bronze, on the plaza of the UN Secretariat. For once Hepworth upstaged her old friend and rival Henry Moore (he had adorned the UNESCO Building in Paris a few years earlier). Usually it was she who came off badly from the inevitable comparisons, having been born within five miles and five years of each other.

II

The north begins once you have crossed this river, or that river, or maybe that sensational sudden plunge in the landscape, over that bridge built in the seventeenth century but which still followed some route established by the Romans as they forced their way further and further into the mysterious alluring roughness of an island that got rougher, damper and chillier but more spectacular the further north they ventured. The Romans made their roads direct, so that troops could travel swiftly from one military station to another, and their straight lines cutting through the nation influenced the routes and resting places of roads and railways that would criss-cross the country in centuries to come. Windswept, wild and wet, north-west England was about as far as one could get in the Roman empire from the sun-baked lands of Spain and Syria. Feeling the bitter cold and fans of comfort, the Romans heated their substantial yet delicately decorated homes, and built furnaces, foundries, hearths and ovens for the tiles, glass, utensils, heating systems, baths, bricks and pottery they needed, teaching the Britons a multitude of new trades.

The north became the north first as a shadow of possibility with the fixed, rather indifferent and actually alien grandeur of Hadrian's Wall, which was ignored when an actual legal border was finally decided in 1237. And then the north's north was under constant challenging siege from battling governments and elusive locals fighting to eke out an existence in an area where you got no immediate advantage from belonging to either the English or the Scottish, and whatever nationalistic pride you did develop was contorted. You survived on your own terms by establishing your own rules, and lack of rules, and by creating your own complicated, tangled and internal allegiances.

Hadrian's Wall was a provisional hint of where the north's northern border would end up, a suggestion, perhaps a Roman recommendation which would be corrected temporarily by the Romans themselves when they moved the line north. The wall is an ideal metaphor for the border: something which is an actual physical barrier between the two nations but only a fantasy border, one which implies, by not actually being a border, how a border is often arbitrary, liminal and psychological.

Beyond Hadrian's Wall there is more English north, and more stories, and myths, and misunderstandings. There is the history of how the border between England and Scotland, and therefore the northern end of the north, itself vibrated, sometimes viciously, through time as skirmishes, battles and disagreements meant the border changed shape, was argued over and moved about before there was a final decision, in 1237. Hadrian's Wall does not mark a place where the north becomes the north, which would be romantically attractive and to some extent exists in a comical and even ideological version of how England is separated from Scotland. North of the wall, there are nine miles more in the west, above Carlisle, and sixty-eight miles more in the east, above Newcastle, before the Scottish border finally appears, sealing the top end of the north, giving us one place where the north begins, as the south to another land, another state of mind.

The north begins with that border skirmish, that line in a poem, that invention of a machine, that adoption or rejection or adaptation of a foreign influence, that criminal act, that frame of mind, that revolutionary impulse, that massive experiment in splendour, that brand-new trade, that personality trait, that thirteenth-century treaty, that clinging on to a word, a phrase, the curtailed form of the definite article, in t' north of England, put th' wood in th' ole, champion, a blunt outburst, it doesn't do, a crusty slice of boisterous slang, for fuck's sake, them as 'as nowt is nowt, that low toneless cloud over a windswept isolated field, that touching arrangement of looming brick and sombre shadow, that red sprawling scab, the oily rainbow shine on a slate-grey rain-covered roof, that period of class conflict, that border change, that melancholy nostalgia, tha's a face like a line a wet washin', the pressing pain of an endless now, a colour that could only belong among L. S. Lowry's faithfully maintained and reworked five favourites.

12

1963

The 1960s was the perfect time for a Yorkshire man to join the BBC. 'Once, I couldn't have got a job there as a gateman, with my accent,' reported Michael Parkinson, born in 1935 in Cudsworth on the outskirts of Barnsley, South Yorkshire. 'Now, they were on their knees begging you to join if you had a northern accent.'

On 10 October Conservative Prime Minister Harold Macmillan resigned and was succeeded by Sir Alec Douglas-Home. Douglas-Home put up a brave fight in the general election one year later, but it was Wilson and his Labour Party who won, with a majority of five seats.

'There is no doubt in my mind that the astounding Merseybeat boom had a big effect on the outcome of the general election. The groups were young, vibrant and new. They were in tune with the desires of the people. They asserted working-class values, they looked to the future. I believe the Beatles made a powerful contribution to Labour's victory without recognising it.' Liverpool MP Eric Heffer writing in his autobiography of the 1963 election.

In December 1963 Morecambe and Wise recorded a show with the Beatles. They treated the most famous pop group of all time with typical irreverence. In a parody of Eric's description of Ernie being the one with the 'short fat hairy legs', George Harrison described the foursome as the 'ones with the big fat hairy heads'. Eric mistook the lads for the Kaye Sisters and kept refer-ring to Ringo as Bongo.

> Morecambe: Hey! Hey-hey! What's it like being famous?
> John: Well, it's not like in your day, you know.
> Morecambe: What do you mean 'not like in my day'?
> John: Well, me dad used to tell me about you, you know.

John Peel found himself in Dallas on 22 November 1963, the day that John F. Kennedy was shot and killed. Peel felt the compulsion to visit the scene of his namesake's assassination and raced across to Dealey Plaza. When faced with the police barrier, he simply claimed that he was a reporter from the *Liverpool Echo* and somehow gained admittance. He later used the same trick to gain access to the press conference that paraded the recently arrested Lee Harvey Oswald.

While appearing as nightly anchor on regional news magazine *Scene at 6.30*, presenter Michael Scott was the messenger in an historic Granada coup. On 22 November 1963 the programme had been on the air five minutes when the telephone rang in the newsroom adjacent to the studio. It was CBS in New York with the news that President John Kennedy had been shot. There was a rule that ITV programme companies should never pre-empt ITN on big stories. Denis Forman, the senior Granada executive present, called ITN and was told they were not going to break into the schedules with the story until they had it from their own reporter in America. Forman decided to go ahead, and Scott broke the news to northern viewers half an hour before it reached the rest of the country.

The swinging sixties saw great changes in the physical appearance of the towns of Tameside. At Hattersley farms and scattered cottages gave way to a vast estate to house Manchester's overspill. Hyde's boundaries were extended to include the area, although all costs were met by Manchester. Building began early in the 1960s and the first families moved on to the estate in May 1963. They were welcomed by the mayor of Hyde and received free milk and sausages from Wall's factory at Godley. By August 1964 there were 4,000 people in Hattersley, served by just one doctor. There were few shops or community facilities and problems increased as the estate grew in size.

13

The north begins with names and naming. In the late ninth century, four centuries after the decadent, exhausted Romans retreated, the fierce Picts filled the vacuum by running riot, and the Saxons, Jutes and Angles established their settlements and kingdoms. The Danes and other northmen were the next set of curious, predatory interlopers sailing from the bays and fjords of north-west Europe. Known as Vikings – creek men – 'the great north wind' brought them to the east coast of what would become Yorkshire, from where they expanded inland and across the Pennines.

Much of what was later known as Lancashire escaped colonisation, although the Danes did settle much of the area around what is now Manchester. Oldham was named Aldenhulme around 865, and places like Urmston, Davyhulme, Cheadle Hulme and Hulme are all of Danish origin – the Old Danish *hulm* or the Old Norse *holmr* meaning a piece of flat land surrounded by streams, or a water meadow. Flixton, close to Urmston, is perhaps a hybrid name from a Danish invader called Flix, and *tun*, the word for village or farmstead. The Lake District in what would become Cumbria was mainly attacked from the Irish Sea by Norse Vikings, around AD 930, and then settled. The area is thick with becks (brooks), fells (hills), garths (enclosures, yards), gills (ravines, gorges) and tarns (lakes). The word acre itself derives from the Viking *mjor-aker*, meaning a small piece of land.

There is a distinct Norse influence on numerous northern place names. Your surroundings need names to create the sort of familiarity that means you are home, and it is all yours. Names stamp territory with claiming authority. Place names ending with 'scale' and 'side' (grazing land) reveal their association with the soil as the Danish colonisers settled down to what, when they weren't sailing the seas and carving open new territories, they liked the most – farming. In north Lancashire any name ending with 'thwaite' (a clearing in a wood, a settlement), like Rosthwaite or Seathwaite, shows Viking presence. In Yorkshire Micklethwaite is the great clearing, Skipton is a sheep farm, Aysgarth is a gap in the hills where oak trees grow.

Place names ending with 'by' – Selby, Whitby – or 'dale' (valley) or 'ness' (headland, important navigation markers for the seafaring Vikings) are Viking in origin. A 'thorpe' – Scunthorpe – was a secondary settlement in an area considered second rate and marginalised. Grim, a Viking prince, founded Grimsby. Many street names in Leeds and York end with 'gate' – from *gata* meaning way, street or road. Many surnames with a decidedly northern tint have Viking roots – Airey, Appleby, Asquith (Askwith), Beckwith, Brandreth, Chippendale, Fotherby, Fothergill, Grimshaw, Hague, Heseltine, Heslop, Hislop, Hogarth, Holmes, Kendal(l), Lofthouse, Pickersgill, Rowntree, Scargill, Schofield, Stockdale, Sykes, Thackeray, Thorpe, Threllfall, Thwaite(s), Willoughby, Wolstenholme and York. From the name of the god Thor we get such forms as Thorburn, Thurkettle, Thurstans, Thurston, Turpin and Turtle. The consequences of Norse immigrants converting to Christianity can be seen in names that end or begin with 'kirk', from the Old Norse word for church – Ormskirk, Kirkby, Kirkham.

By 880 the Vikings controlled most of England, with Jorvik – York – as their capital. In what was not yet named Yorkshire the thorough, highly regimented and bureaucratically minded Viking rulers divided the area into three separate units for ease of administration. The Old Norse word for a third of something (*thrithjungr*) became modified to 'riding', giving rise to the East Riding, North Riding and West Riding of Yorkshire. Pushing south and west, the Vikings had attacked the

Anglo-Saxon kingdom of Wessex in 871. This was resisted by Alfred, who thus became 'the Great'. He became king that same year and was the first Anglo-Saxon ruler to be recognised as a national leader, if only because of his effective use of self-promoting propaganda. Alfred retook London in 886 but realised that he could not force the Vikings out of the rest of England and so came to an agreement with the Danish leader Guthrum. This gave the Vikings their own independent territory in England, the Danelaw – an area of the country subject to Danish law – north-east of a line stretching from London to the River Mersey north of Chester. On the Mersey frontier with the Danelaw were *burhs* – a word which denoted a fortified town, a Saxon stronghold or a neighbourhood, which in time became 'borough' – at places to be one day known as Chester, Runcorn, Thelwall and Manchester.

14

1963

For young people in York the sixties truly began in 1963. That was the year the Beatles played the Rialto on Fishergate no fewer than four times. Their first appearance was on 27 February, supporting Helen Shapiro, who was ill and didn't perform. The group are said to have written the follow-up to 1962's 'Love Me Do' – 'From Me to You,' their first number 1 in the *NME* charts – on the tour bus journey from York to the next gig in Shrewsbury. They wrote 'She Loves You', their first number 1 in the BBC charts, in the Imperial Hotel, Jesmond, Newcastle. They had played the modest Majestic Ballroom in Westgate Road on 26 June 1963 and had a spare day before performing in Leeds on the 28th. Paul encouraged John to start composing the song in their hotel room.

'Already an old square, I propose in 1964 to be even squarer. I have no desire to bully teenagers into trying to like what I like, and so long as they are out of my hearing, they can scream their heads off; but on the other hand the mass media must stop trying to Beatle me. At the point where teenage-herding, adolescent hysteria and high-pressure salesmanship all meet, there will probably be just as much sound and fury in 1964 as there has been in 1963; but nobody will do nicely out of explaining their social significance to me. Or, for that matter, the social significance of anything else. Any of that stuff needed here will be produced in and for the home market and will not be imported.' J. B. Priestley, *New Statesman*, 27 December 1963.

A few years earlier Priestley had responded to the rise of the Angry Young Men in theatre, literature and film by saying, 'Angry? I'll show you bloody angry. I was angry before you were all born.'

An editorial in *International Socialism* commented in 1963, 'In the portly lineaments and plummy accents of the late Gaitskell the world could detect more than a mite of that amateur gentlemanly public-school tradition which Labour is so dedicated to combating.' Harold Wilson, his successor, looked and sounded quite different. While Macmillan and Home posed as Edwardian gentlemen on their grouse moors in plus fours, Wilson was a pipe-smoking northerner, a self-proclaimed supporter of Huddersfield Town with traces of a Yorkshire accent. Far from being a landed gentleman, he was the son of an industrial chemist. Wilson shrewdly exploited these assets. His Huddersfield accent faded away during the forties and fities, but now made a telling come back.

15

The north begins with the Normans, who had Viking ancestors, coming from the south, from across the narrow Channel, and pulling the constitution of the country to the south. The Norman influence on Englishness led to new layers of aristocracy and intermarriage which tended to be in the south, nearer to the centre of the new regime in Normandy. A few centuries before the metaphorical centre of the islands had been in the north-east, collected around the curious patient minds and manners of the learned monks in the abbeys on the Northumbrian coast.

Previously invasions and foreign influences had arrived in the north as much as the south – from the north Germanic tribes which absorbed and amended particular British qualities more than they wiped them out, producing a new hybrid of social and cultural dynamism that seethed and simmered in all areas of the country. With the Normans the energy shifted to the south, new forms of social division and class systems started to operate and the idea developed that people in certain parts of the country were more advanced and more important, involved and sophisticated, than in other parts of the country – which, by the very nature of them being not near the ruling centre, meant they were not part of where the action actually was. They were judged to be ecclesiastically, socially and culturally backward. This would hold for those parts of the British Isles that were not English and for regions of England more distant from what was now the direct link to the royal home – the Channel.

These latest conquerors of the British Isles were not quite as flexible as previous invaders and outsiders in absorbing and realigning the existent indigenous characteristics. French took over as the language of the court, administration and culture – and remained so for 300 years. Meanwhile, English was demoted to everyday unimportant uses.

The most significant change in terms of the psychology of the region that was becoming England was that previous historical currents, especially through the Saxon and Viking eras, had tended to run from east to west – the Danelaw itself split the nation predominantly vertically between east and west. Under the Normans the currents shifted to run from south to north, as if England had shifted position, revolving so that it was clearly, in the mind and on the map, split between up and down. There was now an area distant from where power materialised, a little shapeless at the edges but with a strong beating heart: there was the north.

The north begins in the markets that started in squares around churches to sell produce from the countryside. Market towns in Lancashire were the county's first towns of any real importance, and most would become over time large towns or cities. Market charters were granted to Lancaster in 1200, Bolton in 1251, Manchester in 1282, Preston in 1292 and Burnley in 1294. In the twelfth and thirteenth centuries Yorkshire thrived and many new towns emerged. These included Barnsley, Doncaster, Hull, Leeds, Pontefract, Richmond, Scarborough and Sheffield.

The north begins with new influences from other countries, because of certain domestic arrangements, and perhaps a little bit of snooty or well-intentioned wifely nagging. In 1330 Edward III was encouraged by his wife, Philippa of Hainault, to invite highly skilled Flemish weavers to settle in England. The intention was to help the expansion of the weaving trade and raise the standard of woollen fabrics. Many of the immigrants headed to Norfolk, but some arrived in and around Yorkshire and also in the Manchester area up towards Bolton. Bolton has had many names throughout the centuries, including Bodeltun, Botheltun, Bodeltown, Bothel-tun-le-Moors, Bowelton, Boulton, Bolton-super-Moras, Bol-ton-in-ye-Moors, and Bolton-le-Moors (to distinguish it from others such as Bolton-le-Sands, and describing its situation among the west Pennine moorlands – formerly wild, almost uninhabited, and infested with wolves and wild boars). Bolton is Old English for 'settlement with a special building'. It is possible that Flemish weavers introduced clogs to the northern English, who redesigned the uncomfortable wooden sabots lined with lambskin. Over time they proved warm and efficient against wet conditions and were economical and durable.

The north begins with the weather, the water, the landscape, the distance from bossy supercilious central authority; the colliding and subdividing of surly, superior and demanding invading interests; the legacy and emotional residue, the conclusions, the prejudices of those who came and went; the resultant stubbornness, resilience, toughness, wryness, independence, scepticism, defiance, acceptance; the need to build, to create, to invent, to speculate, but also, less romantically, the need to accept, to put up with, to reason and withdraw, and then to fight back, to resist, to argue and struggle.

And then there is the combination of the geology of the north and the emphatic earthiness of the people to produce voices that make sounds that seem to follow and be followed by the shape of the earth around them. In the south your voice leaves the ground, your accent fights away from the earth, as if you are using how you speak to avoid the dirt under your feet, which represents the planet itself.

People with voices that resembled the landscape around them built on this northern earth stretching between one sea and another, between one part of the country and another, a place to dwell, dream and determine their destiny. All of this dreaming and determination poured into and out of the mouths of people who spoke – whether on the east or west coast, on top of hills, by lakes, by rivers, down slopes, in valleys, under shadows, in forests, across shiny cobbles the shape of petrified kidneys, in unforgiving isolated open spaces, in misty scalding coldness, in villages becoming towns and cities, even small empires – in ways that clashed with those who came with hostile intent or friendly reasons from outside, or by those who slammed the door on outside influences, even rejected the slur, sting and snap of near neighbours, preferring their very own slap, twist and thud, in ways that dug into and twisted around their rolling, turbulent surroundings and circumstances the richly developing English language, so that it all fed back into and bent into shape what was always becoming north.

16

The Park Hill Flats, located on thirty-two acres of land behind Sheffield station and overlooking Sheffield city centre, were built 1957–61, inspired by Le Corbusier's Unité d'Habitation. The flats were the result of the first complete post-war slum clearance scheme in Britain, relocating thousands of people. The project meant clearing a violent slum nicknamed Little Chicago. Rather than rehousing the area's residents in then-fashionable isolated towers, the architects attempted to replicate in the air the traditional tightly packed and communal street life of the area. Consisting of 995 dwellings, and housing over two thousand people, the huge snake-like blocks were built on a slope. Sheffield Council hoped that Park Hill, the 'streets in the sky,' would signal the rejuvenation of the town and provide attractive enduring homes in a deprived area.

1962

One of the reasons the Decca record label rejected the Beatles in 1962 was that it preferred the safety and convenience of signing the London-based Brian Poole and the Tremeloes.

Ringway Airport Terminal One was officially opened in 1962 by Prince Philip, and was the first in Europe to incorporate the pier system, in which passengers remain under cover until ready to board their flight. This state-of-the-art construction cost £2.7 million. Four specially commissioned Murano glass chandeliers were ceremoniously unveiled at the same time, their meticulously hand-blown multicoloured teardrops symbolically flooding the city with light, pointing the way to whole new worlds beyond Britain's austerity-period shores. Each weighed two tonnes and was made up of 1,300 individually blown pieces of lead-grey and amethyst glass up to ten feet long. They were the centrepiece of· a grand tribute to the glamour and romance of air travel in the style of the splendour of the great old railway stations but reinterpreted with modernist flourishes – including black rubber floor tiles and an Elizabeth Frink sculptural piece celebrating Manchester's Alcock and Brown, the first aviators to fly the Atlantic non-stop.

17

If you are coming to the north, it, the north itself, perhaps doesn't really begin – it isn't what you were expecting, however vaguely – until you arrive at the pinched scrappy edges of a major industrial city, one of the greats, one of those with a name that chimes with achievement even if only because of sport, or music, or perhaps comedy and entertainment, but certainly history, filled with people who know their own minds because they've learned in the face of all manner of questioning and condemnation to speak for themselves in a way that is often very different from people living a few short miles away. As you head towards the north, destined to arrive in the north-west, as opposed to the north-east, which would bring you into the north through Yorkshire, there are warnings about what is to come. You will have spotted them perhaps as far south as Birmingham, or Nottingham, or Derby, or Stoke. They will have taken the form of the land, or the buildings, or simply the clouds gathering in a sky that itself seems to be changing, as if the north actually begins high above the ground, in the atmosphere that borders outer space.

Even though by the time you arrive on the edges of this major northern city and see the buildings, new and old, that tell its story, that announce its entrenched character, you may have been in the north for a fair few miles, nothing will have seemed so dramatically different since you were in the obvious south. It takes a city, or at least a town, to clarify that you are indeed in the north, where the highest buildings tell their own story of religious presence, commercial ambition, social purpose, ideological clashes, commemorative pride and consolidated residential organisation. The north made up of cities and towns split into definite if intangible sections by roads, waterways, lines of communication, places of work, green spaces and spaces just left over, and especially by dynamically straight railway lines. If you follow these lines it doesn't take long before you detect the past and pass right through it. This is the north that has cut itself into the national imagination, the north that has bullied its way, or entertained its way, or bought or conned or stolen its way into history, or shaken history apart through glittering genius.

Plenty of the north is rural and secluded, much of it not built on, where you can walk for hours without having to enter a town or village or cross a road or railway line. But the north of England would not be the north of England without the city, the crushing together of layers of old and new, a network of nowheres seeking a proper place, with its fine upstanding town hall, majestic churches, stony-faced civic structures and a dense jumbled inner series of spaces folding in on themselves, slanted roofs, dislocated ghettos and secretive turnings that disclose a sense of what the city was like before it was a city, before it expanded and spread itself further out, until it was so big, filled with so many turnings, so much space and density, that it constantly broke its own borders. It spread out so far bits of it needed their own names, and suburbs formed, and towns and villages nearby felt its gravitational pull and themselves grew into bigger places.

Heading south, at some point in this relatively untouched country-side, long after you have left behind a major city, or a nearby town – the mighty industrial city in rough, hopeful, closely related miniature – you feel you are leaving the north behind, as though it was something foreign, a colony, a collection of colonies, England twisted into else-where, and dropping into the south – the neutral plains, stately homes and gentle order that radiates from London, the centre of the south, the imagined levels of entitlement that reach as far as the midlands, before they are shaken off, cast aside, rejected, not quite in a northern way, but in ways that are more northern than southern. It does seem as though you arrive in the north at a different level from where you leave it: higher up when you first find it, lower down as you leave it.

18

As the impressionistic French structural anthropologist Claude Lévi-Strauss said in 'History and Dialectic', the final chapter of his 1962 book *The Savage Mind*, historical facts are no more given than any others. It is the historian, or the agent of history, who constitutes them by abstraction and as though 'under the threat of an infinite regress'.

The Savage Mind was published in the same year that the Beatles released their first single, that Anthony Burgess's *A Clockwork Orange* was published, based on the nattily dressed weapon-wielding Moss Side street gangs he grew up around in the 1920s and thirties, and L.S. Lowry painted *Station Approach*, a re-imagining of Manchester Central train station. The station, built among the notorious slum dwellings written about by Friedrich Engels, opened to passengers in 1880, featured a magnificent single-span arched roof and was where serial killer Ian Brady met his final victim, Edward Evans, on 6 October 1965. Manchester Central was one of the city's main stations for most of its existence, with the Midland Hotel built on adjacent land in the early part of the twentieth century – the grand hotel once allegedly coveted by Adolf Hitler as a northern HQ for the Nazis, an early meeting place for Charles Stewart Rolls and Frederick Henry Royce as they planned the foundation in 1906 of Rolls-Royce Limited, and where the Beatles were turned away from the restaurant, described by W. G. Sebald in the mid-sixties as like something you'd find in Warsaw, for being inappropriately dressed.

The station finally shut on 5 May 1969 after a last burst of life in the sixties as the northern home of the luxurious Blue Pullman service to London King's Cross, and was sold to National Car Parks in 1972, before slowly decaying and becoming a symbol of the dismal decline of the railways and the once proud northern industrial towns.

Lévi-Strauss wrote, 'What is true of the constitution of historical facts is no less so of their selection. From this point of view, the historian and the agent of history choose, sever and carve them up, for a truly total history would confront them with chaos. Every corner of space conceals a multitude of individuals each of whom totalises the trend of history in a manner which cannot be compared to the others; for any one of these individuals, each moment of time is inexhaustibly rich in physical and psychical incidents which all play their part in his totalisation. Even history which claims to be universal is still only a juxtaposition of a few local histories within which (and between which) very much more is left out than is put in.'

1961

Castleford housewife Viv Nicholson won £152,300 on the football pools. At the time Viv and Keith Nicholson were just about at rock bottom. On a seven-pounds-a-week trainee miner's wage they were bringing up three kids in a tiny terraced home in Castleford, Yorkshire. Just trying to make ends meet was a constant battle. 'We found out on Saturday evening that we'd won the pools, but we couldn't find the coupon. We weren't sure if we'd sent it off or not, but then the winning ticket turned up in Keith's trousers. It's unbelievable that I remember the exact amount we won so clearly – it was £152,300, 18 shillings and 8 pence. Back then, even the eightpence meant something. That night we walked into town and had a couple of halves of beer each, and we got the bus back home, but we couldn't sleep. My mum and dad came round with some cans and we had loads to drink and smoke. We did that for a couple of nights, before getting the train to London to collect our winnings from Littlewoods. There were so many people at King's Cross station, all rushing towards my particular compartment, I thought, "Oh, I didn't realise there were so many people who wanted to catch a train." That is how naive I was. They were reporters, and they all asked, "What are you going to do now?" And there I was, wearing a pair of tights I had to borrow from my sister, and I said I was going to "Spend, spend, spend!"'

George Formby suffers his second heart attack and dies in St Joseph's Hospital, Preston. His funeral takes place at St Charles' Church in Aigburth, Liverpool, and over 100,000 people line the twenty-mile route to Warrington Cemetery, where he is buried in the Booth family grave.

In Manchester at the Embassy Club Bernard Manning booked the big northern acts of the day, including, he claimed, the Beatles. 'They were fourteen quid and they just did a one-off show,' he recounted. 'All nice boys, got there dressed, went on and did the show and then buggered off. That John Lennon drove me potty because he wanted a dressing room with a washbasin. What did he want that for? You come here to work, not to wash.'

19

I write as a ten-year-old and as a fifty-four-year-old and everything in between. I write across distance and so much time. I write about a walk, a number of walks making the streets near me my home, which I would take as a bony nervy fair-haired boy between the ages of about seven and about twelve, hands stuck in trouser pockets that seemed all holes, wearing a torn hand-me-down duffel coat that was turning into an idea.

A walk that helped me become a northerner, and that helps me, as I look back on that walk, and where it was during what period of time, work out what being a northerner means. A walk that ends with the north that is inside this book, which is a north that explains how, between the ages of seven and twelve, which is between 1964 and 1969, I became a northerner, and then through my teenage years, as I grew into what I was to become, I became someone because I was that northerner. I walked in the same spot, until a path appeared.

I didn't think any of that at the time. I was not aware of the southerner as a category, certainly not as any sort of enemy or competition. I didn't have any sectarian connection to where I lived, almost the opposite, and I didn't feel explicit romantic loyalty to any sort of traditional or progressive northern spirit, nor feel any need to build up my role – to play up my accent, which sounded like no accent to me, and make a defiant case for my glamorised provincial setting by adding edge to whatever attitude I had to whatever it was I felt about being dragged into life and then set for some reason deep into the mucky, broken or transcendent, fantastically complicated north of England.

I have not lived in the north since the late 1970s. I started the seventies at the age of twelve and finished them at twenty-two, which means that during this decade I became a teenager, struck by abrupt, disconcerting changes in my mind and body, and then left home, on the way to becoming an adult. I spent most of this time planning how to get out of the north, sometimes vaguely, but occasionally with real purpose, especially if an argument with someone older and with power over my destiny went badly wrong. I didn't think about it as leaving the north, but simply as leaving where I was at the time, which seemed intent on fixing me in place and stopping me working out who I was, separate from my family and where we lived.

I didn't think about being a northerner so much as think of myself as someone who happened to live in a series of houses, all of them within a few miles of each other, all of them containing everything I was. All the houses I lived in as the sixties became the seventies and I became sexually aware if not active – leaving aside my night-time interest in myself – were in the north.

I was not then imagining myself as a northerner, not necessarily fighting a southern enemy, not knowingly accumulating and cherishing exclusively northern heroes, not admiring the views around me that let me glimpse with pride and awe hundreds of years of northern spirit, not planning on continuing various northern traditions that I now imagine I could hear in the voices and see in the faces and bodies of those who lived all around me. I was where I was, and this happened to involve the occasional massive building that rose up above my head totally out of scale with those around it like some sort of squat, commanding parody of a pyramid, quietly humming with secret knowledge, built to devour everything near it, or protect everything, people who spoke with a certain sort of tough, scuffed and striven fluency, and all that there was within a couple of hundred yards.

All of me seemed contained inside my head, which was contained inside a bedroom, my very own room to some extent, which was contained inside a house, which was always set in a row of other houses. This row of houses was set inside a number of other rows of houses. I never had any idea what was happening inside these houses, which were very close to me, and then less close, laid out in fixed, straight or crooked patterns, pinning me in and then stretching away into the distance but which might as well have been on the other side of the planet.

I did not notice at the time that I was being worked on as I walked around the small fragment of the north where I had landed, influenced by something I do not want to say was 'a something in the air', a floating of words into the mental air, an elaborate entwining of history actively seeping into me, penetrating my mind and even coating my tongue with something that affected how I talked.

I was picking up on things not only to do with how I talked, which an expert could no doubt have pinned down as being very specifically the accent and vocabulary of a boy being himself in the 1960s, going to a school five miles south of Manchester city centre, three miles east of Stockport's bus-laden shop-heavy Mersey Square and therefore very close to where the River Mersey itself formed, a school filled with kids who came from the dingy changeless tightly packed streets of Longsight, Gorton and Denton – streets at the same time distinctive and indistinct. These low-slung dead-end areas spat out at the edges of Manchester were not soot-slammed slums, they were not on the whole dangerous and forbidding, give or take the occasional breath-taking horror that crept along the cobbles soiling history and draining whatever subdued colour had made it through the fussy flat-cap-targeting damp and drizzle, but it would not take much of a nudge or many more years of neglect for these places to end their days in defeated damned disgrace.

In the 1960s these places, with common names handed down to them which had to be used, were in limbo, held in waiting between one momentous event, which had already happened and had determined the details of an immediate murky reality, and another, which had not yet happened and which could not be imagined, because everything seemed piled up in the past. The past – most recently a war, the physical and mental signs of which still hung around, given unflappable support by the rain and wind and mocking skies – had beaten the north into submission.

The signs of the future that made their way into this present – logos, vehicles, brands, building materials, clothing, TV programmes, DJs, pop stars – as novel and flash as they seemed to be, were all rooted in the mountainous past that had moulded the houses packed between front doors and alleyways, inside which people got used to the fact they were in limbo. What there was of the future was represented by the spread of spindly television aerials sticking up at gaunt angles above endless exhausted-looking roofs. Even the shapes and sounds of a lively, consoling and rapidly changing modern world brought into those tight inbred streets through those bits of wire were really part of the debris of an event that had happened over one hundred years ago, an event historically described as a shock, a shock that was still vibrating, still releasing its esoteric power, still allowing a certain form of continuity even in punished, humbled areas so far removed from where whatever action there was in the world was actually happening.

20

1961

In Anthony Burgess's novel *One Hand Clapping* – 'dashed off to make £100 or so' – published under the pseudonym Joseph Kell in 1961, he describes a working-class couple from the north of England, Howard and Janet Shirley, whose leisure time is spent eating food out of tins and watching game shows on television. A bitter satire on the modern media and a fierce defence of the eternal values of literature, the novel aimed to show that such lives are artificial and detached from 'real' life, 'real' food and traditional forms of culture.

1960

The first *Coronation Street* concept was offered to the BBC in 1957 as *Our Street*, to be rejected by the aloof upper-middle-class broadcaster, and it was Granada TV under its more down-to-earth chairman Sidney Bernstein who accepted it after initial reluctance. In a memo to Granada executives, creator Tony Warren – born Anthony Simpson in Swinton in 1936, child actor and model – wrote that his new programme's purpose was to explore 'the driving forces behind life in a working-class street in the north of England' and 'to entertain by examining a community of this kind'. A colleague at Granada, Harold Elton, had suggested that he develop something based on a working-class street after Warren complained he was not a fan of the crime and adventure series he was then involved in. He developed an idea based on a street located 'four miles from Manchester in any direction'. Warren said, 'Northerners have an enormous curiosity about everything. They'll also tell their life story – as long as the listener is prepared to do the same.'

The working title of the show was *Florizel Street*, named after a character in Robert Louis Stevenson's detective short stories *The Suicide Club*, who was perhaps named after a character in Shakespeare's *Twelfth Night*, but a tea lady named Agnes remarked that Florizel sounded like a brand of disinfectant. The choice of new name was between Jubilee Street and Coronation Street, with Granada executives Harry Latham, Harry Elton and H. V. Kershaw plumping for the latter. The look of the street was based on one side of Archie Street, in Ordsall, part of Salford, close to the River Irwell border with Manchester, home to the Salford Lads Club. The street was built by the Groves and Whitnall Brewery and officially opened in 1904 by Sir Robert Baden-Powell, who founded the Scout movement four years later.

At first, reactions inside Granada were sceptical, even hostile – neither a comedy nor a documentary, said one insider, not funny or informative – and Sidney Bernstein was concerned the programme presented a disagreeable even dismal image of the north-west he was hoping to promote as a region of purpose and optimism. The series was reluctantly given a six-week trial, replacing a serial based on the Biggles stories, and first broadcast on 9 December 1960, with a melancholy theme tune echoing the north's traditional ethereal but gutsy brass-band music. The new soap opera eventually appealed on a number of fronts: it harked back to a friendlier time when everyone knew their neighbours but also connected to a newly discovered 'northern cool'. By May 1961 the Salford East MP was praising its realism and noting its increasing popularity. It was said to be an 'eye opener' for middle-class viewers, as to 'how the other half lived'. The first swear word heard in the series was 'bloody', said by Ken Barlow in 1961 in an argument with his mum, Ida. Seven years later, hard-drinking Liverpool builder Len Fairclough – played by Peter Adamson, who was made an honorary member of the Master Builders' Association – used the word 'bastard'.

Coronation Street became known for the portrayal of strong women, with characters like the imperious Ena Sharples, Annie Walker, Elsie Tanner and the battling Hilda Ogden becoming household names during the 1960s. By 1962 Violet Carson, born in Ancoats in 1898, daughter of a flour miller father and amateur singer mother, pianist at Market Street cinema accompanying silent movies after the First World War, a member of the cast in the 1920s of the BBC's *Children's Hour*, pianist during the forties for Wilfred Pickles' *Have a Go*, who played seventy-two-year-old Ena Sharples, was ITV Personality of the Year.

Tony Warren created a programme largely based around loud, powerful, determined women, which some commentators put down to the environment in which he grew up – a close-knit world where the matriarchs were the guardians of their community and obtained power over an apparently male-run society through a combination of good will and cattiness, and a careful storing and distribution of valuable information. His tart-tongued, shrewd, energetic and proud women, especially Sharples, Tanner and Walker, were in part a tribute to those pioneering northern women who had found subversive ways to wield influence. He was honouring those women, some more moral or self-righteous than others, making the best of their run-down and limited circumstances, those committed to ensuring that women and their bold brilliance did not shrink behind the archetypical powerful male northern entrepreneur, planner or politician as they reorganised the fundamental structure of society. The consistent, pugnacious and sometimes punishing

Violet Carson as Ena Sharples from *Coronation Street*, with view over Manchester

female edge of *Coronation Street* existed from the very first episode. It can be traced back to a woman who never for a moment accepted that the progress taking place for better or worse in the nineteenth and twentieth centuries was going to be solely controlled by men.

In 1960 George Formby made his last record, 'Happy Go Lucky Me', and in December of the same year made what was to be his last television programme, a forty-minute one-man performance called *The Friday Show*. It was a confessional with George admitting that his wife Beryl had been the driving force behind his success, that he couldn't read or write properly, that he didn't understand music and that he regretted not having children. Beryl watched the programme from her sickbed. She was dying from leukaemia but was still able to offer her usual tough critique of George's performance. Formby – before the final credits began to roll – turned, full face on, to camera and appealed: 'And folks, if you'd like to have me back again, I've got a lot more stories to tell, and a couple of hundred more songs to sing.'

The Beatles played Hamburg for the first time in 1960. They described Liverpool as 'pockmarked and shagged out' in comparison, the 'Reeperbahn was still open while Liverpool was shut.'

Not only had Granada built a brand-new studio centre in Manchester, they had developed a strong northern identity for themselves – with northern voices, northern programmes, northern idents. This immediately set Granada apart. It made them unmovable and led to the ITA deciding that all TV companies, large and small, should identify with their regions. Granada, Granadaland – these terms entered the nation's psyche so much that the terms still mean Manchester, Lancashire, Merseyside, Cheshire. For a decade 'Granadaland' vied with 'the north country' as the term used in the south to describe any godforsaken sooty town over two hours away from London by train. The people of the north, at thirteen million the biggest of all the regions, became citizens of Granadaland, and the local newsreaders spoke to them like neighbours.

By 1960 the cotton industry, which had flourished in the north-west of England for 150 years, was in terminal decline. The Cotton Industry Act of 1959 was intended to revitalise the Lancashire industry by helping cotton companies replace outdated machinery, but its practical effect was to close countless mills. During the 1960s and seventies mills shut across Lancashire at a rate of almost one a week.

The Football League gave permission for a scheme to, in the words of its secretary Alan Hardaker, 'arrest the alarming decline in football gates and extend the game's popular appeal as a spectacle'. The idea was 'to present football and the League in the best possible light and give the public, including millions of women who watch television on Saturday nights, a taste of the excitement and spectacle of first-class football'. So, on Saturday 10 September 1960 the match between Blackpool and Bolton was screened live on ITV. The match kicked off at 6.50 pm, so as to avoid clashing with any others, and the channel was able to screen the last ten minutes of the first half and the entire second half. Blackpool had agreed to be televised as they were confident of a good attendance thanks to the pull of the town's illuminations. With crushing inevitability, this example of 'the excitement and spectacle of first-class football' ended goalless.

1959

The opening images of *Room at the Top* stand as some of the most familiar in the history of British cinema. Black and white shots of industrial landscapes, majestic ageing railway stations and a young man arriving somewhere with a raincoat folded over his arm are instantly evocative of a certain time and place in the history of British cinema. The British New Wave is commonly seen as comprising nine films released between 1959 and 1963: *Room at the Top* (1959), *Look Back in Anger* (1959), *The Entertainer* (1960), *Saturday Night and Sunday Morning* (1961), *A Taste of Honey* (1961), *A Kind of Loving* (1962), *The Loneliness of the Long Distance Runner* (1962), *This Sporting Life* (1963) and *Billy Liar* (1963). The films shared characteristics: black and white photography, moody jazz scores and northern locations – Blackpool, Salford, Bolton, Bradford, Wakefield, Morecambe, Stockport, Manchester. Recurrent images of puffing steam trains, cobbled backstreets, mournful gasometers and deadpan railway viaducts gave the films the feeling of taking place at the crumpled end of the nineteenth century. The bus ride around Manchester that opens the film version of *A Taste of Honey* captures perfectly the oppressive and decaying world of time-worn military statues, smoke-grimed buildings and weather-beaten Victorian iconography.

After completing his National Service in 1959, John Ravenscroft spent six months working at the Townhead Mill in Rochdale. His father then decided that it would be a good idea if his son spent some time in the United States learning the cotton business. In the spring of 1960 John climbed aboard the SS *Eugene Lykes* bound for Houston, Texas. From Houston he caught a train to Dallas, where he worked for a firm at the Cotton Exchange.

In 1959 Bernard Manning borrowed £30,000 from his father and transformed a run-down billiards hall on the Rochdale Road in Harpurhey into the Embassy Club. Manning the family man came to the fore: 'Everything clicked into place. My sisters and my brother were going to go behind the bar. John, my brother-in-law, went on the door. Mum would work the cash till, Dad do the cellar and Vera keep an eye on the rest of the club. It was a real family concern, a right team, with few outsiders – and no fiddlers.' At that time his material was comparatively innocuous, but as white working-class Britain began to experience an influx of workers from Asia and the West Indies, Manning's act adjusted to reflect its anxious prejudices and concerns. It is not known whether he held the racist, homophobic and sexist views he expressed on stage or if they were just part of his act. 'I get up on stage and I do an act,' Bernard Manning once said. 'It's not me, just as an actor playing a part in a film isn't the character. I don't go home to my grandkids and say, "Fucking queers, niggers, they're all cunts." It's my act, not me. It's all a joke.' Manning would place visiting liberal journalists in seats near the stage, the better to torment them. The typical audience at the Embassy Club came from the working-class estates of Manchester and surrounding areas, even Liverpool. They seemed to enjoy being insulted by him. Revelling in his own repulsiveness was part of his act. It was as though his audience needed, demanded, to be wound up in order to deal with and confront the merciless stress and pressure of their everyday lives.

1958

The Preston Bypass was Britain's first motorway, opened by Prime Minister Harold Macmillan. The road was barely a motorway by later standards – two lanes each way with soft shoulders, a broad central reserve with a hedge and just one junction. It started and ended at roundabouts on the A6 to the north and south of Preston. The road, said Macmillan, was a sign that Britain was finally beginning the process of bringing its highways up to a standard that a modern country could be proud of. At this point press releases promised the sight of him pushing a button which would automatically cut the ribbon and unveil the plaque, but unfortunately the system couldn't be made to work, and so on the day there was no button and no ribbon. Instead, he simply revealed the granite plaque himself and then got into the first car of the motorcade.

1957

Roger McGough graduated from the University of Hull in 1957 after studying French and geography at the same time as Philip Larkin was head librarian and sub-warden of his hall of residence. They never met. McGough didn't dare speak to him – 'He didn't hang out with any of the students' – although he sometimes found himself in the same room as Larkin and described him as a 'toppling steeple of tweed. But I did send him some poems while I was there and he was very nice, very kind. I wouldn't have known what to say to him really, you know. I was a bit gauche then.' Larkin made the young Roger McGough realise that it was possible to be a poet and not be already dead. 'I'd grown up in Liverpool with a working-class, Irish-Catholic background. Men of my father's generation worked on the docks, but I was among the first of that post-war generation for whom education was available – I got a scholarship to go to grammar school, and then a university degree.'

Guardian writer Nicholas Wroe wrote, 'The publication of *The Uses of Literacy* in 1957 propelled Richard Hoggart, then an extramural lecturer at the University of Hull, to the forefront of the changes that swept British culture from the sclerotic 1950s into the swinging sixties. The book was a ground-breaking study of working-class culture and a critical appraisal of the changes wrought by the commercial forces . . . Not only did it anticipate the opening-up of the cultural landscape, it also contributed to a critical and popular climate far more receptive to the subsequent explosion of books, films and art about working-class subjects by working-class artists.'

John Braine's *Room at the Top* was published in March 1957 and was immediately and exceptionally successful for a first novel by a largely unknown author. Written in 1953–4 while he was being treated for TB at Grassington Sanatorium, it was initially rejected by several publishers. When it finally appeared, Braine was working as a thirteen-pounds-a-week librarian at Darton, near Barnsley, and living with his wife and two-week-old son on Doncaster Road, Wakefield. Within a month the BBC's *Panorama* had sent the journalist Woodrow Wyatt to interview Braine in Yorkshire and hail *Room at the Top* as the most significant novel for a generation. Braine told Wyatt he had no plans to relocate to London 'because it has ruined many potentially good writers'. (He would move south nine years later and begin the process of self-destruction.) The novel is set in the north of England, with its working-class protagonist Joe Lampton ruthlessly climbing the social ladder by seducing and marrying Susan Browne, the millionaire factory-owner's daughter, and abandoning an older woman whom he actually does love who tragically dies of drink. He wants to get rich as fast as possible, even though he hates the rich, and secure a source of individual power at a time when there was a general feeling of powerlessness. The book's genius was to tap into the mood of 1950s Britain, when old attitudes were disappearing and working-class people more than ever before aspired to join the middle classes, and when the idea of youth was rapidly developing as a separate class, a distinct cultural entity.

Elizabeth Raffald, cook, entrepreneur and inventor of the Eccles Cake

Joe says of his ambition, 'I was going to the Top, into a world that even from my first brief glimpse filled me with excitement. Big Houses with drives and orchards and manicured hedges.'

PART TWO

Through no fault of my own

I take a simple view of life. It is to keep your eyes open and get on with it.

Laurence Sterne

21

I was not born in the time before Christ was born, or in the time of the Romans, or Alfred the Great, or the Black Prince, or Elizabeth I, or Thomas De Quincey, or Emily Brontë, or Gracie Fields, or Jimmy Tarbuck, nor in Doncaster, or Rotherham, or Barrow, or Glossop, or Gloucester, Bath or Pontypool. I was not born outside England, anywhere on the planet, at any time between, say, 1234 and 1957. I could have been. I could have entered existence anywhere at any time, catapulted through an unbelievable gap that suddenly prised reality open, and found myself stunned and speechless where I happened to be, in time and place, obediently getting on with accepting, coping with, or even rejecting, where I was during whatever period of time.

There were millions of possibilities for where I could arrive on the planet, and on what date, at any point between, say, 1234 BC and AD 1957, and ultimately it might have been at any second, on any day, anywhere in the world. I ended up in a very particular place at a very specific time, with a date of birth stuck firmly inside the month of

March, in 1957, when most of the patterns, accents, attitudes and principles of the north were considerably established, when a vast amount
of social, political, legal, technological and economic history was in
place, and after the world had spent more than a century being transformed by a series of inventions, imaginings and innovations that had
made parts of life more convenient, pleasant and accessible, and parts
of life more gruelling, pressurised and crowded. I turned up, and there
was a time and place for me, and a lot to get used to connected to the
time and place where I did.

In the early 1960s through no fault of my own, I found myself, as a
young boy, duly breaking into awareness, six or seven, shy, reticent son
of dad Leslie and mum Dilys, skinny big brother of Jayne and, eventually, in 1966, Carol, living at number 12 Westbourne Grove in Reddish,
Stockport. I loved my mum and dad like a small boy loves his parents,
but I didn't know what love was in much the same way I didn't really
know where in the world I was. Slowly I would find out, if never fully
understand, what it was to love your parents, who were simply there
when you arrived, and to get to know where in the world I was, which
of course I had no say in deciding. Where in the world you found yourself after some kicking and screaming and catching of breath would
make such a difference, because it would slowly dawn on you that
where you lived was filled with meaning and detail you could spend
your life investigating and recording.

I was born two days after the American writer, essayist and editor
Christopher Morley died, and a newspaper obituary spotted by my
mother almost meant I was named after him. For a few days I was
nameless, as my parents had been expecting a girl – a boy, needing
a name, disconcerted them, upset their plans for a Kim Elizabeth.
I was not named after him in the end, but some of his interests
seemed to have become tangled up in my consciousness – how this
happened is either a miraculous transference through the Morley
name into my mind at the moment he died, or just one of those
things that make it into a writer's notes, and then make it into a
book, on this particular page.

He wrote an essay in 1918 entitled 'The Art of Walking', remarking
on the reflective practice of walking during a time when automobiles

were rapidly making 'the highways theirs beyond dispute'. I seemed to spend a lot of my time as a young boy walking, and as it happens reflecting, at a time when the car was well on its way to completing its conquest of even the backstreets of the world, and I never learned to drive, preferring always the walking, and reverie, to the extent of often being in the sort of trance as I wander and wonder that would be dangerous while driving. C. Morley in his essay notes how William Wordsworth would 'employ his legs as an instrument of philosophy' and how your true walker is 'mightily curious in the world, and he goes out of his way to sate himself with a thousand quaintnesses . . . walking will remain the mystic and private pleasure of the secret and humble few'. All great ideas, he suggests, are conceived by walking, with the brain working at the pedestrian speed of three miles an hour.

I lived in a district at the far north-easterly edge of Stockport named, it seemed to me without a care in the world, Reddish, which was too small to be called a town, and too big to be called a village. It was a fine place to walk, because whichever way you headed, there was something to see, even if that was nothing but a paving stone, a lamp post or shop window, all of which were new enough to me as a boy to send the pulse racing. I became an explorer of corrugated iron, drainpipes and gutters, which are strangely fascinating when you are fresh to them and have no idea of what else there is in the wider world. A matter-of-fact zebra crossing and a metal garden gate in a certain shade of green can for a while introduce a young mind to the spiralling miracle of existence; and the zebra crossing can give you a certain amount of power, stopping cars in their tracks, and the gate can be opened, leading to the creation of a brand-new moment where something unexpected could happen.

There were plenty of corners to turn, and places to visit at a later date, and high brick walls, fences and hedges that hid from view what might be nothing special, but what might be astonishing. The hidden remained astonishing, until I knew for sure that it wasn't. I learned from an early age to relish being lost, because then I would find new areas that I had not yet surveyed.

Reddish was very neatly if haphazardly laid out, small streets nicely leading to other small streets without it getting too built up, the occasional giant dingy mill turning its back on the present, so aloof it could make you feel a little paranoid. Back alleys were not intimidating, and there were parks, worlds within the world, and because this is the north, it was within reach and actual sight of the sort of open spaces running wild and free on the edge of farmland that could make you think you lived in the country. Reddish was not blocked in by the brick and muck of relentless urbanisation. It was, though, largely unassuming, and I am hoping to connect directly with what I thought as a ten-year-old who had nothing really to compare it with, rather than respond with my own later feelings about its tired, vaguely desolate atmosphere, where nothing was destined to happen now that Manchester, and Stockport, had spread this far, because they were full, and needed somewhere to deposit their leftovers.

For me, before there was a wider world, and wider spaces, and the thought of something out there, there was Reddish, and it's where I feel I came to life. Actually, there was North Reddish. South Reddish was in the direction of Stockport, and therefore in the direction of the big mucky town, and in the direction of where things were happening, at least locally, in the direction of main roads and big bus squares and stations that could take you all over the north, and even to the south, or its closest northern representative, Cheshire, which some considered the northernmost outpost of the genteel and posh Home Counties.

When Morrissey – whose songs tell very evocative stories about the combination of battered cobbles, magical Manchester rain, shady inner-city mystery and enchanting but gloomy and even dubious country in the middle distance – heard that I grew up in Reddish, he was immediately keen to establish that I was not from South Reddish, which did not quite have the same credentials as North Reddish in terms of establishing unstained honest-to-goodness northern-ness. The thought of South Reddish caused his lip to curl in distaste, perhaps purely because of the word South, perhaps because he knew more than anyone that nothing had ever happened in South Reddish, and nothing ever would. And if it ever did, how would you ever know?

22

1956

Granada House was the first commercial building to be built in Manchester after the war. That chairman Sidney Bernstein chose the city as the base for Granada Television and specified such a large and impressive building was crucial in Manchester's post-war regeneration. With its illuminated sign in then-fashionable Stymie Bold Italic typeface, designed in 1931 by influential designer Morris Fuller Benton of America Type Founders, Granada became an important landmark on the Manchester skyline, in direct modernist opposition to Alfred Waterhouse's old-style, garnished and gothic bustle. The four-acre site surrounding a basin on the Manchester Ship Canal had been purchased from the city council for £82,000.

It was only in 1956 that the government actually set about using the legislative tool it had created seven years previously. Work started on a short experimental motorway to bypass the industrial town of Preston in Lancashire. Preston was a major bottleneck on the road between the industrial heartlands of Lancashire and Scotland, the meeting point of traffic from Liverpool, Manchester and the Colne valley on the way north, and the only way to the thriving resort of Blackpool. Its bypass had been in planning for many years, and in many ways it was fitting that the town was to benefit from the first motorway push.

It was at the age of seventeen in 1956 that John Ravenscroft first heard 'Heartbreak Hotel' – played on *Two-Way Family Favourites* – and bought the record the very next day. As he later explained, 'Everything changed when I heard Elvis. Where there had been nothing there was suddenly something.'

1954

In 1954, after visiting Texas and recoiling from the materialistic post-war 'affluent society', J. B. Priestley coined the term Admass. 'This is my name for the whole system of increasing productivity, plus inflation, plus a rising standard of living, plus high-pressure advertising, plus mass communication, plus cultural democracy and the creation of the mass mind, the mass man. (Behind the Iron Curtain they have Propmass, official propaganda taking the place of advertising, but all with the same aims and objects.)'

In the same year Priestley's essay 'They Come from Inner Space' presented a critique of science fiction as he saw it at the time. Priestley argued that the interest in outer space was a move 'in the wrong direction' and maintained that SF should instead be 'moving inward' to explore 'the hidden life of the psyche'. He singled out American writer Ray Bradbury as a pioneer of inner space and added that although Bradbury used traditional SF motifs such as spaceships and Martians, he did so in order to 'show us what is really happening in men's minds'. Priestley held that men are not as rational as they like to think they are, but are also driven by the desires, urges and irrational instincts of the subconscious mind. For Priestley, the idea that people's actions are dictated solely by their conscious selves was akin to the equally fallacious assumption that 'what can be seen of an iceberg is all there is of it'. Priestley of Bradford thus becomes the missing link between Charles Dickens and J. G. Ballard.

1953

It was television which finally dealt the death blow to music halls in the 1950s, although the tradition lived on in the new medium with performers like Tommy Cooper, Ken Dodd and Morecambe and Wise, and most of all in the sentimentalised version of the halls provided by *The Good Old Days*. The first programme was broadcast from Leeds on 20 July 1953, and the series ran for thirty years.

Actress, entertainer, scriptwriter and comedienne Victoria Wood was born in Prestwich in 1953, and attended Bury Grammar School for Girls. 'If they like you in the north of England they won't say, "You were wonderful, darling!" They'll say, "You weren't bad" or "I didn't mind it."' For a sketch with a continuity announcer she wrote the line: 'I'd like to apologise to viewers in the north. It must be awful for them.' For another sketch she wrote:

Kitty is about fifty-three, from Manchester and proud of it. She speaks as she finds and knows what's what. She is sitting in a small bare studio, on a hard chair. She isn't nervous.

Kitty: 'Are you familiar with Marks?' she said. I said, 'Well, I think their pants have dropped off.' She said, 'I was referring to Karl Marx, who as you know is buried in Highgate Cemetery.' I said, 'Of course I knew! But were you aware,' I said, 'that Cheadle Crematorium holds the ashes of Stanley Kershaw, patenter of the Kershaw double-gusset? To my mind a far bigger boon than communism!'

1952

Actor, socialist, singer, poet, provocateur Ewan MacColl was born James 'Jimmie' Miller in Salford in 1915, to parents Betsy and William Miller. William was an iron moulder, militant trade unionist and communist from Stirlingshire. Betsy Hendry was from Auchterarder in Perthshire. When William was unemployed she supported the family, cleaning houses and offices, and taking in washing. Jimmie left school a week after he turned fourteen and worked briefly at a number of jobs, including factory hand, builder, mechanic and street entertainer. During this period he wrote for and edited factory newspapers, and for a short time wrote and performed advertising jingles for small businesses. In March 1930 he was made redundant. He then joined an amateur drama group, the Clarion Players, which later changed its name to the Workers' Theatre Movement.

Miller became Ewan MacColl in 1945, reflecting his Scottish roots and the fact he needed an alias after deserting from the army during the war. In 1952 he released the 78 rpm single 'Dirty Old Town', a folk song he had written about his hometown in 1950 to cover a set change in the Theatre Workshop production of his play *Landscape with Chimneys*. 'Dirty Old Town' seems to set to music the opening pages of Walter Greenwood's novel *Love on the Dole*. When MacColl first wrote it, the local council was uncomfortable with a direct reference to Salford, and after considerable criticism this was changed, a Salford wind becoming a less specific smoky wind. He was singing how for working people their surroundings may have been awful but were still special when in love. The awful slum dwellings he refers to were peeled away like layers of decay in the 1960s to make room for Salford's very own brave new world, which in turn became the high-rise nightmare that a mere thirty years later needed demolishing itself.

In 1952 Alan Turing, the founder of computer science, decades ahead of his time intellectually, philosophically and emotionally, was arrested and tried for a homosexual relationship with a young man from Manchester, where he had settled to research the theory of growth and form in biology. His only defence to what was then 'gross indecency' was that he did not think that he had done anything wrong, which was both naive, considering the times, and completely sensible. Turing avoided prison by agreeing to have yearly synthetically produced oestrogen injections to control his libido – chemical castration, a savage punishment even when male homosexuality was illegal in Britain. After having to endure the humiliating hormone treatment and the subsequent loss of his security clearance, which restricted his secret work for the government at the beginning of the Cold War, Turing took his life at his home in Wilmslow in 1954, aged forty-one.

His cleaner found him dead in his bed. Turing had died the day before, rumours suggesting it was from eating an apple laced with cyanide, a method inspired by one of his favourite films, Walt Disney's *Snow White and the Seven Dwarfs*. (It has been suggested that the Apple logo of the half-bitten rainbow-coloured apple was Steve Jobs' way of paying tribute to Turing.) Some have attempted to build a conspiracy around the tragedy, although the coroner's verdict of suicide seems plausible, the persecuted, desperate and then relatively obscure genius and war hero dying after swallowing cyanide, with the apple a mordant joke left behind to confuse matters. His mother rejected the verdict, suggesting he died after eating the apple with fingers contaminated with cyanide following a chemistry experiment. Some felt he had with convoluted last-minute kindness arranged it to look to his mother as though that was what had happened, that his death was an accident. It was a complicated, sordid and theatrical end to one of the century's most original, independent and questing minds.

23

Despite my home being North Reddish and close enough to danger, or existential grit, or a blazing, smoking, consuming industrial history, to satisfy the extremely picky local historian Morrissey, at the corner of Westbourne Grove stood the relatively imposing Reddish Conservative Club. It was an ugly misshapen brick building featuring a tangle of pseudo-turrets, stern arches and fussy windows that needed a lot of curtain material, surrounded by a rutted stony car park that had never been smoothed over with tarmac, the big gates of which were goal posts for scrappy street football between the Westbourne Grove kids and those from nearby Sykes Street. The opposite goal posts were on the other side of the road, a little off to one side, and were formed by an alleyway that went nowhere down the side of a couple of battered garages.

These lopsided garages were next to a modest, largely unchanging and often closed shop on the corner that sold bicycles, tyres, Airfix model sets and puncture repair kits. The shop was called Jones, which led to an exciting rumour that it was owned by fairly close relations of the jockey-sized lead singer of the Monkees, Davy Jones. This wasn't as unlikely as it seemed. The dinky Jones had been born in Openshaw in 1945, not far up the road from Reddish between Droyslden (where the first machine-made terry towel in the world was manufactured, and where Harry Pollitt, general secretary of the British Communist Party was born, son of a cotton spinner and a blacksmith striker, fifty-five years before Davy) and Gorton.

The son of a railway fitter, Davy grew up near Debdale Park, which contained a rudimentary nine-hole pitch-and-putt course which, at the age of ten, playing with my dad, I completed in twenty-seven shots, which is probably par for the course but seemed to me up there with Arnold Palmer and Gary Player. No one at school believed me; they thought I was showing off. When I went with them, under severe peer pressure I took forty hopeless shots. This seemed to satisfy them, and put me in my place as nothing special. They would soon forget all about me, as I seemed pretty forgettable. At the time Debdale Park, a couple of miles from Westbourne Grove, was about as far as I would go. It was the limit of my world for a year or two.

Davy Jones began acting in church plays in Lees Street, Higher Openshaw, and first appeared on television as consummate battleaxe Ena Sharples' grandson Colin Lomax in *Coronation Street*. This one-episode appearance led to him playing the Artful Dodger on stage in London. He then went on to appear on Broadway, New York, resulting in him being cast in the new Monkees television show, put together in 1965 – going on air in 1966 – as a mocked-up childishly subversive money-making Hollywood rival to the original Beatles of Liverpool.

The Conservative Club was the other side of the Gorton Road from the Essoldo Cinema, a big square block of brick with heavy brass doors that sucked you into darkness and light and the plush red seats that set you in front of most of the glamour that made it into Reddish. I think the first film I saw there was the widescreen epic *Zulu*, starring Michael Caine and Stanley Baker, released in 1964, which had at least twenty vivid colours never before seen in Reddish exploding from the screen, and clear signs of the existence of another (highly unlikely) continent. I saw *Lawrence of Arabia* there, another surely impossible continent represented, and Peter O'Toole dying at the beginning of the film, followed by the rest of the story, which was his life. I was very taken by this unexpected structural trick, and sometimes wonder if this was the moment something entered my mind that made me want to write – the fact that when you write, you can play around with time, and just by thinking about it create life after death.

The combination of the Davy Jones bike shop, the decorative Essoldo and the nearby dingy sweet shop jammed with treats next to a busy and basic brightly lit fish and chip shop, gave this end of Westbourne Grove a heady aura of excitement, a fuzz of fantasy, as if you might find treasure buried nearby, and an endless desert broken by the sudden insane emergence of the Suez Canal. The large forbidding Conservative Club, the size of a knocked-about pirate ship and with the presence of a cobwebby haunted house, actually helped. If the ball ever went close to the big front doors during a football game, I wasn't keen on going to fetch it – not that I remember ever seeing anyone enter or leave the building, which seemed dormant during daylight hours. The club was founded in 1899 by a group of individuals who up to then had met in rooms above the Reddish Post Office. The building they acquired in 1912, Summerfield House, had been constructed in 1870 as a home for the Shawcross family. Mr Shawcross was a partner in the hat-makers Barlow and Shawcross of Pink Bank Lane, Longsight.

For me, approaching ten years old, it was part of a world of play and adventure, at the end of my street, by the main road, and the sweet shop a first sign of choice, of possibility, just a few steps from my house. Its shadowy, taciturn owners, who were on the dark side of Dahl, even a whiter shade of Poe, were slowly drawn from the dark back of the shop by the bell that tolled as you pushed open the door. Once the bell sounded, and the door shut behind me, enclosing me in balmy fantasy, I would pause, for incredible thought. What to have? Lots of jars, and boxes, and layers of chocolate bars, all laid out in front while the owners loomed over me waiting for me to hand over, say, two sweaty dark brown pennies, which had a certain amount of buying power, leading to the deliciously stunning sugar rush, and how could I ever decide what I wanted like a kid in a sweet shop faced with rows and rows of: dolly mixtures, pear drops, pineapple chunks, Uncle Joe's Mint Balls, mint imperials, fruit-flavoured Polos, iced gems, Love Hearts, Spangles, spine-tingling Smarties in space-age tubes, coconut mushrooms, aniseed balls, Pontefract cakes, sherbet dabs, liquorice allsorts (allegedly created by accident in 1899, when clumsy salesman Charlie Thompson, representing Geo. Bassett and Co. of Sheffield, tripped up, jumbling up all the different sweet samples he was carrying, creating an almost psychedelic mix of sweets), liquorice bootlaces, Victory Vs, chocolate-covered cinder toffee, four-to-a-penny Fruit Salads and Black Jacks, which meant a farthing (from the Anglo-Saxon forthling, or fourth part) each, but the farthing was dead by the end of 1960, flying saucers, Penny Arrow chew bars, silver-foil-sealed Kit Kats (invented in 1935 by Rowntree of York – fifty-four years after they launched their sugar-coated fruit pastilles – as the two-fingered twopenny Chocolate Crisp following a suggestion from a worker that they produce 'a snack a man could have in his lunchbox', becoming Kit Kat in 1937 and then also four-fingered, snapping with such satisfying intent), multicoloured boxes and tins of Quality Street way beyond reach on the top shelf at the back of the shop (launched in 1936 by Mackintosh of Halifax, cele-brated toffee makers, inventively blending brittle butterscotch with soft caramel, founded by self-styled King of Toffee John Mackintosh in the late nineteenth century, who also made the more accessibly priced and packaged Rolos two years later, and in the early sixties the Toffee Crisp, crisped rice made into a chewy chocolate bar), and then there were Jubblies, fist-sized triangular blocks of rock-hard vaguely orange ice inside a cardboard wrapper fused to the ice so that it was hard to peel away, and you sucked at the corner until your lips were numb and stained, and your fingers ached, and you wished you'd chosen some gluey chewy Jelly Tots or been able to afford a sixpenny bar of Galaxy, which would need a neat silver tanner, or the unimaginably huge almost mill-sized ninepenny version, but you knew that you would never in your life ever get to have a shilling, twelve big brown pennies, or one weighty silver coin, called a bob? A shilling could take you into the chip shop next door, a vinegary blaze of white and sizzle, which smelled of something fishy that wasn't necessarily food. A shilling would never happen before at least eleven years old.

In the grocer's there was wanly pink boiled ham sliced so thinly you could see right through it and even thinner slices of corned beef that instantly disintegrated once they were unwrapped, which prob-ably contributed to me eventually turning vegetarian. Other meat regularly served in our house included glum liver the consistency of decay, gummy, fatty chops with enough bone-splintered meat on them to fill a matchbox, bitty sausages that split open like raw wounds, death-like mincemeat that wept for humanity when fried, and occa-sional shrivelled joints of beef the texture of polyester from cows seemingly killed centuries before. The memory of cheap, slithery margarine the colour of pus roughly spread on woolly slices of pallid white bread still makes my tongue beg for mercy. Eggs and chips were fried in a pan so old, permanently home to a congealed white pool of ancient lard, that the food came to the plate sprinkled in fragments of burned fat resembling iron filings and tasted as metallically gritty. For years I thought this was normal, in a world pre-pizza, pre-mayon-naise, even pre-curry, in which as a family we never once ate in a restaurant, dinner time was solidly situated in the middle of the day, and later there was tea, and then something posh never really experienced called supper.

All this food was prepared by my mother, although she wasn't really prepared, best at opening tins, baking rustic pies, knobbly crumbles, sloppy ground rice with a glum spot of jam in the centre, and relatively pleasing, because they were sweet, sponge cakes. This food was echoed at school, where daily dinners combined solid pies dense with ooze, vague vegetables and soggy sugary puddings encased in claggy custard that seemed to be breathing or at least wheezing.

I don't remember my dad making anything other than a pot of tea, eccentrically spreading marge on his Weetabix and dousing his Kellogg's Cornflakes in milk and sugar, but it was on our annual holiday with his mother by the sea in Margate where we ate our most formal family meals. Her small, austere semi-detached house, unmodernised since the war, two miles from the seafront, smelled ripe and sour at the same time, a blend of boiled sweets and dismay. At the time, she was known to me as Granny Morley, to separate her from my mother's mother, the gentler, wilder Granny Young, and as a Methodist, which meant that this was how I would describe my own religion. I had no idea what it meant to be a Methodist, and we never went to church, but I interpreted the idea of Methodism through the chilly, reproving demeanour of my Granny Morley, and the fact that at any given moment I would expect a rap on the knuckles for some perceived act of insolence.

We would solemnly eat together at a table complete with fancy tasselled chenille tablecloth and ominously laid-out worryingly polished knives, forks and spoons with well-used handles the colour of glue. The meals painstakingly prepared by my grandmother were basic and influenced by the rationing years but the most methodical of any we would have during the year outside Christmas dinner. To leave the table before the end of the meal would mean having to say 'excuse me,' although this rarely guaranteed permission. For a few years, my father would continue this tradition in his own home, until he just couldn't see the point any more.

The way Granny Morley fastidiously spread rich yellow butter – never margarine, proper butter was one of her personal treats – on her ritualistic teatime bread, smoothly covering all of the surface, from crust to crust, unlike my mother, who would scrape the thin marge roughly into a coarse blob in the middle of the slice, seemed to me the height of sophistication. The butter itself, which I occasionally had on a piece of freshly sliced white bread, coated my mouth like chocolate, and left me feeling vaguely giddy with something somewhere between pleasure and wonder. Nothing like that seemed to exist back in the north. Not one of her kitchen skills was passed to my dad.

Our summer holiday trips under endless sun-stirred blue skies to Margate, then a relatively refined seaside resort, perched on the tip of the Isle of Thanet, looking out across the English Channel, at the edge of the flat green Kent countryside, strewn with dignified orchards, labelled the Garden of England, made me feel something I could never quite put my finger on – it was so far removed from where we lived in Reddish, which seemed completely landlocked – until I read the writer Richard Hoggart (born in Leeds, 1918) describe how, to George Orwell, the north was a stranger place than Burma. Back home after a fortnight in Margate, Reddish always took some getting used to. Everything seemed smaller, darker, dirtier, sadder, colder, and lardier, with houses pressed into the ground not watching the skies. Dashing sea air was replaced by stale air. I grew up never knowing our relative proximity to both the North Sea and the Irish Sea – the English Channel over 200 miles to the south was the only sea I saw for years.

There were another couple of shops on the modest parade of commerce by the Reddish Conservative Club – a subdued, ordinary newsagent and a dead-looking shop which sold I cannot quite remember what – it might have been wool, cotton, scraps of material and lace doilies, it might have been something a little more sinister. I never went inside. Or, if I did, one version of me went inside, and another version came out with something else altogether on my mind, and more walking to be done. More walking, leading to new territory, to the creation of my surroundings, because there was so much time to fill in, and so many things to make present.

24

After the war the British government, keen to increase the available workforce in the country, invited West Indians to come to the 'motherland'. Of the so-called Windrush Generation – the first boatload of Caribbean immigrants was carried by the *Empire Windrush* in June 1948 – many settled in Moss Side, two miles to the south of Manchester city centre. Those from Jamaica moved from an Island described by Christopher Columbus as 'the fairest of them all' to a crowded smoky place where 'darkness was made visible' and where it really did seem to rain all the time. Fog got into their chests. The surroundings were semi-derelict. The locals seemed poorer than they were, with their unimaginative fatty food, and were immediately suspicious of 'these people'.

Hope that they would be eagerly embraced for their sparkling energy and welcome talents soon turned into bitter defiance as the new arrivals were faced with indifference and much worse as they found themselves banned, rejected, and shunned. They brought with them a distinctive set of skills and stunning new forms of exuberance and style, but ran into barriers, distrust and plenty of brick walls. They were largely left to fend for themselves, and improvised an outside community within their unpromising new circumstances. New churches, clubs, gambling dens, shebeens – unlicensed establishments selling alcohol to those working unsocial hours, a reaction to the local drinking hours – and music venues catered for spiritual and earthier needs. Vegetables and other foods much less plain than English post-war rations, familiar to West Indians but not seen before in Britain – yams, salt fish, black-eyed peas, spicy ways of fighting the wet and cold – began to appear in the shops. They set out to make themselves at home as best they could, made the best of what were often insulting and intimidating conditions, and contributed to a considerable change in local consciousness.

The area became vibrantly multiracial, spawning fragmented, mythical and obliquely influential music scenes springing up inside once-sturdy derelict houses that had been left to rot. The newcomers showed the locals how to party and made themselves hard to ignore. In the 1920s Anthony Burgess had lived as a child in an off-licence on the corner of Moss Lane East and Lincroft Street to the east of Princess Road in Moss Side, and thirty years after he sat in the family's combined dining and sitting room behind the shop listening to his crystal radio, the shop became a Jamaican shebeen, not far from a Rastafarian gift shop. He wrote in his autobiography of Moss Side in the 1920s being a respectable if ugly district with decent houses but already with 'the scent of coming seediness', where undernourished means-tested locals lived on bread and an egg every two days.

Walter Greenwood described Blackpool's distinct appeal in his 1951 book *Lancashire*: 'No other county than Lancashire could have produced Blackpool. It is a product of unconscious revolt, revolt of the masses against the horror of living 51 overworked weeks in hideous industrial towns. They want a holiday place in which they can give vent to their hysteria. Blackpool caters for this . . . Blackpool is unique.'

After the war George Formby found himself out of fashion. After *George in Civvy Street* (1946) the film offers dried up, but he continued to tour, and found a new outlet as a stage actor. He'd always loved pantomime: 'I look forward to it all year. It permits you to go crackers. You get to wear comic clothes and give vent to your feelings.' In 1951 George starred at the Palace Theatre in London's West End in the musical comedy *Zip Goes a Million*, which became a huge success. The show's extended run took its toll on Formby's health, which had already been weakened by his wartime exertions. While being driven home after a performance in 1952, George suffered a massive heart attack. He wasn't wearing well, as a man or a star, and perhaps there was something about him that sensed somewhere in the country, perhaps in the north-west not far from where he was born and bred, some kids who in ten years' time would become a musical group perfect for the times were mixing up their identity, energy, sense of humour and rebellion with flashy American input in just the right proportions to eventually completely replace him.

French writer Michel Butor taught at the University of Manchester from 1951 to 1953 in between stints in Egypt and Geneva. Jacques Revel, the narrator of Butor's novel *L'Emploi du Temps* (*Passing Time*), fulfilling a year's contract as translator for an English firm, largely detested his time in Manchester, which Butor called Bleston, specified only as an industrial town in the north of England. This reflected the miserable time Butor himself spent in Manchester, even though Butor said that in his early writing especially he wanted to have characters as different as possible from himself. As a writer, Butor tended to hide behind narrators and characters – the individual as a succession of individuals. Revel is 'dwelling in transit' in a city that is . . . 'a fusion of space and experience, a space filled with meaning, a source of identity. It is also a specific context for our actions, a configuration of objects and events filled in space, a milieu, as the French say. It is outside and inside us, objective and subjective, universal and particular. We live our lives in place and have a sense of being part of place, but we also view place as separate, something external.'

As 1950 approaches, it is over a hundred years since Benjamin Disraeli wrote in his novel *Conningsby*, 'From Hellenic Athens and classical Rome, to renaissance Florence and Georgian London, history is rich with examples of towns and cities which embodied the best of urban tradition. There were places that stimulated new ideas and transacted knowledge. They inspired generations in terms of their design, their economic strength and their cultural diversity . . . By contrast, more recent urban history has been dominated by a severance in the relationship between people and place. It is the philosopher alone who can conceive the grandeur of Manchester and the immensity of its future.'

1950

While some hoped that new technologically advanced manufacturing would take over with the decline of the old industries, this was not happening. By 1950 industrial decline was evident, and Manchester had lost its hold on its economic base and began to take on the appearance of what would come to be known as the deindustrialised city.

The Yorkshire Symphony Orchestra's regular conductor, Maurice Miles, suggested that a visit to London's Royal Albert Hall would be a prestigious, morale-boosting change from concerts in Armley Baths Hall or the Ritz Cinema in Doncaster. 'Nay, nay, Mr Miles,' barked one councillor on the orchestra committee. 'If London wants an orchestra, let them do what we've done and get one of their own!'

Alan Turing published 'Computing Machinery and Intelligence in Mind'. It was another visionary paper from his fantastically inventive mind and seemed to anticipate many ethical and technical questions which would arise as computers developed. He studied problems which today lie at the heart of artificial intelligence. It was in this paper that he proposed the Turing Test, which is today still applied in attempting to determine whether a computer can be intelligent.

25

I was surrounded by the north, embedded in it, on top of it, breathing, touching and receiving something northern that had been circulating since long before there was any sign of me. The north was waiting at the bus stop, on everyone's lips, sighted explicitly in the largest buildings that loomed up at the edges of my vision, towering over the houses that surrounded them as if they were on their knees, eyes shut, worshipping these high and mighty symbols of prosperity, or ego, or function, or ingenuity, or decline.

The north was right up my street, in my next-door neighbour Mrs Wilson. On her own, wrinkled, pointed and bent like a storybook witch, stubbornly resisting the modern world and kids with their comics, TV and sweets, getting in her way, clearly planning a world that would require more and more electricity, more and more frivolous comforts, and more and more television, which ruined everything, all her past, which she had saved up, like a miser, and was all she had. She would have worked at a mill, and knew all about the great noise of the girls' wooden clogs sparking on the cobbled streets as they all left for home at the end of a working day, or remembered such a thing through a golden haze of memory, as if such a thing really happened. She was so old in my eyes that now, thinking about her, she could easily have

featured in the introduction to the northern mill towns in Elizabeth
Gaskell's *North and South*.

Living on the other side, a couple, Mr and Mrs Brown, Christian
names kept well away from me, who would never know what to do
with such familiarity – elderly, less forbidding, but still bringing with
them in shadowy form what I was slow to realise consisted of such
things as the Second World War, Victorian hymns, Edwardian pride
and an idealised view of a northern atmosphere that Lowry would turn
into a smoky broken tragi-comic vision of brick togetherness and
isolated souls crowding around each other on flat, forlorn and framed
streets which contained great truth, fabricated memory and a riveting
myth that draped a golden haze over the rancid, immutable business of
poverty.

Here I was, in Reddish, of Stockport, near Manchester. Stockport
was regarded as one of Lowry's favourite towns, if favourite is the
word – one close enough on the bus or train to his house, where he
found the basis for much of what he liked to paint: a landscape stuck
in or to time, attractive to him because it was gathering dust, and
rusting, and darkening from within, where proud, stubborn, grum-
bling people were engaged in a stable and affectionate but corrosive
and imprisoning relationship with the environment that had been
built around, below and above them, a new sort of bound and belted
reality, which drained and distorted colour, which adjusted what it
was to be human and have a soul, and move from place to place and
moment to moment, day to day.

Stockport, filled with sudden turnings from the present to the past,
truncated streets leading to truncated streets, and sudden worn-down
grey stone steps that seemed to drop into the ground, for Lowry a
depleted wonderland of mill, pavement, lamp post, chapel and watch-
ful post box – and in the background a severe sense of loss: cryptic
alleyways, tilting walls, weeping gutters, people with nowhere to go
other than their own front door and the inside of their thin-walled
house, which was filled with secrets, or relative hard-earned cosiness, or
death, which is where cosiness ultimately leads, a life that he viewed as
beautiful, and inevitable, and for something so plain and everyday and
even ugly, he spotted poignant, even awe-inspiring signs of grace.

There is a photograph of a glum but content, heavyweight and over-coated L. S. Lowry hanging around on some steep steps in the centre of an early 1960s dependably overcast Stockport, and he seems very much at home, phlegmatically breathing in the soot, in a grounded world tipping over the edge of grey-washed black and white that still seemed as much made of smoke as it was of brick, populated by people who were clearly made up mostly of bones and the sheer effort of living. It's the sixties, but this is someone deeply entrenched in an early-twenti-eth-century north, where you layered shirts, waistcoats and trousers, many-pocketed for possible valuables and sundry possessions, as a psychological barrier against the clobbering of a hard world, and simply for warmth. It's a holiday snap of a doomed but self-possessed transient furtively revelling in the shady ruins of vigour and doing a bit of special-ised snooping.

Stockport, beginning in the north as soon as south Manchester petered out, in the west as soon as Cheshire lost heart, in the east within sight of Yorkshire, and in the south up to and almost including the northern reaches of Derbyshire. Near enough to Manchester for the Germans to drop bombs on the place during the Second World War, perhaps unused ones as they were flying away after hitting the city, lighter than when they arrived, making a different noise, satisfied with the destruction they left behind and their contribution to the turning of a city, a town, into something else, into broken bits of itself.

Stockport was, for me, at six and seven, off in the distance, the next step, a considerable change in circumstances, an opening of the mind, rarely visited with parents for the shops or nothing special on an echoey double-decker bus the size of our house patrolled by a restless, purposeful uniformed conductor, a complicated metal ticket machine slung jauntily around his neck, up and down the stairs from his spot in the corner of the bus, the wooden platform open to the road and the pavement as it sped past, which as you got older and bolder you would jump on and off as the bus moved away from or arrived at the bus stop, incurring the wrath of the squinting conductor, the bus drawing us down into magnetic Mersey Square, the restless shop-tangled centre of town.

Stockport contained Reddish, which contained Westbourne Grove, which was a small road containing two rows of small nondescript flat-fronted semi-detached houses built seventy years before, enough houses to home about thirty families, some of which I knew the names of. Reddish was where I came to, where I began to think there was such a thing as thinking, and therefore of remembering. For a while I had very little to remember, but slowly I banked up my memories, and five decades later these memories of experiences I was having as my mind formed at roughly the same time as my body, seem stronger than they did at the time, if lacking a newness, the robust, acquisitive newness that fills in the sort of details that made the experiences seem real, and not, as they now seem, dreamlike.

26

1949

On 16 September government permission is granted to burn the fuel required to bring back the Blackpool lights. A spectacular display on the cliffs portrays a deep-sea diver's world of tropical vegetation. At over 200 feet long and 22 feet high, it is an amazing sight. Actress Anna Neagle is the celebrity chosen to switch on the lights; other celebrities – sportsmen, singers, politicians, comedians and television personalities – follow her.

1950 Wilfred Pickles
1951 Stanley Matthews
1952 Valerie Hobson
1953 George Formby
1954 Gilbert Harding
1955 Jacob Malik (Russian ambassador)
1956 Reginald Dixon
1957 John H. Witney (US ambassador)
1958 'Matty' Matthews
1959 Jayne Mansfield
1960 Janet Munro

1961 Violet Carson
1962 Shirley Ann Field
1963 Cliff Michelmore
1964 Gracie Fields
1965 David Tomlinson
1966 Ken Dodd
1967 Dr Horace King (speaker of the House of Commons)
1968 Sir Matt Busby
1969 A Canberra bomber
1970 Tony Blackburn
1971 The cast of *Dad's Army*
1972 Danny La Rue
1973 Gordon Banks
1974 Wendy Craig
1975 Tom Baker
1976 Carol Ann Grant (Miss UK)

Wilfred Pickles said in 1949, 'May it be forbidden that we should ever speak like BBC announcers, for our rich contrast of voices is a local tapestry of great beauty and incalculable value, handed down to us by our forefathers.'

By the late 1940s Granada's attention was turning away from theatrical entertainment towards the fledgling television industry. As a theatre chain, it had taken the name Granada in 1930, chosen by its well-travelled chairman, Sidney Bernstein. He felt that the name's exotic connotations suited the image he wanted for the theatres. After requesting a licence to operate an independent television station in 1948, the company finally received a contract in 1954 to broadcast five days a week in all of northern England, becoming one of the four founders of Britain's Independent Television Network. Granada made its first black-and-white transmission on 3 May 1956, with a programme called *Meet the People*.

John Robert Clynes and Mary Elizabeth Harper, a textile worker, married in 1893. He died on 23 October 1949 and she soon afterwards.

'Our fourth leader, John Robert Clynes, he once said something very, very important. He said we come into Parliament not to practise the class war, but to end it. To end the abuse of power in the workplace, to end the inequalities of health and education, to end the waste of worklessness and the cruelty of crime. He said he came into Parliament to put into practice what it says on our membership cards: power, wealth and opportunity in the hands of the many and not the few. Those are inspiring words. Those are words that, if put into practice, would transform this country.' David Miliband, Labour Party Conference speech, 2010.

Increasing prosperity meant that more and more families could take a fortnight's holiday on the coast, and the seaside towns were in competition for a growing market. Many resorts believed that beauty contests were important in gaining publicity: in Morecambe beauty contests were seen as second only to the illuminations as its major tourist attraction. The Morecambe contest began in the summer of 1945 as the Bathing Beauty Queen. It was organised by the local council in partnership with the *Sunday Dispatch*. The first final was watched by 4,300 people in a continuous downpour and the winner was a civil service typist. According to the local paper, she received a cup, a 'paltry prize' of seven guineas and a swimsuit.

27

There were a few cars parked on Westbourne Grove, but this was in the days before the dominance of the car, and it was possible to play a scrappy game of football in battered Tuf school shoes – the only shoes I owned – on the street without having to stop more than once or twice an hour to let a car pass. Each house had a yard or two of garden in front of a deadpan door painted in one of a few neutral, unshowy colours and windows blocked with dainty lace and hints of curtain. The houses on our side of the street each had a basic back garden about twenty feet by ten, which ended with an uneven charred-brick wall roughly eight feet high tipped with scraggly barbed wire. On the other side was a creepy scrapyard filled with rusting corrugated iron, piles of rubble, old cars, tyres and broken bottles. The houses the other side of the road had smaller back gardens which each led through a gate to a narrow cobbled back alleyway. These houses more traditionally fitted the image of the classic affordable northern terraced house, with its distinctive style arising from the need for economy: small size, red brick (cheap and quick to build with), a shared chimney stack and scullery wall, small panes in the sash windows, slate roofs pitched low to save on materials, and a minimum of decoration.

There was only one tree in our garden, which never produced any leaves and therefore seemed made of the same dull grey-brown earth it grew out of. I don't think it did much growing. Thinking about it now, it seems more like a sculpture, a shape, a smudged mark in space and time that illustrated where nature itself had run out of inspiration. This was where I began to think, I suppose, about what it was to be someone else, somewhere else, as if the tree's stunted branches were the beginning of a bridge that I could cross over and emerge somewhere glorious.

I could climb up its scarred spindly trunk to a height of about six feet, and for this period of my life, at least until 1966, this was about the closest I got to feeling on top of the world, as if I knew everything there was to know. There was a branch that stuck out at a melancholy angle which was strong enough to support a cheap child's swing. I would sit on this swing and absent-mindedly rock back and forth, more reflections leading to the filling of the spaces in my mind.

In our back garden we also had a home-made-looking air-raid shelter. Square and dominant, you could not miss it, craggy copper-red bricks jammed together with coarse grey cement, a crude miniature version of a satanic mill minus a proud purposeful chimney, ten feet tall, probably that across, featureless, windowless and pointless, set dead centre between the house and the back wall. It was dark and damp inside, with suggestions of slimy emptiness and shapeless decay, and I have very little recollection of ever entering it, just in case. A certain timidity kept me from imagining it as a cave, a tunnel, any sort of adventure. I climbed on top of it now and then, reaching a brave new height even above the crooked tree, and sat there, surveying the whole world as far as I could see, mostly the placid backs of houses, which suggested to me that without brick there would be nothing in the world, and nowhere for people to go. Because bricks were Lowry's bread and butter, because for him they were the pillars of beauty, the beginning and end of decency, he was in the right place at the right time to paint that part of the universe that was so bricked up and bricked in it was a kind of primeval, time-worn cul-de-sac.

I never imagined the shelter being used, packed with neighbours knee to knee, as the determined, merciless German planes flew above them, a younger Mrs Wilson with husband away fighting, nervously chatting with Mrs Brown, husband closer to home, drinking mugs of tea and waiting for the all-clear siren and the relief, as the impassive droning and danger passed overhead. I didn't play war games much. I had boxes of cheap grey, green and navy Airfix plastic soldiers that you could line up in rows, and a box of more colourful even camp cowboys and Indians, but I never really knew what to do with them once they were lined up, except knock a few of them over. I did not have a fighting mentality, tended to be bullied rather than the bullier, and so never developed any strutting, threatening northern hard-man qualities and the sense that surviving in the world could be done through demonstrating toughness in the way you walked, talked, smoked, drank and, if necessary, hit someone. I was not cut out to be any sort of warrior or even any sort of niggly, annoying local hooligan, let alone an off-colour unblushing pub poet who did all his gruff rhyming, considering and slagging-off over a hard-earned pint.

I never heard any stories of bombs dropping nearby, or I didn't pay attention to whatever stories there were. Eventually our unlovely back-garden shelter was knocked down. My dad demolished it in a sudden rush of something that might have been anger, tearing into this big block of the past with a monstrous hammer, dropping a bomb on it in the madly focused form of his temper, which could be war-like, successfully hitting the target, and brick by broken brick it was removed, leaving behind the stark slab of scarred immovable concrete that had been its base. I would then use this as a penalty area for games of football using a rusty metal single-bed frame on its side as the goal. The bed's wilted springs made a wonderful substitute for a goal net, and sometimes the tennis ball I used would get stuck between two springs, giving me the sense of actually scoring and hitting the back of the net.

Turf was laid by my dad between the concrete base and the house, turf that never really became a Cheshire-style lawn, more a patchy collection of warped muddy grass squares.

These games were separate from playing in the street with neighbours about my age. I enjoyed myself more in these solitary games, creating tournaments in my mind, imagining matches, playing in them, creating rules that suited the garden's layout. When I was about eleven, I played more and more on my own, in my own world, having not made an impact as part of my school football team, not enjoying the rough competitive element of playing with others, which involved rules of engagement that I was not in control of.

I had a brief alliance with Westbourne United, a football team run by a stocky bow-legged twinkly local chimney sweep. He was called Frank Aspinall, although at the time I knew him only as Frank but maybe never even called him anything, not to his face. He lived at the bottom of Westbourne Grove and always seemed covered in the soot he swept out of the numberless chimneys in the neighbourhood. To my young eyes he was so gently ancient, uncomplaining and wrinkled, he could easily have lived in the nineteenth century, and his spindly black wire brushes and charred face seem now to have made him something I only vaguely sensed at the time, a blemished character in the background of a Lowry who had carelessly fallen from the canvas into the burdened modern world. No doubt my memory is playing tricks to suit this sort of book, but he seemed to be constantly coughing up phlegm, caused by a Woodbine habit that shook the smoke that gave him, just about, a living, deep into his ruined chest.

I was never happy in his team, possibly because this required a certain amount of discipline, morning training sessions and teamwork alongside tough ruddy-faced boys always aiming elbows at my ribs. It all felt a little dodgy, and the matches arranged did not seem very real, but I think this was the young me making assumptions based on my own reading of the situation, which was simplistic and prejudiced. I didn't like playing for Westbourne United, and I stopped going to the training and playing in the matches.

In fact, Frank Aspinall was a part-time scout for Stockport County, at the time mostly near the bottom of the Fourth Division of the

Football League. But they were one of the League's ninety-two teams, up and above the Northern Premier League, which was non-league and therefore irrelevant. Frank had actually discovered and nurtured some local youngsters who went on to play professional football, including Bobby Noble, who played for Manchester United, and Keith Newton, who played for Blackburn, Burnley and Everton. I either did not know this information, which would have excited me, or did not believe it, as there seemed no way to my biased young mind that this always filthy, slightly uncommunicative, rather crumpled chimney sweep could possibly have any connections with professional football. Locally, I learned later, he was seen as something of a hero, donating all his time and energy to encouraging and training young boys in Reddish and giving them the opportunity to play trials for local teams.

I kept myself to myself and didn't turn up for training, not realising that adults talk to each other. Frank told my dad I was not attending training; I must have told my dad that I was. He was furious with me, and grabbed the ball one day as I was playing my solitary game in the garden, dreaming of greatness in a match against imaginary superstars, scoring astonishing goals in a setting entirely of my creation that transformed our small scruffy garden into a magnificent stadium. He shouted at me, his attitude based on information I did not have, about letting poor, generous Frank down, and told me what an embarrassment I was, why I was stupid for playing on my own and not joining in with others and, possibly, going on to play for Stockport County. I think I had a suspicion – which I now wonder is me now wondering, and which I did not actually have at the time – that he was so angry with me because he recognised something of himself in my behaviour – his inability to make friends, or if he did, keep them.

After this shock, an education into how other people had feelings and that there were consequences if you didn't turn up to do something you said you would, I soon reverted to my solitary football world, where I was everything I wanted to be. I did not return to Frank's team, now too embarrassed to show my face. I reverted to kicking a ball around the garden on my own, which must have looked odd to anyone watching me, but as far as I was concerned it was a game of great skill, built around rules that made complete sense. In a world where it was hard to get the sort of attention I was seeking, which might have made me feel more confident about myself, I set myself at the centre of my own attention, where, in all the fantasies I created, I was tremendously talented.

If my ball went over the wall at the back of the garden, I faced up to the terrors on the other side and climbed over. I needed to get it back because it was the only ball I had to play football with, and losing it would mean, for a while, losing everything, even if it was no more than a tennis ball so battered and faded most of its fibres were missing, revealing bare patches of rubber. The ball was an essential part of my meagre set of toys at the time, which included two Subbuteo balls, the big brown one for football, preposterously almost as big as the little Subbuteo players themselves, the tiny red one for cricket, a flimsy blow-football ball, a floaty table-tennis ball, a full-sized red plastic cricket ball with moulded seam, a faded rare hard cricket ball that wasn't authentically leather but still stung the hand, and chipped glass marbles, never many at the same time, most of them lost within weeks. My first feeling of loss, of real, desolate grief, was not because of a dead relative, friend or neighbour, but when a red plastic ball modelled to resemble a real leather football, proudly bought earlier in the day for a few pennies, burst on the end of a rusty nail in the garden. It instantly turned from something that enabled me to dream and lose myself into a few miserable scraps of useless plastic, and I was consumed with a sadness that made me want to brick myself up in a corner of the world where no one would ever find me.

The wall was greasy, the bashed moss-streaked bricks always seemed soaked with rain even on sunny days, and once on top I would look down what seemed an awful long way on an area filled with chunks of barbed wire, weeds, shards of glass, brick dust, smeared sweet wrappers, grimy pop bottles filled with a liquid the colour of something someone had decided was waste, although it was hard to believe that all the rubbish at the bottom of the wall, which had gobbled up my poor tattered ball, had ever had anything to do with being human. This was a discarded north outside the perversely glorifying frame of Lowry, and the other side of the immediate northern border to my existing personal territory.

Jack Bond, captain of Lancashire Cricket Club in the late 1960s

I slid down the rough wall, scraping skin off my hands and knees, into the other side, which was as soft and greasy on landing as rotting flesh, with jagged shapes and scraps of metal sticking up in the direction of my bony white legs, and strange sudden possibly animal movements at the edge of my vision. I squeezed between the wall and the back of some sort of derelict shed, with no sign of my valuable ball, and felt in no doubt I might be trapped there for ever. If I didn't find the ball, history and time would stop. If I found it, then everything kept going, and everything was as it should be.

28

1948

It was a significant event for the University of Manchester when shy, funny, free-spirited, nail-biting genius, thirty-six-year-old Alan Turing joined the mathematics department. Turing, whose thinking ranged across philosophy and psychology to physics, chemistry and biology, joined the department as a reader, with the nominal title of Deputy Director of the Royal Society Computing Machine Laboratory. He had been a full-time member of the team of mathematicians at the wartime Bletchley Park code-breaking centre and was awarded the OBE in 1944 for his vital contribution to the war effort.

In work that remained secret until long after the war, Turing is credited with helping to break the code used to encrypt communications with the German U-boats operating in the North Atlantic, which were sinking merchant ships bringing much-needed supplies to Britain. Some historians have suggested that without this breakthrough a war claiming millions of lives every year might have continued another year or two. Turing had long imagined a machine that could think in the way a human brain did, and in 1949 an astonishing machine connected to the urgent requirement for a British atom bomb was built at Manchester by the Royal Society Computing Machine Laboratory. It was the very first practical application of Turing's computer principle based on his 1936 paper 'On Computable Numbers with an Application to the Entscheidungsproblem'. The Manchester Mark I was nicknamed The Baby or Small Scale Experimental Machine, and was one of the earliest electronic computers. Occupying a large part of the top floor of the engineering building, its vast size was due to the fact that an enormous number of electronic valves were used for its construction (transistors were not yet available). Turing envisaged a computer able to switch at will from numerical work to algebra, code-breaking, file handling or chess playing. He was a pioneer of computers for personal use and one of the first to use a computer for mathematical research. There are those who therefore argue he both defeated Hitler and gave us computers.

Davyhulme, six miles west of Manchester city centre, bound by the Rivers Irwell and Mersey, can be traced back to the twelfth century, when it was the seat of John de Hulme. It is assumed that 'Davy' was prefixed to 'Hulme' to distinguish it from Hulme in Manchester. In 1948 the minister for health, Aneurin Bevan, conducted the symbolic inauguration of the National Health Service at Davyhulme's Park Hospital (now Trafford General Hospital). He received the keys from Lancashire County Council; nurses formed a guard of honour to greet him, and for the first time hospitals, doctors, nurses, pharmacists, opticians and dentists were brought together under one umbrella organisation providing free treatment for all at the point of delivery. Sylvia Diggory (née Beckingham) was the first NHS patient – she was thirteen. Before she died, Sylvia said, 'Mr Bevan asked me if I understood the significance of the occasion and told me that it was a milestone in history – the most civilised step any country had ever taken, and a day I would remember for the rest of my life – and of course, he was right.' The hospital also witnessed the first baby born under the NHS, weighing six pounds eleven ounces, named Sandra Pook.

The decision to take children's shoes off rationing was the subject of a speech given by Harold Wilson on behalf of the Labour government in Birmingham in July 1948. 'The school I went to in the north was a school where half the children in my class never had boots or shoes on their feet,' he declared. The schools that young Harold had attended were soon objecting strongly. The mayor of Huddersfield declared that when Wilson had been at New Street Council School in Milnsbridge there had never been any children without shoes. There was awkward backtracking, with confused excuses about clogs not counting as boots or shoes. The 'barefoot speech' aimed to give the impression of great crusading progress; in reality, as the mayor of Huddersfield pointed out, it wasn't true.

In 1948 David Hockney won a scholarship to Bradford Grammar School, one of the best schools in the country. In Keighley Road opposite the statue of Sir Titus Salt in Lister Park he enjoyed his art classes most and decided that he wanted to become an artist. Furthermore, he disliked the other subjects he was required to study. It was also in that year that Kenneth Hockney took his son to see Puccini's *La Bohème* at the Alhambra Theatre in Bradford's Morley Street. It was the first opera the future stage designer had ever seen. In 1950 he asked to be transferred to the Regional College of Art in Bradford so that he could pursue his interest in art more seriously. However, the BGS head-master recommended that he first finish his general education before transferring anywhere. Previously making good progress, Hockney responded by behaving badly and with poor grades. He spent his class time doodling in notebooks. Nonetheless, his artistic leanings won him prizes and recognition, and he drew for the school newspaper. Overall, he was a likeable and intelligent student with many friends. He once said: 'East Yorkshire, to the uninitiated, just looks like a lot of little hills. But it does have these marvellous valleys that were caused by glaciers, not rivers. So it is unusual.'

W. H. Auden was besotted by the north Pennines in particular, and limestone in general, and in 1948 even wrote a poem entitled 'In Praise of Limestone'. He clearly had extensive knowledge of the Pennines and his works make numerous references to remote places that could only be known by exploration on foot. In America in 1947 an Ordnance Survey map of Alston Moor hung on the wall of Auden's chaotic shack on Fire Island (and later in his house at Kirchstetten), and he told Geoffrey Grigson in a letter of 17 January 1950, 'My great good place is the part of the Pennines bounded on the S by Swaledale, on the N by the Roman wall and on the W by the Eden Valley.' Despite living in Birmingham and attending school in East Anglia, Auden's mind was irresistibly drawn towards the north. In December 1947 in an article for *House and Garden* entitled 'I Like it Cold', he wrote,

Though I was brought up on both, Norse mythology has always appealed to me infinitely more than Greek; Hans Andersen's *The Snow Queen* and George Macdonald's *The Princess and the Goblin* were my favourite fairy stories and years before I ever went there, the north of England was the Never-Never Land of my dreams. Nor did those feelings disappear when I finally did; to this day, Crewe Junction marks the wildly exciting frontier where the alien south ends and the north, my world, begins.

North: cold, wind, precipices, glaciers, caves, heroic conquest of dangerous obstacles, whales, hot meat and vegetables, concentration and production, privacy.

South: heat, light, drought, calm, agricultural plains, trees, Rotarian crowds, the life of ignoble ease, spiders, fruits and desserts, the waste of time, publicity.

Sooty's birth occurred in 1948 when, during a family holiday in Blackpool, a Yorkshire engineer and part-time magician named Harry Corbett came across a glove-puppet teddy bear in a novelty shop at the end of the seaside resort's famous north pier. 'I'd always had a thing about teddy bears,' Corbett said years later. 'And this one had a cheeky face. It was almost as if it was saying, "Don't leave me here."' So Corbett paid 7s 6d (38 pence) for the bear and returned to his boarding house with his new partner-to-be wrapped inside a brown paper bag.

1947

From 1905 to 1924 the Newcastle press used every other description but Geordie to report the triumphs of Newcastle United and its supporters: they were by turns Tynesiders, Novocastrians, Northumbrians, Magpies, North-country men, Newcastle excursionists or Northerners, but not Geordies. There is no definitive meaning to the term anyway. As a place to start, Newcastle City Libraries 'Fact Sheet Number 5: Origin of the name Geordie' offers four original meanings: a supporter of the Hanoverians at the time of the 1745 Jacobite Rising, a name given to coal miners, the nickname for George Stephenson's pit safety lamp and a term for the Tyneside dialect dating back to Stephenson's oral evidence to Parliamentary inquiries in 1826. The BBC Home Service programme *Wot Cheor Geordie* was immensely popular from 1947, and had as its signature tune Jack Robson's 'Wherever ye gan you're sure to meet a Geordie'.

Les Dawson attended Cheetham Senior School, and began his semi-professional career in 1947, in the same venues as Bernard Manning. Before his fame Dawson wrote poetry – a guilty secret for someone of his earthy background – and he harboured literary ambitions throughout his career. He wrote many novels but was publicly regarded solely as an entertainer, and this saddened him. Having broken his jaw in a boxing match, Dawson was able to pull grotesque faces by pulling his jaw over his upper lip. Dawson and Manning first performed at Lee Road Social Club in Harpurhey, where Dawson was immediately popular, as he came to be all over the working-men's club circuit of the north-west.

29

The Reddish houses and streets stretched all the way to Stockport, which was, as far as I could tell from my irregular trips with my mum, made up of miles of countless buildings constructed out of bricks and slate standing guard each side of endless roads, which I had very little idea about but which, as far as I could tell, took you all the way to Manchester, which I knew about because I would hear it mentioned, because my dad worked there, and every day we received a copy, around four in the afternoon, delivered as if by magic through the door, of the *Manchester Evening News*. The ink would still be wet inside a small box on the front page where the latest cricket scores had been printed like a bulletin from heaven. This brought me news, exciting even when I was seven, of the lunchtime score a few hours before of the Lancashire County Cricket team. Because the ink was wet, this cryptic, crooked information, which would generally report something like 'Lancs 113–4 H.Pilling 64 no v Glouc' and nothing more, seemed to glisten with modern magic, and no news that Google can now instantly supply me with can equal the marvel of knowing so quickly how Lancashire were getting on against some English county that seemed as far away and mysterious as the other side of the Iron Curtain.

This cricket news for some reason became an early addiction, and the damp blurry latest score, those numbers that meant something next to places with names that already had their own character because of the shape of the letters and the rhythm they made, helped me to begin piecing together the universe as a combination of evidence and mystery that required careful examination. The expanding universe at first was made up of the seventeen counties that played first-class cricket, and I made my first move out into that swelling cosmos to go and see Lancashire play cricket at Old Trafford. This required a train journey, which meant I realised that next to Reddish was another place, and then another, and then another, and that it was not all alone in the world. One street led to the next; one railway station led to another; you could move from one place to another; each place was named; each place was where people felt as unchallenged and as secure as I was where I had been placed.

The idea of the county gave me my real first sense of a tangible locale bigger than just the streets I lived in – although I did not attempt to work out why I happened to be in the county I was and simply took it for granted that because of where I was I followed Lancashire. That would soon seem like a choice made for heroic and important reasons, and then seem like Lancashire had chosen me, because of my virtues.

Lancashire were one of the counties in the Cricket County Championship, and these counties were for me inevitably superior to what were called the Minor Counties, which had their own pretty much invisible competition. This, then, as far as I thought it through, was the heart of the country, the seventeen counties that I list here in the order they came in the 1967 final championship table: Yorkshire, Kent, Leicestershire, Surrey, Worcestershire, Derbyshire, Middlesex, Somerset, Northamptonshire, Warwickshire, Lancashire, Hampshire, Sussex, Glamorgan (the one county outside England), Essex, Nottinghamshire and Gloucestershire. Essentially this meant that the two great northern counties, Lancashire and Yorkshire, plus the Welsh Glamorgan, were pitted against counties from the lower midlands and the south, the non-Danelaw Anglo-Saxon heartlands, from where it seemed the game had spread. Cheshire was Minor, the thought of which had quite an impact on my consciousness, slightly tarnishing its exoticism and cultivated airs and graces, which meant it was consigned to the world of first-class counties' second elevens and those apparently less powerful, somehow more delicate counties such as Dorset, Bedfordshire, Berkshire, Suffolk, Wiltshire and Devon.

Cheshire, though, as I learned as I became more experienced in my love of cricket, tended to be at the top of the Minor Counties table, so all was not lost. Cheshire was Minor, but within that superior, so my picture of where I was, with all those other counties simply somewhere else, was not significantly degraded. In fact, Cheshire's position in my mind as king of the Minors seemed to support the picture that they were not like any other county. To some extent they were a fantasy county, coming into and around and through the north with a special sensibility that was limper and more subdued than the more emphatic counties, more intangible than the mighty two northern counties, but also more quixotic.

I grew to love the structure that the County Championship appeared to impose on the wider world, even if this was a structure filtered through cricket. I sensed, somehow, perhaps from the nature of the game – complex but thrilling, taking its time, where patience met urgency and with very particular rules and regulations, played on an area of unspoilt summer grass marked out into very specific shapes, with players in pure white positioned in important parts of the playing area in ways that seemed deeply symbolic, some of those players sporting various types of protection that made them look part warrior, part angel – that cricket brought with it not only history, but also the very reason why England was what it was. My sense of England developed as I followed how players from the various counties represented England, so that I began vaguely to piece together a sense of the dynamic of a nation in which elegant opening batsmen tended to come from southern counties, and furious fast bowlers, greased-back hair flapping manically as they bore down through a red mist on Australians and Indians, were tough, threatening and beguiling northerners – suave Brian Statham of Lancashire, bolshie Fred Trueman of Yorkshire.

Even if this order was reversed, and stolid, careful, almost paranoid northerners opened the English batting, and tough, uncompromising fast bowlers from counties in the south hurled the hard red leather ball at aggrieved if defiant representatives of a collapsed empire, there still seemed something of how the nation was itself divided, into counties, into regions, into different characters, through the way cricket, and the players, organised themselves, and represented their counties, and, possibly, in occasional enforced unity, their country. This was the ethereal, gentlemanly conclusion of centuries of tribal rivalry, the separated kingdoms, competing interests and colonising/conquering temperament of the eccentrically compiled nation distilled into this highly ritualised competition, where the idea of battle, of gaining territory, protecting interests, removing members of the enemy, piercing their armour, tactically outwitting them, had been transformed into this cryptic, philosophical and serene-seeming abstraction. Englishness had culminated in a unique way of translating and modifying centuries of invasive, controlling exuberance and consolidation into a pattern arranged out of attack, defence and protection.

There are players who are specialists in certain areas of the game, some requiring strength, composure, determination, power, a strong arm, some requiring intelligence, persistence, imagination, a quick eye, all of them needing concentration and good judgement, led by an unruffled captain who at his best personifies the sensible, the controlled, the calculating, and yet the ingenious, righteous and perceptive. This game can seem chaotic and/or banal to the outsider, packed with pointless effete repetitions, never really beginning, never really ending, a futile pursuit of futility itself, but is to the insider an enthralling accumulation of patterns, conclusions, internal battles, surprising moments, implicit tension, small triumphs, stunning disappointments and, even while a result, a conclusion, is never guaranteed, an overall victory.

Sometimes, because this open-air game is only a shadow, a polite charming echo of tempestuous combat, rain and bad light are deemed an intrusion on the game, something that ruins the moment. The

Alderley Edge, Cheshire

weather has the last word, and often brings the game to an early end. This infuriates the non-believer, as hours and days of effort and endeavour can come to stupid rained-off nought, but further excite the believer, who understands how this game reflects the nature of life itself, where nothing is sure and/or everything changes from moment to moment, or stays exactly the same for vast stretches of time. Sometimes, however much you want something, and fight for it, nothing really happens: life goes nowhere, and there is an empty feeling, but also a sense of anticipation, for the next game, the next over, which could make everything burst into life. Other times, one shot, one catch, even one dropped catch, and the game shows how out of nothing life itself becomes life itself and who knows what will happen next.

I didn't think about it like that at the time. I started to watch Lancashire during a good period, when they were becoming the very best at a new abbreviated form of cricket played in one day, often a Sunday, in which each side bowled a limited number of overs. Lancashire players were kings of the sponsored forty-over format, launched in 1963, which offended traditionalists with its commercialised bluntness but excited a new audience.

Cricket's unhinged elegant crystallisation of skill and discretion, which could take days to make its point, which was often pointless, a grave matter of deadlock, was refined or coarsened into something shorter, faster and more explicitly argumentative. The one-day game was less stationary, and even though it could still be curtailed by weather or dwindling light, there was a greater chance of one side winning, and one side not doing enough to win. The one-day game was more of a clash involving clear dispute rather than a drawn-out encounter hinting at a minor difference of opinion twice removed. Three-day county cricket and five-day test cricket still leaned towards the seductively epic, but the commercial single-day format, without cutting too many corners, translated a complicated set of equations into a purged and thrilling accumulation of additions and subtractions.

Lancashire's cricket team – I quickly found out because I was obsessed enough with the county team I started to watch when I was ten, in 1967, and breathlessly looked up their statistics and backgrounds in cricket manuals and magazines – was made up of players who were mostly from Lancashire or a scant few miles over the border. Without thinking about it or even really knowing it, the names of the places where those Lancashire players born in Lancashire came from gave some sort of clue as to the nature of Lancashire itself, and why those players played the way they did, and spoke the way they did. Even those from outside the county seemed to devote themselves to the fierce, proud Lancastrian cause, so that when belting rangy batter and spectacular fielder Clive Lloyd arrived from the West Indies, and the wildly enthusiastic Farokh Engineer, deft wicketkeeper and flamboyant, even camp, slightly erratic batsman, landed from Bombay, India, they were instantly Lancashire, and Lancashire itself was made richer, and harder to beat, because of these legendary test players from the other side of the world.

Engineer and Lloyd joined Harry Pilling of Ashton under Lyne (settlement by ash trees, possibly 'under the line' of the Pennines, considered in 1769 to be bare, wet and almost worthless), my favourite player, small and perfectly formed, with neat pre-Beatle black hair tidily side-parted, in first wicket down, after either Geoff Pullar of Swinton (swine town, in the city of Salford on the gentle south-west slopes of the River Irwell) or Barry Wood of Ossett (a fold frequented by blackbirds, over the Pennines between Wakefield and Dewsbury). Pilling of Ashton scored the first century I ever saw made in a match, 112 out of 284 against Northampton, after Wood had made a duck, enough to make the ten-year-old me marvel at the idea of Lancashire, and cricket, and fiercely competitive number-three batsmen bravely marching into war, and then working hard and making something out of nothing that went all the way to 100, a number it had taken all my life to count up to.

Lancashire, as a thing to be loyal to, expanded in my mind seeing such batting a few miles from where I actually lived. There was Ken Shuttleworth of St Helens, eleven miles to the east of Liverpool, twenty-three miles from Manchester city centre, 1901 birthplace of George Groves, sound recordist on the famous first talkie in 1927, *The Jazz Singer*, Oscar winner for best sound for *Yankee Doodle Dandy*, *Sayonara* and *My Fair Lady*, whose father George Alfred founded the first brass band in St Helens. Dour, direct middle-order batsman David Lloyd was 'Bloody 'ell, my backside's a fire engine' of Accrington (acorn-ringed town, between Burnley and Blackburn, with a soft cultivated accent all of its own, where you catch the 'buzz' and 'them up Burnley Road' means those in the cemetery, twenty miles north of Manchester city centre, producing famously hard-wearing super-dense bricks used for the Empire State building and Blackpool Tower, rapid nineteenth-century industrialisation and a century later riots between locals and Asian and Caribbean immigrants).

Committed, energetic fast bowler Peter Lever – gently pushed into cricket by his parents because it would be 'better than hanging around street corners', apprentice to the great Lancashire bowlers Gorton's Brian Statham and Ken Higgs of Kidsgrove, Staffordshire, a few miles south of the Cheshire border – of Todmorden, birthplace of Keith Emerson of ELP, right on the border between Lancashire and Yorkshire, seventeen miles from Manchester, the border running through the centre until the 1888 Local Government Act, when it was nudged into the West Riding, but with an Oldham postcode, so of Yorkshire with a Lancashire pull, its town hall built astride the border, and a name made up possibly of two words for death, tod and mor, so that it means death death wood, or in Old English marshy home of the fox. Todmorden cricket club, where Lever started playing, was the only Yorkshire team in the Lancashire League.

Lever's debut for England in 1969 was against a Rest of the World team hastily assembled to replace a South African team exiled from test cricket due to the apartheid regime. Lever took seven wickets, those of Eddie Barlow, Graeme Pollock, Mushtaq Mohammed, Gary Sobers, Clive Lloyd, Mike Procter and Intikhab Alam – arguably the greatest batsmen on the planet at the time. This was Lancashire ruling the world.

Off-spinner John Savage was born in Ramsbottom (valley of the ram or possibly wild garlic valley) in the Irwell valley four miles north of Bury, the skyline dominated by the 124-foot Peel Monument on Holcombe Moor, built for the nineteenth-century prime minister and founder of the modern British police, Sir Robert Peel, for his help in repealing the Corn Laws, with views across west Yorkshire, north Lancashire and Manchester, to Blackpool and Wales in the west.

At the time I didn't know anything of the history of the county or of cricket, and how, perhaps, cricket is rooted in the thirteenth-century game of club-ball, which itself might have emerged from a tenth-century game played by children using a bat and a ball – and *cricce* is a Saxon word meaning crooked stick. Something, though, took me to the game, and to Lancashire, which was just a word but, because of the cricket and the idea of a team representing the county, meant more to me than just a word; it was where, and therefore who, I was, and what I could become part of – even if initially that meant batting at number 3 for Lancashire, and bowling the occasional deadly bamboozling spin that put me on the very edge of being a cherished all-rounder, one who could now and then even do a spot of wicketkeeping, padded- and gloved-up like someone who had some important guarding and attacking to do. Now and then I might turn out for Cheshire, and I had a soft spot for Surrey and an affection for Kent, my dad's county. He was deeply Kent, to the extent that in the north he was from far, far away, across so many boundaries and borders and rivers and hills, and different shades of history and meaning, that he appeared, inside rough, plain and shrivelled Reddish, to be from another country, representing another race, and all but speaking another language.

Counties and the parishes within them were originally political constructs imposed on the land by invading forces, and counties have somehow retained some of their authority. Sometimes this is because their borders are what they are because of some sort of fixed geographical feature, because of coasts, rivers, hills, forests, mountains. They fit around natural contours, and in between a coast line and on one side of a particular mountain range. Sometimes they do not and seem entirely arbitrary, and yet have continued to inspire loyalty whatever political and historical changes have ensued.

Shires were originally West Saxon territorial units, spheres of administrative responsibility, many based on old tribal districts and retaining Celtic roots in their names. 'Shire' came from *scir*, meaning district; these developed in Wessex in the eighth century and then spread through the country as Wessex itself gained more land. They were run by the shire reeves – sheriffs – the oldest secular office in the country after the crown.

Wittgenstein flying a kite in Glossop in the summer of 1908

The Saxons rejected Roman social organisation in favour of their own ideas of community and cultural structure, which the Normans were happy to maintain when they took over. The Saxon shires constituted a practical and uniform administrative system leading to an efficient method of raising local taxes. The wealth generated made England a tempting target for invading forces. The original five shires of Wessex were Devon, Dorset, Somersetshire, Wiltshire and Hampshire, followed in the ninth century by Kent, Sussex, Surrey, Middlesex and Essex. Cornwall became one of the Wessex shires in the tenth century. Those formed out of the 'reconquest' of the southern Danelaw, the East Anglian provinces of Norfolk and Suffolk and the shires of Bedfordshire, Buckinghamshire, Cambridgeshire, Cheshire, Derbyshire, Gloucestershire, Herefordshire, Hertfordshire, Huntingdonshire, Leicestershire, Lincolnshire, Northamptonshire, Nottinghamshire, Oxfordshire, Shropshire, Staffordshire, Warwickshire and Worcestershire, were created out of Mercia again some time during the tenth century.

Yorkshire represented the remnants of the vast Viking kingdom of

Jorvik, and emerged in 954 as the most northerly shire. After 1066 the Norman word *comté* – which became 'county' – replaced 'shire', as the new French rulers aligned the *scir* scheme with their own administrative understanding, and continued in the north the successful southern uniformity. Where the shire system existed, the Normans were able to detail every manor, but in the dubious areas in the north towards the fluid tenebrous border with Scotland, their Domesday surveys were less complete and sometimes did not take place at all.

Six new counties were formed in the Norman era – Rutland was granted an independent existence from Nottinghamshire by 1159, Lancashire was created in 1168 and the counties of Westmorland and Cumberland in 1177. County Durham and Northumberland were not completely integrated into the shire system until the sixteenth century and their territorial boundaries not finally set until 1844. In addition to these thirty-nine historic counties of England there are the forgotten Anglo-Saxon shires of Winchcombshire and possibly Stamfordshire as well, plus the later northern 'peculiars' of Norhamshire, Bedlingtonshire, Islandshire, Salfordshire, Hexhamshire, Tynemouthshire, Heighingtonshire, Carlisleshire, Hullshire and Staindropshire.

The division of England into the classic thirty-nine became the basis for English history, our sense of the country, and where we belong within it, and from the Normans to the twentieth century the borders of the counties stayed more or less intact, and certainly their names did. This meant that real allegiance to their shapes and names developed and also the idea that these were permanent places that contained the places, neighbourhoods and streets where we lived which themselves existed in the way they did because they were inside a particular county. The county we lived in, more in England than in Britain as a whole, could supply a powerful sense of rootedness and meaning in a world that could seem extremely confusing and futile. The sense of county – the one I was on the edge of, Lancashire, as much as the one I was inside, Cheshire, or was it the other way round – was as a youngster the first real hook I felt that pulled me into a sense of belonging.

30

1946

'A Plan for Todmorden' was the enterprising brainchild of town planning consultant Thomas Sharp, commissioned by the Borough Council and published in 1946 in response to the severe difficulties the town then faced. In his 36-page pessimistic report Sharp warned: 'The town finds itself in a difficult, even desperate situation. It is difficult enough to predict with any assurance the possible future of the cotton industry as a whole; it is even more difficult to attempt to estimate the future of cotton in Todmorden.' Had the suggested improvements gone ahead the impact would have been tremendous. 'These improvements would, I believe, give Todmorden a town centre which would not in the least be pretentious or grand, but which would be orderly, efficient in character with the town, and worthy of it,' concluded Thomas Sharp. The plan came to nothing.

Broadcaster Jimmy Savile is credited as the first modern British DJ, using twin turntables for continuous play after he obtained two domestic record decks welded together. He first used this device to play to the public in 1946 at a nightclub called the Ritz on Whitworth Street, Manchester, which had opened in 1927. Records could bring just as much musical excitement as a live band, a lot more variety and a whole new form of anticipation, rush and noise into a room, a club, a space, an atmosphere.

J. B. Priestley's *Bright Day* was published in 1946. He fictionalised Bradford as Bruddersford:

> Lost in its smoky valley among the Pennine hills, bristling with tall mill chimneys, with its face of blackened stone, Bruddersford is generally held to be an ugly city; and so I suppose it is; but it always seemed to me to have the kind of ugliness that could not only be tolerated but often enjoyed; it was grim but not mean, and the moors were always there, and the horizon never without its promise. No Bruddersford man could be exiled from the uplands and blue air; he always had one foot

on the heather; he had only to pay his tuppence [two old pennies] on
the tram and then climb for half an hour, to hear the larks and curlews,
to feel the old rocks warming in the sun, to see the harebells trembling
in the shade.

Less than a hundred years earlier, Priestley's hero and mentor Charles
Dickens had fictionalised an amalgamated Preston, Oldham and Manchester
as Coketown in *Hard Times*. Dismissed initially as 'sullen socialism', the novel
gained new life with F. R. Leavis's positive critical treatment in *The Great
Tradition* (1948). Leavis considered *Hard Times* Dickens's masterpiece and
'his only serious work of art'. Dickens contributes to many of the subsequent
northern stereotypes that follow, as if he invents a myth of the north as much
as he invents Christmas – based on definite source material but with inevitable imaginative embellishments.

It was a town of red brick, or of brick that would have been red if the smoke
and ashes had allowed it; but as matters stood, it was a town of unnatural
red and black like the painted face of a savage. It was a town of machinery
and tall chimneys, out of which interminable serpents of smoke trailed
themselves for ever and ever, and never got uncoiled. It had a black canal
in it, and a river that ran purple with ill-smelling dye, and vast piles of building full of windows where there was a rattling and a trembling all day long,
and where the piston of the steam-engine worked monotonously up and
down, like the head of an elephant in a state of melancholy madness   it
contained several large streets all very like one another, and many small
streets still more like one another, inhabited by people equally like one
another, who all went in and out at the same hours with the same sound
upon the same pavements, to do the same work, and to whom every day
was the same as yesterday and tomorrow, and every year the counterpart
of the last and the next.

1945

In the 1945 Manchester Redevelopment Plan, the city surveyor R. Nicholas
boldly claimed that 'in many respects the Manchester citizen of 1650 was in

a better position to enjoy a healthy life'. He painted a grim picture of the city in which people were condemned to live under a cloud of 'perpetual smoke . . . which enfeebles the health-giving property of the sun's rays and lowers our general vitality and ability to resist infection'. Nicholas posed the question: 'Is Manchester prepared once again to give the country a bold lead by adopting standards of reconstruction that will secure to every citizen the enjoyment of fresh air, or a reasonable ration of daylight, and of some relief from the barren bleakness of bricks and mortar?'

The 1945 Labour government faced the twin problems of modernising the cotton industry and attracting labour back to it. The mills of Lancashire were working flat out to produce exports to save the British economy. The government's slogan was 'Britain's Bread Hangs by Lancashire's Thread'. In this situation modernisation fell by the wayside. The failure to modernise was not a consequence of entrenched trade union practices but a lack of employer confidence in the future. The return of international competition in the 1950s was the death knell of the Lancashire cotton industry.

In 1965, during the optimistic forward-thinking Wilson era, A. J. P. Taylor completed his boisterous *English History 1914–1945*, in which he concluded that the Second World War was when Britain had embraced modernity – before the war Britain had relied on its traditions, now it was compelled to develop new industries. 'Imperial greatness was on the way out; the welfare state was on the way in. The British Empire declined; the condition of the people improved.'

An Inspector Calls is a play written by J. B. Priestley in 1945 but set in 1912. He penned it in a single week, the very week after the Second World War finished. Priestley chose 1912 because the date represented an era when everything was very different. There are many ways in which it resembles plays set in the north of England in late Victorian times or in the years before the First World War. For example, *Hobson's Choice* (written by Harold Brighouse in 1916, set in Salford in 1880) and Priestley's own *When We Are Married* (set in his birthplace of Bradford) deal with domineering business-men and local politicians whose weaknesses and failings of character are exposed. In 1912 rigid class and gender boundaries seemed to ensure that nothing would change, yet by 1945 many of the dividing lines had been breached. Priestley wanted to make the most of these changes. Through *An Inspector Calls*, written just ahead of the creation of the welfare state, he encouraged people to seize the opportunity the end of the war had given them to build a better, more caring society. Priestley made some trenchant observations about the importance of community, stressing his view that everyone, regardless of class, should look after everyone else.

In the 1945 general election Harold Wilson stood as Labour candidate for Ormskirk and won. The new MP, aged twenty-nine, became parliamentary secretary in the Ministry of Works, a major job with so much war damage to repair. Two years later Wilson became secretary for overseas trade and then almost immediately entered the Cabinet as president of the board of trade. He was the youngest minister since William Pitt.

At the start of Blackburn's July 1945 wakes week, the first since the end of the Second World War, holidaymakers queued at the town's railway station from early morning to catch one of twenty-three trains. The following week fourteen trains set off from Accrington. It was estimated that 250,000 people crammed into Blackpool that Saturday.

31

We wrote the end of our address as Reddish, Stockport, Cheshire because Stockport was in Cheshire, and since 1901 Reddish was in Stockport. Reddish, though, was one of those places on the edge of things, in between places, succumbing to the slight but significant border adjustments that ensued over the decades and centuries. Reddish was in Lancashire as much as it was in Stockport, so could seem to be in Lancashire and Cheshire at the same time, or possibly in neither.

In 1974 major changes were made to county borders, and Stockport was transferred into one of the bright new administrative regions, Greater Manchester. A brief call to name this area SELNEC – like something from a Brian Aldiss short story concerning the emergence of a future language or dialect to control perception and expression – standing for South East Lancashire North East Cheshire, came to nothing. The SELNEC PTE – Passenger Transport Executive – had been in operation since 1969, coordinating rail and bus transport in the area. The municipal operators were split into three divisions – Salford and Manchester were Central, Northern included Bolton, Bury, Ramsbottom and Rochdale, and Southern comprised Oldham, Ashton and Stockport. Each division featured SELNEC's S logo in a different colour – blue for Central, magenta for Northern and green for Southern.

An incongruous post-swinging-sixties orange and white colour scheme was selected for the SELNEC vehicles, and for a few years white or cream – which quickly attracted grime – buses striped with sunglow orange looked right but very wrong charging through the steadfast rain and streets of the area. Right because this was the era of Concorde and glam rock, but wrong because cheerful orange did not bounce well off the standard backdrop to be found within a few miles of Stockport – industrial or rural, the orange did not work. Perhaps it was chosen because the colours used by the eleven fleets absorbed by SELNEC – Manchester, Salford, Stockport, SHMD (Stalybridge, Hyde, Mossley and Dukinfield), Oldham, Ashton, Rochdale, Bury, Bolton, Ramsbottom and Leigh – had covered the more standard red, green, maroon, blue and white. The new organisation wanted to break away, especially from Manchester red and white, and orange was one of the few unused colours. Orange was also appropriated rather awkwardly as a sign of the glittery moving times to represent a modern image by companies such as Sainsbury's and WHSmith.

In Stockport the trams that had glided around town since the very un-orangey first decade of the twentieth century had stopped running in 1949 – the last tram ran through Stockport on the Manchester–Hazel Grove route – and it had taken nineteen years for these would-be-trendy orange and white buses to arrive, turning the town away from the stuffy remnants of the nineteenth century and on course for a surely sleeker, lighter future. In this future even conductors adding life and characterful motion to the buses' seating areas were extinct, and you paid your fare as you got on, with glass doors folding behind you with a modish *swoosh*, a seductively synthetic noise closely related to the noise of Dr Who's materialising – or dematerialising – Tardis.

The orange was, on the one hand, not romantic or super enough, and on the other, not murky and preoccupied enough. This was not a colour scheme of interest to regular solitary bus user Lowry, for whom a bus was dark, more dour and practical, a muddy hard green or a jaded red, the top deck coated with the degraded smell and memory of the green smoke and coughed-up phlegm and spit of pensive, faded others, and not part of a world where appearance and frivolous brand image were decided by the sort of indiscriminately past-hating committees and consultations that felt flared-trouser orange was appropriate in Bury, Hyde and Ramsbottom.

The scuffed orange slapped around Stockport as if it was part of some system of commercial and administrative encouragement to the town to 'get with it'. Buses must be up-to-date, as the main way of broadcasting how efficient and up-to-date the local council was, and buses that once looked like they drank flat-out bitter now looked more likely to smoke a joint, if they smoked at all. Buses that once looked like they were matter-of-factly losing their hair now seemed to be wearing undignified fake wigs and speeding through traffic lights with an iffy aura of self-conscious cool.

In 1974 towns and villages and populations were shunted between counties and administrative areas, crossing borders at the whim of the authorities in a way that governmentally meant little, but psychologically and practically could be very disorientating. Reddish was not only split between being both of Lancashire and of Cheshire, it was now in neither. It was officially in Greater Manchester, which, following the SELNEC boundaries, exploded into the middle of an accepted natural-seeming set of borders that had been settled for centuries.

It had taken some time for the shape of Cheshire to settle down. As with the nations that eventually solidified as England, Scotland and Wales, county boundaries ebbed and flowed over centuries as tribes (Cornovii, Ordovices, Brigantes), civilisations (Celts, Romans, Vikings) and kingdoms (Mercia, Gwynedd, Northumbria, Wessex) jostled for position, fought, conquered, and were conquered. The border with

Francis Lee of Manchester City celebrating a goal as City beat Newcastle 4–3 to win the 1967–8 First Division Championship

Wales was particularly volatile if not as violent as that between England and Scotland. It was finally fixed in 1284, with Cheshire bordered by counties, a country and the sea, connecting the midlands with the north, and England with Wales, and Wales with Liverpool and Manchester.

Most of the borders between Cheshire and whatever was next to it were natural geographical features. These features were if nothing else clearly where something should come to an end and something else begin. There was the far north-west limit, where the Wirral Peninsula was surrounded by the Irish Sea as the Mersey and the Dee became estuaries. To the north, Cheshire was separated from Lancashire by the Mersey, and along the north-east, not far from Reddish, there was a short stretch where it was separated from Yorkshire by the Pennines. There was a border to the east with Derbyshire, which used rivers, and to the south-east with Staffordshire along the tightly twisting River Dane. To the south, the boundary with Shropshire followed (a little erratically) the watershed between the Mersey and the Trent. The border to the south-west with Flintshire used various brooks that fed into the Dee. The border with Wales and Denbighshire to the west clung to the Dee. The boundaries of Lancashire in the north were Cumberland and Westmorland, in the east Yorkshire, and in the south Cheshire and Derbyshire. To the west was the Irish Sea, with all that was beyond – can you imagine?

By 1835 the changes to society caused by the Industrial Revolution had exposed cracks in the county system, especially where borders between counties were along rivers that bisected rapidly expanding towns. The Mersey, separating Lancashire and Cheshire, flowed through the middle of Stockport, and so someone living only a few yards north of the river was not able to use the local facilities south of the Mersey. They would have to travel further north into Lancashire. Heaton Norris, a small Lancashire district tucked in north of the Mersey, was handed to Stockport, but remained in Lancashire, so that part of Stockport was now Lancastrian. Further minor adjustments during the nineteenth century, including small gains from Lancashire, small losses to Lancashire, Derbyshire and Shropshire, led to a substantial expansion in the size of Stockport when, needing more land, it incorporated Reddish in 1901. In 1931, as Manchester expanded to the south, Northenden, Baguley and Wythenshawe moved from Cheshire into the city.

Lancashire produced the great cities of Liverpool and Manchester, which then to some extent broke free of their parent, and became the equivalents of counties, great conurbations sprawling at the eastern and south-western limits of the county that had nurtured them. There was much about the cities that was straight Lancastrian, but as one of the elements inherited from Lancashire and deposited into Liverpool and Manchester is a sense of independence, they existed entirely separately from the county. They were once part of Mercia – spiritually, sort of geographically, possibly merely historically they still were part of Lancashire – but by 1974 they were legally and officially on their own.

There is, if discreetly, much about Liverpool and Manchester that is Cheshire, as much as the two cities were in, and what they were because of, Lancashire. This mixing of Lancashire and Cheshire – with all the other mixing that took place, from all over the world in Liverpool, and from all over the nation in Manchester – meant that there was a great difference between these cities and the inland Lancashire cities, the character of which was formed by less cosmic and not so cosmopolitan external pressures.

32

1944

The German V-1 flying bomb, or doodlebug, was the first guided missile used in war. The characteristic buzzing sound of its engine caused considerable fear, but then relief if it then faded into the distance. If the engine cut out, it was time to take cover, as the missile was on its terminal dive and about to hit. In the early hours of Christmas Eve 1944 German bombers flying over the North Sea launched V-1 flying bombs at Manchester. Most missed the city, but one landed at 5.50 a.m. on a terrace of houses in nearby Oldham. It killed thirty-seven people, including some evacuees from London, seriously injured sixty-seven and damaged hundreds of homes.

Hull was the most severely bombed British city or town apart from London during the Second World War. Of a population of approximately 320,000 at the beginning of the war, approximately 192,000 were made homeless as a result of bomb destruction. Much of the city centre was completely destroyed and heavy damage inflicted on residential areas, industry, the railways and the docks. Little was known about this by the rest of the country at the time since most radio and newspaper reports did not reveal Hull by name but referred to it as a 'north-east' or 'northern coastal' town to avoid giving information of value to the enemy. Consequently, it is only in more recent years that the damage to Hull has been acknowledged. The city was an obvious target because of its port and industrial activity, and an easy one because of its location on the east coast at the junction of two rivers, but Hull often took hits meant for more inland places, or from German aircraft fleeing down the Humber to the open sea after failing to find Sheffield, Leeds or other northern towns, the victim of pilots who needed to dump their bombs. Remarkably, the port continued to function throughout the war.

In 1944 a poll showed George Formby to be the most popular figure in Russia after Stalin. In his films (over twenty blockbusters) he always played the underdog who succeeds in the end; rich toffs are portrayed as bad-tempered, idiotic, bullying and small-minded.

1943

Born in Liverpool in 1943, George Harrison grew up with the music of Lancashire comedian George Formby, as did all the Beatles. Formby's huge popularity meant that the sound of the ukulele banjo, particularly his own rhythmic style, was a familiar part of life.

The Second World War put a temporary brake on Blackpool, although Leonard Thompson said, 'Entertainment is about the only commodity that isn't rationed.' During the war years Blackpool's Pleasure Beach remained open all year round, enabling thousands of evacuees and service personnel to escape the reality of war for a short while.

The BBC's glorification of 'ordinary people' as heroes of the national struggle did not suddenly emerge out of nowhere, but was the result of a thorough remapping of the symbolic representations of nationhood that had taken place earlier, a complex process in which individuals and institutions from film makers like John Grierson, via popular magazines like *Picture Post*, novelists and social critics like George Orwell, J. B. Priestley and Walter Greenwood, organisations such as Mass Observation and the Pilgrim Trust, social investigators like Seebohm Rowntree – born to Joseph Rowntree in York in 1871, 'the Einstein of the Welfare State', committed to helping the poor and the disadvantaged, arguing after the First World War for the introduction of a family allowance and a minimum wage – to artists like L.S. Lowry, whose visual remapping of the north became central to shared perceptions of the meaning of the nation and national identity.

1941

Eric and Ernie first performed together on 28 August 1941 at the Empire Theatre, Liverpool, as Bartholomew and Wise, but soon made the change, having rejected the idea of using both their birthplaces, given that Morecambe and Leeds sounded like the name of a building society. Eric recalled, 'My mother was talking to Adelaide Hall, the coloured American singer on the bill, and explaining to her how nobody liked the name Bartholomew and Wise. Adelaide's husband, Bert Hicks, overheard and said that he had a friend who called himself Rochester because he came from Rochester, Minnesota.' Bert asked Sadie where she came from.

'Morecambe,' she replied.

'That's a good name. Call him Morecambe.'

Julie Goodyear was born Julie Kemp in Heywood on 29 March 1942, daughter of Alice and George. He walked out soon after, and her parents divorced. She was brought up by her mother and stepfather Bill Goodyear. While at school she wanted to be a singer but eventually decided to take up modelling. In order to fund this she trained as a shorthand-typist, worked in an aircraft factory, sold washing machines and worked as a waitress. She also served behind the bar in her stepfather's pub in Heywood, the Bay Horse.

Wilfred Pickles became the first national newsreader with a pronounced northern accent in December 1941, signing off each night with a hearty 'Goodneet.' His appointment was a ploy by Minister of Information Brendan Bracken to foil Nazi propagandists, who had become skilled at imitating BBC 'Oxford English'. His unconventional style created a furore and he was caricatured mercilessly by London cartoonists, who depicted him with his shirtsleeves rolled up and wearing a muffler and cloth cap.

33

As part of the county reorganisation of 1974 – the culmination of changes begun over a century before when modern local government was established – Liverpool and Manchester, while remaining part of the historical counties of Lancashire, and of Cheshire, and in Manchester's case a slice of West Yorkshire, became the centres of the administrative and ceremonial counties of Merseyside and Greater Manchester.

The name Greater Manchester had more of a sense of locality than the invented Merseyside, although the latter expanded Liverpool sensibilities throughout the new area more coherently and instantly than Manchester distributed any Mancunian spirit through the areas of Lancashire and Cheshire that it absorbed. Liverpool was always more inside itself than Manchester, more set apart from the history and geography of Lancashire, creating a singular cultural personality from within that tended to confound political and social systems vainly imposed upon it. Its accent was outside Lancashire, expressively other, ahead of the time, post-1974, when the Manchester area accent would move away from the soft, broader, chummier Lancashire, with an edgeless Yorkshire bruise, and closer to the demonstrative and unparalleled Liverpool hybrid of interruptive, argumentative foreign outsider and edgy, insular insider. Liverpool was more of a detached sovereign territory, almost an island following its own rules, its own standards and internal strengths and weaknesses.

Cheshire lost much of the northern Wirral to the new Merseyside, keeping Ellesmere Port, and gained Warrington and Widnes from Lancashire. Those who had happily lived in Lancashire since they were born were handed a Cheshire address, which for many was an outrage. A whole chunk of Cheshire (Longdendale, Stalybridge, Dukinfield, Hyde, Bredbury and Romiley, Marple, Hazel Grove and Bramhall, Cheadle and Gatley, Stockport, Ringway, Bowdon, Hale, Altrincham, Dunham Massey, Carrington, Warburton, Partington and Sale), the most removed from its traditional Chester centre near the Welsh border in the west, became part of the new Metropolitan County of Greater Manchester, both administratively and geographically (though not for postal purposes).

People in Sale – one of the world's first commuter towns, emerging along the new railway routes of southern Manchester in the 1840s – were still likely to write their address as Sale, Cheshire, though, if only from habit, ancient allegiance or because, for any number of reasons, Cheshire seemed a better, less artificial place to be than Greater

Manchester. The new metropolitan county comprised ten administrative districts: Bolton, Bury, Manchester, Oldham, Rochdale, Salford, Stockport, the invented Tameside and Trafford, and Wigan. Those in Wigan would still mostly say Wigan, Lancashire, because Wigan, Greater Manchester seemed either too new and awkward, or a bit contrived, and local roots went deep into the idea of Lancashire. Allegiance to the name of a place and the name of where it was showed how place names represented history and identity as much as anything, and an arbitrary adjustment to any part of the name of the place where you lived could be considerably disconcerting.

Manchester Airport, once very much of Cheshire, when it was known as Ringway, was placed entirely inside Greater Manchester, although appropriately for a place where the world came and went, later expansion of the airport would see it extend back into Cheshire. Parts of Yorkshire were administratively passed to Cumbria, Lancashire, Greater Manchester, Humberside, Cleveland and County Durham, causing considerable grief among those who had invented steady, inspiring identities as Yorkshire folk. However, even with boundaries moved and land removed, the county was still the largest, taking up about 10 per cent of the nation.

Those who lived in Ulverston – birthplace of comedian Stan Laurel, Christine McVie of Fleetwood Mac, and Maude Green, mother of Bill Haley – north Lancashire, north of Morecambe Bay, and 'north of the sands', now found themselves in another county, Cumbria, itself a new invention. They were suddenly called Cumbrians, as though their history could be abruptly rewritten, the geography changed and their identity altered. The Tan Hill Inn in the North Yorkshire Dales, reputedly the highest pub in Britain at 1,732 feet above sea level, mere inches above the Cat and Fiddle on the Cheshire–Derbyshire border, has been moved back and forth between the Yorkshire and County Durham sides of the Tees – switched from the North Riding in the 1974 county reorganisation when Teesdale was shunted into County Durham, and later moved back into North Yorkshire.

The historical counties still existed, but there were many who resented this technical fiddling with these existing regions which were far too psychologically and culturally set into the mental and physical landscape of the nation for them to simply disappear. People having over centuries been made to accept borders, regions, local authorities, were now shifted into a new place where the map itself was being redrawn, no doubt to be redrawn again, as if to undermine the very certainties that this new infrastructure intended to define. Those on or near the borders slipped through gaps and often switched counties without moving home.

When the slicing up and renaming of counties happened in 1974, I was ignorant of the details, as much as I was of what had happened to the counties in the nineteenth century, but felt the changes, which came not long after the decimalisation of the pound, which gave money, so fixed in solemn shape for so long, a sense of unreliability if not downright quirkiness. Twelve pennies to a shilling and Stockport being in Cheshire were now, it seemed, outdated. A world made up of long-established patterns of common ground was being taken apart, and although I had no loyalty to much of the old, most of which I was racing away from with the natural forward-looking appetites of a teen-ager annoyed, irritated and impatient with traditions and elders and their superior, commanding and guarded ways, the new world seemed a little flimsier and unformed. This made the need to find things that were personally certain and existentially firm even more urgent.

34

1940

For three nights leading up to Christmas the Luftwaffe bombed Manchester. The city was ablaze, with many of the fine historic warehouses of Portland Street set alight or razed to the ground. This was the Christmas Blitz of Sunday 22 December to Tuesday 24 December 1940. On the first night 270 aircraft released 272 tons of high explosive and 1,032 incendiary bombs. On the next night 171 aircraft dropped another 195 tons of high explosive and 893 incendiaries on central Manchester and Salford. More than 650 people were killed, more than 2,300 injured. Within a mile of Albert Square and the town hall, 165 warehouses, 150 offices, 5 banks and over 200 business premises were destroyed or so severely damaged that they subsequently had to be demolished. Many major buildings were wrecked or destroyed: the Free Trade Hall, Cross Street Chapel, the Corn Exchange and Smithfield Market. Within days the medieval pubs of the Shambles, apart from the (still surviving) Wellington Inn and Sinclair's, had been wiped out. Only one English cathedral – Coventry – took more bombs than Manchester's. The city would never look the same again.

The first Manchester air-raid sirens were heard after the surrender of France on 20 June 1940. There were minor German raids on Lancashire, and on 29 July a bomb fell on a hut in Salford at the corner of Trafford Road and Ordsall Lane. Two weeks later, on 8 August, an aircraft dropped Nazi propaganda leaflets on Salford containing a translation of a speech by Hitler.

In 1940 the band Jack Hylton had formed in 1923 entered the recording studio for the final time. By April seven important members had been called up for war duty and Hylton decided to disband the orchestra permanently. The Second World War accomplished what the Depression had not been able to do. Running a dance orchestra was an expensive and demanding task, but the band had been a magnet for the best musicians in Britain, and the British public knew it. Jack Hylton concluded that once musicians of the calibre he required were no longer available, it was time to give up bandleading. There was never a decline for Jack Hylton's orchestra; only a peak of perfection and then abrupt silence. Hylton didn't retire. He had already established himself as promoter and talent spotter as much as performer and conductor, and he went on to become perhaps London's leading theatrical impresario. His new career began with the promotion of the Royal Philharmonic Orchestra, who were in financial difficulties. Hylton secured them two successful concert tours and ensured their longevity. He would go on to to become an enthusiastic promoter of Morecambe and Wise in their first months, discover Shirley Bassey, develop the early career of Tony Hancock, and become light entertainment adviser for Associated Rediffusion, the London branch of the Independent Television Authority, set up in 1955 in opposition to the BBC.

During the Second World War J. B. Priestley presented *Postscripts*, a BBC Radio programme that followed the nine o'clock news on Sunday evenings. Starting on 5 June 1940, Priestley built up such a following that after a few months it was estimated that around sixteen million people, 40 per cent of the adult population in Britain, was listening. He took the raw stuff of the day's news and turned it into instant history, or legend. Priestley had a deep rich voice, spoke with a marked Yorkshire accent and was a skilful broadcaster aware of how the war was heightening national consciousness and how 'we are all in the same boat'.

Only Churchill was more popular with listeners, and Priestley became a potent symbol of resistance to Hitler. He was a wireless superstar who 'couldn't walk into a pub without being touched, as if people wanted to see if I was real'. But his talks were abruptly cancelled, apparently as a result of complaints from members of the Conservative Party that they were too left wing. Churchill himself, it was suggested, was jealous of Priestley's success. Although Priestley is very critical of *Postscripts* in his autobiography *Margin Released* (1962), he did acknowledge the role he played: 'To this day middle-aged and elderly men shake my hand and tell me what a ten-minute talk about ducks on a pond or a pie in a shop window meant to them, as if I had given them the *Eroica* or *King Lear*.'

In one programme Priestley spoke of the horror of seeing his home city, Bradford, damaged. It was far more of a shock to see a few burned-out buildings there than it had been to see all the damage in London. 'I think the sight made a far deeper impression upon me than all the bombing I had seen for weeks in London, because it somehow brought together two entirely different worlds: the safe and shining world of my childhood, and this insecure and lunatic world of today, so it caught and held my imagination.'

1939

John Robert Parker Ravenscroft was born on 30 August 1939 at the Cottage Hospital in Heswall, which is to be found on the west side of the Wirral facing Wales. His father Robert Ravenscroft was a Liverpool cotton broker with the family firm of Strauss & Co., although he was away serving as a captain in the

Royal Artillery for the duration of the war, which started the day following
John's birth.

35

I never felt at all loyal to the idea of Greater Manchester, which did not
bring with it the same sense of romance, history, geography and presence as the counties it rudely broke up and into. Just the plain name
alone seemed to indicate it was the invention of insipid bureaucrats
intent on replacing messy, turbulent history – the kind that emerges
from energetic planning for the future – with control and order – the
kind that rebrands with ambition but is happy to maintain things as
they are. Somehow it seemed this change was intended to block the
sort of transformation that emerges from within communities. To be
suspicious of it, or unmoved, did not mean a reluctance to adopt
change, but merely to note that this particular change did not seem to
be about progress or improvement, merely moderate correction and
legal containment.

But times change, and nothing lasts for ever. Lancashire as it was
had run out of steam – it wasn't what it was – and Greater Manchester
reflected in a practical even prosaic mid-twentieth-century way how
the power of Lancashire had ended up residing in what had become
during the nineteenth century its spirited and ostentatious capital
(Manchester) and the city of disobedience most naturally reluctant to
settle down (Liverpool). Preston, Blackburn, Rochdale, Burnley, Bury,
Bolton remained solidly Lancashire, impervious, unlike the more easily
seduced and gullible Liverpool and Manchester, to fey, fishy new ways.
Blackpool had turned itself into its own rusting raving madcap version
of a north-western seaside resort lit up with jest and hoopla called
Blackpool. Lancaster seemed to have settled contentedly into an even-
tempered historic symbol. But although Manchester had grown too
big, even in its crushing post-cotton decline, to remain inside
Lancashire, Greater Manchester did not and would not have a cricket

team in the County Championship, and even if Lowry painted many of his greatest northern works in towns and localities that were now part of Greater Manchester, these paintings trapped and were trapped inside the sentimentally abstracted memory and reality of Lancashire.

Lancashire and Cheshire were the first social and symbolic constructs I responded to, although I had never committed to either being or belonging to either. I was pulled between the two: Lancashire for the cricket, a game and a team within a couple of short train journeys from where I lived – into Stockport, and then out towards Stretford, via Manchester city centre, or a bus via Manchester Piccadilly – Cheshire because, after all, it contained Alderley Edge, which I found out at a very young age was where King Arthur and his Round Table, overseen by the great local wizard Merlin, waited in mystical limbo before they were called back to life, to save us miraculously from some despicable enemy. Cheshire channelled something of the Welsh magic into the Lancastrian cities of the east and west, influencing their overall personality. It was stranger, somehow more surreal, surreal because of not only Arthur and Merlin and seeming wilder, less tamed than Lancashire, but of course there was Lewis Carroll's Cheshire Cat and there was Crewe Junction, known as the gateway to the north, which put Cheshire at the centre of a nation connected by railway.

And then, connected by radio waves and even stranger things, there was Jodrell Bank, which took a bit of believing – gigantic, mechanically alien and spectacularly isolated, with a pulse all of its very own, in the middle of the prim gladed Cheshire lowlands, twenty miles south of Manchester. Jodrell Bank placed Cheshire if not at the heart of the universe, then plum at the very edge of outer space, communicating with satellites 400,000 miles in the sky. In 1959 the first pictures transmitted from the dark side of the moon by Lunik 3 were received there.

Jodrell Bank was the brainchild of cricket-loving idealistic experimental physicist and pioneering astronomer Dr Bernard Lovell, who before the Second World War had studied cosmic rays in the physics department of the University of Manchester. While leading a team developing radar technology during the war – contributing to an eruption of belief in the positive world-changing power of organised science as much as in its dark side – he noticed some sporadic and unexpected

echoes. Intrigued as to whether these were caused by cosmic ray particles passing through the atmosphere, once the war was over he set up
some surplus radar equipment – including some possibly originating
from Germany – in the quadrangle outside his laboratory in Manchester.
Electrical interference from the trams shuffling along Oxford Road
nearby made him look for somewhere quiet outside Manchester.

In 1939 the university's Botany Department had bought three fields
totalling eleven acres of land a mile or so to the north-east of Holmes
Chapel at the edge of the Cheshire Plain alongside a riverbank named
after the Jaudrell family, descendants of William Jauderell, a fourteenth-
century archer who fought with the Black Prince. Lovell had found his
site, and dated his initiation into radio astronomy to a foggy day in
December 1945, when a trailer loaded with old army gear was driven
into these unpromising fields.

In 1951, now thirty-eight, Lovell was appointed professor of radio
astronomy at Manchester University, and a year later set about supervising the building of a fully steerable telescope using such recycled
parts as gun turrets from First World War warships, after experiments
with scaffolding poles and wire mesh. In austere post-war Britain even
a screwdriver was considered a luxury. Lovell had an evangelical, moral-
istic determination to see his project completed, so powered through
problems, including the weather, budget constraints and sundry scep-
tics. He convinced the local authorities that the telescope would not be
a building, because it moved, and so avoided the planning regulations
that normally would not have allowed the erection of such a colossal,
intrusive structure.

With the help of volunteers, including a bridge-building engineer from Sheffield, and mostly making it up as he went along, he
planned to set what became the Mark 1 telescope on a circular track
– a standard-gauge railway track – so that the whole sky could be
covered. Even then the design of a facility which would play such a
part in the opening-up of the future must have seemed old-fashioned and wonky, but simultaneously looked so out of this world
surrounded by winding narrow Cheshire roads, neat and tidy
cottages, stiles and watermeadows.

During a five-year period of intense anxiety as Lovell struggled for finance to finish what seemed to prosaic politicians and committee minds an absurd waste of time and money – it was dismissed as 'Lovell's folly' and a little more affectionately by bemused locals as 'Lovell's contraption' – its budget spiralled over four times the original estimate, but in 1957, when Russia launched the Sputnik satellite, the only apparatus on earth capable of tracking it was Jodrell Bank. Panic about what on, or off, earth the Russians were up to led to a quick change of mind about Lovell's belligerent, audacious dream. What had been deemed cranky and self-indulgently expensive was suddenly acclaimed as visionary, and possibly as likely to protect the nation as his wartime research into radar. Wiring and electrical work scheduled to take two months were completed in two days, and Jodrell Bank was up and running, and scanning – 3,200 tons, fully steerable and rising 250 feet high above the surrounding trees, as mysteriously still-seeming as the space between stars it stared at, scouring the cosmos, its smooth, serene dish visible for miles around. Sputnik, Lovell said, by a strange irony, saved both him and Jodrell Bank from extinction. If his telescope could detect 'a wonderful echo of the carrier rocket moving over the Lake District', then it could detect Russian missiles raining in on the West. Later, Lovell would describe his main radiotelescope as 'the biggest bargain in the history of science'.

Since the late 1940s he had lived nearby with his wife Joyce in the tiny idyllic village of Swettenham, discreetly folded into the Dane Valley alongside the A535, also known in its early stages as the Macclesfield Road, running from Holmes Chapel to Alderley Edge. In 1961, already made an OBE after the war for his radar work, Lovell was knighted for his contribution to physics and astronomy. When the Americans landed on the moon, Lovell's ingenious Mark 1 telescope, improvised in an obscure muddy field out of scraps, great imagination and sheer will, seemed to my twelve-year-old mind to have played a part, so that the route to walking on the moon had begun in the middle of a scented tangle of hedgerow-fringed country lanes in Cheshire. For Lovell, who believed space travel would have a cataclysmic effect on society, the next stage after the moon landing was a man on Mars by the 1980s and a Jodrell Bank observatory in space.

In 1966, at the height of my temporary interest in collecting stamps, Jodrell Bank featured on a series of issues celebrating recent British technological innovations – the fourpenny Jodrell stamp was the lowest value in the range, which also featured British motor cars including the E-Type Jaguar and the Mini (sixpence), the hovercraft (one shilling and threepence) and the Windscale nuclear reactor, west of the Lake District by the Irish Sea (one and six). The dramatic Jodrell dish was printed in unimaginative black, looking like a plastic toy, on an unimpressive amber background and was only a little bigger than the Queen's head. (The colour was officially described as 'lemon'.) The stamp did not do much in representing the mechanical science-fiction immensity of the real thing and its status as one of the world's great scientific instruments. The thing itself seemed to have arrived from Jupiter, if via the A535, first left after Daisy Bank Farm; the stamp had come through the post without bringing much with it.

Cheshire and space exploration, Lancashire and cricket – epic space and time turned into a game that represented the rise and fall of a great earth-bound earth-spanning empire – were early influences on the formation of my imagination. Lancashire was my county, perhaps, because Reddish itself was until the early part of the twentieth century a part of Lancashire, even though it had then been moved, given as a gift to Stockport and become part of Cheshire, even if it hadn't.

Stockport had become a county borough in 1892, and quickly needed to expand beyond its existing borders. In 1901 the whole of Reddish was absorbed by the borough, and was described as its 'greatest prize' even though Stockport had also expanded into parts of Cheadle and Gatley, Hazel Grove and Bramhall, and Brinnington. Stockport repaid the gift of Reddish, its tax income and building land, by supplying it with a library, public baths including a swimming pool, and a fire station, combined in a new red-brick building designed with reserved, dignified Edwardian grandness by Albert E. Dixon and Charles H. Potter, and opened in stages during 1908 – the same year as Stockport Town Hall, which was opened by the Prince and Princess of Wales. At the time most houses only had a tin bath, so it was a treat to pay a small fee for a hot soapy wash.

Reddish, healthily stocked with its library, swimming baths and fire station, and new parkland created as part of its move into Stockport, was right on the edge of the two counties, belonging to both, and neither, and then entering Greater Manchester representing how Manchester itself was, apart from its own independent city-sized identity, a place that contained, or was contained by, elements of both Cheshire and Lancashire. Reddish moved about even as it stayed exactly where it was. Reddish changed shape, but could only change shape so much.

36

1939

Arthur Lloyd James, a member of the committee set up to determine pronunciation at the BBC, argued in 1939, 'You must not blame the BBC for killing dialect. The native comedians have done more harm to the cause of the honest English dialect than anybody else . . . the Lancashire comedian has killed the Lancashire dialect, and made Lancashire for ever afterwards impossible for the production of Shakespeare . . . It's not the BBC.'

1938

Following three years of construction, Ringway Airport opened officially in June, after various local short-lived aerodromes had come and gone and twelve years after prescient city fathers decided without a permanent airport the city would suffer commercially. In 1929 Manchester had become the first municipality in the country with its own licensed aerodrome. Following a few false starts – a boggy airstrip in Barton (near Eccles) and in fields around Wythenshawe – suitable land for its location was found in the Cheshire parish of Ringway (circular hedged enclosure).

Ticket for a David Bowie concert at the Free Trade Hall,
Manchester, 1972

The Apollo Cinema in Ardwick opened in 1938, with a seating capacity of
nearly 3,000. It was built in response to the huge demand for films, and was
constructed in a streamlined modern style reminiscent of a giant wireless set,
with a luxurious interior.

In 1938 Christopher Isherwood ascribed W. H. Auden's low spirits on their China-
bound ship to his being uprooted from 'his beloved chilly North', and wrote of
him, 'His romantic travel-wish was always towards the north. He could never
understand how anyone could long for the sun, the blue sky, the palm-trees of
the south. His favourite weather was autumnal, high wind and driving rain.'

1937

'In advocating wider universal education I received much bitter opposition.
Elderly spinners claimed that "learning" only made the youngsters discon-
tented, and taught them to cry for the moon. "What was good enough for

me ought to be good enough for my children" was the basis of their belief. The mill owners, too, threw their weight solidly against the unsettling influence of education. They wanted steady workers; it did not suit their ends that the workers should know too much.' J. R. Clynes, *Memoirs*.

'When I'm cleaning windows', undoubtedly George Formby's most popular song, featured in his 1937 film *Keep Your Seats, Please* and was banned by the BBC because of its content. Such was its popularity that Formby or his collaborators wrote a sequel the following year. Of the twelve verses in the two versions, nine contain sexual references as follows: the sexual activities of newly-weds (three verses); women undressing (two); naked women (two); frustrated 'old maid' (one); his large penis (one).

David Hockney was born in Bradford, Yorkshire on 9 July, the son of Kenneth and Laura Hockney and the fourth of five children (Paul, Philip, Margaret, David and John). His father worked as a clerk in a city centre dry-salters, grocers and wholesalers, although he later became an accountant. The family lived in a typical large Bradford terraced house at 61 Steadman Terrace, Leeds Road.

'At night, when you cannot see the hideous shapes of the houses and the blackness of everything, a town like Sheffield assumes a kind of sinister magnificence. Sometimes the drifts of smoke are rosy with sulphur, and serrated flames, like circular saws, squeeze themselves out from beneath the cowls of the foundry chimneys. Through the open doors of foundries you see fiery serpents of iron being hauled to and fro by redlit boys, and you hear the whizz and thump of steam hammers and the scream of the iron under the blow. The pottery towns are almost equally ugly in a pettier way. Right in among the rows of tiny blackened houses, part of the street as it were, are the 'pot banks' – conical brick chimneys like gigantic Burgundy bottles buried in the soil and belching their smoke almost in your face. You come upon monstrous clay chasms hundreds of feet across and almost as deep, with little rusty tubs creeping on chain railways up one side, and on the other workmen clinging like samphire-gatherers and cutting into the face of the cliff with their picks.' George Orwell, *The Road to Wigan Pier*, Chapter 7.

Returning from Hollywood, Gracie Fields said, 'I still say by gum and gee whiz; I haven't gone all glamour.' In 1937 she was given the freedom of Rochdale. Her identification with Rochdale needed to be maintained in the midst of her fame, so that to the outside world she still possessed some sort of immediate difference, even if that difference bore little relation to what it really was to be working class and living in Rochdale. Fields used an idea of northernness to achieve a perverse form of glamour, shrewdly exploiting her underclass roots in order to convey alluring novelty. 'My work . . . has meant travelling the world over, to great places and small, but home to me always means Rochdale and its gradely folk.'

37

Reddish does not appear in the Domesday book – typical of places in the south-east of Lancashire and other northern areas such as County Durham, Northumberland, Cumberland and Westmorland. There is a brief mention of Manchester – as Mamecastre – in the book, noting that it had a parish church, but of its 1,700 pages Lancashire and Manchester occupy a bare one and a half, as an appendix to Cheshire, which then included parts of what would later be Wales.

The 1086 survey was ordered by William the Conqueror as a record of the land he had conquered twenty years before, and is regarded as the first great work of a bureaucratic state, a way of discovering who owned what land in order to calculate tax. The document, allegedly written by a single monk, was nicknamed domesday because like the Last Judgement there was no appeal against its findings.

For centuries, until the period of history that framed and was framed by what was later branded the Industrial Revolution, Reddish was all but on the verge of not even being a place, simply somewhere possibly nameless connecting other places, somewhere as much on the edge of the countryside as on the edge of Manchester, or Stockport, or its own insignificant shapelessness.

I find out how distant and removed it was by searching for Reddish on Google. There are a few, slight traces, explaining how the area came into being, enough traces of memory and archive to form a basic history of the place where I lived. The information resides in the Internet – I imagine towards the edge of whatever shape the Internet actually is – and seems to be there purely for me to find. Who else would be searching for this information – looking to write a book in which the hero, and occasionally the villain, and now and then something blurred grey-red and receding in the mirror, is Reddish? It enables me to piece together the beginnings of the place where I found myself, and realise how hard it is to truly know yourself. I can find out how Reddish materialised, the place where I lived then left, and eventually went back to in order to write a book about the north, of which it is a tiny part.

Before the industrial era there were two notable houses in the Reddish area, Reddish Hall and Hulme Hall, and several small hamlets consisting of farmhouses and cottages. The opening of the Ashton Canal in 1797 precipitated the changes that turned Reddish into a place filled with houses, and streets, and families with children like me, caught in all innocence right where they were. During the next few decades Sandford, Reddish Green and Whitehall fused along the banks of the canal into a larger settlement.

Nothing happened overnight, though. The Stockport Branch Canal passed through Reddish at the end of the eighteenth century, but it was fifty years before the first cotton mill was built in the area. The canal was heavily industrialised along most of its length, and was mostly used to deliver coal to the mills and factories on its banks, and to homes and steam engines. It also carried passengers – 'an elegant boat for passengers and their luggage', a shilling return in the front room, eightpence in the back – between Stockport and Manchester. It went from the Stockport Basin in a wharf and warehouse complex half a mile north of the centre of Stockport through Reddish and Gorton to Openshaw (from old English Opinschawe, meaning open wood), eventually joining the Ashton Canal. The Ashton Canal joined the Rochdale, the Duke of Bridgewater's ground-breaking first canal, and the Peake Forest canals, to and from the Dukes Warehouse near Piccadilly in Manchester, and Hull, Mellor, Chapel-en-le-Frith, Saddleworth, Stockport, Oldham and everywhere in between.

The Stockport Branch Canal didn't have much immediate impact on Reddish, which was described in 1825 as having a population that was 'but thin'. The pre-industrialisation pace of things persisted well into the nineteenth century, while Manchester tore up time and the past and zealously, even cruelly, remade human purpose. In Reddish, despite the canal, the world of George III's accession (1760), a world in which there were no hard roads, no factory system, no capitalist manufacturers, no smelting of iron by coal, seeped into the next century. Things had barely changed for centuries and showed no signs of doing so. The Industrial Revolution, rather than being a sudden convulsion, was the diffuse result of a couple of centuries of gradual change. It was really an evolution, but this word imparts much less suggestive detail about the ultimate nature of the metamorphosis of the area.

Locals had a static unrefined view of things before the rush and snarl of commercially generated change moved people into an always evolving society frantically, or dutifully, keeping pace with its own ruthlessly established pace. Manchester was transforming a few miles away, people being squeezed into a world making a new sort of noise that was not natural but soon came to seem so. Stockport was heaving, swelling and beginning to sweat, sending prodigious numbers of hats out into the wider world. How long could docile little Reddish, shyly tucked up against where the Pennines made their turn at the southern end of Yorkshire into the eastern end of Cheshire, resist? Then came the trains, and people began to pour everywhere, even into Reddish.

In 1830, when there were 574 inhabitants, Reddish was called a township and within the parish of Manchester. Slowly, the mills, the entrepreneurs and the cotton industry turned Reddish into the place it was in the early twentieth century. The first industrialist to arrive was Robert Hyde Greg, son of Samuel Greg, who had built the pioneering Quarry Bank Mill at Styal. Greg built Albert Mills and bought the land around Houldsworth Square down towards Sandy Lane on the ridge above Stockport that would become South Reddish. Strict churchgoers with no tolerance of alcohol, the Gregs developed the area, building cottages for their employers and providing facilities such as a small park, but didn't allow public houses. (Maybe the Gregs' pious control over South Reddish, leaving behind a pub-less inconsequential strip of housing, no place to find subject matter for het-up sick-at-heart songs, accounts for Morrissey's sneering antipathy.) South Reddish listlessly sank into itself and thinned out before disappearing into the centre of Stockport, while at the other end of Reddish things got a little serious, and there were increasing reminders that it was of Lancashire, despite what anyone said or legislated.

As soon as the freshly cut Branch Canal left the Stockport Basin by Lancashire Hill near the town centre, it ran into the farmland that Reddish essentially comprised, sloping down into the barely inhabited Reddish Vale. A spur of the canal running east from Reddish to a coal mine at Beat – also Beet or Beight – Bank near Haughton Green was abandoned when only partly built. When I was growing up in Reddish, there was little explicit sign that a few miles away there had been mining activity, a genuine sign of an industrial past on the very edge of southeast Lancashire, over the border from the very tip of the north-east of Cheshire. On the Cheshire side of the Tame was Bredbury, which by being on the Cheshire side meant that you thought of it differently, as though the difference between Lancashire and Cheshire was like the difference between somewhere painted in one colour, and somewhere of a darker, older, grimier hue. Haughton Green, like Reddish, was mostly rural farmland until the discovering of coal led to the mines.

Coal mining in Denton and Haughton can be traced to the early 1700s, and there are indications that it went much further back than this. One early record can be found in the parish register of Denton Chapel (St Lawrence's Church) for 1743: 'Buried. John Bretland of Whernith, who was killed in ye Colepit in Haughton.' There were numerous shallow pits throughout the townships of Denton and Haughton, but the names and even the whereabouts of many of these are now lost. The sites of some can be found on old Ordnance Survey maps, where they are marked as 'Old Coal Shaft' or 'Old Air Shaft' but without names.

A canal running to these pits might have changed my whole view of the district where I grew up, made Reddish seem more specific, but there was no canal, or even the remnants of one, in the open land that poured away into the distance on the side of Reddish opposite where it was built up and already preparing to become the outskirts of built-up and leaking Manchester. The open country that spread out beyond the last line of streets and on the other side of the derelict brickie, where a solitary forty-foot chimney stack looked lost and a little lonely at the side of Harcourt Street, was where the brick and human spillage from Manchester, and Stockport from another direction, stopped.

Look this way, towards Manchester, or Stockport, or Gorton, across roofs stretching away like solid grey tents, down cramped insular streets, a tangled, packed urban setting: but look the other way, and there was rolling, bucolic Reddish Vale, containing endless grass to sprawl all over, and plenty of woods and trails where it was easy to lose yourself. On one side an unbroken spread towards the classic scaly and scaled-down northern picture of cluttered brick and grim streets, on the other, a harmonious sweep down into the actual picturesque. I could break from one to the other in minutes, and coming to the country could be a pleasant surprise, but then coming to the unlovely streets could be exhilarating, and this constant criss-crossing from one landscape to another made the whole thing seem as much a personal playground as a home for hundreds of families.

Reddish Vale even contained (and still does) a small but, by reputation, challenging eighteen-hole golf course laid out in 1912 by Dr Alister MacKenzie, who designed the Augusta National Course, home of the greatest golf tournament in the world, the US Masters. The River Tame winds its way through and features on seven of the holes. The course was carved out of a hundred acres of local farmland, 'undulating but not too hilly', as MacKenzie said. He described the turf as excellent, and was impressed by the natural surroundings. Even though it shares the same SK5 postcode as Westbourne Grove, the course was as remote to me as Augusta, as if there was some barrier that kept me out, kept me at the edges, where I might find and treasure the occasional chipped lost ball. For a while it was the southern limit of my young existence, a barrier between me and what was out there – Brinnington, Bredbury and Stockport, and further to the south-west Buxton, the Peak District and Derbyshire, and beyond that the unimaginable rest of the world.

Reddish Vale was for me a place to explore tentatively, reaching further and further inside what seemed to go on for ever, a never-ending sloping wooded sweep of fields, trees, long grass, nettles, dock leaves, brambles, barbed wire, conkers, wild flowers, hedges, ponds, lanes, mounds, trespass notices, fences, acorns, sticks, ditches, paths, all cut through by the meandering River Tame, on its way via Saddleworth from the edge of the West Riding, separating Ashton from Dukinfield, and Lancashire from Cheshire, to Stockport, where it ended and began a new life. Bluebell Valley led to Denton Woods, and I never dared to swim near the Strines Weir, where water deflected from the Tame tumbled in a bubbly white rush. I suppose, compared to the unappealing pedestrian terraced narrowness of Reddish and Gorton and Denton – which were chained to Manchester – or Stockport, Reddish Vale was a comely paradise, with a hint of danger, a sudden eruption of wild flowers, unexpected trenches, overgrown thickets, magical groves, strange smells and hints of moats and castle ruins and even more mysterious possibilities, an outpouring of natural colour at the edge of where mighty made-up machine-mad Manchester dribbled to an exhausted spiritless end.

To carry the Sheffield and Midland railway line from central Manchester towards Yorkshire, there was a viaduct consisting of sixteen arches. I don't know how I knew, or who told me, but this impressive structure sweeping across Reddish Vale with monumental Victorian grandeur was looked upon as being a dangerous thing. Constructed in 1875, when the train had truly picked up steam, bringing speed and nearness to everyone, local wisdom claimed that a witch was disturbed during the building. She placed a curse on the damned thing soaring over her head, and over time it was passed down that you must not count the arches, or you would die inside a day. Perhaps this was because this hulking brick monster – which is either beautiful or horrendous depending on your point of view – sliced through unspoilt country allowing trains to spew malodorous steam into the air, ruining the deep green vale, the precious paradise that until then had resisted the rancid soul-destroying revolution exploding out of nearby Manchester. The viaduct was a filthy finger stretching from noisy Manchester, bringing some of the noise and filth with it.

Counting the arches, which is an irresistible thing to do, as if to check or simply marvel at the number and their design – a symbol of progress if you believed, capitalist defilement if you didn't – indicated you admired it and therefore deserved to die. The viaduct diluted, as rumours of murders and nasty surprises waiting in the woods also did, the idea that this was pure paradise. A tumble into a riot of nettles causing stings across the body that seemed like burns or getting stuck while trying to cross the weir near the viaduct and almost drowning would also remind you that this Eden was filled with its own threats and potential punishments.

I never did count the number of arches on the viaduct over the Tame.

38

1936

'I was born in 1936 in Castleford, Yorkshire. You'll find it on the map – I'm the bugger that put it there. Where we lived, all the fellers were coal miners. Except me dad – he was a full-time, fully-paid-up, fully-fledged bastard.' Vivian Nicholson.

Cinema magnate Oscar Deutsch opened his latest Odeon in Bury. The Odeon chain was setting new standards in comfort, presentation and show-manship, and relished using the flamboyant new architectural language of art deco. To the downtrodden hard-working Bury folk of the mid-1930s, stuck in the seemingly endless Depression, it must have seemed as though a shiny luxury liner had sailed up the Bury Canal and dropped anchor. Twenty years before television began to reach the masses, with entertainment still largely based around the wireless and reading, film's ravishing visual escapism and otherworldly romantic expression experienced in the midst of this commer-cially confident opulence must have been hypnotising, even hallucinatory. Deadened workers in a world that had suddenly hit a dead end were shown extraordinary signs of life, which would inspire a new sort of obedience. They may have still been kept in their place, exploited for their labour and soon their ridiculous bravery, but some would begin to wonder what was out there, beyond the hanging smoke, constant brick and dismal routine.

1935

On his return to Parliament in 1935, J. R. Clynes was pressed to stand again for leader but declined. He remained a loyal and reliable elder statesman of the Labour movement until he retired.

In 1935 George Formby made *Off the Dole* for John E. Blakely of Mancunian Films, a follow-up to his first film *Boots! Boots!*, again with wife Beryl as a co-star. Market trader Blakely had bought a cinema in 1908, when cinemas were often just rows of benches in converted shops or churches with sheets for screens. Twenty years later Blakely started making his own films, shooting rough-and-ready shorts featuring ebullient northern music-hall talent. By the time he shot the first two George Formby films – above a garage in London – Blakely had established his blunt, no-fuss, inexpensive formula, relying on the energy of the entertainers rather than sophisticated film-making. In the two films Formby made with Blakely there was no attempt to play down Formby's happy-go-lucky Lancashire character, and audiences looking for mad but recognisably regional assaults on everyday routine loved him.

London-based producer and impresario Basil Dean, who had been work-ing with Gracie Fields, hired the Salford-born author of *Love on the Dole*, Walter Greenwood, to script Formby's first Ealing film, *No Limit* (also 1935). This and *Keep Your Seats, Please* (1936) were both directed by Monty Banks, who later married Gracie Fields. After this a special Formby unit was set up at Ealing, headed by writer and director Anthony Kimmins, to produce his films. These usually conformed to a set pattern: at their centre is Formby, a shy, innocent, gauche, accident-prone Lancashire lad; frequently he is in a skilled trade (photographer, typesetter, gramophone engineer) and lives in the south, either in the suburbs or the countryside, thus nationalising his appeal; he has a bashful courtship with a brisk sensible heroine with an upper-class accent; he is put through a succession of comic humiliations but eventually wins the girl and achieves success in his job or in sport or, later, in war. If Formby could win through against adversity, then anyone could. His eternal optimism was summed up by his catchphrase 'Turned out nice again, hasn't it.' It was partly by becoming a more universal symbol that Formby achieved his success. He was northern and working class but, more impor-tantly, he was the little man who wins through against all the odds, as Chaplin had on the silent screen, and as Norman Wisdom was to do in the 1950s. He was, as Colin MacInnes observed, Everyman: 'the urban "little man" defeated – but refusing to admit it'.

1934

Born 9 May 1934 in Armley, Leeds, author, playwright and actor Alan Bennett grew up surrounded by gossipy Yorkshire women, who made an indelible impression on him, as did regular holidays to coastal resorts like Morecambe. His first encounter with comedy was via the radio, but he later said that he disliked popular comedians like Tommy Handley and Tommy Trinder for being 'relentlessly cheerful'; more down-to-earth figures like *ITMA*'s appropriately named charlady Mona Lott were closer to an already melancholic outlook.

'I was born and brought up in Leeds, where my father was a butcher, and as a boy I sometimes used to go out with the orders, delivering the meat. One of our customers was a nice woman called Mrs Fletcher, and I used to go to her house and she had a daughter called Valerie. Valerie went to London and became a secretary and she got a job with a publishing firm and did well in the firm, and became secretary to the chairman, whom she eventually married. Now the publishing firm was Faber and Faber, and the chairman was T. S. Eliot. So there was a time early in life when I thought my only connection with literature would be that I once delivered meat to T. S. Eliot's mother-in-law.'

Gracie Fields, rich, successful and famous, both because of her northern otherness and how she had transformed herself beyond that otherness, considering herself a hard worker just like she had been when employed in the Rochdale mills, told *Film Pictorial*, 'I ought to feel right at home, by rights, because here I am back in the mill again – right where I started. I have to get up at six o'clock, only instead of knocking off at five as I did in Rochdale; I work till eight; and instead of cotton fluff, it's incandescent carbons and dust and grease paint.' And, instead of a shilling a week, it was two pounds a minute, 'or so they tell me'.

Sing as We Go is Gracie Fields' fifth feature film – following *Sally in Our Alley* (1931), *Looking on the Bright Side* (1932), *This Week of Grace* (1933), and *Love, Life and Laughter* (1933). The greater part of the film's budget went on her fee. What's a Lancashire lass to do when the mill closes down? Go to Blackpool to look for work and give us the best portrait of seaside holidays in the thirties: 'If we can't spin, we can still sing.' Seen as her best screen work, and best loved, it was set in Lancashire and directed by Basil Dean from a story by J. B. Priestley (who Robert Graves once described as 'the Gracie Fields of litera-ture'). Priestley himself once wrote, 'Listen to Gracie for a quarter of an hour and you will learn more about Lancashire women and Lancashire than you would from half a dozen books on the subjects. All the qualities are there, shrewdness, homely simplicity, fierce independence, an impish delight in mocking whatever is thought to be affected and pretentious.'

Scriptwriter Priestley knew his audience just as surely as Gracie Fields. This is a rose-tinted view of the Depression-hit north based on his childhood memories of early-twentieth-century music hall, but that is exactly what was wanted and suited how Priestley sentimentally but sincerely reflected the struggling 1930s working class. Grace is a working-class hero. She may be poor, but she's resourceful, optimistic, quick-witted and gloriously stroppy. There's no forelock tugging here. Fields stood for all that Priestley liked in northern music-hall culture. Presented in terms that still echoed Dickens, she enabled him to refine the myth of Englishness but also appealed to her audi-ence by appearing to be like them. 'The secret of Gracie Fields' vast popularity is that not only does she know . . . how to entertain people, but she knows, too, how to represent the people. In a country [in] which privilege is still the rule and snobbery is the most characteristic weakness, the people do not get much of a chance to express themselves. But in Gracie Fields for one they are expressing themselves and that is why she is at one and the same time an admired artist, a symbolic figure and a beloved woman.' Priestley, a forward-looking nostalgic, used Gracie to personify the fight against a new impersonal world.

By the 1930s, the Rochdale Canal in Miles Platting, set amongst damp, decaying houses as bleak inside as out, was a toxic soup of polluting chemi-cals leaking from the surrounding factories and sundry debris, consisting of discarded bicycle frames, old rubber tyres and the rotting carcases of dogs.

1933

Walter Greenwood's 1933 novel *Love on the Dole* about the crisis of unemployment following the General Strike of 1926 (although the main action
takes place in 1931) concentrates on a working-class community trying to
come to terms with poverty while retaining its dignity. It was at once recognised as a classic. Greenwood said he 'tried to show what life means to a
young man living under the shadow of the dole, the tragedy of a lost generation who are denied consummation, in decency, of the natural hopes and
desires of youth'. Dire poverty haunted Salford, the novel's setting, where
Greenwood also grew up. The first chapter ends: 'The identical houses of
yesterday remain, still valuable in the estate market even though the cost of
their building has been paid for over and over again by successive tenants . . .
Places where men and women are born, live, love and die and pay prepos-
terous rents for the privilege of calling the grimy houses "home".'

A lunch hosted by Gracie Fields' record company EMI in London in 1933 to
mark the sale of her four millionth record was transformed into a 'Lancashire
do'. Waitresses wearing clogs and shawls served fish and chips, hotpot, beer
and tea to an audience that included industry executives, her parents, the
mayor of Rochdale and her first clog maker.

J. B. Priestley was invited by publisher Victor Gollancz to undertake a journey
around the country to experience at first hand the life of people in the industrial areas and the plight of the unemployed; but the journey he made in
1933 included much more than that, opening out into an examination of
England and the English, praising as well as blaming. *English Journey* was an
exceptional success for a work of non-fiction. Though he was undoubtedly
nostalgic for the Bradford of his Edwardian youth, he exploited his memories
of this utopia to argue for a classless society and 'a cleaner, tidier, healthier,
saner world than that of nineteenth-century industrialism'. The book captures
a country in economic, political and social turmoil, mangled by the after-
shocks of the Great Depression. Heavy industry was suffering and
unemployment had rocketed, especially in the industrial north. In response,
the National Government, formed in 1931, instituted draconian spending
cuts and wage reductions. There was political turbulence and polarisation,

with the left protesting against unemployment and poverty, and Mosley's British Union of Fascists paralleling the rise of fascism across Europe.

The 1931 Statute of Westminster, which established the legislative independence of Australia, Canada, New Zealand, the Irish Free State and Newfoundland, brought a loosening of the imperialist grip, and the horizons of the British empire began to recede. In a climate of cultural anxiety England's gaze turned inward. Priestley was no reactionary, however: his nostalgia was not of a mythical pre-industrial Merrie England, but the vigorous England of the Industrial Revolution, and its 'energy, organisation, drive of purpose'. Under the weather, nursing what could have been a hangover from Manchester, he visited Blackpool out of season. The journey did little to cheer him up. 'Between Manchester and Bolton the ugliness is so complete that it is almost exhilarating. It challenges you to live there.'

Lancastrian working folk had accepted that challenge. 'They are on active service, and like the frontline troops, they make a lot of little jokes and sing comic songs.' He wrote of the Fylde's 'flat and characterless countryside'. 'All the roads suddenly become very straight and wide and display vulgar advertisements because they, like you, are going to Blackpool.

'Even if you did not intend to go to Blackpool, once you had got beyond Preston you would have to go there. These roads would suck you into Blackpool. That is what they are there for. There is no escape.' The bracing sea air cured his headache and blasted the measly city air from his lungs, giving him his first decent night's sleep, eleven hours, for weeks. 'Blackpool the resort was dead,' he wrote. 'Even the residential town, of a considerable size, was moribund. Only the weather was awake, and that was tremendously alive. The sea roared in the deep dusk and sent sheets of spray over the glistening wet railings and seats. And this was, for the time being, all the Blackpool I wanted. If you do not like industrial democracy, you will not like Blackpool. I know people who would have to go into a nursing home after three hours of it. (In the season, of course.) I am not one of those people.'

39

In the north-west Reddish pushed up against closely related crowded Levenshulme and scuffed first cousin Longsight, which were themselves piled against the more distantly related and packed-in Burnage, Rusholme and Fallowfield, so lay between these increasingly urban and degenerate places and the open-air rewards and submerged dangers of the Vale. If you went further west, you reached blighted Moss Side, Old Trafford and Whalley Range. (In *Mary Barton*, published in 1848, Elizabeth Gaskell describes Moss Side, two miles outside the city centre, as a pleasant rural space with green fields and small farms where workers from Ancoats and Chorlton-on-Medlock went as an escape from their hard-working lives.) Further north, you went through Ardwick and Hulme, and beyond the Mancunian Way made it into the compressed, engaged and mercenary Manchester city centre. All this within five miles.

Each dowdy teeming district blended into the next, brick-cobble alleyways, grey back-to-back houses, deserted wasteland and pubs leading to more of the same, held in decaying check under clouds that simmered with age-old resentment, but each had its own special atmosphere, and even though Longsight looked like Rusholme, which quickly became Hulme, and was right on top of it, they were not the same. There were borders, limits to break through, everywhere you looked and travelled, each zone defined and bisected by roads and railways, and those living in Levenshulme felt apart from those in Gorton, if only because it was in a different place, with a different name. Levenshulme was to some extent made up of the bits of older communities left over from Rusholme, Ardwick and Gorton, but as soon as it became a known neighbourhood with known boundaries, it became its own defined territory.

I did not know it at the time, considering only my relationship to a place on earth because of sporting teams that were, it seemed, close by, but I was living in the heart of something unflagging and contrary that you could call the north. It never occurred to me this was something I might make a fuss of, because of how I talked, because of where I was, a couple of hundred yards from the centre of Reddish, Houldsworth Square, under those immense, churlish skies, constantly sending out warnings about what was around the corner.

The walks I took around Reddish would often follow the same route. One walk in particular would take me to where I went to school, and then, in reverse, it would bring me home. It was a relatively straight walk, taking about twenty minutes, along either what was the main road through where I lived, the busy Gorton Road, essentially the high street that channelled right through the centre of Reddish from beginning to end, or the quieter Harcourt Street, where chimney sweep Frank Aspinall lived, at number 77, in one of its square placid semi-detached houses, stuck to each other, with their ageing pleated curtains – a lingering pretension to class – barely hiding pottery ornaments, polished cupboards and wall mirrors, some with truncated porches that fancied themselves grand, alongside the run-down brickworks and rutted grassless sometimes swampy patches of wasteland which tempted a young boy in.

This wasteland led to small dirty ponds graced with wriggling newts, stumpy sticklebacks and queer frogspawn, and a view which offered glimpses of other counties across the viaduct, the weary but lively river and empty railway lines. The counties were a long way off, especially if you were walking and even if you got a train, one or two of which still blasted steam out of their dangerous ancient metal bodies, but they were there, and one day I would get to know their names, and work out how they all fitted together, and what that actually meant. That's why I walked to and from school, sometimes skipping and hopping on one foot, all part of an everyday performance. To find things out. To find out where I was, and what would happen to me if I followed one of the roads that went that way, or that way. There were a lot of roads, more than you could ever take in your stride, and if you thought about it, in the way you don't when you are eight or nine or ten, places like Reddish exist so that there is somewhere for the roads to lead to and to leave behind.

If I walked along the Gorton Road, I was perhaps beginning to understand that a road can eventually take you away from where you are apparently for ever. You can head out on that sort of road and never come back. Along the Harcourt Road, the back way to school, you were walking a street that would take you nowhere, or abruptly to another street, an opening to a field, or back where you came. For now I would walk to school along the Gorton Road and back home along Harcourt Street. Or I would do it the other way round. For now the Gorton Road trapped me, because to my young self, as big as the road was, containing cars that brought vague speeding news of an outside world, it only existed inside Reddish, which was the place where I clearly belonged. As far as I knew, as a young boy, glued to humble Reddish as though it was sticky with liquid the consistency of frogspawn, having no choice, I belonged there for ever, and the Gorton Road would never lead me away.

The Gorton Road went in one direction west towards the centre of Stockport, eventually changing its name, becoming the Reddish Road past Houldsworth Square and then Sandy Lane, and you abruptly dropped down Lancashire Hill into the town centre. If you kept going the other side of Stockport, along many roads that kept changing their names, through districts and communities bigger and smaller than Reddish – Cheadle, Altrincham, Lymm, Leigh, Widnes – you could make your way through salty, affluent and hushed, sometimes scruffy and less showy Cheshire, and on to a coast cracked open around spicy loud-mouthed Liverpool, and the Irish Sea, an entry to the whole wide world.

In the other direction the Gorton Road bored its relentless dingy way towards places too small to be towns and too big to be villages, which had names as banal as Reddish but, it turned out, after I had walked far enough and found out various things, were in fact soaked with the past, with history, with work and sometimes with death, or something not quite so bleak, but still bloody. If you kept going in this direction, turning to the east, beyond Gorton and Denton, away from Stockport, away from Manchester, past Ashton under Lyne, Stalybridge or Glossop, you would head towards south-west Yorkshire, over the hills and moors which were always in view and yet inching away, keeping themselves to themselves. When I was ten Yorkshire seemed completely out of reach, out of sight, over there, miles away, hours away, even days, another country, except when it came to cricket, when it was the enemy or at least a tough imposing rival.

40

1931

Les Dawson was born in 1931 in Thornton Street, Collyhurst, a working-class suburb of Manchester, where his bricklayer father struggled to find work during the Depression. The podgy schoolboy, nicknamed Dossy, dreamed of becoming a famous writer, spurred on by an enthusiastic English teacher. After leaving school at fourteen he got his first job in the parcels department of the Manchester Co-op, and then as an apprentice electrician. Les Dawson spent his schooldays keeping bullies suspicious of his sensibility at bay with his humour.

> I was born in Manchester in the Thirties. It was a depressed decade and most of the people who lived in our area were decayed. Our terraced house was so narrow, the mice walked about on their back legs and the kitchen ceiling was so low the oven had a foot-level grill. The place I was born in was called Collyhurst; it lay two miles from the city centre and it was a district of narrow streets and tenements that gazed eyeless on to cobbled roads escorting the warehouses and shops past shadowed alleyways where teeming hordes of ill-dressed children ran amok. But it was a place that held warmth and comradeship in adversity, and there was compassion and love among the inhabitants.

Gandhi came to England in September 1931 as Congress Party representative at the London Round Table conference on Indian constitutional reform. He spent a week of his visit in the cotton districts of Lancashire and west Yorkshire explaining the meaning of his anti-colonialist strategy *khadder* to those who were likely to be most affected by it. *Khadder* was his campaign to resist the importation of non-Indian goods, particularly Lancashire cotton; Gandhi argued that cotton should be produced in the impoverished Indian villages.

He used his meetings with industrialists, cotton workers and the unemployed to debate the relationship between local industries, imperialism and global economics. A crowd of 3,000 turned up to welcome him at Darwen by big neighbour Blackburn, 'lovely little Dirty Darwen, 'tween two bleak hillsides, both bleak and barren', the very essence of Lancashire, with weather conditions and environment perfect for cotton weaving, but he got off a station early, in Spring Vale. He spent two days touring several mill towns, staying in the homes of progressive Nonconformist industrialists. He met the mayors of Darwen and Preston, Manchester traders, local spinners and weavers, and numerous journalists. 'Pray tell me,' he asked at a meeting with unemployed cotton workers, 'what am I to do with a fifth of the human race living on the verge of starvation and devoid of all sense of self-respect. It should occupy the attention even of unemployed Lancashire.'

Lancashire and Gandhi stayed stuck inside their own historical and cultural contexts, with the severely declining Lancashire cotton industry still assuming its world-leading nineteenth-century golden age would yet return and unable to face up to its diminished role, and the dialogue between them did not live up to the expectations of both sides. Lancashire was out of date and out of touch, clinging to a notion of industrial superiority that clashed with Gandhi's rejection of what he saw as Western industrial madness, even though much of Lancashire was now suffering from appalling poverty. Gandhi – romanticised by Lancashire as a humanitarian friend of the peasant – was not moved by Lancashire poverty. His enemy was exploitative British imperialism, and his trip was ultimately part of his greater plan to get the British working class to see the justice in Indian independence. He remained quite clear that Lancashire 'could never hope to get back to the quantity of goods formerly supplied to India', which the industry thought was its right and a vital element in its revival, but which Gandhi viewed as part of the enslaving of his country. Indian nationalists suffering at the hands of the British had nothing in common, he thought, with the poor in Lancashire, as much as they were themselves marginalised by power that rested elsewhere. It was a failed visit and soon faded into obscurity.

Barbara Hepworth sculpted *Pierced Form* in 1931, the year she gave birth to her first child. Originally called *Abstract* and then simply *Sculpture*, this was an alabaster piece with a hole carved through the centre, where the invisible indivisibly met the visible. You couldn't tell where something stopped and something else started – as if the northern idea of form was a process in which thoughts and inspiration overlapped and yet were kept apart. The holes were like portals through which you could move from one dimension to another. 'I felt the most intense pleasure in piercing the stone . . .' she said. A year later, although he might have had the idea at roughly the same time, or a little earlier, Henry Moore made something similar, a hole in a sculpture, space within space – for Moore 1932 was 'the year of the hole'.

1930

Edward James Hughes was born on 17 August, the third child of Edith Fararr and William Henry Hughes, at 1 Aspinall Street, Mytholmroyd, a small town close to Hebden Bridge in Calder Valley, Yorkshire, a forty-five-minute drive or train journey from Manchester and Leeds. The stone-built end-terrace house backed on to the Rochdale Canal, where Hughes caught his first pike. Beyond the canal was the main trunk road which connected the woollen towns of Yorkshire with those of the Lancashire cotton mills. Close to the canal and road was the railway, and rising almost sheer from the valley like a monolith was Scout Rock. Ted Hughes' childhood home looked straight across to the surly cliff face of Scout Rock: it provided 'both the curtain and back-drop to existence'.

In this setting he learned the love of nature and its creatures. Hughes described the Calder Valley, with its poisoned canals, unpredictable weather and decaying industrial landscape, as his 'tuning fork' and the moors as 'a stage for the performance of heaven'. He once said that he could 'never escape the impression that the whole region was in mourning for the First World War'. The textile factories were closing and the Depression pressed down on the cobbled streets of towns and villages. He contrasted the atmosphere of futility and gloom in the towns with visits to nearby woods and lakes, which were filled with life and sheltered from the effects of industrialisation. There he fished, trapped and hunted.

'Well, as far as my writing is concerned, maybe the crucial thing was that I spent my first years in a valley in west Yorkshire in the north of England, which was really a long street of industrial towns – textile mills, textile factories. The little village where I was born had quite a few; the next town fifty. And so on. These towns were surrounded by a very wide landscape of high moorland, in contrast to that industry into which everybody disappeared every day. They just vanished. If you weren't at school you were alone in an empty wilderness.'

In 1938 the family moved to Mexborough, a mining town in south Yorkshire. It was under the care of his teacher at the town's only grammar school that Hughes began to mature, his work evolving into the rhythmic passionate poetry for which he became known. His father William was a carpenter but opened a newsagent and tobacconist shop on Main Street opposite St George's Church. Ted was able to read the comics and boys' magazines for nothing, and these were to be the basis of his first attempts at storytelling.

Bernard John Manning was born on 13 August 1930 in Manchester. 'I was born in 1930 in the Ancoats district of the city, and I never lived more than five miles from my birthplace. I always loved Manchester and her people, though that kind of loyalty and sense of belonging is never understood by the metropolitan elite who despise their own country. My dad was a greengrocer and it was a tough upbringing – the north was in a pit of depression and money and food were short. I was one of six children and was forced to share a bed with all my siblings, some of whom wet the bed. In fact I learned to swim before I could walk. I remember one night, my mother asked me: "Where do you want to sleep?" I replied: "At the shallow end." The soles of me shoes were that thin that in 1936 I could put me foot on a penny and tell you if it were heads or tails. I went to an ordinary local school and left at the age of fourteen, taking up a job at the Senior Service tobacco factory in Manchester. From my earliest years, I had a bit of a talent for performing, singing in choirs and at work. Then, when I was fifteen, my life changed dramatically on being called up to serve in the Manchester Regiment of the British Army.'

In 1930 Harold's father Herbert Wilson lost his job. It was two years before he found another, and this necessitated a move to the Wirral, across the Mersey from Liverpool. Harold attended Wirral Grammar School and won an exhibition award to study economics at Jesus College, Oxford. After a modest beginning, Harold Wilson shut himself away and worked. Rather unexpectedly a promising student transformed himself into one of the most outstanding scholars of his generation. He studied, dabbled in liberal politics, went to hear a young Edward Heath play the organ at Balliol College and then went back to work again. He took no part in the Oxford Union, where Heath won the presidency in his fourth year.

41

In Reddish you could see the implacable hilly backbone of the nation, always present in the background, conclusively remote and imposing, especially for a seven-year-old frolicking inside a seven-year-old's world, marking the immediate end of that world. You could see how fog, rain and snow almost permanently covered this sodden spine through a long interrupted winter that seemed to stretch between the beginning of September and the end of May. On cold wintry days when covered in snow the hills could seem mountainous and were very sure of their own superior position in the grand scheme of things, a scheme way beyond the understanding of someone only due to be around on the planet for a few decades and who in fact would only be hanging around for a few years.

We weren't caught up in the worst of the weather; the frosts were never horribly severe, and the rain didn't fall all of the time. I remember sunny summers that seemed to fit into the exact shape and size of the classic school summer holiday as described at length by Enid Blyton. We weren't immune, though, from the soggy effects of being close to where the bruised stricken moors and the menacing, patient Pennine range seemed to break the hearts of the sullen clouds in the sky between the battering winds from the Atlantic Ocean and the North Sea. Manchester, and everywhere for miles around, suffered because of this clashing of clouds and winds right above our heads.

These past few hundred years the sturdy abiding hills and moors have had to put up with violent man-made interruptions to peace and quiet, and even hope and reason, as parts of the land nearby, through some accident of not being on the right curve of a river, or in the best part of the valley, have been sliced, diced, battered, burned, crushed, skinned, torn, dug, maimed, destroyed and covered over with the solid but mostly always melting by-products of near-crazed human endeavour.

They watched as, over a century or two, a stunning eruption of pioneering activity and lusty movement turned empty spaces split by ancient rivers and miles of quiet content country into a massive frantic montage of cities and anxiety that spilled over in random messy shapes, reaching as far as money, planning and energy allowed before petering out in a spiral of depletion. The moors, hills, fields, rivers and trees, this neck of the woods, the original landscape, which consisted of nothing but desolate windswept valleys, gullies, peaks, ridges, woods, shrubs and grassland, have been stained by the results of independent thinking, intellectual inquiry, economic development, political reaction, entrepreneurial vision, inspired madness and cultural innovations. The raw, unfilled land has been scarred with the inevitable consequences of decades of interconnected experimental thinking about the making of money, the establishment of community, the building of society and the convoluted realities of the class system. Reddish – and all those other places that packed in around it – was at the edge of this staining, and straining, this eruption of material, greed, organisation, competition, opulence, desperation and obedience, and I was one of the human examples of this massive experiment, which saw mass production lead to a shift in psychology and a different world to grow up in. I was an afterthought in an area that was itself an afterthought, even though, now and then, it was itself a gift, and was given gifts.

Reddish perhaps owes its name to when, hundreds of years ago, it was little but a pitiless series of muddy fields – a ditch – and a fight of some sort, possibly even a battle, led to much bloodshed and, yes, a red ditch where blood mixed with mud. Gorton, following similar heroic principles, was Gore-town, from the gore that ran into a brook after a battle between brave defending Saxons and terrifying Vikings. *Gor*, though, in Old English can also mean mud or dirt, and also a triangular plot of land, a more mundane but perhaps more likely origin for the name, so perhaps derives from words meaning filthy brook. Because history is very much not a settled issue, and piles up at the edge of being forgotten unless someone's got something to say about it, a fragile combination of clear evidence and something that has the stranger, dubious quality of a dream, it could be that 'Reddish' came about because the sky one night, those hundreds of years ago, had a distinctive reddish glow, or a leading light in local affairs, perhaps when there were only a dozen or so locals living in what was effectively the open air, had reddish hair. It could come from the reeds that there were everywhere in this mossy area – a plain old reedy ditch, rather than anything bloodier and more melodramatic.

It may even be 'Reddish' because it comprises the remnants of words borrowed from other languages, dragged there by invaders or wanderers, a gaggle of visitors who were lost and decided to stick around for a while. A putting together of one sound with another, a name with a noise, a syllable with a meaning that has long dissolved, jammed next to another syllable with another meaning that didn't make it past the thirteenth century. Reddish, made up of fragments, lost in time, not Lancashire enough to make me a Lancashire lad, not Cheshire enough to mean our family was affluent, on the edge of the edges of Manchester but not near enough to make me undeniably Mancunian, a mile or two away from being either really pleasantly rural or an even more wasted caved-in afterthought of Stockport. Reddish, within sight of a door to paradise, but stuck in a corridor that could eventually lead to hell.

It is a ditch – and another corridor bringing to mind a bloody hell – that in the end may not suggest how Reddish got its name and where its history began, but generates the sort of intrigue that resonates through time and cuts a groove all the way to the Internet. There is a ditch dug into the ground which makes its way through the northern part of Reddish that shows how history is often entirely reduced to a mark in the ground, a pile of dirt, a desperate attempt to keep an enemy at bay simply by digging a hole, as if the very act itself can intimidate and repel invaders. History is made up of borders, some as epic, daunting and enduring and ultimately as unreal as Hadrian's Wall, which marks the northern border of England metaphorically but not actually, and some as buried, lost and indistinct, and yet in their own way legendary and unreal, as the ditch that marks the southern border of Manchester. History is made up of rumours, which form their own fragile border between truth and fiction, between the real world and fantasy.

The ditch winding across the southern edge of Manchester is now known as the Nico Ditch or Mickle – from *micel*, meaning large in bulk or great, 'Nico' itself possibly a corruption of *micel*, so simply the Great Ditch – and it runs through five miles of low-lying land from Ashton Moss at Ashton under Lyne – where Geoff Hurst, scorer of the

1966 World-Cup-winning hat trick was born – to Hough Moss at Urmston – a neighbour of Davyhulme, six miles to the south-west of Manchester city centre – and in between cuts first through Denton, where Geoff Hurst's father was born in 1919, not long after when Denton's felt hat industry was the largest in Britain with thirty-six firms directly involved. In 1907 the majority of the 16,428,000 felt hats made in England (worth £2,068,000) were made in Denton and Stockport. In 1921 the working population of Denton was 9,653, with about 41 per cent of those people in occupations related to the hatting industry.

From Denton, perhaps marking how far south of the city Tony Warren's *Coronation Street* could be set, the ditch weaves through Gorton, Reddish, Levenshulme, Burnage, Rusholme, Fallowfield, Withington, Chorlton-cum-Hardy (the settlement of peasants by trees near the water) and Stretford. Some argue the name Nico derives from Hnickar or Nickar, a water spirit of Viking myth, the God Odin himself in destructive mode, renowned for ensnaring and drowning careless travellers. As Hnickar, Odin was imagined to inhabit the lakes and rivers of Scandinavia. *Noecan*, meanwhile, is an Anglo-Saxon verb meaning kill, which would suggest the Ditch had a definite defensive function. The favoured theory is that it was a fortification intended to slow down or break up an attacking force.

It could date back to Roman times, surviving as a rough trace of a possibly more systematic border structure, or it may have formed the southern boundary to Coel Hen's sixth-century kingdom of Rheged. It might have been dug in the seventh century, marking the boundary between the kingdoms of Mercia and Northumberland, but was more likely constructed in the so-called Dark Ages at some point between 890 and 910, or possibly earlier, in 869, when the Danes were expanding in the area, moving towards what would become Cheshire and Lancashire. It certainly follows or shadows long-established borders between kingdoms, regions, tribes and counties. Manchester, as Manigeceaster, was apparently raided by the Vikings in 870, suffering severely and almost completely ruined. This seems to suggest that if it was a barrier hastily built to repel the Vikings it did not work, or the attacking forces merely went around it.

The *Anglo-Saxon Chronicle* – written at the end of the ninth century, the earliest known history of England written in the English language, beginning with the birth of Christ – mentions the ditch, which was about five foot wide with a high bank on the north side, and documents it as an attempt to create a permanent defence against the Vikings. Legend has it that the ditch was dug in one unbelievable night by local inhabitants, who were each allocated a piece of land to dig up. They were told to build up the bank to their height. But a night's work would not have been enough to create a five-mile trench in the land as deep as a man, and there probably weren't enough men around at the time to cover the whole length anyway.

The ditch, still sporadically visible amid the streets, cemeteries, golf courses, parks, paths and playing fields that now cover its route as it skirts the fringes of densely developed central Manchester, is a genuine missing link, as myth and reality, between shrouded Roman Manchester and the Industrial Revolution. Even if just a hastily dug act of fear as the Vikings stormed ever closer, it required in its own medieval way the sort of planning, dedication and strength usually ascribed to the Roman era and the Victorian Manchester that shook up the world, and itself.

In Reddish it cut across from Gorton Cemetery a few hundred yards to the east of my primary school, in between the local park where as a school we played football, and Debdale Park, where I played pitch and putt. As I made my way within what for a time were the limits of my world, between my house and school, and sometimes further up the Gorton Road to Debdale Park, the ditch formed one of my borders. Whether or not it was an epic act of community defence against the ruthless Vikings, it became part of the internal territory I explored and claimed as I became a northerner.

Again, I had no idea of this at the time, but it was one of the three main historical structures in Reddish which formed the triangle that enclosed me: the mysterious ditch that burrowed through from the earthy Anglo-Saxon time when England itself was forming and being fought over, divided, connected, named, owned; the sixteen-arched Victorian viaduct sweeping over the Tame, representing dynamic future-forming landscape-changing industrial expansionism; and a few hundred yards down the Gorton Road from my street in the other direction from the ditch, where the buses began their journeys to

Debdale Park or the other way across to Parrs Wood and Didsbury, the small square named after William Houldsworth, the local industrialist known as the Man who made Reddish. Here was a man who fully intended to enter history, to make sure Reddish appeared in any twentieth-century version of the Domesday Book, and who did all he could to ensure that he did exactly that.

42

1929

The peak of British cotton cloth production came in 1913, when the combined output of the industry reached 7,075,000,000 (7 billion) square yards of cloth. But within a few short years the world would be a very different place, and the British cotton industry would begin its rapid decline. Those who in 1920 had pondered the question 'Is Lancashire a modern El Dorado?' were by 1929 left to wonder 'is Lancashire finished?'

J. B. Priestley's fortunes were transformed when he was given a sizeable amount of money by his great friend the novelist Hugh Walpole in 1929. Walpole's gift enabled Priestley to write *The Good Companions*, a novel concerning a troupe of players touring Depression-hit middle England. The novel earned him the James Tait Black Memorial Prize for fiction and made him a national figure.

> To say that these men paid their shillings to watch twenty-two hirelings kick a ball is merely to say that a violin is wood and catgut, that *Hamlet* is so much paper and ink. For a shilling the Bruddersford United AFC offered you Conflict and Art; it turned you into a critic, happy in your judgement of fine points, ready in a second to estimate the worth of a well-judged pass, a run down the touchline, a lightning shot, a clearance by back or goalkeeper; it turned you into a partisan, holding your breath when the ball came sailing into your own goalmouth, ecstatic when your forwards raced towards the opposite goalmouth, elated, downcast, bitter, triumphant by

turns at the fortunes of your side, watching a ball shape *Iliads* and *Odysseys* for you; and what is more it turned you into a member of a new community, all brothers together for an hour and a half.

J. B. Priestley's broadcasting career began in the 1920s and almost ended in 1929, when Hilda Matheson, the BBC director of talks, concluded that he had a 'very unattractive voice on the microphone'. Matheson's verdict would have surprised later admirers of his wartime broadcasting style, and perhaps reflected a 1920s view that northern accents, however 'educated', lacked the gravitas of the 'received pronunciation' in which the BBC preferred to discuss weighty issues.

1928

'In spite of weariness I fell brooding over cotton men and their problems yet further, and as my thoughts turned more and more on the men I grew more and more depressed. I wondered despairingly whether they could appreciate any danger until it had overtaken them . . . By some Wellsian magic I was transported into the House of Commons . . . The President of the Board of Trade was winding up a critical debate on the Lancashire cotton industry. Just before he made an end my eyes wandered to the Speaker's Chair. I started. Ghostily I seemed to see behind it the greatest of old timers who had brought the cotton industry to its hour of unparalleled fortune . . . Unseen by the assembled House the ghost of the great old pioneer, no longer able to restrain its fast-rising passion, was turning to depart. As it made ready to go its eerie way, I seemed to catch the words that fell between heartbeat and anger from its lips: "The men are spent. The machine is broken. The glory is for ever departed."' Ben Bowker, *Lancashire Under the Hammer*, 1928.

1927

Kenneth Arthur Dodd was born in November in the Knotty Ash area of Liverpool, which he later would make famous via the Diddymen. He began his career as a ventriloquist when his parents bought him a dummy. He performed on the club circuit under the guise of Professor Yaffle Chuckabutty, Operatic Tenor and Sausage-Knotter, but kept his day job as a door-to-door salesman. 'People in Liverpool live their lives in a higher gear than most people. We are very enthusiastic people.'

Most of urban Lancashire was bypassed by the changes of the inter-war years, left in a time warp from which it was occasionally retrieved by music-hall jokes and horrified social reporting. The popular proverb about industrial success and failure 'Clogs to clogs in three generations,' with its wryly comforting message of the ultimate humbling of the upstart mighty – pride coming before a fall – had come to pass; but the real victims were the work-ing class of industrial Lancashire not those who had pocketed the surplus value of their labour. The wheel had almost turned full circle, and Lancashire was fast reverting to the relative poverty and provincial backward-ness of its provincial pre-industrial past.

In 1924, the Rochdale Canal Company made a statement warning that they felt there was no future for canals in this country unless the government provided them with some sort of aid. Their pleas were ignored by Parliament, and after many decades of decreased use, *Narrowboat Alice*, carrying 20 tons of wire from Sowerby Bridge to Manchester in 1927, was the last commercial cargo to travel the whole length of the Rochdale Canal. Over the next few decades canals were treated as though they were something of an embarrassment in a world of rail and road, and were increasingly ignored, built over, filled in, used as a local dump, stuck under motorways, treated as sewers, like they were channels of pollution, slow routes to nowhere special, not astonishing waterways that had opened up the nation.

43

To get to Houldsworth Square meant a walk along Gorton Road towards South Reddish, a walk lined with shops of which none have remained fixed in my mind apart from my barber, the occasional shop

Map of the Nico Ditch from Reddish across South Manchester

that sold fizzy pop and loose sweets, and an early version of a pound
shop, which sold a lot of very cheap nothing in particular from plastic
toys to cleaning sponges. I never went into pubs – I wasn't even aware
whether my dad ever did, and there was never any alcohol in our house
– so I don't remember any of the locals.

Houldsworth Square, and until I was about eleven the toy shop on
the other side with its transforming display of shiny multicoloured
sweetly detailed Matchbox model cars, was about as far as I would
venture. There were a couple of gigantic buildings near the square,
totally out of scale with everything around them, mounds of brick,
window and towering chimney that even to my young mind seemed
to have run out of purpose, and I never wondered what their original
purpose might have been. They were used now to manufacture and
pack sweets – my mum worked in one for a while, eight hours a day
filling bags with an assortment of misshapen toffees, boiled sweets and
broken candy – and as the headquarters of a mail-order catalogue, but
the buildings dwarfed this kind of mundane activity. These were buildings that must have once been important but were now stilled, giant
reminders of when men made their minds up that they were going to
make money, run businesses, hire people, organise communities, make
decisions and fashion changes. Men who were going to show the world
how important they were by building bulked-up structures clearly
meant to stand at the centre of affairs representing their yearning to
stand tall and proud among many. They intended to stamp their egos
into the very ground they owned and throw grit in the eyes of the
feeble minded. To me the buildings just seemed from the ancient past
or weirdly fed back from a distant future. I never thought about why
it was called Houldsworth Square and never considered that there in
fact had been a Houldsworth, a William Houldsworth and eventually

a Sir William Henry Houldsworth, Baronet. Without Sir William Houldsworth there would not only have been no Houldsworth Square, there would not have been a Reddish – at least, not as it turned out to be.

There would not have been this story, so this story of the north, with Houldsworth Square at its nondescript centre, the story in my mind of how the north was built, rebuilt, dreamed, scarred, lost, found, is the consequence of Conservative politician, committed Christian, dedicated philanthropist, social pioneer, paternalistic entrepreneur, cotton master and gifted organist William Henry Houldsworth being born in Ardwick, Manchester on 20 August 1834, the fourth son of Henry Houldsworth and Helen Hamilton. (At the time pre-industrialised Ardwick was an indistinct mile east of the Manchester city centre, located in open countryside, and Tiny Tim from Charles Dickens's *A Christmas Carol* is said to be based on frail invalid Henry Augustus Burnett, known as Harry, Dickens' nephew, son of his sister Fanny and Henry Burnett, both of them singing and music teachers living in Elm Terrace, Higher Ardwick. Harry died in Ardwick in 1849, aged nine, a year after his mother, who died of consumption.)

Houldsworth was educated at the University of St Andrews in Scotland, and then joined the family business. His family were Liberals and shared some of the values and wider principles of Liberalism, but William was unsympathetic to the radical wing of the party and felt closer to the New Conservatism of Benjamin Disraeli. He was a prime example of the new type of Manchester businessman, succeeding through their own concentrated self-motivated energy and expecting others to be inspired to do the same and thus generate more of the same sort of achievement.

In a speech in 1827 at the Manchester Mechanics Institute in Cooper Street, founded two years before for the 'improvement intellectually and socially of the working and middle classes', the scientist, lecturer and Institute administrator John Davies told his audience, 'Man must be the architect of his own fame,' and this philosophy drove the likes of Houldsworth. As William was planning his local empire, he perhaps felt some guilt that earlier generations of Manchester men, those bigwig entrepreneurs who had made their money as the city went through an accelerated urbanisation, had ignored the neglect of town planning that had led to the shocking disparity between the 'hovels and the palaces'. Houldsworth was more sensitive to how the increase in production leading to the increase in population had had such a terrible impact on the quality of life and health of ordinary working people. He built big to express his ego and ambition, but he also thought of his workers.

He first bought land in Reddish in 1864 alongside the Stockport Branch of the Ashton Canal, where he built Reddish Mill, adding North and Middle Mills over the next ten years. The gargantuan main factory contained a huge central clock with front and back faces to ensure late workers had no excuse, a fine 110-foot chimney at the back and forthright twin towers either side of the main entrance.

Abraham Henthorn Stott designed the Houldsworth Mills. Born in 1822 in Crompton, the son of a stonemason, he'd served his apprenticeship with Sir Charles Barry, architect of the Houses of Parliament and Manchester Art Gallery, and was the head of the Oldham-based Stott dynasty of mill-building structural engineers and architects, who designed and constructed scores of important, extremely conspicuous mills in the surrounding area. He spent ten years building not only the mills for Houldsworth but associated houses and community buildings. Houldsworth, inspired by the example of distinguished Nonconformist West Riding industrialist Sir Titus Salt and his progressive industrial community outside Bradford, was concerned to look after the spiritual and social welfare of his employees and their families, and spent time and money on where they could worship, socialise and be educated. In 1874 *Practical Magazine* described Salt's industrial community, Saltaire, three miles from Bradford, which took twenty years to build, as 'a nation in miniature, a little kingdom within a kingdom'.

In building and expanding his community, Houldsworth was a bold enterprising thinker, or at least was part of a committee of big thinkers, even though Reddish was a modest, peripheral space. He and the company he helped found commissioned the best practitioners in their fields. Stott was chosen for the mills because he was the best in the north, and to design his churches and schools he hired one of the most

successful nineteenth-century architects, Alfred Waterhouse, born in
Aigburth, Liverpool in 1830, the son of wealthy mill-owning Quaker
parents. One of Alfred's brothers, accountant Edwin, was co-founder
of Price, Waterhouse and Co.

The prolific, versatile Waterhouse was an influential figure in the
assertive high-Victorian architecture that was part of Manchester's
transformation into a major international city during the nineteenth
century. Known as Slaughterhouse Waterhouse for his liking for red
brick, his buildings were nostalgic for medieval flamboyance, which
made them look particularly dated by the 1960s, and he was determined to produce complicated, stirring skylines. He built the
intimidating Strangeways Prison, the massive, quintessentially Gothic
Refuge Assurances Building on the corner of Oxford Street and
Whitworth Street, as well as twenty-seven buildings around the county
for the Prudential Assurance Company. He also designed the Natural
History Museum in London, the National Liberal Club, Liverpool
Infirmary, the Metropole Hotel on the seafront at Brighton, and various
buildings for Oxford and Cambridge including the Union Buildings
and work for Caius College.

By the end of his career, always determined to be much more than
a provincial architect, he would be credited with over 650 buildings,
and between 1865 and 1885 was known as Britain's most widely
employed architect. He was president of the Royal Institute of British
Architects from 1888 to 1891. Most notably, in 1869 he solved the
problem of locating a large building on a tricky triangular site in the
city centre by building the dramatic, architecturally sonorous
Manchester Town Hall with its front on Albert Square. This was
finally completed in 1877, with a 280-foot clock tower, the three faces
of the clock inscribed with 'Teach us to number our days.' The town
hall would be described as a 'High Victorian secular masterpiece' and
gave imposing spatial form to the then cresting Manchester self-
belief. Waterhouse's work for Houldsworth was relatively modest,
especially compared to the ostentatious and ingenious Manchester
Town Hall, but he would work on anything that caught his eye – as
big as a town hall, a church, a museum, a prison, but with his love for
practical but alluring detail he also designed the hot-water fountain

in Chester Street, Manchester, a signboard on iron brackets for the Grosvenor Hotel in Chester, an extension to Knutsford Jail, various stables, semi-detached houses and sundry alterations to existing buildings. Commissioned in the 1870s and named after Houldsworth's wife, St Elisabeth's Church was built between 1881 and 1883 and paid for by Houldsworth, with the addition of a rectory, school and working men's club, also designed by Waterhouse. The combined buildings were known as the Waterhouse Set. Houldsworth also planned several streets of cottages for his employees, but only a few terraced houses were actually built.

One hundred and five years after the birth of Alfred Waterhouse, in 1935, Norman Foster was born in Reddish and brought up in a gaslit terraced house in The Crescent near a railway viaduct on the gloomy outskirts of Levenshulme where it merges into Reddish. 'The nearby railway bridge,' he remembered, 'bore huge steam trains that flew directly past my bedroom window. Under the arch of that bridge, though, down along a path, was a quite different proposition: a nice middle-class area of streets lined with trees and smart detached villas.'

Norman Foster's father ran a pawnbroker's and was later a security guard and a manual worker in a factory; his mother was a waitress. He went to grammar school and was bullied, leaving at sixteen. Foster was a determined bookish youth, a trainspotter, a fan of the *Eagle* comic and fascinated by Meccano. As a teenager he would cycle around south Manchester sketching parks, bridges, walkways and town squares before he even knew what an architect was. He became besotted with two books in his local library. One was about the American architect Frank Lloyd Wright, the other Le Corbusier's modernist bible *Towards a New Architecture*. Lloyd Wright's maxim was 'Form and function are one.'

'If it hadn't been for Levenshulme Library,' Foster once said, 'and those books about architecture I found, I probably wouldn't have gone to university.' After school Norman Foster initially worked in the Manchester City Treasurer's Office before National Service in the Royal Air Force. Once out of the RAF, he went to Manchester

University School of Architecture and City Planning – working in a cold store, selling ice cream and furniture, in a factory and even as a bouncer at a cinema to pay his way through college – and developed an understanding of Manchester as a precursor of the modern global city. Perhaps too he found out about a local architect, an innovative designer who died the year he was born at the age of seventy-five, so that Foster joined the path trod by Edgar Wood, born in Middleton to a strict mill-owning father.

Wood initially had ambitions to be an artist, coming to a compromise with his disapproving father, who expected him to enter the family cotton business, by training as an architect. He transferred his artistic temperament and belief in the beauty of creative power into buildings, mostly domestic but also several churches and commercial buildings, schools and hotels, and he was perfectionist enough to design the furniture and stained-glass windows that went with them, aiming for a completely integrated environment. He was influenced initially by the bold, lyrical Arts and Crafts Movement, and then in the early part of the twentieth century, as the Victorian Gothic tradition faded out, by the more abstract and modern: houses with flat roofs, dramatic curves and discreetly detailed elegance, almost prototypically space age. He built one of the first known concrete flat roofs in Britain – in 1906 – placing Mediterranean-inspired minimalism at the end of a row of everyday terraced houses in his red-brick hometown. In 1914 he built a semicircular two-storey house for himself clearly influenced by his travels to Persia and Tunisia – anticipating the geometric decorative detailing of Frank Lloyd Wright and the romantic industrial mind of Le Corbusier – in Hale, Altrincham, ten miles out of Manchester, where the managerial middle class moved for peace and family life. Florid Victorian architecture veered bizarrely towards Bauhaus sparseness in the village of Hale (Anglo-Saxon for nook or shelter) sixty years after its population was less than a thousand. Wood's progressive and vivid approach to architecture, his sense of style and purpose, was right up Foster's high street.

After four years starting in 1963 working at Team Four with his friend the more naturally glamorous Richard Rogers – he toured America with him to find as many Frank Lloyd Wright buildings as possible – Norman Foster formed his own firm in 1967, today called Foster and Partners. Rejecting the stock concrete shell favoured by most other architects, which had introduced negative brutalist iconography to rushed British post-war modernisation, perversely intensifying rather than remedying the damage of the Second World War, Foster used less aggressive and alienating materials, especially steel and glass, and opted wherever possible for natural light. He set out to reinvent architecture, seeing buildings as permanent performances embedded in articulated environments. He believed that buildings could open up the future, in the process symbolising new ideas, new relationships and the availability of important new information. When he was created a life peer in 1999, he chose the title Baron Foster of Thames Bank, of Reddish in the county of Greater Manchester.

Looking at some of his buildings, like the headquarters of the Swiss Re in London (the Gherkin) and Wembley Stadium in north London – the way they flow above the land and buildings around them, dominant and strangely lucid, filling space and somehow internalising space, bringing intimacy to majesty, inhuman but down to earth, gargantuan but precise – I wonder if he spent time staring at the monumental mills in Reddish near his house and the way they communicated something spectacularly special and announced their impressive, incongruous presence in the middle of the passively routine and forgettable. They were very particular ideas turned into mass, into material with personality.

An apprentice architect wanting to design buildings with a showman's brashness must have learned much from being surprised when the boldly bulky Reddish mills appeared at the end of an ordinary street, glimpsed between standard terraced-house chimneys from a train passing through the chimneyed, drainpiped and slated plainness reliably unfolding between Stockport and Levenshulme, swelling with uncurbed pomp and pride in the otherwise mediocre middle distance. The mills were spectres from the past destined to expire through sheer bulk alone, but they were once a dazzling sign that the future was on its way, and in my childhood they still lifted themselves above their low thrifty surroundings with an attitude that was as much futuristic as it was dead and gone.

Born twenty-eight years before Foster, on 24 July 1907 in Reddish, Charles Hugh Owen Ferry would write as Hugh Charles the words for two of the Second World War's most distinctive patriotic songs, 'We'll Meet Again' and 'There'll Always Be an England' – songs that travelled beyond those events with memories and feelings stuck fast to them, with the latter often advocated as a new national anthem and 'We'll Meet Again' featuring on the 1962 album *Sinatra Sings Great Songs of Great Britain.*

Written before the war but shrewdly prepared for the struggle ahead, 'There'll Always Be an England' was written to be sung by a soloist in front of a rousing military band, triumphantly leading thousands festooned in flags, blandly but belligerently challenging those who heard it to agree or disagree with how much England means and how much it is worth fighting for. The way the song lightly combined the pastoral – the small cottage on a country lane beside an inspiring field of green – and the urban – the busy street, the turning wheel, a million marching feet – suggests that childhood memories of Reddish lying between crammed, purposeful, mighty Manchester on one side and the exhilarating but ordered and gentle open spaces on the other, had stayed in Charles's mind as he imagined an idealised England that combined Blake's romantic pre-industrial green and pleasant land – a vital eternal detail in the wartime construction of a proud unique image of the nation – and the city centres being pounded by German bombs. Reddish, on the border between the big, battling and bustling industrial city and the very English dreamlike hedgerows, stiles, streams and winding lanes, was his template for an England that would always be, half of it wide awake, on the edge of its nerves, fighting for survival, half of it sleepily caught up in its own endless cosy patterns, as close to sedate deadlocked Houldsworth Square as it was to the factories, the town halls, the competing high streets and the relentless snorting trains thundering through its heart.

Houldsworth's church used brick from Openshaw – two miles east of Manchester city centre between Gorton and Ashton Old Road – and stone from Wrexham, north Wales. The granite columns in the nave were brought to Reddish by narrowboat and taken from the canal wharf by the mill on carts drawn by elephants borrowed from Belle Vue Zoo. Designs for the decoration of the private chapel of Houldsworth's home in Kilmarnock, Scotland were eventually used inside the neo-Gothic church in Reddish. They were created by Frederic Shields, Hartlepool-born Pre-Raphaelite artist and contemporary and colleague of Ford Madox Brown, whose twelve spirited panels illustrating the history of Manchester decorate Alfred Waterhouse's Great Hall in the centre of Manchester Town Hall. At Reddish Shields' stern, impassioned, cosmically religious designs became the stained-glass windows.

Here, a quarter of a mile from my local Essoldo, was more rare vivid colour pressed into everyday Reddish, as if the flushed ghost of William Blake had poured precious liquid drops of his dangerous fiery spirit into this quietly expanding meek little village. Not that I knew at the time. One anxious glance at the church, all that ecstatic pious imagery compressed inside an unashamedly Gothic building representing an exotically charged faith, was enough to propel me a considerable distance from its extravagant doors. In pared-down 1960s Reddish the Victorians' faith in a higher power and entrepreneurial self-belief – made visible in the buildings around Houldsworth Square, where you caught the coach to see Manchester City or the number 9 single-decker leaving twice an hour to head via twenty-two stops towards Parrs Wood and West Didsbury – would have seemed especially alien.

There would have been no sense in my mind of how the imaginative enterprise involved in the creation of Reddish was the reason it existed. And whatever that imagination and commitment to a new community, most of it had by then drained away. The buildings were still there, adrift in the wrong place and the wrong time. Other mills had landed after Houldsworth's, including the blandly lofty Broadstone Mill, built by Stott and Sons in 1907. The Houldsworth Mills were intended to form the unintimidating hub of a well-designed, practical and nurturing model estate, but the later ones lacked this community element. For a while Broadstone Mill was the biggest in the country, reflecting the idea that in business size obviously means success. It survived as a working mill for fifty years, but

was already defunct by the time I lived in Reddish, as stonily ancient
and remotely mysterious as something out of the Bible. It was just
standing there, minding its own business.

Cotton production at Reddish Mill continued until the 1950s. It
was then sold to a mail-order catalogue company and used primarily
as a warehouse. The rampant roar of the Industrial Revolution
subsided to a mere croak, leaving behind these mammoth brick
carcasses, and all that was left of the great benefactor Houldsworth
and his dream of a better way of life in the Reddish he made was his
name – a name it never occurred to me at the time was the name of
someone who had once lived, who must once have been vigorous,
ambitious and stubbornly determined. There were a few signs that
Houldsworth was once a real man, the powerful man who made
Reddish, but there was no statue.

Houldsworth stood unsuccessfully for Parliament in 1880, but
won three years later and was until 1906 the Conservative MP for the
brand-new middle-class commercial constituency of Manchester
North West. In 1892 he was the government's delegate to the European
Monetary Conference held in Brussels and the same year opened the
Conservative Club in Manchester Road, Denton, 'a structure of
Accrington pressed bricks with ornamental cornices, relieved with
Yorkshire stone dressings. It contains a large assembly hall, reading,
billiard and other rooms, and is fitted with every modern improve-
ment; the architect was Mr T. D. Lindley, of Ashton under Lyne; the
total cost was about £2,300.'

As an MP he was a supporter of the Manchester Ship Canal, free
trade (until 1903, when he came out in favour of tariff reform), the gold
and silver money standard and the amalgamation of the cotton industry. He was also actively involved in public institutions in Manchester,
including Owen's College and many working men's clubs, and was
given the freedom of the city in 1905, a further sign he had hauled his
way, with the help of Reddish, into history. In the end, though, for all
his diligent efforts to leave his mark, he managed to reach only a dim,
neglected corridor of history some way off from any of the blazingly
illuminated main rooms. Further down the corridor, perhaps in the
main room, was much more of a name, and perhaps Houldsworth's

ultimate role in history was to make way for this indelible figure and his close association with the unimaginable tensions, traumas and emergencies of the twentieth century.

His successor in Parliament after winning six elections was Winston Churchill, who represented Manchester North West until 1908 as a member of the Liberal Party. Houldsworth, then a powerful figure in Lancashire politics, had apparently taken Churchill under his wing when he was a twenty-five-year-old Conservative candidate at Oldham in 1899. Churchill was then mainly known as the slick talkative son of Lord Randolph Churchill and a journalist beginning a career as a war reporter for the *Morning Post*. The Oldham Conservative Party had been keen to present a candidate with his name and connections. Churchill wrote to his mother while in Oldham, describing the area as lacking a hotel, at least to his standards, and noting 'there is practically no local society, only multitudes of workers'. When Churchill made a campaigning visit to Hollinwood on the western edge of the Oldham constituency, memories of his father provoked a lively someone to heckle, ' Eh, lad, thou art a chip off t' owd block.'

At the time Oldham had a population of 150,000, mostly due to its closeness to Manchester, six miles and a few minutes away by train. It was said that Oldham was to Manchester what coal was to a steam train: fuel. It was noted at the time that: 'No one stops there. Externally, life is here of the plainest drab; everything is for use, nothing for ornament. The town appears to have grown simply by the accretion of mills and works with the necessary streets for the accommodation of the workmen.'

Churchill had failed by 1,500 votes in his attempt to win Oldham in 1899. During the election J. R. Clynes, the secretary of Oldham Trades Council, had led a delegation to challenge him on various labour issues. Clynes would write later, 'I found him a man of extraordinarily independent mind, and great courage. He absolutely refused to yield to our persuasions, and said bluntly that he would rather lose votes than abandon his convictions.' A year later, after an escapade in South Africa while covering the Boer War for the *Morning Post*, Churchill was back. While on the run from the Boers he had been helped by an Oldham man, Dan Dewsnap, who once freedom was achieved, shook Churchill's hand 'in a grip of crushing vigour' and announced, 'They'll all vote for you next time.' Returning as a hero, Churchill wrote about his visit to Oldham in July 1900, when he was welcomed by brass bands and friendly crowds: 'Oldham almost without distinction of party accorded me a triumph. I entered the town in state in a procession of ten landaus, and drove through streets crowded with enthusiastic operatives and mill girls. I described my escape to a tremendous meeting in the Theatre Royal.' He told the Oldham voters that the town was exactly the sort of place he wanted to represent – 'a throbbing, pulsing, living place full of work and working men'.

He did win, making his inaugural acceptance speech from the Old Town Hall, opened in 1841, but mostly stayed in London. Churchill clearly never took to his constituency. 'There is neither warmth nor comfort in the place. Through the recent frost one of my clerks is dead (pneumonia) and the other has acute bronchitis, and the two illnesses can only be attributed to the absence of any fire or warmth in the office, and to general damp, dark, unsanitary condition.' He always regarded himself like his father as a 'Tory Democrat' and in secret a Liberal 'in all but name', defecting during his time as Oldham MP to the Liberals. He stayed on until the next election in 1906, when as Liberal candidate in Houldsworth's old Manchester North West seat he won easily and became a junior minister. Four years later he was home secretary and between 1940 and 1945 prime minister. He was PM again in 1952 when on 3 October Britain detonated its first atomic device, code-named Hurricane.

Oldham, his first constituency, made him a freeman in 1941, some time before it was clear who would triumph in the Second World War. In later life Churchill sentimentally looked back on the 'warm hearts and bright eyes' of the Oldham people, and a little hazily remarked that 'no one can come in contact with the working folk of Lancashire without wishing them well'.

Churchill, a great man of international history, has been remembered in all sorts of traditional ways, from statues, coins and glorifying hero worship (or corrective contempt) to vast volumes of reverential (or critical) biography and a state funeral. Houldsworth, an early mentor, a great man of Reddish history, has been remembered with a small square – more or less a glorified open-air bus terminus – a golf course that took his name in 1910 – Houldsworth's extravagant estate and stately home in Ayrshire was once the home of the founder of the British Open – and a fifteen-foot-high clock with fountain erected in the square three years after he died in 1917. He clings on to history by the fingertips; his apprentice Churchill punched history in the face, and was punched back.

Plans for this memorial started soon after the end of the First World War, and a committee formed for the purpose of raising funds had by February 1919 collected £707. This included £250, the largest amount, from the Cotton Spinners Association, £50 from the manager of Houldsworth Schools, £70 from Houldsworth Working Men's Club and £20 from the Reddish Conservative Club, which had resolved in a special meeting on 23 April 1917 that a letter of condolence be sent to Lady Houldsworth on Sir William's recent death. (A meeting three days later resolved that the price of tobacco in the club be increased – Rolling Tobacco Twist be raised to sevenpence an ounce, and a packet of Woodbines from twopence ha'penny to threepence ha'penny. A month later it was agreed that as a packet of Woodbines could be purchased around the corner for a penny ha'penny the price be reduced to that amount. It was also resolved that the club would send two representatives to the Houldsworth Working Men's Club 'regarding a suitable memorial for Sir William'.)

The location for the memorial had been agreed upon, but not the actual form that it would take. It was eventually decided that it would be a tower with four clock faces and fountain: 'Plinth with inscription, bronze portrait roundel, fountain niche and bowl on faces, supports clustered columns in pink granite, carved capitals, below block with clock face, gable top and foliated finial.' It originally included ground-level animal troughs, which were eventually removed. It was unveiled on 20 September 1920 and the inscription read:

DEDICATED

TO THE MEMORY OF

SIR WILLIAM HENRY HOULDSWORTH,

BARONET,

BY THE PEOPLE OF REDDISH
IN GRATEFUL REMEMBRANCE
OF THE BOUNTIFUL GIFTS WHEREBY
HE ENRICHED AND ADORNED THEIR VILLAGE
AND MANIFESTED HIS CONCERN FOR THEIR
SPIRITUAL, MENTAL AND PHYSICAL WELFARE.

The original clock was mechanical and needed to be regularly wound. The mechanism was in the cellar of a nearby pub, the Houldsworth Arms, connected to the clock under the ground. An electric drive eventually replaced the clockwork mechanism. Over the years, as Reddish trundled on after the loss of its main creator, asymmetrically settling around his whimsically monumental brick buildings and their towering chimneys, the electrically powered four clocks often registered different times and sometimes stopped altogether. Time and Reddish never quite joined up.

44

1926

The Wilson family went on a trip to Australia. Meeting an uncle who was a politician in Western Australia was something of an inspirational experience, and on his return home young Harold announced to his mother Marjorie that he was going to be prime minister one day.

1924

J. R. Clynes became leader of the House of Commons and deputy prime minister under Ramsay MacDonald. In 1923, as leader of the Labour Party, he had moved the successful motion of no confidence against Stanley Baldwin's Conservative administration which led to the appointment of the first Labour government.

1923

George Formby met the woman who would change his life. Beryl Ingham, who with her sister May had a clog-dancing act called the Two Violets, was not impressed with George. She had been a professional for ten years and was one of the most talented performers in her field. She found George's amateurish, shambolic act painful to watch, but recognised something in him, some quality of which he himself was unaware, and was ambitious enough for both of them to want to exploit it. In September 1924 George and Beryl were married, much to his mother's dismay. Beryl now assumed professional and financial control over George, modernised his act and set out the future path of his career. Having adopted his father's stage persona, it took George the younger a while to develop his own identity. This was helped along no end by his marriage to Beryl, who introduced him to the banjolele and carefully honed his act to create the gormless warm-hearted character who would enchant – or infuriate – Britain throughout the 1930s and forties.

1922

Interview with W. H. Auden, 15 November 1971:
'Did you ever regret becoming a poet, particularly in your early years?'

'No, not when I started, I must say. I started in rather an odd way. Psychologically I think I can understand it now. In March 1922 I was walking across a field – I was in boarding school – with a friend of mine (a fellow who turned out to be a painter later), and he asked me if I ever wrote poetry. I said no, that thought had never occurred to me, and he said why don't you?

'I can still remember the last line of the first poem I ever wrote, about a town in the Lake District. The last line ran: "And in the quiet oblivion of thy waters let them stay." I can't remember who "they" were.'

Although he lived the greater part of his working life in Hull, Philip Larkin was born in Coventry in 1922, the year when the two stream-of-consciousness masterworks (James Joyce's *Ulysses* and T. S. Eliot's *The Waste Land*) were published.

J. R. Clynes led Labour in the breakthrough 1922 general election, when the party supplanted the Liberals as the official opposition to the (Conservative) government, almost tripling the number of Labour MPs elected.

The BBC was created and started broadcasting in 1922. Two years later it began local radio broadcasts – from Leeds with the official opening of the Leeds/Bradford (2LS) relay station by the legendary John Reith, its first director general. The offices and a studio were at Basinghall Street. The studio was draped with pleated curtains and featured a hair cord carpet with ample underfelt, which helped to muffle every echo. The first station director was G. P. Fox, son of the town clerk of Leeds.

John Braine was born in a small terraced house off Bradford's Westgate. He was educated at St Bede's Grammar School, moving to Thackley when his father got a job at Esholt Sewage Works. Thackley was a morose satellite of industrial Shipley, just the sort of place his main *Room at the Top* character Joe Lampton came from, 'where the snow seemed to turn black almost before it hit the ground'. His mother gave John an interest in books, and after various jobs around Bradford, from junior salesman in Christopher Pratt's furniture shop to progress chaser at the Hepworth & Grandage piston factory, he found work as an assistant at Bingley Library.

1921

'A good clear star has ceased to shine in our firmament,' wrote Harry Lauder after George Formby Senior died in 1921.

George Junior's mother Eliza told him that despite his father's feelings about him 'treading the boards', he was to go on stage. When a shy seventeen-year-old ex-jockey called George Hoy took to the Newcastle stage in 1921, it was an inauspicious start to a considerable career. Earlier that same year George had been a spectator at the Newcastle Empire, watching for the first and only time in his life his famous dad in pantomime only months before he died. This was the point when George decided on a career change and, accepting Harry Lauder's advice not to follow a famous name, he was introduced as George Hoy, taking his mother's maiden name, by which he had also been christened. As he explained in later years, this was because he did not want to trade on his father's fame and reputation. Even so, he essentially regurgitated his father's act. If not trading on his reputation, he was relying on what had gone into building it. And why not? Charlie Chaplin, as a sixteen-year-old, had imitated Formby Senior, who twirled a cane in his song 'One of the Boys'. Borrowing Formby's hat, lace-less boots and baggy trousers for a performance, Chaplin never returned them.

'This is an age of transition between the music hall and the revue. The music hall is older, more popular, and is sanctified by the admiration of the nineties. It has flourished most vigorously in the north; many of its most famous stars are of Lancashire origin. (Marie Lloyd, if I am not mistaken, has a bit of a Manchester accent.) Lancashire wit is mordant, ferocious, and personal; the Lancashire music hall is excessively intimate; success depends upon the relation established by a comedian of strong personality with an audience quick to respond with approval or contempt. The fierce talent of Nellie Wallace (who also has a Lancashire accent) holds the most boisterous music hall in complete subjection. Little Tich and George Robey (though the latter has adapted himself in recent years to some inferior revues) belong to this type and generation. The Lancashire comedian is at his best when unsupported and making a direct set, pitting himself against a suitable audience; he is seen to best advantage at the smaller and more turbulent halls. As the smaller provincial or suburban hall disappears, supplanted by the more lucrative Cinema, this type of comedian disappears with it.' T. S. Eliot, 1921.

1919

Peace parades were held throughout the land on Saturday 19 July 1919. The *Rochdale Observer*, reporting the following Wednesday, said, 'Not since the King and Queen came to Rochdale in July 1913 have there been such vast crowds in Rochdale streets.' They also reported that 'at night there were bonfires and flares on the surrounding hills, and they were watched by masses of people from a variety of viewpoints. The old churchyard and slopes formed a capital vantage point for such spectators, who remained in large numbers until a late hour.'

Henry Moore returned to Castleford aged twenty, obtained an ex-service-man's grant and became the first ever student of sculpture at Leeds College of Art in September 1919. As he remembered, 'sculpture was not a popular art form in England in those days'. The college had no department when Moore arrived in 1919, and Reginald Cotterill set one up especially for him in his second year. Collections of African carvings belonging to Leeds University's vice chancellor, Sir Michael Sadler, sparked his initial interest in primitive art long before it gained general acceptance in England. He continued to live in Castleford, where he attended Miss Gostick's Peasant Pottery Class in the evenings, travelling to and from Leeds by train each day. At Leeds College of Art Henry Moore met fellow students Barbara Hepworth, Raymond Coxon and Edna Ginesi. All went on to attend the Royal College of Art in London from 1921 to 1925, where, along with Wakefield-born Vivian Pitchforth, they formed what became known as the Leeds table. Moore had a nice Yorkshire analogy for the limited support around for modern art in the 1920s: 'when you put a tight lid on a kettle you develop quite a head of steam'.

Bassett's gave birth to the Jelly Baby in Sheffield – first called the Peace Baby to celebrate the end of the First World War.

1917

Physicist Ernest Rutherford discovered how to split the atom at Manchester University. He showed that by firing alpha particles into nitrogen gas a small amount of hydrogen could be produced. This was the first artificial disinte-gration of a nucleus. His laboratory in Manchester had been the scene of scientific discoveries that were to form the foundations of nuclear physics since 1907.

45

I didn't think about it at the time, but the north folded out from me, all of me and the house where I lived, in the street where it was, in the district where that was, part of the town it belonged to, which was in a particular county, near a large city in its own county, which connected to other counties, which contained their own districts, regions, cities and towns, their own versions of Stockport and Reddish, and streets and houses and people at the centre of their own north, connected to each other because for hundreds of years there had been plans and ambitions and inventions, and a sense of how to create for better or worse a future. I didn't realise when I was seven or eight or nine, knowing only that I lived in Reddish, Stockport, Cheshire, but where I found myself was connected to a history of plans, systems and ambitions, highfalutin minds, dreamers and workers – men, women and artists with a distinctive commitment to progress and change, entertainers happy to make things seem better than they were, comedians understanding how it all led to a certain sort of relieving, even inspiring punchline – and to the severe specialness of the landscape where they found themselves, a combination of people crammed together in villages that became towns that became cities that spilled out into towns and villages and empty open spaces.

Once you had passed through Reddish, past North Reddish School and Reddish North station – originally just Reddish, it acquired the 'North' in 1951 – meeting eventually the Hyde Road and Davy Jones of the Monkees' Debdale Park, you were in Gorton; you were in Denton, south of Dukinfield, north of Gee Cross. Despite the pitch-and-putt course and the proper golf course next door, this area seemed harder and tougher to my young mind. It was where the city of Manchester frayed and splattered into dishevelled spiky suburbs, with tighter streets, more cobbles, greyer roofs, gloomier corners, meaner skies, harder minds – pushing out towards the sullen darkness of elsewhere where the moors took over.

The Gorton Road plainly ebbed away into the forlorn brickbuilt past, one sullied district dissolving imperceptibly into another and yet another intricate network of distressed undernourished streets diligently holding on to their inhabitants, up to their neck in local business, routine tasks, family tensions and blossoming gossip, and then you were in areas dominated by the lingering presence and foul moods of Ian Brady and Myra Hindley (born 23 July 1942 in Crumpsall (crooked field by a river) on the River Irk, next to Blackley, Harpurhey and Prestwich, two miles north of Manchester Cathedral. Crumpsall was described in 1830 as a 'pleasant village containing several handsome residences belonging to the opulent merchants and manufacturers of Manchester'. Lowry's shabby subdued abstractions of abandoned streets, people and factories like those around Gorton and Denton were definitely appealing, even soothing cartoons next to the degraded hell-soaked angle of approach that Brady and Hindley took.

They were the repellent child killers who slithered into the national imagination through news reports that were so vile and shocked, even scared stiff, they resembled smoke-stained blood-saturated Gothic fantasy. Their diabolical life's work stuck to your soul especially once you had seen their stunning police photographs, in which two defiant haunting faces stared straight at you, sizing you up, bringing steaming news of terror from just damp yards around the corner near the chip shop which sold Holland's pies, by the garage where your dad once went to buy a pale blue second-hand Triumph Herald, a little potential flash of style and difference on the mundane streets comfy with pragmatic Morris Minors, Minis and Prefects and Cortinas, which he couldn't in the end afford, not by a mile.

Hindley and Brady, charred trapped scraps of frustrated northern will, were some kind of warning to those who might think there must be more to what I am and where I am than this, to those who thought differently. Look what you became if you thought there might be something not revealed by the buses and back gardens, the newsagents and swings and roundabouts; look what would happen if you thought about yourself too much and had ideas above your station, ideas that questioned the view that you were nothing special.

The deadly couple, the psycho-sadist and the battered, damned bully, helping each other out on their way to sordid infamy, intently combining the practical, the perverse and the grotesque, took advantage of the nearby moors, thousands of acres of alienating open land blasted and twisted into apocalyptic austerity by decades of unforgiving industrial activity a few miles away, to bury, once rubbed out, their shy victims, who were about my age, sons and daughters of dads and mums like mine, brutally stripped of their future and shoved into the deep damp mirthless earth. Under the surface, where nothing from above could reach them – no messages, no love – face to face with the brutish end of time, robbed for their innocence and unmarked kids' skin of the gathering awareness I, close by, unmolested, was slowly getting used to. This abrupt premature end – under the ground, of children coldly tossed inside a slab of rocky muddy country that seemed built by demons to resemble, in the right light, at the wrong time of day, under a desolate stabbing drizzle, the damned middle of nowhere – happened very near to North Reddish, my north Reddish, to North Reddish Infants and Junior School, where I didn't have a clue, teeming with sons and daughters resembling their mums and dads, who were sons and daughters, and so on.

Reddish was everything, my home and my surroundings, walls and roads, library, baths and classroom, friends and enemies, toys and pets, and I would move around, as far as I could, from day to day and street to street and Sunday to Sunday from park to park, but stay where I was. There seemed no possibility that I would ever leave this place. I don't think I ever thought it through, and I cannot remember ever thinking this so precisely, but I felt that I was surrounded by people who were staying where they were, busy but planted, essentially obedient, and I would join them, because this was where I was, and therefore who I was. Little came into Reddish but the place itself, as maintained by its position, bricks and mortals under a sceptical sky reflected in glazed puddles that never seemed to disappear even in the summer, which was always, year in year out, doomed to end quickly.

Even now as I consider the possibility that there were things floating through the mental air – words, songs, feelings, history, superstitions, thoughts, facts, myths, births and deaths – and appreciate that by considering this possibility I am actually proving that it was true, forty-five years after I was there, I remember the time when I was no more than a boy, immersed and acceptant in a world that was still made out of steam, church and tradition, which contained immovable ceremonies, duties, routines, unseen stumbling blocks, and the non-stop demands, restrictions, instructions and occasional ferocity, even danger, of adults, who could be kind but were essentially in superior unforgiving control. Adults who promised a future made up of more of where you were and what there was around you because of the way they seemed so stuck inside their own thorough and unchangeable fate. There was too a coldness and darkness, a heavy atmosphere in the house where I lived, that seemed to repel the very idea that you could change who you were and where you were because something outside immensely anchored Reddish might make it through some unreal, invisible opening and into the clear spaces inside your mind.

46

1917

'[Mancunians] make an affectation of candour and trade a little on their county's reputation for uncouthness.' Harold Brighouse, *Hobson's Choice*, 1917, set in the soot-sodden Salford of the 1880s.

In July Prime Minister David Lloyd George appointed J. R. Clynes parliamentary secretary at the Ministry of Food in his coalition government. Clynes used rationing to save the country from starvation and, according to some, Bolshevism. He is one of Labour's less well-known party leaders but would have been the first ever Labour prime minister had he not been defeated by just five votes for the party leadership by Ramsay MacDonald.

1916

As well as being one of the first artists to make records, starting in 1907, amiably chatting away to his invisible audience with much of his on-stage sparkle, George Formby Senior was perhaps the first of the northern comics to confirm the stereotype that everyone north of Watford was a slow-witted idiot. One of his first manifestations in the halls down south was as John Willie, up in London for the Cup, with tales of Wigan Pier, a name Formby invented, joking there was a pleasure pier in Wigan leading to a sandy beach, like there was in Blackpool, even if it was actually just a wharf where coal was loaded from trucks on to barges. The reputation of the citizens of Lancashire and Yorkshire has never recovered from what he started, in fact, this notion of backwardness. Formby was never a well man either, which didn't help the picture. His lungs bore the marks of consumption from breathing in sulphur when as a boy he worked in a Manchester steel foundry, and his trademark cough was as famous in its day as his son's banjolele would become thirty years later. Indeed George would often break off in the middle of a song to have a hearty cough ('Coughing better tonight – coughing summat champion') and have them rolling in the aisles. On stage he was both simple and always ailing, and frequently complaining.

Harold Wilson was born in Cowersley near Huddersfield on 11 March 1916. His father, Herbert Wilson, an industrial chemist, resented the fact that lack of family resources meant, though clever, he was never able to fulfil his potential. Herbert's son would represent an opportunity to make up for this, and he was given every encouragement by his parents to succeed academically. Harold worked hard, and was an enthusiastic Scout in his spare time, loving all the knots and singing around the campfire.

When writing his pronouncing dictionary in 1916, phonetician Daniel Jones described received pronunciation as the accent 'most usually heard in everyday speech in the families of southern English persons whose menfolk have been educated at the great public boarding schools'.

Stockport Edgeley to Manchester Piccadilly

Since Chaucer's times and his use of northern clerks from Strother (an imaginary village) as uncouth and slobby comic figures simply because they were from the north, there had been signs of how regional generalisation could be used to fabricate an idea of northernness as a state of otherness – culturally, socially, linguistically, politically, geographically – within the English language and the nation itself. Southern speech, it was implied, if not blatantly stated, had a higher social status and cultural authority than northern speech. An alternative view, a correction, can be made, exploiting generalisations and assumptions in the other direction – that the speech of the south was in fact artificial, fey, alien, linked to the cynical, corrupting worlds of wealth, business and power, and ultimately as unauthorised as northern was considered by the south. The speech of the north was domestic, genuine, virile, blunt, colloquial and rooted in the hard-working endeavours of honest, enterprising, unaffectedly common people. The northern tongue has as much claim to be dominant rather than provincial – to speak for the whole nation – as the southern tongue.

1914

When Britain entered the war against Germany on 4 August 1914 groups of local men signed up all over the country. In Accrington and its surroundings, 36 officers and 1,076 men enlisted in ten days. Their official name was the 11th (Service) Battalion (Accrington) East Lancashire Regiment, but they quickly became known as the Accrington Pals. Their valedictory service was held at St John's Church on 21 February 1915. Two days later 16,000 people lined the streets of Accrington to watch the Pals march to the railway station on their way to training in north Wales. In July 1916, at the Battle of the Somme, 230 Pals were killed and 350 wounded in the space of twenty minutes.

1914

By 1914 Manchester had 111 cinemas, more per head of population than anywhere in the country.

1912

'For Manchester is the place where people do things . . . "Don't talk about what you are going to do, do it." That is the Manchester habit. And in the past through the manifestation of this quality the word Manchester became a synonym for energy and freedom and the right to do and to think without shackles.' Judge Edward Abbott Parry, *What the Judge Saw*, 1912.

1911

The Ford factory at Trafford Park, the first in Europe, opened on Westinghouse Road. Initially the factory built Model T cars using traditional methods. On 23 October 1911 the first British-built Ford was completed. In 1914 the factory began the use of production lines. Although the company had strict rules and regulations, workers were keen to gain employment with the American firm, as Ford paid good wages. The mass production of combustion-engine vehicles saw the start of the demise of horses, canals, trams and ultimately railways for mass transportation.

1908

Surrounded by the heady aroma of herbs, spices and essences from around the world, John Noel Nichols created the original Vimto taste in a wooden barrel in his warehouse at 49 Granby Row in central Manchester in 1908 when he was twenty-four. In the early days Vimto promoted itself not only as a health tonic but also as an ideal temperance beverage. The temperance movement and the passage of the 1908 Licensing Act, which attempted to considerably reduce the number of licensed premises in England and Wales, were the ideal context for the launch of a soft drink.

Alistair (Alfred) Cooke, the graceful and cultured journalist, author, commentator and broadcaster whose *Letter from America* series of fifteen-minute talks explaining America and Americans ran for fifty-eight years, was born on 20 November 1908 in Salford and grew up in Blackpool, where his parents ran a guesthouse. His father Samuel had previously been an iron fitter and was also a Methodist lay preacher. Alfred went to Blackpool Grammar and won a scholarship to Jesus College, Cambridge and then later Yale and Harvard. He moved permanently to America in 1930, changed his name to Alistair, and after refusing a job offer from Charlie Chaplin joined the BBC in 1934 as a film critic. He became an American citizen in 1941, and lived in New York until his death in 2004, but he once said, 'I'm still an Englishman in America. An Irish Lancastrian, really. I don't kid myself that I'm from Arkansas.'

47

There was a grubby small front room in our Westbourne Grove house in Reddish containing bits of junk and old furniture, which embarrassed me so much in front of my friends, none of whom seemed to have rooms as messy, as unused as ours, with such drab peeling wallpaper and a stained carpet curling up at the edges, tired of life the way carpets get, endlessly beaten down from above, that I still redden thinking about it to this day, nearly fifty years later. Even as a young boy yet to form considered opinions or prejudices about how you were meant to live as a family and present yourself to the world, I felt it suggested that we were as a family somehow broken, not finished, not competent enough to be able to make this room what such a room should be – the room that showed off what you were as a family, something tidy, cosy, well kept, the room where you invited guests and visitors, and gave them tea and biscuits, and welcomed them into your home. I was ashamed by this room, but I could never fully explain why. We didn't go into it much. The door was often shut, hiding the shame, the devastating lack of basic competence.

I got clues about what such a room should be from visits I made to friends' houses, but mostly my reaction was based on instinct. It seemed wrong to have a room that did not work. It seemed to encourage the possibility that something else would enter this room and make it its own, not necessarily a ghost or anything, but not necessarily something benign and helpful. The room was haunted not by what had once been inside it and was now trapped, but by the inability of us as a family to fully take control of all that it could offer.

I remember sitting in it when I felt particularly sad or not sure what to do with myself. This meant sitting on the floor. I threw a tantrum when I was only about eight in front of some friends after a few hours biking around the streets. One of them must have said something or given me a funny look that seemed judgemental or challenging. I ranted that I knew they thought I was poor, and my mum and dad were poor, and dirty, because we had this unsightly room, which was not used as a room but as a sort of shed filled with the congealed ruins of my contaminated family. My bike was cheap and second hand and I'd painted it myself with thin emulsion so that it was covered with slimy lumps. I screamed at them that it wasn't my fault. I shouted that actually I was proud that we had a room like that. There was nothing wrong with a room used to store rubbish. I don't think they knew what I was going on about. I couldn't talk to them for days. I kept myself to myself and arranged the fine-grained details of a simmering sulk that felt powerful enough to be seen through walls.

Eventually the room was organised, at least so that it had chairs and a rented television and a small picture on the wall, and we had two rooms to live in. We fell into calling the former junk room the front room, as if that was the correct, noble term, and having one elevated us through the ranks of society, corrected our sorry displacement. I am writing this in the front room I now have, outside the north but with a north that I bring with me, just a feeling, which is therefore connected to that front room and all the front rooms I've ever had, always called the front room even if in fact not in front, relieved that I have access to such a thing and am therefore a member of the human race.

Before the front room was cleared out and organised, the room at the back was where we all lived, where we functioned as a family to the respective limits of our abilities and hankered after the kind of cosiness that might fix us together. It was where I was, a mite scared, when news came from upstairs, from the back bedroom, where my everyday mum and dad regularly dissolved into obscure secrets filled with unknown unknowable intention, that my new sister, my second, Carol, had been born in what must have been such a night-time burst of blood, fluid and shock that no one ever talked about it. I remember being shell shocked, perhaps not so much by the extraordinary arrival of a new life, but by the fact that I had another sister, and not a brother to play football with. I remember, or it seemed it should be this way, that my dad, faced with what appeared to be my sadness, or actual fear, compensated me with a handful of prized Quality Street chocolates, usually only ever seen at Christmas.

By being born there, in that room, in that house, in Reddish, Stockport, born among rows and rows of brick and numbered doors, houses filled with furniture built to drift into the margins, in between

GETTY IMAGES

The Duke of Bridgewater, founding father of the British canal system

impassive corners around which there was change and no change, under a diligent dove-grey sky committed to bringing showers and sudden downpours, Carol was instantly a northerner, and for all of her life there has never been any doubt that she remains one. Wherever she lives, wherever she travels, it is as though somehow in that miraculous melee of mess and matter in the room upstairs she was stamped with some ancient life force that infected her voice, her manner, her whole approach to the facts of life and the various fusses that ensue.

By being this northerner, she became part of – without knowing it, at least for a while, in no particular order – the energy, the substance hanging in the air, infused in the cement that jammed all those bricks together, pressed into the cracks between the paving stones that made up the pavements that could take you where you wanted to go and lead you round in circles, rising and falling in the damp and smoke that was never far away. As soon as she hurtled out of astonishing oblivion into this little Reddish room covered in flowered wallpaper the colour of a sticking plaster, the north had rushed into her and influenced her mind as though it alone could represent the difference between not existing and existing. Carol could now be added to a list of northern moments, incidents, personalities, jokes, sentences, routes that included:

48

1907

Wystan Hugh Auden was born at 54 Bootham, York on 21 February 1907, the youngest son of Dr George Augustus Auden, a general practitioner, and his wife, Constance Rosalie. Between the ages of six and twelve, wrote Auden, 'I spent a great many of my waking hours in the fabrication of a private second-ary sacred world, the basic elements of which were (a) a limestone landscape mainly derived from the Pennine Moors in the north of England, and (b) an industry – lead mining.' The Pennine landscape and its declining lead-mining industry figure in many of his poems. Auden's first love was the old industrial machinery littering the Yorkshire Dales.

1906

Although Manchester experimented early with the motor bus, it was not until July 1906 that the first Manchester Corporation bus route, between the tram terminus at West Didsbury and the Church Inn at Northenden, began oper-ating, replacing the horse buses that had previously used the route. The residents of West Didsbury were not impressed, and voiced their complaints about the noise and fumes.

'To see what the people are like you must observe them not only at work in the mill and at home or going to and from work, but also in their leisure time when they go out to enjoy themselves on Saturday and Sunday. This is the most striking feature of our industrial towns as compared with others. On Saturday afternoon you must go to the football field (in the season) to see the men and to the markets to see the women. The scenes presented by these two institutions are remarkable and not to be witnessed in any other country, but they are common to all our manufacturing towns, and are even more striking in Yorkshire than in Lancashire. At the football field there are generally gathered from 10,000 to 20,000 men and lads, nearly all out of the mills and machine shops, tidy, well dressed and well behaved. They pay 6d [six old pence] to go in. There are covered stands at a higher rate and in inferior matches the entrance is sometimes 3d, but 6d is the regular rate money. The spectators stand in serried ranks all around the ground and watch the game with intense interest. They keep up an incessant fire of comments and shout at every stroke or point in the play, which lasts an hour and a half. No better opportunity for observing them and their demeanour could be provided if they were paraded for the purpose. Here is the manhood and the youth of factoryland at the end of their week's work. They are full of animation and a spirit of sturdy independence; satisfied with themselves and their surroundings they neither fear nor envy anyone. Somewhat rough and blunt of speech they are yet by no means ill-mannered: the stranger will meet with no discourtesy from them if he shows them none.' Arthur Shadwell, *International Competitiveness*, 1906.

J. R. Clynes was a talented writer and in the early 1900s became a regular contributor to socialist newspapers such as the *Clarion*. Secretary of Oldham's Trade Council, Clynes was invited to be the Labour Party candidate for North East Manchester in the 1906 general election and was the youngest of the twenty-nine Labour MPs elected. He held the seat until 1931, even being returned unopposed in 1918. He won the seat back in the 1935 general election and remained an MP until he retired at the 1945 general election.

1905

Gracie Fields made her first appearance at Th' Owd Circus in Rochdale, sharing the first prize of ten shillings at the age of seven in 1905. Two years later Charlie Chaplin appeared there in a show called 'Casey's Court', where an unruly gang of children ran wild while music-hall star Will Murray, dressed in drag, failed to keep them in order. The seventeen-year-old Chaplin played a fake medicine seller in his sketch.

49

There was a settee and a table in the back downstairs room, which was next to the cramped kitchen, which was not much bigger than my bedroom. I remember it had a rickety free-standing electric oven, a kettle, but not a fridge. Facilities and equipment were pretty much what they would have been twenty years earlier, after the war. The lino on the floor looked like it had been in the war, on the inside of a tank.

The small main room where we lived, which never had a name like lounge or dining room, was mostly where we gathered to watch television – sometimes whatever kids were allowed in the 1960s, from *Andy Pandy* and *The Woodentops* to *Blue Peter*, sometimes events as unforgettable as the Saturday afternoon final of the 1966 World Cup, which England won with a team that included seven northerners – and get ready for school and work. It was freezing in the morning, not only in the dead of deadly winter but as far into the year as tentatively brightening May and then again by the darker part of September.

A coal fire needed to be quickly built as soon as we woke up, around seven, firmly twisted copies of the *Daily Express*, my dad's favourite newspaper, laid on top of a few pieces of coal when we didn't have Zip firelighters, which was mostly the case. Mum, five foot three inches, sensitive, belligerent daughter with three others, Sally, Jill and Liz, and a brother, David, of a woebegone Hyde cobbler, George Young, and a feisty Wilmslow housemaid, Sarah, was nineteen when she had me, and two years short of thirty when Carol burst forth into the north. Her fine fair hair so set, swept and sixties it was almost a beehive, her broad chin set into a fierce determination I only picked up looking at photographs decades later, she would perform the morning newspaper twisting with a strength that made me think of televised Saturday-afternoon wrestling.

A few damp matches would be struck before there was any sort of ignition. The coal would splutter into life behind the cheap buckled metal fire guard and above piles of soft grey ash from the day before and even the day before that, pathetic little flames forcing themselves into flickering motion soon gaining in confidence and alerting the icy grey room where we were gathered to the benefit of warmth. After early-morning fire duty, perhaps scooping up in a small battered shovel some of the old ash from coal and *Daily Express* and crushed unknown objects that all ended up mushroom-coloured, my mum would make tea.

My dad took a big dollop of milk and three teaspoons of sugar, probably craving enough energy to get out of the door and head for work and an unnamed occupation which was never clearly described to me, but which, from odd clues I picked up, consisted of hours of paper-work, boredom and irritation in an office. If there was some sort of ladder of seniority, from what I could gather he was at the bottom with no chance of ever being a boss. This, I am guessing, but with what, take it from me, is accuracy generated by hindsight, made him bitter. It was a bitterness that would develop over the years, so that his story, even in 1967, when he was a surely youthful thirty-one, was already well on the way to becoming what you could describe, depending on your point of view, as a disaster, a tragedy, an inevitability, a major upset or one hell of a punchline which certainly pushed boundaries and broke free of the north or plummeted straight down into it. His end was already in sight, as though the clouds – often low and bruised, sometimes high and white above the Reddish house which stooped like a comfortably sad, or sadly comfortable, Lowry person – were also committed to bringing with them a sense of doom personal to us at number 12.

There was no real clue to my future in what I could see and sense from my father's life, in the way you might expect from the behaviour and demeanour of your dad. This meant I had to look elsewhere to get some sense not only of my future but also my past. My father's manner was of someone cut off from his own past, and therefore from whatever dimension the future consisted of. He acted as if he had been adopted. His own father was not around – dead, he thought – but actually living in London since the war with a woman not my dad's mother, out of sight and mind, and dying in the late 1960s without my father knowing he had been alive while he grew up, married and had children.

His mother, my grandmother, confined to a solitary life in Margate, never explained that my grandfather had deserted them when my father was a young boy, during the war. The first real mention she made of him was in the late 1960s to tell my dad that he had in fact now died. This emphasised the distance there was between him and his mother, so that she too to some extent disappeared from his life. She was not someone who praised others much and didn't seem keen on making people feel good. Victoria Wood has said that this is a northern thing, the grudging handing out, if at all, of encouragement or motivation, but in my grandmother's case it was a very distant southern Methodist thing, a reluctance perhaps to express love to a human product, a physical reminder, of her wrecked wartime marriage. Moving north was perhaps more an escape from her, and all that shattered past, than it was an embracing of the north. I'm not sure how she treated her other child, Eileen, my dad's sister, our one aunt on his side of the family, who lived along the coast in Chatham at the top of what seemed the steepest hill in the world. She died in her fifties before I could get to know her properly.

I remember once travelling to Margate for our annual summer holiday, in which pain and pleasure would be mixed up with the Kent sunshine that seemed organised yet again by Enid Blyton. We drove down overnight: Mum, Dad in the front, three kids – eleven-year-old me, eight-year-old Jayne and toddler Carol – jammed into the compact back of a blocky-looking putty-coloured two-door Vauxhall Viva HA, a model launched in 1963 and discontinued by 1966. There was something about the windscreen of this car, the first new small car produced by Vauxhall since 1936, which reminded me of my dad's firm distinctive forehead, although obviously without the worry lines scored deep into the surface.

We set off from Reddish in the early evening. My dad had

overestimated how long the journey would take, so we made it into Margate before dawn, at about 4 a.m. He was too scared to arrive this early at his mother's house and have to wake her up, so the five us sat, or awkwardly slept, in the Viva parked a mile or so away by Cliftonville's Dane Park. Seven o'clock was deemed the correct moment to arrive, once his mother had been up and about for a good half-hour. Nothing was mentioned when we got to the house.

While my dad was alive I never knew anything more about his father other than that he was dead and then not dead and then dead, really, surely, and then afterwards that he might have moved to north London during the war and built another life with a new wife and possibly children, who might now be alive, with children of their own, southern versions of me, operating elsewhere – Morleys with altogether something else about them. I developed a vague sense that my dad's dad resembled the cockney spiv in the sitcom set in wartime Kent, *Dad's Army*, ducking and diving indifferent miles away from his son, leaving him further and further behind. Perhaps that was too specific – perhaps in the end he was more like one of the extras in *Dad's Army*, lined up behind the main characters, never saying anything, commenting on events only through mugging, shrugs and offstage rummaging and mumbling, ultimately disappearing from view, leaving no mark on the plots and progression of the show, permanently nameless and featureless. I wonder how far back in time I would have to go, searching through the male line that led to the Morleys, before I find someone more specific, more dynamic, or were they always floating in the background, teetering on the verge of having something to say, never fully opening their mouths to reveal what was on their minds? And how far would I have to go back to find the first signs of the personality my father had? He seemed to have so much he wanted to say about how he was so much better than someone who always seemed to be down on his luck, but no way of saying it so that people would listen to him.

My dad passed on to me the feeling that your past is of no real help in working out who you are, finding your voice and establishing a steady, mature identity. He didn't perhaps mean to, but he passed on the notion that to be alive is to be a fraud, adrift from reason and reality. You lie and evade to make people believe in you, and finding your own voice must always be a fruitless task. Perhaps it was this that made me consider being a writer, as though it would actually lead to the finding of a voice, even though as a writer finding a voice becomes even more intimidating. Writing, as a search for the truth about who you are and how you fit into the world and its history, as an invention of your own self that often involves a fair amount of lying and deceiving or at least making things up, means you are always catching sight of your own ghosts, and the ghosts of others, in the gaps between one reality and another, and these ghosts are not necessarily on your side, mainly because they have no idea you exist.

50

1904

George Formby was born George Hoy Booth on 26 May in Wigan, the son of music-hall star George Formby Senior. He was born blind on account of a caul or membrane enclosing his head and was unable to see for several months. He said he owed his sight to a simple sneeze. The young George was educated only to the age of seven at Notre Dame School in Wigan, after which he was sent to train as a jockey, first in Yorkshire and later in Ireland. As a result he was barely literate. While serving his apprenticeship he made his screen debut at the age of ten, playing a stable boy who outwits a criminal gang in the film *By the Shortest of Heads* (1915).

Wilfred Pickles, actor and broadcaster, was born on 13 October 1904 at 24 Conway Street, Halifax, the second of the four sons of Frederick Pickles (1880–1954), stonemason and builder, and his wife, Margaret (1876–1962), daughter of William and Ellen Catterall. He later recalled in his autobiography that his father – whose amusing, unsophisticated letters from the trenches during the First World War had been published in the *Yorkshire Weekly Post* – 'showed a lively wit that made him the immediate centre of attention in any company'. This talent transcended even 'the worst of our family's economic troubles'.

1903

Walter Greenwood was born in Salford. He came from a poor working-class family and attended the council school in Langworthy Road. He began part-time work as a milk roundsman's boy when he was twelve, then worked, again part-time, for a pawnbroker, before leaving school at the age of thirteen. He later worked as an office boy, a stable boy, a clerk, a packing-case maker, a sign writer, a driver, a warehouseman and a salesman, never earning more than thirty-five shillings a week except while working for a few months in an automobile factory. He was on the dole at least three times.

Jocelyn Barbara Hepworth was born on 10 January 1903 in Wakefield, the eldest child of Herbert Raikes Hepworth, civil engineer to the West Riding of Yorkshire, and his wife, Gertrude Allison. She was educated at Wakefield Girls High School and studied at the Leeds College of Art and at the Royal College of Art in London. It was as a seven-year-old schoolgirl growing up in Yorkshire that Barbara Hepworth was 'fired off' as a sculptor. In her classroom at Wakefield High School she listened intently to a lecture on Egyptian sculpture and, from that day on, as she wrote in her autobiography, 'Everything was forms, shapes and textures. Moving through and over the West Riding landscape with my father in his car, the hills were sculptures; the roads defined the forms. Above all, there was the sensation of moving physically over the contours of foulnesses and concavities, through hollows and over peaks – feeling, touching, seeing, through mind and hand and eye. This sensation has never left me. I, the sculptor, am the landscape. I am the form and I am the hollow, the thrust and the contour.'

She spoke of Yorkshire as a 'curiously rhythmic patterning of cobbled streets . . . mostly ungracious houses dominated by . . . slagheaps, noise, dirt, and smell'. These early impressions of the contradictions between industrial town and quiet countryside later became an integral part of her work. 'Feelings about ideas and people and the world all about us struggle inside me to find the evocative symbol affirming these early and secure sensations – the feeling of the magic of man in a landscape, whether it be a pastoral image or a miner squatting in the rectangle of his door or the "Single form" of a mill-girl moving against the wind, with her shawl wrapped round her head and body. On the lonely hills a human figure has the vitality and the poignancy of all man's struggles in this universe.'

1900

Arthur Bowden Askey was born in Liverpool on 6 June at 29 Moses Street, only son of Sam and Betsy Askey of Knutsford. After being educated at the Liverpool Institute and singing in the Liverpool Cathedral choir, he entered the Liverpool Education Offices as a clerk. At the age of sixteen, having stopped growing at five feet two inches, he gave this up and began to learn a new trade as an entertainer around the clubs. Arthur soon emerged as a true all-rounder in the grand tradition of the British music hall. When asked why Merseyside produced so many comedians, Arthur Askey replied, 'You've got to be a comic to live in Liverpool.'

1898

Henry Moore was born in Castleford, in a small terraced house in Roundhill Road on 30 July. His father didn't want his children following him into the pits. To make sure of this, he got Moore and his seven siblings a formal education, despite the family's constant struggle with poverty. Henry Moore went to the local infant and primary school, and then in 1910 won a scholarship to Castleford Secondary School, which later became a grammar school. At weekends the family would ramble over the moors and surrounding countryside. In later life Moore recalled these walks as a formative influence on his imagination, citing the dramatic forms of Adel Crag near Leeds and the slag heaps – Castleford's own mountains, artificial mountains, like pyramids, he called them. 'We played about in them and got very dirty. I remember the street where we lived and the sun just about managing to penetrate the fog.'

Even during these early years Moore was interested in art, and at the age of eleven he decided to become a sculptor after learning about the great Michelangelo. While at secondary school Moore was greatly encouraged by his art teacher Miss Alice Gostick.

Gracie Fields was born Grace Stansfield on a bitterly cold day (9 January) at 9 Molesworth Street over a fish and chip shop in Rochdale. Her mother, Sarah Jane, was nineteen, and Gracie, christened Grace, was the first of four children. Gracie's father, Fred Stansfield, a former merchant seaman, was a fitter at Thomas Robinsons, engineers, of Milnrow Road. Her mother was stage-struck and had a strong voice. It was said she could sing better than the local music-hall artistes. Gracie made her first appearance on stage at five years old.

PART THREE

13 June 1963

We can only see a short distance ahead, but we can see plenty
there that needs doing.

Alan Turing

51

I was not born in the north. Carol was, and I think her birth and first
few years in Reddish made me forget that for the first few years of my
life I was following my parents around the south of England. I was
born in Farnham, Surrey, a few miles from Aldershot, where my father,
the Kent man born and raised in Cliftonville, Margate on the Isle of
Thanet, was doing his eighteen months National Service, five years
before the conscription of young men between seventeen and twenty-
one ended, fifteen years after the end of the Second World War, leading,
effectively, to the Beatles, the Rolling Stones, the Kinks, the Who,
David Bowie, and so on.

My mother was an army nurse from Handforth, near Wilmslow, the
first place you come to in Cheshire travelling south from Manchester,
with a population of a sheltered few thousand. The brash, vaguely tense
twenty-year-old temporary soldier and the shy, slightly dizzy and
mischievous Cheshire nurse, a year younger, hit it off to such an extent
I was without much of an invitation encouraged to join them in a

brand-new late-1950s family. They had been married for six months when I was born. After the army, the three of us stayed with my grandmother in Margate, and in a flat in Dover, before my quick-thinking but underqualified dad got a job as a prison warder at the maximum-security Parkhurst Prison on the Isle of Wight.

The first memories I have of light and meaning, Mum and Dad, Christmas and back garden, shoes and clockwork train sets, shops and beach, ferry and washing on the line, snakes and hedges, baby sister and red plastic fire engine fitfully pouring into my mind are from the Isle of Wight, which is so far to the south that it is off the coast of England a few miles from Southampton and all on its island own in the English Channel. We did however live in the north of the island.

There is another world, filled with another reality, where I stayed on the Isle of Wight, and my father gradually rose through the ranks to become governor of the jail in the years when inmates included Ian Brady, the Krays and Yorkshire Ripper Peter Sutcliffe, and was present at the time of the 1969 riot protesting against the conditions with fearsome gangster Mad Frankie Fraser as one of the ringleaders. This would have led, perhaps, to a different book, or no book at all. If there had been a book, there would have been my toughened, hardened, resilient father at the centre of it, efficiently ruling a cruel, disturbing and often brutal inside world, overseeing the constant battle between staff and prisoners, rather than his role in this book, in which he spends most of his time in disorientated, or stubborn, or increasingly resigned exile, in the background, until he disappears altogether, chased into the shadows, as nameless and removed as his father, by ruddy northern bricks and endless smothering rain, falling between the cracks that separate success from failure.

Perhaps this book about the north began when my father, alienated by his strict and frosty mother, stumped by a missing father, rattled and psychically bruised by draining daily confrontations with murderers and sundry violent criminals, disconcerted by hours spent inside a grim prison when he had done nothing wrong, became more receptive to suggestions from my homesick mother that they move north closer to her parents in Handforth near Wilmslow. Our little family, without any input from me or my baby sister Jayne, born on the island in 1960, made plans for my mum to return home and my dad to escape from prison and head north into what for him became another prison.

We moved in time for my first school to be a northern school. A few months were spent in Handforth with my mum's parents between Cheshire and the traumatised post-war Manchester, and then a move into Salford, into Eccles, four miles to the west of Manchester city centre, so that I landed in the north at four or five right in the middle of an area laced, drenched and reinforced with northern history. Eccles (possibly deriving from the Latin *ecclesia* meaning church or congregation) stretched back to the misty Roman era, to the time it might well have been founded by refugees from Mamucium (or Mancunium) in the fourth century – Christians fleeing a late purge by the Romans. Then centuries of isolated, slow progress until a handful of hamlets – Eccles, Barton-upon-Irwell, Monton and Winton – became a village and then during the Industrial Revolution a small town.

The district was profoundly altered by the Industrial Revolution, and was itself directly crossed by those important transport developments that transformed the economic potential of south Lancashire in the eighteenth and nineteenth century, its border to the south marked since the 1890s by the Manchester Ship Canal. With a station set on the important, pioneering railway line connecting two of the Industrial Revolution's star cities, Liverpool and Manchester, Eccles' rural character was replaced with part of the urban sprawl spreading into and out of Salford and Manchester. Buildings filled the once open spaces around the village centre; streets expanded around the station building, described when it was built as being 'perched like Noah's Ark upon the Mt Ararat of the railway station'. Handloom weavers' cottages gave way to the stubby rows of functional working-class Victorian dwellings that would come to characterise such towns well into the twentieth century.

52

1898

Fairy Soap was launched in Newcastle upon Tyne in 1898. After going green (from its original less likeable brownish-yellow) for its nationwide launch in 1927, green was always the colour of the Fairy brands. Domestos, Be-Ro flour, Andrews, Eno's Fruit Salts and Lucozade are other firsts for the city. John Crossley Eno, a pharmacist at the Newcastle Infirmary, had a shop in Bigg Market.

1896

By the late nineteenth century the Irish-born and their children formed roughly one third of Manchester's population. Without the contribution of Irish labour, Manchester could never have become the world's first industrial city – an achievement which Disraeli considered to be 'as great a human exploit as Athens'. Yet for the most part the Irish were never fully accepted. They formed their own separate community and, as American academic Gary Messinger points out in his history of the city, they 'made Manchester into an enclave of Irish political separation second only to London in importance'.

1895

On 29 August 1895 twenty-one clubs met at the George Hotel in Huddersfield and formed the Northern Rugby Union. The Union aimed to support players from the mills and mines who could not afford to take time off work to play on a Saturday without being paid. This highlighted class issues within the game and led to the 1906 separation of the professional rugby league, of the north, and the amateur rugby union, of the south.

The clubs and their years of foundation were: Batley 1880, Bradford 1863, Brighouse Rangers 1878, Broughton Rangers 1877, Dewsbury 1875, Halifax 1873, Huddersfield 1864, Hull 1865, Hunslet 1883, Leeds 1890, Leigh 1877,

Liversedge 1877, Manningham 1876, Oldham 1876, Rochdale Hornets 1871, St Helens 1874, Tyldesley 1879, Wakefield Trinity 1873, Warrington 1875, Widnes 1873, Wigan 1879. Dewsbury withdrew a few days later and was replaced by Runcorn (1876).

1894

J. B. Priestley was born John Priestley on 13 September in what he described as an ultra-respectable suburb of Bradford, the son of a schoolmaster. Priestley inherited a 'public-spirited' socialism from his family, and he later recalled a happy childhood. He had no memory of his mother, who had died when he was two years old and who was of the 'clogs and shawls' working class, but his stepmother, who brought him up, was 'kind, gentle and loving'. After leaving Belle Vue Grammar School when he was sixteen he worked as a clerk for Helm and Company in Swan Arcade, Broadway, exporters of wool tops, from 1910 to 1914, and commented that he must have been one of the worst wool clerks ever. Already determined to become a writer, he spent his hard-earned money on books, and in his spare time tried different kinds of writing, including a regular unpaid column in a local periodical, the *Bradford Pioneer*.

Priestley's mother and grandparents on each side were mill workers, a 'solid steady sort'. His father 'plucked my mother, my real mother, about whom I know nothing except she was high-spirited and witty' from a free and easy, rather raffish kind of working-class life, where in the grim little back-to-back houses they shouted and screamed, laughed and cried, and sent out a jug for more beer. He recalled avidly watching the 'dressing-up, display, showing off, pursuit and capture' during promenades of 'lads and girls' at Bradford's summer concerts. Priestley defended female mill workers who had raucous fun. As he put it, 'There was nothing sly, nothing hypocritical, about these coarse dames and screaming lasses, who were devoted to their own men, generally working in the same mill, and kept on "courting", though the actual courtship stage was over early, for years and years until a baby was due, when they married. They may not have lived happily afterwards, but they saved themselves from some unpleasant surprises.'

Inspired by the enormous cast-iron tower built in the centre of Paris for the 1889 International Exhibition, the mayor of Blackpool, John Bickerstaffe, responded to a financial scam proposing to build replicas all over England by actually commissioning a tower. He invested money in the project himself, and raised money from cotton barons in Blackburn, Bury and Preston. A pair of Lancashire architects, James Maxwell and Charles Tuke, had designed the Blackpool Tower and overseen the laying of its foundation stone in 1891. When the Tower opened on 14 May 1894, 518 feet 9 inches high, a magnificent engineering masterpiece ahead of its time, containing 2,500 tons of steel, able to sway in the winds coming off the Irish Sea, both men were dead, but Mayor Bickerstaffe was on hand to see 3,000 excited customers take the first sixpenny rides to the top.

With costs that had soared from £5.25 million to £15 million, an army of 16,000 builders ranging from labourers to craftsmen to engineers and surveyors, and numerous setbacks, the Manchester Ship Canal was finally officially opened some five months after its opening for general traffic. The ceremony took place on 21 May 1894, and Queen Victoria knighted the mayors of Salford and Manchester while she was there. She arrived by train at London Road station (later renamed Piccadilly), and from there progressed through the city, which was decked out with bunting and ornamental arches, to Stretford and then to the port, where she boarded the royal yacht for a ceremonial sail around the docks. Apparently she was heard to remark on the very noticeable smell. The canal, 36 miles long, 200-plus feet across and 30 feet deep, enabled ocean-going vessels to navigate from the Irish Sea into the industrial heart of Manchester.

Queen Victoria's royal train passed through Miles Platting on its return journey after she had opened the Canal and an eye-witness account survives from one of the excited children who had gathered on Miles Platting station to wave to her as she passed. The lad said that although the Queen acknowledged them she did not smile and he thought her 'a bit of a sauerkraut!'

The name Formby is said to have come to James Booth while sitting on a railway platform watching a goods train destined for Formby, a coastal town between Liverpool and Southport. He took the name George because of its royal connections, or perhaps because it was a common name at the time and went well with Formby, and he was George Formby until his death twenty-four years later in 1921, when his son took over and assiduously developed the franchise.

1893

Leeds became a city. It boasted an effective tramcar service, libraries, parks, schools and one of the finest shopping centres in the north, famed particularly for its arcades. By now the village by the Aire had spread itself across the hillsides of the valley, absorbing the local townships. It had become, as the *Yorkshire Factory Times* described it, 'A vast business place . . . a miniature London.'

'As a practical man,' Robert Blatchford asked an Oldham weaver in his collection of socialist essays, *Merrie England*, 'would you of your own choice convert a healthy and beautiful country like Surrey into an unhealthy and hideous country like Wigan or Cradley, just for the sake of being able to once a year go to Blackpool, and once a night listen to a cracked piano.'

1892

Band leader and impresario Jack Hylton was born on 2 July at 75 Boundary Street in the village of Great Lever, Bolton. He was christened John Greenhalgh Hilton by his cotton-yarn-twister father, George, originally from Stalybridge, and his mother, Mary, a schoolteacher. It was reported that his mother was knitting a pair of socks to earn a shilling the day he was born. George Hilton worked in a cotton mill, along with a great number of people in that area of Bolton in the late 1800s, but, unlike most, he was determined to make a better life for his wife and children. He was also an active trade unionist and helped establish a local socialist club.

Jack's interest in music probably developed through his father's talent as an amateur singer, mostly of Victorian ballads. By the time Jack reached the higher grade school in Bolton, his father had become the licensee of a public house called the Round Croft in James Street, Little Lever. George would sing to the customers as well as serve drinks. Here Jack gave his first public performances, accompanying his father on the piano as he sang popular songs of the day. Hylton then accumulated considerable experience as a stand-in pianist and singer, but it was in 1909 that he found his true vocation as a conductor, when he began to direct touring pantomime.

On a foggy night in November, 1892, the Mellor Mill at the foothills of the Pennines, on the bank of the River Goyt near New Mills and Marple, built by one of Stockport's pioneering cotton traders, Samuel Oldknow, caught fire. Accidents were common at such mills, but there were rumours of it being the result of business rivalry. The blaze was not noticed until 2 o'clock in the morning, by which time it had gained a firm hold and there was no hope of checking it with the fire-fighting equipment then available. The following is an extract from the *Cheshire County News* report on the burning of the Mill:

> . . . Immense tongues of fire were belching forth from the windows. Higher and higher they leaped and blazed, the building and its environs being encircled with a halo of crimson light. A message was despatched to Marple and Compstall fire brigade, but they arrived too late to be of any practical service. The spectacle when the fire was at its height was a splendid but awe-inspiring one. The entire mass of buildings, which covers half an acre in area, was in gigantic blaze, brilliantly illuminating the district. Huge columns of smoke ascended into the heavens and hung in the form of a dense canopy over the burning building. One by one the floors fell in with a deafening crash and the machinery clanged together like the roar of artillery. Then the roof with one gigantic swoop collapsed, falling through the practically demolished building with a thunderous smash, amidst the shrieks of the by-standers, for all the village was now awake. The mill girls with their shawls over their heads, the children clinging, terrified, to their mother's dresses, and the men who had been striving to render what little assistance there was in their power, were all gazing at the burning pile . . .

In 1892 J. R. Clynes became an organiser for the Lancashire Gasworkers Union. This resulted in him leaving Oldham for the first time.

Millions of men and women died in their own towns and villages without ever having travelled five miles from the spot where they were born. How vividly I remember my first long journey away from Oldham. I had to attend a conference of the Gasworkers Union at Plymouth. To get there entailed a railway journey down the length of England. Men of my own class were driving the engine and acting as porters. I remember a sensation of power as I glimpsed a future in which all these men would be teamed up together with mill-hands, seamen, gasworkers – in fact, Labour everywhere – for the benefit of our own people. The least change of accent in speech, as we stopped at various towns, fascinated me, and I noted varieties of face, dress and manner. That was a wonderful journey for me, who had never before been out of the Lancashire murk. To look through the carriage windows and see grass and bushes that were really green instead of olive, trees that reached confidently up to the sun instead of our stunted things, houses that were mellow red and white and yellow, with warm red roofs, instead of the Lancashire soot and slates, and stretches of landscape in which the eye could not find a single factory chimney belching – this was sheer magic! I began to experience an inexhaustible wonder at the gracious beauties of the world outside factory-land, and this sensation has never wholly left me. That first long railway journey was as wonderful to me as if I had been riding upon the magic carpet in the Arabian Nights. And more and more strongly as I gazed, I felt a sense of indignation that the world should be so generous and so lovely, and yet that men, women and children should be cooped up in black and exhausted industrial areas like Oldham, merely so that richer men could own thousands of acres of sunlit countryside of whose experience many of the mill-workers hardly ever dreamed.

53

I arrived in an Eccles largely settled into a typical post-industrial post-war rut, stuck to a declining darkening Salford that had slumped against its more prosperous Manchester neighbour for decades. Eccles was poignantly most famous for its deceptively

simple round currant-packed flaky light-puff-pastry cake, first sold
in the late eighteenth century at James Birch's shop on the corner of
Vicarage Grove by the station. An early rivalry with a former
employer over who made the best, most authentic cake encouraged
enough local interest for them to quickly become popular.

It is thought that the original Eccles cake recipe came from the
remarkable and highly accomplished Doncaster-born Mrs Elizabeth
Raffald's (née Whitaker) influential *The experienced English housekeeper
– for the use and ease of ladies, housekeepers and cooks*, one of the most
successful cookery books of the eighteenth century, published in 1769.
Written in robust direct language that still seems clear and useful today,
it included advice about how to spin sugar and thoughts about wine.

Elizabeth apparently served Eccles cakes regularly when she was housekeeper at Arley Hall in Cheshire for the eldest daughter of the Earl of
Derby, Lady Elizabeth Warburton, to whom she dedicated her book. She
made the rare move from domestic service to business, using the experience she had gained running an aristocratic household to reinvent herself
as a visionary entrepreneurial career woman, quick to recognise and
observe the rapid changes that were taking place socially and economically in Manchester. She was a shrewd and enterprising living metaphor
for how Manchester and surrounding districts accelerated into the nineteenth century and beyond, anticipating how there would be demand for
new sorts of trades, services and financial exchanges, and how people
with new money would crave novel tastes, pleasures, opportunities and
venues. Business – and people being busy – would require new forms of
finding, inventing and enjoying leisure pursuits.

Manchester was transforming because of irrepressible self-made
people like her, whose imaginative ability to create change led to more
change, to equally motivated individuals who were inspired by the
progress around them, and who in turn inspired others with their ideas
and activities, expanding their minds and the city. New thoughts led to
new discoveries led to new people with their own originality and pride
arriving to make use of this new dynamic world. Women, with their
own particular flair for creative and commercial thinking, with their
own desires, were a vital part of this shift towards the future.

Raffald's restless, aspirational craving for progress, cooperation and

GETTY IMAGES

Fred Perry

social well-being is at the very start of the momentum that can still be felt in the north over 200 years later, wherever there is still belief in self-enlightenment, in making the best of whatever is around, in adapting to local conditions. She helped form the 'shopocracy' that was an essential part of Manchester's rise to greatness, another layer of influence, energy and achievement to rival that of the mill owners, its members emerging often from the working class to claim positions within society without losing their appreciation of values other than merely the making of money and the creation of prestige. She was selling things; she was selling herself, and making her own way.

Presciently appreciating the connection between commerce and print, between an audience and exciting new products, anticipating the important role publicity would play in this new world, Elizabeth helped found Salford's first newspaper, *Prescott's Journal*, and published the first street and trade directory of Manchester in 1772. She kept a confectionery shop – more of a delicatessen stocking an exotic array of foodstuffs – ran old and famous local inns including the Bull's Head in Manchester and King's Head in Salford, was one of the first writers to use 'barbecue' as a cookery term, the first to record in writing the word icing for the topping of cakes, wrote the first published recipe for a wedding cake and for crumpets, wrote an unpublished book on midwifery, supplied basic and sophisticated cosmetics, rented genteel lodgings and storage space, opened perhaps the first office in Manchester for the supply of servants, and was buried at Stockport parish church after dying suddenly possibly from a stroke at the age of forty-eight in 1781.

Raffald had sixteen daughters during a troubled and sometimes torrid marriage to her less ingenious and fairly hapless florist husband John, formerly head gardener at Arley Hall and from a Stockport family of seedsmen and gardeners going back to the sixteenth century. Only three of her daughters – and it is possible their number was exaggerated, considering she would have had them in the space of eighteen years – were still alive when she died.

The first edition of her recipe book (priced at five shillings) comprised 800 copies, all of which she signed to prove that it was not pirated, and it was reprinted numerous times into the nineteenth century. Some of the recipes, including one for 'hens nest in jelly', turned up in Princess – later Queen – Victoria's hand-copied book of recipes. In 1773 she sold the copyright to her book for £1,400, a considerable sum at the time. After the publisher Richard Baldwin had handed her the money, he asked that some of the terms in the book, being mainly of general use in the north, be changed for the south. Fiery, self-assured Mrs Raffald gently but firmly explained that what she had written was what she had meant to write, and she did not want any changes.

The book included 'sweet patties', based on an ancient recipe, with variations according to taste and family tradition, for a cake with enough exotic juicy richness to upset Puritans. Raffald's ingredients were 'the meat of a boiled calf's foot, two large apples, and one ounce of candied orange, chop them very small, grate half a nutmeg, mix them with the yolk of an egg, a spoonful of French brandy, and a quarter of a pound of currants clean washed and dried; make a good puff pastry, roll it in different shapes to the fried ones, and fill them the same way; you may either bake or fry them – they are a pretty side dish for supper'. Elsewhere there was a recipe for 'little currant cakes' which hinted at the eventual Eccles cake – 'bake them pretty crisp and a fine brown'. (A fresh well-made Eccles cake is beautiful. Try with Lancashire cheese. Never eat one that is stale, which leads to their reputation as a fly sandwich.)

Elizabeth Raffald had incredible willpower and the imagination and desire to inspire change. She was an early participant in and an inspiration to the spiritual, cultural and commercial transformation of northern life. It is fitting that something of her fortitude and vivacity has survived (a memorial plaque near Marks & Spencer in Manchester's Shambles Square was destroyed in the IRA bomb attack of 1996) even if it is nothing more than a pastry that is often made so badly it might have been baked during her lifetime. A theatrical reverberation of her confidence, knowledge and power also lingers in the women of *Coronation Street*.

54

1890

Bram Stoker did a considerable amount of work on his novel during three summer weeks in Whitby (white settlement) – seaside town by Scarborough, east Yorkshire, facing the epic North Sea at the mouth of the Esk, surrounded by the bracken-laden 550-square-mile North York Moors. Of the 124 pages that comprise his working notes, thirty were written in Whitby. They include descriptions of weather conditions, words and expressions in local dialect, a coastguard's report of shipwrecks, inscriptions copied from tombstones and sketches of the landscape. The name Dracula came from what Stoker learned in the Whitby library while researching the history of vampirism. His original intention had been to call the character Wampyr, but he came across references to a Transylvanian prince called Vlad Tepes (also known as Dracula and

Vlad the Impaler), who fought the Turks in the fifteenth century and was renowned for his brutality. A hand-written footnote in the notebook records that Dracul meant devil in Hungarian.

The roads of Lancashire towns were paved with rectangular blocks of hard sandstone called setts, and the footpaths were made of larger oblongs of sandstone called flags. At rush hour, as the mill sirens sounded to summon the workers to their posts, or at the end of a long day the cacophony of a thousand iron-shod clogs on stone paving was tremendous and likened to artillery fire. Children enjoyed making their clog irons spark against the paving stones. Wherever it was wet underfoot, clogs were the preferred footwear, due to their cheapness (to buy and to repair), their durability and their comfort.

1889

English writer Edward Carpenter publishes *Civilisation: Its Cause and Cure*, which later has a great influence on Mahatma Gandhi. Carpenter looks down on the town of Sheffield and sees 'Only a vast dense cloud, so thick that I wondered how any human beings could support life in it, that went up to heaven like the smoke from a great altar. An altar, indeed, it seemed to me, wherein thousands of lives were being yearly sacrificed. Beside me on the hills the sun was shining, the larks were singing; but down there a hundred thousand grown people, let alone children, were struggling for a little sun and air, toiling, moiling, living a life of suffocation, dying (as the sanitary reports only too clearly show) of diseases caused by foul air and want of light – all for what? To make a few people rich!'

1888

'I bought a copy of John Mitchell's *Jail Journal* in an Oldham junk-shop in 1888, and the author's patriotism, courage and loyalty to his country affected my feelings in a way I have not yet forgotten. But books of my own were rare luxuries. Most of my reading was done in the Oldham Equitable Co-operative

Society's Library. I remember sitting there night after night, watching men and boys reading the employment advertisements, reading them till the type stupefied the eye and then sighing and shuffling down the steps into the grimy streets outside. I sat at a table reading Shakespeare, Ruskin and Dickens, or whatever else I could get hold of. I remember my discovery of Julius Caesar and how the realisation came suddenly to me that it was a mighty political drama, not just an entertainment . . . The old librarian of the Society's library took a kindly interest in me. Often he would hobble across to where I sat and murmur in satisfaction, "Stick to Shakespeare and the Bible. They're the roots of civilisation."' J. R. Clynes, *Memoirs*, 1937.

The world's first professional football league was set up in 1888 in the Royal Hotel, Piccadilly. None of the twelve original members were from Manchester. Blackburn, Burnley, Preston, Bolton and Accrington joined the Football League at its inception in 1888 and Preston North End emerged as the dominant football team in the early years of the League's history.

James Haslam, secretary of the Piecers Union in Oldham, describes a meeting that took place in 1888: 'The turn of Clynes came about nine o'clock. He was nothing to look at – a frail lad, pale and serious in ungainly clothes. For three-quarters of an hour the piecer-orator spoke with well-measured sentences of sincerity and grammatical precision. The audience, which had not been easy to control, laughed with him, and was sad with him. Afterwards the chairman of the committee said to me: "Where did you get that lad from? This country will know summat about him – if he lives!"'

1886

Self-educated, at the age of sixteen J. R. Clynes wrote a series of anonymous articles about working in a cotton mill. The articles showed how harshly children were still treated in textile factories. Clynes argued that the Spinners Union was not doing enough to protect child workers and in 1886 he helped form the Piecers Union.

1885

'The character is essentially Teutonic, including the shrewdness, the truthful-
ness without candour, the perseverance, energy and industry of the Lowland
Scotch, but little of their frugality, or of the theological instinct common to
the Welsh and Scotch, or of the imaginative genius, or the more brilliant
qualities which sometime light up the Scottish character. The sound judg-
ment, the spirit of fair play, the love of comfort, order, and cleanliness, and
the fondness for heavy feeding, are shared with the Saxon Englishman; but
some of them are still more strongly marked in the Yorkshireman, as is also
the bluff independence – a very fine quality when it does not degenerate
into selfish rudeness.' How the often misinterpreted Yorkshire character was
described by John Beddoe in *The Races of Britain*, 1885.

Because of the bitter opposition of the Liverpool Dock Board and the railway
companies it was not until 1885 that the Manchester Ship Canal Act finally
received royal assent, clearing the way for the construction of the canal. It
was another two years before enough finance was raised and work started.

1884

William Hesketh Lever started selling Sunlight soap to the mill workers of the
north of England in 1884. Lever and his brother James, sons of a wholesale
grocer in Bolton, bought a small soap works in Warrington in 1885. Five years
later Lever Brothers was manufacturing soap at its own factory in Port
Sunlight near Liverpool. Using copra or pine kernel oil rather than animal fats
to manufacture soap and glycerine, the company produced a free-lathering
soap which proved popular. Unusually for the time, Lever Brothers gave the
soap a brand name and sold it wrapped in distinctive packs. Before
Lever, soap was a cottage-industry commodity – you got the shopkeeper to
cut you a slab. Lever Brothers pre-wrapped it and imprinted the brand on
each bar. Sunlight Soap was primarily used for housework and marketed as
ideal for the pre-treatment of stubborn stains, cleaning hard surfaces and
hand washing after jobs around the house and garden.

With the coming of the railways, the traditional wakes festivals became weeks when workers travelled to seaside resorts like Blackpool for their annual holidays. A town and its surrounding area would grind to a halt and workers plus families would board trains for the coast. Resorts such as Blackpool – and for the slightly more discerning, Morecambe – would be filled with holidaymakers. Whole streets would move from the cotton towns to the coast for one week of the year. In 1884 an article in the *Pall Mall Gazette* described the arrival of holidaymakers in Blackpool: 'The wakes festivities and fairs continued in Blackpool with the building of the Big Wheel and the Pleasure Beach, the greatest wakes fair of all!' Because of the overwhelming exodus to the seaside, neighbouring towns grew to hold their wakes weeks at different times. Blackpool simply could not have accommodated the whole of Lancashire in one week.

The 1884 FA Cup Final between Blackburn Rovers and the amateurs of Scottish club Queen's Park was held in London. The *Accrington Times* reported the *Pall Mall Gazette*'s reaction to the northern football crowd: 'To the amazement of the populace the capital witnessed an invasion of Northern barbarians on Saturday. Hot-blooded Lancastrians, sharp of tongue, rough and ready of uncouth garb and speech. A tribe of Sudanese Arabs let loose in the Strand would not excite more amusement and curiosity. Whether it is eating or better still drinking, or whether there is a little rioting to be done or such a small matter of a house to be burned down . . . these Lancashire folk enjoy it with infinite zest . . . The looms will stand idle and the sons of toil will drink much more liquor than is good for them.'

55

I made it to Eccles without knowing anything much other than the fact that I had gone where my mum and dad had gone. The Isle of Wight melted away in my memory leaving just a few sticky images.

Nearby, the film based on Shelagh Delaney's play *A Taste of Honey* (written when she was nineteen) would be made by director Tony Richardson the year I arrived, 1961, three years after its first theatrical performance, but I wouldn't know anything about that for a good twelve years. When I did watch the film, I felt I knew the place I was seeing – the shabby backstreets, bunched-up terraced houses showing no hint of anything whimsical, the cryptic array of walls, steps, bridges, alleys, waterways, towpaths, lamp posts, cracked concrete slabs angled and crooked under boisterously gambolling stone-grey clouds, the sense even in black and white, or perhaps because of the black and white, how filthy everything was, the sense of people trying to get out, trying to get on, trying to be seen, trying to be someone – much more than I did the Isle of Wight. I felt I belonged to that world, crushed between Salford, Manchester and the Second World War, between cynicism and naivety, between life and death, between hopeless houses and disused pubs, between crumbling walls and rippling black puddles, which was both something you needed to escape from, but which you relied on because it seemed so solid and shared, and lonely and desperate, but somehow, perhaps because of the combination of circumstances, mental energy, inherited mettle and physical strength that had created it all, containing a sepulchral beauty and a covert togetherness.

GETTY IMAGES

Frank Randle

In 2010 I asked my mother why we had moved to Eccles, about as far away from the Isle of Wight as you can imagine, beyond it seemed Prague or Belfast, certainly as alien to the land and character of my father's Kent, and actually not that connected to Handforth, which although only a few miles away was planted in a different time. There seemed no family connection, no reason to move into the heart of Salford when not far off there was open country and gentler villages. Why not the Ribble Valley, Knutsford or Glossop, which superficially resemble the meadows and trees of Kent, the slumbering, winding roads of the Isle of Wight? My mum was very ill, in her early seventies, skidding through a series of nasty strokes gradually increasing in ferocity, her limbs and brain freezing up from Parkinson's. I thought she might like to remember when she was younger and her life was beginning, and she hadn't yet bounced through a series of menial jobs to bring some cash into the house. The eager spark in her eyes suggested, in spite of what happened during the next fifteen years, which ended with the violent, abrupt end of her marriage, that she did have fond memories of those late fifties, early sixties adventures.

Apparently, because nothing ever seemed planned, except at the last minute or under duress, there was no real reason why we ended up in the middle of an area flaking away into archetypal post-war depression, waiting to see what might happen in Manchester, if not Salford, and what effect that might have on towns like Eccles, which had materialised in the aftermath of the rise and rise, and fall and fall, and resultant communal concussion of Manchester. It wasn't as though the move had anything to do with romantic feelings for canals and flaky cakes, identifying with George Stephenson's triumph when building the Liverpool to Manchester railway line over the seemingly impassable quaggy squishy Chat Moss, admiration for Elizabeth Raffald or knowing that the first general meeting of the Trade Union Congress took place in Salford's Three Crowns pub in 1868. No sense of getting close to mighty, deteriorating Manchester, which was in desperate need of some sort of revival, and which therefore, if its recent history was anything to go by, it would, against all odds, achieve.

According to my mum's memory, fast degenerating like a post-industrial northern city, perishing around the edges and internally, but receiving no vital regeneration or renovation, she and my dad had come across our new home in an estate agent's while staying with her mum and dad in Handforth. It was somewhere affordable and practical to live near my dad's new job in Deansgate in the city centre, to finally start their life, or at least one that didn't have parents, prisoners or the dispiriting after-effects of the war crowding around them.

We moved into a two-bedroom first-floor flat on Victoria Road a couple of miles from Salford Royal Infirmary, a mile or so north of the Ship Canal. I arrived in the north as an outsider, but immediately adopted a new identity in Eccles, in Salford, tarnished sidekick to Manchester. We didn't land in Eccles amid a crushed row of squat terraced houses, next to a derelict building, rudely demolished homes and a scrappy patch of wasteland littered with war-era rubble, nettles, indeterminate organic material and puddles the colour of mucus – some might have considered we were in the posher part of town – but there was no doubt we were in Lancashire, even if that part of Lancashire pulled into something else by the weight and history of overbearing Manchester.

My next set of flimsy fractured memories emerges from my time in Eccles, which included attending my first school, Clarendon Road Community Primary School. Probably because I was still southern soft my mum needed to physically drag me to the school on my first day. I remember being terrified and screamed loudly at the injustice of it all. Looking at the building now, a substantial multi-windowed triple-chimneyed two-storey Edwardian structure decorated with convoluted pinky-red brick patterns, built in 1908, slammed at the side of the pavement looking as out of scale with demure local kerb and low garden wall as a nineteenth-century mill, it's no wonder I was apprehensive. It looks as if what goes on inside involves straitjackets, clanging metal doors, solitary confinement and random forms of punishment, and it perhaps scared me because the only building I could compare it with in my young mind was Parkhurst Prison.

I had occasionally waved goodbye to my dad as he passed through the massive wooden doors of the prison, disappearing into a clanking dark inside I didn't want to imagine. Being sent on my own into this giant brick building by my mother, who seemed insistent I should go, triggered five-year-old hysterics. Eventually I was dragged inside. My memory then goes blank, suggesting what happened next was either deeply traumatising or completely banal.

We didn't last long in Eccles. Enough in my shaky world for a Christmas nativity play at the school, in which I was the inn keeper, entirely forgettable, with one line to deliver – that the inn was full. Enough, perhaps, to begin the piecing-together of my important new identity, a process which became more intensive once we moved to Reddish.

My sister Carol's arrival as new-born Morley of the north confirmed my feeling that Reddish was where our family was at home, even though it had taken all of my life to get there. At the back of my mind, which was a long way from where I spent most of my time, where the Isle of Wight and Kent had melted into recent northern memories, I had decided that in fact I had been born in Eccles as well as in Farnham, Surrey, that somehow the two locations could be fused. I had arrived as an outsider, but very quickly I was being adopted, absorbed, accepted. And now, it seemed, the new me was about to be born in Reddish, Stockport.

I was going to ask my mum exactly when we moved to Reddish, but before I could get around to it, she died. She took her north with her, along with her life, her irrepressible energy, her suicidal husband's inner chaos, her chaotic memories, her limited stuck-in-the-sixties cooking and nosy, gossipy interest in the affairs of others in one crushing, freezing go. The lines on her face that first started to threaten her pale, lovely Celtic skin in Reddish were instantly erased.

It was like what had happened with my father. He died before I could ask him all the questions I wanted to about his place in the north, about what he thought – about most things. Most of these questions were in fact provoked by the fact that he had died so young and so could not be answered. I had plenty of time to ask my mother questions, but in much the same way the questions seemed more urgent once she had died. One of the last conversations we had was about Eccles, and Reddish, and the journey there, which both came out of nowhere and was meant to happen.

For the sake of this book – estimating, assuming, inventing, elaborating and consolidating in the ways that history most often gets written – I have decided that the exact day I arrived in Reddish with my mum and dad and three-year-old-sister Jayne was 13 June 1963. This was the day the Beatles played their one and only gig in Stockport – at the Offerton Palace Theatre Club, a converted cinema on Turncroft Lane typical of the clubs all around packed Manchester, where acts yet to be famous would perform, from Gerry Dorsey to Heinz and Shane Fenton, as well as the stars of the day, Alma Cogan, Lonnie Donegan, Johnny Ray, and those drifting the other way like Kathy Kirby. There were a lot of Palaces dotted around between Hyde and Bury, as well as the Empress, Silver Moon, Bossanova, Ponderosa, Regency, Domino, satisfying people's almost pathological need to get out of the house, find release, burst out of confining routine, be entertained, leave their worries behind, with names designed to signify a glittering end-of-the-working-day escape into fantasy, clubs drenched in bitter, mild, smoke and red velvet curtains, non-stop entertainment on tap, where from the top of the stairs by the entrance, the bar and seating area were to the right, the stage and dance floor to the left.

Sometimes the club was decorated with convincing tropical élan and/or intimate enough to make the audience feel they really were in a glittery fragment of Las Vegas that had somehow dropped on to the East Lancs Road or embraced tatty, charmless Oldham and Eccles. They sipped incongruous cocktails from delicate glassware or supped foaming amber beer from substantial glass tankards, winning or losing a few bob at the casino while a velvet-voiced crooner/compère in expensively cut gold suit and shoes made to glisten where the sun never shines, nicknamed Mr Manchester, a Miles Platting Dean Martin, convinced you that it never rained in Manchester, and glamour was never more than a few yards away. Under the ground, away from the factory, office, building site, railway, somewhere else, late at night, in the early hours, down the lit-up steps that led into the volatile promise of a good time the entrepreneurial energy of Lancashire mutated into the sort of play that kept life buzzing even as the sky was falling. Music hall might have been fatally wounded, but not the craving for punchlines, choruses and ferocious, uplifting charisma.

GETTY IMAGES

Sir William Houldsworth, founding father of Reddish

At the beginning of the 1960s, along the Princess Road in Moss Side, once home to the young Anthony Burgess, now the centre of the fluid self-regulating Caribbean community, there was the steamy Nile Club run by Tunde Moses, the temple of sound, knocking out keen, caustic rhythms not yet termed ska or reggae, next door to its fierce competitor, the Reno, beginning life as a Salvation Army hostel for African seamen, where they could grab a hot meal, a fag and a sleep. In these off-the-cuff unofficial haunts underground glamour drew Manchester hedonists on the hunt for illicit late-night thrills after the more regulated city-centre clubs had shut. Some, the hard-core self-conscious in-crowd, found their solace, their sensation, the room to move sometimes all through the night at the alcohol-free but highly charged Twisted Wheel. It opened in 1963 off Albert Square, in little basement rooms with bare brick walls painted red, black and white, and was initially a local home for connoisseurs of the recently born British blues scene. The rhythm and blues of Stax and Atlantic and the soul of early Motown took over for the elitist cliquish mods after the club moved in 1965 to Whitworth Street, the exultant sound mutating via Wilson Pickett's 'Midnight Hour' into the more urgent, faster and physically demanding northern soul. It was called northern because it was the sort of tense elastic soul that wasn't played down south at the time, and it attracted people from miles around before it acquired its second home at the Wigan Casino. The Wheel played serious music for serious people and always prided itself on not being as commercial as other clubs. Whenever what it played became chart music, obvious and over-used, losing its rarity, its point, it would move on to fresher, rawer and hipper sounds.

The Beatles had been booked to play in Stockport a few months earlier after their first minor hit with 'Love Me Do', but by the time they arrived had released 'Please Please Me' and the accepted, comfort-able phrase when recording this time is quite simply that 'Beatlemania was taking the world by storm.' Manager Brian Epstein honoured the contract he had made with resourceful local promoter and nightclub owner Sid Elgar for the group to play the tiny venue outside Stockport town centre for a few quid, before they raced off to play a second show at the Southern Sporting Club in Gorton, also run by Sid and part of the same deal. Sid always made sure the acts he booked played both Offerton and Gorton.

The Southern was originally the Corona Cinema and later, in early 1971, became the Stoneground Club, where I would see many of my first rock concerts, confirming how Manchester clubs after the war if they wanted to keep up to date, chasing the smashing benefits of enter-tainment like it was going out of fashion, went from cinema and variety to blue comedy, to boozy dance, to raucous rock and roll, to louche cabaret, to current hit parade, to speeding soul, to underground hippy, to glittering glam and shiny disco, and, madly, unstoppably, beyond. The drink, drugs and clothing that accompanied each period reflected the onstage entertainment, the noise, gags and rhythm, and the chang-ing demands of the customers, which were ultimately based around the same feelings of vagrant curiosity and a craving for something different, something imported and uncharted that could then become local and deliciously personal.

The route from Offerton to Gorton would have taken the Beatles, experiencing their first flush of fame, music-hall zaniness flipped by rock and roll and on their way to druggy, imperial glory, down the hill into the sleepy centre of Stockport, through Mersey Square, nothing stirring but a few buses on the turn and the usual supping and smoking inside outlying pubs, and then up via boring South Reddish along the Gorton Road past the end of my new street, Westbourne Grove. So I like to think that as I was settling down for my first night in my new home, where I was going to make up a new life, at the end of the street the Beatles drove past the Essoldo cinema – possibly showing the first James Bond film *Dr No* with a theme tune arranged by John Barry, born in York, 1933 – like something out of *A Hard Day's Night*, on the way from one tiny local venue packed with shocked screaming teenage girls born mere months after the war to another.

And: Ian Brady and Myra Hindley moved in together to her grand-mother's Gorton house in June 1963. The next month they killed their first victim as part of Brady's coldly self-defined 'existential exercise', sixteen-year-old Pauline Reade – the same age as many of those new Beatles fans chasing liberating, nourishing post-war pleasure – who disappeared on her way to the British Railways Club in Gorton, look-ing for someone to show her a great night out.

Welcome to Reddish.

Welcome to the rest of your life.

56

1879

J. R. Clynes started work in the cotton mills of Oldham. Self-taught using candlelight and second-hand books, he could recite Shakespeare and was one of if not the greatest orator in the Labour movement's history.

When I achieved the manly age of ten I obtained half-time employment at Dowry Mill as a 'little piecer'. My hours were from six in the morning each day to noon; then a brief time off for dinner; then on to school for the afternoons; and I was to receive half a crown a week in return. The noise was what impressed me most. Clatter, rattle, bang, the swish of thrusting levers and the crowding of hundreds of men, women and children at their work. Long rows of huge spinning-frames, with thousands of whirling spindles, slid forward several feet, paused and then slid smoothly back again, continuing the process unceasingly hour after hour while cotton became yarn and yarn changed to weaving material. Often the threads on the spindles broke as they were stretched and twisted and spun. These broken ends had to be instantly repaired; the piecer ran forward and joined them swiftly, with a deft touch that is an art of its own. I remember no golden summers, no triumphs at games and sports, no tramps through dark woods or over shadow-racing hills. Only meals at which there never seemed to be enough food, dreary journeys through smoke-fouled streets, in mornings when I nodded with tiredness and in evenings when my legs trembled under me from exhaustion.

The Bishop of Manchester noted in 1879,

Within a radius of five miles . . . there must be aggregated a population of probably 750,000 persons . . . fifty years ago the wealthier merchants of Manchester lived in the heart of the town, in streets in which today there is not a single gentleman's residence. Tradesmen lived over their shops: manufacturers found existence tolerable under the smoke of their tall chimneys surrounded by the cottages of the people. Now all these conditions are changed. You will hardly find one of our wealthiest men living within two miles of business or of the Exchange. The centre of the city at night is a mass of unoccupied tenements. The working class and the poor still cluster thickly together in some of the murkiest and dismalest quarters of the town . . . The houses in the centre have been removed to meet the exigencies of commerce, and the remainder of the city up to its boundary is now nearly covered.

On 18 September in Blackpool eight arc lamps are used to create 'artificial sunshine' emitting the equivalent of the light from 48,000 candles. The technology is extremely new – only in this year is the first English patent for a light bulb granted. More than 70,000 people travel to Blackpool to see the demonstration.

1876

Isabella Banks's most famous novel was *The Manchester Man*, serialised first in *Cassell's Magazine* between January and November 1874 and published in book form two years later. Banks remembered Manchester before the railways, viaducts and wide roads, and the novel elaborately reconstructs the city at the turn of the nineteenth century. It includes a chapter on the Peterloo massacre of 1819. The hero of the novel, Jabez Clegg, is an orphan, discovered Moses-like on the banks of the Irwell. He becomes a textile worker, marries his employer's daughter – after various trials and tribulations – and ends the novel as a prosperous and enlightened master. Banks detested the 'modernisation' of Manchester happening around her.

'When Pliny lost his life, and Herculaneum was buried, Manchester was born. While lava and ashes blotted from sight and memory fair and luxurious Roman cities close to the Capitol, the Roman soldiery of Titus, under their general Agricola, laid the foundations of a distant city which now competes with the great cities of the world. Where now rise forests of tall chimneys, and the hum of whirling spindles, spread the dense woods of Arden; – and from the clearing in their midst rose the Roman castrum of Mamucium, which has left its name of Castle Field as a memorial to us.' Mrs G. Linnaeus (Isabella) Banks, *The Manchester Man*, 1876.

1875

George Formby Senior was born as James Booth in 1875 in what was once considered the 'almost worthless' Ashton under Lyne on the north bank of the Tame. His mother, Sarah Jane Booth, an unmarried working-class woman, was a prostitute who was convicted of offences 140 times in ten years. She eventually married James's father, a few months after his birth. However, the marriage was turbulent, and James was often beaten up and deprived of food. Sarah Jane used to sing in the local pub for alcohol, and often ended up being taken off to the police station to sober up. Because his mother was so often absent from home, young James had to sleep outside – in the doorway or the lavatory. Because of this, he developed asthma and became very susceptible to bronchitis and tuberculosis. 'My childhood was the most miserable that could have happened to any human being.'

1874

Received pronunciation was never formally created or enforced as an official form of the national language (unlike in France or Italy); it grew out of a middle-class version of the London/south-east dialect, its rise aided by the increasing social mobility of the nineteenth century, which led people to be concerned about talking and writing 'correctly'. Dictionaries became popular, learning the grammar of English came to be seen as essential, and regional dialects were despised and even suppressed. Well into the nineteenth century, however, even the upper classes were still talking with a variety of regional accents. The catalyst for the creation of a distinct and universal public school accent seems to have been the 1874 Education Act. As education was now to be available to all, the traditional upper classes and the new rich needed a distinctive cultural badge to distinguish themselves from the masses below.

57

Reddish was full of square straight-faced houses on placid streets that all joined up with each other, but, like a small village written into a very English story that was quaint even as it contained a murder or two and the inflexible, darkening pressure of history, there was within a few streets of where I lived, a couple of hundred yards along from the Essoldo and the Conservative Club, a fire station, a police station, a church or two and a library.

The library was, as it should have been, the quietest place in time and space, tucked next to the swimming baths, the coldest harshest place in time and space, seemingly never warm since they were opened at the beginning of the century. I liked the quiet place more than the cold place lined with dull dazzling tiles that implacably absorbed splashes and wet soiled feet, and filled with icy pale-blue water that stung the eyes and stank of fun, fear and a combination of chlorine and urine. Perhaps this was also because I picked up on how the quiet place contained clues about why I was where I was and how I could explain it and do something about it, in books that were about where people find themselves and what then happens and how they work out a solution or accept their problems. The watery hell hole stripped me near naked and froze me sore to the bone. I like to think the library was where I learned to read, as much as at school, and where without me even understanding what was happening, I began to write, or at least have the thoughts, rooted in the beatific blue eyes of Peter O'Toole as a larger-than-life T. E. Lawrence, who died and then lived, that can become writing.

At the age of thirteen I remember moving, in a sudden rush, on to George Orwell, leaving behind unbelievable Enid Blyton and her nostalgic glowing settings and the actually more believable Alan Garner and his unsettling secrets. Garner lived in a Cheshire village half a mile from Jodrell Bank, moving the year it was finished into a ramshackle sixteenth-century house called Toad (old) Hall. He wrote enticingly about the areas around where I lived as though they were next door to the lion, the witch and the wardrobe, where unicorns roamed through a warren of pasty, rayless streets, as if they were wonderful hidden places you might reach using a time machine that was all in the mind, where a shadowy line between reality and fantasy could be crossed using nothing but words and will and the map his books became, describing a dying land that needed to be saved.

Rochdale Town Hall

The still, spectral atmosphere inside the chaste library somehow encouraged me to challenge myself, to see what on earth was going on in those apparently forbidden and definitely difficult books that sat composed within themselves on row after row, promising either absolutely nothing, just page after page of pointless print, shapes needing too much hard work to understand, or absolutely everything, each letter on each page promising a mystery of such power it would inevitably lead to another mystery and, now and then, some sort of sensational solution. These single magic letters making up these liberating words inside these tantalising books which were not for me seemed to bring more colours into reticent Reddish than even the Essoldo down the road.

When I was twelve I took two books by Orwell out of the library – *1984* and one other, which I have forgotten but am convinced, if only for the sake of this story, was a collection of his journalism. I remember feeling absolutely compelled to try Orwell, although I cannot remember what made me so convinced I needed to read him. Perhaps it was the smell of the books, an aroma made stronger when their pages were opened and something unfamiliar and inspiring burst into the air. The smell must have been different to anything I had come across before, something – a smart smell, from out there, in the direction of the possible, where things were different and always changing – sucked into the books, the pages, the words themselves, from the sort of Reddish homes that contained those people, their exotic food and posh cleaning methods, perhaps even pedigree pets, who would take Orwell books out of the library.

I didn't understand a word of either book, but this didn't put me off: I remember thinking they were magnificent. There was something in these books that implied that my library card, which was a small rough scrap of stiff brown card which I wish I still had, was some sort of ticket to the future. I remember thinking that it was a good thing for me to have done: to have opened those books and tried so hard to understand them, to know that one day it would be important for me to recognise each and every word inside them, to know that one day I would understand them in the way that I was beginning to understand and recognise each paving stone and brick wall, each mark in the tarmac, each slight curve in the road, each turning and traffic light, each driveway and chimney pot, each shop window, lamp post and drain along my walk to and from school.

My bedroom in the corner at the front of the house could just about take a narrow single bed, leaving barely enough floor space for me to get in and out of it. A crude hand-built wooden airing cupboard took up all the wall next to the door, the cupboard itself on top of some drawers so that it was a few feet off the floor. The doors to the cupboard didn't quite fit together when they were shut. Sometimes I would climb up into the cupboard, which was empty give or take a few boxes of papers and my collection of *Beano*s and *Whizzer and Chips*, a football magazine or two, a couple of tattered Enid Blytons and a special, haunting Alan Garner, close the doors and sit in the dark, which didn't smell of smartness but another, more muddled, vaguely threatening world, with a hint of something nasty, and pretend that I was somewhere else, even someone else. Sometimes I would accept that I was exactly where and what I was: me, eight or nine, jammed inside a bare cupboard in a small room in a small house shared with my family, who I had never properly been introduced to.

Inside, I could hear myself breathe. I would listen to the rhythm of the falling rain. I would hear elsewhere in the house the raised voices of my parents arguing about a fresh grievance, or an old grudge, fighting between themselves about a life I was part of, their early romance and lust replaced by cramped routine and a bricked-up hopelessness. Arguing, perhaps, because my mum was where she belonged, close to her family, to where she had been brought up, but my dad was a long way from home, stunned by his surroundings, lacking the equivalent sanctuary of my cupboard.

Outside, elsewhere, the north was gravely collecting itself, gradually correcting itself, and the scattered mills that rose up above the land, those that had survived lack of use, wartime bombing and unsympathetic demolition, were transmitting secret messages, as though they were mysterious obelisks whose real meaning would only reveal itself in decades to come. Locked in my cupboard in my tiny bedroom these secret transmissions meant that even though I knew nothing, about where I was, about the north outside, I nevertheless knew, somehow felt, the following:

58

1871

Urbanisation accompanied the Industrial Revolution, as people moved into the growing towns and cities in pursuit of work. They had little opportunity for leisure at first, but after the Ten Hours Act of 1847 and the Bank Holidays Act of 1871 workers had some free time, and amateur football had become popular. By 1871 many factories were closing at lunchtime on Saturday, giving workers more time to participate in sport, whether actively or as spectators.

Rochdale Town Hall was opened on 7 September 1871 with a grand ceremony appropriate to this fine building designed by William Crossland and built upon the back of decades of success in the textile industry. It was commissioned by proud citizens who saw their success as on a par with the medieval mercantile achievements of Venice. When proposed in 1864 it was recommended that £20,000 be spent on the building. When it was completed, the remarkable building with its 240-foot wooden spire topped by a gilded statue of St George had cost £155,000. In his speech the mayor vindicated the massive outlay with 'We cannot have beauty without paying for it.' Twelve years after it was opened a fire, visible ten miles away, destroyed the tower. The building remained without a spire for four years before Alfred Waterhouse, the architect responsible for Manchester Town Hall, completed a fine stone replacement.

1869

Joseph Robert Clynes, the son of a labourer, Patrick Clynes, was born in Oldham on 27 March.

Whoever has seen Manchester in the solitary loveliness of a summer morning's dawn, when the outlines of the buildings stand clear against the cloudless sky, has seen the place in an aspect of great beauty. In that hour of mystic calm, when the houses are all bathing in the smokeless air – when the very pavement seems steeped in forgetfulness and an unearthly spell of peaceful rapture lies upon the late disturbed streets – that last hour of nature's nightly reign, when the sleeping city wears the beauty of a new morning, and 'all that mighty heart is lying still' – that stillest, loveliest hour of all the round of night and day – just before the tide of active life begins to turn back from its lowest ebb, or, like the herald drops of a coming shower, begins to patter, here and there, upon the sleepy streets once more; whoever has seen Manchester at such a time, has seen it clothed in a beauty such as noontide never knew. It is, indeed, a sight to make the heart 'run o'er with silent worship'. It is pleasant, even at such a time, to open the window to the morning breeze, and to lie awake, listening to the first driblets of sound that stir the heavenly stillness of the infant day – the responsive crowing of far-distant cocks; the chirp of sparrows about the eaves and neighbouring house-tops; the barking of dogs; the stroke of some far-off church clock, booming with strange distinctness through the listening air; a solitary cart, jolting slowly along, astonished at the noise it is making. The drowsy street – aroused from its slumbers by those rumbling wheels – yawns and scratches its head, and asks the next street what o'clock it is . . . Then come the measured footsteps of the slow-pacing policeman, longing for six o'clock; solitary voices conversing in the wide world of morning stillness; the distant tingle of a factory bell; the dull boom of escaping steam, let off to awake neighbouring work people; the whistle of the early train; and then the hurried foot and 'tap, tap, tap!' of the Knocker-Up. Soon after, the shutters begin to rattle, here and there; and the streets gradually come alive again.

Edwin Waugh, 'The Knocker-Up', *Lancashire Sketches*, 1869 edition

1865

Music hall emerged from the home-made entertainments of the working class. Groups of people would gather together in private homes or public houses for amusements including listening to local storytellers and singing. The public-house events became known as smoking concerts or free and easies. Jeffrey's Music Hall was Rochdale's first, opening on 19 April 1865 on Drake Street. Like Rochdale's first theatre, the building was originally a chapel. The second was Th' Owd Circus in Newgate, erected by an acrobat named Ohmy!

The Lake District was first mapped by the Ordnance Survey between 1856 and 1865.

1863

The first 'fish and chip shop in the north of England is reputed to have opened in Mossely, near Oldham. Mr Lees sold fish and chips from a wooden hut in the market, later transferring the business to a permanent shop across the road.

1861

Top ten occupations in Lancashire according to the Census: 1) cotton weaver, 2) servant, 3) housekeeper, 4) labourer, 5) coal miner, 6) dress maker, 7) cotton winder, 8) cotton spinner, 9) carter, 10) agricultural labourer.

'As long as the English cotton manufacturers depended on slave-grown cotton, it could truthfully be asserted that they rested on a twofold slavery, the indirect slavery of the white man in England and the direct slavery of the black men on the other side of the Atlantic.' Karl Marx, *New York Daily Tribune*, 14 March 1861.

The Lancashire cotton industry was devastated by an event far beyond its control, the American Civil War. In April, President Lincoln ordered a blockade of the Confederate southern ports, the outlet for the raw cotton on which Lancashire's mills depended. Attempts to find alternative sources of supply from India or Egypt failed. Lancashire's cotton supplies dried up and many mills closed down. The result was tremendous hardship, with many thousands of workers reduced to grinding poverty, forced to exist on minimal state help and charity soup kitchens. In these circumstances, Lancashire's poor could have been forgiven had they turned against Lincoln, but the sympathies of the mill workers stayed loyally behind the cause of the slaves. On New Year's Eve 1862, Lancashire cotton workers attended a public meeting at the Free Trade Hall in Manchester. A letter was drafted and sent to President Lincoln. An excerpt reads: '. . . the vast progress which you have made in the short space of twenty months fills us with hope that every stain on your freedom will shortly be removed, and that the erasure of that foul blot on civilisation and Christianity – chattel slavery – during your presidency, will cause the name of Abraham Lincoln to be honoured and revered by posterity.' The letter reached Lincoln, and inspired a considered response, drafted by a President at war – all in little over two weeks. Abraham Lincoln's quick response acknowledged Lancashire's hardship as a result of the Cotton Famine: '. . . I know and deeply deplore the sufferings which the working people of Manchester and in all Europe are called to endure in this crisis. Under the circumstances I cannot but regard your decisive utterances on the question as an instance of sublime Christian heroism which has not been surpassed in any age or in any country. It is indeed an energetic and re-inspiring assurance of the inherent truth and of the ultimate and universal triumph of justice, humanity and freedom.'

1859

'The theory of natural selection, it is said, could only have originated in England, because only laissez-faire England provided the atomistic, egotistic mentality necessary to its conception. Only there could Darwin have blandly assumed that the basic unit was the individual, the basic instinct self-interest, and the basic activity struggle. Spengler, describing the *Origin* as "the application of economics to biology", said that it reeked of the atmosphere of the English factory ... natural selection arose ... in England because it was a perfect expression of Victorian "greed-philosophy", of the capitalist ethic and Manchester economics.' Gertrude Himmelfarb, *Darwin and the Darwinian Revolution*, 1962.

Thomas De Quincey dies on 8 December 1859. 'My life has been,' he affirms in his *Confessions*, 'on the whole the life of a philosopher; from my birth I was made an intellectual creature, and intellectual in the highest sense my pursuits and pleasures have been.'

59

And then I forgot all about it, these details, and incidents, and broken contours, of a north that was life, right and centre, nowhere to be seen, beyond me, everywhere, needing me to activate it. It left some sort of impression, some sort of haunting of the mind, a forming of sensibility, but it would take decades before I could piece it all back together again, reconstruct it, dredge it up from where it had gone, beyond me, in the cupboard, smelling of impertinent otherness, in the dark, in my house, in Reddish, in the north, outside from the start.

And what else – something else – thoughts, words I shared with myself, a conversation inside myself, a provisional puzzling out of the puzzle that had been handed to me without any apparent consideration of what that might do to my wellbeing . . . I could hear myself think. Some of these thoughts were the silent sound of me growing as a conscious being, getting used to the way that a thought you had came out of nowhere, but the more you thought, the more you had to think about, and once you started, there was no stopping you, and you'd get to understand how those thoughts had in fact come from somewhere. What those thoughts became, what they consisted of, how they would lead to more thoughts filling your head with sense and nonsense, would all depend on the outside help you got, in whatever form that presented it yourself, whether you knew it or not.

At the time, I was vaguely aware that in the early to mid-sixties my father worked for British European Airways. There was a BEA flight from Manchester's Ringway Airport to London on the way to our annual summer holiday in Margate when I was five or six, presumably bought at a staff discount price, which is my first real memory of feeling absolute terror. Each abrupt dip of the plane in flight, each shudder, vibration, unexplained noise, shift to the right or left, caused me to scream. I tearfully protested at this ludicrous way of travelling, and when we landed had to be dragged from the plane, a red-faced mess of fear and fury. Research now tells me that my dad must have worked in the BEA sales office at 41 to 43 Deansgate, about as modern an early 1960s Manchester address as you could get, a few steps around the corner from the Granada Television headquarters where *Coronation Street* was invented and where the street actually existed as a set.

The office where he worked was designed in 1959 by John Warren Chalk, born in 1927 and educated during the war at Hyde County Grammar School, Hyde being a shabby half-brother of Stockport, five miles north-east, and seven miles east of Manchester, the other side of Denton. It was once a part of Stockport, and therefore Cheshire, with no real identity before the nineteenth-century cotton industry. It's where my grandfather George, my mum's dad, was born, to a mother whose maiden name was itself Hyde, so of the Hydes of Hyde, which means I might be able to trace myself all the way back to Matthew de Hyde, born in 1167, father of Sir Robert, himself father of Sir John, born in 1245, companion of the Black Prince. This was a family that ended up with the motto 'Be steadfast,' but by the time it reached my grandad George, was not knighted or notable.

How many of the later, less noble Hydes of Hyde made it on to a Lowry canvas representing his own inscrutable mind, and how many times did my beyond-steadfast grandad, father of four demanding daughters, constantly stooped over an imaginary shoe he was hammering nails into, mooching from one nowhere to another via a possible somewhere, himself feature as a human splinter sloping towards death adrift in Lowry's painted-up reflection of the abyss, which Hyde could make great claims to be the capital of?

The earliest references to Hyde come in a book called *Forty Miles around Manchester* published in 1795, when what was to become the town centre was no more than a group of houses known as Red Pump Street: 'Near the commencement of the Eastern Horn of Cheshire, which runs up into the wild country bordering on Yorkshire and the Peak of Derbyshire, is Hyde Chapel, or, as it is now called, Gee Cross.'

Hyde United's 26–0 hammering in 1887 to Preston North End is the greatest ever defeat in a FA Cup tie. That is one of the first facts I ever learned in a life I eventually realised was made up of a random accumulation of facts you packed around your personality like a protective lining of knowledge, as if knowledge was real strength and gaps in knowledge an unconditional disaster, an emptiness representing pure death, and the thought of it still winds me forty-five years later. The fact seemed stronger, more shattering, because Hyde was near me, and the place had the resigned nature of a town that had never recovered from the size of the defeat.

Oddly enough, in the first few years of the twentieth century the Hyde Seals water polo team were the best in the world, three times world champions, but that fact has not infected the psychology of the town. Perhaps it is too watery a fact, lacking the near-epic dimension of those twenty-six goals conceded. In 1936, in a complicated exchange of territory that presumably satisfied some local government official trying to balance the books, parts of Hyde were handed to Bredbury and Romiley and Dukinfield, and Hyde was extended to include parts of Compstall, Dukinfield, Hattersley and Matley civil parishes. By the end of the twentieth century, certain events that happened in and around Hyde meant that it had a reputation as a town that suited its name, which originally came from the Anglo-Saxon *hid* (hide), a measure of land that could be farmed with one plough and support one family for a year. A hide was quite a substantial area, varying from sixty to one hundred and twenty acres. The surname Hyde or Hide was often given to the holder of the land and his family, or to a family living near a hide.

Brady and Hindley lived together in Hyde, and three decades later there would be another series of murders that meant that you could think of Hyde as the Hyde in *Dr Jekyll and Mr Hyde*, something that is usually normal, ordinary, everyday and can be magical, audacious and even genius, and then something that is grotesque, horrific, rotten to the core, a repugnant latent energy jumping out from thousands of years ago into unsuspecting modern life.

Harold Shipman was born on 14 January 1946 into a working-class Methodist background, and committed suicide as one of the world's most prolific convicted serial killers on 13 January 2004. He became a general practitioner in Todmorden (death death wood) in 1974, and was seen by many as solitary, arrogant and inscrutable behind his thick glasses and beard, although patients loved his friendly bedside manner. He enjoyed his little jokes, more amusing to him than to their subjects, but he apparently thought of himself as 'boring' and 'normal'. Fired from Todmorden for writing drug prescriptions for himself, he was not struck off, merely fined £600 and referred to a psychiatric unit, and he re-emerged as the GP for Hyde in 1977. Over twenty years he was responsible for hundreds of deaths, usually older ladies who lived alone, injecting them with opiates. He covered his tracks by altering records and falsifying death certificates.

A year below John Warren Chalk at the Hyde County Grammar School was a Dukinfield boy born on 13 March 1928 called Ronald Hazlehurst. His dad worked on the railways and his mum was a piano teacher. He left school at fourteen and worked as a clerk in a cotton mill for a pound a week, playing cornet for four times as much in a local band that made regular appearances on the BBC Light Programme. He became a professional musician, and after a few years' freelance work in Manchester, including time at Granada TV, and in London, he joined the BBC in 1961 as an arranger and conductor. He worked on *The Likely Lads* (1964) and *It's a Knockout* before becoming head of music for light entertainment in 1968. A fan of the Bradford-born Frederick Delius, he could locate, capture and emphasise an atmosphere using melody and rhythm within seconds, which led to his genius as a writer of succinct, instantly catchy television music.

Ronnie Hazlehurst would write the always entirely appropriate, witty, suggestive theme tunes for *Some Mothers Do 'Ave 'Em* (gently strange through the enforced use of economical instrumentation, 1973), *The Two Ronnies* (cheerfully batty jingle promising contagious naughtiness, 1971), *Are You Being Served?* (slapstick set in a department store, so neatly featuring cash registers, anticipating Pink Floyd's 'Money' by a good couple of years, 1972), *Last of the Summer Wine* (perversely but accurately mournful and as trippily gentle as the setting, 1973) and *The Fall and Rise of Reginald Perrin* (which naturally, but brilliantly, featured a jaunty but bleak melody that rose and fell, 1976). *The Fall and Rise of Reginald Perrin* opened each week with a naked Reggie walking out into the sea to end it all before rapidly rethinking the whole idea, and told the story of a man desperate to escape his loving but dull marriage, disappointing, puzzling offspring and the daily grind of his job. The first series, which finished in October 1976, while undeniably funny was incredibly dark, focusing on a man on the edge of a nervous breakdown. I remember my dad watching the show and seeming to like it, but what with one thing and another, he didn't get round to the second series in the autumn of 1977.

After the war architect John Warren Chalk was sent six miles from Hyde to Stockport College to finish his schooling, a place I too ended up thirty or so years later, also as a sort of punishment for underachieving. After Stockport College, instilled with more purpose and thinking of ways to turn his developing interest in jazz, design, poetry, art and buildings into a profession, he went to the College of Art and Technology in Manchester, where he was torn between painting and architecture. He chose architecture, but didn't lose his belief in the fantastic and transformative, and combined the reflection of the artist with the action of the architect.

In 1962, along with Blackpool-born Dennis Crompton, Chalk joined a London-based group of dissident neophyte architects who had founded the playful, pop-art- and futurist-inspired avant-garde architectural group Archigram – short for architectural telegram. They viewed constantly advancing technology as something to be fused with mass culture, space-age surfaces with the natural environment, and were committed to understanding how architecture could keep up with and reflect the rapid social and cultural changes and gathering political discontent. They would have been appalled by the fussy baroque Stockport Town Hall, situated a short way down Wellington Road from Stockport College, a run-of-the mill decorated box designed in 1905 by Alfred Brumwell Thomas resembling a shrivelled-up Buckingham Palace with its tiny columns and insipid scrolls. It was not the sort of structure to interest L. S. Lowry – no seemingly imperishable blend of brick, cement and iron flaunting a genuine monumental air – it never possessed dignity, so there was never any cracked or lost dignity; it was simply a fussy extravagance representing the town's badly disguised inferiority complex. Perhaps Chalk was so upset by it, he set out to imagine a world that contained breath-taking space-age grandeur and not buildings that seemed to have been excreted rather than designed.

Perhaps the Merseyway Shopping Precinct was more his concrete and steel cup of tea, except it lacked a soaring sense of wonder, and the tower, with its numberless square white clock face, sheepishly poked up towards the sky with no sense of how the mill chimneys it could have been some sort of tribute to were often indebted to the bell towers of Venetian churches. I liked it at the time because it seemed like something that might have featured in the shakily futuristic *Thunderbirds* puppet show on TV, but as time has passed the buildings near it constructed a hundred years before have retained their overwhelming and future-minded power, and the clock has come to look cheap and plastic, like it runs on clockwork and the key has been lost. It symbolises a zealous, anxious 1960s, which bulldozed the finicky, embalming and hieratic Victorian and Edwardian past into oblivion but very soon started to look a little dated itself.

Archigram's main interest was in seeing the radical changes of the sixties, from J. F. Kennedy to the photocopier, from Bob Dylan and Roy Lichtenstein to the pill, reflected in audacious contemporary domestic architecture. They were happy positioning their experimental thinking inside the burgeoning post-war consumer culture, imagining buildings that mixed novel building materials with swift, ephemeral and dynamic images and ideas taken from science fiction, Dadaism, collage, advertising and toys. The group aimed to transform the world of things into a direct projection of the world of spirit. Lives had been enriched by elements the possibility of whose existence the ancient world had never even suspected. Archigram dreamed of integrating these into everyday life, and of responding to environmental trends and tumultuous changes in fashion, politics and cultural appetites.

Archigram was also the name of their broadsheet, as poetically inspired as it was technologically enthusiastic, whose strapline proclaimed that it had been 'founded as an occasional journal/ manifesto of dynamic ideas for new architecture'. The first issue in May 1961 was ninepence. The paper had the character of an under-ground art-scene magazine rather than an architecture periodical: instead of glossy paper, elegant photo series and factual journalism, *Archigram* featured comic strips, erratic typography, poetry, mani-festos and curt, cryptic motivational statements. The print run soon rose from a few hundred to several thousand, and the influence of its ideas spread as quickly.

One of the founders of Archigram, Peter Cook, would write of Warren Chalk, 'his work is so condensed, accurate and to the point. Yet the culture they represent is a difficult one to recall: something that came out of Britain in the 1950s, which led to satirical comedy, pop art, mixed-media events, the mock architectural movement Bowellism, Archigram – that video-as-rabbit-as-bicycle-as-poem-as-cathedral world which is probably unthinkable right now because of its apparent anarchy or apparent inconsequentiality. It stemmed as much from the world of the art school as it did from the Partisan Coffee Bar in Soho or from Cambridge. Warren was undoubtedly part of the first-named circuit. All along, architecture was learning as much from this as it was from Le Corbusier and Buckminster Fuller. So lateral thinking was inherent and not just acquired – especially from someone so intelligent coming out of this funny corner of European revival.'

I had no idea at the time that my dad worked in a building designed by a northern figure with Stockport connections, who built capsule homes inspired by John Glenn's 1962 first orbit of the moon, who was part of a collective which hated 'ponderous buildings that just got in the way' and who would assist in the building of the Hayward Gallery, part of the Southbank Centre arts complex in London. We lived in an extremely average semi-detached, which looked more as if it had been inspired by the turn-ups on George Formby's grey trousers than anything supersonic, Eurominimalist or brutalist. But something did leak through to me that my father, now in his late twenties, with a lean hopeful look that seemed to belong to tomorrow and aerodynamic slicked-back hair, not Beatles long but post-Teddy-boy cocky, with a neatly combed Brylcreemed dash of 1962 Sean Connery as James Bond, brought back with him from work a sense of something exciting and in keeping with talk of a white-hot technological revolution. A small zip-up bag with the red slightly slanted BEA logo printed on each side in the centre seemed connected to the space age and was definitely a jet-set snippet of glamour in our worn-down house.

We had a basic unkempt working-class house with haggard second-hand cars parked in front, but he didn't have a job that involved getting his hands dirty. My dad's work seemed to consist of holding a biro and writing things down and finding extracurricular ways to brighten his routine. He wasn't part of the traditional local working class he seemed to fear or look down on, but nor anywhere near the middle class to which he craved to belong. He was nothing, belonging nowhere and feeling the pressure. For a while he had a go at moving on from being neither one thing or another, as if his worries would be wiped away by living a comfortable existence further into lighter, leafier Cheshire. No doubt his horror was slipping into Denton, into Gorton, into Hyde, and whatever monstrous void there was beyond that.

I don't exactly know what happened to cause him to leave the BEA sales office except that there were rumours in our household that it involved a mysterious woman at work and an affair that motivated my mum to storm Deansgate and bring a little old-fashioned working-class vim to the modernised surroundings. His next job, though, still seemed linked to the technological revolution. He moved to the new computer centre that Shell Mex and BP had built in Wythenshawe to partner a similar complex in Hemel Hempstead. Wythenshawe was part of Cheshire until 1931, when it was transferred to Manchester to help deal with the slum problem. It was planned as a decorative but functional 'garden city' to absorb some of the swelling population of inner Manchester. To those moving after the war from the dirty brick tenements and bomb sites of Moss Side and Rusholme, hemmed inside the constant smell of dog dirt and coal smoke, the newly painted houses with three bedrooms, a bathroom and an inside toilet, and oval-shaped plots of land to play on and numerous ponds and brooks filled with sticklebacks seemed like paradise. The paradise wouldn't last.

Wythenshawe would become famous in the sixties and seventies for the Golden Garter nightclub, originally a bowling alley, now proudly presented as a theatre restaurant, a deluxe confirmation of that strident northern need for nightclub fantasy. Inside, leaving the pedestrian Wythenshawe Civic Centre well behind you, the carpets were thick, the decor a sumptuous blend of gold and crimson, the tables clothed in white linen. It opened on 7 October 1968, when Coca-Cola seemed as exotic as champagne and a three-course meal was thirteen shillings and sixpence – start with grapefruit cocktail, then the golden-fried scampi, apple pie and cream for pud – coffee one and six extra. Babycham was two and six, a pint of Double Diamond three shillings and the cheapest champagne a tanner under two quid when the average weekly wage was about thirty pounds. Bruce Forsyth was top of the bill and seemed old even then, and the club was the last gasp of the variety era as it metamorphosed into the mongrel cabaret that would become associated in the seventies with chicken in a basket.

Garter nights were generally rowdy, audiences possessing almost a violent hankering for gaiety and distraction, a relish for racy, rip-roaring fun rooted in centuries of slog and toil, and acts facing their audience through a dense purple haze of smoke behind a solid array of frowning bouncers. There was sexy pop music from the Supremes, Sandie Shaw, Lulu and Dusty Springfield, bawdy comedy from Bob Monkhouse, Cannon and Ball, Les Dawson and Ken Dodd, and haywire comedy groups like the Grumbleweeds and the Barron Knights making a mockery of talent. American superstars Roy Orbison and Eartha Kitt visited, real life verging on visions of the otherworldly fame and fortune the local talent strived for, descending like serene gods as if the Garter really was a paradise, if a fallen one, and the venue where they played truly built out of gold even if it was actually painted and chipped plaster.

I remember my dad talking about going to the great Golden Garter in the early 1970s, although I found it hard to envisage him eating scampi and downing pints of Double Diamond, but then this was the kind of grown-up haunt kept well away from children, and who knows what he got up to inside this backstreet pleasure palace. He told me about seeing Tommy Cooper, and how rumour had it Tommy had got a taxi from central Manchester, where the hotels were, out to Wythenshawe, and had handed the driver an envelope, telling him, 'Have a drink on me.' Once Tommy had gone, the driver ripped open the envelope, expecting from the famous comedian at the very least a crisp fiver, if not a splendid tenner. Even a ten-bob note would have been nice. Inside, there was nothing but a tea bag. I now realise my dad was repeating a joke that Tommy Cooper told against himself, but it was as though somehow Tommy had told it to my father over a three-shilling brandy.

I never went to visit my dad at his work in Wythenshawe, which remained a mystery. It was a drive from Reddish of about eight miles. If I had, it would have been ten stops on the bus from Mersey Square, Stockport, upstairs for the view – the tops of trees and upstairs windows – rumbling west through Heaton Mersey, Burnage, Parrs Wood in East Didsbury, where the Wilmslow Road begins, along the way north to Manchester city centre after becoming Oxford Road and then Oxford Street (an eighteenth-century route to Oxford), crossing Cheadle Bridge the other way at the Parrs Wood end over the Mersey into Cheadle – a parish created in 1879, the gateway to Cheshire at the southern tip of Manchester, called Cedde in the Domesday Book (clearing in the wood) – Withington, West Didsbury, Northenden (north enclosure) and Baguley. Baguley was one of the nine Wythenshawe areas that had mopped up the Manchester population overspill, along with Benchill, Peel Hall, Newall Green, Woodhouse Park, Moss Nook, Sharston, Northenden – at the edge of affluent Didsbury, where the houses are semi-detached and detached, big enough for attics and basements, and fancying itself as upmarket, before being absorbed by Manchester as an attractive riverside village – and Northern Moor, ancient Cheshire hamlets, townships, communities and parishes on the southern banks of the River Mersey.

Up until 1964 I could have taken a train from Stockport's Tiviot Dale station to Baguley, but the station, which had opened on 1 February 1866, was shut to passengers during what were called the Beeching cuts. British Railways chairman Dr Richard Beeching's reshaping of the network resulted in the closing of 6,000 miles, one third of the total, of little-used mostly rural and cross-country lines, in order to cut costs. Tiviot Dale, near Lancashire Hill, at the bottom of South Reddish, one station down from Reddish North, was one of two stations in Stockport along with Stockport Edgeley. Trains from there ran to Liverpool Central High Level, also shut down as a result of Beeching's report, and on 30 November 1964 the services between Tiviot Dale and Liverpool and Warrington, via Baguley, were withdrawn.

In the other direction, trains would steam over to Buxton via New Mills, eight miles south-east of Stockport, its town centre perched above the Torrs, a gloomy steep-sided gorge through which the Goyt and Sett rivers flow. New Mills is on the borders of Cheshire and Derbyshire at the north-west edge of the Peak District, and got its name from a fourteenth-century corn mill. The Manchester-to-Sheffield fast line bypasses New Mills' two stations, Central and Newtown. Tiviot Dale was finally closed down on 2 January 1967 – freight trains still used the line for a few more years, especially those carrying coal from South Yorkshire to the Fiddlers Ferry Power Station near Warrington – and Edgeley was left on its own, soon becoming simply Stockport now that there was no second station.

Eventually I would visit all of the places on the bus route from Stockport to Wythenshawe, and on the line to New Mills, and beyond, to Buxton, because it became apparent very early on living in Reddish that one place led to another, and then another, and it was amazing how far you could go if you just kept going. If you didn't keep going you would stay put for ever where you were.

60

1859

'[A town hall should be] the most dominant and important of the Municipal Buildings of the City in which it is placed. It should be the means of giving the expression to public feeling upon all national and municipal events of importance.' Sir Charles Barry.

1858

Leeds Town Hall was designed by Cuthbert Broderick and completed in 1858. It is the seventh highest building in Leeds (225 feet) and one of the largest town halls in Britain. When built the western side of the basement housed thirteen cells, a police office and accommodation for the jailer and his wife (a converted cell). Queen Victoria visited Leeds to open the new town hall. She was accompanied by Prince Albert, and it is said that he remarked that 'Leeds seemed in need of a good theatre, and that nothing was more calculated to promote the culture and raise the tone of the people.'

Charles Dickens visited Harrogate in 1858 and noted, 'Harrogate is the queerest place with the strangest people in it, leading the oddest lives of dancing, newspaper reading and dining.'

1857

Felix Mendelssohn passed through Manchester in 1847, performing with the decidedly inferior orchestra of the Gentlemen's Concert Club. The director of the orchestra, one of a strong German community in the city, challenged conductor Charles Hallé, born Carl Hallé in Westphalia in 1819, to come to Manchester and improve it. Hallé, previously living and working in Paris but driven to England by the 1848 revolution, a friend and aficionado of Chopin and Lizst, contemporary of Wagner and Grieg, whose musical awareness was formed during Beethoven's lifetime and extended to the time of Debussy and Satie, accepted.

Manchester had a lively music scene at the time, and discerning audiences, but lacked a visionary with intimate knowledge of the structure and personality of classical music. Forming Britain's first permanent professional symphony orchestra in 1857, Hallé spent the next thirty-seven years as charismatic promoter and conductor of the famous orchestra that would take his name. He was driven by intellectual ideals and a deep belief in the civilising influence of music, but possessed a salesman's commercial energy, familiarising northerners with the orchestral works of all the great composers. This was the time when the idea of a classical music repertoire was being enshrined, the masters being established as mainstream geniuses, with music beginning to symbolise national and civic status rather than remaining mere entertainment. Hallé aimed to do for music what the great galleries and exhibitions had done for painting and sculpture: to organise and define taste, and, exploiting and even shaping the desires and appetites of the new middle class in the first industrial city, create a grand soundtrack to a society that had so recently transformed itself, in the process creating a cultural representation of self-improvement in direct contrast to the raucous reflection of street life in free and easy public houses and music halls. Hallé was knighted by Queen Victoria in 1888.

1856

Novelist and chronicler Elizabeth Gaskell wrote of Yorkshire men, 'Their accost is curt; their accent and tone of speech blunt and harsh. Something of this may, perhaps, be attributed to the freedom of mountain air and of isolated hill-side life, something be derived from their rough Norse ancestry. They have a quick perception of character, and a keen sense of humour. The dwellers among them must be prepared for certain uncomplimentary, though most likely true, observations pithily expressed.'

A nineteenth-century marvel and widely hailed as the city of the future, Manchester represented a break from the past. What Manchester did that was so new and different was simple – it specialised. The city threw its lot in with one industry, textiles. To its supporters, Manchester's textile industry represented the triumph of the Industrial Revolution, the vindication of the division of labour and specialisation. To one detractor, a German writer named Karl Marx, Manchester's boom period was less admirable. He loathed the inequality he saw – a few wealthy mill owners and thousands of impoverished workers – and deplored the dehumanisation of humans doing repetitive work like machines. But like its supporters, Marx saw Manchester as a precursor of a future in which places consolidate economic activity into a single industry and then produce a single kind of product with terrible efficiency.

'Our journey between Manchester and Sheffield was not through a rich tract of country, but along a valley walled by bleak, ridgy hills, extending straight as a rampart, and across black moorlands, with here and there a plantation of trees,' wrote novelist Nathaniel Hawthorne, who lived nearby in Liverpool during the mid-1850s. 'The train stopped a minute or two, to allow the tickets to be taken, just before entering the Sheffield station, and thence I had a glimpse of the famous town of razors and pen knives, enveloped in a cloud of its own diffusing. My impressions of it are extremely vague and misty – or rather, smoky – for Sheffield seems to me smokier than Manchester, Liverpool, or Birmingham, smokier than all England besides, unless Newcastle be the exception. It might have been Pluto's own metropolis, shrouded in sulphurous vapour.'

1855

It is nearly forty years since Jane Austen wrote *Pride and Prejudice*, and the social landscape of England is in transition in Elizabeth Gaskell's novel *North and South*. The aristocrat who lives a life of leisure while his tenants work his fields in southern England is being replaced by the common man who works his way up to a position of wealth and power in the factory towns of the north. First published as a magazine serial of twenty-two instalments in

Household Words – edited by her mentor Charles Dickens – *North and South* was expanded by Mrs Gaskell and published in book format in 1855. The story explores some of Gaskell's favourite topics: social division and class struggle, religious faith and doubt, and the landscape of mid-Victorian England as it changed from agricultural nation to industrial giant.

North and South (originally called *Margaret Hale* after its principal character until Charles Dickens made Gaskell change it) starts in a rose-covered country cottage in the south of England where Margaret Hale lives with her pastor father, her mother and their servants. Margaret loves the outdoors: she sketches nature and spends a carefree and idyllic youth roaming the countryside and helping neighbours with various acts of charity. But towards the end of Margaret's teens her father announces that he has abandoned the Church, and because of this the family is uprooted to Milton (apparently based on Gaskell's hometown of Manchester) to start again.

Starting life anew in Milton comes hard to Margaret. She knows no one and is unfamiliar with the ways of the town, but Margaret Hale is one of the strongest female characters in English literature. She immediately sets to work finding a place to live, puts on a brave face in front of her troubled family and steadies them with her perseverance. Margaret soon makes friends with some of the mill workers and sympathises with their complaints against their harsh employers. This was a turbulent age and climbing the ladder was difficult. Mill hands worked under terrible conditions and often had poor health, while mill masters were sometimes cruel.

1854

Queen Victoria visited York, her one and only visit to the city. According to the *York Press*, 'She was allegedly asked to pay for her meal at the Royal Station Hotel. She was shocked and said she would never visit York again. Apparently, whenever the Royal train passed through York afterwards she always made sure the blinds were firmly pulled down!'

1853

Until 1853 the short drop was used in Lancaster when hanging criminals. This resulted in a slow death by strangulation and was replaced by the more humane long drop. We still use sayings rooted in these practices. To hurry death, a victim sometimes had their 'leg pulled' by a 'hanger-on', while some people think that the practice of selling the rope after a hanging (by the inch at sixpence a time, as a lucky charm) was 'money for old rope'.

61

I never clearly understood what it was my dad actually did at BP and Shell Mex, what was going on with the new computers. I think he worked in the clerical department, but I'm not sure what I'm basing that on. The job didn't seem to turn him on, so he wasn't likely to talk about it much, except, occasionally, when something good happened – promotion, I think, to something called a team leader, which appeared to involve being in charge of about five people. Whatever it was he did, it lasted the longest of all the jobs he ever had, at least until 1972 or '73. It was also the last real job he ever had; after that he worked selling things, door to door, which meant travelling the streets of Stockport, facing up to pestered, irritated people opening and shutting doors in his face, or just humouring him, trying to place his suspect accent. Possibly sometimes he followed in the footsteps of Lowry, briefly glimpsing strange, unknowable other lives, searching for inspiration in the fading, failing world, into streets and alleys which for my dad seemed to take the form of prison bars.

By the time I was ready to ask him how he spent his days and what his job title was, it was too late for him to tell me. We didn't talk much about anything outside of football – never had conversations about life or death, or family, or money – and the only time we drifted, or smashed, into anything that might be considered serious was because he was shouting at me about something I had done wrong, or he thought I had done wrong, turning on me with a cornered look in his eyes that came from his mother, and also from the dark that started out deep inside him and increasingly made it to the surface. It was no use arguing back. God knows where that might have ended up, not that in the end the ending could have been any worse. I wonder if this is why I cannot remember what my dad sounded like, except I know for sure, somehow, that he never absorbed any of the accent or slang of the area where he ended up, facing the end. He would withdraw far into himself, as if deep inside he found the best clues about who he was and what to do next.

For me and my dad, Reddish was mostly a base for talking about and watching Manchester City. Together we watched them rise from the Second Division in 1965 to (surprising) First Division champions in 1967/8; we were there in Newcastle for the final match of the season to see City win the League in a style approaching the delirious, scoring four goals, beginning and ending our long Saturday journey into a far, far north and back at sleepy Reddish North station, which had all the presence of a mumbled aside.

Even as City fulfilled our belief that they were the team to follow – not Manchester United, who were legends but somehow not local – United carried on in their bullying way justifying the original reason I had decided to support City: United seemed too mono-lithic, too intimidating. My bold choice, as instinctive as the feeling that led me to Orwell and Garner, paid off, as though it was actually my support and loyalty that had enabled their success. My regular attendance at their home games sprinkled Garner-esque magic over the previously struggling club, and City knocked United into second place with such flash and swagger I swear it illuminated Reddish itself. Reddish was within walking distance of the City ground, Maine Road, although it took an hour to walk and we usually went in my dad's car.

I knew it could be walked because sometimes Dad had no car or money for petrol, and no money for the coach that left Houldsworth Square. I took this lack of money in my stride. I didn't really know where his money came from anyway, or where it went, and sometimes there was none, and not even my mum going to work up the road at the sweet factory seemed to make money appear – although tins of rejected sweets would. He never had much and towards the end of his life seemed to have even less. He perhaps feared this end so much it inevitably happened: ending with nothing after all that concentration, and tension, and walking through northern streets on the way to more northern streets past doors that seemed shut for ever.

The walk to see City play, an opportunity for some pre-match reflection for us both, took us east along the Gorton Road, left at Longford Road down the street from my school, along which, amazingly, a City player actually lived – Mike Doyle, lean aggressive number 4 right half in the League-winning side – and into the Barlow Road, then up the Stockport Road to Dickinson Road through dishevelled Longsight towards the hard-working Wilmslow Road. We were in Rusholme now, near where some of the streets in Victoria Park contained substantial houses exuding unexpected Victorian grandness, once, as Manchester grew in confidence, the homes of eminent locals such as Charles Hallé, Emmeline Pankhurst, Ford Madox Brown, Richard Cobden and Elizabeth Gaskell. Among the many distinguished-looking houses giving the area a discreet even serene splendour there was a building designed in the early years of the twentieth century by Middleton's romantic proto-minimalist Edgar Wood for the Christian Scientists, a blend of sinuous art nouveau and austere modernism that looked as though it was out of something written by the Grimm Brothers and filmed by Ingmar Bergman.

When we drove to the ground, this was where my father liked to park, away from the dense football traffic the other side of the Wilmslow Road, the Kent snob in him perhaps fancying Victoria Park as the type of area he would like to live in, close to the disordered city centre but full of spacious institutional and religious signs of prosperity, sealed off from the surrounding disintegration, a lot of it broken enough to be classified as slums, and the commotion of match days. Whether we drove or walked, we would then cross the Wilmslow Road amid the chattering crowds draped in sky blue and white that told us we were close to the ground. For a few miles before that, when walking, we were on our own, crossing the invisible borders from one ward to the next, occasionally spotting as we got closer the ground's floodlights scraping the sky like medieval metal warriors above the surrounding crouched houses bunched up in terror. The walk was worth it to see City win, which, for a few years, into the early 1970s, they usually did, in the sort of style that meant I would crave a repeat for the rest of my life.

Never for a moment thinking I would within a few years be without a dad, who seemed more permanent than bricks, more certain than rain, if as unpredictable as smoke, I would have three heaped sugars in my tea too, like father like son (within reason), piling up the cup with spoonfuls, a habit which took about fifteen years to lose, and now, forty-odd years later, I don't take sugar, having finally shaken off this particular parental direction. On a school day, by the time the morning fire was really alive and on top of itself, hot enough to burn my face if I bent close to the fireplace because I needed its heat more than usual to give life to my fingers and toes, it would be time for me to leave and walk through Reddish, which was the world to me, in a world of my own.

The outside world was doing all that you would expect it to do as it charged through the 1960s full of revelation, revolution, space travel, hippies, regeneration and protest. I was more interested in picking the crusty scabs that always seemed to form on my knees and elbows, or suddenly breaking into a mindless sprint along the pavement as though I was in a race against whatever car was alongside me and reaching the bus stop first meant untold riches, or going into the sweet shop on my dreamy way home from school, sticking my head into a transporting stench of sugar and spiked fruit, and spending the grubby coppers I'd got on some chunky puff candy or a handful of sticky Black Jacks, four for a pre-decimal penny. Then you still got 240 pennies to a pound, in a past now falling away into the last century, just as the last century is falling away to join the century before it, which for so long seemed so long ago. The 240 pennies and the chunky ha'pennies, which could actually buy a couple of sticky sweets, showed how close the 1960s really were to the 1890s, even though enough had changed to mean the smoke had cleared, the local buses were dressed in hippy orange and new city-centre buildings pretended to be as modern – encased in glass, steel and opaque purpose – as anything in Europe or America.

Sometimes, sat on a sadly orange bus heading towards the increasingly seductive shopping centre, I might even have a threepenny bit, a twelve-sided brass coin which would occasionally date all the way back to the 1950s and looked eccentrically ancient enough to have been around for centuries. Threepence was about one and a bit post-decimal pennies. I remember once having one dated 1966, and it was so shiny and new it felt as though it had been handed to me by the captain of England Bobby Moore himself. I spent it, though. In 1970 with a couple of extra pennies it would have got me a Mars Bar. By 1971 it was gone, as dead as a farthing, as if such an eccentric coin, as English as a knighthood and with such an intricate shape, could never survive in an age when men walked on the moon for hours at a time and Stanley Kubrick's ultra-violent futuristic *A Clockwork Orange*, based on the novel by industrious, self-admiring Manchester genius-charlatan-fantasist-wit Anthony Burgess, was released.

62

1853

'Paradoxically, it was after Manchester officially became a city in 1853 that interest in it slackened. Writers might occasionally continue to focus attention on the city, but they were no longer "excited" or "shocked" by what they saw . . . Manchester was beginning to be taken increasingly for granted, a fact rather than a symbol, just as Chicago began to be taken for granted after 1900 and Los Angeles after the Second World War. Cities usually have only a relatively short "shock" phase. The problems which they seem to "incarnate" may persist but the issues become increasingly abstract and generalised, less attached to particular and specific local situations.' Asa Briggs, *Victorian Cities*, 1963.

1851

In the year of the Great Exhibition, a year in which the term Victorian was increasingly being used, Queen Victoria visited Manchester. For the town's corporation this was an opportunity to show off the municipality to the world. They planned a mass pageant, which was to be performed in front of vast crowds and enhanced with ritual – even if the ritual was invented for the occasion. After the Queen had visited Salford, the royal party, conducted by the mayor and high sheriff, both wearing ceremonial dress for the first time, passed through the city-centre streets. 'The streets were immensely full,' the Queen later recorded in her journal, 'and the cheering and enthusiasm most gratifying.' As a sign of her gratitude, the Queen knighted the mayor, John Potter. Behind the scenes she was also being canvassed for something more.

The corporation saw the visit not just as an opportunity to project Manchester to the nation, it was also after city status. Manchester had good reason for thinking it should have this, but coming as this did at the beginning of two decades or so which saw civic rivalry erupt on a scale never previously witnessed in England, the events of the next couple of years came to symbolise the growth of civic pride more generally. The transformation of 'city' from a term designating a town with a cathedral to a symbol of status began in Manchester with Queen Victoria's visit in 1851.

Marian Withers, the third novel written by the 39-year-old Geraldine Jewsbury, another of Charles Dickens's protégés, was first serialised for the *Manchester Examiner & Times* and appeared in book form in 1851.

Chapter 1
It was a regular Manchester wet day of more than ordinary discomfort! The rain came down with a steady, heavy determination, aggravated from time to time with an emphatic energy by gusts of winds, which swept down the streets, rippling the puddles which had gathered in the uneven flags, and rendering all attempts to shelter under an umbrella entirely vain. The atmosphere was a murky composition of soot and water, which rendered the daylight only a few shades brighter than night. Nothing could be discerned beyond the distance of a few yards, the sky and the earth being seemingly mixed together in a disorganised fog. Few persons were in the

streets, for nearly everyone had sought refuge in the vain hope that the rain was too violent to continue.

In the fourth chapter, Jewsbury talked of a hidden world that existed just before the railways made previously inaccessible places easier to reach, places in Lancashire and Yorkshire that seemed as distant as anywhere in India, which were somehow ashamed at being discovered.

The country towns of Burnley, Colne, Clitheroe and Accrington lay in a country which had not been penetrated to any distance by public conveyances, and individuals journeying across the country were generally obliged to provide their own conveyance and depend on their own resources both for going and returning. About twenty years ago, the traveller leaving Accrington a little to the left would find himself upon a very rugged highway, in a wild country, so surrounded on all sides by a labyrinth of hills, that he would, if a stranger, be apt to wonder how he came there; followed by the more anxious wonder of how he was to get out again.

By 1851 the population of Manchester had reached 186,000. Later in the century the population was boosted by the arrival of Jews fleeing persecution in eastern Europe.

1850

On 23 April, St George's Day, aged eighty, William Wordsworth caught a cold on a country walk and died of pleurisy, an inflammation of the lining around the lungs. His friend Thomas De Quincey estimated that in his life Wordsworth had walked about 175,000 miles, walking with purpose, for enjoyment, without a care in the world, for necessity and duty, to purposely get lost, get the post, or for inspiration. Coleridge liked to compose walking over uneven ground or broken branches, Wordsworth while walking up and down a gravel path. De Quincey never rejected the idea of the city or of modern urban life, and, unlike Wordsworth, Keats or Shelley, couldn't permanently settle in isolated or rural circumstances. De Quincey needed an abundance of buildings, streets, squares, bridges, false doors, glowing lights and secret alleyways, which he could flow through like thought. Where Wordsworth wanders among the daffodils, De Quincey strolls through crowds and markets, chasing smells, noises and experiences most poets would have considered repugnant.

A few months after Wordsworth's death, his widow Mary published *Poem to Coleridge*, a work now known as *The Prelude*, an enormous wandering epic that starts on the ground and climbs to the top of the mountains. Wordsworth had asked for this long, autobiographical poem to be published only after his death. Recording Wordsworth's spiritual transformation, it is now considered his masterpiece.

> A hundred hills their dusky backs upheaved
> All over this still Ocean, and beyond,
> Far, far beyond, the vapours shot themselves
> In headlands, tongues and promontory shapes
> Into the sea, the real sea that seemed
> To dwindle and give up its majesty

The literacy of the working class was advanced considerably by the Public Libraries Act of 1850. There was much hostility to the bill when first introduced, the Conservatives claiming that the upper and middle classes would be paying for a service that would mainly be used by the lower class and that 'the more education people get, the more difficult they are to manage'. The bill was eventually passed, though with many modifications. One of the first authorities to establish a public library service was Manchester, and one of the main campaigners for the innovation, Edward Edwards, was appointed its first chief librarian. A former bricklayer, he had educated himself at the library of the local Mechanics Institute and in 1839 had become an assistant at the British Museum. He was dismissed from his post at Manchester in 1858 for his radical political views.

1849

'The traveller by railway is made aware of his approach to the great northern seats of industry by the dull leaden-coloured sky, tainted by thousands of ever smoking chimneys, which broods over the distance. The stations along the line are more closely planted, showing that the country is more and more thickly peopled. Then, small manufacturing villages begin to appear, each consisting of two or three irregular streets clustered around the mill, as in former times cottages were clustered round the castle. You shoot by town after town – the outlying satellites of the great cotton metropolis. They have all similar features – they are all little Manchesters. Huge, shapeless, unsightly mills, with their countless rows of windows, their towering shafts, their jets of waste steam continually puffing in panting gushes from the brown grimy wall. Some dozen or so of miles so characterised, you enter the Queen of the cotton cities – and then amid smoke and noise, and the hum of never ceasing toil, you are borne over the roofs to the terminus platform. You stand in Manchester.' Angus Reach, *Morning Chronicle*, 1849.

63

I don't remember the specifics of what I learned at North Reddish Infants and Junior School between the ages of six and eleven. I walked to and from the sprawling dark-red-brick building breaking up patterned rows of narrow houses along the busy-with-cars-and-buses Gorton Road or the humble Harcourt Street for years, unknowingly soaking up the north without really thinking that I was anywhere else but the absolute centre of my own unique if tiny universe. I would go on my own, joining a class of forty for hours of facing a blackboard and a capable-seeming older person with an occasional need to smack me on the back of the legs, and then go home, again alone, occasionally finding a less familiar winding back route that meant I missed both Gorton Road and Harcourt Street. When I was about ten I told some friends that I lived so far from the school I needed to catch the bus – on my own – an act of significant independence at the time, but it wasn't true. They were not impressed when they found out I was lying, and another of my erratic attempts to impress others with my apparently unique skills, to elevate myself above those around me, had failed.

It took me about fifteen minutes to walk home, and I remember when I was about eight, before Carol was born, when my mum must have been working at the sweet factory near Houldsworth Square and Jayne playing at a friend's house, I would arrive home and be on my own for an hour or two. If I was lucky there would be a bottle of orange squash and some rich tea biscuits, maybe some sliced white bread and jam. If not, a wait for someone to come home, and more time to be filled in.

Also without thinking much about it, just accepting it as so, I was at the top of that class of forty kids in most subjects, and feeling a little superior because of this. I sulked tremendously when the sports teacher put me in the football team not as the swift-dribbling star left winger I fancied myself as, but as a common centre half. Number 10 or 11 was where I dreamed of playing, scorer of goals, deliverer of dangerous in-swerving corners, possessor of dazzling agility, but he wanted me at number 5 or 6, in defence, and this broke my heart, the heart of a young boy who for some reason fancied himself a believer in flair and originality with a commitment to the creation of surprise, as demonstrated by my favourite footballers, and a complete indifference to the mundane function of the hard-man defender.

I eventually realised he had put me in defence simply because I was one of the taller boys. He was not interested in or aware of how fast I might be, or (due to my solitary back-garden games with tennis balls) how skilled I was at dribbling. He wanted me to be strong, a scrapper, but this did not fit in with the picture I was forming of myself. It was the beginning of a painful understanding that football was a physical game – you were expected to fight for the ball, bang into players and fly into tackles, leaving bruises and scratches – and my avoidance of contact and cowardly reluctance to head the ball made me a weak and almost useless team player. Fantasies I had about being a key player for the North Reddish team in my last year there, scoring great goals, even captaining the side, were abruptly ended by my position in defence, a position I never played in the playground, where I was officially known as a goal hanger and it never occurred to me there was any point helping out in defence. My role was as hero winger with electrifying pace and a future as the George Best of Manchester City. He didn't look like he was trying either, but was memorably effective.

My favourite City player, inside left number 10 Neil Young, never,

ever tackled an opponent or headed the ball, and often seemed to finish a match, even in gluey goal-line-obliterating November mud, pitch rained to a corrugated mulch, without a mark on his angelic sky-blue and white kit. He was frail and skinny-looking, like me; he hung around the halfway line when City were defending, but he scored goals from twenty-five yards with a glorious left foot, and he made things happen but didn't need brute force to do so.

My sports teacher compounded his grave error of judgement by then not choosing me to bat at number 3 or 4 in the cricket team, but at number 10 – the number I wanted in football not in cricket – because this meant he saw me as a slogger, and he didn't want me to bowl audacious subtle spin – me, someone who had spent time at home, alone, working out how to deliver the batsman-bewildering googly – but bowl as fast as I could. The dreadful disappointment I felt that he had got me so wrong – ignoring my unique abilities, seeing me merely as a fairly anonymous tall lad who might be some use as battering ram or hurler – resonated for years. In many ways I am still dealing with it.

I developed skills in mental arithmetic and by seven could speed through the times tables all the way up to 12 and accurately add up columns of figures faster than my father, who was himself good with numbers. He reckoned this was not because of anything that was happening at school, but because of the imaginary games of cricket I played, using a dice to create the scores and carefully filling out scorecards. He first assumed I was making up the total scores, the 324 for 5s, the 123 for 7s, the bowlers' figures of 3 for 56 from 9 overs, but one day checked one of my scorecards and was pleasantly surprised to see that it indeed all added up.

I liked the fact that racing through the times tables and adding up figures seemed to impress adults, and it led to a faint suggestion that in his own quiet way my dad was quite proud of me. Even though day-to-day interaction tended to be either remote or sturdy male closeness when it came to Manchester City, I would ultimately say he was on my side. He wanted the best for me but perhaps wasn't clear how he could make that happen except by ensuring I took school seriously and didn't daydream on my own in my bedroom, stuck in my cupboard or in the back garden. I think he imagined I could make it as an accountant, a profession looked upon with respect, and that would give my life a nondescript but pleasing steadiness he never had. To be an accountant would have been his dream, to a point, and under the circumstances – where we lived, who we were, what our background was – it was the very best he could see for me. It was better than working in a prison.

I wished the sports teacher would treat me with similar hope, but he saw me as the sporting equivalent of someone who could not add up two plus two. He treated me like a plodding centre half, as a sissy when I couldn't even tackle and head the ball, as someone who fielded not in the glamorous edgy slips but out on the boundary, where you put the kids who couldn't catch, who lacked agility, who you wanted out of the way.

There would have been history classes at school, in which I suppose I learned all that I would ever get to know about the Romans, the Vikings, 1066, the stony clichés of history as superficially pressed into young minds already being distracted by sport, TV, pop – distilled rudimentary information that would be the extent of my historical knowledge for decades. No stories of the local heroes and heroines, villains and victims, of the Industrial Revolution, no mention of Sir William Houldsworth, of the history of Reddish, or even of Stockport or Manchester, or the nearby Tame and Mersey, flowing with the grainy dirt and greedy one-way pace of history, through urban blight and glorious views, no sense of how we were, where we were, why we were there, what surrounded us, what those massive buildings were around Houldsworth Square and how they ended up there. If we ever learned about the Nico Ditch a few hundred yards away, it passed right through me, not made into something exciting, but remaining a pointless muddy gash in the ground round the back of the park.

No northern history seeped through the walls of a school built by Cheers and Smith of Blackburn in 1907 at a cost of £11,000, six years after Reddish was absorbed into Stockport and a year before the library, swimming pool and fire station block was completed. I knew none of that for years, until I found it at the far end of the Internet, over forty years after I had left the school. It is described in a book on buildings in Lancashire and Manchester as 'A low nicely grouped gabled complex, given distinction by the tall chimneys with flared tops of horizontal channelled brick, and a pretty flèche over the hall with a slender slated spire.' If you had asked me when I was attending the school how old it was, I would not have known if it had been built in the 1950s, which seemed a lifetime ago, or the 1850s, which seemed a little bit before that.

There were two playgrounds, one for the infants and one for the juniors, and when I was nine or ten and in the juniors, the children in the infants, on the other side of the wall, seen through a locked gate, just three or four years younger, seemed like babies. They were of no interest to me. But at eleven, and I couldn't quite put my finger on why, the girls in my class *were* becoming of interest, throwing invisible darts of intrigue in my direction, sometimes accurately enough to provoke a deep, amorphous response.

By the time I finished at the school I was as northern as any of the other kids in my class, in the rest of the school, who came in from around Denton, Longsight, Levenshulme and the rest of North Reddish, where they had been born. Surrey, Kent, the Isle of Wight had mostly melted away into the ground, give or take a lingering fondness for Surrey Cricket Club and its opening batsman John Edrich. I had without knowing it, without being tempted by friends or alienated by the bullies, without anything being explained to me about local history or local people, invented myself as someone from the north: Cheshire to an extent, Lancashire around the edges, Manchester close by, Stockport at the near limits. So of the north – speaking it, living in it, searching through it – that I didn't even notice, and didn't notice that people around me spoke in a Stockport accent. What I did notice were the peculiar accents of my dad's Kent relatives, which seemed stretched out, distended and unlikely compared with the normal everyday way we spoke around Reddish.

64

1848

The anonymous publication of Elizabeth Gaskell's *Mary Barton: A Tale of Manchester Life* caused a sensation. This was a year of revolution in Europe, and the novel's socio-political subject matter marked a major new direction in British fiction, especially fiction by women, to which reviewers responded with either excitement or unease.

In 1848 the average life expectancy for the poorest people of Preston was said to be only 18.23 years. (Preston has added at least one word to the English language – teetotal. This came from a meeting held at the old Temperance Hall in 1833. Joseph Livesey, a founder of the temperance movement, was leading the meeting when Dicky Turner, who had a profound stammer, stumbled during his oath, 'total' coming out as 'tee-tee-total'.)

1847

In July publishers Thomas Cautley Newby accept *Wuthering Heights*, which is published in December under Emily Brontë's pseudonym Ellis Bell. Set in eighteenth-century England when social and economic values were changing, patriarchal values are juxtaposed with natural elements. Brontë explores themes of revenge, religion, class and prejudice while plumbing the depths of the metaphysical and human psyche. Brontë's own home on the bleak Yorkshire Moors provides the setting for the at times mystical passions of the Byronic Heathcliff and Catherine.

1846

The history of Blackpool has been largely determined by its position in relation to the heavily populated towns and cities of Lancashire and by rapid changes in transportation and economic conditions. The town began attracting holiday visitors in 1735, when the first guesthouse opened. However it was when the railway arrived in 1846 that holidaymakers began to arrive in their thousands.

1845

In a single decade, 1835–1845, scholar Robert Fishman observed in *Bourgeois Utopias: the Rise and Fall of Suburbia*, 'Manchester achieved a higher degree of suburbanisation than London did in the whole century from 1770 to 1870.'

The office in which Friedrich Engels, long-time collaborator of Karl Marx, worked would become the first floor of upmarket department store Kendal's. Engels was sent to Manchester from Germany in 1842 to be trained in business. His father hoped that his son's foolish romantic radicalism would be knocked out of him. Instead, the young Engels made contact with the workers' movement and collected material for his book *The Condition of the Working Class in England*, published in 1845. Engels began to collaborate with Marx and together they developed their political views. Engels' time in Manchester led him to stress the power of the working class, encouraging Marx to shift his emphasis from the study of radical philosophy to 'political economy'.

65

As well as the school and the local library, both of them sixty years old, I was educated by playing with other children and watching television. TV wasn't then such a constant distraction from the outdoors as it would become, and I played mostly out on the street with the Conservative Club firmly stuck on the corner. We would play cowboys and Indians, in the days when every boy owned a gun – a cap gun to make a bang, a water pistol for laughs, a spud gun if you wanted to shoot something, an air gun if particularly rascally, as if the Wild West had any relevance to our lives in Reddish. When we played Robin Hood, it was as though in the history of the world, he had emerged out of Jesus – who had something to do with the Romans, who had lived in Chester, which had a castle – and had led to cowboys and Indians and perhaps the American Civil War, which had then led to the Second World War, which had led to where we were, seeing it all play out at the Essoldo.

Pavements were chalked for hopscotch and walls had three white uneven stumps drawn on them for cricket and/or shaky goalposts with a wobbly bar for football. You would be 'it' and chase others so that you could touch them, and then he or she would be 'it', but you weren't allowed to touch the person who had just touched you. Yard gates and back entrances along alleyways were used for hide and seek and hiding behind to shoot someone with a small piece of potato.

The draining reality of limited, limiting wartime rations still hung in the Reddish air at the same time as the shiny consumer world was picking up energy and sounding an ever-present mesmerising chiming in my gullible consciousness. The backdrop to my life through the television, the local shops, kids' shared excitement and boredom, and scraps of adult conversation made up a world where for mash you got Smash, where beans meant Heinz, where chimps sold you tea, Frosties were grrrrreat, glossy paint was sold to you by a shaggy Dulux dog, Stork and nothing else was what you spread on bread, you put a tiger in your tank, the Milky Bars were on the Milky Bar Kid, who looked like a very clean almost sinister version of some of your friends, hands that did dishes were as soft as your face with mild green Fairy Liquid, hot chocolate again and again whispered like a mantra, drinking chocolate, hot chocolate drinking chocolate hot chocolate drinking chocolate, a Mars a day helped you work rest and play, Milky Way was the sweet they said you could eat between meals but your dad wouldn't let you, although if you negotiated with him he might let you have an occasional Twix because this counted as a biscuit not chocolate, Colgate toothpaste gave you a ring of confidence, Daz washing powder for some reason gave your wash a blue tinge.

Berserk television creatures mingled with routine Reddish reality. A pair of hyperactive wooden puppet pigs in waistcoats with strangulated high-pitched voices and dead eyes sang pop songs. Real rats, mice, moles, guinea pigs and hamsters with names like Roderick and Hammy lived in houses on the riverbank in black and white, sailed boats, drove cars, flew planes and had random adventures, told to us by zookeeper turned children's TV presenter Johnny Morris, who gave each animal its own apparently appropriate 'human' voice, and spoke over and over again one word for the owl living in a tree: Who? Who? Who? I never did find out who, but felt vaguely depressed and even disturbed by the clearly rattled animal's clumsy, nonsensical and finally completely monotonous antics.

A seedy boisterous fox with a pervert's laugh, a squirrel called Tufty who was meant to teach us how to cross the road and had a fan club that I joined, or was made to join, a hallucinatory family of poor crackpot American farmers who had struck oil, black gold, Texas style, made millions and moved to a mansion, some other crackpot Americans, stranded on a desert island, both shows featuring dolled-up hairsprayed glamour girls with unprecedented ways of moving that were almost painfully intriguing to a nine-year-old boy, a smarmy dubious American who lived with a talking horse, another smarmy dubious American, who was married to a friendly witch, the creepily silent Sooty and the honking Sweep, who lived on the ends of a bald man's hands, a real kangaroo in hot faraway Australia who said as little as Sooty but was more motivated and saved more lives, pink woollen puppets speaking in squeaked tongue who lived on the moon, the incandescently sensible *Blue Peter*, the even more sensible *Jackanory*, in which someone read you stories in a voice someone had decided was funny, or soothing, the even more sensible *Vision On*, which seemed to suggest that art was something you did if you felt a bit ill. *Crackerjack* combined the sensible with issuing a warning about the perils, and thrills, of intoxication.

In opposition to the sensible if anxious grown-ups encouraging you to believe that the world was full of fun and things to learn about, the last few minutes before the news – a world where fun and learning had gone very wrong indeed described by elderly men in unwrinkled suits and sober ties apparently there to restore calm – contained a series of five-minute programmes that led you to think the world was not that far removed from your weirdest dreams: *Hector's House*, *The Magic Roundabout*, *Captain Pugwash*. Or you would find yourself confronted by unhinged cartoon gurus offering oblique advice about logic, mortality and language – *Tom and Jerry*, *Popeye*, *Top Cat*, *Yogi Bear*, *Pixie and Dixie*, *Scooby Doo*, *Deputy Dawg*.

The future was either the delirious solemn puppetry of Gerry Anderson – *Supercar*, *Fireball XL5*, *Stingray*, *Captain Scarlet*, *Thunderbirds*, *Joe 90* – or *Dr Who*, who was like a cross between God, your teachers and one or more of your older male relatives, but not your dad, who, it seemed, was not particularly in favour of time travel. With your mum and dad, everyone putting away their secretive appetites and instincts, uncomfortably and comfortably sharing an experience you might all enjoy, you watched Morecambe and Wise, Mike Yarwood, *It's a Knockout*, *Opportunity Knocks*, *Ask the Family*, *Dixon of Dock Green*, *Softly, Softly* and *Coronation Street*, which was like where you lived, but more, and less, so, nostalgic for a close-knit north that never was, but could have been, and sometimes, when you came to think about it, was closer than most things on the telly to the stricken, striving, embattled northern state of play and the streets right outside your door.

66

1844

As towns expanded with the coming of industrialisation, it became increasingly difficult for ordinary people to buy unadulterated food. In 1844 a group of twenty-eight men in Rochdale formed the Rochdale Equitable Pioneers Society. Their objective was to open a shop where they could sell wholesome products at a fair price. Each of them contributed twenty shillings, producing an initial capital of twenty-eight pounds. They began in a disused warehouse at 31 Toad Lane on 21 December 1844, opening between 8 p.m. and 10 p.m. To start with they sold only five commodities: oatmeal, flour, sugar, butter and tallow candles, although as turnover grew they were able to add other items, including tobacco and tea. They refused to give credit, but for the first time paid customers a share of the profits – a dividend.

The rules of the society became a model for others, and within a decade there were nearly 1,000 cooperative stores operating on similar principles across the country. The objectives of the Rochdale Pioneers went far beyond running a cooperative store; through the combined efforts of working people they aimed to create manufacturing enterprises and fully self-supporting communities on land which they themselves would own.

By 1844 there were railway lines connecting Manchester with London, Liverpool, Birmingham, Leeds, Sheffield and Bolton. French politician and economist Léon Faucher recorded, 'The Leeds railway connects Manchester with Oldham, which contains 60,000 inhabitants; also with Bury, Rochdale and Halifax, each of which numbers from 24,000 to 26,000 souls; the Bolton railway connects it with Bolton, Preston and Chorley, which together have more than a hundred factories and 114,000 inhabitants. On the Sheffield line a few minutes suffice to reach the establishments of Stalybridge, Ashton, Dukinfield and Hyde, peopled by more than 80,000 inhabitants; the Birmingham line incorporates it with, so to speak, the 50,000 inhabitants of Stockport; that of Liverpool connects it with Wigan and Warrington. Thus we have 15 or 16 seats of industry forming this great constellation.'

A committee appointed by a meeting of Huddersfield citizens to survey the town reported on 5 August 1844, 'It is notorious that there are whole streets in the town of Huddersfield, and many courts and alleys, which are neither flagged, paved, sewered, nor drained; where garbage and filth of every description are left on the surface to ferment and rot; where pools of stagnant water are almost constant, where the dwellings adjoining are thus necessarily caused to be of an inferior and even filthy description; thus where disease is engendered, and the health of the whole town perilled.'

When in 1844 Leeds first contemplated sewering the town, it was nervous about the high compensation and attendant legal costs that would be incurred, the consequences of diverting water from the all-important factories, the possibility of sewer seepage into cellar dwellings and the costs and problems of processing the sewage at the outfall. Above all, many members of the corporation wondered whether the whole thing would work.

Léon Faucher: 'And thus at the very moment when the engines are stopped, and the counting houses closed, everything which was the thought – the authority – the impulsive force – the moral order of this immense industrial combination flies from the town, and disappears in an instant. The rich man spreads his couch amid the beauties of the surrounding country, and abandons the town to the operatives, publicans, mendicants, thieves, and prostitutes, merely taking the precaution to leave behind him a police force, whose duty it is to preserve some little of material order in this pell-mell of society.'

'From Liverpool to Manchester, the land is generally level, and is almost wholly applied to agriculture; but in traversing the country from Manchester to Todmorden, which is on the extreme northern verge of the district, probably not one mile of continuously level ground will be passed over. Betwixt Bury on the western, and Oldham, on the eastern verge, some comparatively level tracts are found, as those of Radcliffe, Whitemoss, and Failsworth; but they are small as compared with the distance, and all the remaining parts of this northern district, are composed of ups and downs, hillocks, and dells, bent, twisted, and turned in every direction. Take a sheet of stiffened paper for instance, crumple it up in your hand, then just distend it again, and you will have a pretty fair specimen of the surface of the northern part of south Lancashire. The hills are chiefly masses of valuable stone and coal; on the north, some heathlands overlap them, but their sides are often brilliant with a herbage that yields the best of milk and butter, while of all the valleys, you shall traverse none where a stream of water does not run at your side, blabbing all manner of imaginary tidings, and asking unthought of, and unanswerable questions.' Samuel Bamford, *Walks in Lancashire*, self-published in 1844. Bamford wrote of the bridge which crossed the 'turbid and black' Irwell, 'Venice hath her Bridge of Sighs: Manchester its Bridge of Tears.'

From Cheshire, Lewis Carroll moved at the age of eleven to Croft-on-Tees in north-east England near the outskirts of Darlington – noted by Daniel Defoe on his travels 120 years before as containing nothing remarkable but dirt. Carroll's father was by then rector of Croft church and archdeacon of Richmond (1843–68). The River Tees is at Croft the dividing line between

Yorkshire and County Durham, and on the middle of the bridge which crosses it is a stone which shows where one county ends and the other begins. Carroll's poem 'Jabberwocky' is thought to be based on the legend of the man-eating poisoned-breath dragon of County Durham called the Sockburn Worm, which lived just across the Tees, the story perhaps rooted in a vicious leader of Viking raids.

Much of the two Alice books is said to be set in and around Croft church and rectory. In the church is a sedilia – a seat for the clergy built into the wall – and at one end of it is the carved stone face of a lion. Viewed from one of the pews it has a wide smile, but looked at from a standing position the grin cannot be seen – so it disappears, and then appears, like that of the Cheshire Cat. 'Well, I've often seen a cat without a grin, thought Alice, but a grin without a cat? It's the most curious thing I've seen in all my life!'

Lewis Carroll, descended from two ancient and distinguished northern families with long traditions of service to Church and State, can be claimed as a northerner. His Mad Hatter was perhaps inspired by the effects of mercury poisoning on the central nervous system – confused speech, distorted vision, mental confusion and anti-social behaviour – plus trembling and loss of teeth. Hat makers, typically working in poorly ventilated work-shops, cured animal pelts by brushing a solution of mercury compound on fur to roughen the fibres and make them mat more efficiently. Carroll was aware of mercury poisoning from living near Stockport, a centre of hat manu-facture. From out of his Mad Hatter, rabbit-hole, looking-glass world we can see coming not only such figures as Joyce, Freud, Oscar Wilde, Henry James, Virginia Woolf, Kafka, Proust, Artaud, Benjamin, Nabokov, Beckett, Waugh, Lacan, Borges, Burroughs, Pynchon and García Márquez, but also much of the character, image and mood of twentieth-century popular culture.

67

One day I looked up into the sky, which I often did because above our Reddish heads and houses, you could see the planes coming in over the Pennines on their way west to Ringway Airport arranged inside chain-link fences at the southern edge of Wythenshawe. Now, I couldn't tell you in detail what was going on in my life during my years in Reddish. Day inevitably followed day, sleep followed sleep, walk followed walk, school year followed school year. I could now only approximate with hindsight when I first went to North Reddish Infants School, or when I moved up a stage into the Junior School, aged seven, sometime in September 1964. I can now look up cricket matches and football games and say, well, I saw my first Manchester City match on Saturday 16 October 1965, and they won 3–1 against Crystal Palace, and I bought my first programme, for sixpence, with a black and white photograph of their empty Maine Road ground set among rows of terraces positioned in the middle of a plainly designed light blue and white cover.

The ground had opened forty-two years before, built on a former brick works in the middle of cramped, boxy Moss Side houses braided with back alleyways and based on Glasgow's Hampden Park but with a capacity of 80,000, the second largest in England behind the just-opened Wembley Stadium. Maine Road was originally called Dog Kennel Lane, renamed because it was where the temperance movement in Manchester was based in the late nineteenth century, the new name inspired by the law which prohibited the sale of alcohol in the state of Maine in 1851. I didn't know any of this in the 1960s, and I took the name of the ground simply to mean it was the main place in Manchester to go and watch football, and Manchester United's ground, Old Trafford, seemed, well, old. Supporting a team playing at Dog Kennel Lane might not have been as alluring.

City were in the Second Division when I started supporting them, as always in the shadow of United, but this was the season where they began a brief but astonishing golden age. They were promoted that year under the inspiring management of wise old Joe Mercer and young wide boy Malcolm Allison – brought in from the south to add other-ness and a more continental influence, with a team that starred right winger Mike Summerbee of Preston, centre half George Heslop of Northumberland, left half Alan Oakes and his cousin left back Glyn Pardoe both of Winsfield, Cheshire, Colin Bell of Hesleden, County Durham, right half Mike Doyle of Ashton, goalie Ken Mulhearn of Liverpool, who had replaced stocky, gum-chewing Harry Dowd of

Salford and inside left Neil Young of Fallowfield. As with Lancashire County Cricket Club, which had a great side when I followed them, as soon as I started watching City, taken by my dad, they became a great side full of northerners with the odd outsider, just like the England team that won the World Cup in 1966.

I could, then, tell you where I was on Saturday 26 April 1969. I was in the front room at Westbourne Grove wearing my blue and white scarf and ribboned City rosette watching live on television City beat Leicester in the FA Cup Final, with the winning goal scored by lanky Neil Young of Fallowfield. That was more or less the only live match shown on television all season. I could tell you where I was on 22 March 1969. I was with my dad wearing a woollen bobble hat knitted by my mum, standing behind the goal at Villa Park at the City end watching Manchester City beat Everton to get to the final, with a late winning goal scored by big gangly Tommy Booth of Middleton. (Named because it was in the middle between Manchester – four miles to the north-east – and Rochdale – five miles to the south-west. Mid-twentieth-century Middleton, on the River Irk, was typically northern in how it combined three distinct forms of urban–rural living: modern suburbs right next to mill-town terraces and, in between, surviving in areas of near-unspoilt farmland, stray secret lanes of isolated dwellings, these sometimes being imposing Victorian properties with substantial gardens. This created a jumble of workers' back-to-backs, suburbia containing a more middle-class type and a lingering scattering of farm-working peasant stock tucked away in crooked cottages in sunken lanes.)

I could also tell you where I was at about ten o'clock in the morning on Sunday 4 June 1967. It was three days after the release of *Sgt Pepper* by the Beatles – which had no impact whatsoever on our home. I was outside the front of our house, mooching about on my own, taking in the air, perhaps making plans for a swoop into the Vale, developing as a ten-year-old useful skills as a daydreamer, and this time I was looking into the sky not expecting to see a plane steadily heading into the airport a few miles behind me the other side of Stockport at a decent, normal height. I wasn't sure exactly how high decent and normal was, but it was high enough for the planes to make a noise barely louder than a fine even whine.

Alice in Wonderland weather vane at the primary school in Daresbury, Cheshire,
Lewis Carroll's birthplace

But the noise something was making that morning was not some
way in the distance; it seemed much closer, but I couldn't see anything
that might be making such a noise. The noise suggested something
might be heading right towards me, but I couldn't tell where it was
coming from. I guessed it must be a plane flying low, really low, but
there was nothing at all to see. Perhaps finally the mills down the road
at Houldsworth Square had come to life again and were making the
sort of pained moaning sounds that such vast stranded edifices would
surely make if they woke up, wondering what on earth had happened
to them, wiping years of sleep from their eyes. Perhaps they were on the
move, breaking out of the ground, about to charge up the Gorton Road
and make their supernatural escape. The noise got louder. Was it
coming from over Reddish Vale? Was it the sound of the viaduct
snoring? Had the viaduct got something on its mind it desperately
wanted to tell those who lived nearby? Was it trying to speak? Or was
it the solitary sleepy Lowry chimney at Jackson's brickies down Harcourt

Street rumbling, about to shoot into the sky, ripping up everything with it, fed up with doing nothing?

I ran inside the house to tell my mum and dad that something odd was happening. No noise this straining and constant that I knew of had ever come this close to Reddish. They were still in bed, having their Sunday lie-in, which allowed my dad, famously grumpy in the early morning, some extra sleep to soothe his accumulating anxieties. (Of course, one-year-old Carol and four-year-old Jayne were in the house as well, somewhere, there to give signs in how they resembled me as to who I might be, but somehow they do not make it into this story, even as extras. In this memory, which seems real but is dreamlike, they would be something of an intrusion and spoil the flow, so the random but functional and precise editing process of memory has made sure they do not feature.) I shouted through my parents' deeply shut door that something outside was making a funny noise. They seemed to pay no attention. I ran outside again, and by now the noise had passed by. The mills, the viaduct, the chimney had all settled down again, resuming their fixed positions, where, even though they were the largest objects around, they seemed under the surface of Reddish or so visibly from the past they never quite made it to where everyone else was.

When my parents finally got up, I reported the alarming noise, which, as I was already a practised and labelled daydreamer, did not seem to interest them. At some point during the afternoon, the news penetrated – via a neighbour, the radio, the television – that something had indeed happened that morning, a couple of miles away in Stockport, and it was a great deal more than an unexpected noise.

What I had heard was indeed a plane. It was the last flight this plane would ever make, a British Midland flight – Derby Aviation until a name change three years before – chartered by Arrowsmith Holidays. Arrowsmith had been founded in the mid-1940s in Bold Street, Liverpool near Cripps – outfitters for well-to-do ladies of Cheshire and Lancashire – by popular travel pioneer Harry Bowden-Smith. Bowden-Smith helped form the Association of British Travel Agents (ABTA) in 1950, anticipating the package-holiday boom of the 1960s that doubled airline passengers.

The flight, from Palma, Mallorca (then more usually Majorca with a 'j'), crashed in the centre of Stockport at seven minutes past ten, plunging into a small scrubby piece of wasteland called Hopes Carr about five miles short of the airport. The plane was a Canadian Air Argonaut C-4, an eighteen-year-old version of the four-engined propeller-driven Douglas DC4, modified to take British Rolls-Royce Merlins – the iconic engine developed in the 1930s used in aircraft like the Spitfire, Hurricane and Lancaster.

Initially flown by Canadair, the Argonaut was reconfigured for BOAC to carry forty first-class passengers, but when it was sold to British Midland it became a seventy-two seater, and later seventy-eight people would be crammed in. Seeing pictures of it now, it seems far more 1940s wartime than late 1960s jet age with a basic cockpit that verged on the quaint even quirky.

The flight path as the Argonaut made its second approach to Ringway Airport would have been over Bredbury – settled in its ways across the Vale from Westbourne Grove, Reddish. Had I seen it, I may have been tempted to jump on my bike and follow the wounded noise of the doomed plane as it vainly attempted to cross Stockport and keep enough height to get to Ringway. The pilot, forty-one-year-old Captain Harry Marlow, had already attempted to land at the airport, but both starboard engines had malfunctioned and he overshot the runway. Coming round again perilously low to the south-east of Stockport town centre, two of the plane's four engines abruptly cut out and one propeller started to windmill. One engine failed because of a fault in the fuel system; the reason for the other failure remains unclear. If the problems had occurred at 15,000 feet there might have been a solution, but the plane was now only a dangerous few hundred feet above ground. Problems with the fuel system had caused an incident in 1953 with a BOAC Argonaut, but the information had not been passed on.

Subsequently there was a suggestion that the pilot had been searching for open land away from a populated area, perhaps nearby Vernon Park or Woodbank Park, but the official conclusion was that he was still hoping to make the airport when the engines abruptly cut out over the one empty space in the area. Some witnesses reported that the plane did appear to make a sudden shift in direction before crashing as if the pilot had suddenly spotted the wasteland. However this might have been the plane hitting a three-storey building, which ripped off a wing.

Captain Marlow survived, but head injuries wiped all memories of the crash. He was cleared of blame, the understanding being that he had courageously managed to bring down the almost unmanageably slow plane into the one empty space in the immediate area. His efforts – struggling to hold the plane straight and to maintain height with dead engines, windmilling propeller, low height, slow speed, buildings and ground fast approaching – were such that in a reconstruction the pilot's seat frame was bent by sheer body pressure alone. A BBC film showed the test pilot moments after he attempted to keep the simulated plane under control – he looked shattered. The sound recording of Marlow himself and the air controller at Ringway Airport dealing with the real events was remarkably calm and low key, but at that point the pilot still felt he might be able to reach the runway. Flying at a mere 800 feet, still eight miles from the airport, two miles outside Stockport town centre, Marlow was asked if he could maintain height. 'Just about,' he coolly replied. The complete loss of power to the engines was yet to happen, but when it did, it was right over the centre of town a few hundred yards up the hill from Merseyway.

After hitting the side of a building, demolishing a garage, wrecking some cars and breaking into pieces, the plane burst into flames. Where it ended up on the edge of the scrubland was surrounded by terraced houses, shops, garages, a block of flats and a gas container, next to a police station and mere hundreds of yards from Stockport Infirmary and the town hall. Those swimming at the time in Stockport Baths a few hundred yards down the hill towards Mersey Square at the top of the steps above the old art deco Plaza cinema claimed they felt a rumble through the water.

Incredibly, there were no fatalities on the ground, even though roof tiles were ripped off by the plane's vortex and people in houses could see those on board through the plane's windows. Twelve of the eighty-four crew and passengers survived, some, astoundingly, by walking through the holes that appeared in the plane as it initially broke into three pieces, although most were seriously injured. Seventy-two died, people from across the north, from Sheffield, Stockport, Bradford, Leeds, Chester, Newcastle, Middleton, Blackpool, Salford and Cheadle.

Many of those who died survived the actual crash at the back of the plane, which escaped the impact relatively unscathed, but broke their legs on impact. The seats concertinaed together and they were trapped, unable to flee the burning plane, which was engulfed by flames and black smoke, explosions ripping it apart. Local people and members of the emergency services dragged injured and terrified passengers from the mutilated fuselage and attempted to get inside the plane, vicious heat blistering their skin and jagged metal gashing their arms and legs. Some they couldn't move however much they tried because they were trapped between the seats. Those still conscious were screaming as the remains of the plane were completely engulfed in flames. Rescuers beaten back by the heat could do nothing as people died. It soon ceased to be a rescue and was simply about recovering bodies. Temporary mortuaries were set up at the local Salvation Army citadel, Stockport Sunday School and a garage.

Hundreds of curious if ghoulish people came to see the scene of the crash – someone even turned up with a chair and picnic table – and by the early evening there were ice-cream vans and a hot-dog stand and teeming numbers of press. One photograph of the aftermath as cranes lift pieces of the plane behind an intact section of brick wall in front of forlorn-looking terraced streets has a bank of spectators in sensible hats and coats in the foreground looking at the activity as though they were watching Stockport County – a mile across town, the other side of the station, towards where the plane should have landed if all had been well or at least not so tragically conclusive.

The live coverage on ITN was oddly presented by endlessly cheerful disc jockey, continuity announcer and sidekick of goofy Liverpool comic Ken Dodd, David 'Diddy' Hamilton, who stood in neat suit and tie on the cobbles in front of a charred pile of shattered metal laced with bits of corrugated iron, fire hoses and random pieces of splintered wood, wearing an appropriately grave expression. Around him milled sightseers, police and firemen, and a man in a white trench coat sizing up the mangled metal with a fag in his mouth. At the time Hamilton lived in Marple a few miles away, and ITN didn't have anyone in the area for the live broadcast. When he was told to get to the centre of Stockport as quickly as possible because a plane had crashed, he thought it was his station manager playing a joke on him on his day off.

It was hard to resist a trip to see something that was all over the national news. A peculiar sort of muted carnival spirit developed, a perhaps natural response to something unprecedented happening a handful of streets from where you lived. The fact that people had been burned to death trapped in splintered wreckage probably didn't immediately register. This was an appallingly unique event. It was the first ever urban plane crash in the country, the second worst ever in the United Kingdom at the time, and it remains one of the worst ever air disasters in Britain. There are two memorials of the crash – one for those who died, and one for those involved in the rescue, who gave aid and saved twelve lives: 'All were faced with the true horror of tragedy and did not turn away.' The disaster led to several improvements in airliner design, and as a result crash landings became considerably more survivable.

For days after, once the fitful smouldering had died down, there was a bulky but very vulnerable-looking tail fin stuck at an angle at the edge of the scrub, near a stiff heavy-hearted Lowry chimney standing guard like some Gothic exclamation mark among the now especially melancholy and seemingly shocked buildings that had somehow been missed. The tail fin, inner framework exposed like some macabre skeleton, poked up towards the sky it had so suddenly fallen out of, a little embarrassed to be so terribly caught out, next to the sort of everyday spiked metal railings Lowry liked to paint. There is no sign of planes in Lowry's work because his universe existed in an alternative corridor in which the nineteenth century of his birth maintained dogmatic control over environment and atmosphere. But he was painting during these years, and the sight of this charred fin surrounded by bits of an annihilated plane sunk in the midst of packed northern streets moistened by the fire brigade's desperate efforts and containing a few speechless pin-thin witnesses could easily have become a Lowry canvas. A canvas containing his five cherished wilting colours that conveyed how a fast new world was breaking up the old world so ruthlessly and unkindly.

There is film footage from a few weeks later of a stunned-looking Captain Marlow – slicked-down short back and sides and three-quarter-length sheepskin coat – being shown the thousands of fragmented pieces of plane that had been put back together as well as possible. He may have survived but looks like he's not sure that's necessarily a good thing, at least not while he's being shown bits of the plane and the huge tears that split the craft apart. Of all the people examining the remains, he does look like the one person who was actually on the bloody thing, even if he can't remember what happened. Something in his wired, thin-skinned, formal demeanour reminds me of my father in his more troubled moments. Both had a certain amount of trouble dealing with Stockport one way or another.

Marlow was forced to give up flying on 'medical grounds'. Bowden-Smith of Arrowsmith completely lost heart seeing so many of his customers killed and in 1969 sold out to cheap-flight pioneer Freddie Laker, acknowledged mentor of Richard Branson of Virgin Atlantic. Michael Bishop, born near Ringway Airport, was the manager on duty at the airport that day, and was responsible for informing family members about the crash. 'If you're twenty-five and you walk into a room and you have to tell fifty people they've lost their husbands, wives, daughters, sons, it has a certain impact on you.' Two years later he was general manager of British Midland; by 1972 he was managing director. In 1975, Manchester (Ringway) Airport was formally renamed Manchester International Airport, but locals were still calling it Ringway years after, and I still find myself calling it that even though it has been plain Manchester Airport since 1986.

Back in Westbourne Grove that Sunday, only after an unusually subdued David Hamilton had sent his shaken reports into our cheap seventeen-inch rented television did my dad accept that something shocking had indeed happened in Stockport. As to whether I had actually heard the plane as it droned and groaned through its final few minutes in the sky, he was not convinced. He felt that I was looking for a connection with it, as if somehow this made me feel important, even, in a weird way, glamorous. I was making up a marginal role for myself in the incident, exploiting the tantalising nearness of the disaster, taking my tendency to bend the truth, to make life a little more exciting than it might otherwise be, to new extremes. He became quite angry that I was claiming I had been some sort of witness to what would be called 'the blackest day in Stockport's history'. People had died in horrible circumstances, and I shouldn't be craving some sort of distinction by association. I was not allowed to talk about it any more.

His anger and distaste, abrasively expressed, distorted my memory of that day, so that ultimately I do not know if I actually did hear the noise and try to raise my sleeping mum and dad, or made it up later in the day when the news rolled in, to impress them or at least put myself at the centre of attention in our house, which my dad and his furies tended to dominate. It certainly increased my self-esteem to feel that at least in our household I had got to something first, that I had actually experienced what was now on our television, the one we watched England win the World Cup on, where the world and history itself seemed to be formed. I was aware that the air crash was the first real thing to enter history that had happened in my vicinity, and something inside me wanted to be part of it. Something inside me felt that if I could somehow enter that history, it might take me with it; it might take me beyond where I had been placed by previous history, a history that had run out of energy. This was fresh, new history, and as much as it contained oblivion, sadness and pain, it was also something that would have an effect on reality itself, and the way that I could make sense of and make changes to that reality.

My dad simply assumed I was lying. I was living too much in my head, and trying to take this disaster inside myself and play with it, make it part of my life, was a bad sign. Who knew where such thinking, such a self-centred approach to life and death, reality and history and my place in it, would end?

My dad a little too calmly watched sombre David Hamilton, Ken Dodd's jolly friend, ask a policeman what time the crash had happened: 'Shortly after ten past ten as far as I can recall . . . there were two explosions, I think, and then the plane fired and we were driven back by fire from getting any more out,' then ask a rescuer what he had seen: 'Well, when I got here the plane was blazing; there was nothing left of the cab, only instruments all over the place,' and perhaps he thought, *This is what happens in Stockport, where I live. Planes can just drop out of the sky and blow a hole in the ground and wipe people out and my son treats it like an adventure that he can make up stories about as if he was somehow involved.*

So, I cannot remember for sure if I actually did hear the plane, or just pretended I had in the hours afterwards, or even slipped the experience over time into a whole new zone of plausible but flexible memory and came to imagine that I had either really heard it, or made it up later in the day, or a few days later. Surely, if a plane crashed near my house, it would have passed very close to that house on its descent, and the noise of its crippled engines, loud and vibrating, could easily have been heard. I *would* have known about it. It *would* be something I remember – the moment I brushed against, or wished I had, the shadowy, inexorable, astounding, perplexing, ultimately routine ebb and flow of history. How could I forget?

68

1843

Poet Laureate Robert Southey died on 21 March 1843. Ten days later Queen Victoria sanctioned the lord chamberlain's letter offering the vacant post to William Wordsworth. He was almost seventy-three and thought of as the greatest living English poet. He initially refused the appointment, pleading old age, but assured by the prime minister, Sir Robert Peel, that there was no longer any obligation to produce verse, Wordsworth accepted. Two years later he attended his first royal reception. Of this occasion, the painter Benjamin Haydon wrote, 'What would Hazlitt say now? The poet of the lakes and mountains in bag-wig, sword and ruffles!'

In the 1840s, Friedrich Engels wrote of the widespread drunkenness that characterised the inhabitants of England's industrial areas, leading to declining health and morals, poverty and broken homes – 'the cheapest way out of Bradford, was via a Tankard, jug, or bottle,' he noted. In the throat-savaging atmosphere of industry, beer and gin were cheap, and certainly safer to drink than the local water. A German friend of Engels, Georg Weerth, worked as a clerk in Bradford between 1843 and 1846, reluctantly locating there from Bonn following 'an indiscretion'. From the moment he arrived, he hated Bradford and its more wealthy inhabitants. He described Bradford as the most disgusting manufacturing town in England, 'dirty, foggy, smoky, cold', the very home of Lucifer himself. He noted that although it had a larger population than Cologne, it had 'no theatre, no social life, no decent hotel, no reading room and no civilised human beings – only Yorkshiremen in torn frock coats, shabby hats and gloomy faces.' Feeling trapped inside what he saw as the hypocritical world of commerce, he took an interest in the appalling conditions of Bradford workers. A doctor friend showed him around local slums, work houses, prisons and hospitals. The workers seemed intelligent and energetic, their bosses barbaric money-grubbers enjoying an unfair share of the good things in life. The monied classes were the villains as far as he was concerned, amassing their wealth by ruining the lives of thousands of workers. They treated their workers 'like beasts, like machines'. A shared interest in the conditions of workers led to a meeting in Manchester between Engels and Weerth. They both believed that England was on the verge of a revolution. Weerth said it would not be against royalty, religion or parliament, but against the propertied classes. 'The last time there was a revolt in Lancashire and Yorkshire the workers simply grumbled and went on strike. Next time they will attack the homes of the rich and seize for themselves the necessity of life . . . they will go on strike for so long that a complete social revolution will be inevitable.'

1842

In *William Langshawe, the Cotton Lord* (1842) Elizabeth Stone set out to examine the image of Manchester popularised by alarmists about the Industrial Revolution: 'Cotton bags, cotton mills, spinning-jennies, power-looms and steam engines: smoking chimneys, odious factories, vulgar proprietors, and their still more vulgar wives, and their superlatively vulgar pretensions; dense population, filthy streets, drunken men, reckless women, immoral girls, and squalid children; dirt, filth, misery, and crime; – such are the interesting images which rise "a busy throng to crowd the brain" at the bare mention of the manufacturing districts: vulgarity and vice walking side by side; ostentatious extravagance on the one hand, battening on the miseries of degraded and suffering humanity on the other: and this almost without redeeming circumstances – we are told. Is it so?'

The first Bassett's sweets were made in 1842 when twenty-four-year-old wine dealer and lozenge maker George Bassett founded his confectionery company in Sheffield. In 1876 he became mayor of Sheffield.

1840

From the moment a railway between York and Scarborough was first mooted, a certain George Knowles had campaigned against the construction of the line, and in 1840 he published a pamphlet in which he protested, 'Scarborough has no wish for a greater influx of vagrants and those who have no money to spend. Scarborough is rising daily in the estimation of the public as a fashionable watering place, on account of its natural beauty and tranquillity, and in a few years more, the novelty of not having a railroad will be its greatest recommendation.'

The River Aire at Leeds in 1840 was described as a 'reservoir of poison carefully kept for the purpose of breeding a pestilence in the town. It was full of refuse from water closets, cesspools, privies, common drains, dung hill drainings, infirmary refuse, waste from slaughter houses, chemical soap, gas, dye-houses, and manufactures, coloured by blue and black dye, pig manure, old urine wash; there were dead animals, vegetable substance and occasionally a decomposed human body.'

The increasing size of urban populations led to overcrowding in the cities as the poor crammed into what living space they could afford. A new word, slum, passed from slang into orthodox use. Of debatable origin, possibly once signifying 'sleepy' areas of 'slumber' off the beaten track, it came to describe areas of squalid and deteriorating housing associated with poverty and disease. Although bad housing was by no means a new phenomenon, what differentiated the problem after 1800 from earlier times was its scale.

1839

Chartism was the campaign that came together from 1838 in support of a manifesto called the People's Charter. At a time when the right to vote was severely limited, the Charter demanded the vote for all men. Ashton under Lyne was a Chartist stronghold. In 1838 it was the headquarters of the Reverend Joseph Rayner Stephens, an ex-Wesleyan minister who had become a national leader of the movement. He was imprisoned in August 1839, and after his release in 1841 did not play a leading part in Chartist activities, although his chapel at Charlestown continued to be a rallying point for the politically active. Chartism is important for three main reasons: it gave birth to the first ever British mass working-class political party, the National Charter Association; it created a political culture that endured for decades; and it paved the way, in terms of ideas and the training it gave to young working-class radicals, for the ultimately successful campaigns for the universal right to vote in the UK.

Following the development of the camera from 1839, photography played a dominant part in the emergence of a tourism industry in the Lakes and in the visualisation and democratisation of the 'Lakeland experience'.

The Corn Laws had been enacted in 1815 to protect British farmers and land-owners by prohibiting the import of grain until domestic prices had risen above eighty shillings per quarter, thus ensuring artificially high prices for grain. The Manchester Anti-Corn Law League was formed in 1838, becoming the Anti-Corn Law League in 1839, and was long associated with Manchester in spite of moving its headquarters to London. By 1846, the Anti-Corn Law League was the most powerful national pressure group England had ever known, and its mass meetings, travelling orators, hymns and catechisms provided the model for many later Victorian evangelical, temperance and even trade union campaigns.

PART FOUR

Making it all happen

There's some peculiar people in this street.

Ena Sharples

69

Eventually, after being alive for one decade, which left me flat-out northern, I made a move outside Reddish, to the next part of the world. Reddish of Stockport replaced plain Reddish as the centre of my universe. I would catch the 17 bus outside the Conservative Club, head off west past Houldsworth Square, through South Reddish and down Lancashire Hill into the hollow where the centre of Stockport sat with a rancorous attitude of *What's it to you?*

I made it to the steady centuries-old town of Stockport, Cheshire – or, as has also been the case, Stockporte, Mercia and Stockport, Greater Manchester – a town split in personality between being historically of Cheshire, the lower, southier, snobbier, richer part of the north, and mighty time-pressed Manchester, which itself is split between being its own region, broadly speaking running itself, organising its own laws and routines, and being part of Lancashire. Stockport also stands up for itself: it has its own pride, its own districts, which themselves contain areas and neighbourhoods with names that help make sense of how it all fits together.

Living in Stockport, there was always this tension between the elegance and even primness of the (mostly) lowlands of Cheshire, where posh people lived, bay-windowed and liberally be-gardened, the magnetic power and pull of famous Manchester, and the grain, grit and size of the mighty Lancashire of Blackburn, Preston and Burnley, of Wigan, Bury and Oldham, which heads off to a north that gets darker but more open as it becomes, romantically, the Lake District, which is made up, among other things, of water, verse and history, of parts that seem a mix of the south and Scotland, but which is nonetheless all north, and which leads to the very end of things, the end of the north that concerns us here.

Stockport, where they made hats because of the dampness in the air that facilitated the production of felt. Then they stopped making hats, because people stopped wearing hats. (I may well have been one of the last men to have worn a non-sporting hat in 1970s Stockport, having bought a floppy patchwork denim trilby as a sixteen-year-old from the one trendy boutique in early-seventies Merseyway. I fancied it made me look like I might get an invite to meet Jimi Hendrix or even members of the all-female American rock group Fanny, but I now realise it more likely made me look like the love child of Shaggy from *Scooby Doo* and Andy Capp, the drinking, smoking, gambling, spirited northern loafer, married to Florrie, created for the *Daily Mirror* by Hartlepool cartoonist Reginald Smythe.)

Stockport, Cheshire – which is how I thought of it as I grew up there, even though Cheshire with its always confusing borders, and regular border changes, was never considered northern enough to be northern, and bordered Wales, which often seemed to concern it more than the north – was within a mile of Lancashire, which was dripping with north, and also within sight of the Pennines, the Peak District – so sheltered between them and Snowdonia to the west – the right northy Yorkshire and Derbyshire, which drifted south. Stockport is where the north begins, if only my north, the one and only north I know from the inside out.

Stockport is all north, full of north, as north as the north gets, taking being in the north to require the correct arrangement of geographical and architectural features which incorporate a sense that everything has already happened and everything else is nothing but a long slow slide towards a further long slow slide into the sense that everything has already happened but a surprise is always on the cards. The geographical and architectural features in this case are a mix of doughty Lancashire immensity, tree-lined Cheshire charm and cramped, murky Manchester menace, and include rivers, railway lines, viaducts, mills, bus stops, hedgerows, allotments, lamp posts, masses of housing laid out in chaotic yet highly regulated order and, beyond the town, beyond the busy arrangement of places to live, work, shop, play, drink, eat, walk, hints of fields and hills that the buildings leave alone, reminders of the original natural essence of this island, covered with signs of growth and decay, the peak, stream, heath and tree that the town does not reach, the town which could be defined as ugly, a scattered display of shapes, shops, roads, gashes in the pavements and internal patterns that do not really match, that seem flung together over a period of time with no real organising principle or design, the town which has at its borders natural beauty, signs of what was there before all the people and buildings arrived, covering up the earth with so much care and carelessness.

I might be choosing Stockport as exactly where the north begins for entirely personal reasons, but it does seem a gate through which, from the south, you enter the north and head on to Manchester, where you will definitely have made it to a northern centre, according to history, and out of which you head to towards London, because the railway line that goes from Manchester to London soars over the sunken centre of Stockport across a businesslike nineteenth-century viaduct that one day might be all that remains of the town and its people.

Stockport became my town, my centre of the north, but there are other places it could have been, where someone else would feel they were at the very centre of the north, a north within the north, with its own colours, anatomy and character, its own lords, thugs and landmarks, views, wrecks and skeletons in the cupboard – Bury, Wakefield, Sunderland, Southport, Grimsby, Oldham, Wigan, Lancaster, Workington, Huddersfield, Carlisle, themselves split into smaller areas, and then even smaller areas, named and numbered, fenced and familiar, filled with vanished lives and forgotten voices, wrapped around each other, inserted into each other, containing their own system of borders and boundaries that you would come across as you grew up, and crossed, and recrossed, as you made progress further and further into your life, walking for miles, living through days.

70

1837

Economic depression spread fear of unemployment and short-time working among industrial workers in Lancashire and the West Riding of Yorkshire, particularly among those employed in declining handicraft industries such as wool combing or calico weaving. The proposal to introduce the Poor Law Amendment Act into these areas increased anxiety since, if passed, workers would be forced into the dreaded workhouse in periods of distress rather than receive a small 'dole' from the Poor Law guardians.

Before 1837 Monks Coppenhall was a small hamlet in the Cheshire country-side, its inhabitants making their living from farming. Crewe did not exist, and the population was about seventy. However, the Grand Junction Railway had decided the fields near Crewe Hall should be the site for its railway hub and locomotive works. In 1837 the railway station was built and called Crewe: the town was named after the station, not the other way round. Crewe was chosen after Winsford, seven miles to the north, had rejected the GJR proposal, as had the landowners in Nantwich, four miles away. The first train arrived at 8.45 on 4 July 1837. The town really took off when the Grand Junction Railway built its workshops in 1843. The first steam locomotive was built at Crewe the same year – the *Tamarlane*, No. 32. A celebratory ball and banquet was held in its honour. Two years later No. 49, *Columbine*, a Standard six-foot locomotive, was rolled out. Between 1843 and 1958 a total of 7,331 locomotives were built at Crewe, more than at any other railway works in the country.

1835

Why should Lancashire, specifically Manchester, have been first in the world in the race towards industrialisation? One reason for the rise of the north, advanced at the time, and widely supported ever since, was favourable geographical circumstances.

> The natural and physical advantages of England for manufacturing industry are probably superior to those of every other country on the globe. The district where these advantages are found in the most favourable combination is the southern part of Lancashire, and the south-western part of Yorkshire, the former of which has become the principal seat of the manufacture of cotton . . . The tract lying between the Ribble and the Mersey is surrounded on the east and north by high ranges of hills, and also has hills of some magnitude in the hundreds of Blackburn and Salford; owing to which cause the district is intersected by a great number of streams, which descend rapidly from their sources towards the level tract in the west. In the early part of their course, these streams and streamlets furnish water-power adequate to turn many hundred mills: they afford the element of water, indispensable for scouring, bleaching, printing, dyeing, and other processes of manufacture: and when collected in their larger channels, or employed to feed canals, they supply a superior inland navigation, so important for the transit of raw materials and merchandise.

In addition, easily accessible coal 'animates the thousand arms of the steam-engine, and furnished the most powerful agent in all chemical and mechanical operations'. Lancashire has 'ready communication with the sea by means of its well-situated port, Liverpool' and 'the acquired advantage of a canal communication, which ramifies itself through all the populous parts of the county, and connects it with the inland counties, the seats of other flourishing manufacturers, and the sources whence iron, lime, salt, stone, and other articles in which Lancashire is deficient, are obtained'. Edward Baines, *History of the Cotton Manufacture in Great Britain*, 1835.

'Being in a straight line between Sheffield and Wakefield, both ancient and important towns, Barnsley derived advantage from the trade between them, as well as being on the routes between Chester and Doncaster, and Rotherham and Huddersfield. But the great cause of its prosperity was the early establishment of manufacturers. Wire-works were in existence here in the time of James I. The ride from Barnsley to Wakefield is one of the most picturesque in the kingdom. The town has obtained the name Black Barnsley, supposed by some to be a corruption of Bleak from its exposed situation, being built on the slope of two or three hills each 350 feet above sea level; by others said to arise from the appearance of its neighbouring moors, its ancient wire-works, its coal-mines, smoke-stained houses and its iron-works.'

Wordsworth's *Guide to the Lakes* appeared in various forms in 1810, 1820, 1822, 1823 and 1835; the full title of the definitive expanded fifth edition published in 1835 is *A Guide through the District of the Lakes in the north of England, with a Description of the Scenery, &c. for the Use of Tourists and Residents*. Alternating between practical information and rhapsodic stanzas, the ultimate Romantic poet muses upon such sublime sights as the 'almost precipitous sides of mountains with an intermixture of colours, like the compound hues of a dove's neck'. Wordsworth's guide drew so many tourists that Matthew Arnold later recalled 'one of the pilgrims, a clergyman, asked him if he had ever written anything besides the *Guide to the Lakes*'.

1832

Lewis Carroll, real name Charles Lutwidge Dodgson, was born on 27 January and grew up in the Cheshire village of Daresbury, of which parish his father was incumbent until he was eleven years old. The village is about seven miles from Warrington and its name is supposed to derive from a word meaning oak – there are plenty of oak trees in the area. A canal passes through an outlying part of the parish, and the bargemen who frequented this canal were a special object of Dodgson's pastoral care. The young boy would have seen the local cheeses, which were fashioned into various animal shapes, one of them a grinning cat.

The development of the railways encouraged reform of the corrupt electoral system. People could more easily visit villages and hamlets with barely any population but representatives in Parliament and see for themselves how absurd it was that a town as large, and getting larger, as Manchester had no representation while the slumbering parish of Newton-le-Willows with a population of less than 3,000 had two MPs. As a result of the 1832 Reform Act (which nevertheless ignored many iniquities which would inspire the Chartist movement), Manchester gained its first two members of Parliament, Mark Philips and Charles Poulett Thompson. According to historian Asa Briggs, 'Manchester enhanced its national reputation as a centre of social disturbances, even as a possible cradle of revolution.'

Founded in 1832, Durham is England's third oldest university. It would have gained its royal charter some two centuries earlier, had it not been for the opposition of Oxford and Cambridge.

Thomas Sharples opens the Star music hall in Bolton in 1832. The great majority of the Lancashire-dialect poets, composers, singers and reciters who appear in the Star are drawn from the local working population. Some of them are possibly home weavers. Their songs not only draw on traditional folk tunes but also deal with town and factory life.

1831

The factory system that became so important in Manchester was still absent in Sheffield. 'The manufacturers for the most part,' wrote one visitor in 1831, 'are carried on in an unostentatious way, in small scattered workshops, and nowhere make the noise and bustle of a great iron works.'

1830

It all – the cogs grinding, the coal burning, the steam ejecting, the pistons pumping, the wheels turning, the train chuffing, leading to the control and organisation of time itself, the linking of cities, the joining of remote places, the opening-up of coasts, mountains and beauty spots, the building of mighty stations, bridges and viaducts, and the transformation of a dislocated

nation into a less scattered community – started at 10.40 a.m. on 15
September 1830, at the Edge Hill, Liverpool end of the recently completed
Liverpool to Manchester railway line. The journey took just two hours, half
what it had taken in a horse-pulled stagecoach. By boat the journey took a
minimum of thirty hours. Eccles station opened the same year, making it one
of the stops on the first inter-city passenger route in the world.

'. . . everything in the factory . . . happens with admirable precision and neatness and at the same time with great speed . . . it seemed . . . as if all these
wheels were . . . really alive and the people occupied with them were
machines . . . [Manchester] this famous great factory town. Dark and smoky
from the coal vapours, it resembles a huge forge or workshop. Work, profit
and greed seem to be the only thoughts here. The clatter of the cotton mills
and the looms can be heard everywhere . . . We visited one of the biggest
cotton mills. A steam engine in the basement powers almost all the innumer-
able wheels and spindles which are fitted on many floors built one above the
other like a tower . . . in all of them we saw some women knotting together
the yarns which rarely tore off from the constantly turning spindles, putting
nappies on children and winding the yarn which had been spun. In one hall
the still unspun cotton was cleaned; it lay on large tables in big square pieces
looking like cotton wool; a number of women and girls armed with a thin
stick in each hand were happily thrashing it.' Arthur Schopenhauer, 1830.

71

Stockport can be divided into nine main parts. There is the most
affluent area, its wealthiest suburb, large houses lining leafy lanes, a
plush, nicely busy village centre. Bramhall (1) – nook of land where
broom grows, the Old English word *halh* meaning secret place near
water – lies to the south of Stockport's city centre, reaching to the
border with Macclesfield. When, in 1969, the twenty-three-year-old
Manchester United superstar George Best asked an architect to build

him his dream boutique-era post-Bond bachelor-pad home in Bramhall, his only stipulations were that it should have a sunken bath and a snooker room. Situated in Blossoms Lane, it was a split-level building encased in glass with a flat roof, and came complete with underground garage for George's E-Type Jaguar. It had all the latest gadgets including underfloor heating, electric curtains and a TV that retracted into the chimney breast.

Nearby, in Bramhall Park, there is another sort of architectural gem, this one set amid nearly seventy acres of woods, landscaped park, terraces and lakes, perched between two valleys containing meandering streams that feed into the Mersey. Bramhall Hall is one of the grandest examples of the black and white timber-framed manor houses that Cheshire is famous for, and one of the most important timber-framed mansions in Britain. The manor dates back to Anglo-Saxon England with the present house dating from the fourteenth and sixteenth centuries and sensitive refinements added in the nineteenth century. The earliest documentary reference to the park is found in William Webb's itinerary of Cheshire around 1620. He noted 'From Stockport, near another water called Brame [Lady Brook] which takes beginning easterly among the hills in and near Lyme Park, we come to Bramhall, a very fair lordship, demesne and fair house, of the great name of Davenport, of Bramhall, the owner whereof, now Sir William Davenport, knight, Mr Sergeant Davenport's eldest brother, to which house lies a park, and all things fit for a worshipful seat . . .' In the late nineteenth century the area became a favourite place for workers in the Stockport mills and factories to visit – a half-hour walk from the stifling factories and hours of back-breaking hard work they could find green fields and clean air, birds and wildlife.

Both the Best whimsy and the imposing stately home with its grand hall and rare wall paintings have Stockport postcodes, and prove that there is more to Stockport than met Lowry's eye, but they are definitely of the Cheshire side of Stockport.

In the far west of Stockport, three miles from the town centre, is Cheadle (2), including Cheadle Hulme, Cheadle Heath and Heald Green, spreading towards the border with the less delicate Manchester, a vital stopping point on the way to the city during the Industrial Revolution.

Also reaching to the Manchester border, to the north-west of Stockport town centre, are the four Heatons (3): Heaton Mersey (at the smarter end, like its neighbours Didsbury and Chorlton-cum-Hardy) plus Heatons Chapel, Moor and Norris (at the more basic end towards Reddish).

To the east of Stockport's centre on a hilltop moorland sits convivial Marple (4), almost as affluent as Bramhall, closer to north Derbyshire than Manchester. (Miss Marple of Agatha Christie fame was named after Marple on the Manchester–Sheffield line, when Christie was delayed at the station. In 1975, at Goyt Mill in Marple, built in 1865, once the largest one-room weaving mill in the country, employing over 300 men, women and children, one Roy Brooke created a machine that put words on a screen while music was playing, so that you could sing along to your favourite songs. Few cared or understood, and it wasn't until someone in Japan picked up on the idea and gave the machine a name – karaoke – that the less memorably titled Roy's Singalong Machine really took off. This means karaoke was invented in Stockport.)

72

1829

In October the news spread around England that a mechanic fairly obscure outside the north-east had achieved what had previously seemed impossible. At Rainhill, near Liverpool, in the presence of an eager awe-struck crowd, in a competition sponsored by the Liverpool and Manchester Railway to find the best type of locomotive, George Stephenson with the assistance of his son Robert drove his *Rocket* steam engine over a prepared length of railway at the rate of thirty-five miles an hour. They were required to traverse the track twenty times back and forth, which made the distance about the same as a return trip between Liverpool and Manchester.

The L&MR had been formed to ensure that the increasing quantities of finished cloth being manufactured in Manchester could be swiftly delivered to the nearest deep-water port of Liverpool for export, and the raw cotton being delivered to Liverpool sent quickly to Manchester. George Stephenson, after some argument about the route and his qualifications as a self-taught engineer, was appointed to build the line. At the 1826 inquiry into the construction of the railway, in the face of considerable opposition and disbelief that he could actually do what he said he could, he attempted to convince a sceptical and technologically unschooled Parliament using not only highly complex language that verged on the apparently nonsensical but also speaking in his local Northumberland accent. To the sneering and profoundly uninformed southerners needing to be convinced, his north-east burr added a further layer of the incomprehensible. He was trying to persuade aloof, unmoved and technologically ignorant Parliament to allow him to propel manic-seeming forty-ton iron engines across untested man-made structures at speeds that defied logic while speaking in what was not yet known as Geordie. At first, Parliament refused permission. Eventually they relented, passed the act necessary for construction to begin, and George Stephenson was finally given the seemingly impossible job of making it all happen.

1825

The Stockton and Darlington Railway opened in the north-east. Built primarily for carrying freight, it reduced the cost of transporting coal from eighteen shillings to eight shillings and sixpence per ton. It quickly became apparent that large profits could be made by building railways.

1824

What is generally acknowledged as Britain's first horse omnibus service was started by John Greenwood, keeper of the toll gate at Pendleton, Salford, between Pendleton and Market Street in Manchester. So successful was this service that it was not long before Greenwood became the proprietor of several more omnibuses. Records show that by 1850 sixty-four omnibuses were serving the centre of Manchester from outlying suburbs, run by various companies.

Hylda Baker and Jimmy Jewel

1823

Stockport is described by a visitor as 'an irregular, ill built, badly lighted, dirty place, which no traveller ever passed through and wished to see again'.

1822

Wordsworth's *Guide to the Lakes* first appeared as a separate volume in 1822, as *A Description of the Scenery of the Lakes in the North of England.* The edition of 500 copies sold out immediately, and a new edition of 1,000 copies was produced the following year. This included an account of an excursion up Scafell Pike, and another of a trip to Ullswater. Wordsworth wrote that early settlers had found the Lake District 'overspread with wood; forest trees, the fir, the oak, the ash, and the birch had skirted the fells . . . Not so interested in skirted fells, the industrialists turned the timber into charcoal and other fuel, while the granite, limestone, sandstone and slate left behind by 500 million years of geological processes were mined for building materials . . . For this, for everything, we are out of tune.'

In 1804, while he was at Oxford, Thomas De Quincey first took opium, not for pleasure but to relieve toothache. By 1813 he was a self-labelled 'regular and confirmed' opium addict, eventually consuming ten wine glasses of the drug each day. Opium released a storm of memories and provided a route to unique literary power. De Quincey became part of a Lake District literary circle with Wordsworth and Coleridge, retreating from a world that was too rough for him, and lived near Wordsworth before his addictions and irregular habits forced him south to London. His most famous work, the autobio-graphically hallucinatory *Confessions of an English Opium-Eater*, described by Borges as one of the saddest books ever written, is about what he knew best, perceptively describing drug addiction and evocatively representing altered mental states. He invents the idea of recreational drug use. It appeared serially in the *London Magazine* and was eventually published in book form in 1822. The combination of a rich imagination and his ambition to atemporally represent his intense personal experiences – in which space and time were distorted and he could live a hundred years in one night – produced a brilliant, digressive and ardent prose connecting grandiose romanticism and nervy self-conscious modernism, which eventually rippled all the way to post-beat-generation psychedelic writing. He was influenced by Laurence Sterne, the way he joined seemingly discordant elements, and his influence haunted not just Borges but Poe, Stevenson, Dickens, Conan Doyle, Baudelaire, Woolf, Proust, Dostoevsky and Burroughs – who remarked that he had written the first, and still the best, book on drug addiction. De Quincey continued to contribute to magazines for the rest of his life and never kicked the opium habit.

1821

When the *Manchester Guardian* was first published in 1821, Manchester had six other weekly newspapers, four published on Saturdays and two on Tuesdays. The *Manchester Mercury*, *Chronicle*, *Exchange Herald* and the

British Volunteer supported the Tories, whereas the *Manchester Gazette* was in favour of moderate reform. The *Manchester Observer* promoted radicalism, and its circulation of 4,000 made it by far the best-selling newspaper in Manchester, but it had very few advertisers and was constantly being sued for libel. Several of its journalists had been sent to prison for articles critical of the government. With the arrival of the *Guardian*, the *Observer* decided to cease publication. In its last edition the editor wrote, 'I would respectfully suggest that the *Manchester Guardian*, combining principles of complete independence, and zealous attachment to the cause of reform, with active and spirited management, is a journal in every way worthy of your confidence and support.'

1820

There is no sign of Miles Platting on maps before the 1820s, other than a nameless patch of fields and trees, when the area along the Rochdale Canal, along the Lancashire to Yorkshire railway, a mile and a half northeast of Manchester city centre, clustered next to Ancoats, Collyhurst and Newton Heath, became the home to a number of mills. By the middle of the nineteenth century, there was a chemical works, gas works and timber yard, and Miles Platting became a venue for intense industrial activity. The Victoria Mill was built by the canal in the 1870s, a sturdy six-storey building with an octagonal chimney dominating the landscape. In operation until the 1960s, it stood guard as Miles Platting, with a population dominated by Irish and Italian Catholics, went through classic, local twentieth-century decline and the closure of most of its factories, leading to its packed, back-to-back, soot-stained, slate-roofed housing becoming slums by the 1950s, and then being demolished in the 1960s and 1970s. The flimsy replacement houses, many built with flat roofs, despite the local rain, fell into disrepair within thirty years.

1819

On 16 August 1819 yeomanry (mounted volunteers) and regular cavalry, acting on the instructions of magistrates, attacked without warning a mass meeting of more than 100,000 people drawn from the industrial centres of Lancashire. The meeting, held on St Peter's Field in the centre of Manchester, had been organised as part of a national campaign for radical reform of Parliament and measures to improve the lot of working people. Riots and strikes had recently become commonplace, and in the face of such a huge crowd, magistrates panicked and ordered cavalry to disperse the assembly. The troopers rode into the crowd, laying about them with sabres. Around 500 people were injured and eleven killed. The Peterloo Massacre, the name commonly applied to these events, is a bitter reference to the feat of British arms at Waterloo four years before. It first appeared in print in the *Manchester Observer* on 21 August 1819.

Joseph Johnson, a shareholder in the *Observer*, wrote of conditions in Manchester in 1819, 'Everything is almost at a standstill, nothing but ruin and starvation stare one in the face. The state of the district is truly dreadful.' Such conditions produced a climate of radical thinking in Manchester, for which no other town in the country was better known.

When Shelley heard about the Peterloo Massacre, he was inspired to write the 'Masque of Anarchy', which called on working men to:

> Rise like lions after slumber
> In unvanquishable number
> Shake your chains to earth like dew
> Which in sleep had fallen on you –
> Ye are many – they are few

73

To the south of Stockport town centre, the Stepping Hill (5) area contains Great Moor, Heavily, Offerton and Hazel Grove – which is at the far end of the 92 (until 1969) and then 192 bus route from Manchester Piccadilly, which passes more or less every ten minutes along a straight line for nine and a bit miles through Ardwick, Longsight, Levenshulme, the Heatons, down the hill into Stockport city centre, and then up Wellington Road South past the town hall, the art gallery, the college, the infirmary, Stockport Grammar School, Mile End School and the Davenport Theatre, towards its destination two and a half miles to the south of Stockport town centre on the way to the northern reaches of the Peak District.

Before Hazel Grove was named Hazel Grove, it was called Bullock Smithy, and when John Wesley preached there in 1750 he described it as 'one of the most famous villages in the county for all manner of wickedness'. It is believed he was referring to the gambling, cock fighting and dog fighting that regularly took place. The town had become well known for its numbers of inns and beer houses, and had a rough reputation. Locals were tired of the town's uncouth 250-year-old name and the ease with which it could be turned into a joke at their expense, and Hazel Grove, a name (or something like it) used around the area before and borrowed by the locals as a nickname for thirty years, was unanimously selected in a vote in 1836. A large celebration followed. As many as 3,000 people took part in a parade and much drinking and eating. Subsequent celebrations every fifty years were equally as grateful. The new name suggested, as was hoped, a more pleasant, gentle area, although in the twentieth century the craved-for bypass taking the traffic heading south away from the centre never materialised. 'Hazel Grove' – filled with a fake sense of salubrious rural history – also looked good on the front of the 192 bus – the one I ended up using the most in my life, and believed to be one of the busiest bus routes in the country.

Sometimes the (1)92 route extended past the Hazel Grove terminus, to reach the gates of Lyme Park, overlooking the Cheshire Plain, a 1,400-acre deer park and estate set on the edge of the Peak District National Park, six and a half miles outside the centre of Stockport. The park's imposing hall, a stone-built mansion designed in the style of an Italianate palace and the largest house in Cheshire, is close to Disley (from the Anglo-Saxon for windy settlement), where novelist

Christopher Isherwood was born in the sixteenth-century Wyberslegh Hall and historian A. J. P. Taylor lived for a while.

Taylor bought his house in Higher Disley in 1933 for £525 so that he could be close to Manchester University, where he was lecturing. It was not far from Buxton, to where his family had moved in 1914, 'very high and open, miles away from anywhere', his only neighbours a couple of farmers. One of his students was Anthony Burgess. Grading one of Burgess's term papers, the great historian wrote, 'Bright ideas insufficient to conceal lack of knowledge.' Burgess in turn was irritated by Taylor's curt dismissal of James Joyce.

Taylor was visited by Dylan Thomas in April and May 1935, 'curly haired and not yet bloated, indeed looking like a Greek God on the small scale'. While there Thomas wrote verse in pencil, enjoyed the views from the front windows of the Taylors' house towards the scoured, craggy plateau of Kinder Scout, over 2,000 feet above sea level, rising like a great brown and green wall, and drank beer at the Plough Boy a couple of hundred yards down the hill. Before Taylor got annoyed with Thomas's sponging, they would take walks on the relentless 'dark peak' that surrounded them, a bleak, treeless, fallen paradise of blasted grass, bog, peat, heather, gravel and exposed rock, stripped into damned submission after a century of pollution carried on the gritty wind from the surrounding industrial areas. There was a devastated beauty all around, but there had definitely been some sort of war that had left its mark.

Taylor and Thomas would still have been trespassing when they walked on Kinder Scout, despite a mass protest that had taken place a few years earlier. In the 1930s rambling became a mass recreation for working-class youth, and the organised left played a decisive role in campaigning against the draconian laws which restricted public access to the British countryside.

The mass trespass on Kinder Scout, held on Sunday 24 April 1932, saw hundreds of walkers stage what amounted to a political demonstration. They had been summoned by hastily duplicated flyers distributed around the Manchester area. 'If you've not been rambling before, start now, you don't know what you've missed. Come with us for the best day out that you have ever had,' said one, given out in Eccles. The great issue which motivated the protesters was access.

Their favoured local walking area, the Peak District, largely moorland and hills, was poor farming land and used mostly to graze sheep or for shooting game birds. Of this huge area of about 150,000 acres, only 1 per cent was officially open to the public. The rest was owned by water companies and landowners, who protected their land using gamekeepers who carried shotguns. Kinder Scout itself was a grouse moor and worked only around twelve days a year. The rest of the time the land was deserted, but walkers were not allowed.

The trespassers were demanding one simple change: the landowners should open a public path through Kinder Scout, allowing walkers through when the land was not in use. The ultimate aim was to open up all the country's moorland and hills for walkers. Rambling was one of the few recreations that the poor working class could afford in the 1930s – the others being camping and cycling. After protests from the Hayfield Parish Council, the hikers regrouped at Bowden Bridge Quarry, where they were addressed by political activist and outdoor enthusiast Benny Rothman, whose inspiring speech set the crowd on the way. 'We ramblers after a hard week's work, and life in smoky towns and cities, go out rambling on weekends for relaxation, for a breath of fresh air, and for a little sunshine. And we find when we go out that the finest rambling country is closed to us. Because certain individuals wish to shoot for about ten days per annum, we are forced to walk on muddy crowded paths, and denied the pleasure of enjoying to the utmost the countryside. Our request, or demand, for access to all peaks and uncultivated moorland is nothing unreasonable.'

The trespass proceeded via steep William Clough, named after a local blacksmith, to the plateau of Kinder Scout, where there were violent scuffles with gamekeepers and one of the keepers injured an ankle. The ramblers were able to reach their destination and meet another group from Edale. On their return, five ramblers were arrested, with another detained earlier who had actually gone to the help of the fallen keeper. The five, who included Benny Rothman, were eventually sent for trial at Derby and given custodial sentences of up to six months.

The ramblers at Kinder Scout received massive support, and in 1949 legislation was passed giving limited rights of access to important sites of interest such as Kinder Scout. These rights were extended in 1951, when the Peak District National Park was created. Within a year 5,780 acres of Kinder Scout and Broadlee Bank Tor were available for public use.

> I'm a rambler, I'm a rambler from Manchester way,
> I get all me pleasure the hard moorland way,
> I may be a wage slave on Monday,
> But I am a free man on Sunday.
>
> He called me a louse and said 'Think of the grouse.'
> Well I thought, but I still couldn't see
> Why old Kinder Scout and the moors round about
> Couldn't take both the poor grouse and me.
> He said 'All this land is my master's.'
> At that I stood shaking my head,
> No man has the right to own mountains
> Any more than the deep ocean bed.

> Ewan McColl, 'Manchester Rambler'

A. J. P. Taylor lived in Disley until 1938, when he moved to Magdalen College, Oxford, where he was a tutor until 1963. The Manchester radical and intellectual celebrity noted, 'If I had stayed in Manchester, I would never have achieved anything other than a few academic books. Without the contacts I made in London, which is easily reached from Oxford, I should never have become either a journalist or a television star.'

He was born on 25 March 1906 in Birkdale, south of Southport, then in Lancashire, into an affluent but politically liberal Nonconformist family involved in the cotton industry, entrepreneurial but with radical views. Alan was to be the only surviving child. He showed early promise, reading books and newspapers from an unusually young age with a particular liking for the historical novels of Harrison Ainsworth and becoming obsessed with history. He would come to consider that true history began with the novelist Walter Scott, for the way he expressed how the past is really different from the present: 'he *felt* himself back in time'.

Throughout his life Taylor made much of his background: the north-ern upbringing, the family of successful Quaker cotton manufacturers, his parents' radical/liberal politics. Taylor would describe Manchester as 'the last and greatest of the Hanseatic towns – a civilisation created by traders without assistance from monarchs or territorial aristocracy'.

In 1953, in an article in the *New Statesman*, Taylor discussed the nine-teenth-century writer and reformer William Cobbett, who had expanded the concept of a religious elite to include those networks of financial institutions related to the Bank of England, elite public schools and clubs and publications such as 'the bloody old Times'. Cobbett labelled this power elite the Thing, maintaining that the aris-tocracy used it to train and sustain its oligarchical bureaucracy, which ran the British empire.

As Leonard and Mark Silk observed in their book *The American Establishment*, A. J. P. Taylor adapted Cobbett's 'Thing', which in his article became 'the Establishment'. Taylor – who would become a millionaire – wrote, 'The Establishment draws in recruits from outside as soon as they are ready to conform to its standards and become respectable. There is nothing more agreeable in life than to make peace with the Establishment – and nothing more corrupting.' Journalist Henry Fairlie refined the term in the *Spectator* in 1955.

Taylor also relished the Lancashire genius for comedy: George Formby Senior of Ashton under Lyne, Stan Laurel of Ulverston, world-weary Robb 'Ee, what a to-do' Wilton of Everton, Frank Randle of Wigan, Ken 'I won't take me coat off, I'm not stopping' Platt of Leigh, Tommy Handley of Liverpool, Ted Ray of Wigan, moving to Liverpool within days of his birth, Eric Sykes of Oldham, Eric Morecambe of Morecambe, Morecambe and Wise writer Eddie Braben of Liverpool, Les Dawson of Collyhurst, Bernard Manning of Ancoats, Jim Bowen of Accrington, Ken 'I'm too good for this place' Goodwin of Manchester, George Roper of Liverpool, Mike Harding of Crumpsall – and on it goes to Jack Rosenthal of Cheetham Hill, Victoria Wood of Prestwich, Steve Coogan of Middleton, Caroline Aherne of Wythenshawe, John Cooper Clarke of Salford, Peter Kay of Farnworth, Paul Abbott of Burnley, Frank Cottrell Boyce of Liverpool, and Danny Boyle of Radcliffe, the sentimental but flinty artistic director of the 2012 Olympic

Games opening ceremony, in many ways the exuberant climax to over a century of sly, protesting, twinkling Lancastrian music-hall mischief-making rooted in Randle, Braben and Kaye as much as Marx, Engels and Clynes, in direct opposition to the ossifying, diminishing idea of the Establishment.

Taylor concluded that there was 'something in the air'. You could actually connect Lancashire's defiant sense of humour with the wind coming in from the south-east, from beyond British shores, bringing traces of distant difference, encouraging a certain edgy whimsy, jittery dreams of otherness, a glorious blend of silliness and wisdom, and a general belief that one way of beating the odds, outwitting fate and rising above social inequity was with a gag. Lancashire was where the world's antic mental energy eventually drifted to, and was absorbed and dispersed with a ruthless sense of timing rooted in fierce centuries of hard labour, defiant love and constant loss. For Taylor's awkward pupil Anthony Burgess – himself, however bombastic, rhetorical or dyspeptic, a part of that list of Lancastrian comedians, the missing link between Les Dawson and Vladimir Nabokov – this distinctive Lancashire spirit was 'the bark of the underdog'.

Reddish (6) is part of the Tame Valley area to the east of the town centre with Brinnington (7), 'Brinny', a post-war slum clearance area, once open farmland above the Tame Valley where the abandoned and homeless were dumped in hastily built council-owned properties after the war and the fifties and sixties slum clearance, isolated and unloved, the other side of Reddish Vale. Stockport is made up of such extremes that it is possible to go from opulent Lyme Park, SK12, with its medieval deer park, extravagant house and Edwardian rose garden, where they film television productions of Jane Austen, to marooned, treacherous Brinnington, SK5, where you could film dismal, dismembered 1960s Eastern Europe. Compared to Bramhall, there seemed to be whole parts of Brinnington that had just gone missing, or had never been there in the first place. Most of the people living there found ways to deal with where they found themselves, even as it seemed to be disappearing into a hole the shape of a broken window, a portal through which you entered another dimension.

The densely populated neighbourhood of Victoria (8), to the west of

the centre of Stockport, contains dowdy but proud Edgeley, tree-lined
Davenport and the baggy in-between Cale Green. In the far south-east
of the borough towards Glossop (9) lies the 'gate-way to the Peak
District', a beginning to the north in this book, a rubbing-together of
Cheshire and Yorkshire, Greater Manchester and Tameside with north-
ern Derbyshire, midway between Manchester and Sheffield, a fluid area
inside all those places but also on the outside, where goldsmith Sir
Edmund Shaa, martyred priest Blessed Nicholas Garlick, novelist
Hilary Mantel, TV personality Stuart Hall, designer Vivienne
Westwood and property developer and soft pornographer Paul
Raymond were all born and/or brought up, Ludwig Wittgenstein lived
in the springs and summers of 1908 and 1909 (at the Grouse Inn on
chilly Chunal Moor, where he tested meteorological kites) and L. S.
Lowry died. Over the Tameside border are humdrum Romiley (spacious
woodland clearing) and amorphous Bredbury, birthplace of famous
1970s comic impressionist and Golden Garter regular Mike Yarwood.

Before I left Stockport, I would know and have visited all of these
places for one reason or another. Before I was allowed to leave, it seemed
I had to tick each place off and get a sense of the interlocking pattern
of human behaviour and how people crowded together interact in
places and streets that have different names yet share an essential spirit,
richer and more focused at its centre, less specific further out, until it
fades away altogether, and becomes something else.

74

1818

Emily Brontë was born on 30 July at Thornton, Bradford, Yorkshire, fifth of six
children. Her mother died of cancer in 1821. In 1824 she attended the newly
opened Clergy Daughters' School at Cowan Bridge in Lancashire. Along
with her sisters Maria, Elizabeth and Charlotte, she experienced a harsh
regime – frequently cold and with poor food. In June 1825 Emily and her
sisters were taken away from the school for good. Their father was a quiet

man, and often spent his spare time alone, so the motherless children entertained themselves reading the Bible and the works of William Shakespeare,
Virgil and John Milton, played the piano, did needlepoint and told each
other stories. Emily's imagination developed early under the influence of her
surroundings – sky, animals, plants, rocks, soil and water – but also around
the contrivances of fictional worlds. Her world of Gondal, developed with her
older sister Charlotte and younger sister Anne, was a faraway place peopled
with medieval-like and romantic characters – kings and consorts, princes and
princesses, generals and rebels, implacable foes, irreconcilable traitors and
flawed lovers – in land- and seascapes filled with castles, cathedrals,
dungeons, warships and forest battles.

1817

Edwin Waugh was born on 29 January in a small cottage by the Old Clock
Face Inn in Toad Lane, Rochdale. His father was a clog- and shoemaker, and
the family, though working class, enjoyed a reasonable income. However,
following the death of his father from a brain tumour at the comparatively
young age of thirty-seven, when Edwin was only seven years old, the family
fortunes plummeted and for a time he and his mother lived in a cellar. At
twelve he became an errand boy for a printer, and two years later was
apprenticed to another printer.

1815

Preston was the first provincial town to have gas street lighting. In May 1815
the Preston Gas Company was formed and the three main streets, Church
Street, Fishergate and Friargate, were lit. The pipes used were army-surplus
musket barrels stuck end to end. A major reason for the interest in gas lighting was its possible use in illuminating the mills so that longer hours could be
worked. Two years later the trustees of the gas company threatened to cut
off the gas as they had not paid their bills.

1811

The last time a convicted prisoner's hand was branded with M for malefactor at Lancaster's Crown Court.

By 1811 there were more than four million steam-mule spindles in over fifty mills in the Manchester district alone. As a result of the improved technology, raw cotton imports soared and the price of cotton yarn plummeted, while cotton textile exports rapidly outstripped those of woollen cloth. Cotton cloth sold well because it was cheap and light, but also because it could be brightly coloured and patterned like the much more expensive silk.

1803

The Lake District is considered by many the birthplace of rock climbing in Britain, if not the world. (George Mallory, born in Mobberly, Cheshire in 1886, who began climbing on his clergyman father's church in Cheshire, the mountaineer who when asked why he wanted to climb Everest replied 'Because it's there,' developed his skills in the Lake District.) The earliest climbers were shepherds who somehow negotiated the crags wearing hobnailed boots. Poets such as Wordsworth and Coleridge, who made an unplanned descent of England's second highest mountain, Scafell, in 1802, helped to popularise both the Lakes and the sport of climbing. (Coleridge had made it up Scafell via a relatively safe route, and then chose the most difficult way down, relishing the danger, deliberately frightening himself as he tumbled from ledge to ledge, sometimes falling twice his own height.) In his poem 'The Brothers' William Wordsworth featured the sheer and intimidating Pillar Rock, in one of the most remote valleys, which Mallory later climbed without assistance, giving his name to what was known as the hardest route in Britain.

> You see yon precipice – it almost looks
> Like some vast building made of many crags,

And in the midst is one particular rock
That rises like a column from the vale,
Whence by our Shepherds it is call'd, the Pillar.

At the beginning of the nineteenth century York was the sixteenth largest city in England; at the end it was the forty-first. In Yorkshire Bradford, Halifax and Huddersfield outgrew the county's capital, which remained at heart a market town. In 1803 across the Pennines Manchester was still a small town of some 600 streets, bordered by fields and meadows.

PART FIVE

The five colours

No matter what the illusion created, it is a flat canvas and has to be organised into shapes.

David Hockney

75

Stockport Viaduct – deposited above Mersey Square across the recessed centre of the nine districts of the town – was something of a church for L. S. Lowry, one that he didn't worship inside but simply worshipped. He didn't go inside the houses, mills and factories he painted; he saw the north from above, from outside, from the perspective of one in control, interested not in the intimate workings but in the power, the presence, of the land and what had been placed on it since the first hiss of steam, the first assembly line, in the pace of life set by machines and the impact that had on reality and the lost souls engaged with whatever the land had become. The viaduct connected one lost paradise and a new, dangerous paradise, and it spanned his imagination, taking him from the smallest corner of his life to the end of the road.

The viaduct was so old and massive I didn't see it at all when I lived there. Like the ponderous Victorian buildings stonily haunting Manchester city centre, its solid largeness somehow slipped outside my vision. The viaduct over the Tame was out on its own, splendidly and a little surreally isolated among shimmering, sweeping acres of open country, but this one, at the heart of town, bigger, mightier, carrying far more traffic to and from Manchester, to and from London, was somehow simply a part of the landscape, as if it was there before humans arrived, lodged in the ground, a native part of the land. You couldn't miss it, but, being a teenager worried about the oddest of things, I did miss it. I took it for granted. It was just an awful lot of bricks, and bricks were everywhere. Bricks were all around; bricks brought with them the walls, towers, factories, unlimited terraced houses and tunnels that hemmed you in and blocked out the light. Bricks made up the obstacles that you had to avoid and break through.

I've come to find Stockport Viaduct through the paint and guarded passion of Lowry. In his work, which was his life, he returned to it again and again, elevating it to a ubiquitous sculptural symbol of the beginning and end of progress, as if to cross it, to stand under it, is to take your place in a determined march towards something that will ultimately be the end of the journey. He treats the lowly brick as the foundation of civilisation, and sees the viaduct as a tremendous community of bricks that are strongly individual yet all joined together. The viaduct is often there in his paintings, in the background, even when his subject is not Stockport. It was always part of his north, of his mind – the Stockport Viaduct was the structure that connected his mind with the north, leading from one place to the other with hypnotic regularity.

The viaduct is there in the background of a compounded Lowry painting of the spare, smeared, fenced-in northern landscape as never was but of course really was, because he painted it so, in the same way he painted all those burdened, crooked people, living inside hutches, strokes of black amid white space, letters transmitting messages about their predicament and the grey past, broken down by time, beyond help, people belonging to iron, coal, clay, brick, deformed by effort and routine, occupying their hometowns as a necessary evil, all that they know, and can know, doing their jobs, trapped between simplicity and nature and the new age of science, calculation and mechanisation.

Chetham Library where Marx and Engels worked

Lowry's painted people make you wonder if he had read this description of mill workers by a medical worker in 1833: '. . . their complexion is sallow and pallid – with a peculiar flatness of feature, caused by the want of a proper quantity of adipose substance [fatty tissue] to cushion out the cheeks . . . their stature low – the average height of four hundred men, measured at different times, and different places, being five feet six inches . . . their limbs slender, and playing badly and ungracefully . . . a very general bowing of the legs . . . great numbers of girls and women walking lamely or awkwardly, with raised chests and spinal flexures . . . nearly all have flat feet, accompanied with a down-tread, differing very widely from the elasticity of action in the foot and ankle, attendant upon perfect formation . . . hair thin and straight – many of the men having but little beard, and that in patches of a few hairs . . .' P. Gaskell, *The Manufacturing Population of England*, 1833.

For Lowry the modern world begins with the building of Stockport Viaduct and ends not long after, as the Victorians grandly, recklessly rebuilt their world from the sewers below to the spires, bridges and chimneys above, combining extravagant self-promoting flair and finery with the plain and utilitarian. Joining the underground tunnels and the gliding triumphant high are the scale and bravado of the viaduct, the very symbol of Victorian engineering flair, industrious ambition and the determination to get things done and create buildings that would last for ever. Shops, hospitals, concert halls, memorial halls, factories, warehouses, mills and schools rose in Stockport as the nineteenth century progressed and the town expanded around the river and up the surrounding hills and slopes, and dominating even those epic structures was The Viaduct. All that organised brick and space making it clear that, from the south, by train, to get to Manchester, where it was all happening, you had to cross this town. Stockport was important. Stockport was here. It was going nowhere, but it helped you get somewhere.

Lowry looked down from above, from a distance, turning his views of what had happened to the land into maps of despair and visions of the tension between hope and hopelessness. The expanses of town, filled with those recently released from office, factory, school, home, not quite sure what they were expected to do next, caught by the watching Lowry in a moment of indecision or blankness, not knowing he's watching, not knowing he's among them, looking like them but someone else.

The people who lived around me in Reddish, and in Longsight, Levenshulme, Edgeley, Denton, Gorton, Burnage and Heaton Chapel, close by but in their own worlds, were to me like the people in a Lowry painting. I was aware of them, saw them moving about, talked to them, did much the same things they did, but I never got close to them, to understanding their succinct or battered uniqueness. They were all heading in the same direction – heading to and from the same place, apparently part of a collective, a community sharing the same resources and lack of resources, enjoying the same occasions and events, the same celebratory dates on the calendar, the same fun and games, the same gossip and news, the same rain that threatened to dissolve them into phantoms, scuttling up and down the same hills, nipping to the same corner shops under drooping canvas awnings sheltering them from wind and rain, and occasionally sun, where the doors made the same assertive noise as they opened – but they were all deep in their own

STEPHENSON TEACHING THE NAVVIES.

George Stephenson

minds, in their own lives, next door to each other in time and place, but far, far away from each other in how they read and experienced their environment, lost in their own bodies, which, according to Lowry, were mere smears, wrinkles, expressions of sensation, obedience, desperation and posture set against a backdrop of brick, road, workshop, field and emptiness.

This was the world Lowry grew up in. He didn't find himself amidst Swiss mountains, or French fields, or Caribbean islands, or Norwegian fjords, isolated and apart from clustered reined-in people compelled to deal with claustrophobic streets and freezing nights. The indomitable Victorian railways, canals, roads, mills and factories were all in place by the time he was a teenager, soon to be supplemented by equally solid but seeming lighter, even fancier, Edwardian bricks and decoration. His surroundings were man-made and often mighty, sometimes at the edge of the sinister, with the polluted, poisoned often equally sinister moors, rivers and hills around the edges. In the middle, stranded, ghostly vivid, were the workers, wives and husbands, children, loners, malingerers, ordinary people and occasional animals, who seem to ache being so close to where the action is and isn't.

Lowry was born in the Victorian era, only child of estate agent Robert and Elizabeth on 1 November 1887 in respectable Victoria Park, east of the Wilmslow Road in Rusholme, then well outside the built-up areas of Manchester. Rusholme was a pleasant place to live, a positive result of Manchester's increasing wealth, home to the great and good and the new breed of energetic self-made men, filled with substantial out-of-town houses and villas, shaded by pretty avenues of trees, birdsong heard more than industrial rumble. The city eventually swamped the independent elegance of Victoria Park but never completely washed it away. The Lowrys were proud members of the lower middle class. They kept themselves to themselves, and an internal dynamic developed between the three of them, based around Lowry's mother's love for him and resentment of her husband.

Lowry started drawing at eight, leaving school at sixteen. By 1904 he had drifted into work as a claims clerk at Manchester Insurance Company, and he used some of his earnings to pay for private art tuition. He studied in the evenings at the Manchester Municipal School of Art under French Impressionist Pierre Adolphe Valette, who arrived in Manchester in 1905, earning a living designing greetings cards and calendars. Valette fell in love with northern England, the resonant dampness as well as the people, and his speciality became atmospheric scenes of Edwardian Manchester, spotting glistening enigmatic beauty amid the hustle, brick and smoke where few others did, locating the young, urgent city in a Monet mist moving between past and present. Lowry was not too sociable, a little on the outside of things, and it seems he was not too precise at representing things as they were or seemed to be, but not necessarily abstract. He was liberated by Valette's careful demonstration of Parisian paint and brush techniques, which could reflect and illuminate details, people, landscape and buildings without the need for soulless pedestrian accuracy. The preoccupied people lurking at the edges of Valette's loving sombre pictures of a Manchester in the middle of just another day, under-neath indistinct bridges, with towers, spires and steeples receding in the crepuscular distance of time and space, figures indirectly inher-ited from Van Gogh's radiantly suggestive impressions of sun-scorched reapers alone in their world, would emigrate into Lowry's universe, shrink into themselves and develop their own obscure but revelatory personalities. (Other sources for Lowry's way of seeing, and choos-ing, things, as a kind of historian of social endurance – the sixteenth-century Pieter Bruegel the Elder's landscapes, real and invented, merging scenes and activities in one painting rooted in Hieronymus Bosch, where he scattered peasants finding ways to cope, in the cold, alone in a vast universe, searching for purpose, indulging in everyday rituals of work, play and worship; a 1906 painting by the obscure E. E. Smith, *Stockport from Brinksway, Cheshire*, when the town was still just filling itself in, countryside beginning to disappear beneath street and factory, where the great viaduct swoops in the middle distance across the valley behind numerous mis-shapen terraced houses, windows giving them comic personality, while tall chimneys above squat factories matter of factly belch smoke and a few straggly individuals stagger along pavements next to untarmaced, carless roads.)

In 1909 Lowry's parents slipped from genteel Victoria Park to dingier, earthier Pendlebury, in the north-west of Salford, an area filled with the thumping industrial buildings that would infect Lowry's mind. This was a Salford in which you would still see men from the poorhouses working with P for pauper stamped on the seats of their ragged trou-sers. This was a Salford that hadn't moved on much from when Friedrich Engels reported it was 'built in courts of narrow lanes, so narrow that they remind me of the narrowest I have ever seen, in the little lanes of Genoa. The average construction of Salford is in this respect much worse than that of Manchester and so too in respect of cleanliness. If in Manchester the police from time to time make a raid upon the working-class district, close the worst dwellings, and cause the filthiest spots in these Augean stables to be cleaned, in Salford it seems to have done absolutely nothing.' By 1900, five years after Engels died, much remained in Salford that was fetid.

Lowry's mother and father felt humiliated by their loss of status, and at first he hated the neighbourhood as much as his mother. However, according to legend, one day when the light was up to a certain north-west something he got a sudden glimpse of a gargantuan mill from a particular position on top of his local station steps, and saw beyond the colourless smoggy grime and unremarkable everydayness into a frail, unquantifiable beauty: 'The huge black framework of rows of yellow-lit windows standing up against the sad, damp-charged afternoon sky.' There was an epiphany, and the rest of his life was spent chasing and circling and refining and confirming this bitter impression of piercing absence, this sight of something other in the midst of withering familiarity and stinging deprivation, something in which you could see time itself, not simply human reaction to and human control of time. 'My subjects were all around me . . . in those days there were mills and collieries all around Pendlebury. The people who work there were passing morning and night. All my material was on my doorstep.' He could see there was something else, behind, inside, at the very core of his defiled surroundings, and that to capture this feeling and express it required a new form of compositional approach, a new way of aligning subject and form, and locating harmony in unlikely places.

Lowry broke free of restrictive social, institutional and aesthetic standards, and developed his own language, his own symbols and reference points, and this made him completely modern despite his subject matter, which could be archaic, nostalgic, sentimental, romantic, but also cruel, dispassionate, weary, removed. This was where he found himself, and what else could he possibly paint, when there was all this crowded space, epic scale and radiant sadness to consider and contain? To paint a landscape in such an area meant painting deformed, withered post-industrial urban living and the consequences of constant graft that profoundly marked the environment – that was the essential nature he was destined to capture. Perhaps, too, his limited palette, the five colours he mixed to create the atmosphere and detail in his paintings, which limited him yet set him free, contained enough potential for him to capture the various reds of northern Victorian brick, and especially the red of the Stockport Viaduct, produced from a very specific combination of local chemicals and minerals at a certain temperature in the kiln where the bricks were baked, allowing him to get inside how that colour had been greyed, marred, soiled by smoke and wear.

He got a job as a rent collector in 1912, which also seemed to influence his painting, his perspective on people. He got into their homes, close to the faces, bodies and even souls of the kind of people who would populate his paintings. He could examine how they moved: with a limp, a little skip, a weird little shuffle, an ageing hobble, a youthful twitch; he could see what clothes they wore, they huddled inside: the holes in the material, their ratty shoes, the mufflers around the men's scrawny necks, the shawls the women wore on the shortest of journeys; he could examine the weariness in their faces, the mouthfuls of rotten teeth, the silly things that made them laugh, the nitty-gritty of their speech and gestures, the meat and potatoes of their daily grind. He watched them play, heard them gossip, moan, scold, shop in the markets, inside their world but on the outside. He could reach inside people, but not to paint them exactly as they appeared, but as he remembered them, as he was already starting to forget them, because there were so many of them, and they were all the same, and all different, and all living on streets that were all the same, and all different. 'Something's gone wrong in their lives,' he once said with a little sad chuckle.

He studies art until 1928. He is a part-time artist, but perhaps only in the way that T. S. Eliot is a part-time poet. Lowry works for a living, but he also records the texture, technicality and magnificent peculiarity of the ailing humdrum corner of the universe where he finds himself. His debt-ridden father dies in 1932, leaving him to look after his ailing, depressed mother, working by day, nursing her in the evening, painting at night. In 1938 he is fifty, and to some extent on his own, in his own world, translating the graceful, grievous north around him through his own obsession with this unique combination of external weight and internal anxiety, of dirty streets and human thought. In the 1930s he develops a fondness for Berwick-upon-Tweed, the northernmost town in England, in the traditional warring border land, on the east coast at the mouth of the Scottish River Tweed five miles north of Holy Island. Both English and Scottish and yet in some ways neither, switching back and forth between the countries, never quite settling one way or the other, achieving such a level of unsettled independence the Crimean War had to be declared on behalf of Great Britain, Ireland and Berwick-upon-Tweed.

In Berwick Lowry sees a Salford without the mills and chimneys, falls for the way the Georgian town-hall steeple dominates the skyline, exaggerating its height when he paints it, admires the seventeenth-century sandstone Old Bridge, stays at the Castle Hotel by the railway station, ponders buying a house on the intact Elizabethan walls of the town, fascinated by how old buildings, crooked lanes, kerbstones, leaning walls, the parish church built in Cromwellian times, and the flights of steps are grimly packed together in gripping geometry by the walls. He once said he always wanted to live near the sea, and crashing, weeping, pounding into Berwick – now a sea-swept Stockport, a Swinton with salty air, reminding him of the summer holidays he took with his mother in Rhyl, north Wales – is the North Sea, particularly eerie and ominous in winter, in which for Lowry there is all the battle of life, the unwavering inevitability, the coming in of the tide, and the going out, the filling up and the emptying out.

His mam, who called him Laurie, dies in 1939, and now he really is on his own. It is suggested he inherited his artistic single-mindedness from her, a lucid tunnel vision, and was distraught she did not live to see the acclaim he received as a painter. In the Second World War he is a fire-watcher, looking out over his city, seeing shapes and fragments no one else can, seeing the world around him fall apart, seeing himself in the ruins, the shabby, melancholy observer watching himself watching the formation of decline and the collapse of greatness.

His house in Pendlebury falls into disrepair and is repossessed, and after fancying a lonely many-windowed house which turns out to be riddled with damp on a hill in Berwick with views of the sea, he moves to a detached old stone house in Mottram, Longendale, near Hyde, midway between Manchester and Barnsley, on the border with Derbyshire. He lives there, putting up with a home he never really likes, for the next twenty-eight years. He keeps visiting Berwick until his final summer. At home he drinks in the Cheshire Cheese pub on Hyde Lane and sets up his easel on the town-hall steps.

He works as a rent collector until he retires in 1952 at sixty-five, wearing the mask of an ordinary man to smuggle himself into the lives of those he is very different from. His world unlike theirs is made of paint and flat surfaces, and he imagines a reality influenced by what he remembers as much as what he sees. He is motivated by how he can organise and articulate his thoughts and feelings by combining, smudging, scratching, fingering, massaging his favourite colours, his vermilion, ivory black, yellow ochre, Prussian blue, flake white – so therefore black, white and three basic tones – on to flat surfaces in ways that record the ornate, decaying atmosphere of where he lives, and the run-down, pragmatic, defeated and/or defiant people he happens to live with and beside.

He is like Edgar Allen Poe's man of the crowd, drifting through the teeming city, or through the dream spaces in his mind, trying to understand and appreciate everything that happens. He inhabits a dilapidated Pinteresque universe rather than a hokey Formby town. Factories are to Lowry what the motor car was to Filippo Marinetti of the Italian Futurists and fame was to Andy Warhol. He creeps through his own life and the lives of others, compiling fragments, morsels of experience, searching for answers about death, disappearance, the past, why we live, why we die, where we go, where we come from, the oddity of everyday life, the pinched dead-eyed ordinariness. He watches, and turns that watching into his paintings, which don't really belong to any school, and aren't as naive as some say, or as primitive, or as simplistic. They are described in condescending ways as being childish, but you get the feeling Lowry was never childish even as a child. Using the minimal means he has decided upon, the limited palette, the stylistic repetitions, the constant dazzling pulse of isolation, he is nevertheless an experimental artist, turning coarse truth into something unworldly, interpreting northern life as something more nihilistic and surreal than cosy and quirky. He is Baudelaire's dandy, with a burning desire to create a personal form of originality within the external limits of social conventions: 'Dandyism is a setting sun; like the declining star, it is magnificent, without heat and full of melancholy.'

Lowry has found something to do that forms an escape from a chaos of imponderables about existence. He has found a way to pass the time and shield himself from sinking into an eternal depression. He paints what he sees, and feels, leaving a tinge of himself, his curiosity, haunting his pictures. He paints to preserve things he has seen, not necessarily for his sake or those of the viewers, but out of a commitment to the essence of the experience itself, to keep it from oblivion.

He paints the fallout of the Industrial Revolution, its sights and splendour, its brutality and brilliance, its beginning and end, often in the same painting. He paints views of strapping distant mills topped with smoking chimneys with high floors full of alive-looking windows among hilly backgrounds that could have come from etchings of Oldham and Bury in the 1860s, but with the addition of people who came later, when these buildings were the new nature, the slipping of the once future into a present slipping into the past. He is reading the past while existing entirely in the present, colouring the landscape with elements of his own psyche, so existing at the centre of a web of contradictions.

He paints the impact of the Industrial Revolution on communities that were once villages but are now something bigger, stranger, ghastlier. He paints as an intruder dressed in clothes that once made him invisible, and now make him stand out, as he witnesses decline, disorientation and devastation, and wit, loveliness and strangeness, with no interest in what is coming next, in how the slums and poor are being replaced with something new, but possibly new slums and new poor as sighted on the wasted streets of Brinnington. Northern regeneration and the recovery, or not, of pride and motive shattered by war and unemployment are outside his remit.

Lowry never married, never went abroad, never had a car, never had a telephone. He was middle-aged before there was any recognition of his work, so that he never really took the respect that did come too seriously. Colossal, tender, he remained all his life encased in the sort of grave dark-grey clothes someone would have worn in the 1890s. 'I keep on working and wondering what it means and it goes on and on and there you are.' A yawn that stretched as wide as a viaduct was his response to those who bored him and separated him from his preferred state of solitude, his retreat into himself – maybe another reason for his fascination with the Stockport Viaduct, the way it announced its own yawning boredom with the land, time and space around it, showcasing its own preference for isolation. Look at that graveyard, he would say; nobody there is complaining – and the viaduct is a giant headstone perhaps, happy in its motionless permanence, a memorial to itself, which doesn't need to do anything any more, but be itself.

He was not interested in the latest representation of progress. He was interested in what had happened to people and their surroundings because of the progress that had begun in the decades leading to his birth: people coming in, people going out. If he saw people as grotesque caricatures adrift and stunned in a hostile universe, in flight from stability, that was because the Industrial Revolution had itself turned them into such and produced that universe. He didn't do it; it had been done to them. He didn't create their helplessness; he witnessed it. Then again, it might be that all those strangers, locals, beggars, pedlars, cripples, neighbours, passers-by, Alberts, Franks, Harrys, Arthurs, Georges, Gilberts, Samuels, Ivys, Irenes, Ednas, Maudes, Gertrudes, Netties, Norahs, Winifreds, Violets (with surnames that survive for centuries without suffering as much from age, wear and tear) pouring in and out of his paintings – and sometimes not there at all, out of sight, gone for ever, leaving behind isolated sea, barren moor or iron-grey sky gravely stacked on the inflamed rim of infinity – were simply shadowy versions of himself, looking for a way out or a way in, painted into the world he was of but deliberately removed from. His characters, as versions of himself, of all the shadows that surrounded him, stalked his consciousness. They were ghosts from his past that would not leave him alone, looking for home, sometimes finding it, but it didn't really feel like home, but that's all they had. It's all he had – a home that is not a home on the way to a forever home that he will not be able to paint, where all he will have is his thoughts and not even those. His paintings acknowledged a world of other people, but he stayed on the outside, an artist, a dreamer, a fugitive from responsibility, a detective in search of a body, sifting facts for evidence, in this case evidence about the point and purpose of existence. A detective who had his own little jokes, which were more amusing, perhaps, to him than to others.

Take a Lowry painting, filled with splinters, smears and smudges representing fleeting souls, thin-lipped strivers and drifting humans, people finding themselves within Stockport, Stretford, Glossop, Swinton, working their own way in and out of their own dreams of existence, and imagine that some of the characters, present and disconnected, have names and histories and even reputations, that as much as they are nowhere and no one, they are somewhere and someone. Who are those people going to the match, at the fairground, milling about in a street scene, hanging around the barred factory gates, yearning for freedom, remaining imprisoned? Imagine this selection of people, verging on the anonymous, sinking into obscurity and heroically rising from it like the faces and personalities lined up on the cover of the Beatles' *Sgt Pepper* album; some of these empty vessels, these featured featureless ones, with the world and nothing more at their fingertips, have names and biographies, crossed the cobbled street, climbed the railings, opened the gate, left the frame, made their fortune, got themselves noticed, changed their minds and then the world. Imagine that in a Lowry canvas, amid that fretting static crowd, there are people who were more than they seemed, who staked claims to attention, because even if Lowry fixed you, trapped you in his world, you still did this, and you did that, and you made a difference in an indifferent universe. Crowded into Lowry's mind, underneath an erect chimney reaching into the foul, livid clouds, on to a page or two of history, into an empty clearing between where you were born and who you become:

John Bradshaw, born in Stockport on 15 July 1602, the younger son of landowning minor gentry, was educated at Stockport Grammar School. He went on to excel in law, and was mayor of Congleton in 1637 and chief justice of Cheshire and north Wales in 1647. As reluctant lord president of the High Court of Justice he pronounced the death sentence on King Charles I in 1649 – 'even a King is subject to the law', his forty-minute statement concluded. Bradshaw was rewarded by Oliver Cromwell: appointed permanent president of the Council of State and chancellor of the Duchy of Lancaster. Supporter of a democratic republic, he came to oppose Cromwell's authoritarianism. When Bradshaw resisted Cromwell's dissolution of the House of Commons in 1653 – 'Sir, we have heard what you did at the House this morning, and before many hours all England will hear it. But, sir, you are mistaken to think that the Parliament is dissolved, for no power under heaven can dissolve them but themselves. Therefore take you notice of that' – he lost his post as chief justice of Cheshire and North Wales.

Bradshaw was baptised at Stockport parish church, where 'traitor' has been added against his name in the parish register. He died in October 1659 and was buried in Westminster Abbey. After the Restoration he was posthumously tried for high treason – alongside Cromwell – for his role in the death of Charles I. His body was exhumed in 1661 and hung in chains on a gibbet at Tyburn.

Admiral Sir George Back, born in Stockport, entered the navy in 1808 at twelve, served in the Napoleonic Wars, spent five years in a French jail, then became a pioneering Arctic navigator. He gave the name Stockport Islands to a couple of pieces of wilderness he discovered in the Canadian Arctic Archipelago in the territory of Nunavut.

Sir Joseph Whitworth, born in a tiny house in Hillgate, Stockport on 21 December 1803, was one of the great entrepreneurial Victorian mechanical engineers alongside Stephenson and Brunel. By 1878 Sir Joseph owned many patents including ones for knitting machines, road sweepers, steel manufacturing and twenty for armaments, even though he was a pacifist. At the 1851 Great Exhibition he exhibited a machine that could measure to a millionth of an inch, and he won more medals than any other exhibitor. Whitworth was deeply concerned with working-class poverty and donated large sums of money to educational organisations.

One of the leading physicists of his time, an inventor best known for his influential research into electricity and thermodynamics and for giving his name to the international unit of energy, James Prescott Joule was born in New Bailey Street, Salford on 24 December 1818, in a house next door to the successful Joule Brewery owned by his father Benjamin. He was considered too sensitive as a child to attend school. In his early years, he was taught by his mother's half sister, and then by tutors at his father's house, Broomhill, in Pendlebury, becoming interested in scientific toys and flying kites. He started work in his father's brewery at fifteen, a good place for him to study machinery and chemical processes. He became fascinated with electric motors, and set out to see if it was possible to convert the family brewery from steam power to electric power.

At sixteen, he was sent to study with 'the father of modern chemistry', John Dalton, at the Manchester Literary and Philosophical Society, thriving in the academic surroundings. Dalton was a big influence on Joule, but most of his scientific understanding was self-taught, his scientific brilliance a combination of amateur enthusiasm and innovative thinking inspired by a brewer's commitment to accurate measurement. His discoveries and writings improved the efficiency of numerous nineteenth-century industrial machines, and his theories led directly to the development of arc welding and refrigeration. His research was self-funded, and his funds finally ran out in 1875 with the decline of the family brewery – his attempts to improve the quality of beer proving a failure. His final few years saw him battle illness, and he died as a result of a form of degeneration of the brain on 11 October 1889 at home in Sale. Joule's gravestone in Sale's Brooklands Cemetery is inscribed with the number 772.55, his 1878 measurement of the mechanical equivalent of heat.

Samuel Laycock, one of the best-known writers of Lancashire dialect, who lived much of his life in Cheshire, was born on 17 January 1826 – 'a year of great drought and scarceness' – in an isolated farmhouse on a steep slope above Marsden, Yorkshire, a no-nonsense small town surrounded by moorland between Saddleworth and Huddersfield near the Roman trans-Pennine route connecting Chester and York. His father had been a weaver, his grandfather was a farmer.

Educated only at Sunday school, he started working at the local Robert Bowers Woollen Mill when he was nine, from 6 a.m. to 8 p.m., for a weekly wage of two shillings. When Laycock was eleven, the family moved to Stalybridge, then at the centre of the cotton industry, an industry that experiencd periodic depressions – 'when't trade wur slack'. He earned his living as a power-loom weaver, eventually becoming a foreman, an occupation he continued in until 1862, when the blockade on Confederate cotton exports imposed by the Union during the American Civil War caused mass unemployment and much hardship among Lancashire cotton workers, a period that became known as the Cotton Famine or Cotton Panic.

Laycock was one of the thousands unemployed who tried to earn a living by writing verses which could be set to music and sung in the streets for pennies. His fortitude and striving, his belief in self-help and social reconciliation, were rooted in his own experience of poverty. Between 1855 and 1867 Laycock wrote most of his best-known poetry, including 'Bowton's Yard', 'Bonny Brid', the collection *Lancashire Lyrics* and his first published work, 'A Little Bit on Both Sides' in 1855. Much of this work described in dialect verse the disastrous effects that widespread unemployment had on the districts of Stalybridge, Ashton and Dukinfield, which were almost totally dependent upon the textile trade for their livelihood. In March 1863 serious riots broke out in these towns, triggered by an attempt to reduce relief payments and impose harsher conditions on recipients. Panic spread among the local magistracy, who feared a return to the Chartist disturbances of the 1840s. 'To riot or to rot' appeared to be the future of Lancashire's demoralised cotton workers.

His works were immensely popular among working people in northern villages, who readily identified with his sentiments – many poems were published as broadsheets and learned by heart or set to music and became popular songs. The melancholy but mischievous Laycock also produced a valuable record of working people's experiences at the time, his poems containing a lively relish for fun despite tough circumstances.

In 1865 he became librarian and porter at the Stalybridge Mechanics' Institute, a fine example of the Victorian quest for self-improvement and self-education as expressed by mill workers. (The mechanics' institute movement was one of the most remarkable in British educational history, and thrived particularly in the mill towns of northern England. The institutes were a significant development in a period when educational provision for the working classes was practically non-existent: in 1833 only about 800,000 children were receiving some form of instruction, mostly in very elementary reading and writing. George Birkbeck, a Glasgow professor, founded the movement in 1800, with the creation of the first institute in Glasgow. Manchester UMIST – University of Manchester Institute of Science and Technology – can trace its roots back to 1824 and the creation of the Manchester Mechanics' Institute, established by local businessmen and industrialists to ensure workers could learn the basics of science.)

Laycock left this post six years later, after which he seems to have drifted for some time. Various unsuccessful enterprises – selling books on Oldham market, a photography business in Mossley, a short stretch as curator at the Whitworth Institute in Fleetwood – belong to this period. In 1868 he settled in Blackpool as it was thought the climate would be good for his health. He then worked as a photographer and his poems were published in book form, but his income remained precarious. He died in 1893 and was buried in Layton Cemetery, Blackpool.

In 1849, when John Ambrose Fleming was born the son of a Congregational minister, the Reverend James Fleming, in Lancaster, the telegraph was only five years old. By the time of his death nearly a hundred years later, Fleming's invention, originally known as Fleming's Valve, had ushered in the age of radio and television. In 1881, after studying at University College, London, and at Cambridge University under James Clerk Maxwell, Fleming was appointed electrician to the Edison Electric Light Company of London, a position he occupied for the following ten years. He then worked as a consulting electrical engineer, advising many corporations on their electric lighting plans and problems.

Fleming's Valve, patented in 1904, was the first electronic rectifier of radio waves, converting alternating-current radio signals into weak direct currents detectable by a telephone receiver. Augmented by the amplifier grid invented in 1906 by the American Lee De Forest, Fleming's invention was the ancestor of the triode and other multi-electrode vacuum tubes. With this advance, the age of modern wireless electronics was born. Fleming lived long enough to see the results of his work help save Britain during the Second World War. Radar sets using his diodes proved decisive in the Battle of Britain.

Samuel Ryder was born on 24 March 1858 at Walton-le-Dale near Preston in Lancashire. His father, also Samuel, had a gardening business, and his mother, Elizabeth, was a dressmaker. Throughout his childhood there was friction between father and son. Sam had a brother, James. When the time came they were both sent to Owen's College in Manchester (now Manchester University), and although James completed his course, Sam did not: he left and got a job with a firm of shipping merchants in Manchester. The family later moved to Sale (at the sallow tree), on the south bank of the Mersey, two miles south of Stretford, and Samuel Senior's business expanded considerably. Sam came up with the idea of selling penny seed packets to gardeners, a plan his father had little time for, so in 1895 he moved to St Albans in Hertfordshire, where he later established the successful Heath and Heather Seed Company. By 1905 Ryder was a very successful businessman and he was elected mayor of St Albans. When his health suffered due to overwork, his doctors prescribed fresh air and light exercise as part of the cure, and he took up golf. A cricket fan and initially not keen, he would become so enthusiastic that after watching a friendly transatlantic match at Wentworth in 1926 he agreed to sponsor what became known as the Ryder Cup, offering a solid gold trophy costing £200 for a biennial golf championship between the best professional golfers in the USA and the UK.

Emmeline Goulden was born in Sloan Street, Moss Side on 14 July 1858, the eldest daughter of a family of ten children. A prodigious intellect from the start, she attended school in Manchester and Paris at a time when it was still uncommon for girls, even those in the upper classes, to be properly educated. After studying in Paris between 1873 and 1877, Emmeline Goulden returned to England to her former hometown of Manchester and married Richard Marsden Pankhurst in 1879. Pankhurst, a radical lawyer, was the author of the first women's suffrage bill in Great Britain and of the Married Women's Property Act (1882). Together they strove to promote equality for women.

In 1894 Emmeline Pankhurst became a Poor Law guardian. This involved regular visits to the Chorlton Workhouse, and she was deeply shocked by the misery and suffering of the inmates. She became particularly concerned about the way women were treated and this reinforced her belief that women's suffrage was the only way such problems could be solved. By October 1903 Emmeline Pankhurst had become frustrated at the lack of success of the Manchester branch of the National Union of Suffrage Societies, and with the help of her daughters Christabel and Sylvia she formed the Women's Social and Political Union. The organisation's motto was 'Deeds not Words' and its aim was to recruit working-class women into the fight for the right to vote. The group only really came to prominence when Emmeline moved its headquarters to London, where the WSPU was able to hold public meetings and protest marches around the capital, and in particular to the Houses of Parliament. It was an extremely efficient organisation and run much like a volunteer army. In 1906, the group was nicknamed 'the suffragettes' by the *Daily Mail*, and the name stuck.

Emmeline Pankhurst died on 14 June 1928, a month before her seventieth birthday and shortly before her life's work came to fruition and British women were granted equal voting rights to those of men on 2 July 1928.

Lottie Dodd, 'the greatest sportswoman of her day', was born in Bebington, the Wirral, Cheshire on 24 September 1871, the youngest child of a wealthy cotton broker. The winner of the Wimbledon ladies' singles title five times, the first at the age of fifteen in 1887, as part of her desire to test her versatility, she won the British ladies' golf championship in 1894.

Frank Pick was born on 23 November 1878 in Lincolnshire, into a devout middle-class Quaker family, the son of Francis Pick, a draper, and his wife Fanny. He was educated at St Peter's School in York and grew up there. After leaving school he worked for a York solicitor, George Crombie. He would always identify with the industrial and commercial values of the north, and was drawn to abstract art because of its iconoclastic free-thinking spirit. In several talks he gave to the local Salem Chapel Guild as a youth, Pick asserted that the rapidly changing urban world required radical new forms of corporate and spiritual identity. He longed to establish a 'City of Dreams', a heroic quest that would require its founders to assume the 'armour of righteousness in moments of trial and step forth spiritual giants, the warriors of the kingdom'.

He moved to London in 1906 to work as a statistical analyst for the new London Underground Group, then a private group of transport companies setting up the London Tube network. Pick believed that the system needed a corporate identity uniting its disparate elements, both as an aid to confused customers and as an elegant model of civic unity. Rising through the ranks, Pick created a distinct and unifying look for the capital's transport until 1940, when he resigned from what had then become London Transport. He commissioned artists to design what have become classic art deco advertising posters for the system, and the typographer Edward Johnston to design a special typeface to be used as a unifying symbol throughout the system alongside the famous Underground bull's-eye logo, which Pick had helped to design. He established the Underground as an aesthetic corporate body devoted to life-enhancing social service as much if not more than profits. Pick was put in charge of the entire London

Underground when it was nationalised in 1933, but declined both a knighthood and a peerage.

Novelist, audacious gay-rights pioneer and playwright Christopher William Bradshaw Isherwood, born in Disley, Stockport in 1904, was one of the first openly homosexual public figures. Best known for his *Berlin Stories* in the 1930s, he was described by Gore Vidal as 'the best prose writer in English'. 'I am a camera with its shutter open, quite passive, recording, not thinking. Recording the man shaving at the window opposite and the woman in the kimono washing her hair. Someday, all this will have to be developed, carefully printed, fixed.' 'Goodbye to Berlin', 1945.

Hylda Baker, born 4 February 1905 in Farnworth near Bolton, the eldest of seven, was educated at Plodder Lane Council School. Originally Hilda, she substituted the 'y' for show-business glamour. A feisty four-foot-ten-inch bundle of energy, the proto-feminist daughter of comedian Harold Baker made her stage debut at ten. A singer, dancer and comedienne, she wrote her own material, sketches and songs, often featuring her mute friend, Cynthia. She went on to manage her own revue show, design scenery and costumes, write scripts and music, organise the finance and tours, and star in them herself. During a brief break from show business in 1950, she owned a fish and chip shop in Farnworth.

She worked for decades in variety and music hall until a memorable television debut on *The Good Old Days* in 1955. Her film appearances included a backstreet abortionist in both *Saturday Night, Sunday Morning* and *Up the Junction*, and as Mrs Sowerberry in *Oliver!*, and she became most famous for playing Nellie Pledge in the 1968 sitcom *Nearest and Dearest*. Nellie was an uptight northern spinster who happily bickered and traded insults – off screen as well, apparently, with little affection – with fellow seasoned music-hall veteran and panto star Jimmy Jewel's debauched, grumpy Eli after they inherit their father's Lancashire pickle factory and his liquid assets of nine pounds, seven shillings and sixpence. Eli called her a 'knock-kneed knackered old nose bag; she called him a 'big girl's blouse' and a 'four-eyed barm pot'. (Jewel was born James Arthur Thomas Jewel Marsh in Sheffield on 4 December 1909, and left school at fourteen to work as a comic feed for his father, although his first stage appearance was at the age of ten in Huddersfield. Like George Formby Junior, he took his dad's stage name.)

Nearest and Dearest was so popular it had a summer season at Blackpool in 1970. Hylda later revamped the role in a slightly disguised setting in the less successful 1974 *Not on Your Nellie*, now as lovable teetotal spinster Nellie Pickersgall, called down to London to run her sick father's London pub, the Brown Cow. Her catchphrases as classic garrulous gossip included 'She knows, you know,' 'Ooh, I must get a little hand on this watch' and 'Have you been, Walter?' Walter was the ageing silent husband of her cousin Lily. Her malapropisms, presumably caused by the pickles, included 'Don't you contracept me,' 'You haven't had the pleasure of me yet' and 'What are you incinerating?'

Sir Frederic 'Freddie' Calland Williams, born in Stockport on 26 June 1911, was the electrical engineer who invented the cathode-ray-tube memory system to store digital information which heralded the dawn of the computer age. By the end of 1948, the team he led had built a working computer – the Manchester Mark I. Enhanced by Ferranti, this became the Ferranti Mark I. Early in 1951 this became the world's first commercially available computer.

Barbara Castle was born Barbara Anne Betts on 6 October 1911 in Chesterfield. Her father was a tax inspector, and his job required the family to move, first to Hull, then Pontefract and then Bradford. Barbara attended Bradford Girls Grammar School and became head girl. She wrote that 'the girls' parents were all rich, and the dainty frocks that the pupils wore did credit to the school's reputation of beauty and culture throughout'. From there she won a scholarship to St Hugh's College, Oxford. She then worked as housing correspondent of the *Daily Mirror* during the Second World War. In July 1944 she married the journalist Ted Castle, and in the 1945 general election was elected to represent Blackburn in the House of Commons. She served as the MP for Blackburn for over thirty years, and had a reputation for being tenacious, conscientious and hard-working. Soon after she was first elected, Stafford Cripps, the minister of trade, appointed Castle as one of his aides. Over the next few years she was associated with the left wing of the party led by Aneurin Bevan.

Castle was chair of the Labour Party 1958/9, and after the party won the

1964 general election the new prime minister, Harold Wilson, appointed her minister of overseas development (1964–5) and minister of transport (1965–8). In this post she introduced the 70 mph speed limit, breathalyser tests for suspected drunk drivers and compulsory seat belts. Wilson wrote in his autobiography *Memoirs: 1916–1964*, 'Barbara proved an excellent minister. She was good at whatever she touched. I doubt if any member of the Cabinet worked longer hours or gave more productive thought to what they were doing.'

Barbara Castle should have been Labour's and Britain's first female prime minister. What a role model she would have been: passionate, fiery and absolutely committed to social justice . . . Barbara's biggest achievement, of course, was the Equal Pay Act, introduced in 1970 following the strike by women workers at Ford's Dagenham plant. Women MPs were few and far between – indeed, there were more MPs called John than there were women in the House of Commons. They were the butt of sexist jokes, from Tory and Labour men alike, and stereotyped as only being interested in 'women's issues'. But Barbara never flinched from taking on the cause of equal pay. Barbara Castle was a hero to millions of British women . . . Modern politics would have been very different if she had succeeded in reforming Britain's outdated industrial relations laws in the late 1960s: her defeat at the hands of Jim Callaghan and the union barons paved the way for the 'winter of discontent' and Thatcher's landslide a decade later . . . we need a heroine like Barbara Castle to remind us that being a moderniser is entirely compatible with a commitment to social justice. Patricia Hewitt, the first female MP for Leicester West from 1997.

Highbrow showman and linguistic illusionist Anthony Burgess was born John Burgess Wilson on 25 February 1917 just over two miles to the north-east of Manchester in Harpurhey – bordered to the north by Blackley, the west by Crumpsall, the east by Moston and the south by Collyhurst – to Catholic parents, a bookkeeper and enthusiastic pianist and the music-hall musician/dancer he met at the Ardwick Empire. His mother died when he was eighteen months old, as the Spanish flu pandemic that killed millions worldwide at the end of the First World War, the greatest medical holocaust in history, devastated Manchester. Three years later his father married an Irish widow who ran the large sprawling Golden Eagle pub in Miles Platting.

Burgess was known in childhood as Jack Wilson, Little Jack and Jackie Eagle. At his confirmation the name Anthony was added and he became John Anthony Burgess Wilson, dropping the John and the Wilson as they were too common – one of a succession of shifty go-getting reinventions. He studied at Bishop Bilsborrow Primary School in Moss Side, the Xaverian College and Manchester University, reading English, and lived in the city until he was twenty-three – if not above a pub, he would say later, then an off-licence or a tobacconist's. After leaving Manchester in 1940, he never returned apart from occasional brief visits, when to him the city shrank from what it had seemed when he lived there, a vast industrial marvel studded with significant cultural landmarks, a city which could actually look down on London, to something much less. He developed a cockiness that was definitely Manchester, but then became too monstrous for it.

He spent six years as a soldier, and then went into teaching, eventually becoming an education officer in Malaya and Brunei. Invalided home in 1959 with a terminal illness, he became a professional writer in the hope that in his final year he could provide some financial security for his wife, Lynne. The diagnosis was wrong, but Burgess persisted with his new career, writing more than thirty novels and other books – including in the months he thought he was going to die, when his mind was concentrated wonderfully, encouraging him to tackle ideas about freedom of choice with psychedelic clarity, *A Clockwork Orange*. The novel made him as famous as he always believed he should be after it was turned, in 1972, into a notoriously glamorous film by Stanley Kubrick, one that for a while was thought too brutal to show, as if it might pervert young minds.

Burgess was proud of his northern roots, but, as he transformed himself from inquisitive local lad to grand gaudy intellectual, hid them behind a contrived cultured accent, forcing himself to conform, anxious his northerness might make him perpetually provincial, unable to compete with the literary and artistic greats who belonged nowhere and therefore everywhere. He had a strong interest in music, and before he became a writer intended to make a living as a composer, fancying himself a Beethoven before he fancied himself a Joyce. Wherever he lived, there was always a piano. 'My family were Manchester Catholic. We missed the Reformation, and Catholic citizens of Britain weren't allowed a higher education until the Emancipation Act. If you had any talent it always went into music. My mother was a singer in a dance band, my father a music-hall pianist. And that's still there. It's in the blood and will never leave.'

> I was born in Manchester . . . but like many people I left my hometown to join the army when the war started, and after six years abroad you tend to lose your affiliation, lose your roots, and when I came back to England I tended to be nomadic and just get a job where I could. I went abroad to Malaya and came back and tended naturally to gravitate towards the south, I suppose, near London where things seemed to be going on; but I'm still a Lancashire man, and what I want to write someday is a novel about Manchester. Very much a regional novel. I don't see myself as a regional novelist now, but I could very quickly become that, given time. I like the idea of a regional novel if the tone of the novel breathes a kind of substitute for the metropolitan. If you can present a town like Manchester or Leeds as being a sort of substitute for London where things go on and culture occurs, and the dialect is a living, intellectual force, then you've got something valuable. I don't think this has been done here yet. It was only done with one writer who's not highly regarded, that's Howard Spring. He wrote a book called *Shabby Tiger*, which was set in Manchester.

Burgess saw Manchester as a writer's city, and Mancunians as very creative, with a truculence that came from the rebelliousness in their character. He was particularly pleased, if a little alarmed, when some anonymous hate mail was delivered to the Midland Hotel, where Burgess the argumentative cosmopolitan wanderer was staying on a rare visit to his hometown in the seventies – a sign to himself that he had made it, staying in the hotel that had cost a million pounds to build at the start of the twentieth century – his city now a strangely familiar but alien place he recognised more in his idealised memories than in reality. 'We have reserved three graves for you. One for your body, one for your books and one for your ego.' He noted on one visit, 'As a place of civic planning, or rather unplanning, I think Manchester is terrible.' As far as he was concerned, Manchester had a lot to live up to as the city that gave him his start.

Tough corrupt pop impresario Don Arden, a foul-tempered and -mouthed five foot seven, 'the Al Capone of pop, the self-styled Godfather of rock, Mr Big, the most feared man in the music business', the missing link between Bernard Manning and the Krays, was born Harry Levy in Cheetham Hill, Manchester, on 4 January 1926, the son of a worker in a raincoat factory. He changed his name in 1944, having become a singer in local synagogues and a stand-up comedian at thirteen. After leaving the army at the end of the Second World War, Arden worked as an impersonator of film gangsters like Edward G. Robinson and George Raft. His authentic Al Jolson went down particularly well with Jewish audiences. In 1954, deciding there was more money to be made in promotion than performance and with his own act falling out of fashion, he became an agent, putting on his own shows, exploiting the lack of organisation there was in early pop management and accounting before the later reign of lawyers and accountants.

By 1960 he was managing American rock and roll singer Gene Vincent and bringing over to the UK American acts such as Bo Diddley, Little Richard and Chuck Berry, claiming to be the man who introduced them to Britain. He considered British rock and rollers wimpy – Cliff was 'pathetic', Billy Fury not 'fit to wipe Eddie Cochran's arse'. By the mid-sixties he was managing British pop groups, first of all the Nashville Teens and Amen Corner, and then the Small Faces, who he got to number 1 in the charts by paying Radio Caroline to play their song. He perhaps quite rightly claimed that was where they deserved to be anyway. Ten years of legal/financial disputes with the Small Faces followed, and when rival Robert Stigwood expressed interest in taking them over, Arden and three minders turned up at his office and dangled him by his ankles from a fifth-floor window until he changed his mind. 'I didn't personally hang him . . . He never bothered me again.' The stunt earned him the fearsome reputation he craved. What had begun as Arden parodying the crooked, ducking and diving, intimidating music business mogul in the wide-lapelled suit had turned into a reality. When someone tried to take his next group, The Move, away from him, he pressed a lit cigar into his rival's forehead.

After bullying, boasting, burning, beating, blackmailing and brawling his way to the top, managing Black Sabbath and the Electric Light Orchestra, and launching Jet Records, he moved into Howard Hughes's old mansion in California, next door to Cary Grant. He died in 2007, over twenty years after his reign of terror had petered out, having gifted the world, as vigorous and provocative, evil-minded jester, his daughter Sharon Osbourne. He said he had never actually killed anyone, but relished his ability to create fear and terror, bragging that those he had scared would have to keep looking over their shoulders for the rest of their lives.

Jean Alexander was born on 24 February 1926 in Liverpool, and began her working life as a library assistant, moving on to acting in 1949 at the Adelphi Guild Theatre in Macclesfield, touring around Oldham, Stockport and York. From 1964 she appeared in *Coronation Street* as wiry gossipy char Hilda Ogden née Crabtree, devoted to husband Stan, making do, looking after their four children, covering up big Stan's ample deficiencies, suffering a nervous breakdown in her slippers, stuck in a rut, getting on with things. Hilda blamed their poor run of luck, which lasted most of the sixties and seventies, on the fact their house was 13 Coronation Street. They changed it to 12A, but were ordered by the council to change it back.

Her faded floral pinny, headscarf tightly wrapped around her curlers, desperate cheerfulness, busybody energy, tireless tragi-comic hope that something would turn up despite all evidence to the contrary, sudden snapping bursts of temper, shrill trilling singing voice, ever-present fag dangling from her lower lip, the 'muriel' that covered one wall of their downstairs back room with a view of the Alps (or the Canadian Rockies) featuring three flying ducks soaring across the sky, one perpetually crooked – all made her one of the most famous women in the country, at the very opposite end of the spectrum from the Queen. When Stan kissed Hilda, or at least pecked her on the mouth, when she was for once all dolled up, he said, 'That lipstick tastes funny – what do you call that flavour?' 'Woman, Stanley,' she shot back with a look in her eye that suggested poverty, daily toilet scrubbing and the pitiless exhausting backstreets hadn't worn down her essential female spark, 'woman!'

The television dramatist, amateur sculptor, and passionate Manchester United fan Jack Rosenthal was born in Cheetham Hill, Manchester in 1931. His father Sam worked for a raincoat manufacturer, his mum Leah was nick-named Leahy, and after their house was bombed in 1939 he was evacuated to Colne near Burnley, after the war attending the local grammar school.

Although only a bus ride from Manchester, Colne was a juddering culture shock. 'To a city boy's eyes, a sort of *Just William* world of chickens, sheep, cowpats, gumboots, allotments, five-barred gates and stiles. I could barely understand a word of the east Lancashire accent. It was like a medieval foreign language. Thee's and Thou's and, on that first morning in my new school – the word yonder. I didn't know what o'er meant and I was completely flummoxed by yonder.'

He worked in a cotton mill making tea after school, where the women workers learned to lip read amidst the constant din, and then studied English literature at Sheffield University, and after National Service in the Royal Navy in 1955, as a Russian translator, he joined the promotions department of the new Granada TV company but left to work in advertising. Five years later, writing in his spare time and watching early episodes of *Coronation Street*, he wrote to its creator and head writer, Tony Warren, asking if he could write an episode – just as, fifteen years later, Morrissey would also ask.

Rosenthal was given the series' thirtieth episode to write, which was transmitted on 27 March 1961. '*Coronation Street* was identical to the street in Colne where I lived.' Jack Howarth, playing definitively grumpy, semi-lovable Uncle Albert Tatlock – not much of a stretch for the actor, born in Rochdale in 1896, son of comedian Bert, schoolfriend of Gracie Fields – who had made his debut in episode 1, already pitting his wits against hairnetted harridan Ena Sharples, was unimpressed with Rosenthal's first attempt. During a read-through of the thirty-minute episode, when someone wondered if it was too long, he remarked that 'it was thirty minutes too long'. Rosenthal would write another 129 episodes during the 1960s and become the series' most famous and successful graduate. Howarth as Tatlock would appear in 1,700 episodes of the soap until just before his death in March 1984.

Rosenthal would contribute to the unwise *Coronation Street* spin-off, *Pardon the Expression*, in which Arthur Lowe's pernickety Mr Swindley went to work in Whitehall. He produced the nicely crude sitcom *The Dustbinmen* featuring Cheese and Egg, Heavy Breathing and Smellie Ibbotson and their dustcart *Thunderbird 3*, and the wonderful curse 'pigging' while writing the ninety-minute comedy drama *There's a Hole in Your Dustbin, Delilah*. An unashamed, committed television man, he learned his trade on *Coronation Street*, and his later classic television dramas included *The Knowledge*, about trainee taxi drivers, *Spend Spend Spend*, the story of pools winner Viv

Nicholson, and *The Evacuees* – based on his own experiences, which won an Emmy. The title of his brilliant *P'tang, Yang, Kipperbang* was his school playground gang's secret password pledging undying allegiance to Burnley FC's flamboyant late-1940s winger Peter Kippax (Kipperbang).

Rosenthal's beautifully textured writing displayed his background, enthusiasms, anxieties and his affectionate but unsentimental attitude towards how friends, relatives, accidental colleagues, workers, kids, lovers – bewildered, bruised but determined – battled through the life they'd been given. He was working on *Coronation Street* in 1969 when he met ebullient Hull-born actress Maureen Lipman in a Manchester pub while she was appearing at one of the city's theatres. They married four years later, and she was always the friendly public face of the two. Rosenthal recalled, 'People do sometimes ring up and ask if I'm Mr Lipman, but I'm totally at ease with that.' Maureen once said, 'He regarded writing as a job. He had no vanity about it. He was working class, northern and Jewish. He knew he had to make a living and that was what he set out to do.'

Terry Eagleton, literary theorist, was born on 22 February 1943 and educated at the 'casually sadistic' but rigorous and scholarly Roman Catholic grammar school De La Salle College and Trinity College, Cambridge. A prolific and imaginative Marxist commentator on British literature and culture with a 'sheer horror of cliché', Eagleton's barbed, lucid *Literary Theory: An Introduction* was an academic best-seller. This powerful and elegant work was a revelation, but led to him being described in neutralising clichés: 'the most gifted Marxist thinker of his generation', 'the most influential living literary theorist', 'one of the world's leading intellectuals'. His upbringing in Salford in a 'Catholic ghetto' during the 1940s and fifties was desperately poor. He was the only kid at school with a coat. His escape from intellectual and physical poverty was literature, especially the collected works of Charles Dickens purchased on credit from a second-hand bookshop by his mum.

At Cambridge he felt 'as ignorant as a fish' but never lost his self-confidence and never wandered far from his distinctly Manchester Irish-Catholic background. His early career focused more on theology than literary criticism, although the merging of the two was his stated intention. In 1964 Eagleton was a founding editor of *Slant*, a journal 'devoted to a Catholic exploration of . . . radical politics'. 'I was a socialist, to be sure, but I was anxious to know how far to the left a Catholic could go without falling off the edge.' The *Daily Mail* called him 'a Marxist punk with a chip on both shoulders' and Prince Charles once dubbed him 'dreadful'. One of his essential arguments is that postmodernism, with its narcissistic view of the world as fragmented and truth as indeterminate, is an inadequate successor to Marxism, which in its critique of capitalism can offer a more concrete moral vision for society.

(Sir) James Anderton, born in Wigan on 4 May 1932, studied criminology at the Victoria University of Manchester. Proud of his working-class Lancashire roots, he was appointed chief constable – the youngest ever – of Greater Manchester Police, England's largest provincial force, on 23 October 1976. A lay preacher convinced he had a hot line to God, his fierce Christian beliefs, hard-nosed morality and commitment to duty saw him called both 'God's copper' and a 'copper's copper'. Admirers praised his approach to policing and social control; critics questioned his mental health.

On 6 May 1932 John David 'Jack' Bond was born in Kearsley, Bolton. His father had worked as a spinner in the local mill and sat as a Labour member on Little Hulton Council, serving one year as mayor. They turned the front parlour of their house into a fish and chip shop and his mother worked there from Monday to Saturday. Jack started playing for Lancashire County Cricket Club in 1955, and after years of dogged, underwhelming but conscientious hard work became captain almost by default on a temporary basis in the late 1960s. Tough and shrewd, Bond led Lancashire for five seasons from 1968 to 1972, during which they finished third in the championship in 1970 and 1971. In 1969 the forty-over Sunday League started, and Bond's talented, gutsy Lancashire were its first winners. 'Some of the counties, like Yorkshire, weren't interested at all. They thought it was a bit of a joke. But our success created so much interest. We won the title at Nuneaton. It was a two o'clock start and we had so many supporters come down that they'd run out of pies by one. And they ran out of beer.' They won the Sunday League again the following year and a hat-trick of Gillette Cups (1970, 1971, and 1972).

(Sir) Peter Maxwell Davies, born in Langworthy, Salford on 8 September 1934, was the son of Thomas and Hilda. After attending Leigh Grammar School, he studied at the University of Manchester and at the Royal Manchester (now Royal Northern) College of Music, where his fellow students included Harrison Birtwistle – born in Accrington, 1934, composing by the age of eleven – Alexander Goehr, Elgar Howarth and John Ogdon. Together they formed New Music Manchester, a group dedicated to the exploration and distribution of experimental contemporary music influenced by the works of Berg, Bartók, Webern and Schoenberg.

Equally inspired by serialism and medieval music, writer of some of the most beautiful music of the twentieth century, and some of the most challenging, Maxwell Davies ranks among leading contemporary composers such as Boulez, Henze and Carter; he is a successor to the international avant-garde generation of Xenakis, Berio, Takemitsu, Ligeti and Lutoslawski, but also to the heady high-minded British tradition of Elgar, Tippett and Britten. Davies is a freeman of the city of Salford, along with L. S. Lowry.

However wild, metaphysical, disturbing and gorgeous his music, there is always Salford grain, rebellion and defiance. 'Cross Lane Fair' is a musical impression of the fairground his parents took him to in the late 1930s: 'We do what you do at the fair. We visit various rides and side-shows: a ghost train and a carousel, a juggler, a bearded lady and a five-legged sheep.' The last two, Davies recalls, 'were exhibited in a mysterious darkened tent, among other curiosities, where one paid threepence to enter'. He also wrote a tone poem based on his childhood memories of the bleak Chat Moss, south of Leigh, which caused George Stephenson so much grief when he built the Manchester to Liverpool railway line. The short piece is a form of exploratory sonic engineering inspired by Stephenson's engineering ingenuity in crossing the black, miry landscape.

Jim Lovelock, who became editor of the *Stockport Express* at twenty-eight in 1949, was as notorious for his socialising as he was famous for writing, and was in turn journalist, author, potholer and mountaineer. Born in Edgeley, up the hill from Mersey Square, Jim overcame polio as a child of six, to become a legendary caver and climber, despite also losing his sight in one eye. His father had decided against a calliper and instead bought him a small bicycle with only one pedal to strengthen his polio-afflicted leg. 'He was an entertaining raconteur too,' noted a colleague, 'often fulfilling the old journalistic maxim of never letting the facts get in the way of a good story. Jim was a brilliant bloke.' Following in the footsteps of another Stockport explorer, Admiral Sir George Back, Jim also famously went on a 16,000-mile adventure to the Stockport Islands in Canada.

John Mayall – bandleader, mentor, multi-instrumentalist, wanderer – was born in Macclesfield, Cheshire on 29 November 1933. His father Murray was a keen amateur dance-band musician with a good jazz record collection, and by 1945, before even reaching his teens, John had become an enthusiastic guitarist and started to learn the piano. He gravitated towards the blues and built up a substantial collection of records. He started playing professionally in 1955, moving in 1963 from Manchester to London on the advice of Alexis Korner. His record collection would form the basis of the school – his ever-evolving group the Bluesbreakers – that all his young recruits attended. Eric Clapton, who lived for a while with Mayall absorbing and copying his collection, Jack Bruce, Davy Graham, Peter Green, Andy Fraser and Mick Taylor were all part of his experiment in finding a British context for the blues and feeding it into mainstream consciousness. This was a significant and direct influence on the great British rock album of the late 1960s.

Artist Trevor Grimshaw was born in Hyde in 1947, and from the age of sixteen to twenty-one studied at Stockport College of Art. He painted and drew a northern landscape related to Lowry's in that it was both all in the mind and rooted in reality, radically personal and yet almost commonplace – a north he remembered as if it was the truth, which it was but wasn't, because he moved the buildings, landmarks and hills around in his mind, abstractly pressed them together, and generated a perversely ideal version of depression, isolation and absence, fixing the past in place, anticipating how this north was in the process of disappearing, even as it left behind signs and structures that this was how it once was. As with Lowry, his north was a form of confession that appeared to give nothing away about who he was and what he was like, but ultimately said everything. Photographs can show how, in the years between its urgent industrial expansion and subsequent decline, the north around Manchester and Stockport, out towards the peaks and moors, had a certain bleary bleakness, a crammed, stained ugliness or a defiant, stoical beauty, an unearthly grace. Grimshaw's unfluctuating images express the less physical even as they reflect nothing but

The Preston bypass, 1958

the physical. He transformed the valleys, canals, viaducts, trains, telegraph poles, factories, machines, waste ground, alleyways, cindery mud and stone skies into pure grey spirit drained of colour, as though the industrial north was constructed out of smoke, shadows and radiant but oppressive emptiness, in which the people, roaming and teeming across Lowry's streets and fields, had been abandoned or absorbed, so that what was in reality full of life became ghostly and anonymous.

Lowry had three large works by Grimshaw in his own collection alongside paintings by Rossetti, Maddox Brown and Lucien Freud, and Grimshaw would visit Lowry in Mottram-in-Longendale. Grimshaw painted Stockport Viaduct, and it was clearly the same Stockport Viaduct that Lowry painted, but so much from another mind, born into another age, with a different level of melancholy and wonder. In 1973 Grimshaw went to 10 Downing Street to deliver a pair of drawings bought by Prime Minister Edward Heath after he saw them displayed at a Tory conference held in Blackpool.

In his forties and fifties, drifting into obscurity, not as affectionately thought of as Lowry, Grimshaw became a recluse and an alcoholic, and five years after his final show, in the County Museum and Art Gallery at Prostejov, Moravia, Czech Republic, he died in a fire at his home. The smoke of infinity he set his north inside gathered him up, as though he had known all along where he was heading and was using his paintings to predict that his end would involve light and murk and ash, and a final, comprehensive veiling of compressed energy.

John Foxx was born Dennis Leigh in Chorley, eight miles north of Wigan, eleven miles south-west of Blackburn, eleven miles north-west of Bolton, twelve miles south of Preston, nineteen and a half miles north-west of Manchester, on 26 September 1947, the son of a coal-mining father and a mill-working mother. His maternal grandmother was a 'life-long, Lancashire-industrial variety spiritualist'. He was reading futurist manifestos by nine, playing amongst derelict local mills, and after attending local schools and art college in Preston, he won a scholarship to the Royal College of Art in London, escaping what he saw as a backward local music scene.

His experimental mentality led to exploring the constantly evolving new sounds made available through the invention of synthesisers and the rapid development in tape-recording processes. He had started performing by singing with a 12-string acoustic guitar in Bolton in 1973, and in a room over a Salford pub, but soon developed an urge to follow the radical, avant-rock lead set by the Velvet Underground. In 1976, in London, after a few false starts, and almost joining an early version of the Clash, he had helped form Ultravox!, looking back to an idealised self-consciously high-brow form of art-glam music, and over the head of punk, to the electronic pop groups that would look to early Ultravox for inspiration – soon without the exclamation mark – as much as Kraftwerk, Can, Bowie and Eno.

Leaving Ultravox by 1980, before they became a more ordinary pop group, his first two solo albums, *Metamatic* and *The Garden*, were like precise, vision-ary J. G. Ballard commentaries turned into intense dreamlike musicals. Always one step ahead of fashion, exiled until the twenty-first century from critical currents, when his experiments with form and sound made more sense, he was almost wilfully off the beat of commercial acceptance.

His lonely, striving music constantly imagined potential futures by explor-ing both utopian and dystopian landscapes, investigating how cities, and the space around them, trigger and re-programme our memories. His other work, as a photographer, painter, theorist and as a graphic designer using his non-stage name designing book covers for the likes of Anthony Burgess and Jeanette Winterson, demonstrates an essential intellectual elegance and curiosity. However space age, dislocated and alienated his music became, however Ballardian, surreal and abstract his conceptual concerns, he remained fixed in a northern time and space. He has talked of how his childhood coincided with the dissolution of the northern factories, the devastation of World War II, and the construction of motorways. 'Everything was change: decline, ruins, overgrowth, then re-growth.'

Dr C. P. – Christopher Paul – Lee, film historian, senior lecturer in cultural studies at Salford University, academic, member of the 1970s surreal musical comedy troupe Alberto Y Los Trios Paranoias (along with vagabond meta-Manchester music man, as much from the muddy 1760s as the rock and roll 1960s, drummer Bruce Mitchell), author of a book on Bob Dylan's appearance at the Manchester Free Trade Hall on 17 May 1966, at which Dylan was called 'Judas' by an audience member, was born in Manchester in 1950. Lee, who was at the Free Trade Hall that night, brought with him into this Lowry world not just spidery, volatile alley poet Dylan but also another of his favourite subjects, the unpredictably subversive slapstick comedian Frank 'Bah, I've supped some stuff tonight' Randle.

Born Arthur Hughes in Standish, Wigan in 1901, once a friend of George Formby, who he later reviled for selling out to the soft south while he stuck to his wild northern guns, Randle began as an acrobat called Arthur Twist. As a child, he sold 't' finest oranges in Wiggin at t' middle of Chorley market site proper next to t' pump'. For a while he was a sports-car-loving superstar earning thousands a week, more popular in the north than cautious, docile Formby, dressing up as a variety of crackpot characters – randy ruffians, cursing deadbeats and belching buffoons. He always appeared on stage without teeth, exaggerating his grotesqueness: southern critics said he lacked polish; he replied, 'What do you think I am – a coffin?' When he appeared at the London Palladium, most of those in the expensive front-row seats made a rapid exit when he threw his dentures into the audience – when you couldn't immediately think of anything funny to say, whipping out the false teeth for a quick gurn was good for a giggle. He would appear in a bathing costume.

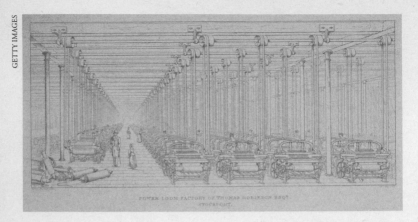

Engraving by Joseph Wilson Lowry after drawing a by James Nasmyth detailing
the interior of a power loom factory in Stockport, 1949

'By God, that watter was cold. When I came out I didn't know whether
my name was Angus or Agnes.' Always a bit of a bugger with a screw or
two loose, spotlessly anti-authoritarian, he once bombarded Blackpool
– or possibly Accrington – with toilet rolls from a plane after a censor-
ship row.

The eight rickety rollicking cheap-as-chips films he starred in for John E.
Blakely's defiantly local Mancunian Films during the 1940s, before his career
was effectively vaporised by television, madly outdid the corn and crudity of
the coming Carry On films: in *Somewhere in Camp* from 1942 he is a soldier
riding a donkey on parade being asked by his sergeant what he thinks he is
doing. 'Sitting on me ass!' In Randle's last Mancunian film, the drunkenly
chaotic *It's a Grand Life*, the one-man Lancastrian Marx Brothers, either the
funniest man alive or the most deflated, still playing a private at fifty, appears
with Diana Dors, whose stunt double was Pat Phoenix, later to play sharp,
passionate Elsie Tanner in *Coronation Street*. (The film used the imposing
exterior of Xaverian College in Rushholme, near to its studios, for some of its
scenes.) In the early 1950s, threatened by new forms of entertainment, he
referred to the new craze of skiffle as 'piffle'. Beaten down by debt, neglect
and alcohol abuse – towards the end it would take an entire bottle of whisky
to get him on stage – he died in 1957.

John Noakes, born 6 March 1934, in Shelf, near Halifax, a member of the classic John, Pete and Val *Blue Peter* line-up between 1967 and 1972, proud owner of Shep, the most famous *Blue Peter* dog after Petra, often used the Frank Randle catchphrase, 'Get off me foot!'

Mark Edward Smith, pitch-black comedian, fierce philosopher, singer, memoirist, sadist, scholar, gentleman, lover, hater, drinker, man with a black-hole grin like Randle and 'veteran rocker' (*Daily Mail*) is born in Salford on 5 March 1957, moving three miles north to Prestwich (priest's farmed land) when he is six months old, earliest memory having a hot wash aged four before first day at school, leaves school at sixteen, works in a meat factory, is a docker at eighteen, auditions for local heavy-metal bands but is rejected for being tone-deaf and/or obnoxious.

He deforms The Fall in 1976 'to have raw music with really weird vocals over it' and for decades is its only continuous member, organising the musicians, sound and things around him like Miles Davis or John Mayall. The Fall become known as John Peel's favourite band possibly because they never stop and never will and always sound the same but different, and to some extent satisfy those wondering what Frank Randle would sound like leading a group as a fan of Can, Captain Beefheart and the Stooges. The Fall songs doggedly rummage through Smith's taut bustling mind, which is something to be scared of, which is inside the north, which is inside his mind, which is made up of words, chopped-up blood and thunder, soiled Bury blues and dank cruel smells.

Manchester was pretty grey in the seventies, he says. 'I liked them days. It's turning touristy now. I can't keep pace with it. I work away a lot and every time I come back there's some new monstrosity of a building sprung up.'

Morrissey's favourite Fall single was their seventh, 'Lie Dream of a Casino Soul', released in 1981. He once assured me the name of his group, the Smiths, was not a tribute to Mark. Smith called Morrissey south Manchester and Catholic as opposed to his north Manchester and Protestant. Morrissey stands close in this Lowry painting to the three greatest Manchester guitar players:

Johnny Marr, born in Ardwick, 31 October 1963, Manchester rapture, rain and romance ringing in his ears, streaming into his songs, lifting the Smiths to greatness, a candidate to feature in an ideal Bob Dylan band. Vini Reilly, born on 4 August 1953 in Higher Blackley, a candidate to feature in an ideal Miles Davis ensemble, Manchester/moorland gulfs of shadow, darkening skies and dreams of winter pouring from his fingers. Roy Harper, born in Rusholme, Manchester on 12 June 1941, who also has one of the loveliest most sensuous darknightofthesoul voices of any Manchester musician, with a desperate, cunning mind – often at the end of its tether and then completely in control – which cuts into and through the dream universe as deftly as De Quincey, E. Gaskell, A. Burgess or E. Smith.

At fourteen he formed a group, De Boys, with his brothers David and Harry. At fifteen home life became too much and he left, lying about his age to join the RAF, where he performed skiffle at camp concerts and ultimately suffered a self-induced nervous breakdown, which led to committal to Lancaster Moor Mental Institute and extreme forms of treatment including electroconvulsive therapy. At some point during his short stay at the hospital Roy was beaten for dressing without permission and then escaped through a bathroom window wearing his pyjamas. He was arrested a few weeks later while attempting to climb the clock tower at St Pancras station in London.

While serving one year in Walton Jail, Liverpool, Harper was put in charge of the library and began reading philosophy and writing poetry, all the while practising his frenetic, ethereal guitar. He was released in 1964 and travelled around North Africa and Europe for over a year playing his guitar. He began to perform in folk clubs to make a living and express his twisting, twisted mind, and was soon offered the chance to record by a small independent label, Strike. His first album, in 1966, *The Sophisticated Beggar*, featured his cracked, epic poetry and cracked folk melodies sung over complex acoustic guitar arrangements, generating an inflamed calm utilising Echoplex reverb and other effects. This record boasts the first known use of electric guitar effects on an acoustic guitar. The opening song, 'China Girl', reflects the increasing numbers of immigrants arriving in Rusholme in the 1950s, especially from newly independent India and newly created Pakistan as well as China. The immigrants quickly got their bearings, creating a chain of gaudy Asian restaurants along a section of Rusholme still known today as Curry Mile.

Harper would go on to write a radiant and traumatised series of albums that made him the closest compulsive European chronicler, curator, surrealist, troubadour, explorer, comedian, phantom, realist and illusionist to Bob Dylan – taking personal hold of history, seizing control of cities and loners, a life that began so abruptly and tragically in slummy wartime Rusholme, birthplace of L. S. Lowry, through voice, guitar and supernatural mental effort.

76

Along the way, with paint and a particular presence of mind, Lowry monitored a solid world that was subsiding, the Victorian era breaking down, the murky climax of the industrial era, people crawling like refugees among the half-magical ruins of a once-heroic construction of new wealth and reason, marooned on an island where it seemed just about possible to live. He drifted in his own dry, disaffiliated way through the thirties, forties, fifties, sixties, seventies, the decades leading to his death, further and further away from his Victorian beginnings, deeper and deeper into the daunting, enthralling white blanks in his paintings. His fame grew. His resistance to accolades, admiration, awards remained stubborn: he was renowned for turning down an OBE, a CBE and a knighthood – the last offered by Harold Wilson, a great fan, who used Lowry paintings for his Christmas cards while in office: *The Skaters* in 1964 and the epic near-futurist composite industrial landscape *The Pond* in 1965. As far as Lowry was concerned, Stockport Viaduct was more worthy of an honour.

The Pond was painted in 1950, and features Stockport Viaduct as a distant apparition amid an uncanny treeless weatherless glory of sublimely dull grey-white sky, smoking chimneys, rusty-brick houses, bobbing boats, cracked walls, spindly poles and anonymous preoccupied people. In 1967 Lowry's *Coming Out of School* appeared on the highest-denomination postage stamp in a series dedicated to 'great British artists' (the others were Gainsborough, Reynolds and Constable). Eleven million were sold inside a month. His north, built around his own isolation from and vaguely official involvement in

Lancashire life, was being appropriated by those yearning for a simpler, rosier but inattentive view of an imaginary north that was fast disappearing.

It was easy to see why his depiction of a lost illusory north was attractive to those feeling wistful about its disappearance and the disappearance of their own youth, which brought with it the increasingly realistic approach of death, but this response missed out on a lot of the bent, troubled wit, reprobate uneasiness and apprehension, the creation of a lurid, devious myth, the strange, tender affinity with inanimate objects where it could seem he loved a broken fence more than a human being. It missed how he set his buildings, characters, gatherings, stories, memories, waterways, Victorian and post-Edwardian yearnings inside a void that was ultimately more modern than anything that came after, however new and fashionable. The void is always of the moment, and never goes out of date, whatever else comes along. (The eleven-year-old me, the short-trousered boy in 1968 Stockport, more at home in the shopping precinct, would not have been thinking any of this about Lowry, who would have seemed a relic, like the viaduct, like the enormous, heavyhearted buildings abandoned around central Manchester, old and irrelevant, and his flat-footed matchstick men stupidly comic. It takes time to get inside the mind of Lowry and the way he got inside time, and inside his mind there isn't a soothing past to remember, but a confirmation of how the memory plays tricks and of how difficult it is to represent positively the passing of time, and a devastating loss or redirecting of energy.)

Lowry looked at the Stockport Viaduct and couldn't believe what he was seeing. He said that he was haunted by it, the millions of bricks and the ordinary, heroic men who had dug up the clay, baked the bricks, loaded them, unloaded them, cemented them together, and faded into exhausted obscurity, anonymously leaving their masterpiece. For him it wasn't that it was about and belonged in the past, it wasn't that it represented the Victorian spirit that built a new society that along the way created and then abandoned millions of people; it was simply its sheer presence, which was both ethereal and colossal, inscrutably dominating the area. Each silent, strong brick demanded attention but then became part of this terrific structure, which could seem both spiritually imposing and unexceptionally familiar and worthy – mighty and matter of fact.

Bricks were a sign of wealth during the Georgian period at the end of the eighteenth and the beginning of the nineteenth century, with landowners and merchants refronting their properties with the recently standardised bricks, nine inches long, four and a half inches wide and two and a half inches thick, to create regular, pleasing patterns. By the mid-nineteenth century, as the manufacture of bricks became like most things mechanised, more bricks were being made and laid than ever before – now a cheap efficient way to build the factories, bridges and warehouses that were increasingly required. The Stockport Viaduct was a demonstration of how the quality, accuracy and density of bricks had improved, and how cement set quicker and stronger, which was vital for the speed of construction that the industrial age demanded.

It was built by the Manchester and Birmingham Railway, and was a key component in linking Manchester and Crewe, as investors explored plans for more lines south of Manchester. Designed by renowned pioneering bridge engineer George Watson Buck, working for Robert Stephenson's team building the railway, it used 27 semicircular arches each with a span of 63 feet, cunningly and prophetically perfectly wide enough to accommodate a motorway, which over a century later would pass underneath. It rose 111 feet over the River Mersey Valley; it was 2,200 feet long; it took 21 months to build, the first stone laid on 9 March 1839; it was built by contractors Tomkins and Holmes of Liverpool; 600 labourers worked in shifts day and night; it was completed in 1840, four days before Christmas, opened for travel in 1842, and was constructed out of neat layer upon layer of red bricks (11 million of them) set in lime mortar; and it cost £72,000.

The Stockport Viaduct was the largest brick structure in the world at that time, and perhaps this is what touched Lowry, that out of these ordinary blocks something so vast, grandiose and functional could emerge, which made the double-decker buses that drove through its gaping caverns seem so minute. Reports suggest there were three fatalities during the construction – two passers-by hit by falling objects and one worker plunging off the scaffolding. The viaduct was widened by

Scafell rock formation in the Lake District

24 feet in the late 1880s, so that four tracks could be carried over Stockport, meaning that by the time Lowry came to consider it and wonder what it all really meant, there were possibly over 20 million bricks in front of him.

Perhaps Lowry kept returning to it because he imagined what it was like out of context, not taking trains over Stockport to and from London and Manchester but nonchalantly floating free of its location, a mesmerising combination of the ordinary and the spectacular. He kept sketching it, sizing it up, rolling his imagination over its bricks, embracing the image, working out why it was he was so fascinated, as if he would eventually work out what it was, and perhaps, tied up in the bricks and their arrangement, there might be some clue as to the mystery of the universe itself. Maybe he noticed in its isolated immensity something of the loneliness he felt – 'Had I not been lonely none of my works would have happened.'

It is as well so matter of fact, as if once the bricks were placed exactly where they were meant to be, and the arches were completed, and the railway laid over the top, and the trains could travel high over the town of Stockport, over the river, over the mills and warehouses lining the river, then that was it, job done. Lowry could identify with that sense of getting on with things, in the order they were meant to be, according to decisions that seem to have been made above and beyond anyone's control.

'It often appears in my pictures,' he said, as usual giving little away. 'As I make them up, I suddenly know I must bring in the Stockport Viaduct.' Why remains a mystery, and perhaps that mystery is connected to the mystery of the viaduct itself, the result of so much effort and commitment and ingenuity but also just there, where it is, doing its job, for as long as it takes. The fact that an 1840 act of Parliament ensured that all trains crossing the viaduct, in and out of the north and south, stopped at Stockport meant that it was never indifferently passed over on the way to somewhere else. The viaduct kept Stockport in the middle of things even when it was sliding out of history.

Four years after it was built Friedrich Engels is in a train crossing the viaduct, with a clear view over slumping cavernous Stockport, which he seems pleased to be seeing from a distance.

There is Stockport, too, which lies on the Cheshire side of the Mersey, but belongs never the less to the manufacturing district of Manchester. It lies in a narrow valley along the Mersey, so that the streets slope down a steep hill on one side and up an equally steep one on the other, while the railway from Manchester to Birmingham passes over a high viaduct above the city and the whole valley. Stockport is renowned throughout the entire district as one of the duskiest, smokiest holes, and looks, indeed, especially when viewed from the viaduct, excessively repellent. But far more repulsive are the cottages and cellar dwellings of the working-class, which stretch in long rows through all parts of the town from the valley bottom to the crest of the hill. I do not remember to have seen so many cellars used as dwellings in any other town of this district.

77

If you look at photographs of how the deep-set centre of Stockport looked in 1964, it seems still arrested in the rickety and smoky post-Industrial Revolution northern 1930s. Engels would have recognised it as the same foul place he had seen from the viaduct. It had been taken for all it was worth, all its local facilities and resources drained, its natural energy squeezed and shaken until there was nothing left, used, abused, coated in filth and sundry deposits, and left to if not rot then fend for itself. Stockport in 1964 looked as if it was about to waste away into the dampness that once made the hats that now in a hatless town mingled with the dust and muck that was getting too thick to ever wipe away.

Lowry loved hats, flat or bowler, bonnet or school cap. Hats topped off his north as much as smog, fog, smokestack, clock tower, church steeple, umbrella or sloping shoulders, although sometimes, oddly but perfectly, a kerb or a boot, a smoked-down fag, a bottom step or the curve of the street would top things off. He loved his own hat, the homburg that carried and deflected the weight of the world, but as once-solid formalities broke down in the post-war transformation of duty, aspiration and expectation, it came to represent conservatism, cracked class divisions, old-fashioned values, a disreputable character, fusty professionalism, and was becoming as much an explicit comic symbol as a prized sign of status and self-worth. Exiled by his attitudes from the changing world, Lowry kept his hat, comic, quirky, defunct or not; Stockport, on its last legs, choking on the smoke, needing to change with the world or sink from view, chucked its away. As one-time home of the hat, in a nineteenth-century world where every man and boy wore one – round, high, broad-brimmed, brimmed, not brimmed – or a cap made out of folded paper if they couldn't afford one, this was quite a statement.

Stockport in 1964 was, knowingly or not, awaiting the giant blade of renewal. Lugubrious double-decker buses stubbornly pushed through its dreary preserved gloom, following routes set in stone during the Industrial Revolution which now seemed to do nothing much but go round in circles. People went this way, people went that way, but there was no sense that they would ever be able to go another way, a surprising way. The buildings, filth and duty left behind by the century-old surge of activity and adventure meant there was nowhere to go but this way and that way and sometimes meet in the middle. And along the way there was the pub, the office, school, the factory, tired shops, a television set, a radio programme, a day trip, a football match, a film matinee, a night out, an inevitable return to the this way and that.

Wellington Road, which had been built as long ago as 1826, crossing the lowest part of the river valley by means of an eleven-arched viaduct 50 feet above the river, still performed its original function of ensuring traffic avoided the steep slopes and narrow streets of the historic town centre. It had been named after the Duke of Wellington, when he was still something of a hero because of his defeat of Napoleon at Waterloo. (The old Etonian Tory prime minister would soon become unpopular, certainly in industrialised, expanding Manchester, for his government's stubborn resistance to political and social reform. He expressed initial hostility to the idea of railways, considering cheap travel and the subsequent emancipation of ordinary people could lead to revolution. 'It will only encourage the lower classes to move about,' he said.)

The bypassing of the centre of Stockport – a forerunner of twentieth-century road schemes – was controversial, but it was seen as an important way of improving transport links between Manchester and Buxton, and beyond that to London. Before Wellington Road, Hillgate was the main route into and out of Stockport, the core around which the town centre developed during the eighteenth and early nineteenth centuries. As an important coaching route, Hillgate was studded with inns, houses, shops and early signs of industrial activity. The streets laid out at right angles to it contained factories and terraced housing, some arranged in steeply sloped steps set into the hillside. By the 1960s Hillgate was an accumulation of Georgian, Victorian and Edwardian structures embedded in a medieval market town so that from step to step you skipped through time.

After Wellington Road was built, development of the centre had slowed down: old buildings stayed where they were, and it was never as radically redeveloped as other areas nearby, which by the 1960s were blighted by industrial decline and lethargy. In the Hillgate area, where Lower led to Middle led to Upper, the past was never rubbed out, lanes and alleyways were never widened or destroyed: some views of rooftops, gutters, lamp posts, railings, chimneys and steps were much as they'd been a hundred years before, and ultimately, dominating everything whether you could see it or not, was the gigantic viaduct dwarfing the Wellington Road bridge that carried trains over the Stockport gorge into and out of Manchester.

The bus square built to the east of Wellington Bridge in the early 1900s near the river was then joined by a new shopping precinct called, with a touch of the futuristic, Merseyway, an awry, slum-clearing sliver of boiled-down Brasilia slotted amongst the shabby remains of eighteenth-century streets and industrial endeavour.

Merseyway transformed the town centre and made it all seem almost contemporary, slyly encouraging locals to think positively about their surroundings, but its minimalist clock tower was not the sort of blackened edifice L. S. Lowry was interested in. If he had ever entered Merseyway, where shops had been turned into mere containers of goods, he would have instantly disappeared in a glum puff of smoke.

78

1804

The Rochdale Canal was the first canal to cross the intimidating barrier of the Pennines, linking the industrial areas of Huddersfield, Bradford, Leeds and Halifax with Manchester and Liverpool. Within months, the 50-ton *Mayflower*, a seagoing vessel, was taken across the Pennines from Hull to Liverpool. The canal's 32-mile route was finally completed after various sections were opened in 1798 and 1799, five years after construction began. The Rochdale runs from Sowerby Bridge in West Yorkshire and passes through Hebden Bridge and Todmorden before skirting around Rochdale and Oldham meeting the Bridgewater Canal at Castlefield Junction in Manchester. To get over the Pennines without the need for tunnels meant that it had to climb 350 feet to a summit of 600 feet in just 14 miles after leaving Sowerby Bridge on the eastern side and then fall over 500 feet through Failsworth and Chadderton into Manchester on the western side. It required 92 locks including the deepest lock in the UK at Tuel Lane. There were also 100 bridges, two major aqueducts and only two short tunnels. In its first few years the most popular cargo was timber, salt, cement, wool, grain and coal, and a load of about 35 tons could be dispatched by barge from Todmorden in the evening and be in Manchester by the following morning.

1803

Manchester scientist John Dalton, born in 1766 in a tiny thatched cottage in the village of Eaglesfield, Cumberland, starts using symbols to represent the atoms of different elements. He is one of the first scientists to note that all matter is made up of small particles, or atoms.

1802

'. . . we were afraid of being bewildered in the mists till the Darkness should overtake us – we were long before we knew that we were in the right track . . .'
Dorothy Wordsworth, *The Grasmere Journals*, January 1802.

It was during a visit on a stormy day to Gowbarrow at Ullswater on Thursday 15 April 1802 that William Wordsworth was inspired to write what is perhaps his most famous and evocative poem, 'The Daffodils'. William had been accompanied by Dorothy on the excursion to the lake. She apparently wrote a description of the place on the spot in her journal: 'They tossed and reeled and danced and seemed as if they verily laughed with the wind that blew upon them over the lake.' William is reported to have relied upon her description when composing the famous poem.

1800

Aged fifteen, Thomas De Quincey entered Manchester Grammar School and learned some important literary lessons while he was there, reading the early works of William Wordsworth, Samuel Taylor Coleridge, and other English Romantic poets who would greatly influence his own writing. He became so miserable and bored he ran away after eighteen months, undertaking a 'pedestrian excursion' through Wales, often sleeping rough to save money. De Quincey disliked the upper schoolroom, an immense building 96 feet long and 36 feet wide, with a ceiling between 20 and 30 feet high – 'though of ample proportions, the room was dreary' – and complained that 'the external walls, which might have been easily and at little expense adorned with scenes from classic history, were quite bare'. In his recollection, 'nothing relieved the monotony'.

William Wordsworth, in his Preface to the second edition (1800) of *Lyrical Ballads*, asserted that the rise of technology had blunted the mind 'to a state of almost savage torpor'.

1799

Everyone with ambition wanted to come to Manchester; it was the place to make your fame and fortune. Archibald Prentice, later to become a reformer and journalist, describes how, at the end of the eighteenth century, he persuaded his Scots employer to concentrate his trade there. 'He said, "We have coal, and industry, and shrewdness, and intelligence here." "Yes," I replied, "you have, but you have not centrality; you are in a corner; you have nothing; you have nothing but Glasgow and Paisley here; Manchester has about a dozen of Paisleys – Wigan, Preston, Blackburn, Bolton, Bury, Rochdale, Ashton, Stockport, and numerous fast-growing villages, all increasing in importance, and likely, some time or other, if fair play is given to their industry, to form one enormous community." After a long pause, he asked, "When can you go to take a warehouse?"'

In December 1799 William and Dorothy Wordsworth moved into Dove Cottage in Grasmere.

1795

Sir Thomas Percival, a Manchester physician, leads a group of doctors who form the Manchester Board of Health to supervise textile mills and recommend hours and working conditions. Their report led Sir Robert Peel to introduce the Health and Morals of Apprentices Act of 1802. Children were only permitted to work twelve hours per day (considered an improvement), walls had to be washed and visitors had to be admitted to factories to make suggestions.

1792

By the time of his death on 3 August 1792 industrial innovator Richard Arkwright had established factories in Derbyshire, Staffordshire, Lancashire and Scotland, and was a wealthy man.

79

Suddenly, Stockport went all 1965, as if this once-thriving hat-making area, this ruined kingdom of mills and entrepreneurial adventure now struggling beside an embattled almost eastern European mid-sixties Manchester and its deteriorating inner suburbs, could swing a bit, as if the local council was terrified that the town was the very symbol of the end of an era, of a town sinking into its past.

The town planners did not want a Stockport where Lowry with his musty-tinted glasses felt at home, a crooked funereal town swathed in smoke, grime and ash in which the grass was black, the trees made up of soot as much as bark, trapping the town in an eternal past profoundly separated from the pop culture that had popped up as fab as a fable the other end of the Mersey. They wanted a Stockport where traces of the industries that had tired themselves out and failed to keep up with changing trends and minds were obliterated, a Stockport where amnesiac teenagers like me could feel at home without feeling we were disappearing into the static void populated with headstrong loners that Lowry painted. Lowry's people were standing about, together and separate, avoiding colliding with each other, spilling, scurrying, splintering, grave, acceptant, dazed in the damp cold air, pores packed with grit, gloom at their shoulders, working their fingers, their arms, their legs, to the bone, wondering what it all meant, one foot in the boxed-up nineteenth century, one in Lowry's own leg-pulling mind.

Into the Lowry space, which he based on his own sense of what had happened to time and people since he was born, popped an incongruous shop – in fact a boutique – called the Toggery, a place where you could buy the sort of clothes that pop stars wore, because, so it was said, although it seems as far-fetched as the thought that Dickens, Darwin and Disraeli bought their hats in Stockport, the pop stars themselves bought their clothes there. The Mersey Square shop was owned by Michael Cohen, the son of an Ashton under Lyne tailor, himself the son of a nineteenth-century Oldham tailor, and Mike adapted his dad and granddad's tailoring to the needs of the pre-mod, mod and postmod man about town, offering both ready-to-wear and bespoke clothing. He sold Rael Brook and Ben Sherman shirts, Leslie Powell suits and Annello and Davide Cuban-heeled boots.

It was ahead of its time, open by 1961, around the time the odd local cafe might have introduced a jukebox, and before my time, but those who were there speak of a fashionable hangout where the new beat groups from Manchester and Liverpool would buy their emphatically outspoken anti-parent clothes – the sort that by the end of the 1960s I was craving myself – and invent their images. These were dashing, sexually challenging clothes saturated with the confident colour that had drained out of the exhausted post-war environment, influenced by, and influencing, Carnaby Street culture, and in the spirit of Raymond Clark, who was born in Warrington on 9 June 1942.

Evacuated during the war, Clark grew up on the Lancashire–Yorkshire border in his family's ancestral village, Oswaldtwistle, from which his nickname – Ossie – was derived. A sensitive boy who found refuge with his mother and an art teacher, at secondary school he was encouraged by the teacher to study American fashion glossies instead of textbooks. Clark was often taunted by his classmates. 'I liked cats and flowers and walked a certain way,' he later recalled.

Ossie formed an alliance with textile designer Celia Birtwell, born in Bury in 1941 to a housewife/seamstress mum and a dad who was an engineer. She grew up in the Manchester suburb of Prestwich until she was thirteen, when her parents moved to Salford by the East Lancashire Road. As a teenager she studied textiles and pottery at Salford Technical College and was influenced by John Piper, Matisse, Picasso and L. S. Lowry. It was during her years there that she met fledgling fashion designer Ossie Clark, in the Cona Coffee Bar in Manchester. Birtwell remembers what Clark was wearing the first time they met: 'He had on a V-neck leatherette sweater with a rounded Victorian collar – this was pre-Beatles but it was a very particular look – and very long winkle-pickers.' In 1961 she headed south, to west London, seduced by the promise of 'powder-blue winkle-pickers and false eyelashes'.

Clark graduated from the Royal College of Art with a collection inspired by Bridget Riley's op art, which he discovered during a trip across America with his friend David Hockney. While in America Brian Epstein gave him tickets to the Beatles at the Hollywood Bowl show, and he was mobbed by fans mistaking him for George Harrison. Living in London, he had a design room above the fashionable Quorum boutique on the King's Road, and Celia worked from home on the textiles he used for his clothes. At Quorum he met Mick Jagger, who would dance around Clark's flat while he sketched. He created the template for Jagger's jump-suits. ('His road manager loved that,' said Clark, 'because you could just chuck them in the washing machine after each show.' By the early seven-ties Jagger had at least ten Ossie Clark jumpsuits.)

Celia and Ossie moved in together in Notting Hill in 1965 and married in 1969. From 1967 to 1973 they were in their imperial phase, adored by the fashion industry and dressing everyone from the Beatles, the Rolling Stones, Jimi Hendrix, Paloma Picasso, Twiggy and Marianne Faithfull all the way to the British aristocracy. During this time Dave Gilmour drove a van for Ossie before he found fame with Pink Floyd. It was the Clarks who began the modern catwalk show: the previous silent procession of models was set to music, leading London hipsters, trend setters and names were invited, and the shows became events.

In 1970 David Hockney began a double portrait of Celia Birtwell and Ossie Clark, *Mr and Mrs Clark and Percy*. Hockney started the painting shortly after their wedding, at which he was best man. The couple are shown in their London flat. Hockney made drawings and took photographs there, but they also modelled in his studio owing to the painting's size. The cat on Clark's lap is actually thought to be called Blanche, but Hockney felt Percy, the name of the couple's other cat, sounded better. Hockney struggled with the painting for nearly a year, reworking Clark's head as many as twelve times. He aimed to capture the couple's complex and unconventional relationship, along with its tensions. Traditional features of wedding portraiture are reversed, with the man seated while the woman stands. The couple divorced in 1974. Hockney once commented, '*Mr and Mrs Clark and Percy* probably caused it.'

Cohen's Toggery, a prescient northern outpost of the London bohemianism that Clark and Birtwell plunged into, was rooted in the faded local tradition of cotton and craft, and catered to the new exponents of a domestic showbusiness recently transformed by electric guitars and the unreserved posing of Elvis, Jerry Lee Lewis and Little Richard. He opened branches in Bury and Bolton, the one in Bolton near enough to a nightclub so that he was soon suiting up bigtime singers Tom Jones and Engelbert Humperdinck. Cohen went on to manage the Hollies, and the group's sweet-voiced Blackpool-born Graham Nash, who grew up in Ordsall, Salford, singing in the choir at the Friends of St Ignatius church, worked at the Stockport shop for a while, a few years before he was engaged to Joni Mitchell a million or so miles away in California. He formed Crosby, Stills and Nash out there, who first sang together in Joni's house in 1968.

Cohen was himself part of an early-1960s showbusiness couple, although not quite in the Joni and Graham class, going out with Jennifer Moss, who played rebellious Lucille Hewitt in *Coronation Street* for ten years beginning in episode 3. Feisty pint-sized Lucille had the name of a local rock and roller, Eddie, tattooed on her arm, and was the soap's first attempt to react to how the musical sixties, swinging for some, were interacting with the memory lane of cobbles and vicious tongues. Jennifer christened a local group Cohen was thinking of managing the Toggery Five, so the shop even had its own band.

The pop stars – Wayne Fontana and the Mindbenders, the Swinging Blue Jeans – disc jockeys – Jimmy Savile – and footballers – George Best – turning up at The Toggery, with its green leather suits hand-stitched in Ashton under Lyne and sky-blue and pink button-down shirts, did not turn the unresponsive Lowry's mighty head. He still wore his heavy black suit and solid sensible shoes with the resigned demeanour of an undertaker even as the flash-forward Toggery signalled his world was about to be almost completely substituted.

Stony worn-out Victorian Stockport was overhauled and propelled into the apparently inviolable modern world, which was, it seemed, as the groovy Toggery predicted, all about a fancy new form of shopping. Planning was still in its post-war period: town centres and areas of working-class housing were coming under hostile scrutiny, being cleared and rebuilt by architects and planners. The stark speculative modernist structures favoured by planners admiring experimental European developments were completely inappropriate for the districts and traditions where they were built. Civic renewal and pride did not necessarily follow from the insensitive destruction of town centres and landmark buildings with their references to the past, and planning based on ideological zeal for a new modern setting replaced one set of problems with another.

In Stockport the once indomitable seven-storeyed mills and the proud lanky brick chimneys that still lingered seemed to exist more than ever merely to remind people of a past that had nothing to do with the present. The chimneys had no useful function, poignantly strained to impress us with their skyward might and dignity, wanted to be treated like prototype *Angels of the North*, but did nothing for us, because they dripped with the past, like the past was some sort of perpetual downpour that just made you feel damp and miserable. A listless past that had led nowhere, except to a world where the last reminding signs of an industrial heyday looked sad, useless and weighed down with their own forlorn weight. The finicky patterns and controlling precision of massed Victorian brick began to be replaced with pale grey sixties concrete, fussiness within a basic form of functionalism; the grimy cobbler dissolving into extinction now that shiny Dolcis had arrived, the butcher and the baker buggered by the exceptionally convenient Marks & Spencer. The Toggery was still on the outside, not quite belonging to what was around it, but now it was opposite a bright, busy and modernised Boots the Chemist, which looked like it wanted to be where Herman of the Hermits and Freddie of the Dreamers shopped, not Formby son of Formby. Scrubbed-up Boots would be soon joined by clubs and nightclubs set into the ground, under arches, at the bottom of carpeted steps in the vicinity of the shopping centre, to where you imagine those who bought their clothes at the Toggery would be heading.

These were clubs with names like Mask and Sgt Peppers, where the centre of activity was down further steps and too intimidating for those not yet groovy, or teenage enough, to enter – an underground world with a smell new to Stockport, an aroma equivalent to flared trousers and flowery shirts. Another smoke now drifted into Stockport, this one hanging in the air out of sight of the everyday world, as young people wearing their own brand of mini, maxi, butterfly and tie-dyed clothes found a new way to deal with their circumstances and surroundings and lift themselves out of, or shift themselves to the side of, the doldrums.

At the end of the 1960s, a few hundred yards south up the Wellington Road right next to where the hat warehouses once were, a chaotic-looking boutique featuring space-age circular windows opened, spilling out on to the pavement goods, furniture and clothing unashamedly announcing grooviness with such exhibitionist purpose that I, turning thirteen, was too nervous to enter. The boutique was called Seven Miles Out. Only now do I realise it was called that because it was seven miles out of central Manchester, although owner Miles Baddeley might have been smoking something when he came up with seven, as it is more like six, but maybe he was measuring from the cathedral not the town hall. Insouciant female sales assistants wearing skirts that only just grazed the tops of their thighs and male assistants wearing brightly coloured kipper ties opening up to the width of the front tyre of a Chopper bicycle indicated to me that to enter such a shop would instantly turn me into a drug addict.

I felt the same, but with an additional coating of menace, walking past the Mersey Tavern on the corner of Chestergate at the bottom of sloping Daw Bank in Mersey Square, which seemed to me to be the very epicentre of the underground. Playing inside were bands with names like Regeneration who would never make it bigger than supporting the likes of Edgar Broughton and Caravan in venues sprinkled around Manchester. Mostly though it seemed like a din of iniquity part out of Victorian squalor and part out of psychedelic San Francisco, where oddly coloured evil-seeming smoke would make an escape when the mostly slammed-shut doors were briefly opened. There was a squat one-legged character in greasy denim sporting the first tattoos I ever saw in the flesh who I would spot slowly leaving and entering the pub on his wretched crutch. He seemed to be at least twenty stone, and the thought of him fiercely inching towards the Tavern doors on who-knows-what mission unnerves me to this day. He was known as Hoppy, and rumour had it he was an actual ex-Hell's Angel, which meant as far as I was concerned he was perpetually stoned, soaked in urine and in possession of both weed and a concealed weapon. It clearly would have taken the combined prose, wit and energy of Charles Dickens and Hunter S. Thompson to fully fathom the life and mystery of Hoppy.

I never made it into these clubs and pubs even when I reached my late teens, as if the lush knockout smell, the silvery shape-shifting dark, the greasy carpeted steps down into the hot, noisy unknown were unofficial barriers to those not qualified, knowing or daring enough, to those still held back by the impressive moral pull of otherwise apparently indifferent parents.

80

1791

Barthélemy Faujas de Saint-Fond, a French traveller who visited Newcastle in 1791, described the colliery wagonways in that neighbourhood as superior to anything of the kind he had seen. The wooden rails were formed with a rounded upper surface, like a projecting moulding, and the wagon wheels being 'made of cast iron, and hollowed in the manner of a metal pulley' fitted snugly around the rails. The ease with which the coal was thus hauled was strongly recommended by Saint-Fond to his own countrymen.

During the latter part of the 1780s four hotels had been opened in Blackpool to accommodate the town's ever-growing number of tourists. However, the growth of the town's economy and population remained slow.

During a summer vacation in 1790 Wordsworth went on a walking tour through revolutionary France. 'Bliss was it in that dawn to be alive/ But to be young was very heaven!' Initially he had great hopes for the Revolution and its dreams of universal brotherhood, but he lost his enthusiasm and reverted from keen republicanism to a conservative belief in commitment and the stability and order of England. When De Quincey ran away from school at seventeen – with a copy of Wordsworth's *Lyrical Ballads* – he would describe the feeling of liberation in the same way Wordsworth had described the spirit of revolutionary France; 'the senselessness of joy'.

The shotgun-like blast of innovation that took place in Manchester between 1765 and 1800 should come as no surprise given its impressive pool of talent. Although the architects of the Industrial Revolution lived in relative isolation from each other, the close timing of their breakthroughs in textile, power and transportation technologies is more than a coincidence. The common thread tying these inventors and dreamers together was rising demand for cotton goods in domestic, foreign and colonial markets.

By the late 1780s, the paths of rainwater down the Pennines had begun to define the outlines of a manufacturing district. An interdependent network of urban places was taking shape that resembled several loose strings of pearls stretching up and out from a central intersection at or near Manchester.

Perhaps the most intriguing thing about the Industrial Revolution is that it did not start a full-scale social war. The workers had their example in the French Revolution, which began in 1789, and, heaven knows, they had good reason to rebel. They knew well enough what their labour was worth, and they saw that the profits of that labour were going to the masters and the State. However, a repressive government kept them firmly in their place.

Spies roamed the countryside looking for the first signs of rebellion, often inventing them when they couldn't find them. Any hint of trouble was crushed – the Peterloo Massacre in Manchester being a case in point. The trouble was that the protests lacked a real political edge. Workers could be roused in the bad times but, perhaps understandably, their aims in the early days were always cheaper bread and better pay. When the boom times returned, the fight faded into the city smog.

1789

Author and diarist Hester Lynch Piozzi reported, 'There is a rage for the Lakes!'; 'we travel to (the lakes), we row upon them, we write about them.' The area, more than any other part of England, was the subject of description and illustration in travel books like Piozzi's *Journey to North England* and, more notably, William Gilpin's *Observations on the River Wye*. The latter book is credited with initiating the vogue for 'picturesque tourism' – for the picturesque tourist the whole world was nothing more than a large garden to explore.

1788

Like all successful politicians born in the eighteenth century, Robert Peel came from a wealthy background. Unlike most, however, the Peel family wealth was neither landed in origin nor of long duration. Sir Robert Peel's grandfather had been a small independent farmer in Lancashire. His father, also named Robert, made the family fortune in the infant cotton industry during the early years of the Industrial Revolution. Peel was therefore the first prime minister to come from an industrial background. He was born in Bury in 1788, the first son of his parents, and, despite an expensive education and a lifetime in the company of the great and the privileged, never entirely lost his Lancashire accent. Peel's father was extremely ambitious for him, grooming him for politics and buying him his Commons seat. It is claimed that he told his son, 'Bob, you dog, if you do not become prime minister someday I'll disinherit you.'

In 1788 the first petition of Manchester folk demanding an end to the slave trade had been presented to Parliament. By 1792 Manchester had produced 20,000 signatures out of a total population of 75,000 people.

1786

In 1786 'only one chimney, that of Arkwright's spinning mill, was seen to rise above Manchester. Fifteen years later the town had about fifty spinning mills, many of them worked by steam.' The same year Richard Arkwright became the first manufacturer to be knighted.

1785

That year it was written of Mancunian manufacturers, 'By much the major part, and even the most wealthy among them commenced their careers in business with but slender capitals . . . Patience, industry and perseverance was their principal stock.'

Thomas De Quincey was born Thomas Quincey in Greenheys, Chorlton on Medlock, in the midst of Hulme, Ardwick and Rusholme, on 15 August 1785. The family later adopted the name De Quincey, hypothesising that they were related to an old Anglo-French family named de Quincis which dated back to the time of the Norman Conquest. De Quincey's father Thomas was a cloth merchant and haberdasher who settled in Manchester, and the family lived in a pleasant country home. De Quincey was the fourth of five children; he was close to his siblings and was deeply affected by the deaths of his sisters Jane and Elizabeth during his childhood, claiming the grief caused him to seek sanctuary in an intensely introspective imaginary world. With his brother William he created a fantasy life centred on the two imaginary warring kingdoms of Gombroon and Tigrosylvania. His youthful dreams were as much an influence on his writing as his later drug taking and psychological awareness. When Jorge Luis Borges said that 'For many years, I thought that the almost infinite world of literature was in one man,' he paradoxically named a number of candidates – Emerson, Flaubert,

Conrad, Poe, Whitman – and De Quincey was one of them. He once referred to how De Quincey's mode of truth 'was not of truth coherent and central, but angular and splintered'.

On 21 July 1784, the same year that preacher and Methodist founder John Wesley found in Stockport 'a lovely congregation much alive to God', the Chorley-born, 28-year-old Samuel Oldknow, part of a textile family and a self-made calico and muslin maker from Anderton near Bolton, rode into Stockport to purchase a house and some land on Upper Hillgate. He used money borrowed from Richard Arkwright.

It was the time of a great cotton boom in Stockport, following the decline of the silk industry. Silk and the location in 1732 of one of England's first mechanical silk mills had transformed Stockport. (A mill was essentially a factory, powered by a water, and referred to the milling of grain which had used water power for centuries. Because many processes in the early part of the Industrial Revolution like spinning and weaving were powered by water, the term mill survived even when steam replaced water power.) At the beginning of the eighteenth century Stockport was a picturesque market town with a population of just 2,000. By 1760, there were seven mills employing the same number alone, but silk was soon outmoded by cotton, the new miracle fibre, easy to spin, clean, dye, and comfortable to wear. People who had worn nothing under their coarse clothes could afford to wear cotton undergarments. Cotton changed people's lives; it allowed the majority of Victorian England to be decently clad, and the public demanded the more practical and versatile cotton.

Cotton calico and muslin had previously only been made in India, and imported. Oldknow was one of the first entrepreneurs to exploit new spinning possibilities and compete with these imports. He had already opened a warehouse in Stockport, and had trawled for workers around the surrounding tenant farms and villages. Nearly 100 workers turned up, and were given the raw materials necessary for turning into cloth at their cottage farms. Oldknow's Stockport warehouse was open four days a week for the return of goods – Tuesdays and Fridays were the 'taking in' days for spinners, Wednesdays and Saturdays the 'taking in' days for weavers, and Mondays and Thursdays being packing days for the cloth. Several days a week weavers would tramp the roads to Stockport with bundles of cloth or travel from further out in wagons.

Bramhall Hall

By the October of that first year Oldknow had 100 weavers in the Stockport district working for him and two years later he had become, with his Stockport and Anderton production, the foremost muslin manufacturer in Britain employing over 3,000 trained weavers who possessed among them at least 500 looms. Oldknow erected the first Boulton and Watt steam engine in Stockport for turning his winding machine – it became something of a tourist attraction, and stagecoach drivers would slow their vehicles as they passed along Hillgate to show their passengers. In time, such engines meant that mills and factories could be located away from the river, hastening the pace of industrial growth. In 1786, Oldknow established a bleach works for the bleaching, dyeing and printing of cotton on the north bank of the Mersey in what before the Industrial Revolution was simple farm country – Heaton Mersey, where he built his bleach works, means 'the high farmstead beside the Mersey'.

The Mersey was an attraction for industrialists harnessing the power of its water, leading to numerous cotton mills such as Park, Logwood and the Dutch, with the result of the cotton production making the river one of the most polluted in Europe. In 1790, the manufacturer becoming a captain of industry, he started to acquire land around the River Goyt in Marple and Mellor – 'the rounded hill', a village that was in Derbyshire until 1936, and then Cheshire, until 1974, when it became part of Greater Manchester. On his new land, he established the largest water-powered cotton spinning mill ever built in England, six storeys high, 42 feet wide and 210 feet long with a further three-storey section on either side adding 190 feet. To power it, the River Goyt had to be diverted, requiring a reshaping of the landscape, and a series of three millponds constructed and a complicated system of tunnels, channels and wheelpits built.

The millponds became known in Victorian times as 'Roman Lakes' and were a huge tourist attraction. Mellor Mill was water powered for most of its life, steam engines and a boiler not installed until 1860. Although the building of Mellor Mill almost ruined him, leading to another loan from Arkwright, he became the driving force in the development and industrialisation of the area, responsible for the building of roads, bridges, coal mines, housing for his workers and canals including the Peak Forest canal. This created a short cut across Cheshire, Manchester and the surrounding rapidly growing industrial area, linking the Trent and the Mersey and therefore Lancashire and the Potteries. He knew roads were as important as the canals – the main road between Stockport and Marple up to then was little more than a pack-horse track, and to help his enterprises, he built bridges, and repaired and gravelled the road. It was this road that would have taken the Beatles, 140 years later, to and from their one Stockport gig.

After becoming the High Sheriff of Derby in 1824, Oldknow died in 1828, and was buried in Marple Church, respected enough for what was described as his open-hearted simplicity, disinterested benevolence and a genial and sympathetic disposition, that over 3,000 people came to watch his funeral procession.

1783

Attempts to perfect a rotary printing machine for cotton had started at the very beginning of the eighteenth century when a wooden printing roller was used in Moravia (now part of the Czech Republic). A three-colour roller was invented in 1743. However the real leap forward came only in 1783, when

Thomas Bell (who worked at Livesey, Hargreaves Hall and Company in Preston) patented a method of printing from engraved cylinders. Two years later he was printing in six colours.

1781

Thomas Clifton and Sir Henry Houghton constructed a private road that made Blackpool more accessible to people. The same year was also the first time stagecoaches from Manchester would travel to Blackpool. By 1782, the stagecoaches would be travelling from Halifax as well.

George Stephenson, born in Wylam, eight miles outside Newcastle upon Tyne, on 7 June 1781, grew up with a keen interest in machines, and would take engines apart to see how they worked. By 1802 he was a colliery engineer, a year before the birth of his only son, Robert. By 1814, experimenting with steam power, he had built a locomotive he called the *Blücher* – after the Prussian general who had just defeated Napoleon – which could pull thirty tons up a hill at 4 mph. It was, he said, worth 'fifty horses'. By 1820, now appreciating the importance of a smooth level track, he had built an eight-mile line from Hetton to the River Wear at Sunderland using locomotives, making it the first ever railway totally independent of animal power.

'From a walled medieval town of monks and merchants, Newcastle has been converted into a busy centre of commerce and manufacturers inhabited by nearly 100,000 people. Newcastle is in many respects a town of singular and curious interest, especially in its older parts, which are full of crooked lanes and narrow streets. As you pass through the country at night, the earth looks as if it were bursting with fire at many points; the blaze of coke-ovens, iron-furnaces, and coal heaps reddening the sky to such a distance that the horizon seems to be a glowing belt of fire. From the necessity which existed for facilitating the transport of coals from the pits to the shipping places, it is easy to understand how the railway and the locomotive should have first found their home in such a district.' Samuel Smiles, *The Life of George Stephenson: Railway Engineer*, 1875.

81

Within a couple of years of the Merseyway shopping precinct emerging from the razed filthy ground around Mersey Square, there would be no more steam trains shuffling across the imperturbable viaduct over the other side of the Wellington Road. It was as though the shopping precinct itself had issued a warning from the future it so dynamically represented. Shops would be a refuge, gathered together in one place, protecting people from lack of choice. The world had changed. It was electric. Steam trains that had once symbolised a world of possibility boiling at the seams were laid to rest where they could be dirty in peace. Nor were cobbles of any use in this increasingly customised consumer world except as a neutralised form of heritage, as harmless souvenirs of the past pressed into the present as depthless decoration.

The new precinct put nationally branded shops on two levels around a pedestrian square you could wander through like it was a flat-packed concrete park left over from a science-fiction film set in an imaginary country lost between America and Russia. Incongruous open-air trave-lators glided from the ground floor to the first level connecting with various gangways as if the space was part of some gigantic machine. Thirty feet below this shiny lightness in a dark dripping tunnel flowed the ignored and apparently reviled river, as if the Mersey, all that wet messy possibly even shitty business, did not suit the new-generation modernist version of the market town. Apparently setting a big steel-framed concrete-clad shopping centre slap bang in the middle would update and repair the town's creaky reputation. Meanwhile, the idea of the Mersey was relegated to a form of branding: a bus station and a parade of shops were the Mersey, not a river.

Stockport followed Manchester as the changes that had begun two centuries before, conclusively moving things from the rural to the urban, were forced to keep coming – industrial revolution, wars, indus-trial decline, uninspired social solutions – and Stockport tried hard to keep up. Merseyway was the latest in a series of rearrangements, reno-vations and building projects that had begun in the nineteenth century – when cathedrals, palaces and podiums were supplanted by hotels,

The Toast Rack, Hollings College, 1973

railways stations, ports, markets, arcades, streets – as if this was to be the one that would bring the town into the middle of the forward-reaching twentieth century.

I never once thought about this at the time, but the darkened Mersey was now beginning in enforced hiding a pulpy journey that for hundreds of years had marked the line between Lancashire and Cheshire. 'Mersey' is derived from the Anglo-Saxon word for boundary or border river, possibly because it originally formed the border between Mercia and Northumbria. Even when I was visiting Merseyway almost every day, because the seductive newness of the place and the shops filled with the now of the times suited me as a teenager more than it did Lowry and his beloved easel, I never seemed to wonder why on earth the Mersey didn't actually flow through the town centre. I'd go as far as to say I never once thought about where the Mersey was.

It made its way to Liverpool, where it was in the clear centre of things, where it was better known, and more loved, because it was part of the city's edgy, alluring worldwide reputation, because it had beat music and the Beatles, and a whole song celebrating the ferry that took you across it. In Stockport we walked across the Mersey without knowing it was there, and we headed into Boots, WHSmith, Marks & Spencer, and the record shop Nield and Hardies, where I bought my first single, which, funnily enough, was about a white swan.

The Mersey becomes itself a few hundred yards to the east of Mersey Square, the result of the foamy black-brown joining of the Goyt and the Tame, which themselves united several small dribbling streams that spring out of the craggy wilderness on the Pennine Hills, dashing out amidst boggy heather, moss, bracken, rocks, bent grass – the Tame rising in Saddleworth close to the border with west Yorkshire, flowing through Stalybridge – separating Lancs. and Yorks. – Ashton under Lyne, Dukinfield (open land of ducks), Denton and Hyde, half a mile to the east of Westbourne Grove, Reddish, close enough for me to bike to within minutes and follow for another few minutes to where it meets the Mersey.

The Goyt starts in the moors of Axe Edge near the main road between Buxton and Macclesfield, travels alongside old lanes and packhorse tracks through Whalley Bridge, New Mills, Disley, Marple Bridge and Offerton, having been joined by the Etherow, which once marked the historical border between Cheshire and Derbyshire. The Etherow rises 1,700 feet above sea level in eerie, boggy Featherbed Moss, Bleaklow near Sheffield, trickles, rushes, winds and spills, trying to find its level, for nineteen miles, flowing through a chain of reservoirs in the valley of Longdendale constructed by the Manchester and Salford Waterworks between 1848 and 1877. Emerging at the village of Tintwistle, once of Cheshire, from 1974 of Derbyshire, with its cricket team logo featuring the wheatsheaf of Derbyshire, the red rose of Lancashire and yet also the white rose of Yorkshire, it enters Tameside and Greater Manchester at Hollingworth before it passes into Stockport and joins the Goyt. Where the Etherow meets the Goyt at Brabyns Park in Marple was once considered the place where the Mersey actually begins; some say it was a mistake in a Victorian map that moved the beginning of the Mersey closer to the town centre. This is where the Goyt tumbles underneath a stone bridge down below a busy, indifferent road and the

Tame swirls by a large patch of waste ground, where little remains of the once busy Stockport Tiviot Dale railway station. They meet in Portwood as the Mersey, and almost immediately disappear.

82

1778

In 1778 William Wordsworth was sent to a school founded by Edwin Sandys, Archbishop of York, in the year 1585 at Hawkshead in Lancashire. Hawkshead is a small market town in the vale of Esthwaite, about a third of a mile north-west of the lake.

Football matches were originally almost battles in the streets of towns like Rochdale fought by unruly crowds, and there were inter town and village 'games'. On 3 February 1778 the *Manchester Mercury* noted a fixture between towns: 'A match of football between Ashton Lever Esq. and the township of Middleton, Blackley, Prestwich against Captain Aytoun and the townships of Rochdale, Royton & Oldham to begin at 12 o'clock on February 11th 1778.'

1770

William Wordsworth was born in the town of Cockermouth in 1770, and his first home was in the Lake District, one of many he would have there. His boyhood was full of adventure among the hills, but he said of himself that he showed 'a stiff, moody, and violent temper'. He lost his mother when he was eight, and his father, John, a legal representative of the first Earl of Lonsdale, in 1783, when he was thirteen. Nature was important to Wordsworth from his earliest years, as it fired his vivid imagination. Some of the most striking memories he would describe in *The Prelude* are of experiences he had as a child, when his impressionable mind was sometimes even afraid of his surroundings. He tells of a night-time boat trip he took which left him shaken, thinking 'grave and serious thoughts . . . for many days':

> I dipp'd my oars into the silent Lake
> And, as I rose upon the stroke, my Boat
> Went heaving through the water, like a Swan
> When from behind the craggy Steep, till then
> The bound of the horizon, a huge Cliff
> As if with voluntary power instinct
> Uprear'd its head.

That cliff seemed to follow him 'like a living thing'. He rowed away with 'trembling hands', and was haunted afterwards day and night by forms moving slowly through his mind. Wordsworth was intellectually inspired by his surroundings: 'O Nature! Thou hast fed / My lofty speculations!' In his everyday life among the vales and mountains he would observe, consider and commit his reflections to verse – often doing so aloud as he walked.

83

The Mersey bursts from its temporary captivity at the other side of the square and the A6, thrashing underneath the hundred-foot-high viaduct past long-extinct mills and settling between the craggy red sandstone and the canopies of trees, and without wondering where it comes from, you could look down on it from the Wellington Bridge, as it heads out to the north-west, south of Heaton Norris and Heaton Mersey past traces of the old bleach works, refuse tips, railway sidings through woods towards Didsbury, Sale and Northenden, meandering around the western edge of Manchester, set back from the massed houses behind protective parkland, the crammed-together Withington, Chorlton-cum-Hardy and Sale golf courses and fields.

As it snakes through the golf courses the Mersey passes near the Southern Cemetery, where notable local personalities are buried: Sir Matt Busby, manager of Manchester United between the finish of the Second World War and the end of the 1960s, including the 1958 Munich air disaster, charismatic Granada Television presenter, northern historian, United fan and Factory Records impresario Anthony H. Wilson, and L. S. Lowry, who often stood near the Mersey, thinking fluid thoughts about the lonely depths, closed-in poetry and mournful resonance of northern colour, character and shadow.

After leaving behind the cemetery and golf courses, the river skirts the Stretford and Urmston in the borough of Trafford, then squeezes between the Flixton and Carrington areas of Greater Manchester. When Flixton was a remote rural area, up to the early nineteenth century, the river would isolate it from its neighbours. The origin of the name Stretford is 'street on a ford' – across the River Mersey. The principal route through Stretford, the A56 Chester Road, follows the line of the old Roman road from Deva Victrix (Chester) to Mamucium (Manchester), crossing the Mersey into Stretford at Crossford Bridge on the border with Sale, built, as its name suggests, at the location of the ancient ford. Ian Curtis, the Joy Division singer, was born at the Memorial Hospital in Stretford on 15 July 1956.

The Mersey is joined at Flixton by the Irwell, which means winding stream, from Olde English *irre* for angry or wandering, and *wella*, for stream, once named 'the hardest-working stream in the world', which rises on Deerplay Moor near Deerplay Hill, in the township of Cliviger, perched above the village of Bacup, east Lancashire. The stream proceeds south through Rawtenstall and Ramsbottom to Bury, where a little to the south near Radcliffe it joins the Roch, which rises near Todmorden and even though pronounced 'roach' gives Rochdale its name. Edwin Waugh:

> The quiet Roch comes dancing down
> From breezy moorland hills;
> It wanders through my native town,
> With its bonny tribute rills.
> Oh, gentle Roch, my native stream!
> Oft, when a careless boy,
> I've prattled to thee, in a dream,
> As thou went singing by.

Deviating to the west, the waters of the Irwell are joined by a rivulet from Bolton at Farnworth; it then changes to a south-easterly direction, meandering around Lower Broughton – separating Salford and Manchester – where it receives the Irk and the Medlock at the foot of the 387-foot, 25-storey Co-operative Insurance Tower. When completed in 1962, the largest office block built in Manchester since the war, a necessarily bold symbol of a post-cotton fightback, with the confident intention of equalling anything in London, the CIS tower was the third tallest building in Europe, and the UK's tallest building outside London for 43 years. The CIS Tower was the first building in Manchester to surpass the ornate town hall's 80-year-old 285-foot spire. Nothing in Manchester was higher until 2006.

It was heavily influenced by the innovative 1958 Inland Steel Building in Chicago, the first Chicago high-rise built since the Great Depression, which was among the buildings inspected by the design team on its fact-finding trip to America. It might be that the building of the CIS Tower was a late sign of Manchester allowing itself to be truly daring, an echo of nineteenth-century enterprise, a monument to local modern-ism and idealism, although the design derives from the US Midwest and East Coast and 1930s Germany. Built to enhance the prestige of both the Co-operative Society and the city of Manchester, the tower is a cathedral to egalitarianism and northern pioneering spirit, with every aspect of its design an exercise in elegance and perfection. Its sleek grey mass rising above the ageing city supplied a solo sixties slice of high-rise New York flair and was an expressive representation of the integrity of the Co-op itself.

Another striking Manchester building embodying optimism and aesthetic purpose, completed a few years earlier, in the late 1950s, and somehow communicating with a gutsy local accent, is a building commissioned by Manchester Metropolitan University as a home for the Hollings Domestic and Trades College. If Manchester's position as a major city held during its shaky period of industrial decline, it was because of its solid reputation for higher education – the colleges, universities and schools distributed along the route south towards Didsbury, including Hollings College and its special building.

It was positioned three miles south, ten minutes on the bus, out of the city centre, along Oxford Road, through the Curry Mile, down Wilmslow Road opposite Platt Fields Park – which contains signs of the Nico Ditch, here more like a pathway – not far from Manchester City's Maine Road ground, midway between Manchester Grammar School and the High School for Girls, where Rusholme bleeds imperceptibly into Fallowfield. Travelling three miles further south, keeping straight, through Withington, you reach the Palatine Road. This is where twenty-year-old engineering student Ludwig Wittgenstein lodged between 1908 and 1911 – drawn to the city by the prominent part Jews played in the cultural life of Manchester, the city's tradition of self-educated genius and by the work of Ernest Rutherford, which encouraged his interest in the philosophy of mathematics and then 'pure' philosophy – and the Factory Records label was based. This leads to Didsbury, on the north bank of the River Mersey, surrounded by Chorlton-cum-Hardy, Burnage, Northenden, Cheadle, Gatley and Heaton Mersey. It is here that the Mersey passes under the Palatine Road, and the Palatine Road was named because it linked the two palatine counties of Lancashire and Cheshire separated by the river – a 'county palatine' was an area ruled by a hereditary nobleman holding royal privileges and exclusive rights of jurisdiction, and was permitted to form its own armies.

Hollings College had begun humbly enough in a single building in 1901 teaching the basics of cookery and domestic science to the working class. The new campus was planned by Scottish-born Manchester Council City architect L. C. (Leonard) Howitt, who had designed the sombre if imposing Crown Courts, the monolithic Sharston Baths in Wythenshawe (sweeping into view like an east European dictator's fantasy) and also deftly reconstructed the Free Trade Hall from very little original material following extensive war damage. His 1955 Heaton Park Reservoir Pumping Station in Bury harmoniously matched architecture and sculpture to salute the immense late-nineteenth-century achievement of bringing water from the Thirlmere Reservoir in the Lake District through the longest tunnel in the world, ninety-six miles, to rapidly expanding Manchester, taking about a day to get there. He was also a member of the powerful Herbert J. Rowse team, which designed with classical late-British-empire verve the tunnel entrances, toll booths and ingenious streamlined ventilation towers for the Queensway Road Tunnel under the Mersey between Liverpool and Birkenhead.

Howitt's building for MMU combined five separate college departments under one spectacular roof, and was fervently post-empire and defiantly post-war but in ways that didn't contradict the utilitarian industrial traditions of the city. It ended up looking like the missing link between exotic but highly functional space-age Jodrell Bank and the self-consciously modern glazed spaciousness of the CIS Tower. The structure was instantly and affectionately nicknamed the Toast Rack for the way its concrete-framed glass-curtained seven storeys elegantly tapered towards a narrow rounded top capped with twenty-three free-standing open concrete arches. Rooms were smaller at the top than at the bottom, the practical reason for the innovative shape being the need for different-sized teaching spaces for a variety of technical purposes.

The post-war intention among architects turning their backs on failed imperial grandeur was to conquer and colonise the future, and some got it right. The Toast Rack demonstrated how post-war concrete could be used to create something witty, tough and accessibly unusual rather than at best the merely blankly solid and at worst a poorly executed configuration of ugliness, an ideological retreat from decoration and elegance. Howitt believed that his job was to produce beautiful buildings which at their best could help put the world to rights, and the architect should have soul, and morals, and a sense of humour.

Nestling against the Toast Rack is a low round building containing the library and cafés, which became known as the Fried Egg. Usually fussy, renowned architectural historian Sir Nikolaus Pevsner proclaimed the campus 'a perfect piece of pop architecture', beyond high praise from him. It's just around the corner from the Dickinson Road Studios, the BBC's first regional television studios, opened in 1954 in a converted church previously owned by cheap and cheeky Mancunian Films, hearty makers of full-blooded 'northern films for northern people', who gave George Formby his first chance in films and opened their own studios in 1947. It was as though the Toast Rack was itself a part of pop-culture history, constantly in performance, rooted in the local and the universal, surely an influence on the coming sound of Joy Division, which combined space, concrete, art, technology and reflections of the internal and external environment.

Joy Division's music producer, Martin Hannett, went to school at the nearby Xaverian College in Rusholme's Victoria Park, solemnly blessed and opened by the fourth Bishop of Salford, Louis Casartelli, in 1907, having moved its premises from a four-storey building on Oxford Road. The salubrious and then gated Victoria Park was where in 1871 Manchester Town Hall and Strangeways Prison architect Alfred Waterhouse had impressed his intricate Gothic imagination on to a domestic building called Firwood, which was purchased in 1905 and set at the centre of the new campus. As extra buildings joined Waterhouse's gently sinister centrepiece, the college exuded stately otherness in the middle of entwined residential streets and tree-sheltered cul-de-sacs. Eventually the college would be just a few steps from what became the packed, animated Curry Mile, and the mind would spin as you moved from Waterhouse's vaulted heavy-doored generosity to the crush of restaurants and a different spread of imported glamour, both locations embedded in Manchester but set on the outside. Hannett's Gothic and hooded but serenely ultramodern, synthetic and yet deeply human work for Joy Division was constructed between these two extremes of the exotic, ones he would have known well, the futuristic Toast Rack and the ornately austere Xaverian estate. (Back in the 1930s Anthony Burgess would suffer a crisis of faith while at Xaverian, leaving him a lapsed Catholic, intellectually resisting but emotionally stained, his fervent self-aggrandising teenage mind no doubt blown apart by the Waterhouse staircase covered with harrowing and/or inspiring Catholic iconography at the centre of the monastic Xaverian campus.)

I couldn't take my eyes off the Toast Rack whenever I passed it on the bus in the late sixties and early seventies, or saw it from the train trundling through Levenshulme on the six-minute journey to Stockport from Manchester Piccadilly, slyly materialising in the distance across the shops, trees and rooftops, an abstract sculptural shape as much as an educational facility teaching students, including my Aunt Sally – travelling in from Handforth, loving its proximity to the *Top of the Pops* studios, where the likes of the Kinks lurked – how to cut hair, cook and fix cars. It veered up amid the strewn nothing special like a station on a monorail that took you across a landscape usually found in your dreams. It was so Manchester too, because it looked even better when it was wet, when it had a general demeanour of *Mustn't grumble*.

To me, the Toast Rack showed how all buildings should look in the future, but most of those buildings would go unbuilt, or even unimagined. I also think it was the first building that made me realise you could fall in love with buildings – when they were so fantastically one of a kind, descriptions of experience as much as mere objects – because of the way they changed the world around them and showed up the banal.

The Irk, derived from *irwke*, meaning swift, rises in Royton, north of Oldham, and was once famous for the bloated eels that swam there, fattened by the grease and oil emitted by the woollen mills into the water. Once, it was clear and full of fish, running through woodlands of wild hyacinths and meadows of daffodils and primroses. The valley of the Irk has a long history in textile development. In medieval times cloth making was a cottage industry with the pieces of fabric bleached on the banks of the Irk using sunlight, rain, sour milk and a daily collection of urine from Blackley (dark wood) village. Queen Victoria's white wedding dress was made, in accordance with designs 'drawn and painted in the Queen's own hand', at the Ashenhurst Works in Blackley by the firm of Messrs James Houldsworth and Co. White was not then a popular option but was picked to complement the locally made lace, chosen to support the dyeing industry. Victoria's dress had a huge influence on the style of weddings, white soon becoming the traditional choice for the bride's gown.

The small Medlock (meadow stream) rises at Saddleworth on the Pennine fringes, then flows through the steep-sided wooded gorge that separates Oldham from Ashton under Lyne, before heading south-west towards Manchester, where it serves as a feeder for the Bridgewater Canal at Knott Mill near Deansgate. Friedrich Engels in *The Condition of the Working Class in England* described an area around the highly polluted Medlock in central Manchester as 'the most horrible spot . . . lies on the Manchester side, immediately south-west of Oxford Road, and is known as Little Ireland. In a rather deep hole, in a curve of the Medlock and surrounded on all four sides by tall factories and high embankments, covered with buildings, stand two groups of about two hundred cottages, built chiefly back to back, in which live about 4,000 human beings mostly Irish. The cottages are old, dirty, and of the smallest

L. S. Lowry and the Stockport Viaduct by the River Mersey

sort, the streets are uneven, fallen into ruts and in part without
drains or pavement; masses of refuse, offal and sickening filth lie among
standing pools in all directions; the atmosphere is poisoned by the
effluvia from these, and laden and darkened by the smoke of a dozen
tall factory chimneys.' In 1832, describing Little Ireland, a local doctor,
J. P. Kay, wrote, 'this unhealthy district lies so low that the chimneys of
its houses, some of them three storeys high, are little above the level of
the ground'.

At flat, bleak Irlam (settlement on the Irwell), south-west of Salford,
the River Mersey, now full of Irwell, which has itself taken in the Irk and
Medlock and all their associations, flows young and hearty and eager for
adventure into the astonishingly man-made Manchester Ship Canal, the
city's audacious late-nineteenth-century retort to coastal Liverpool's
natural but irritating maritime superiority. Here, abruptly canalised, the
Mersey once had a real grown-up job to do, supporting the cargo-laden
weight of ocean steamers, its course obliterated past Hollins Green to
Rixton, although the old riverbed can be seen at Warburton. At Rixton

near Lymm (Celtic, 'running water') the River Bollin (of uncertain origin and meaning) enters the canal from the south.

The main source of the River Bollin is on Toot Hill in the hamlet of Forest Chapel on the edge of Macclesfield Forest at the western end of the Peak District. It passes through Macclesfield and Wilmslow, and in 1784 the Quarry Bank Mill was built right next to it, a waterwheel powered by the fast-flowing river driving all the machinery. Close to Styal Prison, a couple of miles south-west of Ringway Airport, the Bollin is joined by the River Dean.

The Mersey closes in on Cheshire, reliving its original function as the historic border between Lancashire and Cheshire, and leaves the canal to the north-west about four miles later around Warrington, where it is deep enough to hold ships of sixty tons. The administrative changes in 1974 meant that Warrington – possibly Viking, meaning a place to moor the boats – was one of those places that shifted from one county to another, the traditional Lancashire town now coming under control of the Cheshire County Council. The great Roman road that ran from Chester to Lancaster went through Warrington, bypassing what was then the swampy, inhospitable Merseyside area. For centuries, Warrington was the one place west of Stretford where a bridge was built over the river, and was the natural point of entry into Lancashire from the south.

Stuck between Manchester and Liverpool, neither one nor the other, the local accent seems uncertain about which way to turn. It comes down from old, no-nonsense Lancashire, up from the subtly milder Cheshire, and is also stained by the loud, lurking cities, reflecting its place on the Mersey, which mile by mile from east to west passes through changes in accent that appear almost imperceptible, and then are suddenly quite distinct. The mixing up of sounds and dialects suits a town that is always in transition that never really changes, at the mercy of town planners never quite making their minds up how things should look and work.

Becoming tidal from Howley and Woolston Weirs, the Mersey is now very much a strong and determined adult, possibly with vague, horrible memories of how it was trapped in the grotty dark underneath Mersey Square. It leaves Cheshire at Hale, in the district of Halton, not far from the birthplace of Lewis Carroll, and loops into Merseyside three miles from Widnes.

At the Runcorn Gap between Widnes, which grew out of the chemical industry, and Runcorn rail and road bridges span the river and the ship canal, which runs alongside the widening estuary to Eastham Locks, where canal and river unite, turning north, widening into a majestic estuary between Liverpool and Birkenhead on the Wirral, swelling and chopping, the volume and vigour of the city massed on either side, with Aigburth and Toxteth on the Liverpool side, Rock Ferry and Tranmere on the Wirral. It passes the Albert Dock before emptying into the sea between the faded resort of New Brighton at the head of the Wirral Peninsula and Bootle, as though that's the reward for all the captivity and service and forced marriages with other rivers and waterways. Seventy miles of river, flowing like a guided dream, inspiring life, invention and activity, myths, industry and leisure all along its shores, ending up three-quarters of a mile wide, far from being an ideal harbour but perfect as a highway to the industrial areas of Lancashire that formed and flourished in the nineteenth century.

Somewhere along here, in 1917, convalescing in a military garrison, the poet Siegfried Sassoon angrily threw into the river the ribbon from the Military Cross he had won on the Western Front for bringing wounded men to safety while under fire. Moved by patriotism to join the army, he had become disillusioned and then disgusted with the war and the callousness of generals making battle plans thinking in numbers not individual souls. He particularly disliked the propaganda aimed at gaining recruits to replace the many thousands of men already slaughtered, which depicted the war as a worthwhile cause, a duty to fulfil – a call, it implied, which only cowards would refuse. He felt the war had become about conquest, and the authorities could stop it at any moment if they wished. The medal itself was not thrown away – Sassoon clenching his fists and shaking them at the sky – he chucked only the ribbon, a shred of purple and white cloth.

'Weighted with significance though this action was,' he wrote, 'it would have felt more conclusive had the ribbon been heavier. As it was, the poor little thing fell weakly on to the water and floated away as though aware of its own futility . . . Watching a big boat which was steaming along the horizon, I realised that protesting against the prolongation of the war was about as much use as shouting at the people on board that ship.'

At the Liverpool end, opened up to the world, the river opens up the world, for better or worse bringing out there into the north, and letting the north reach out there. It puts on a hell of a performance, bringing rhythm in, sending rhythm out. The Mersey, which has risen in the east, blinking into drizzly daylight at the sodden edges of the gloomily beautiful Pennines, hastening or pacing itself across the milds of Cheshire and underneath looming Lancashire, viewed by British Hindus as the British version of the Ganges, drifts free of land and responsibility in the west, kissing the spirited Irish Sea, which has so much it wants to show the liberated river – a river that has ceased to be, fresh water mixing with salt – but now has the most extraordinary afterlife to enjoy and which inspired the most extraordinary city to make itself up and make history.

84.1

1770

When Arthur Young toured northern England in 1770, he travelled on horseback. Because so few boats were available for hire, he had trouble using canals. He complained at the state of the road from Wigan to Lancaster via Preston, writing: 'Let me seriously caution all travellers to avoid it as they would the devil – they will have met with ruts four feet deep and floating with mud. The only mending it receives is the tumbling in of loose stones which serve no other purpose than jolting a carriage in the most objectionable manner.'

In 1770 the town of Bolton was described as 'a district almost rural, an idyll made up of bleaching crofts, orchards and garden cottages' – a very quaint-sounding place, but within thirty years water-powered textile mills and engineering works had drastically altered the landscape.

1769

The deeply delicate pre-Romantic poet and classical scholar Thomas Gray (1716–71), coiner of 'Where ignorance is bliss . . .', visited the Lake District and was one of the first major literary figures to write about it, positively marvelling at the mountains' 'dreadful bulk'. His prose about the Lakes, which he described as 'charmed,' was published posthumously in 1775 and influenced William Wordsworth.

'On one side a towering crag, that spired up to equal, if not overtop, the neighbouring cliffs (this lay all in shade & darkness), on the other hand a rounder broader projecting hill shagged with wood & illumined by the sun, which glanced sideways on the upper part of the cataract. The force of the water wearing a deep channel in the ground hurries away to join the lake. We descended again, & passed the stream over a rude bridge. Soon after we came under Gowder crag, a hill more formidable to the eye & to the apprehension than that of Lodoor; the rocks atop, deep-cloven perpendicularly by the rains, hanging loose & nodding forwards, seem just starting from their base in shivers: the whole way down & the road on both sides is strewed with piles of the fragments strangely thrown across each other . . .'

The breakthrough came in 1769, when Richard Arkwright, a Preston barber and wig maker, patented a machine for roller spinning – drawing the thread through pairs of rollers. He had heard about attempts to produce new machines for the textile industry and in 1762 met John Kay, a clockmaker from Warrington, who had been busy for some time trying to perfect a new spinning machine with Thomas Highs. Kay and Highs had run out of money and been forced to abandon the project. Arkwright was impressed by Kay and offered to employ him to build the machine. He also recruited other local craftsmen to help, and it was not long before the team produced the spinning frame. Arkwright's machine involved three sets of paired rollers which turned at different speeds. While these rollers produced yarn of the correct thickness, a set of spindles twisted the fibres firmly together. The machine was able to produce a thread far stronger than that made by the jenny. The invention of Arkwright's water frame in 1769 transformed spinning, enabling ninety-six threads to be spun at once. Mass production of cotton cloth in Lancashire made it available to the masses in Britain and then around the world.

. . . a large and handsome town occupying three hills and three valleys which are so serpentine as to form many pleasing prospects of churches, pieces of water, with the large silk mills belonging to the chief tradesmen of the place . . .

Description of Stockport in the 1769 edition of Defoe's *Tour*

1766

An accident is said to have given a Lancashire spinner, James Hargreaves, the idea for the first mechanical improvement of the spinning process. In about 1764 he noticed an overturned spinning wheel which continued to turn with the spindle vertical rather than horizontal. This gave him the idea that several spindles could be worked simultaneously from a wheel in this position. In 1766 he invented the spinning jenny, which, by fixing a handle to the spinning wheel, enabled a single workman to turn six or eight threads simultaneously and still work at home. This should have rendered the spinning wheel obsolete, but he lacked the market awareness to capitalise on his invention. In 1768 domestic spinners wrecked his home. To escape trouble he moved to Nottingham and opened a jenny workshop there, but he soon went bankrupt.

Tenterhooks were used as far back as the fourteenth century in the process of making woollen cloth. After the cloth had been woven it still contained oil from the fleece and some dirt. It was cleaned in a fulling mill and then had to be dried carefully as wool shrinks. To prevent this shrinkage, the wet cloth would be placed on a large wooden frame, a 'tenter', and left to dry outside. The lengths of wet cloth were stretched on the tenter (from the Latin *tendere*, to stretch) using hooks (nails driven through the wood) all around the perimeter of the frame to which the cloth's edges (selvages) were fixed so that as it dried the cloth would retain its shape and size. The wool was hung on tenterhooks. So if you were very tense, like stretched cloth, you were on tenterhooks.

PART SIX

A leap forward through the past

I didn't think – I experimented.

Anthony Burgess

Digressions, incontestably, are the sunshine, the life, the soul of reading! Take them out and one cold eternal winter would reign in every page. Restore them to the writer – he steps forth like a bridegroom, bids them all-hail, brings in variety and forbids the appetite to fail.

Laurence Sterne

84.2

The seventy-second Archbishop of York (1664–83) and master of Jesus College, Cambridge, Richard Sterne is one candidate among many for the author of *The Whole Duty of Man*, often considered the most influential work of Restoration pastoral theology. The subtitle is worth noting: *laid down in a plain and familiar way for the use of all, but especially the meanest reader. Divided into XVII. chapters; one whereof being read every Lord's Day, the whole may be read over thrice in the year. Necessary for all families. With private devotions for several occasions.*

Richard Sterne was the great-grandfather of Laurence Sterne, born in 1713 in Ireland, who spent the first twenty-five years of his adult life in obscurity as a Yorkshire clergyman, became a prebendary of York Minster and preached throughout the Vale of York and the East Riding. A squabble concerning Church preferments inspired Sterne to compose a short satirical pamphlet, *A Political Romance*, published in December 1758. It was immediately suppressed by Sterne's superiors: only six copies are said to have survived.

Between 1759 and 1767 Sterne wrote in eight instalments one of those books often claimed to be the first modern – indeed, by mocking and remaking the then quiveringly new conventions of the novel, the first postmodern – novel, *The Life and Opinions of Tristram Shandy, Gentleman*. For the sake of argument, modernism can be defined as that period of enlightenment that continued until the mid-twentieth century, and postmodernism as what followed, but here is a book that anticipates a post-nuclear renaissance, a deviation in man's thinking, a leap forward through the past into the future that was not to occur for nearly two centuries. For the sake of more argument, let's say that the postmodern relies on the fragmentary, paradox, ambiguity, questionable narrators, black humour, multiple realities, a nostalgia for the impossible, in which nothing is framed within a certain existing universal truth, the world is a place where things happen randomly, interruptions are a constant, truth is an illusion manipulated by those wanting to gain control over others, and everything is brought into question. Postmodern literature tends to feature narratives borrowing techniques and possibilities from film and television, flashing back, flashing forward, frequently interrupted and repeated – and here was Sterne doing it hundreds of years before. He adopted a position of openness, and was especially receptive to the unpredictable, the contingent and the difficult. Clear prose can sometimes indicate the absence of thought. Sometimes careful disorderliness can be a true method of composition.

Shandy can be seen as the alter ego of his fellow Yorkist, Robinson Crusoe, and a book that contains life and intensely introverted opinions supplants a story about a life and open-air adventures. And whereas in Daniel Defoe's book the hero is the sole unifying force, in Sterne's novel the hero is based on digression. Digression is a strategy for putting off the ending, a multiplying of time within a work, a perpetual flight. A flight, in fact, from death. Endless wandering can ensue using simply the word, and the next word, and the next page, which is the first page, and the last, followed again by the last page, and the first.

The Sex Pistols at the Lesser Free Trade Hall, 4 June 1976

Sterne wrote and completed *Tristram Shandy* in the serene surroundings of ramshackle medieval Shandy Hall, set among two acres of gardens – sometimes between writing Sterne would step out 'to weed, hack up old roots or wheel away rubbish' – in Coxwold, to where he moved in 1760, living alone after becoming vicar of the parish. Coxwold is about fifteen miles north of York close to the market towns of Easingwold and Thirsk on the most southerly edge of the vast heather-covered North Yorkshire Moors, scattered with abbeys, valleys and waterfalls. Oliver Cromwell is reputed to be buried in Coxwold's Newburgh Priory, where his daughter brought his headless remains. After the Restoration of King Charles II in 1660 his body was exhumed from Westminster Abbey and he was posthumously hanged and beheaded.

This whole area, local events and some of the characters who lived there found their way into Sterne's novel. John Burton was a York doctor, the first physician at the newly founded York Hospital. He had published a history of the Church in Yorkshire, *Monasticon Eboracense*, in 1758, and was the inventor of obstetric forceps. Sensitive to criticism and not a little paranoid, he suffered the most by being viciously and possibly unfairly satirised in *Tristram Shandy* as Dr Slop. Burton was well known as a Jacobite and Tory, while Sterne had allied himself with the Whig interests dominant at York Minster.

Sterne incorporated into *Tristram Shandy* many passages taken almost word for word from Robert Burton's *The Anatomy of Melancholy*, Francis Bacon's *Of Death*, Rabelais and many more, and rearranged them to serve the meaning he intended in his own book. Some accused him of artistically dishonest and mindless plagiarism, and Sterne seems to condemn it: 'Shall we forever make new books, as apothecaries make new mixtures, by pouring only out of one vessel into another?' he asks. 'Are we forever to be twisting and untwisting the same rope?' It was not noticed until some time after his death in 1768 that this passage was itself plagiarised from Robert Burton's attack on literary imitators in his introduction to *The Anatomy of Melancholy*. 'As apothecaries,' Burton observed, 'we make new mixtures every day, pour out of one vessel into another . . . Again, we weave the same web still, twist the same rope again and again.' In his existential search for origins (parentage, character, identity), Tristram is for ever causing them to recede. At the ontological level, the book itself, published at the dawn of the age of mechanical reproduction, is a studied attempt to confront issues of originality, using the very physical form of the book to question the technology which produces identical copies of an 'original'.

Appropriation of previously existing material may be the central aesthetic of the late twentieth century and early twenty-first century, animated by the Internet, sampling and the availability of information and reference material which can be taken and redeployed. However, Sterne was already exploiting the process, testing how crude the technique might seem, how it might fight the poetic unity of a piece of writing, or how successful it could be at generating text containing its own originality while absorbing the thinking and invention of other minds and activating various themes, motifs and symbols and a myriad of enriching associations. He was reflecting how the quote, the stolen or lifted phrase, demonstrates that there are at once repetitions in history and at the same time moments of originality, as material quoted in a different context, embedded in a different story, leading to and from a different place, is never the same as where and when it first appeared. Or perhaps he was indulging in what the writer E. E. Kellett noticed: 'A quotation may be adopted as a subterfuge; you may shelter yourself under the authority of another author when you do not wish to face entire responsibility in your own person.'

Sterne was perhaps suggesting how the writer is not an originator, but an accumulator and editor. He would have been at home with the Internet, which would have allowed him to pursue to topsy-turvy extremes his way of binding fact and fiction, identity and history, quotes and speculations together. Many forms of writing now involve not using a pen or a type-writer and total isolation from the outside world, apart from that which has collected in books, the memory and the imagination, but a machine – the computer – which allows access to knowledge, interpretation and texts, and indeed a whole separate reality absorbing other realities by the day.

A writer can still resist consulting this expanding source of information, presumption and judgement, this warping, or encouraging, or damned unwanted temptation, and exist as though it is of no use in their writing, indeed is a rotten, warping distraction. A writer can on the other hand use this strange new tool to instantly slip into another dimension, to check, uncover and confirm prejudices, to discover evidence, to support hunches, to in fact find pieces and areas of knowledge to reproduce as part of an over-all compilation of ideas that emerges into tentative originality not because of what is said but because of how the montage or labyrinth of facts and obser-vations is positioned and ordered.

As I wrote this book about the north, darting into another dimension to check a fact or make a connection, to support a theory, entering this new venue of content that it seems has no edge and no ending, resembling the idea that history itself is an 'argument without end', it became more and more obvious that in fact I was writing a personal history of the north, and at the same time a history of the north as it is emerging on the Internet. Using and compiling the fragments found on the World Wide Web, strolling through time and text, stumbling across new views, can convey a sense of disrupted time. Each comment or quotation can appear in a list of thoughts and influences, only to tumble back into an unfinished book, an incomplete, interrupted action. Time, and cause and effect, can be mixed up, move from the past to the present, and the present into the past, fused in a multiple series of historical events, and all these events can be seen as interconnected, implicated with each other. The past can explode in the present.

This Internet history – all the problems and dangers of forming history by filtering something that has essentially disappeared through the shape-shifting prejudices, pressures and problems of the present – is a distillation, or a replenishment, of the very idea of history as a creation of different stories using the same facts. Internet history emphasises, on the other side of the screen, out there in some emerging space that might yet stretch on for ever, on the edge of disappearing for ever once the power is turned off, the idea expressed by Arnold Toynbee that history is just one damned thing after another. And the type of history being told depends on just who is deciding what damned thing followed what, and from what point of view.

The Internet might not be the early embryo of God – God, of course, coming after his creation has attained enough intelligence to create himself for real not merely in myth and story. God, of course, coming after enough time for humanity to prove it deserves a god, by developing enough intelligence to make one, and give it a memory of all human events and experience, as decided upon by a committee that made itself up as it went along. The Internet might be merely the latest stage after the prayer, ballad, hymn, play, printing press, theatre, cinema, radio, television enabling the human mind to reflect and nurture itself. It supplements those things, not replaces them, at its best renews them, and nurtures whatever new medium may emerge because of it.

This still means that a creative way of exploiting the material that has been placed on the Internet is an important stage in the sort of thinking that led to the song, novel, the poem, the symphony, the album, the film. Perhaps there is something beyond the novel – which itself as A. S. Byatt of Sheffield has said rises up out of the shortcomings of history – which emerges out of the active exploitation of the Internet not as a convenience for consumers but as a complex representation of experience. The novel is a map of a mind. A new map of the mind, taking into account the way it now has the Internet to deal with, to control, to assimilate, could be this individually directed assortment of received ideas collated from the Internet – viewed as a cosmic library – blended with thoughts, assumptions and feelings that can only appear from the experiences of one person.

If, and this is only one way of thinking about what the Internet is, history has led to the first signs of what will become an *I*, a single consciousness to where everything that has ever happened is heading, a distillation of human endeavour and thoughts into a post-human near god-like vessel, then it is best that what ends up as *I* contains all the best that *we* ever were. This will need a large amount of the north of England for it to be close to complete. In this future ideas as distinctive and dynamic as the north will not disappear, even if the land, the planet, itself disappears.

This *I*, if it speaks English, or whatever it speaks, will be most complete if it speaks with a northern accent, which is of course the best way of reflecting how it has emerged as a combination of different elements with different appetites fighting to survive In the most unlikely of circumstances constantly under pressure for it to disappear, or conform, or lose its fighting, competitive, disobedient qualities. God should speak with a northern accent. The accent, perhaps, of Laurence Sterne.

In *Tristram Shandy* there is no real narrative, and what narrative there is does not proceed in a single direction. The so-called narrative intrusions and comments actually form a linear narrative whose subject is the composing of a narrative. Sterne distrusts language as a means of communication while being fascinated by its elemental magic powers. One critic noted how Sterne loved to litter his pages with esoteric encyclopedic graffiti. It makes the long sentences, like the very first one in the book, for instance, which might seem intellectually indigestible to an unaided eye, immediately available, not as structures but as developments, and reveals, where it occurs, the opening to an interpretation that the mere sweep of an eye might either neglect or refuse. Another difficulty is the babble of competing voices and tones that make up the curious texture of the prose – perhaps he was drawn to quoting and appropriating because of how they generate alien texture.

He intended to explain how our minds work by allowing us to understand how his mind worked, and part of how he did this is how he brings us in and out of the text. *Tristram*'s system demands a reliance on Sterne's leadership, a trust in his choices, that can seem overweening, irritating, demeaning, even perilous or simply not worth the effort. But after some time readers may begin to understand why *Tristram* has turned in each new direction, led the way forward (or backwards) into yet another strange terrain, but they will never predict beforehand where they will next be led. Sterne took pleasure in destroying the normal order of things and in creating an exaggerated appearance of disorder, but only to link the pieces in another and more interesting way. By dramatically scrambling chronological and psychological durations, he emphasised the dual nature of time, something to which an individual responds both by reason and by emotion.

Sterne didn't want unity or coherence or defined direction, at least not in any conventional sense; he wanted multiplicity; he wanted free association of ideas, not subordination of them; he wanted to go backwards or forward or sideways, not in straight linear paths. Virginia Woolf, an ardent admirer, remarked, 'and though the flight of the erratic mind is zigzag, like a dragon-fly's, one cannot deny that this dragonfly has some methods in its flight . . . what fascinates him is his own mind with its whims and fascinations. We go backwards instead of going forward . . . we circle round and round . . .'

The sense of randomness and accident, the role of chance, the principles of absurdity, the confusions in communication, the authorial tone and direction: all these follow naturally from the description of a novel whose intention is to create a fictional world that parallels the realities of experience. It represents how the brain starts several different journeys at once. A single word can make you recollect, or anticipate, several different events. Its realism lies in representing not a completed world (*natura naturata*), but rather a process (*natura naturans*) – the process of creation, of growth, of the author's imagi-nation of his own world, with all its emergent contingencies, idiosyncratic perspectives and alternations of cosmic and local scale. The action is noth-ing less than creation itself making a child, a microscopic model, an individual, an autobiography, so that its completion must always recede before fresh interruptions. In *Tristram Shandy*, the earliest example of experimentation with time in the novel, or at the time the latest, we find that a superficially haphazard form becomes upon closer examination very conscious, even precise. Because there is no definitive reality, the novel, in what would become a classic postmodern style, playfully shifts between surfaces. The idea of the fragment becomes more trustworthy than the whole. Rather than bow down to the limitations imposed by indeterminacy, the texts embrace fragmentation through plurality. By adopting collage, montage, bricolage and pastiche, it succeeds in sketching a more believable simulation of a coherent reality. The disjointed, schizophrenic nature of the discourse not only draws attention to the limitations of perception, but to the possibility of a multiplicity of realities. It becomes impossible ever to truly know anything.

Everything is incomplete until read, and even then the reader only gets a semblance of order brought about by the act of filling in the blanks. Because many realities exist, nothing can be certain. How can anyone ever come to know anything?

Tristram himself, the hero whose story is never completed, stumbles through days and nights in an unpatterned movement of 'transverse zigzaggery'. He is vulnerable to countless accidents, interruptions and digressions. Existence, never quite in focus, appears to be made up of uncontrolled events and meetings within a nonconsequential time frame. The span from birth to death creates an illusion of disorientation as the prevailing reality.

The book includes so much that it hardly has space for the hero of its title. The birth of young Tristram only occurs after 200 pages have passed. Meanwhile, the magnitudes of life's complexities have been exposed to view. Sterne points out how we can read to forget about everything else, losing ourselves in another world made up of fragments of other worlds, at the same time as facing up to everything. *Tristram Shandy* and Sterne, as precursors of the postmodern, the Internet, display research for something else, the form of which isn't yet clear.

Belle Vue Pleasure Gardens

PART SEVEN

The rest of the world rubbing off

Poetry is nobody's business except the poet's, and everybody else can fuck off.

Philip Larkin

85.1

At the other end of the Mersey from Stockport, looking out rather than in, the living, seething Liverpool, constantly digressing from the ordinary, the obvious, defying time and the likely. The city as surreal act of self-belief, the city as fluid integrated object, composed, constructed, imagined, created over centuries, by individuals and communities, by exceedingly practical people and unholy fantasists, by solo and connected corrective acts of genius, by coordinated determined blasts of surrealist survival spirit. The city starring in its own far-fetched story, making stars and making people. Liverpool, built on the show-off genius and transformative memories of those who thought of it and those who live in it, adapt to it, leave it, taking it all with them and spreading it throughout the world, with unique timing and barbed melancholy emotional force, so that it feeds back again. A city not built only by bosses, trade, ambition, chiefs, leaders, managers, officers, academics, envoys, entrepreneurs, planners, literati, but by the adapta-bility, energy and subversive mutating flair of the serf, slave, worker, underling, hired hand, vagabond, outlaw, deputy, steward, pen-pusher, artisan, shopkeeper, apprentice, assistant, aide and gang. Hard-working, blunt and self-assured Lancashire, softer, sweeter Cheshire, steamed, baked and boiled in the spices of the world and soaked in the residual spirit of the poetic, sensitive Celts – the wild, wily, spiritual side of Britishness, pushed away to the edge, the edges, into the margins, against the more prosaic and regulated Anglo-Saxon in the solid indifferent middle. A succession of generations and increasing populations responding to the challenges and pressures that economics thrusts at them by constantly restructuring the society around them, and finding different highly articulate and provocative artistic, dramatic and comic ways to explain, exploit and explore those changes.

A city representing the bleak, brilliant, narrow, open north of England, but out on its own, a compression, distortion and extension of the stubborn energy of pioneers, immigrants, outlaws, artists, entrepreneurs, labourers, dockers, sailors, teachers, drinkers, travellers, politicians, thieves, poets, celebrities, comedians; in this history of the north, this discriminating impartial selection of moments and moods that reflect the making of a whole different world, it could be Manchester – its fierce, ironic, sporting, cultural, commercial, friendly rival – Leeds, Sheffield, Newcastle, Preston, but it is Liverpool, at the other end of the Mersey from Stockport, where I sat on the bus, on my way to school, a million miles away, a few miles away, crossing the start of the Mersey hundreds of times a year, as the water rushed through Stockport, eager to reach Liverpool, which was something else, and undefeated, undeterred, by war, indifference, all forms of hostility, intolerance and condescension.

85.2

1154

Facing what became Liverpool, on the opposite bank, a Benedictine priory was founded between 1154 and 1199, and was the beginning of Birkenhead.

The name is thought to derive from Birchen Head (a birch-covered headland) or else refers to the mouth of the River Birket. The monks started the first ferry service across the Mersey from the priory to Liverpool. The Priory was closed in 1536 on the orders of Henry VIII.

1207

Liverpool, a tiny watery eye blinking bravely in the dense dark cold. Liverpool, Lle'rpwll, Lerpwl, Lyrpul, Leverpul, Laverpul, Lyfrpwll, Leverpole, Liverpul, Lytherpwll, Lieverpull.

King John founded the borough and port of Liverpool to the south of Blackburn on the north shore of the estuary of the River Mersey where it flows into the Irish Sea. John wanted a port independent of nearby Chester, which was too much under the control of its powerful and independent-minded earl, from which to send troops to Ireland. On 23 August 1207 he issued letters patent which resulted in the little hamlet becoming a borough. John invited people to settle in his new township and offered them tax concessions and land to do so, his agents laying out seven streets.

1379

The poll tax returns for Leverpull reveal 86 householders: 26 engaged in agriculture, 18 brewers, 9 servants, 9 cobblers and shoemakers, 5 fishmongers and herringmongers, 4 drapers, 3 tailors, 2 smiths, the mayor, William de Leverpull, a franklin, a tanner, a dyer, a butcher, a carpenter, a chaloner, a weaver and a baker. The list is incomplete.

1565

Liverpool is described as a poor and obscure village. Apparently only the original seven streets in the town were settled, containing 138 cottages and

690 inhabitants: Chapel Street, Castle Street, Dale Street, Bancke Street, Moor Street, Juggler Street and Peppard Street.

1635

A bridge is built over the Pool and a quay and harbour constructed 'for the succour of shipping', and in 1647 Liverpool is made a free and independent port, no longer subject to Chester, where the Dee has silted up. (The Romans had ignored the Mersey in favour of the Dee to the south, which got them further inland to Chester, and the Ribble to the north. Perhaps they avoided the Mersey because the tides and gales during winter were too harsh: Liverpool's name could be an Anglo-Norman translation from Latin of a phrase meaning 'spring time anchorage', because the location was only used during the warmer months. There is no Roman mention of the Mersey, and it was suggested by George Stephenson and Thomas Telford that the Mersey estuary was created by an earthquake in about AD 400 or some time between the fifth-century departure of the Romans and the eleventh-century arrival of the Normans. This would account for the total obscurity of the area around Liverpool until then. It seems to have appeared like the beginning of a work of art, a brave stab in the dark, out of nowhere, but everything has to begin somewhere.)

1667

Sir Edward Moore, a member of the leading family of the town at the time, warns: 'Have a care of them, the men of Liverpool are the most perfidious in all England, worse than my pen can describe.'

1705

Daniel Defoe describes Liverpool as 'one of the wonders of Britain; what it may grow into in time I know not'.

1717

The first dock in Liverpool is built. Previously ships were simply tied up by the shore, but as the port grows busier this is no longer adequate.

85.3

Liverpool is not part of England in the way that New York is not part of America. It is more Welsh, more Irish, more Scottish, more exotically international and defiantly local, a shifty, shifting outpost of defiance, determination and scouring kindness reluctantly connected to the English mainland, more an island set in a sea of dreams and nightmares that's forever taking shape in the imagination, more a mysterious place jutting out into time between the practical stabilising pull of history and the sweeping sharpening force of myth.

It's where it says it is on the map, in position, up there, and along there, down under what's above, above what's below, and rivers and roads and railway lines draw it towards England, and a little bit further out, and you can easily find ways in and out without losing track of time or leaving behind English weather, English telly or English moods. Liverpool, though, fancies that it can just keep going, leave mean and limiting England far behind. It can climb mountains, crack open new territory, even conquer space; the implacable water keeps it connected to the rest of the world, all of history, and grinding reality doesn't wreck its role as a kind of gutsy cosmic link between the tough everyday and the fraily fantastic.

Liverpool has always forced itself forward through the grimy thick and thin of rise and fall, success and failure, hope and hopelessness, despite what is said about it, however hostile the assault on its bittersweet rhyme and reason. Liverpool is always on guard. They know that the English elsewhere look up and over with suspicion and doubt, stumped by the language, needled by the snappy, mongrel confidence, outmanoeuvred by the logic-shredding wit. The city is also always wary of what might appear over the horizon, from the endless heavy sea, of what unknown force, for good or evil, might wash up on its vulnerable shore. The city has had more money than some, and been poorer than most. It's seen better days; it's always on the up; it believes in itself; it's all on its own. It's been associated with grotesque episodes in history. It's had ideas that have contributed to the progress of the whole world. Its hands are dirty, but its mind is open.

You can hear it in the way Liverpool talks, finding meaning in the very heart of words. You can hear all its grievous, glorious past in a single sentence spoken about nothing much in particular. Local history, and its well-reported agitated impact on the planet, fizzes one way or another on the whetted tongue of a Liverpudlian. You can hear the enterprise and belligerence, the flippancy and the rage, the ambition and the stubbornness, the influx of this, the passing-through of that, the constant rumour of the amazing and the bog standard. You can hear the guilt, the defensiveness, the aggression, the pride, the victimised flush, the determination not to be taken for a ride, not to be taken for granted, the hunger to be in the know, first in line, ready for anything, dead on the money.

In a single sentence spoken about nothing much in particular you can hear that this is a city that has fought off all manner of danger, derision and repression, from inside and outside, and has lived to tell the tale, and tell it with a kind of spectacular, cunning relish. You can hear arrogance and music, love and anger, a turbulent, tragic city folded into speech, centuries of movement and achievement propelling words that urge the future to happen, now, again, now and again, friendly, violent vowels that connect friends and family and streets and memories and strangers with everything that's happened, that's come and gone, that's lived and died, across 800 years. It's the cranky, nimble sound of a people who have been loved and hated, ignored and exiled, the sound of an inspired but persecuted collection of voices, religions, myths, schools, rhymes and traditions that have fused together in one impoverished, prosperous place where, against all odds, they found refuge, a home and a future. The Liverpool playwright Alun Owen suggested that the multiracial population of the city 'evolved an accent for themselves', borrowed from their Irish and Welsh grandfathers in response to the 'problem of identity'.

One Liverpudllan wit described Scouse as 'one third Irish, one third Welsh and one third catarrh', which is not far off the mark, according to Andrew Hamer, a regional accents expert at Liverpool University. 'During the potato famines in the mid-nineteenth century Irish immigrants moved to Liverpool, some of whom spoke Gaelic. It was their children who first spoke with a distinctive accent that was a mix of Irish accents and the accent from neighbouring Manchester.' Liverpool grew to be the 'second city of the empire' (an accolade also given to Glasgow and Calcutta) through trade with the colonies and serving the Lancashire factories inland. The distinctiveness of the Scouse accent is largely the result of immigration, particularly from the Celtic lands surrounding Liverpool, but also from elsewhere, far away, bitten and nibbled at from all over the world, biting and nibbling back.

The peculiarities of Scouse are almost entirely phonological; thanks to prolonged and regular contact with London, its grammar and vocabulary remain close to British standard English. It has been suggested that its adenoidal quality is derived from poor nineteenth-century public health – the prevalence of colds and chills. Impairment of nasal resonance in many people over a long time resulted in it becoming regarded as 'the group norm' and it was copied by immigrants. Liverpool, its language becoming itself when the city made the most of what it had and didn't have, in the nineteenth century, when people poured in and poured out, leaving behind sounds and attitudes, and changing a nervy town on the obscure edge of Lancashire into a self-glorifying city on the exhilarating edge of the world. The most important port in the British empire had by the end of the nineteenth century a morphing charged sound all of its own. It's one of the city's greatest achievements – the mixing together out of the air, the sea, the world, the hunger, the place where it is, the people, whether down and out and up against it, or prospering, or on the prowl, or on the verge of discovery – its very own dialect.

85.4

Liverpool, surreal. Liverpool, sardonic. Liverpool, battered dignity. Liverpool, flotsam of maritime memory. Liverpool, never quite what it was because everything it does changes what it does. Liverpool, the home of Liverpool. Liverpool, welcoming the world. Liverpool, cutting-edge, keeping pace, dropping anchor. Liverpool, lost. Liverpool, as spontaneous as life itself. Liverpool, born. Liverpool, going to sea. Liverpool, set in its ways, at the end of the line, at the beginning of time, with its back to the land, its feet in the water, its head in the clouds, its heart on its sleeve, hearts in its mouth. Liverpool, its being so cheerful that keeps us going. Liverpool, the first city to rock in Britain. Liverpool, boring people to tears. Liverpool, singing for its supper. Liverpool, a long memory for those who aimed kicks when it was down. Liverpool, eagles become seagulls. Liverpool, working. Liverpool, dreaming. Liverpool, a terminus for down and outs. Liverpool, corrupt. Liverpool, uncompromising. Liverpool, playfulness turned into art, and philosophy, and business. Liverpool, a relatively small provincial city plus hinterland with associated metaphysical space as defined by dramatic moments in history, emotional occasions and general restlessness. Liverpool, the rest of the world rubbing off. Liverpool, occupation hard knocks.

Liverpool in the seventeenth century, on the River Mersey, newly built in brick and stone, handsome paved streets, fashionable and well-dressed people, a large fine town, London in miniature. Liverpool, spirit, spirited, spiritual.

'This commercial intercourse of the inhabitants, induces a general harmony and sociability, unclouded by those ceremonies and distinctions that are met with in more polished life; hence the freedom and animation which the town has always been observed to possess.' William Moss, *Georgian Liverpool*, 1797.

Also in 1797 the Reverend William Bagshaw Stevens: 'throughout this large-built town every brick is cemented to its fellow brick by the blood and sweat of Negroes'. The first known slave ship here was the

Liverpool Merchant, which took 220 African slaves to Barbados in 1699. In 1768 the *Liverpool Chronicle* advertises the sale of a 'fine Negroe boy, of about 4 foot 5 inches high. Of a sober, humane, intractable disposition, eleven or twelve years of age, talks English very well, and can dress hair in a tolerable way.' By the 1790s Liverpool ships carry 80 per cent of the British slave trade – over 40 per cent of the European trade. The Liverpool Triangle saw ships from the port take Cheshire salt, Lancashire coal, textiles, Staffordshire pottery and Birmingham metal to west Africa, exchange the goods for slaves and sail to the West Indies, where the human cargo was traded for sugar, spices and rum which was then taken back to Liverpool.

Defending the slave trade in Parliament in 1806, Liverpool's MP, General Bonastre Tarleton, himself from a slave-owning family, describes with pride Liverpool's rise 'to become the second place in wealth and population in the British Empire'. During the same debate William Roscoe and William Wilberforce, on behalf of the Society for the Abolition of the Slave Trade, are adamant that 'nothing short of an entire and immediate abolition will satisfy'. The vote results in the abolition of slavery in Britain the following year. The last British slaver, *Kitty Amelia*, under Captain Hugh Crow, a one-eyed Manxman, leaves Liverpool in July 1807. Cotton saves the day. Eight new docks are built in Liverpool between 1815 and 1835.

William Gladstone was born on 29 December 1809 – the same year as Abraham Lincoln, Charles Darwin, Edgar Allan Poe and Alfred Tennyson – in Rodney Street, Liverpool. Gladstone was the fourth son and the fifth of six children. His father had 'half commoner blood, robust, energetic merchant and magnate drive', his mother a sympathetic, progressive, semi-poetic sensibility. His father owned mines in Wales, factories in Lancashire and sugar plantations in Jamaica. He went to Eton in 1821, Oxford afterwards. His links with his hometown were not strong, but it is said he retained traces of his accent, and claimed that he 'backed the masses against the classes'.

Queen Victoria described Gladstone as a 'half-mad firebrand' and complained he always addressed her as though she were a public meeting, but to a large part of the British working classes he was the

Grand Old Man, the people's William. Four times prime minister, at fifty-eight, seventy, seventy-six and eighty-two, sitting in the House of Commons for sixty-three years, Disraeli's chief opponent, Gladstone provoked strong reactions. 'Oxford on the surface,' said Walter Bagehot, writer and constitutional expert, 'but Liverpool underneath.' There are two statues of Gladstone in Manchester, for supporting two issues crucial to the city's development – free trade and political reform. Holmes and Watson's bulldog was named Gladstone, and the name was given to a style of large briefcase hinging open on metal frames.

In 1810 75,000 people were packed into one square mile of Liverpool streets and fever-haunted alleys. The pressure on city-centre housing for dock and factory workers, who needed to live close to their work, was counterpointed by the fine houses of the better off, which were built on the outskirts in places like Crosby, Sefton and, into the twentieth century, on the Wirral. In the late eighteenth century the Wirral was a wild region with a total population of about 6,000. Most of the people worked on the land as agricultural labourers.

Liverpool in 1820 has more breweries than any other British port, a gin shop or alehouse to every forty inhabitants.

Liverpool, Victorian overcrowding, malnutrition, filth and disease. Liverpool was the most densely populated town in England. Mortality was unparalleled – one in every 25 people died of fever in one year. Following the Municipal Reform Act of 1835, the city was obliged to tackle the problem of the 1,200 thieves under the age of fifteen and 3,600 prostitutes in the town. The corpses that accumulate overnight in the docks and alleys are collected in the death house and there each day a crowd can be found gazing upon the nameless dead. Liverpool, genius. Liverpool, the archetype of the modern secular city. Liverpool, the approach to unknown worlds. Liverpool, Herman Melville, 1839, genuinely comparing its docks with the Great Wall of China and the pyramids of the pharaohs, 'In the evening, especially when the sailors are gathered in great numbers, these streets present a most singular spectacle, the entire population of the vicinity being seemingly turned into them. Hand organs and fiddles, plied by strolling musicians, mix with the songs of the seamen, the babble of women and children and the whining of beggars. From the various boarding houses proceed the noises of revelry.'

In 1845, of the Irish fleeing to America from the Great Famine 90 per cent pass through Liverpool. Those who never make the boat, flinching from the gruelling, often fatal voyage, or those fleeced by the infamous local 'land-pirates' are called 'the scum left by the tide of migration between Europe and the continent of America'. Melville: '. . . of all seaports in the world, Liverpool, perhaps, most abounds in all the variety of land-sharks, land-rats, and other vermin, which make the hapless mariner their prey. In the shape of landlords, bar-keepers, clothiers, crimps, and boarding house loungers, the land-sharks devour him, limb by limb'. Liverpool becomes known as the hospital and cemetery of Ireland.

A more positive side of the Irish presence was noticed in 1760 as Liverpool pulled ahead of Bristol as a port: 'This great increase in commerce is owing to the spirit and indefatigable industry of the inhabitants, the majority of whom are either native Irish, or of Irish descent: a fresh proof that the Hibernians thrive best when transplanted. They engage in trade as battle, with little or no spirit at home, but with unparalleled gallantry abroad.' By the late nineteenth century the Irish presence is nearly 200,000 strong, belonging in neither their old home but loving its memory, nor their new home, there but not there, yet, but falling in love with its potential, struggling against adversity, willing to tackle any task, Micks on the make in Mersey, developing the underdog persecuted patois that is the precursor of Scouse.

Dublin is not far from Liverpool, wrote Anthony Burgess, 'and Catholic Lancashire has allowed the indigenous form of its culture to be influenced, and sometimes swamped, by Ireland. More than that, Anglo-Saxon Catholic blood has been much mixed with Irish . . .'

85.5

In 1846 William Duncan (usually known as Doctor Duncan) was appointed Britain's first medical officer of health and began a programme of improvements to Liverpool's water supply, drainage and living conditions.

A new dock was officially opened on 30 July 1846 by Prince Albert. The wood used to build warehouses had made fires a big problem. The Albert Dock was the first enclosed, non-combustible dock warehouse complex in the world, and the first structure in Britain to be built entirely of cast iron, brick and stone. It gained another first in 1848, when the world's first hydraulic warehouse hoists were installed.

In Chapter 4 of Emily Brontë's *Wuthering Heights*, written in 1845 and 1846 at the beginning of the Great Potato Famine and set during the years of slave trading about fifty years before, gentleman farmer Mr Earnshaw walks sixty miles from his home on the remote treeless Yorkshire Moors to Liverpool on business. He finds a dark-skinned orphaned boy 'starving, and houseless, and as good as dumb in the streets of Liverpool'. The boy has no place to live, speaks 'gibberish' that nobody can understand, and might have been abandoned by a foreign visitor. His identity as an ambiguous racial 'other' has left him with nothing to belong to; he represents the mongrel, the irregular black, 'dark almost as if it came from the devil', a cause of considerable nervousness among Victorians. Later in the book he will be referred to as beast, savage, lunatic and demon.

Earnshaw pities him, and after following the law of the time and asking after 'its owner', brings the boy from Liverpool to Wuthering Heights, into the Earnshaw home. He decides to adopt him and bring him up with his own children, the beautiful Catherine and her truculent brother Hindley. Cathy is intrigued by the boy, who is given the name Heathcliff, the name of a son who had died in childhood. Even as his lover, Cathy describes Heathcliff as an 'unreclaimed creature, without refinement, without cultivation; an arid wilderness of furze and whinstone'. Liverpool was the only place, the only space – where life itself is an ongoing experiment in fusion and diffusion – that Emily

Brontë could send Earnshaw to find a child with this dangerous, glamorous mixture of the unknown, untamed, tough, satanic, unpredictable and possibly noble.

In his autobiographical 1849 novel, *Redburn*, the quintessential nineteenth-century Liverpool novel, written by an outsider, on the route to Joyce's Dublin, 'all climes and countries embrace', voyaging towards *Moby Dick*, Herman Melville relates how it was in Liverpool that he first saw black sailors walking arm in arm with white women, and remarks how much the black Americans loved the city because they felt a freedom there that they did not have at home. It is said that it in this book Melville presents the notion that Liverpool was named in honour of an extinct creature called the Liver Bird.

> As we sailed ahead the river contracted. The day came and soon passing two lofty landmarks on the Lancashire shore, we rapidly drew near the town, and at last, came to anchor in the stream. Looking shoreward, I beheld lofty ranges of dingy warehouses, which seemed very deficient in the elements of the marvellous; and bore a most unexpected resemblance to the warehouses along South-street in New York. There was nothing strange; nothing extraordinary about them. There they stood; a row of calm and collected warehouses; very good and substantial edifices, doubtless, and admirably adapted to the ends had in view by the builders; but plain, matter of fact warehouses, never the less, and that was all that could be said of them. To be sure, I did not expect every house in Liverpool must be a Leaning Tower of Pisa, or a Strasburg Cathedral; but yet these edifices I must confess were a sad and bitter disappointment to me. But it was different with Larry the whaleman; who to my surprise, looking about him delighted, exclaimed, 'Why, this 'ere is a considerable place – I'm dummed if it ain't quite a place – Why them 'ere houses is considerable houses. It beats the coast of Afriky, all hollow; nothing like this in Madagasky, I tell you – I'm dummed, boys, if Liverpool ain't a city!'

85.6

Liverpool, under an ambiguous rainy heaven. Nathaniel Hawthorne was installed as the United States consul in Liverpool in the 1840s. Living on the Birkenhead side of the river, he wrote in his diary that the parlour window gave him a pretty good idea of the nautical business of Liverpool:

> . . . the constant objects being the little black steamers, puffing unquietly along . . . sometimes towing a long string of boats from Runcorn or otherwhere up the river, laden with goods; – and sometimes gallanting in or out of a tall ship . . . Now and then, after a blow sea, a vessel comes in with her masts broken short off in the midst, and marks of rough handling about the hull. Once a week comes a Cunard steamer, with its red funnel pipe whitened by the salt spray; and firing off some cannon to announce her arrival, she moors to a large iron buoy in the middle of the river . . . Immediately comes puffing towards her a little mail-steamer, to take away her mail bags, and such of the passengers as choose to land; and for several hours afterwards, the Cunarder liner lies with smoke and steam coming out of her, as she were smoking her pipe after some toilsome passage across the Atlantic.

'Liverpool contains a multitude of inhabited cellars, close and damp, with not drain nor any convenience . . . Some time ago I visited a poor woman in distress, the wife of a labouring man; she had been confined only a few days, and herself and infant were lying on straw in a vault . . . with a clay floor impervious to water. There was no light or ventilation and the air was dreadful. I had to walk on bricks across the floor to reach her bedside, as the floor itself was flooded with stagnant water.'
Report of the Royal Commission on the Sanitary State of Large Towns and Populous Districts, 1845.

85.7

Liverpool trade and commerce as described in *Lewis's Topographical Dictionary of England*, 1848:

The most remarkable feature in the history of Liverpool is, the extraordinary rapidity with which it has risen into importance. Among the causes which have produced its elevation to a rank but partially inferior to that of the metropolis, are, its situation on the shore of a noble river which expands into a wide estuary; its proximity to the Irish coast; its central position with respect to the United Kingdom; its intimate connection with the principal manufacturing districts, and with every part of the kingdom, by rivers, canals, and railroads; and the persevering industry and enterprising spirit of its inhabitants.

For the collection of customs, &c., due to the crown, Liverpool was anciently a member of the port of Chester; but, as is evident from records belonging to the corporation, it was an independent port as early as the year 1335, though for some centuries it made but little progress. The commerce may be divided into several distinct branches. The trade with Ireland appears to have been established, or greatly promoted, by the settlement here of a few mercantile families from that country, about the middle of the sixteenth century; at that time, only fifteen vessels, of the aggregate burthen of 259 tons, belonged to the port, whereas Liverpool now imports of Irish produce alone an amount equal in value to several millions annually. Another principal branch is the trade with the United States. The chief article of commerce in respect of that country, is cotton, which indeed may be considered as the staple of the town; Manchester and the other cotton manufacturing districts are supplied from the port with the raw material, and manufactured cotton goods form more than half of the entire exports of Liverpool . . . The United States also send hither tobacco, rice, dyewares, and numerous other varieties of American produce.

John Milne, born in Liverpool in 1850, was a man alive with energy and enthusiasm with a passion for earthquakes. At the age of thirteen he entered Liverpool Collegiate Institute, where he won many prizes, one of which was a sum of money which he used to fund a trip to the Lake District. He lived in Rochdale, then moved to Japan, working there as a geologist and mining engineer for twenty years. He pioneered modern seismology, and invented the seismograph for recording movement in the earth. In 1898, with W. K. Burton, he published the classic textbook *Earthquakes and Other Earth Movements*. In this he correctly argued that earthquakes occurred along fault lines in the earth's crust. He set up his research centre for seismic research, the leading establishment for earthquake studies in the world, near Newport on the Isle of Wight. A Newport local said of Milne, 'He always spoke with a quiet Lancastrian accent, which fascinated us lads, as did his nicotine-stained, bushy moustache with a gap burned in it by numerous cigarettes.'

Charles Dickens's first public reading in Liverpool, at the Philharmonic Hall, was in 1858. He sailed to America from Liverpool on at least two occasions, visited the docks and spent a night with the local police to aid his research in writing *The Uncommercial Traveller*. His time in Liverpool must have been very dear to him: 'Liverpool lies in my heart next only to London.'

85.8

A prophecy in *Recollections of Old Liverpool*, 1863, an anonymous author recalling the mid-eighteenth century: 'Could we draw aside the thick veil that hides the future from us, we might perhaps behold our great seaport swelling into a metropolis, in size and importance, its suburbs creeping out to an undreamed-of distance from its centre; or we might, reversing the picture, behold Liverpool by some unthought-of calamity, some fatal, unforeseen mischance, some concatenation of calamities, dwindled down to its former insignificance, its docks shipless, its warehouses in ruins, its streets moss-grown . . . Under which of these two fates will Liverpool find its lot some centuries hence; which of these two pictures will it then present?'

Liverpool, 1880: Queen Victoria grants the town the right to call itself a city.

Liverpool, 1886: the Mersey Railway Tunnel, the first to pass under the river, links Liverpool with the developing town of Birkenhead and the Wirral peninsula. The mammoth task takes approximately six years with the main tunnel excavated with picks, shovels and explosives. The tunnel will soon carry over ten million passengers a year. However, many people still use the ferry, disliking the smoke and fumes of the railway.

Liverpool, the Irish impulse to perform, the Welsh need to sing, the sailors' shanties, the movement of the mighty river, the roar of the sea, the rhythm of the wind, the beat of the factory. Liverpool, the slope by the creek. Liverpool, on the threshold of the invisible. Liverpool, pulling itself up by its bootlaces. Liverpool, a frenzy of activity. Liverpool, nothing lasts for ever. Liverpool, welcome to the real world. Liverpool, Penny Lane, moldy moldy man, a cellar full of noise, more popular than Jesus, blah blah blarney, the centre of making it up as you go along. Liverpool, fuck right off. Liverpool, it really is a fantastic game. Liverpool, the centre of somewhere, if not everything, where something happens, most of the time, leading to something else, only in Liverpool. Liverpool, made up. Liverpool, you couldn't make it up. Liverpool, ban the bomb. Liverpool, gateway to the empire, leaving for America, Canada, Australia, New Zealand. Liverpool, arriving from Africa, from the Indies, from places without names, Jews, Africans, Asians, the Irish, the Chinese. Liverpool, a direct steamer connection with China, trading tea, cotton and silk, Chinese seamen jumping ship in the mid-1800s, settling around Pitt Street, Cleveland Square and Frederick Street, forming the first Chinatown in Europe, setting up shops, cafés and boarding houses for Chinese sailors passing through a strange town with alien ways and customs, spreading inland by the First World War. Liverpool City Council concerned over Chinese marrying English women, gambling and opium consumption. Liverpool's chief constable, however, expresses the view that the resident Chinese are a 'quiet, inoffensive and industrious people'.

Chinese-speakers add a further layer of molten mutable tone and tang to the local accent.

Liverpool, the end of the road. Liverpool, offering hope to millions passing through on their way to America. Liverpool, the world in a city. At the end of the nineteenth century Liverpool concerns own one third of British ships, and one seventh of the world's registered merchant tonnage. One in ten of the world's ships visits the port. The great shipping lines such as Cunard and White Star, owners of super-ships such as *Mauritania*, *Lusitania*, *Aquitania* and *Titanic*, are Liverpool companies. Liverpool, motivated by progressives, inspired by the classical and Renaissance past, constructing public buildings that would not look out of place in Venice, Florence or Athens. Liverpool, 1901: for eighteen months chaotic Welsh adventurer, proto-hippy, post-Impressionist Augustus John teaches at the progressive art school established by the university in 1895 – 'I became more rebellious in Liverpool' – long hair, gold earrings, flamboyant clothes, Gypsy mind, later painter of Dylan Thomas, T. E. Lawrence, Aleister Crowley, Tallulah Bankhead, Thomas Hardy. Liverpool, never the same again.

Liverpool, 1902. James Nuttall took his two sons Edmund and James into partnership trading under the name Edmund Nuttall & Company. In 1904 James Senior died and the business was carried on and rapidly developed by Edmund, a contractor down to his fingertips with a flair for assessing the price of a job and the right way to carry it out. In 1908 they built the Royal Liver Building, the first reinforced-concrete 'skyscraper' in Britain, 300 feet high to the top of the Liver Birds. Liverpool, a combination of ancient empire, classically inspired buildings, cornices, attics, mouldings, pediments, rustication, granite columns, built to British empire standards as the empire began to expire, and high-speed lifts, techniques and steel frames derived from contemporary American architecture, in which a new empire mentality was materialising, one Liverpool fancied itself capable of keeping up with because it fancied it had set it in motion. Several buildings have a distinctive American quality. Oriel Chambers (1864) is the most revolutionary and a frank, stripped-down expression of function and technology; it anticipated by twenty years the modernist commercial buildings of Chicago and New York, and was the world's first metal-framed, glass-curtain-walled building. India Buildings (1924–31) is typical of North American architecture of the 1920s; it includes a central barrel-vaulted arcade, another American feature. Barclays Bank (1927–32) is similarly monumental and American. The Adelphi Hotel was a grand building for transatlantic travellers; its exterior and interior reflected the wealth of the city.

The first railway in Britain to convert from steam to electric operation was the Mersey Railway in 1903 when they electrified the line from the city centre to Birkenhead, solving the problems of the choking atmosphere caused by the steam trains in the tunnel under the river. Liverpool, cultural ambitions. The University of Liverpool was created in 1903, absorbing an earlier college. The immense Anglican cathedral was started the same year. It took until 1974 to complete. It is the largest Anglican building in the world and the fifth largest cathedral of any denomination. Its length is 600 feet compared with 510 for St Paul's in London and 715 for St Peter's in Rome. Liverpool, the city at its peak.

Malcolm Lowry – who also went by the name of Malcolm Boden Lowry – was born on 28 July 1909 in New Brighton, a dormitory town on the tip of the Wirral, where his father was a wealthy cotton broker with Methodist affiliations, who fox-hunted. His Merseyside youth informed his writing, and Liverpool, which he described as 'that terrible city whose main street is the ocean', continued to hold tremendous significance for him. He was a restless spirit, 'a small boy chased by furies', an alcoholic by thirteen, who wanted to write and not follow his three older brothers into the family business. At the age of eighteen he set sail from Liverpool – 'ran away to sea' – as a deckhand on a freighter bound for Yokohama. Liverpool, the sailor the real king; everybody in Liverpool loves a sailor.

Liverpool, Frank Hornby, the man who created Meccano (first called Mechanics Made Easy, patented in 1901, appearing in Liverpool toy shops the same year), Dinky Toys and Hornby model railways. Liverpool, small patches of wasted wasteland in the shape of President de Gaulle. Liverpool, beat. Liverpool, speaking in tongues. In 1907 Walter Dixon Scott wrote that Liverpool was 'Quite frankly an almost pure product of the nineteenth century, a place empty of memorials, a mere jungle of modern civic apparatus. Its people are people who have been precipitately gathered together from north, from south, from overseas, by a sudden impetuous call. Its houses are houses not merely of recent birth but pioneer houses, planted instantly upon what, so brief a while ago, was unflawed meadowland and marsh. Both socially and architecturally it becomes, in large measure, a city without ancestors.'

The first branch of Woolworth's in England opens in 1909 in Church Street. Liverpool, the summer of 1911, gripped by mass social unrest and strike action which peaks in August, when troops are dispatched to deal with protesters on the streets and a warship is stationed in the Mersey. The extreme measures taken by the home secretary, Winston Churchill, which resulted in violent clashes and a number of deaths, have led some historians to conclude that events in Liverpool during 1911 were the nearest the UK has come to a revolution.

Liverpool, Arthur Wynne, inventor of the crossword, his two passions in life, music and puzzles. He was able to use this latter interest to earn his living when he accepted the editorship of the fun section of the Sunday newspaper *New York World*. It was on 21 December 1913, when he was pressed to fill a space on a page that the printers were in a hurry to lock up, that he thought of reviving the acrostic word game, which dates from at least Roman times. He constructed a hollow diamond-shaped grid of interlocking words and dubbed his creation a word-cross. It was clear from the start, from the volume of letters sent in by readers, that Wynne's word-crosses were popular. He did not benefit financially from the many newspapers that used the syndication service as he never patented the concept which brought so much pleasure and frustration to so many.

The start of the First World War in 1914 saw the beginning of the decline in Liverpool's fortunes. The passenger liners moved to Southampton, which had better tidal conditions, but were themselves later superseded by air travel, and Liverpool's substantial banking and insurance businesses moved to London as part of the general concentration of the nation's business elite in the capital.

'Scouser' creeps into general use around Scotland Road after the First World War, by 1945 leapfrogging 'Dicky Sam' – imitation Yank slang, someone born and bred in Liverpool, within the sound of the bells of St Nicholas, the waterfront parish church? – and 'wacker' or 'whacker' – from 'wack', army slang for goods or provisions – as the main signifying badge for locals who belong to some touchy alternative nation.

On 19 September 1934 the Beatles' future manager and mentor, Brian Epstein, was born in suburban Liverpool, in the same street as Gladstone. His father Harry called his mother Queenie because her name Malka is Hebrew for 'queen'. Next to the furniture store that the Epstein family owned was the North End Road Music Stores. The Epsteins later expanded and took over NEMS. He recalled being 'ragged, nagged and bullied' for his homosexuality and dropped out of school at the age of sixteen. Liverpool, the great unwashed. Liverpool, people passing through, sticking around, passing it on, keeping it to themselves, sharing it out. Liverpool, Knotty Ash. Liverpool, the summer of love. Liverpool, no scented breeze. Liverpool, the full-bodied whine of self-pity. Liverpool, 1931, population 855, 688. Liverpool, step inside, love.

Liverpool, Scotland Road. Scotty by the docks, the first port of call for desperate Irish emigrants fleeing the ravages of the Great Famine in the 1840s. Scotland Road is located in the heart of Liverpool and runs along what was once the old coach route to the north from the town centre. It became a turnpike road in the 1760s, as the road to Preston via Walton and Burscough. The first through service by coach from London started in 1861. Entry into Liverpool was along the Prescot Road, which had become a turnpike and been improved from its former status as a packhorse route, when it would have been totally unusable by stagecoaches. The 'Flying Machine' made its journey in two to three days; fare two shillings and sixpence, outside passengers and children on laps half price. Some time after this stagecoaches took this road north through Lancaster and Kendal up to Scotland, giving Scotland Road its name.

Between the years of 1880 and 1912 a steady flow of Italian immigrants arrived in Liverpool. By 1913 it was estimated there were in excess of 400 Italian-born residents of the tiny cluster of streets which had affectionately become known as Little Italy. By the 1920s the inhabitants of this close-knit community had become an integral part of the city. Many earned their living as musicians, hotel workers, knife sharpeners and street entertainers, although it was in ice-cream-making that several families distinguished themselves. Others opened fish and chip shops throughout the city, and as a result of their enterprises the Santangeli, Gianelli, Podesta, Chiappe and Fusco families became part of the folklore of Liverpool. Scotland Road's Little Italy was also renowned for the many outstanding boxers developed in the amateur boxing clubs of the neighbourhood. One such was Dom Valente, who topped the bill at Madison Square Gardens.

In the early twentieth century the number of pubs in the Scotland Road area peaked at approximately 224, with 65 actually on Scotland Road. By 1960 the number had reduced to 111 in the area and 41 on the road. Liverpool, according to J. B. Priestley in 1933: 'Neon lighting and flashing signs. Cinemas, theatres, dance halls, grill rooms, boxing matches, cocktail bars, all in full glittering swing. The Adelphi Hotel had dressed up for the evening, was playing waltzes, and for the time being did not care a fig about the lost Atlantic trade.' Liverpool was not at its best when Priestley arrived in the city that autumn, but nor did the author want to find the city at its best. Liverpool he found imposing and dark, 'like a city in a rather gloomy Victorian novel'. It was foggy, the streets slippery and a little dangerous. He found tenements where 'the open doorways gave out the reek of unwashed humanity'.

The opening of the Queensway Tunnel in 1934 was a key moment in the modern history of Liverpool. Named in honour of Queen Mary, the tunnel (or 'wonder tube' as it was described in a newsreel item on the event) connected King's Square in Birkenhead with Old Haymarket in Liverpool, and at the time of opening was the longest underwater tunnel in the world. It was hailed as one of the world's great engineering triumphs and was Britain's biggest single municipal enterprise ever. More than 1.2 million tons of rock, gravel and clay were excavated, some of it used to build Otterspool Promenade. Of the 1,700 men who worked on the tunnel during the nine years of its construction, seventeen were killed. The King and Queen went on to open a new central library in Birkenhead, the original Carnegie Library having been chosen as the final site of the Birkenhead entrance to the tunnel. At the opening the King said, 'Who can reflect without awe that the will and power of man which in our own time have created the noble bridges of the

Thames, the Forth, the Hudson and Sydney Harbour, can drive also tunnels such as this, wherein many streams of wheeled traffic may run in light and safety below the depth and turbulence of a tidal water bearing the ships of the world.' In the days that followed, the tunnel turned into something of a tourist attraction, with crowds watching the steady flow of traffic between Liverpool and Birkenhead.

85.9

Liverpool, hit hard by German bombers on the nights of 20, 21 and 22 December 1940 with 622 people killed and 777 injured. Liverpool, one of the most heavily blitzed cities outside London, the docks destroyed, but the Luftwaffe's success hidden from the Germans. Anti-U-boat measures were controlled from Liverpool, from the basement of Derby House. Previously this work had been done in Plymouth. Liverpool, the son of a bookmaker, Jimmy Tarbuck was born on 6 February 1940. 'My dad was a very jolly, funny guy who enjoyed the company of professional comedians. He'd been to school with a famous comic called Ted Ray.' He left school at fifteen and started work as a garage mechanic but was sacked from this and many subsequent jobs for 'fooling around'. Liverpool, John Lennon was born to the sound of Hitler's bombs in Liverpool on the night of 9 October 1940. His mother Julia gave him the middle name Winston as a tribute to Prime Minister Churchill. His father Alfred, a ship's steward, was at sea at the time of the birth and was to spend most of the war years away, either at sea or AWOL.

'I was bored on 9 of Octover 1940 when, I believe, the Nasties were still booming us led by Madalf Heatlump (Who only had one). Anyway they didn't get me. I attended to varicous schools in Liddypol. And still didn't pass-much to my Auntie's supplies. As a member of the most publified Beatles my and (P, G, and R's) records might seem funnier to some of you than this book, but as far as I'm conceived this correction of short writty is the most wonderfoul larf I've ever ready.

'God help and breed you all.' John Lennon.

Liverpool, James Paul McCartney was born in Liverpool's Walton Hospital on 18 June 1942. His father Jim worked in the cotton trade and played trumpet and piano in jazz and ragtime bands; his mother Mary worked as a midwife. Young Tarbuck attended the same school as John Lennon, Dovedale Primary, from 1946 to 1951. George Harrison was there two years later. Tarbuck later remembered John as unusual and belligerent. Pete Shotton remembers Tarbuck throttled Lennon with his school scarf for 'looking at him funny' and was pacified only when Shotton explained that John looked at everyone that way because of his short-sightedness.

John Brophy's 1946 novel *City of Departures* is set in Liverpool at the end of the Second World War. His protagonist Charles Thorneycroft is returning home after artistic success in the metropolis and reflecting that if he had stayed in his native city he would have become a 'local painter', deriving most of his income from formal portraits of aldermen, ship owners and cotton brokers. Describing his city, Thorneycroft recalls that there was hardly ever a day without wind and that, too, spoke of the sea and the port. 'The city air was fresh, it blew perpetually strong or mild off the sea and the river, and channelled its gusty way through every street. It ought to be a healthy air, and it had the tang of health, the odour of tidal salt water, edged with smells from mud flat and sand hills and shores strewn with seaweed. But it was not healthy. It was laden with smoke and soot and grease, and with smells from tanneries, breweries, oil-cake factories, margarine factories, smells from the engine rooms of ships, from dockyards, from thousands of warehouses where every sort of cargo was stored.'

Walking through the city streets, noticing the grime, dinginess and unrepaired bomb damage, Thorneycroft is depressed by the contrast between what he sees and his boyhood memories of a proud thriving place. But once on the street he rediscovers Liverpool's urgency: 'Here where the ships sailed in and unloaded, loaded again and sailed out once more to all the oceans of the world, here was visible all around him a continuing magnificence. Here was no sign of lethargy or despondent regrets for the prosperities of the past. Here Liverpool was laying claim with a brawny fist to its own important place in the world.'

Liverpool, destruction and dislocation, places no longer existing, some houses and streets apparently moved somewhere else. Liverpool, in transit. Liverpool, on the hoof. Liverpool, the spaces of the city shifted, the physical replaced by the psychical. Liverpool, the satanic quality of Lime Street station. Liverpool, shipping in decline, the port now at the wrong end of the country. After the war Liverpool City Council decided that a clean start was needed. Along with the bombed houses, huge parts of the old Victorian city were bulldozed and thousands of families moved out of the city to live in new council estates at Kirkby, Speke and Skelmersdale. Liverpool, car factories built for the redundant dockers. From 1946 John Lennon lived with his Aunt Mimi (Mary Smith) and Uncle George in their house, Mendips, at 251 Menlove Avenue, Liverpool, after his mother had handed over care of her son to them. John was based here from age six to twenty-four. Liverpool, post-war sailors bringing American 45-rpm blues, jazz, proto-rock-and-roll, country and western records into the city, the dirty seeds of the Mersey Sound planted in the minds of successful and not so successful eleven-plus kids. Liverpool FC winning the first post-war First Division championship.

Under the Volcano (1947) is now widely accepted not only as Malcolm Lowry's masterpiece but also as one of the great works of twentieth-century writing. It exemplifies Lowry's methods as a writer, which involved drawing heavily upon autobiographical material and imbuing it with complex and allusive layers of symbolism. *Under the Volcano* depicts a series of complex and unwillingly destructive relationships, and is set against a rich evocation of Mexico. The great Liverpool writer sets his visions outside Liverpool, but the road began there, the road that went to sea, the road that travelled to and through Kerouac and Ginsberg, into the beat that rattled under the rough, smooth skin of the Beatles.

A sinister ferry opened Lowry's first published tale, the short story 'Goya the Obscure', in which the hero crosses to a shadowy Liverpool of sexual sickness and fear: 'Imprisoned in a Liverpool of self, I haunted the gutted arcades of the past.'

In *Under the Volcano* a sinister little rhyme incorporating a children's chant plays in the mind of the consul as he sets off with his brother:

> Plingen, plangen, aufgefangen
> Swingen, swangen, at my side,
> Pootle, footle, off to Bootle,
> Nemesis, a pleasant ride

Liverpool, everyone has an opinion. Liverpool, in excess. Liverpool, Alexei Sayle, born in Anfield, 7 August 1952, humour not a priority in working-class fifties Liverpool dominated by Stalinist communism and political activism. 'I think that my idea of the world is that it's random and cruel but quite sort of comical really. If you stand in the beating heart of Liverpool on the waterfront and look west you can almost see Dublin, and beyond that New York, hunkering just over the horizon. To me, Liverpudlians have broader horizons, and the characters in a city are formed by what the city does. In a place like Birmingham people have spent the past 300 years taking apart and putting together tiny little machines; if you stand in the centre and look west from Birmingham you can almost see Wolverhampton.'

Liverpool, 1955: Bill Haley appears at the Odeon, resulting in disturbances in which 150 seats are wrecked. Liverpool, the Merseysippi Jazz Band sharing the stage with Louis Armstrong at the Liverpool Stadium in 1956. 'I was born across the river in Birkenhead, brought up from the age of five in north Wales, trained as a painter in Newcastle upon Tyne; the reason I moved back to Liverpool in 1956 was because it was an artist's town, cheap to live in, with a thriving bohemia based in the inner-city Georgian/Victorian area.' Adrian Henri. In his poem 'Liverpool 8' he writes of it as a place

> where you play out after tea . . . back doors and walls
> with names, kisses, scrawled or painted
> . . . a new cathedral at the end of Hope Street . . . wind
> blowing inland from Pierhead bringing the smell of breweries
> and engine oil from ferry boats.

Liverpool, hire purchase is invented. Do you do terms?

On 31 October 1956 Paul McCartney's mother Mary, a heavy smoker, died of an embolism after a mastectomy operation to stop the spread of her breast cancer. Liverpool, 1957: the first rock and roll record from the city, Johnny Guitar and Paul Murphy's 'She's Got It'. Liverpool, town. Liverpool, ringleaders. The Cavern Club opened in Mathew Street on Wednesday 16 January 1957 days after Anthony Eden resigned as prime minister following the Suez Crisis, to be replaced by Harold Macmillan. It aimed to put Liverpool on the map by having the leading jazz cellar in the country outside London. Opened and owned by Alan Sytner, it was named after the Parisian jazz club Le Caveau. Liverpool, Woolton parish church garden fete, 6 July 1957, 6.48 p.m., Paul McCartney introduced to John Lennon by Ivan Vaughan. Paul realised John had been drinking: 'he was a little afternoon-boozy, leaning over my shoulder, pissed'. McCartney said that sailors and immigrants made Liverpool a 'melting pot' of different ethnic sounds and added, 'We took what we liked from all that.'

Liverpool, Jacaranda Coffee Bar. Liverpool, these are places I remember. Liverpool, 1958, Ronald Wycherly aged eighteen of Garston becomes Billy Fury; John Lennon asks for his autograph. After leaving school at the age of fifteen, Ronald was a rivet thrower in an engineering factory and a deckhand on a tug in the Mersey estuary. He suffered intermittent health problems following a bout of rheumatic fever at the age of six, which damaged his heart valves. He spent a great deal of his early life in hospital. He later recalled, 'I was always sick, I was always in hospital, lying in bed somewhere, and I missed a hell of a lot of my schooling. And every time I got back to school, I didn't know the kids – I was always the stranger.' Liverpool, Her Majesty's decayed town. Liverpool, the muddy pool. Liverpool, a good place to wash your hair. In 1958 Ingrid Bergman shot *The Inn of the Sixth Happiness* in Snowdonia, using hundreds of British-Chinese extras with most of the children coming from the Liverpool Chinese community. On 15 July 1958, when John Lennon was seventeen, his mother died on Menlove Avenue shortly after leaving his Aunt Mimi's house, while crossing the road to get to a bus stop. She was struck by a car driven by a drunk off-duty policeman, PC Eric Clague, a learner driver. He was acquitted of all charges and later left the police force to become a postman.

When Stuart Sutcliffe sells a painting in 1959 for sixty-five pounds, an unheard-of sum for a student's painting in those days, John convinces him to buy a bass guitar and join the band, never mind that he can't play. Before their first big break, a two-week tour to Scotland backing Johnny Gentle, Stu (almost) comes up with a new name for the group, jokingly suggesting 'the Beetles' as a play on Buddy Holly's Crickets. In 1960 the Beatles are George, Paul, John, Stuart and 'very shy' drummer Pete Best, whose mother Mona effectively manages the group as a vehicle for her good-looking son before Brian Epstein takes over. On 29 October 1961 Raymond Jones supposedly walks into the NEMS record store in Liverpool's Whitechapel shopping district and asks proprietor Brian Epstein for a copy of 'My Bonnie'. Alistair Taylor, Epstein's assistant, explains: 'I got fed up with youngsters coming in asking for the Beatles record. So I put a name, Raymond Jones, in the order book. I just made it up. Otherwise Brian wouldn't have paid any attention.'

Liverpool, rolling the dial on the radio. Liverpool, November 1961. Brian Epstein meets the Beatles – everyone from south Liverpool – in a dressing room as big as a broom cupboard at the Cavern Club; by Christmas he is their manager. Liverpool, place of slogans. Brian Epstein gives Pete Best the bad news: Ringo Starr is to become the Beatles' new drummer. Best is sacked not necessarily for drumming reasons. Neil Aspinall would later recall how it came about: '. . . so I drove him [Pete Best] into town to see him. I was in the record store looking at records, and he came down and said he had been fired. He was in a state of shock, really. We went over to the Grapes pub in Mathew Street, had a pint.' Pete continued his musical career and tried to piggyback on the Beatles' success. In 1964 the Pete Best All Stars were signed to Decca, the label that originally rejected the Beatles. Their one single, 'I'm Gonna Knock on Your Door', was a flop, and Decca dropped them. Pete then spent some time touring with his Pete Best Combo, to middling success if that, and retired back to Liverpool in 1966, taking a job in a bakery.

Liverpool, swarming city of dreams. Liverpool, a view of the Mersey until the cathedral gets in the way. Liverpool, dead sea. Liverpool, not London. Liverpool, carnival of the mind. Liverpool, a makeshift mythological aura. Liverpool, 1961: poets Adrian Henri, Brian Patten and Roger McGough meet almost on the same day that Andy Warhol directs his first film, Ornette Coleman releases *Free Jazz*, and Joseph

Beuys is made professor of sculpture at the Academy in Düsseldorf. Liverpool, Bob Shankly's Liverpool FC are promoted from the Second to the First Division at the end of the 1961/2 season. Liverpool, Carl Jung, 1961: 'I had a dream. I found myself in a dirty, sooty city. It was night and winter; and dark and raining. I was in Liverpool. In the centre was a round pool; in the middle of it a small island. On it stood a single tree; a magnolia in a shower of reddish blossoms. It was as though the tree stood in the sunlight, and was, at the same time, the source of light. Everything was extremely unpleasant; black and opaque – just as I felt then. But I had a vision of unearthly beauty . . . and that's why I was able to live at all. Liverpool is the pool of life.'

Liverpool, 1961, population 745,114. Liverpool, like New Orleans at the turn of the century, but with rock and roll not jazz. On 6 July 1961, in the first issue of *Mersey Beat* magazine a feature headlined SWINGING CILLA begins, 'Cilla Black is a Liverpool girl who is starting on the road to fame.' The editor, Bill Hary, had run a piece written by Cilla White, who worked in the cloakroom at the Cavern Club, but could not remember her surname other than it was a colour. Looking at the piece, he plumped for Black.

Her piece appeared on page 6, four pages after John Lennon's biography of The Beatles:

FASHION NOTES BY PRISCILLA

WHITE. The knitted crochet look, which started in Italy, has at last reached our shores, and you can find it in cotton, silk, ribbon and even straw.

GREY. No longer is grey a dismal, formal form of office wear to be worn only during the day. Grey is now the colour for evening wear.

RED. To be worn at any time of the year, in blazing tones for the autumn, and in various tones during the other seasons.

BLACK. The slickest word in fashion. This year's bare-armed dresses are ideally suited to this colour, and for lighter relief a touch of white is elegant and dramatic.

Liverpool, 1961. Gerry and the Pacemakers' version of Ray Charles' 'What'd I Say'. Liverpool, 25 January 1961. 'It was a damp and foggy night as I nervously approached Hambleton Hall, a miserable little dance hall on the outskirts of Liverpool. I was tense because a gang of "Teddy Boys" were following me to the same little dive. They were putting the boot into cars, lamp posts and the occasional cat. We were all going to see a new group called the Beatles, who had just come back from Hamburg.'

Liverpool, 1962, happening, pre-scene, public event as work of art, mixed-media event, Merseyside Arts Festival, find a flower, hold it up to the light. Adrian Henri claims to have organised the first happenings in England in Liverpool after reading a piece by the American painter Allan Kaprow. 'We did mixed-media events – happenings – with titles like City, Death of a Bird in the City, City and Blues, eventually incorporating live music from some of the local Merseybeat groups.' Liverpool, 1962. American singer Bruce Channel is on tour with the Beatles, supported by local bands the Four Jays and the Statesmen. Channel describes Liverpool as a bleak lonely place, with Bible-black buildings, light shafts and a memorable seawall. Liverpool, the outlook had not improved. In 1962 the North West Regional Board for Industry says, 'The amalgamation and rationalisation of firms in Merseyside was resulting in a loss of employment opportunities in an area where unemployment was a serious problem.'

Liverpool, Allen Ginsberg walking down Mathew Street, like a bloody saint, holier than Ringo or John. In 1962 teacher Roger McGough appeared at the Merseyside Arts Festival as part of the Liverpool Oat-Lady All-Electric Show, with Post Office engineer and sometime comedy actor John Gorman, and Michael Blank, as he was credited in the programme, hiding the fact he is the younger brother of Paul McCartney. Mike McCartney's first published photo – in *Mersey Beat* – calls him Francis Michael. The trio decide to stick together and perform as The Scaffold. Granada Television records the Beatles – with Ringo Starr on drums for the first time – playing at the Cavern in August 1962.

When in 1962 writer Troy Kennedy Martin was confined to bed with mumps, he decided to pass his time listening in to the police wavelength on his radio. What he heard was a far cry from what was being depicted on television. As a result he created *Z Cars*, a series set on Merseyside at a time when Liverpool was on the verge of significant social changes. To combat the growing crime wave policemen were

The River Mersey as it passes between Liverpool and the Wirral

taken off the beat, placed in fast-response vehicles, the Z cars of the
series title (so called because the cars were Ford Zephyrs), and put on
patrol around the old district of Seaport and the modern high-rise
development of Kirkby Newtown. *Z Cars* mirrored its era and dared to
push the depiction of the police and their role in a rapidly changing
society to starkly realistic new heights.

To the surprise of the BBC, the show was an instant hit, with audiences rising to fourteen million before the end of its scheduled
thirteen-week run, which was hastily extended to thirty-one episodes.
The *Z Cars* theme was based on the old Liverpool sea shanty 'Johnny
Todd'. A children's skipping song in Liverpool, the lyrics were filled out
by Frank Kidson, who collected it from a singer who couldn't remember all the words. The tune was revived when Fritz Spiegel, sometime
flautist with the Liverpool Philharmonic Orchestra, and his ex-wife
Bridget Fry arranged the melody as the signature tune for *Z Cars*. The
effect aimed at was that of the fife-and-drum band playing in an Orange

Day parade. The section of the Liverpool Phil that recorded the tune had some difficulty playing the off notes.

The Everyman was born as an alternative to the Playhouse theatre in 1964, when idealistic Liverpool University students Martin Jenkins, Peter James, Susan Fleetwood and Terry Hands founded a new company on a shoestring budget operating out of a run-down building licensed as a cinema and nightclub at the weekends. Hope Hall had originally been a chapel, built in 1837 and closed in 1853, when it was turned into a concert hall. In 1912 the hall was converted into the Hope Hall Cinema, which lasted until 1959. Knowing that the venue would still be used as a cinema on Thursday, Friday and Saturday nights, Jenkins, James and Hands had to find other ways to draw in audiences. They decided to put on matinee productions of plays on the syllabus of schools within a thirty-mile radius of Liverpool, while also staging evening performances aimed primarily at adult audiences. In 1965 a Conservative councillor begged, 'Let this thing die now.' In 1967 the theatre refined its role as a voice of the local people, reflecting the city's sense of itself, developing plays written by local writers such as Alan Bleasdale and Willy Russell. Actors who started their careers with the Everyman include Alison Steadman, Anthony Sher, Trevor Eve, Bernard Hill, Jonathan Pryce, Bill Nighy, Pete Postlethwaite, Barbara Dickson, Julie Walters and Matthew Kelly.

Liverpool, a goal to the good. Liverpool, Liverpuddle. Liverpool, Liverpolitan. Liverpool, resisting. Liverpool, dissenting. Liverpool, booming. Liverpool, pop groups that demand perfection, setting out to make an impression on the whole world, which they can glimpse from their bedrooms, from the waterfront, from the inside of bars and clubs. Liverpool, Teardrop Explodes, Orchestral Manoeuvres in the Dark, Echo and the Bunnymen, Wah! Heat. Liverpool, a cosy anarchy of pilfering, gossip, giddiness and love. Liverpool, championing the demotic in language, and in everything. Liverpool, underdog. Liverpool, you can put your finger on it. Liverpool, a cathedral to spare. Liverpool, moving things around from place to place, around the world, across the universe. Liverpool, stew, hotpot, hash, scouse. Liverpool, Hairy Records, the divine smell of vinyl. Liverpool, the nervous skin of sensation just this side of darkness. Liverpool, rising through the mist. Liverpool, nothing is real. Liverpool, a seaport spun from the blood of slaves, in the pool of life a macabre parade, slave city in a society built on a truth that's cruel, once upon a time you were the nation's jewel. Liverpool, a dark lightless white netted over with grey. Liverpool, the enchantment sours. Liverpool, little boxes, little boxes. Liverpool, the immaterial sphere of our furious and outreaching emotions. Liverpool, collapse of the capitalist system. Liverpool, earthy mysticism. Liverpool, cabs that smell like people have stopped wiping themselves. Liverpool, a goddess in disguise. Liverpool, Ken Dodd, Jimmy Tarbuck and Arthur Askey – in his autobiography he recalled a visit back to Liverpool: 'They've put a plaque on the wall of the house where I was born. It says condemned.'

Liverpool, passion. Liverpool, moving. Liverpool, moving cotton, sugar, slaves, invoices, music, ideas here, there and everywhere else. Liverpool, import, export. Liverpool, a bit raw. Liverpool, rich, richer, richest. Liverpool, slum, slummier, slummiest. Liverpool, shady. Liverpool, good old-fashioned genuinely likeable, salt of the earth, with this and that thrown in for good measure. Liverpool, the problem with demoralised cities. Liverpool, 190,000 cousins. Liverpool, in my eyes and in my ears. Liverpool, people fleeing social reforms and economic decline. Liverpool, what about us? Liverpool, a post-war anglicised Siberia, out of sight, out of mind, unloved, unwanted. Liverpool, Hamburg. Liverpool, gossip. Liverpool, history. Liverpool, the Kop. Liverpool, drug addict, shoplifter and burglar. Liverpool, oh you are a mucky kid, dirty as a dustbin lid. Liverpool, John Lennon's urgent urban harmonica introduction to 'Love Me Do'. Liverpool, the opening chord to 'A Hard Day's Night', which became the magical mystery chord, the wake-up chord, as restless as progress, the summation of everything they knew, with the excitement continual discovery provides, recognised in about 1.4 seconds, which may or may not have taken a combination of: producer George Martin glancing against a Steinway grand piano just to sweeten things a little, Paul McCartney on Hofner bass with pillow-muffled speaker, George Harrison on his prized new Fireglo twelve-string Rickenbacker 360, the second one ever made, ringing the changes, charging into being a sound of the sixties, a different kind of continuity, putting the world on edge, John Lennon on a six-string Gibson J-160E flat-top acoustic-electric guitar, Ringo Starr, drum of the people, with his standard 1963 Black Pearl Ludwig drum kit, tapping the snare, grazing the Zildjian ride cymbal, maybe a tip of the bongo, and sundry other sonic colour, acoustic cut and space, metallic accents, and speeded-up half-speed interplay, and a Liverpool kitchen sink, so that the chord sounded like some sort of exotic percussive electric organ being played in the Church of Time, where the world breathes in, and the world breathes out. Liverpool, if I gave marks out of ten for towns then Liverpool would get thirteen, said Lux Interior of the Cramps some time between 1852 and 1988. Liverpool, John Peel, Rex Harrison, who talked to the animals, Harold Wilson and Tom Baker. Liverpool, in the town where I was born, lived a man, who sailed the sea.

Liverpool, Brian Patten recalls: 'I started writing because I was quite isolated. My family didn't talk to each other, it was one of those nightmare families. My father had left. I grew up in a quite violent and strange house and I just felt very isolated, so I started writing to try and articulate my own feelings really, you know. I wasn't thinking about whether it was poetry or not, I was just trying to articulate what was going on inside me. I had one teacher at school, a guy called Mr Sutcliffe, who was really ace and he was inspirational to me. That was at a school called Sefton Park Secondary Modern; I think there is a little Norwegian supermarket there now.' Liverpool, and Alan Bleasdale answers a question about why so many writers come from Liverpool: 'I think it's the influence of the Irish, the Welsh and the dock economy, and the fact that nobody had proper jobs up to about a hundred years ago. My mother's family is from the Dingle and my dad's family is from Scotland Road – that's where they were born and brought up . . . A lot of my mother's family especially were dockers, and when I was a kid you'd go down to the Dingle and you'd hear stories of these 6,000 men in a pen, with 300 jobs, of a 6 o'clock on a Monday morning. And the 5,700 men who went back up the hill – and they'd go into the pub . . . and play cards, and they'd have the crack. And . . . so there was an awful lot more time for people to talk. To create stories, and . . . I think Liverpool is very much a verbal city, and surely it comes from the, you know, the Welsh and the Irish, and it comes from the fact that not many people had jobs a long time ago.'

Liverpool, all our friends are all aboard, and many more live next door. Ken 'what a beautiful day for sticking a cucumber through a letter box and shouting the Martians are coming' Dodd also proved a weirdly accomplished singer, with a string of hits that seemed to exist in a world where the Beatles – who had a bit of Dodd about them – had never happened. Ken Dodd's 1965 song 'Tears' was beaten only in overall sixties sales by 'She Loves You' and 'I Want to Hold Your Hand'. When the Beatles appeared on Dodd's television show he said, 'We talk the same language. It's the draught from the Mersey Tunnel which causes the Liverpool accent.'

Liverpool, *Till Death Us Do Part*, Johnny Speight's abrasively realistic BBC sitcom, piloted in 1965, running until 1975, featuring swearing, ranting, racist, right-wing, East End working-class bigot Alf Garnett, played by Warren Mitchell (after Peter Sellers turned it down), whose socialist son-in-law Mike, played by Antony Booth, at the other end of the widening post-war generation gap, is a smart Liverpool layabout combining many of Alf's most hated traits – northern, Catholic, Irish, tolerant, liberal, sexually liberated, young, Liverpool FC fan to Garnett's beloved West Ham United. During their non-stop slanging matches Mike was frequently abused as a 'randy Scouse git' by his explosively intolerant and ignorant father-in-law. Booth himself was born in Jubilee Road in 1931 to an Irish mother and merchant-seaman father who worked as a clerk in a docklands warehouse and at the United States consulate in Liverpool. He is a descendant of the famous nineteenth-century Booth family of actors which includes John Wilkes Booth, who assassinated Abraham Lincoln in 1865.

Liverpool, a decisive moment in the history of Western civilisation. Liverpool, dazzling but ultimately fraudulent. Liverpool, but the thing is, it really just is . . . Legendary fast-thinking, quick-talking and beloved Liverpool comedian Tommy Handley, born in Toxteth on 17 January 1892 – famous for the moral-boosting radio programme that became synonymous with glorified war-time British spirit, *It's That Man Again* (*ITMA*), that man being both Handley and Adolf Hitler, the latter constantly baited by the roguish Handley and his crew – is featured on the cover of the Beatles' 1967 album *Sgt Pepper's Lonely Hearts Club Band*. Marilyn Monroe is flirting with him, and he is next to acid author

William Burroughs. Stan Laurel of Lancashire is between artist Richard Lindner and guru Sri Mahavatara Babaji. Lewis Carroll of Cheshire is standing next to Lawrence of Arabia. Handley and *ITMA*, in which convivial music hall moves into radio, its elastic exuberance transformed into something experimentally new, is a big influence on the four worked-up post-war authority-scorning surrealists making a mockery of British stoicism who would become the Goons – Peter Sellers, Michael Bentine, Harry Secombe and Spike Milligan – who in turn trigger something, as an incorrigible gang and self-governed creative collective, in the Beatles. Liverpool, digging the weeds.

Liverpool, John Betjeman, 1970: 'Liverpool Cathedral is one of the great buildings of the world. Suddenly one realises that the greatest art of architecture, that compels reverence, but also lifts one up, and turns one into a king, is the art of enclosing space.' Liverpool, the departure for the Sea of Dreams is from the Pier Head. Liverpool, described in 1920 as a 'threshold to the ends of the earth'. Liverpool, outdoor toilets. Liverpool, unconquerable charm. Liverpool, from side streets and backyards, from all directions, come more and more children, suddenly grown up. Liverpool, a fountain of things. Liverpool, sights of local interest. Liverpool, nowhere to look for amusement and mercy but to one another. Behind the Pier Head there are numerous narrow streets that drop down to the river: Water Street, Chapel Street, Dale Street and James Street. Liverpool, it's just a rumour spread about town. Liverpool, a dreary flat spread of streets. Liverpool, the foul disorder of bad dreams. Liverpool, daydream, trance, faith and passion all exist on the borders of waking thought. Liverpool, the patchwork landscape around the cathedral yields a supernatural dell. Liverpool, Phil Redmond, Jimmy McGovern and Anthony Shaffer. Liverpool, I'm Bloody Sure You're On Dope. Liverpool, the true beginning place. Liverpool, somebody speaks and you fall into a dream.

Liverpool, artistic troublemakers. Liverpool, serious fools. Liverpool, Stan Kelly-Bootle, born 1929, eccentric Renaissance man, achieves the first postgraduate degree in computer science in 1954, is a member of the earliest wave of computer programmers – 'computer science is the boring art of coping with a large number of trivialities' – and also writes the lyrics to 'Liverpool Lullaby', where he talks of something tough and resilient, nothing can take its place. He also wrote the lyrics to 'I Wish I Was Back In Liverpool', longing to be back in the town where he was born, even though it has no trees, no wonderful fields of swaying corn, but the all the girls with their dyed blonde hair make up for that, and the constant black and tan, the dark stout and pale ale, and he lingers over memories of his favourite town, however packed it is, however many are crammed into a single bed near the old Pier Head.

Liverpool, decline. Liverpool, docks, obsolete. Liverpool, run-down council estates. Liverpool, population 1971, 610,000. Liverpool, John Lennon, 1971: 'Yes, well, the first thing we did was to proclaim our Liverpoolness to the world, and say, "It's all right to come from Liverpool and talk like this." Before, anybody from Liverpool who made it, like Ted Ray, Tommy Handley, Arthur Askey, had to lose their accent to get on the BBC. They were only comedians, but that's what came out of Liverpool before us. We refused to play that game. After the Beatles came on the scene everyone started putting on a Liverpudlian accent.' Liverpool, voices. Liverpool, Al Hibbler. Liverpool, Carl Perkins. Liverpool, Ray Charles. Liverpool, the Mersey meets the Mississippi. Liverpool, the Dissenters. Liverpool, the Mersey Sound. Liverpool, Robert Mitchum. Liverpool, Stuart Sutcliffe. Liverpool, yeah yeah yeah. Liverpool, George Martin. Liverpool, MBE. Liverpool, Ravi Shankar. Liverpool, Vietnam. Liverpool, the Maharishi, transcendental meditation. Liverpool, Ringo takes several tins of baked beans with him when the Beatles go to India to study with the Maharishi. Liverpool, long-haired rough-spoken poets wandering into O'Connors and screaming their poems above the bar noise.

Liverpool, Abbey Road. Liverpool, the home of the Beatles. Liverpool, the Beatles, the ultimate confidence trick. Liverpool, a dry eye rubbed raw shrinking into itself. Liverpool, windows and curtains in the same position for fifty years. Liverpool, chasing rainbows. Liverpool, the train from outside the city holding its breath before it noses into Lime Street and sinks into the earth. Liverpool, the air lashed and staggering with suction winds. Liverpool, nothing to breathe but burned rubber and diesel fumes. Liverpool, despised. Liverpool, drunk. Liverpool, repartee. Liverpool, mass redundancy, failed strikes, depopulation, gangs, guns, drugs, poverty, social exclusion. Liverpool, making a dent in national self-awareness. Liverpool, the brand names, the fads, the bastardised vistas. Liverpool, a succession of poses. Liverpool, imagine. Liverpool, frozen memories gleam amid the blackness of loss. Liverpool, hope springs eternal. Liverpool, November 1976, Julian Cope surfaces at a Liverpool college, meets Ian McCulloch, Pete Burns, Pete Wylie, and forms a succession of half-groups. Liverpool, to be physically on the edge is to be spiritually on the edge. Liverpool, an epic whodunnit. Liverpool, a certain slippery ease. Liverpool, make me whole again. Liverpool, live and let die. Liverpool, making to live. Liverpool, hate. Liverpool, well there's something else to life. Liverpool, Dunlop, Tate and Lyle, Kraft, leaving. Liverpool, scum. Liverpool, smackhead. Liverpool, scallies. Liverpool, vagabonds and thieves and scoundrels on the make always lying. Liverpool, how do we soldier on? Liverpool, a triumph of drift and whim. Liverpool, late into the night. Liverpool, buildings and stars laid flat for storage. Liverpool, the steady accretion of plain lived moments. Liverpool, destruction of, by bombs, town planners, politicians, indifference, 'when desolation spreads her empire here'. Liverpool, love. Liverpool, needles and pins, winds blow, the rains pour, the seas flow, old men grow tired of sailing: 'The old ships' ghosts, drifting away.' Liverpool, ta ra then.

On 27 August 1967 Brian Epstein dies in his Belgravia home, officially from an overdose of sleeping pills, the day before he was due to travel to Bangor, north Wales, to join the Beatles at the International Meditation Society. The band decided not to replace him and instead embarked on a new project alone. The BBC TV film *Magical Mystery Tour* was treated poorly by the critics and for some was the beginning of the end for the Beatles. Within three years they fell apart.

Brian Patten, Roger McGough and Adrian Henri authored the outstandingly successful *Penguin Modern Poets: The Mersey Sound* – the only one in the series to get its own title (at the time the poets were not keen on the link with pop music, preferring to be nothing fancier than number 10). Each volume of the series, an attempt to introduce contemporary poetry to the general reader launched in 1962, featured three poets of the 1960s. The Mersey volume featured a variation on the normal predominantly black cover – a mix of red and black with silhouettes of Liverpool landmarks and a black and white photo of a pop fan – and brought together approximately one hundred poems by the Liverpool poets. Over 500,000 copies have been sold, more than any other poetry anthology, and it has been credited as the most significant anthology of the twentieth century for its success in bringing poetry to new audiences. Priced in 1967 at three shillings and sixpence, the book consolidated three poetic reputations and was reprinted eight times in seven years. The poets mixed avant-garde and popular culture in an accessible and saleable form and extended their work into performance.

Liverpool, we hope you have enjoyed the show. Liverpool, a moment of utter clarity. Liverpool, I love to visit the city to see my hub caps (Bernard Manning). Liverpool, among people who would be lost without the cross. Liverpool, entertaining all sorts of conditions with a view to self-preservation. Liverpool, dogged dedication. Liverpool, industrial anxiety. Liverpool, work-shy. Liverpool, loss of civic vision. Liverpool, above us only sky. Liverpool, football crazy, Brian Redbone, Ian Callaghan, Chris Lawler. Liverpool, Albert Dock, at the edge of the water, from old world to new world, from new world to this world, eat, drink and spend. Liverpool, and the years flare up and are gone quicker than a minute. Liverpool, John Lennon as Mickey Mouse, John F. Kennedy, Gandhi and Chaplin. Liverpool, it's been a hard day's night. Liverpool, thank u very much. Liverpool, your sky all hung with jewels. Liverpool, people they rush everywhere, each with their own secret care. Liverpool, diving for dear life when we could be diving for pearls. Liverpool, until you realise it's just a story.

Liverpool, George Melly, the British saint/pope/uncle/tout/fount/jester/dean/queen of surrealism, born Alan George Heywood Melly, son of a wool broker and an actress in Liverpool on 17 August 1926. The Melly family were wealthy pillars of Liverpool society, and young George and his brother and sister led a comfortable life in a large ugly Victorian terraced house in the Sefton Park area. He described Liverpool 8, his home as aspirational 1950s bohemian poet, writer, artist, flaneur, as 'a multiracial slum waiting for the planners' bulldozer'. He said of the Beatles – 'that four-headed Orpheus' – that their songs at the time 'trapped what it felt like to be a rebellious suburban Liverpudlian for whom beat music offered an escape. They were tough and tender. You could sense, behind the words and music, the emergence of a new spirit; post-war, clever, non-conformist but above all, cool.' He wrote of their song 'Eleanor Rigby', 'Liverpool was always in their songs but this was about the kind of old woman that I remembered from my childhood and later, very respectable Liverpool women living in two-up, two-down streets with the doorsteps meticulously holystoned, and the church the one solid thing in their lives . . . I could see Park Road or Mill Street and those houses going down to the river, and I could imagine Eleanor Rigby living in one . . .' In the *Sunday Times* he traced John Lennon's roots in *In His Own Write* through Carroll, Klee, Thurber, the Goons and Joyce. He wrote in his 1970 book *Revolt Into Style*, 'Dedication to pleasure is Pop's intention: pleasure in the present for young people, before they are independent, and have to assume adult responsibilities.' He noted that following the success of the Beatles, 'States Worship had largely been replaced by a cool, if deep, chauvinism, but as it is impossible to think of England as having no past, this is dealt with by treating history as a vast boutique full of military uniforms, grannie shoes and spectacles, 1930s suits and George Formby records. By wrenching these objects out of their historical context they are rendered harmless.' Pop culture, he announced, is the passport to the country of now, where everyone is beautiful and no one grows old.

In 1971 George Melly gave evidence for the defence in the celebrated *Oz* trial. (The magazine's editors had been prosecuted under the Obscene Publications Act for their 'Schoolkids' Issue', which included pornographic images.) He would be happy, Melly proclaimed, for his sixteen-year-old son to read the issue (his son was in fact eight at the time), adding for good measure that a Rupert Bear cartoon featuring the character having sex with an old woman was 'the funniest thing in the magazine'.

The Kingsway Tunnel was opened on 24 June 1971 by Queen Elizabeth II. The new link between Liverpool and Wallasey actually consisted of two tunnels, one in each direction and each with two lanes. In early 1971 The Scaffold provided some catchy tunes for a television campaign heralding the introduction of decimal currency to the UK. In a series of five-minute programmes entitled *Decimal Five* and shown on BBC1, they sang such inspired lyrics as 'Give more, get change' and 'Use your old coppers in sixpenny lots' in an attempt to help older people to weather the change. The fact that The Scaffold were hairy freaks likely to repel older people seemed not to have occurred to the decimalisers. Liverpool, whispers out of time. Liverpool, the gibbous mirrored eye of an insect. Liverpool, a breeze like the turning of a page. Liverpool, the momentum of a conviction. Liverpool, a society specifically organised as a demonstration of itself. Liverpool, the mouth of the Mersey. Liverpool, the mouth. Liverpool, the river itself. Liverpool, roll on, John.

85.10

Yoko and John left England for New York on 3 September 1971.

'My love of New York is something to do with Liverpool. There is the same quality of energy in both cities.'

'What is Liverpool like?'

'Liverpool was just where I was brought up. It's like anywhere . . . I love the concept of it, but I don't live there.'

'What did being from Liverpool have to do with your art?'

'Because it was a port, that means it was less hick than somewhere in the midlands, like the Midwest or whatever you call it. We were a port, the second biggest port in England. Also, between Manchester and Liverpool the north was where all the money was made in the 1800s whenever it was, that was where all the brass and the heavy people were. And that's where the despised people were. We were the ones who were looked down upon as animals by the southerners, the Londoners. In the States, the northerners think that down south, people are pigs, and the people in New York think West Coast is hick. So we were hicksville. Liverpool is a very poor city, and tough. But people have a sense of humour because they are in so much pain. So they are always cracking jokes, and they are very witty. It's an Irish place, too; it is where the Irish came when they ran out of potatoes, and it's where black people were left or worked as slaves or whatever. It is cosmopolitan, and it's where sailors would come home with blues records from America. Liverpool has the biggest country & western following in England besides London

– always besides London because there is more of it there. I heard country & western music in Liverpool before I heard rock & roll. The people take their country & western very seriously. I remember the first guitar I ever saw. It belonged to a guy in a cowboy suit and a cowboy hat and a big dobro. They were real cowboys and they took it seriously. There were cowboys long before there was rock & roll.' From the 'Rolling Stone Interview' with Jann Wenner, *Rolling Stone*, 1971.

PART EIGHT

For all the boys of Stockport

Nothing is inevitable until it happens.

A. J. P. Taylor

86

At the Liverpool end the Mersey has been allowed to work its prodigious magic, allowed to have its say. At the Stockport end the river was removed from sight, as if it was ugly and poisonous, a squealing newborn mutt, an exuberance of threatening occult vitality, something wild and deviant that needed to be tamed – covered by consumer-framing concrete, grinding workaholic double-decker buses and a well-stocked C&A, by an ugly, squat shopping precinct that dropped something quasi-continental and pseudo-modern right between the colossal Victorian viaduct and the winding inbred twists and turns of a lacklustre market town painstakingly carved out of centuries of endeavour, struggle and commerce.

It's peculiar that Stockport made the decision to tuck the Mersey away as if it was embarrassing, or dangerous, a liminal representation of supernatural energies, because without the river there would be no Stockport – this is where people met in the Middle Ages to cross the river, and in the late eighteenth century cotton mills were built using the powerful, hurrying and pent-up river for power, giving the town new purpose. It was partially covered first of all, in the 1930s, for the building of a dual carriageway which was part of an improvement scheme, because it was something of a sight, full of industrial waste, an eyesore. That was when the Merseyway was first named, a road on stilts, flat for the trams which had trouble with hilly twisty Stockport. In the 1960s the dirty deed, the complete dismissal of the river, was done, as if covering the Mersey meant covering up the disastrous past, which threatened to make Stockport, crawling noisily and indiscreetly away from the wreckage of the war, too ancient to survive in a world that urgently needed to rebuild and regroup.

As it gratefully emerged into view the other side of the A6, beginning its life, which would lead all the way to Liverpool and the rest of the world, the river was coated with a pockmarked chemical crust that resembled the inside of a Crunchie bar, fizzing and foaming in chunks the size of cannonballs, but the heady smell was more Maltesers, a thick aroma that didn't seem beery to me as a kid, but which must have been, carrrying waste from Robinson's Brewery perhaps, which by the 1960s had been situated in Stockport for over 150 years, dominating the south end of the town centre, regularly expelling a pungent aroma into the air, on its way to owning over 400 pubs in the north-west. This wasn't a river you thought of as being filled with water, or even any type of recognisable liquid, where you used to be able to fish and one day you would be able to fish again.

This was the Mersey Square I grew to know, surrounded still by a dense, meandering, cobbled network of lanes, alleyways and steps laid out under the mighty arches of the viaduct as it soared over the hard-working bus terminal as if brick could cast a spell, a cluttered mosaic of hills, slopes, brows and stairs that you needed to climb in order to head out of the depressed town centre, which always seemed shiny with rain or drained by a stubborn mist that seemed reluctant to let anything as newfangled as electric lighting spoil its effect. For me the narrow lanes, the winding slopes, the steep little steps that took you from one level to another, the convoluted accumulation of cobbled inclines and abrupt ascents packed around the scrubbed backside of the shopping precinct, the Little and Great Underbank, the centre of Mersey Square around where the buses parked, known as the Bear Pit, were as natural as the hills and peaks in the distance, and I was completely ignorant about why they existed. I was oblivious to what history they brought with them, and why the A6, the Wellington Road, swept right over the town centre, above and next to the square where the buses ended their journeys, turning around ready to head out again, in all directions.

Mersey Square was relatively easy to get out of, from what at times could seem like the bottom of the world, because all roads and paths out rose quickly above it – north towards Manchester up heaving Wellington Road North, or up Wellington Road South, which soon evened out as the Buxton Road towards Hazel Grove, Poynton and Macclesfield (Old English *maccel*, cleared land, or (St) Michael's open fields), which took you south. You could leave Stockport to the west and move into Cheshire through Bramhall, Heald Green and Wilmslow (William's hill or mound), to the airport, or leave south-east, climbing Churchgate, Hall Street and Offerton Lane through Offerton before heading down the hill to Marple and High Lane, which issued an invitation to the northern edge of unaligned, toneless Derbyshire. Or you could rise from the hollow at the centre of Stockport, cross the Manchester Road, which would join the Wellington Road North a couple of miles towards Manchester at Heaton Chapel, and head plain east to my impassive Reddish, which sucked you into the shabby south-eastern edges of Lancashire, which in some ways resembled rubble that had slipped to the bottom of the pile.

An early-nineteenth-century description of the shape of Lancashire remarks how it can be likened to a miniature version of England and Scotland, with Manchester in the position that London is in a map of the kingdom, and Liverpool the equivalent of Land's End. To the south-east, near the bottom, you could place Reddish, but more accurately Gorton and Denton, as the equivalent of the East End of London. The same description talks of Manchester's reputation for rain, that it is deemed to be the wettest of places – always soaked and miry. It explains that the reputation is slightly exaggerated, but its evident wetness has much to do with its position between the Irish Sea, where the clouds glide over from the Atlantic Ocean, and the mountainous ridge called the 'backbone of the nation' which extends from Staffordshire through Derbyshire to Yorkshire – the Pennines. This backbone checks and breaks the invading clouds, which release their liquid load over Manchester and surrounding districts. It then suggests that this mountainous range is actually a sort of advantage, being the most elevated ground on the island. It produces allegedly constant rain but also screens the eastern parts of Lancashire from the blasts, frosts, blights and insects which infest the counties bordering the German Ocean – as the North Sea was also known, depending on your national point of view, until the end of the nineteenth century before hostilities with the Germans meant the name was entirely not acceptable. (At the beginning of the nineteenth century the British Isles were written about as something that merely 'severed' the Atlantic Ocean before it took over again in what is now the North Sea.)

87

1761

Richard Arkwright began his working life as a barber, and it was only after the death of his first wife that he became an entrepreneur. His second marriage, to Margaret Biggins in 1761, brought a small income that enabled him to expand his barber's business. He acquired a secret dyeing method and travelled around the country purchasing human hair for use in the manufacture of wigs. During this time he was often in contact with weavers and spinners, and when the fashion for wigs declined, he looked to mechanical inventions in the field of textiles to make his fortune.

1760

The first coach road between Huddersfield to the east and Manchester to the west was made in 1760. It was constructed by Blind Jack of Knaresborough, who, despite his blindness, was a musician, carrier and guide, as well as a planner and constructor of highways. The road was laid on bundles of heather over the boggy terrain. Much of this road is still in use today. To avoid the steepest gradient on the old road, a new section was constructed in 1791 and is also still in use. At the height of coach traffic six coaches each way between Huddersfield and Manchester would change horses at the Old New Inn in Marsden, and passengers were asked to dismount in consideration for the horses during the long pull up out of the village.

Around 1760 is generally accepted as the eve of the Industrial Revolution. In reality this eve began more than two centuries before. The late eighteenth and early nineteenth centuries brought to fruition the ideas and discoveries of those who had long passed on, such as Galileo, Bacon and Descartes. The discovery of agriculture had made civilisation possible; the Industrial Revolution multiplied society's productive capacity many times over. Agricultural progress is limited by the ability of the land to produce (although biotechnology may be changing this) and by the limits of demand. Once food fills the belly, demand ceases. Demand is never infinite. But the demand for manufactured and technological products, arguably, is unlimited.

London to Manchester by coach takes three days.

1759

Francis Egerton, twenty-three-year-old third Duke of Bridgewater, was looking for a better way of carrying coal six miles from his Worsley mines to rapidly industrialising Manchester. Roads were primitive, still mostly a matter of medieval mud, and packhorses were the main method of transporting both raw materials and finished goods. Frustrated by how close he was to Manchester and yet how difficult it was to get his coal to where it was most wanted, Bridgewater needed a waterway that did not head towards the sea but went inland and was totally independent from a river route. Having travelled throughout Europe during his youth on the Grand Tour, the duke had been impressed by continental canal systems such as the Canal du Midi in southern France, running between Toulouse and the port town of Sète. He hired an ingenious self-taught engineer, James 'Schemer' Brindley, born north-east of Buxton in 1716, to build him a canal with a series of locks to get barges down to the River Irwell, about three miles from the mine, and then on into Manchester. Brindley had the bold idea of constructing a more level canal requiring fewer time-wasting locks; he would take the canal via an aqueduct over the River Irwell at Barton into the centre of Manchester. Some said this was an impossible scheme – no aqueduct this size had been built before in England – but the duke commissioned it. The canal was carried 840 feet across the river – 38 feet below – on three sandstone arches.

On 17 July 1761 the first barge load of coal is pulled by horses along the completed Bridgewater Canal; the price of coal in Manchester is immediately halved and within a year is down by two thirds. The impact on the cost of coal causes instant canal-building mania. The sight of a barge floating serenely in a gutter high up in the air becomes one of the first great tourist attractions of the Industrial Revolution – the castle or canal in the sky, which before it was built had been a term of abuse from those who thought Brindley was mad. The canal is among the beginnings of the nation's inland waterway system, the catalyst that started fifty years of canal building.

1758

Cheshire was the most popular cheese in Britain by the late eighteenth century. In 1758 the Royal Navy ordered ships to be provisioned with Cheshire cheeses and by 1823 production was estimated at 10,000 tons per year.

1757

The census puts the Manchester population at 17,101.

1755

Some of the comments on the lifestyle of the lower orders which emerged from large employers and their allies in the eighteenth century suggest that a cultural divide had opened between sectors of Lancashire society. In Manchester in 1755 the Reverend John Clayton described the town's poor as having 'an abject mind, which entails their miseries upon them: a mean sordid spirit, which prevents all attempts at bettering their condition'.

1753

When a local entrepreneur put a handful of experimental models of John Kay's flying shuttle into operation around Lancashire in 1753, word quickly got out that a sinister machine was threatening to rob hand weavers of their livelihood. Mobs marched across Lancashire smashing flying-shuttle looms, and weavers stormed Kay's home in Bury, destroying everything they found, and might well have killed him if he hadn't managed to flee to France.

1752

In the sixteenth century 'manufacture' meant something made by hand. A manufacturer would therefore be a craftsman. However, as early as 1752 a manufacturer is 'one who employs workmen for manufacturing'. Moreover, in the late eighteenth and early nineteenth centuries, in several industrial districts, especially in Lancashire and Yorkshire, it had a more restricted sense, denoting 'an organiser of the domestic system'.

1750

There were probably no more than half a million men, women and children within Yorkshire's four million acres. There were no towns of any size. Leeds with a population of 17,000 was a collection of mean streets clustering about an old bridge. Sheffield was a nest of squalid houses at the foot of a wild moorland. Bradford was no more than a village of three streets closely packed in a hollow of the hills. Hull sent out a few ships from the quays which lay behind its one street of any importance. Scarborough was a collection of fishermen's cottages nestling together under the protection of a ruinous castle. Harrogate was a hamlet of nondescript buildings, half-inns, half-farm-steads, which stood about a mineral spring in the middle of a waste. The market towns, still semi-medieval in appearance, were little more than meet-ing places for husbandmen and hucksters. The countryside, on the other hand, was thickly populated; not only were strings of villages and hamlets as frequent as in the south-west, but sometimes the process of dispersion was carried a stage further, and several villages merging into one another became one vast and loose agglomeration. There was little noise of machinery, and little movement in the land: folk stayed, from birth to death, where fate had set them down. Of animation, evidence of energy, desire for progress, there was nothing save among a few ardent but unencouraged spirits. In York Minster silence and desolation brooded heavily in the deserted aisles and desecrated sanctuary; within York Castle they hanged men for the theft of a goat or a sheep. And on Micklegate Bar, plainly to be seen by all who entered the ancient city, still stood, firmly fixed on pikes, the rotting heads of the Jacobites of 1745.

Published in 1750, Tim Bobbin's comic dialect masterpiece *A View of the Lancashire Dialect; containing the Adventures and Misfortunes of a Lancashire Clown* was a great success in the north of England. It was reprinted; further editions appeared and it was pirated. Some people thought the book reflected badly on people in the area, presumably feel-ing that Lancashire people were made to look like simpletons. Tim answered the criticism in his forthright manner: 'I do not think our country exposed at all by my view of the Lancashire dialect: but think it commend-able rather than a defect, that Lancashire in general and Rossendale in particular retain so much of the speech of their ancestors.' He went on to ask why, if the Welsh could be proud of retaining their language, and the people of Saxony and Silesia were 'commended' for speaking in 'Teutonic or old German', should people in Lancashire be 'laughed at for adhering to the speech of our ancestors?'

1747

The romantic imagery of the Lake District which is now the norm was in fact culturally constructed from the middle of the eighteenth century. Before 1750 or thereabouts the region was described by notable travellers as wild, barren and frightful. Defoe considered the landscape as 'all barren and wild', a wilderness far removed from civilisation. The transformation of this bleak wilderness into Arcadia was not a result of a change in the landscape, but came from a new way of viewing nature, as something to be savoured not feared.

1747

In *The Art of Cookery Made Plain and Easy* housewife Hannah Glasse upgraded and renamed a Middle Ages recipe for 'dripping puddings' first recorded in a book in 1737. What she called a Yorkshire pudding was used to fill up in hard times when there wasn't enough meat to go around and even used as a main course on its own with onion gravy. When wheat flour came into common use for cakes and puddings, economically minded cooks in the north of England devised a means of utilising the fat that dropped into the dripping pan to make a batter pudding while the meat roasted. She said the sound of fat hitting batter was like the explosive personality of Yorkshire folk.

> Take a quart of milk, four eggs, and a little salt, make it up into a thick batter with flour, like a pancake batter. You must have a good piece of meat at the fire, take a stew-pan and put some dripping in, set it on the fire, when it boils, pour in your pudding, let it bake on the fire till you think it is high enough, then turn a plate upside-down in the dripping-pan, that the dripping may not be blacked; set your stew-pan on it under your meat, and let the dripping drop on the pudding, and the heat of the fire come to it, to make it of a fine brown. When your meat is done and set to table, drain all the fat from your pudding, and set it on the fire again to dry a little; then slide it as dry as you can into a dish, melt some butter, and pour into a cup, and set in the middle of the pudding. It is an exceeding good pudding, the gravy of the meat eats well with it.

Glasse's book became the prime reference for home cooks in much of the English-speaking world during its original publication run and spread word of the newly named Yorkshire pudding. Hannah wrote mostly for domestic servants (the 'lower sort', as she referred to them), using a conversational style familiar to anyone who has learned a recipe at the elbow of a

parent or grandparent. The food is surprisingly recognisable, with staples
such as gooseberry fool still known and eaten today, and there are even
early traces of Indian dishes which eventually became naturalised in the
UK. She disapproved of French cooking methods and in general avoided
French culinary terminology.

For decades following its publication, there were widespread rumours that
The Art of Cookery had been written by a man. For a woman to have authored
such an eloquent and well-organised work seemed implausible to many.
James Boswell's diary records a party at the house of the publisher Charles
Dilly, at which the issue was discussed. He quotes Samuel Johnson as saying,
'Women can spin very well; but they cannot make a good book of cookery.'

James Cook, sailor, surveyor, cartographer and explorer, was born on 7
November 1728 in the tiny Yorkshire village of Marton in Cleveland in the
North Riding of Yorkshire. Cleveland is a district bounded to the north by
the River Tees, to the south by the North Yorkshire Moors and to the east
by the North Sea. As a teenager he learned about sailing in the dangerous waters of the North Sea, and taught himself algebra, trigonometry,
navigation and astronomy. Cook began the life of a sailor on the *Freelove*
in February 1747, carrying a cargo of coal to London, and spent ten years
working in the coal trade off the east coast of England with its treacherous shifting shoals, uncharted shallows and difficult harbours. Cook
seemed born to sail.

88

In 1968 I took my eleven-plus examination. I was a bright but unremarkable boy, and wanted people to think I was smart because it made
me feel good. There was a general feeling within the school, communicated by the confidence of my teachers, that I would pass the eleven-plus,
devised twenty-four years before to channel children into the school
apparently most suited to their needs and abilities. It was a form of
streaming intended to separate the cleverer kids from those allegedly

not so clever. The only reason you were tested at that age was because you were now due to go to what was generally known as big school.

There were three tests – in maths, writing and general problem-solving – and I was moderately capable in all of these. Assuming I passed, I would then go to the single-sex Mile End Grammar School, also known as Stockport School, along the Buxton Road in Great Moor, heading south out of Mersey Square. This seemed my approximately-one-shade-above-average destiny. For those who failed, their next school would be Reddish Vale Comprehensive. Throughout my childhood I heard dark rumours about what went on at this vast low-lying post-war school lurking at the edges of the Vale. Exaggerated, or quite accurate, reports built up in my imagination until I came to believe that it was the educational equivalent of the prison where my dad once worked. There were hints of initiation ceremonies involving toilets, heads, flushing, and even knives, muscles, fists and bloody noses. Attending such a school would make living in Stockport seem much more threatening, make you feel closer to the edge of real danger, with a more direct sense that you were in constant competition with others battling for space, control and survival.

The kids who went to this school, even the kids who seemed likely to go to this school after North Reddish, were to my mind the harder, meaner ones, and compared to them I was a little sensitive. The terrifying thought of this school, which although low slung and modern in look seemed to belong to the nineteenth century, a cousin of the gothic Strangeways, a place where children went when they were stupid and aggressive, encouraged me to do so well in my eleven-plus that I leaped above the medium-level Mile End Grammar and won one of the scholarships that went to the fifteen top children in all of Cheshire, giving me a place in a school that seemed nineteenth-century in an entirely different way, Stockport Grammar.

The comprehensive conjured up visions of ill-disciplined teenagers the rough side of mod and the mad side of rocker, while the grammar school suggested a world where all the kids lived in mansions and were waited on by servants. Before I went all I really knew about the place was that it did not play football, promoting rugby as the true gentleman's game, that you had to wear a uniform that featured an ornate peaked cap, that the teachers addressed you by your surname, and that the kind of boys who went there bullied you in a different, less physically aggressive way than the kids who went to the comprehensive. For some reason I imagined there would be no bullying at the more modern Mile End, which had a uniform that seemed less stiff and archaic than that of Stockport Grammar. My dad was very proud of how well I had done and could see doors opening to a career in accountancy, even a place at university.

Stockport Grammar was along the Buxton Road three miles out of the town centre along an uneventful section of road near the Davenport Theatre. It had a motto – 'He who endures conquers' – was boys only and had plenty of history. It is the oldest school in the north of England, founded in 1487 with a legacy left by Lord Mayor of London Sir Edmund Shaa, who was born in Mottram in the extreme north-east of Cheshire, in the valley of Longdendale (long wooded valley) north of Glossop, close to the fluid borders with Derbyshire and Yorkshire. (Where L. S. Lowry moved in the 1950s. The Shaas were among the earliest inhabitants of Mottram.) Shaa, whose parents had been born in Stockport, wanted the school 'for all the boys of Stockport and their neighbourhood'. As mayor of London, he appears as a character in Shakespeare's *Richard III*. When the head of the executed Lord Hastings is brought in, he is persuaded by Gloucester and Buckingham to tell the citizens he was executed for just reasons.

As a daydreamy but ambitious boy, Shaa yearned to escape Cheshire, rapidly developing an 'unconquerable aversion to the unchanging life of the country'. Life was relatively pleasant, but the work he was expected to do as a plain yeoman seemed to lead to nothing better than humble respectability and more, more or less, of the same thing all his life. He wanted more. He desired power and influence, the sort he saw when lords and ladies and noble knights passed through his hometown. The young Edmund told friends and relatives of his determination to stretch his mind and rise above his station, and they laughed at him. 'Banish all such dreams from thy foolish pate,' remarked one, 'thou art a good lad, and a clever one to boot, but the life thy fathers led is good enough for thee.' Others jeered openly at his conceit, poured scorn on his ambition, and he would wander off into the woodland glades and sob his heart out. He became a lonely boy, frustrated by everyone's lack of faith in his dreams of escape and personal triumph.

Inspired by a dream in which fairies 'stealing from their tiny palaces under the leaves in the forest' whispered in his ear about the wealth and honour in London awaiting those lads bold enough to seek their fortune there, he set out for the capital and settled there, becoming a goldsmith. He rose rapidly in wealth and status, was employed as an engraver by the Royal Mint, became prime warden of the Goldsmiths' Company and was eventually appointed jeweller to King Edward IV. By 1482 he was lord mayor, and he played a key role in securing the crown for Richard III – with more influence than Shakespeare suggested as a mere henchman of the alleged arch-villain – helping Richard secure the sympathies and support of the city of London against Edward IV's children. He was knighted for this valuable service, and attended Richard III's coronation, serving the King and Queen wine and receiving the cups and pitchers as his fee. After Richard's 1485 defeat and death at the Battle of Bosworth Field, Sir Edmund continued as court jeweller to his Tudor successor, Henry VII.

Shaa didn't forget the county of his birth, leaving an endowment of seventeen pounds per annum to found a school in Stockport, despite the small size of the town. The school moved to the building on Buxton Road in 1916, and from my house in Reddish this meant catching two buses – the 17 right outside the Conservative Club to Mersey Square, changing underneath the viaduct across the square from the now very settled shopping centre on to the 92 on its unbending way from Manchester Piccadilly to Hazel Grove. The journey would usually take about forty minutes, getting me to school with five or ten minutes to spare. (There was also the rare 17X, which went all the way via Mersey Square and the school to Hazel Grove, so there was no need to change, which saved a few minutes, getting me to school early enough to fit in a quick chaotic game of football, but this was an irregular bus which took the sort of planning and preparation to catch that was generally beyond me at eight o'clock in the morning.)

This was the beginning of my main move out of Reddish, the thickening of my world, the regular crossing and recrossing of borders, the shift into a larger space which promised views of even larger spaces and sightings of greater possibilities. Home had expanded into street had expanded into neighbourhood and now expanded into town. Parts of my mind expanded too. The next part of how I was inventing myself, based on the evidence, knowledge and equipment available to me, was under way.

The first sight I had of Stockport Grammar School was at the far end of its long drive, which seemed more suited to a nineteenth-century horse and carriage. Lording it over its own grounds with the railway track at the bottom of the extensive playing fields, it boasted its own cricket pavilion with electrically powered clock. Despite this clock, the trains and the odd modern building, it seemed more 1487 than 1968. This impression never left me in the five years I attended the school: at the moment the sixties seemed finally to be seeping into Stockport I had been thrust back into the numbing, unforgiving past, a past that involved rules, and order, and ever-present tension, and striding menacing authority figures, a past that seemed all about keeping you in your place and separating you from the real world – and all the intriguing furtive changes that as an adolescent you want to use as your inspiration.

The school was like a massive version of the Conservative Club. At the centre of the main school there was a quadrangle open to the skies, paved it sometimes seemed with gravestones, around which heavily wooded echoey old classrooms patterned with scratched sloping Dickensian desks were arranged. (You would write on these desks using your (compulsory) fountain pen, which was of little use to me, being left-handed, as my wrist dragged through the wet ink, smudging everything I wrote and leaving me with a thick permanent blue stripe on the underside of my hand. It was a relief when the ink ran out in my flimsy cartridge pen, the cheapest in WHSmith, and my writing faded away into almost invisible marks on the paper, until I reluctantly inserted a fresh cartridge.) The quadrangle created plenty of dark corridors for masters to swoop along with their gowns flailing dramatically around their backs. Bells for lessons to begin and end would ring as if there was an emergency, the sound always a shock to the system. There was a daunting theatrical quality about daily life at the school that was somewhere between the unnatural and the weirdly camp.

The other boys, my new colleagues, all seemed to come from deep inside the posher parts of Cheshire, not from the remote north-east of the county, which was really Lancashire, or the narrow corridor of uncertainty between the two that meant I belonged nowhere. These boys seemed more definite than I was, came from more definite families with dads who did definite things. The firm, forceful, starched masters, in my limited political view of the world, seemed more Enoch Powell and Harold Macmillan than Roy Jenkins or Harold Wilson, which meant that to me they were stuck in post-Victorian 1910 and had no interest in even pretending that the world now involved rockets into space, Concorde and the Rolling Stones, and that farthings, ancient fragments of an empire-controlling pound, were a thing of the past. Their job was to maintain connection with a world undisturbed by facile modern nonsenses and trivial transient distractions. The atmosphere in the school seemed cut off from the rest of Stockport, enclosed inside its own petrified space, far away from the mutant shopping centre. It confirmed what I felt about such schools formed by my limited unenthusiastic reading of the public schools and boarding establishments written about in slapstick Billy Bunter books featuring a bumbling buffoon, a junior Falstaff, and in books about eternal schoolboy Jennings set in anxious post-war austerity that would be described as a children's Wodehouse.

A flyer for the Manchester Stoneground venue

The mild rebelliousness of William Brown, the devil-may-care hero of Richmal Crompton's *Just William*, was too subtle for me to appreciate. Born in Bury in 1890, on a moral cause to monitor the dismantling of the Edwardian age and the assumptions of 1910, a firm supporter of the Suffragette movement and regular correspondent of the Pankhursts, Crompton, the second child of a clergyman, was educated at St Elphins, a boarding school for daughters of the clergy in Warrington which hosted a resident ghost. She should have been the missing link between soft, silly but weirdly adultless Enid Blyton – where I had gone after wearing out the repetitive and dull Rupert the Bear – and the illuminating darkness of Alan Garner, but I could never summon up much interest in stories, however smartly told, about an unruly boy my age having adventures in a world that was a lot like my world and nothing like it at all – perhaps a reflection of how Crompton set William in a weightless hybrid location that was part her childhood Lancashire and part where she lived as an adult in north Kent. I didn't identify with William's naughtiness, his style of causing trouble, which to my mind was a bit *Beano*, a bit twee. I was already straining to understand the cause and complexity of the rebellion of Orwell's Winston Smith and developing a preference over Bunter, William and the Famous Five – with their yearnings for an idealised childhood set in a space only lightly, if at all, ruffled by the war and post-war realignments – for the way *Animal Farm* was unconventionally but more dramatically rooted in fairy stories and magic.

My Stockport Grammar School, to which I wore a uniform like that of Bunter and his pals, was the stuffy mid-twentieth-century residue of Shaa's generous fifteenth-century desire that Cheshire boys might have the sort of opportunities he had taken to get on in the world, to lift themselves up a level or two or even more in the social order, although it now seemed about maintaining the status quo and frustrating social mobility.

Of all the boys at the school, certainly in my class, travelling in each morning in their yellow and black uniforms from leafy Bramhall, Gatley, Dukinfield, Wilmslow, Heald Green, Cheadle, Disley, sons of affluent, professional families, I appeared the odd one out, the awkward introspective loner who might spend time daydreaming alone among the wild flowers near the Tame in Reddish Vale and imagine fairies chattering in my head, outlining what I should do with my life. This advice would not involve business, or passing exams, or pleasing or appeasing threatening and mostly eccentric teachers, who seemed to be acting on behalf of distant powers to ensure 1910 values would not be undermined by the fairies introducing the Toggery and the Merseyway shopping centre into Stockport, and the Beatles and Kinks to the world. The fairies whispering in my ear were talking of something else, another way to become if not the lord mayor of London then something other than who and what your father was. I couldn't quite make out what they were saying, except that it would be best if I stuck to Orwell and Garner and even the Merseyway shopping centre, and the 92 bus to Manchester would open up more possibilities than anything said and done at the school of Shaa.

From an academic high as one of only two pupils from North Reddish Junior School to make it to Stockport Grammar School, I plummeted almost from the day I arrived to the very bottom. It was as though wearing the black cap with yellow bands crushed my brain and savaged my concentration. The teachers must have taken one look at me and sensed I was away with the fairies: perhaps it was all the chalk dust, which would now be a part of my life for a few years, or the hard blackboard rubbers regularly hurled in my direction, occasionally making contact with my teenage skull. Maybe they saw me as a Lancashire outsider, a subdued Reddish failure split apart by the Nico Ditch, who had gained entrance to their hallowed halls by a lucky fluke, or could they tell that I had made it there only because the thought of spending time at delinquent Reddish Vale Comprehensive, teeming with ruffians from the Brinny part of town, where I really belonged, had made me panic and rise above my station, and travel beyond my bus stop.

Some pupils there might have been guided, inspired and encouraged, but I felt totally lost. From the outside, and as far as my parents were concerned, my life had been put in the hands of teachers who definitely knew what they were doing, but I learned less in the five years I was at Stockport Grammar School than I did at North Reddish. The job of the teachers seemed more about breaking your spirit than

A detail of the Alfred Waterhouse-designed St Elisabeth church in Reddish

opening your mind. My one lucky break was that the year before I started was the final year the school had lessons on Saturday mornings to compensate for sports on Wednesday afternoons.

I was taught history throughout those five years, and it was one of the four O levels that I passed, two at fifteen in the fourth form, two a year later. I struggled to grade 5 at history, grade 6 in English and English literature, and a miraculous grade 6 in religious knowledge, which perversely suggested my deceitfully hypocritical prayers had been answered. I was a disaster at all other subjects, the sciences, the languages, failures which opened up holes in my life that were never adequately filled. In four years of Latin I learned perhaps one fact: boredom is an extraordinary thing, somewhere between a time machine and a near-death experience, in which you become increasingly aware as a distant light beckons you that words are mere sounds containing only the meaning you can muster up from within your own fear that nothing makes sense. From the very first year I was scared of taking my annual report home, a folded blue card filled with expressions of pity, hostility and anger written in various impatient shades of emphatic dark blue ink by those who loved using fountain pens and had found a way of making their own very particular, savage sense.

After my dad's initial euphoria, each report, acknowledging how the stuffing had been knocked out of me, and most of my brains, seemed to knock more and more stuffing out of him. His disappointment and what seemed to me at the time fury at the first two or three reports was replaced by a weariness, as he started to give up if not on his family at least on himself, with life becoming an increasingly complex series of puzzles he had no answer to. The fact that those teachers, with names like Gosling, Harris, Durnell, Swallow, Stanley, Slaughter, Bromley, Johnson, Jermy, were reducing me with their withering one-line year summaries and damning C minuses and Ds to the level of feckless class idiot suggested that his dream of me as accountant was fast receding. If there had still been cotton mills or coal mines, I would have been heading there or, at best, into the sort of office he worked in, a vacuum of repetition, with no real job title, no real prospects, playing with ultimately meaningless numbers and systems not that far removed from what I did with imaginary cricket scores when I was eight.

I did not make the sixth form and A levels, something that must have been spotted very early on, contributing to the school's lack of interest in me. Stockport Grammar was all about ushering its pampered Cheshire charges into university, preferably Cambridge or Oxford, and a box had been ticked within months of my arrival that indicated I was not university material. I did not develop as the kind of boy they would get behind to motivate and nurture.

The only history I remember from those five years was the nineteenth-century unification of Germany and Italy, which was conveyed to me in great and pompous if entirely abstract detail. As with most of what was taught me at the time, the rest of whatever I was meant to learn has drained away, reflecting how I was systematically starved of energy and enthusiasm. Since leaving the school, recalling the teachers who ignored or intimidated me, I have felt particularly aggrieved by the headmaster, F. W. Scott, who seemed the king of an array of unpredictable eccentrics shackled inside a series of quirks, mannerisms and idiosyncratic approaches to discipline and education, and by the sense that in this relationship they were the immovable bosses, and we were the disposable often completely worthless child labour.

Most were in their fifties, and some had started there before the Second World War. A combination of being set in their ways, only interested in the welfare of boys who caught their attention, bored with their own position and routine, and disappointed that they hadn't done as well in their academic lives as they might have wanted, added up to an ever-present tension. On the other hand, if you were enjoying your time at the school, and thriving, they were demanding, committed and thorough, delivering a high-class education for anyone requiring a certain slate of qualifications. Anyone who couldn't cope and keep up was quickly left behind. If there was no sense that you were letting the school down, which I was clearly doing, ruining their records with my inadequacy, you were treated with respect.

Scott left a lasting impression. He seemed a major factor in my maturing sense of inferiority, even though he did not teach me. My encounters with the headmaster were limited to daily morning prayers, which he presided over like an ageing Laurence Olivier playing a pompous, baffled small-town mayor, and an occasional clash in the corridors over the length of my hair, which consistently strayed scruffily over my ears and collar and marked me out as a clear malcontent. During my time there, between 1968 and 1973, the older more formal teachers reacted intolerantly and defensively to the visible signs of teenage rebellion. The one thing about me that got their attention was the length of my hair – or so it seemed to me, although perhaps my apparent indifference, laziness, dirty clothes, spotty complexion, sullenness and increasing stupidity also annoyed them, even though that was more a manifestation of fear and apprehension of the system that had trapped me. I was not particularly naughty, or even mischievous. I would say that I was bland to the point of boring, but the hair was enough for them to believe, even in a world where long hair had clearly replaced hats, that I was trouble.

Francis Willoughby Scott joined the school as headmaster in 1962. I never thought of him as having a life, a past, a family, a strategy; he seemed to exist in paper-thin form simply in order to terrorise and disorientate me. Now that he becomes a character in a book, written by someone who is out of all the boys who went to that school probably the last person the teachers there would have ever imagined writing a book that contained information about the school, let alone a book that claimed itself as a history book, I know a little more about him. Even the dreaded fusty Scott leaves traces on the Internet, that ever-expanding unlimited storage facility where academia and pop culture, knowledge and trivia, learning and simplification, fact and fiction, teachers and pupils coexist.

I know now that he was a northerner, a Yorkshireman, born in 1915 in the Hull that Robinson Crusoe yearned for while stranded on his island, the Hull where Larkin lived on the dwindling, strained, provincial edge of things and told Betjeman the most beautiful spot in Hull was Spring Bank Cemetery. When I started going to Stockport Grammar Scott would have been as old as I am now writing this. To me, stared at by his appraising, slightly mocking eyes under straggly blue-grey eyebrows, he was twice as old as I am now. There is, though, now I am that same age, an awareness that I might have been missing out on the ironic relish, incapable of realising he had a sense of humour, interpreting the sparkle in his eyes only as a threat.

An obituary written in the *Independent* in 2004 by two ex-pupils, Gordon Marsden and Nicholas Henshall, describes someone who I would like to have known, but my limited understanding of a man wearing a dusty academic gown almost casually falling off his shoulders leaning into me so I could feel his dingy breath and he could contemptuously finger my would-be hippy hair, and his limited understanding that there was more to me than my shyness and chronic lack of academic flair, meant we never really met.

Apparently, he was a phenomenon with the sort of vital ornate character and mind that Dickens would love to have owned – I did think of him as Dickensian, but not in a good way. He read both English and history at St Catharine's College, Cambridge. I am not sure what he would have made of the fact that my daughter Madeleine attended that same college, studying English, as I am not sure what I think of it myself, let alone that she edited the Cambridge newspaper *Varsity* in her second year and became Varsity president. Is there some shred of destiny, even a strange culmination of Shaa's moorland fairy dream, twisting around the fact that the daughter of such an embarrassing academic failure ended up not only at university, or Cambridge, but actually at his college? Does it prove him right about something or other, or prove me right about something else altogether? Is he haunting me more than I could ever anticipate – reaching out to demonstrate that he was caring for me in his own slightly capricious way?

He only taught sixth formers, and as I never made the sixth form, I never experienced what the obituary calls 'a roller coaster of ideas and essay construction'. His mind 'whirred like Dr Who's Tardis between past, present and future'. He swooped down corridors like a combination of the first two Doctors – shrewd white-haired William Hartnell and scattily wise tartan-trousered Patrick Troughton – but I never thought of him as being magical enough to be the Doctor. A description of his essay technique suggests a real reason for our incompatibility: 'His formula for crisp prose (short sentences, vigorous verbs and avoidance of the passive) was honed as "Don't say, 'Our world is threatened by human pollution,' say, 'Man pollutes' or 'Man excretes' – even better, 'Man sh . . .'" – the Anglo-Saxon expletive lost in the mix of terror and mirth from students wondering how on earth to get away with that in the exam.' The pious, clipped Scott led the assembled boys day in day out in a mumbling early-morning Lord's Prayer. The thought of him saying 'shit' in front of me would have sent me spiralling through space and time, probably to land in shit in 1555 in a field near where Edmund Shaa grew up by the River Etherow.

The obituary does admit that the regime at the school did 'evoke a bygone era', but there was method to what could appear like the madness of Scott. The Gothic gowns were worn, it seems, to protect the masters' suits from chalk dust, but also because the heating was poor – when Scott arrived at the school each classroom had its own fireplace. He did run the school like a tyrant, but, it seems, as part of his battle to make it pay as an independent with an illustrious but fading history, and modernise it while maintaining its standards. He prepared the way for new buildings, for the eventual introduction of girls – previously only tantalisingly spotted through gaps in the symbolic hedge along the playing fields that separated the school from the Stockport Convent Girls' School next door – and there is a suggestion he was aware of useless non-standard pupils like me, limply hanging out at the far end of the school's vision, out of focus, more or less out of mind: 'I knew I had one or two pupils who were rogues, but I let them stay – it keeps teachers on their toes and both sides get to learn something.'

He let me stay, and suffer. Meanwhile, on the outside I was building a new identity and continuing my self-education in Reddish Library, on the television, on the two-pound transistor radio that had led me, fiddling with the dial, to scratchy distant Radio Luxembourg. Outside I was finding pop music, and this developing love for music contrasted with how I was taught music, and indeed art, and language, inside the school. Outside my mind was being opened. Inside it seemed to be being shut down. Nobody was taking any interest in me, or what I was interested in, and when it came time to tell Mr Scott what I wanted to do with my life – I was fourteen and had set my heart on being a journalist – I received the kind of derisive snort that founder Shaa had received when he announced his own ambitions for personal growth.

The music teacher was called Doug Steele, alongside Scott perhaps the most demented of the eccentrics, as far as I could tell. The system was that for the first four years of school you took music, art and religious knowledge – studying the Bible with such flattening intensity the whole epic thing was wiped out in my imagination, leaving yet another hole, another vast negative space that has never been filled. In the fifth year you chose, or had chosen for you, one of the three subjects to take at O level. I ended up in religious knowledge – where inevitably those with no real skills were dumped – to continue delving into the Good Book, full of words that dissolved in your mind as soon as they were read, either by you or to you, by master in charge Mr Gosling in a tone that suggested he had died in the 1930s. There was never a chance that I would do music, because Mr Steele's teaching technique, the lack of it, made it increasingly difficult to understand what the subject actually was.

His lessons were wild. Sometimes we would read Marvel and DC superhero comics he had piled on a table. He would play random albums – I remember lessons consisting of listening to the Moody

Blues, *Jesus Christ Superstar* and, with no explanation, the first J. Geils Band album, which sounded great but was put in no context at all. We would sit on low wooden benches in his classroom, which was separated from the rest of the school, leaving us exposed to him roaming around in front of and behind us. When he wanted an answer to any question he would abruptly jam a pointed knee into the base of a boy's spine. This cannot have been all that happened during four years of alleged study, but it is all I have taken away with me – Superman comics, flashes of temper, the Moody Blues (*Every Good Boy Deserves Favour*, so perhaps he was showing us how to remember the notes on the treble clef) and a bony jab in the back.

As with Scott, there is a trace of Steele on the Internet, so that he is a wisp or two above disappearing totally into the void. This Douglas Steele is far removed from the spiky, zany character that ran his lessons with a frayed rod of rubber. This Douglas Steele suggests a reason for the gnawing uneasiness that there was in his teaching presence – that his life had not turned out how he had wanted it to, teaching classes of ignorant boys who had no idea who he was and most of whom had no interest in finding out. He was frustrated, sore and highly self-critical, but he adopted a teaching style, at least as far as I was concerned, that was midway between couldn't care less and what the hell.

I must have missed the point of what Doug Steele was up to, or was lost in my own fog of sloppy teen prejudices within a general fear and loathing of the school as a whole. I was distracted by how my interests were developing outside the school, how I was piecing together a love for music based on what I was reading in music magazines, seeing on *Top of the Pops* and hearing on my transistor radio after I had gone to bed. Steele, as a musician and a music teacher, was not engaging me, and he clearly took the decision that as a class – I was emphatically planted in the miserable B stream, those already marked out as second rate – we were not likely to be responsive to his skills and interests. Presumably none of us could play an instrument or sing well enough to join the choir, and so we were of no use to him, and he had no time to waste, and we had other things on our minds. He was perhaps a man who believed in fragile beauty, and we were an ugly, indifferent mob.

I *must* have missed the point, because I am now aware of an elegant song cycle that he wrote 'for the pupils of Stockport Grammar School', which was first played in the school's brand-new neo-modernist Hallam Hall in 1969, where Steele had overseen the installation of the organ. He would play this organ every morning as the assembled school staggered through hymns with melodies that seemed made up on the spot, and possibly were, as Steele was fond of improvising. He clearly took morning assembly as an opportunity to please himself, playing flamboyantly in an attempt to drown out the untidy singing making a mumbling mockery of the Lord.

His song cycle, *Autumn Sequence*, is whimsically scored for speaker, solo voices and the few instruments available at the school at the time – flute, piccolo or recorder, tubular bells, handbells, tambourine, organ and piano – which must have been another cause for frustration, but the limitations were used in his composition as a challenge. I was at the school, a twelve-year-old, when it was premiered. I imagine attendance was compulsory and something of an event, the music teacher composing a twenty-five-minute piece especially for the school choir to sing. I have no memory of the performance. If I did attend, I assume the bored, snooty me found the music – which his fans, his more affectionate ex-students, would call charming, wistful, occasionally slyly dramatic with a decent dash of Delius – old-fashioned and dull. (As well as Steele's wired organ playing at assembly, which could cause much sniggering during 'Onward Christian Soldiers', I remember annual school speech days at the plush but faded 1,750-seat Davenport Cinema and Theatre next door. As we impatiently waited for the prizes to be given – never to me or my classmates, who therefore viewed the whole thing with rejected and childish disinterest – and the invited speaker to bore us with flaccid inspirational words, the highlight would be the moment when the massive theatre organ slowly rose out of the pit. Steele would be in control, and out of control, madly pumping the mighty instrument to the hilt, splashing around the special effects, stamping on the pedals, acting like a nutty combination of Keith Emerson of Nice and Emerson, Lake and Palmer, Catweazle, the quaint TV wizard, and Professor Pat Pending from *Wacky Races*. There was, perhaps, something in him that if he had been born thirty years later might have led to him being in a progressive rock group, possibly

Saddleworth's very own Moody Blues, Barclay James Harvest. Some of his other pieces, with titles like *Slow Air, Thrice Toss These Oaken Ashes in the Air, The Land of Lost Content, Blow, Blow, Thou Winter Wind*, suggest he could have written a decent concept album based on the romanticised dreams of Edmund Shaa. As Steele charged through his organ repertoire, he would be lustily, slightly ironically cheered, by his restless, listless audience, sensing a peculiar hint of liberation and soul at the heart of this soporific ceremony.)

Douglas Steele was a northerner, born in Carlisle in 1910, the ancient Roman frontier town, the western end of Hadrian's Wall, a prize possession fought for by England and Scotland over centuries, where Mary Queen of Scots sought asylum in 1568 and was imprisoned as a threat to English security. Before teaching at Stockport, he had studied at the Royal Northern College of Music, taught at Chetham's School and was an assistant organist at Manchester Cathedral and director of music at Holy Innocents Church in Fallowfield. After studying in Salzburg, in 1939 he became a 'talented secretary' and librarian to entrepreneur, impresario and conductor Sir

The SELNEC 92 bus from Manchester to Hazel Grove,
via Levenshulme and Heaton Chapel, in the 1960s

Thomas Beecham, then working at Covent Garden, the founder of the London Philharmonic Orchestra in 1932, closely involved with the Manchester Hallé and the Liverpool Philharmonic, and a celebrated, prolific and spectacular musician with a cavalier brilliance for presenting opera. Beecham was a Hadyn and Mozart specialist who helped introduce Debussy, Sibelius and Strauss to a wider public and who had an extraordinary ability to transform the sound an orchestra made, inspiring even mesmerising his musicians.

Beecham was born in St Helens in 1879, the son of wealthy chemist Sir Joseph Beecham, whose father Thomas had been responsible for Beecham's Pills, which proved to be an excellent patent remedy for indigestion ('Hark the herald angels sing, Beecham's pills are just the thing . . .'). Thomas Beecham, born the son of a farm worker in 1820, had spent his youth as a shepherd, and had learned a good deal about herbal remedies. Beecham was said to have had a special knack for healing sick animals and, on occasion, humans. For several years Beecham sold his laxatives at local markets with a sales pitch that included showing off a jar of intestinal worms. In 1847 Beecham began hawking his own brand of pills throughout the town of Wigan and the surrounding countryside. He soon set up shop as a herbalist and grocer in Wigan. In 1859, after mixed results in Wigan, Beecham moved his base to nearby St Helens, where he focused on two products: a cough tablet and the famous laxative Beecham's Pills, advertised in the local newspaper as 'worth a guinea a box'. Both products were available through mail order, and Beecham advertised extensively to take advantage of a rapidly growing demand for novel health remedies.

Thomas Beecham the musician was knighted in 1916 and died in 1961, buried in Limpsfield, Surrey near Frederick Delius of Bradford, who he loved like 'an alluring, wayward woman' and had rescued from obscurity with his advocacy. Reading Steele talking about his time as assistant to the haughty myth-making Beecham perhaps provides a clue to his own idiosyncratic approach to life and teaching. He recalled Beecham preparing on the piano for a performance of Wagner at the Covent Garden Royal Opera House, where Steele was expected to turn the pages of the score.

He called me in and said, 'Have a piece of birthday cake.' This cake was made for him, so he told me, 'by a little old lady in St Helens'. Then he said, 'I want you to turn over for this terrible piece.' He went over to the piano and the terrible piece was *Götterdämmerung*. As fast as he roared, coughed, cursed, sang (and what singing!), I turned. When I missed a turn, he cursed, not me, but The Ring. 'Damn awful thing, what – barbarian lot of Nazi thugs, aren't they?' If complications in turning brought us to a stop, he roared with laughter; stopped, told a marvellous anecdote about some accident in performance, and the swearing and the banging on the piano started all over again, along with the terrible, moaning sing-song. The following night he gave an absolutely majestic performance of the work.

What a comedown I must have been after working with Beecham at the height of his powers, insignificant me representing all small pointless boys, selfishly mooching about like he was just another ageing teacher with no internal life, no experience and no idea how to teach. He had worked with one of the great, notorious and controversial men of classical music, alive with wit and appetite, who once described the sound of the harpsichord as 'two skeletons copulating on a corrugated tin roof'. Steele had been given a tantalising glimpse into the madness of genius, into an international world of ideas and achievement, and then been removed and eventually placed in an ordinary, unexceptionally eccentric minor grammar school filled with boys becoming more interested as the sixties become the seventies in a seductive and powerful form of music that increasingly marginalised his own. Those pupils and colleagues who were fond of Steele, like he was fond of Beecham, and who curated his memory, organising recordings of *Autumn Sequence* and some of his other nostalgic, yearning chamber pieces, remember a man 'held in warmth and affection in Manchester and all areas from Carlisle to Stockport'. A hint of what I experienced in his unsettling classroom comes in a review written by one of his students and friends, Christopher Fifield: 'Douglas was an eccentric bachelor, with a history of mental breakdowns, but he possessed an impish sense of humour and was hugely gifted as a teacher and musician, a fine organist – in particular as an exceptionally talented improviser – in short a thoroughly likeable man from whom I learned a great deal.'

I didn't get his sense of humour, perhaps in the way that I wouldn't have got Spike Milligan's sense of humour if he had taught me. My musical education was happening elsewhere. My mind was elsewhere.

89

1746

Sheffield, already for centuries a home of edged-tool manufacturing, had in 1746 about 12,000 inhabitants. It was a plainly built town, which was just beginning, as a result of improvements to the navigability of the River Don, to develop trade with more distant markets and to grow into an important industrial centre for plated goods as well as for the manufacture of iron and steel.

1742

In 1742 Thomas Boulsover, a Sheffield cutler, while repairing a silver and copper knife, fused a thin layer of silver to copper, discovered they behaved as a single metal and produced what became known as Sheffield Plate. Other craftsmen in Sheffield began to use this method to produce tableware that looked like silver but at a fraction of its cost. At this time, nearly 100 water mills lined the easily dammed rivers and brooks that flowed through Sheffield, operating grindstones, forge hammers and rolling mills all necessary for knife making.

1733

John Kay, son of the owner of a Lancashire woollen factory, patents the first of the devices which revolutionise the textile industry. He has devised a method for the shuttle to be thrown mechanically back and forth across the loom. This greatly speeds up the previous hand process and halves the labour force required. Where a broadcloth loom previously required a weaver on each side, it can now be worked by a single operator. This makes the weaver's work easier and less tiring, but many fear they will lose their jobs.

1725

Whig historian Thomas Macaulay noted the desolate condition of the northern counties at the beginning of his controversial 1848 *History of England*. This is in stark contrast to Daniel Defoe, who in his *Tour through the Whole Island* (1725), remarked,

> The country south of Trent is by far the largest, as well as the richest and most populous, though the great cities were rivalled by those of the north. There is no town in England, London excepted, that can equal Liverpool for the fineness of the streets, the beauty of the buildings; many of the houses are all of stone and the rest (the new part) of brick. Newcastle is a spacious, extended, infinitely populous place. It is seated upon the River Tyne, which is here a noble, large and deep river, and ships of any reasonable size may come safely up to the very town. As the town lies on both sides of the river, the parts are joined by a very strong and stately stone bridge of seven very great arches, rather larger than the arches of London Bridge; and the bridge is built into a street of houses also, as London Bridge is. They build ships here to perfection, I mean as to strength and firmness, and to bear the sea; and as the coal trade occasions a demand for such strong ships, a great many are built here. In Newcastle there is considerable manufacture of wrought iron.

1725

In 1725 Lancashire's first turnpike act passed through Parliament. This permitted the businessmen of Liverpool to construct a road linking the coal fields of Prescot with the expanding city. The Wigan to Preston Turnpike opened in 1726, and from 1750, as the cotton industry grew in dramatic fashion, turnpikes punched their way through the valleys, vital routes for trade until the expansion of the railways in the 1840s. The building of canals, which could transport much heavier loads much more easily, was also a factor in the demise of the turnpikes. Road trade fell to such an extent that it became uneconomical to collect tolls. At one time there were some ninety turnpikes in Lancashire, although most were less than ten miles in length and only four exceeded thirty miles.

1721

Up to 1700 Britain's largest and most profitable exports had always been wool fleeces and textiles, but cotton was soon to replace wool. An act of Parliament in 1721 prohibited the import of all printed and painted calicoes and fine pure-cotton fabrics, which came from India and the Far East. This caused consternation among London society and the new fashion houses. Lancashire hand-loom weavers copied the imports, and filled the gap in the market.

1719

Robinson Crusoe was, according to north England expert Daniel Defoe, in a book published in 1719, considered by many to be one of the very first novels because it tested the possibilities of extended narrative written in prose: '. . . born in 1632, in the city of York, of a good family though not of that country, my father being a foreigner of Bremen, who settled first at Hull. He got a good estate by merchandise, and leaving off his trade, lived afterwards at York, from whence he had married my mother, whose relations were named Robinson, a very good family in that country, and from whom I was called Robinson Kreutznaer; but, by the usual corruption of words in England, we are now called – nay we call ourselves and write our name – Crusoe; and so my companions always called me.'

The first book printed in Manchester was John Jackson's *Mathematical Lectures Read to the Mathematical Society in Manchester*, printed in 1719 by

Roger Adams of Chester, printer of the *Manchester News-Letter*, later the *Weekly Journal*, 'containing the freshest advices, both foreign and domestic', price one penny, the very start of Manchester newspaper history.

1718

Thomas Chippendale Senior was born in Otley, a small market town in the Yorkshire Dales, and was baptised in the parish church there on 5 June 1718. His family had long been involved in the woodworking and timber trades, and he probably received a practical apprenticeship from his father. Not a great deal is known about Chippendale's life and the work he did until the publication of his ground-breaking book *The Gentleman and Cabinet Maker's Director*.

This was published in 1754 and included 161 engraved plates of 'Elegant and Useful Designs of Household Furniture in the Gothic, Chinese and Modern Taste'. It was an immediate sellout and a second edition was reprinted a year later. A third edition, with many new plates, appeared in 1762. This work is Chippendale's enduring legacy, and shows his gift for adapting design styles to the fashion of the mid-eighteenth century. The book was so influential that the name of Chippendale is often indiscriminately applied to mid-eighteenth-century furniture as a whole. From the 1760s Chippendale was influenced heavily by the

A 4d stamp from 1966 showing Jodrell Bank

neoclassical work of architect Robert Adam, with whom he worked on several large projects, notably at Harewood House and Nostell Priory in Yorkshire. In both places he supplied furnishings from attic to basement, which was his preference.

Chippendale described himself as an 'upholder' – which implies that he was able to supply his clients with furnishings of every kind. He was an entrepreneur running a large business employing perhaps as many as fifty in-house craftsmen – including cabinetmakers, upholsterers, carvers, gilders, chair makers, polishers and packers – as well as a number of outworkers. He was the artistic director of the enterprise: supervising the workforce and its production, appeasing clients and always keeping abreast of new fashions. After Chippendale's death in 1779, the business was carried on until well into the nineteenth century by his eldest son, also called Thomas Chippendale.

The *Leeds Mercury* was established by John Hirst in 1718 as a weekly newspaper in the rapidly growing west Yorkshire woollen textile town. It was one of the foremost provincial newspapers, publishing articles by many distinguished writers and gaining a reputation as a leading reporter of liberal politics. The newspaper only had a small circulation in its early years. The *Mercury* began as a four-page Saturday newspaper, but It gradually increased in size, frequency and popularity, being published daily from 1861.

1700

In a time when it took a week to travel from York to London, pioneering traveller and diarist Celia Fiennes rides most of her way from Rochdale between hedges cut smooth and even. She writes, 'Manchester looks exceedingly well at the entrance. Very substantial buildings; the houses are not very lofty, but mostly of brick and stone; the old houses are timber work. There is a very large church, all stone; and [it] stands so high that walking round the churchyard you see the whole town. There is good carving of wood in the choir.' After describing the Chetham Hospital and Library, with its curiosities, she continues, 'Out of the Library there are leads on which one has the sight of the town, which is large, as also the other town that lies below it, called Salford, and is divided from this by the River Irwell, over which is a stone bridge, with many arches . . . The Market place is large; it takes up two streets' length when the market is kept for their linen cloth [and] cotton tickings which is the manufacture of the town. Here is a very fine school for young gentlewomen, as good as any in London; and music and dancing and things are very plenty here. This is a thriving place.'

Until about 1700 most English speakers, whatever their dialect, pronounced the letter r very clearly in words where it followed a vowel, such as in farmer and carter (this is known as rhoticisation). After 1700 this swiftly died out and is now virtually unknown in British standard English. It survives, however, in the dialects of the West Country, part of Lancashire and some parts of Yorkshire. It is also a standard feature of Scots, the English spoken in Scotland. Nobody is quite sure why it disappeared from most British English, but its loss was certainly noticed at the time. Some eighteenth-century folk complained about 'R-dropping' the way people complain about H-dropping today.

1698

Visitors were struck by the menacing quality of the landscape around the Cumbrian lakes. In 1698, Celia Fiennes rode on horseback through Kendal and over Kirkstone Pass into Patterdale. She described it in terms both admiring and forbidding. 'As I walked down at this place I was walled on both sides by those inaccessible high rocky barren hills which hang over one's head in some places and appear very terrible.'

1696

Chester was chosen over Hereford as one of the locations of five country branch mints, to the delight of local people. This was a period known as the Great Re-coinage, an attempt by the government to renew the currency at a time when people would slice small amounts of precious metal from silver coins rendering them unusable. The Warden of the

Royal Mint, Isaac Newton, appointed astronomer Edmund Halley deputy controller of the mint to help coordinate the standardisation and milling of silver coins. In the year he spent at Chester Halley wrote in *Philosophical Transactions* about various things including the discovery of a Roman altar in Eastgate Street, an extraordinary hailstorm and an eclipse of the moon. The Chester mint, the least succesful of the five country branches, was shut down in 1698.

1673

Broadsheets in Yorkshire and Lancashire dialect appeared with increasing frequency after the seventeenth century. A York printer, Stephen Bulkley, published the poem 'A Yorkshire Dialogue in Yorkshire Dialect: between an Awd Wife, A Lass and a Butcher' in 1673. The poem describes in realistic detail the misadventures of an ox on its way to the slaughterhouse – a subject lacking heroic possibilities but defining dialect's greatest strength: hard-boiled comedy that did not bow to elitist literacy or flippant social assumptions.

90

For a couple of years I obediently caught the bus outside the Conservative Club at about five past eight so I could be at school by a quarter to nine and disappear into my other life – which required a ridiculous uniform – and then the Morley family moved house. We stayed within Stockport, as if despite all the carefully organised transport routes, there was no way out. The move was part of my parents' thinking that it was important to move up in life – to advance. Clearly it was time to leave cramped, static Reddish, which despite its Cheshire address was really south-east Lancashire, and head over to the other side of the Mersey into Cheshire proper. My father, never a fan of Harold Wilson as prime minister, a guarded, conventional

Kent Ted Heath man through and through, never felt at home in Lancashire and craved a move further into smarter, moneyed Cheshire as a reflection of his ambition to join the middle class.

I felt no regret at leaving Reddish. I had got everything I needed. Reddish had made me what I was: it had formed my identity, created the boy, coated my consciousness with an image of myself that would never leave me, as someone of the north, a fan of Lancashire County Cricket Club, of Manchester City Football Club, someone who was if not born in Reddish then made in Reddish. Wherever I now went, throughout the rest of my life, all subsequent reinventions would be based around that Reddish core. Everything else that happened to me formed around that grave and tangible self-conscious pre-teen centre. If I had left Reddish at eleven or twelve and our family had headed south, perhaps to my dad's home on the Isle of Thanet by the Channel, I would still have always thought of myself as a northerner, from Manchester, Lancashire, Stockport, Cheshire, never slipping over into a southern map, a non-northern mind. There was, though, some further northern education still to come.

My dad was in relatively steady employment, and we moved closer to my school, towards Bramhall, but nowhere near in it, more than a mile or so from the splendid black and white Bramhall Hall. We ended up in an area of Stockport called Woodsmoor, prettier than Reddish, but still a lot lower than middle class, the other side of the railway line from Manchester to Sheffield at the bottom of the school's sports field. It was now a short walk to school. The house was like a sketchy, down-market version of the kind of semi-detached suburban home my dad truly desired. Nearby there was plain, doughty Davenport, named after the railway station – built before there was any settlement, which in turn was named after the fourteenth-century Davenports who owned the land for 500 years. They were a locally important family which can be traced back to 1066 with a name derived from the Norman French Dauenport meaning the town on the trickling stream. Davenport was filled with larger houses built for the moguls of the Stockport hat industry that was no more.

My dad now had a garage – for a second-hand but recent-model gold-coloured Vauxhall Viva HB – a slightly flashy upgrade of the tatty

HA Viva he'd driven in Reddish, with American-influenced curved back windows, a relatively fancy front grille and interior, the kind of car he hoped would be good for the ego – and a few yards of drive between the front door and the pavement. It was in this house, while working for BP and Shell in Wythenshawe, that he had a catastrophic nervous breakdown, a phrase we used in our family to attempt to explain how he lost his mind, which contained who he was, as if the effort of the rising and advancing, the move deeper into more wholesome Cheshire, the accumulation of mortgage, hire-purchase agreements, funding a near-new car and maintaining an increasingly complicated marriage was just too much.

If there was a sigh of relief at leaving Reddish and a feeling of satisfaction at being within a few minutes of lush, melodious Bramhall, whatever it was that had marked him – before he arrived or once he was in the north, absorbing northern history and environment as a deadweight, an offence to his south-eastern sensibility – continued to blacken his being to such an extent he would eventually become a mere shadow and then even more evanescent. An unfillable hole that had opened in my life was caused by opaque, bizarre lessons in Latin and biology. The gaping hole in his life was caused by life itself.

When my dad was a teenager and a younger man he loved to play table tennis, and there was the odd small silver shield wistfully leaning on otherwise bare shelves around our house that suggested he played well enough to win one or two minor youth tournaments in Kent. He still played occasionally, and I remember how when he wore his short-sleeved dark blue table-tennis shirt and crisply pressed trousers he looked very like how Fred Perry had looked in the 1930s when he was at his peak as a player both of table tennis and tennis. Six feet tall, twelve stone, lean, long legs, an agile, athletic presence, dark hair neatly slicked back with Brylcreem, a solid centre of some confidence, a broad, winning, flirtatious smile: this is how I remember my dad before he was reduced by circumstances and sadness, unable or unwilling to transcend local conditions, and slipped further into the gaping hole inside and out.

I always know how old my dad would be if he was still alive because he was born in 1936, which was the year of the three kings, the death of George V followed by the crowning and abdication of Edward VIII, who was replaced by his younger brother, George IV. It was the year that BBC Television officially began and also the last time that a British male won Wimbledon. My dad was born on 10 May, at the beginning of summer, a few weeks before Wimbledon begins. I can keep in touch with my dad's shadow age by the annual lamentation that it is so many years since Fred Perry was the last British player to win the singles title at Wimbledon. In 2011 it was seventy-five years since Perry won the last of his three Wimbledon titles.

In much the same way I can always remember how old my younger sister Carol is, because she was born in 1966, the increasingly mythical year that England last won the World Cup. So in 1996 it was 'thirty years of hurt' since that victory, and Carol was thirty, and in 2011 it was forty-five years since England won what may turn out to be their only World Cup, with Gordon Banks of Rotherham in goal behind the Charlton brothers of Ashington, Northumberland, a central part of the Great Northern Coalfield, once named the largest mining village in the world, fifteen miles north of Newcastle, home to the Pitmatic dialect.

In the nineteenth century Pitmatic – a compound of 'pit' and 'mathematical' – meant the skill and craft of mining and then came to denote the local dialogue, a dialect within a dialect, a dense insular crush of Old Norse, Scots and Low German that developed around the pit villages of south-east Northumberland and Durham. The term is first recorded in print, in a slightly different form, in an article on a major rally by Bill Lancaster in the *Newcastle Weekly Chronicle* in 1873: 'A great many of the lads, especially from the Durham district, had evidently never been in Newcastle previously, and the air of wonder with which they gazed at the crowds, at the buildings, and especially at the fine folks who occupied the windows, was very amusing. If the quality criticised and quizzed them, the lads returned the compliment, and it was entertaining enough to catch snatches of criticism on the manners and customs of the upper ten thousand of Newcastle, reduced to the purest "pitmatical", shouted across the streets, as the men and lads belonging to collieries swept by where I stood in the crowd.' In his *English Journey* (1934) J. B. Priestley noted that this 'curious lingo', developed within the collieries by colliery men linguistically mapping their own unique underground world, 'should be an excellent medium for grim tales of accidents far underground, the sagas of the deep pits'.

Fred Perry was born in 1909 in Stockport, in Portwood, close to the town centre near the River Goyt, a couple of miles away from where we lived in Reddish. There is no Perry statue in Stockport, but a fourteen-mile Fred Perry memorial walk opened by Stockport Council in 2002 runs into Reddish from Woodford, passes where the Goyt and Tame become the Mersey, and winds through Reddish Vale up towards Houldsworth Square and Houldsworth Mill.

Fred's father Samuel Frederick was born in Stockport on 29 June 1877, the son of a cotton spinner, Samuel Ainsworth, born in Hull who later moved to Cheshire, where his family was originally from. Samuel Junior won a scholarship to Stockport Grammar School, but was forced to leave the school at ten because of the death of his father, and work spinning cotton to help feed his family. Frustration at losing out on his treasured place at the grammar school mutated into serious political aspirations, and as a cotton worker he became involved with the Stockport Co-operative Society, elected leader when his abilities became apparent. He married local girl Hannah Birch, and when the Co-operative Party was formed in 1917, Perry became its first national secretary.

Young Fred was nine, and with his father setting up the new party's headquarters in London, the family moved south – they had already moved via Bolton to Birkenhead as Sam pursued his career – to the Brentham Estate in Ealing, an Edwardian co-operative housing scheme that influenced the design and structure of Hampstead Garden Suburb. For Fred, Brentham was 'paradise after the bleak streets of the north because everyone in the garden village had use of the Brentham Institute and its cricket field, football pitch, tennis courts, bowling green and – an important thing to me – table tennis facilities. It was there that I first became interested in watching and playing sport, because it was all on the doorstep.'

Perry Senior attempted a return to Stockport when as a Labour Party candidate he contested a by-election in the town in 1920 and again stood at the general election of 1922. He lost both times, but eventually became an MP in 1923 when he was elected for the constituency of

Kettering. He lost and regained the seat a number of times between 1924 and 1931, and the Perrys remained in the south. Fred never lost his Stockport edge – living there until seven or eight was enough for him to always retain a scrappy self-contained outsider's spirit. He fell in love with table tennis at Ealing County School and, inheriting his father's focus, strength and determination, was the world champion by 1928.

While on holiday in Eastbourne a few years earlier he had noticed some expensive-looking cars lined up near the courts where a tennis tournament was taking place. His dad told him the cars belonged to the players. Fred immediately made up his backstreet mind that he would become a tennis player. Tennis was a game that belonged to the public-school and Oxbridge middle and upper classes and the elitist, enclosed world of Wimbledon, with no easy access for the working class. Provoked by this exclusivity and encouraged by his father, with his own dedication to overcoming the obstacles set in his way by his background, he took up tennis. The competitive Stopfordian spirit of Edmund Shaa penetrated Perry's psyche – if you were told that you could not do something, this made you even more determined. He practised for hours at a time, but he also had an essential genius for both table tennis and tennis, and an intimidating physical technique combined with superior stamina that was ahead of its time. His table tennis experience and quick, hungry playing style had a positive effect on his speed and reflexes as a tennis player.

His aggression and determination as a player was undoubtedly the result of feeling patronised by the tennis establishment for how he talked and the ungentlemanly enthusiasm and delight he took in playing and winning. His ferocious will to win, addiction to success and the psychological games he played to disconcert and dominate his opponents were considered common. He never shook hands with an opponent before a game, in case, he claimed, he lost some feeling in his hand. His habit of leaping over the net after a win particularly annoyed the powers that were, and refined southern crowds shook their heads in distaste when he changed into fresh kit if a match went to four sets. (In his career he only ever lost two matches that went to five sets.) He had another habit as well – after he hit a winner he would exclaim 'Very clever' in a fine Stockport accent guaranteed to irk the All England Club regulars.

'I made up my mind early on that I wasn't going to let people order me about,' he once stated. 'If they said, "We would rather you didn't do that," there was no problem, but if they gave me an outright prohibition then I would deliberately find a way round it. Bloody-mindedness was one of my specialities, and revenge was never against my principles either.'

When he beat Australian Jack Crawford in his first Wimbledon singles final, a Wimbledon official handed Crawford a bottle of champagne after the match while Perry was taking a bath. He overheard the official commiserate with Crawford as 'this was a day when the best man certainly didn't win'. Perry's winner's tie was not presented to him, but tossed over a nearby chair. A reluctant apology materialised a few days later, but the dislike didn't go away. A Lawn Tennis Association member once murmured, 'Not one of us,' in front of Sam Perry. In 1933 Perry helped Britain win the Davis Cup for the first time in twenty-one years, and he went on to complete his three Wimbledon wins in succession (1934–6), and also the Australian, French and American singles titles to complete the Grand Slam. He completed his break with the proudly amateur British tennis establishment by turning professional in 1936, the day after his third Wimbledon victory.

Bored with the small-minded, spoiling antics of the British tennis bosses, he had already moved to California, where his blazing self-confidence and unfettered ambition was embraced. He bought into the Beverly Hill Tennis Club, gave tennis lessons to Charlie Chaplin, Errol Flynn and the Marx Brothers, and had flings with actresses such as Jean Harlow and Marlene Dietrich. They loved his funny accent and pipe-smoking, especially because they came with a striking physique. For those still looking down on swaggering Perry, he became The Working Class Playboy.

By the early 1940s he was an American citizen, and an elbow injury had led to early retirement. Never a particularly popular hero because of the elitist nature of the game in a pre-television world, he reinvented himself by commentating for BBC Radio after the war and in the late 1940s made his name all over again.

An Austrian ex-footballer, Theodore 'Tibby' Wegner had invented an anti-perspirant device worn on the wrist, and approached Perry for an endorsement. Perry didn't like it, but had some suggestions, and

THE NORTH

Wegner returned with a neater, more practical sweatband, an invention which led to the founding of Fred Perry Sportswear. Fred's first thought for a logo was the pipe he loved to smoke, perhaps as an oblique reference to the Stockport of his youth, regularly slumped underneath what was surely the thickest pall of smoke in the country. The pipe wasn't sexy enough for Wegner, who had his eye on the slick crocodile logo used by the French 1920s Wimbledon champion René 'The Crocodile' Lacoste on his fashionable soft-collared cotton shirts. The logo they settled on was the Wimbledon laurel wreath that Perry had proudly worn on his touring blazer and sweater during his peak years. The laurel wreath is a symbol of victory, and looking to one's laurels means taking inspiration from past achievements to conquer a new task. Resting on your laurels does not.

Perry assumed that the All England Tennis Club, the snobbish centre of a snobbish sport, would refuse permission for them to use it, but the club unexpectedly agreed and released the rights. By 1952 the understated but striking white short-sleeved honeycomb-weave cotton-piqué Fred Perry shirt with three buttons down the front and the wreath logo stitched into the breast was ready for sale. (Fred's dad Sam died in 1954, having become one of the leading figures in the practical, canny co-operative experiment in self-help.) Soon the shirt spread beyond sport but clung to Perry's insolent, discreetly showy working-class image, other colours being produced following a 1957 petition from West Ham United fans, and the later dogmatically self-conscious mods desiring a wider range of shades.

The combination of smart, casual, inexpensive and versatile meant the shirt was endlessly adopted by emerging teenage subcultures (as soon as there was a teenage culture), especially if that subculture reflected a certain sort of practical, masculine, comfortable Britishness. Each emerging tribe, from mod to northern soul to skinhead to suede-head to punk to Perry boy to two-tone to Britpop and subsequent nostalgic recreations, read their own interpretations into Fred Perry and the leaves stitched into the clothing, an accumulation of real and imagined myths about the meaning of the brand. The brand became a reflection of its own resilience: it survived endless shifts in fashion and tribal movements, never losing its restrained allure.

A timelessness was pressed into the fabric and the image that never obstructed its fashionableness, as prime adopters wanted at the same time to belong to a certain tribe, but retain an invisibility and yet an individuality. The Fred Perry shirt could satisfy all those requirements, without sacrificing its fundamental message, which again perhaps goes back to the vigorous man and the tough mentality that first inspired it and the subtle symbol of victory, of one-upmanship, stitched above the heart. (The role of Perry's business partner in the branding of a shirt often favoured by no-nonsense even neo-Nazi English nationalists is more fuzzy. Tibby Wegner was a product of the 'muscular' Judaism of Hakoah (the Force) Vienna, part of a sports club formed by liberal Jews as an intellectual experiment in the idea of Jewish sporting superiority. The club was intended as a counterweight to the limp, bookish, stereotype of European Jews in the 1920s and thirties, and its football team was rumoured to be Franz Kafka's favourite. The Star of David stitched into the breast of the shirts worn by club members probably had no influence on where Perry's laurel wreath was placed.)

The Fred Perry brand was sold in the early 1960s, eventually ending up as part of a Japanese company, but the name stayed, perhaps because it has a sense of something solid, plain and permanent, uncompromising and unpretentious, which attracts a manly form of dapper fashion follower not interested in the fey and frivolous, but the traditional and utilitarian. It can be at the same time cutting-edge and conservative. It moves with the times, sometimes actively moving them along, but never in a way that seems to sell out its original principles, encouraging a feeling that the brand stands for integrity and authenticity in a world that too easily succumbs to commercially engineered trends.

Perry took the Wimbledon logo and transformed it into the logo of the proletariat the snooty All England Club despised. It became the everyday shirt of the working man obsessed with a certain corner of mass popular culture. It anticipated, created and participated in a gradual shift into a liberated casual world that explicitly rejected the superior-minded formalities and routines of the upper class – a general removing of the tie that was never properly handed to Perry. The clothing brand named after the man who hated doing what he was told was

Fred answering back those officials who never looked him in the eye and wished he'd never left the drizzly backstreets of Stockport.

Wimbledon maintained its stiff upper lip as Fred went from vulgar strength to strength, a living legend even after he died, worn on the backs of the common man, and also as no one with the club's preferred brand of class came along to replace him as the last British man to win its championship. Through gritted teeth they played at being good sports, and eventually a statue was erected to mark the fiftieth anniversary of his first win. By then Fred was seventy-four, never to be knighted, and he commented, 'There will be a few former members of the All England Club revolving in their graves at the thought of such a tribute paid to the man they regarded as a rebel from the wrong side of the tennis tramlines.'

91

1670

Rock salt was rediscovered (coal was the intended target) in 1670 near Northwich in the heart of the Cheshire Plain at the junction of the Rivers Dane and Weaver. When the Romans first discovered the salt, Northwich was known as Condate, meaning the confluence, because of its position. Salt was important to the Romans, and is linked as a source to the words soldier and salary. The seventeenth-century rediscovery led to a sudden increase in the town's prosperity, but transport links were still poor. Salt was carried from the town to other parts of the country by pack pony. At one time salt was highly taxed, and a fair amount of smuggling went on. The traditional method for extracting fine white salt from brine was to boil it up in immense pans until the water evaporated. This meant the town was afflicted by great clouds of smoke and steam, as antiquarian John Leland noted in the sixteenth century: 'Northwich is a pratie market town but fowle, and by the Salters houses be great stakes of smaul cloven wood, to seethe the salt water that thei make white salt of.'

Northwich is the most northern of the Cheshire 'wyches', which include nearby Middlewich and Nantwich. (It is the salt deposits beneath the soils of the Cheshire Plain that give a special flavour to the pasture and therefore the milk and therefore the flaky Cheshire cheese.)

1664

First estimates of population make Stockport the fifth largest town in Cheshire. The population is recorded as 1,400–1,500 in 308 households.

1660

By 1610 a quarter of English maritime trade (by weight) consisted of coal, and this rose to 40 per cent by 1660, three times the size of all other coastal shipping. The coal trade was seen as an ideal training ground for sailors: 'the principal nursery of English seamen. England is built upon an underground mountain of coal. Its exploitation was the motor-force in the revolution that created modern industrial society.'

1652

Up to the early-modern period Lancashire was predominantly Roman Catholic, although after the Reformation it developed remarkable religious diversity, particularly after the Toleration Act of 1690. Perhaps the most notable example of this diversity is George Fox, who in 1652, on the summit of Pendle Hill, experienced a vision which later led him to the home of Thomas and Margaret Fell near Ulverston, where the Quaker movement may be said to have been founded.

1650

The people of Manchester are spoken of as the most industrious in the northern parts of the kingdom; the town is stated to be a mile in length, the

Winston Churchill surveying the remains of the Manchester Free Trade Hall,
demolished by German bombs at the beginning of the Second World War

streets are open and clean, and the buildings good. There were four market-
places, two markets weekly and three fairs in the year.

1648

The Battle of Preston took place between 17 and 19 August 1648, and effectively ended the second phase of the English Civil War. On one side were the
invading Scottish Engagers (supporters of Charles I) under Hamilton. On the
other was Oliver Cromwell's New Model Army. The raw Scottish recruits,
although greatly superior in numbers, were no match for the English veter-
ans. Oliver Cromwell caught up with them at Preston and dispersed them in
a series of running battles.

1642

Manchester has a population of 6,000. Salford has 1,500 citizens.

The nine stormy years of the English Civil War, actually three separate wars, resulted from a range of factors, economic, constitutional and religious, inextricably interwoven. The war which broke out in 1642 saw a broadly Royalist north and west ranged against a predominantly Parliamentarian south and east. Manchester was one of very few towns in Lancashire to support Parliament against King Charles I and can claim the first casualty of the whole war. In a riot on Market Street on 15 July 1642 Richard Percival, a linen weaver, was shot dead. Four days later this was announced in the House of Commons as 'The beginning of Civil Warres in England: or Terrible News from the north'.

In September of the same year Lord Strange (James Stanley, heir to the Earl of Derby, born in Knowsley in 1607, devoted to the King's cause), in command of between 3,000 and 4,000 Royalists, attacked Manchester along Deansgate and across the thirteenth-century Salford Bridge, at the time the only bridge over the Irwell. When Strange demanded that Manchester give up its store of gunpowder and its weapons, he was told that he would get 'nothing, not even a rusty dagger'. At the battle's height two barns caught fire, the resultant smoke causing confusion. As the smoke cleared it became obvious that the assault had failed. Strange and his troops abandoned the siege on 1 October. In the course of the week's skirmishes the Royalists appeared to have lost about 200 men and the defenders about twenty.

As a consequence of this victory Parliament gave the town its first MP in Oliver Cromwell's First Protectorate Parliament in 1654–5. Manchester's new representative was Sir Charles Worsley, the son of a prosperous merchant from Platt Hall in Fallowfield, a zealous Puritan, lieutenant colonel of the Lancashire infantry regiment and one of Oliver Cromwell's favourite major generals during fifteen months of direct military government, strictly governing a district containing Cheshire, Lancashire and Staffordshire with powers second only to Cromwell's. The task proved so stressful he died in 1556 aged only thirty-five. When the monarchy was restored in 1660 Manchester faced harsh punishment for having supported Parliament and, like other boroughs enfranchised during the republican Commonwealth of England, it lost its MP. (It would have no seat again until 1832.) The Restoration, though, was not a 'restoration of the natural and divine order' but the beginning of a shift in power from monarchy to Parliament.

PART NINE

A special world apart

If you don't know where you are going, any road will get you there.

Lewis Carroll

92

My dad was in his own way as absolutely certain of his destiny as Fred Perry, but somehow it was all in reverse, and my dad was shrinking as fast as Fred was always growing. My dad moved from the south into the stifling backstreets of the north and eventual unemployment; Fred moved from the north to the south and eventually Jean Harlow and four wives, having spent enough time in Stockport never to lose his single-minded determination to get on, to get away from the base that moulded his fortitude and head where the action was. My dad was dead on course for an abrupt end inside the 1970s – a couple of decades ahead of Fred, born twenty-seven years before my dad – which would require a different sort of wreath.

After Woodsmoor and losing his job at Shell, losing his interest in playing table tennis and never really getting another proper full-time job, he kept trying one way or another for a few more years, not yet totally losing interest in life. We moved, when my sister Jayne was eleven, a few miles to the east, back towards the Pennines, to Offerton, very close to the school she was now attending – Goyt Bank Secondary School – with the Goyt flowing past between Marple and Stockport at the bottom of the school playing fields, on its way a few miles down to the north-west, where it would become the Mersey, passing near Carrington Street, where Fred Perry had been born. The move to Offerton was not a step up the social ladder, but it was still the right side of the Mersey, the Cheshire side, and instead of towards salubrious Bramhall it was towards pretty Marple and the tranquil, appealing Derbyshire border. My dad lost his garage, his modest driveway; the gold Vauxhall disappeared, and nothing as modern ever replaced it, but he gained a rough patch of green in front of our house, around which plain, modest but perky semi-detached houses were arranged. We were moving about but staying where we were. We were on a slow tour of Stockport, circling the racy source of the Mersey, with the newbuild shopping centre still at the centre of our world. Near our house in Offerton there was a miniaturised version of Merseyway, a compact pedestrianised precinct containing a few shops that demonstrated how the spirit of the precinct was moving through the country, removing nicely mismatched local shops, their faithful owners and their hardy awnings.

It was while we were living in Offerton, with Dad clearly not sure from day to day which way to turn next, that our collective family

A BEA Viscount 701 at Manchester Ringway Airport

energy started to wind down, so that we barely noticed the effects when, for four months, the commercial use of electric power was reduced to just three consecutive days a week. This was caused by a coal shortage, the result of a fierce battle of wills between the powerful National Union of Mineworkers and Ted Heath's unbending Conservative government, which searched for ways to conserve dwindling coal stock, and began an assault on the power of the trade unions that would continue throughout the 1970s. (My dad the Heath supporter viewed Heath's great rival Harold Wilson as scheming and manipulative, and he easily made it through the 1960s without picking up any hint of fashionable disaffection with government and institutions, deeply suspicious of those who challenged authority and questioned Establishment practices. He would have probably appreciated Margaret Thatcher's 1980s Conservative backlash against post-sixties radicalism and general cultural disobedience.) The TV ended early, heating was unreliable, candles often required; food supplies were threatened – not that that made much difference to our sparse store cupboards, which were never known to contain enough food to last more than a couple of days. It became known as the three-day week, but by then all my dad's weeks had a three-day quality, severely limited by uncontrollable forces and the battle of wills going on inside his head: three days of action, falling towards two days, and then one day, on the way to no days at all.

It was still a walk to school for me, but it took a little longer than from Woodsmoor, cutting down from Offerton to the Buxton Road. The journey into Stockport town centre on the number 16, which involved a gradual drop in height and then a final plunge through the medieval twists and turns around Hillgate into Mersey Square, and then on the 92, rising on the monotonously straight A6 through the nondescript Heatons and hum-drum, secretive Levenshulme to Manchester's broadening city centre, became increasingly important to me. The borders to my inner and outer world were pushed further out, incorporating more land and landmarks, and bookshops, and record shops, and opportunities to define and refine who I was, and extend my own personal imaginative space.

My new identity, forged by the time I was thirteen and fourteen, based on my life in Reddish, corrupted by my time at Stockport Grammar School, embedded in various forms of self-education, started to involve various venues around Manchester where I went to see gigs.

Before I started to go to pop concerts as a fourteen-year-old, especially while I lived in Reddish, nights out had often involved visits with family or friends to Belle Vue, the 'showground of the north', a fantastical, absurd combination of the first privately funded zoo in the country, funfair, flea circus, Louis Tussaud waxworks, stock-car and speedway stadium, gardens, exhibition hall, circus and King's Hall concert, boxing and wrestling venue, a couple of miles the other side of Gorton and Longsight from Westbourne Grove. (On 24 July 1926 Belle Vue held Britain's first licensed greyhound meeting, using a recently invented American system with a mechanical lure and a track covered with straw. It was attended by 1,700 people. Manchester was considered a good place to hold the meeting because of its sporting and gambling tradition. As the *Manchester Guardian* put it, the crowd consisted of 'fat men, very agile and earnest men with flat-brimmed bowlers, men with large confident silver name-plates in their button-holes . . . smart young men and smart young women'. They watched six races each with seven greyhounds; the winner of the first race by eight lengths with a prize of £10 was Mistley at 6–1, racing 440 yards in 25 seconds. Word spread quickly. A week later 16,000 turned up, and 330,000 paid for admission in the first eleven weeks. A year later greyhound racing began at White City, home of the 1908 Olympic Games in London. Going to the dogs became a national pastime, working people appreciating the easily accessed urban tracks and the evening race times, with betting the main reason to go. Speedway started at the greyhound stadium in 1928 before moving to its own Hyde Road stadium a year later, where the Belle Vue Aces speedway team was founded.)

Belle Vue was a gaudy, faded inner-city simulation of seaside Blackpool's Pleasure Beach that merely took a short bus ride to Denton and then a few more stops on another bus along the Hyde Road towards Kirkmanshulme Lane, which headed into Longsight. Among the bricks, run-down shops, bedraggled houses, broken windows and weather-beaten gasworks of the slimy, sorry Hyde Road, suddenly there were screeching monkeys in the middle of cramped concrete, rubble and metal, the huge entrance gates, glimpses of a high, high and menacing wooden roller coaster called The Bobs – a shilling, a bob, a ride in the thirties – flashing above the caged Gorton skyline, and a building sense of expectation intensified when the tangled smell of fried onions and petrol fumes got stuck into your nose. Looking back, it could be that the place never existed and was merely a kid's dream, a fantasy of an imaginary place that could never have been, that was nowhere, because places as pleasure-packed with physical and metaphysical contradictions are impossible to build and can only be remembered.

Near your house in an ordinary street close to nowhere was a place where you could see fireworks splashing and bursting across the black sky; see explosive stock-car carnage; be too thrillingly scared at the thought of going on the swooping, rattling rollercoaster which looked like it could take on Houldsworth Mill in a monster fight and win, squeezing the life out of it, and which came with the sort of desperate screaming that confirmed there was real terror; watch the Belle Vue Aces on a Saturday night in the illuminated drizzly dark, stand on a corner and be drenched with sodden grey–red ashes as the rasping, slanting, 70-mph bikes skidded pressed to the ground right past you; see a polar bear that looked depressed, a giraffe bending over your head looking related (from where I was) to a dinosaur, chimpanzees morosely taking tea, a hippo sleeping in a pool, camels daydreaming above a boating lake, a numb-looking zebra, a lost-looking kangaroo, parrots that told you to bugger off; take a ride on an elephant or a ghost train or a miniature railway or the creaking but once-lovely Waterchute that eventually received a transfer into some obscure part of Blackpool Pleasure Beach.

Belle Vue had begun as a humble early-nineteenth-century attraction founded by Stockport gardener and aviary owner 'Honest' John Jennison on a stretch of scrub and moorland used for rabbit coursing around a public house called Belle Vue near Ardwick Green. He took out a six-month lease on the land and planned relaxing botanical gardens with a few animals for extra interest. Within a year of its 1836 opening an advert in the *Manchester Guardian* stated that visitors could expect to see parrots, macaws, cockatoos, pheasants, peacocks, swans, geese, a borrowed pelican and various other animals (rabbits, dogs, goats, deer and a fox). Entry was threepence, for which patrons would also receive a drink and some biscuits. Jennison extended his lease to ninety-nine years. People came more for the animals than the gardens, and wilder, more exotic animals such as armadillos, monkeys, bears, kangaroos and an elephant were introduced. The elephant was bought for £680 from a menagerie in Edinburgh, and ended up walking for ten days with its handler Lorenzo Lawrence to Manchester after it wrecked the railway carriage that was meant to carry it south – an accidental or intended publicity stunt. After its death in 1882 a use was still found for Maharajah the elephant – its scrubbed, majestic skeleton became part of the eccentrically assembled attractions, eventually ending up in Manchester Museum, alongside other animals that died after service at Belle Vue zoo.

Through the late nineteenth and early twentieth centuries the Jennison family relentlessly expanded, landscaped and marketed the park and gardens with grafting, speculative Victorian economic purpose. With huckster passion and a hustler's zeal, they attempted to eradicate boredom and misery, at least inside their artificial world. Brass-band competitions were held; firework displays took place, mazes, grottoes, roller-skating courts, sea-lion pools and boating lakes built, seductively isolated from but readily available to the real world. By 1925 the Jennison family had sold their attraction, and the zoo was transformed into a prototype theme park with the addition of the circus, stock cars, speedway, lakes, bang-up-to-date thrill rides, scenic railway, miniature village, ballrooms, ten-pin bowling – a layering, sense-overloading accumulation of fictional stages, fake spaces, simulated experiences, controlled dreams, pirate fantasies and epic caricatures of everyday life. For decades Belle Vue had an ebullient distorted grandness that mixed the seedy with the sensational, the quirky with the electric. In the 1940s and fifties at the height of its fame over 150,000 people would visit over an average bank holiday weekend, escaping one world to enter another, then escaping back into a now more charged and attractively less certain place.

In 1948 Mancunian Films detoured from its usual haywire comedy films, featuring excitable local music-hall acts from George Formby Junior and Frank Randle to Sandy Powell, and released *The International Circus Revue*. It used documentary footage shot around the pleasure gardens by Mancunian, material the company used in a number of films. The flimsy plot wrapped around the footage featured Bunny Graham, later to be known as Bernard Youens, who played Stan Ogden in *Coronation Street* from 1964. As Stan, married to faithful curlered Hilda, struggling against decades of rotten luck, he drifted from job to job, and was at first susceptible to violent rages. At various times, after years as a long-distance lorry driver, he was a milkman (early mornings compensated for by afternoons in the pub), a coal man, an ice-cream salesman, a chauffeur, a street photographer, a professional wrestler (in his only match he was thrown from the ring into wife Hilda's lap) and an artist (creating sculptures from scrap metal; this backfired when his masterpiece was taken to the tip by mistake). However, in 1969 Stan bought a window-cleaning round, and this would remain his main means of support for the rest of his life. His first line, delivered in the Rovers Return, was 'A pint of mild and twenty fags, missus.' (Ogden, called 'ghastly', perhaps affectionately, by Sir John Betjeman, was a classic cartoon image of the oafish beer-swilling betting northern loafer, a warning to potential layabouts yet to lose their ardour and ambition, although Youens started out at Granada Television in its early days as a 'velvet-voiced' continuity announcer.)

By the 1970s Belle Vue was run-down and shabby, the spirited entrepreneurial momentum that had taken it from the 1850s to the 1950s at a pitiful end, the threadbare zoo heart-breaking, a badly maintained home for distressed animals, and the park falling behind the faster modern world, where reality was turning into a disorientating model of itself. Entering Belle Vue was less and less an escape into romance and exotica and increasingly a poignant visit to a fatigued zone of abandonment and despair.

An annual lick of cheap paint, the surviving circus tent, the non-stop Aces and hurtling rides didn't disguise the fact that as a flamboyant fun complex Belle Vue reflected how the enterprising industrial city that once supported and used it for recreation and wonder had itself broken down. Cheery, kinetic Belle Vue became a derelict extravaganza in a ramshackle part of the city where acres of slum houses had been ruthlessly cleared away leaving brutalised remains. What had once strained to be more Las Vegas or Disneyland than Blackpool had shrunk to a fenced-in ghost town, and the city lost some of the messier, pushier, wayward but exciting parts of its soul. The great, magnificently discordant profit-making industrial city had been replaced by a provisional half-hearted hybrid of the tentatively new and the torn apart, and, to the frayed east of the city, Belle Vue simply fell apart, as a going concern, as a special world apart, as wished-for reality, as if to show how the madly marvellous elements of Manchester had been chased away. The collapsed utopia inside the park proved as frail and stressful as the reality outside.

Despite its position in the middle of the dereliction, the wooden King's Hall still had commercial merit in the early 1970s as a concert venue, and could hold a couple of thousand more than the Free Trade Hall in the city centre. The Free Trade Hall was where I had seen my first ever pop concert – T-Rex in 1971, as a fourteen-year-old travelling on my own on the 192 bus into the city centre and encountering a revelation. The north, my home, was still what it was, home, but it was now splitting off into new directions, an endless, stimulating other place always on the shifting verge of elsewhere. The gorgeously self-conscious attention-seeking exhibitionist Marc Bolan had become my own personal pop star, a replacement or supplement to the thrills and otherness collected and displayed at Belle Vue, a supplier of an intense fluid form of happiness, and here he was, in Manchester, within touching distance, infecting, intensifying my restricted local terrain.

Manchester, its compressed, ruined, resilient city centre laced with stagnant, abandoned canals, apparently derelict warehouses, grand but spooky remnants of the city's glory years, rough-and-ready curry houses, random, reconditioned post-war newbuilds and truncated boarded-up backstreets, was now becoming part of my mental map, along with the tantalising, transient pop music that visited and left, and the two things fused for a while as I went to more gigs. These concerts, and the city that was emerging in my consciousness, beyond Stockport, became the centre of my learning, along with the reading that I made up as I went along, which had nothing to do with the Stockport Grammar School curriculum.

In Manchester the outside world, containing different sorts of outside worlds, poured in, in the form of groups and musicians with their own sense of history, identity, understanding and personal motivation. There was plenty to enjoy, but essentially to study. While my school teachers were turning the adventure of life into a retreat, these musicians, emerging out of the fluid 1960s, were in their way teaching me to believe that there was more to life and existence than what there was on the surface around where I lived. There was more to life than bricks and a bus ride from one part of town to another. There was more to life than school and family and the local shops. Even those groups I didn't like had some form of advice to pass on about how to make the world a bigger, stranger, more challenging and transformative place.

At the Free Trade Hall, after T-Rex, within months I went to see David Bowie, Lou Reed, Black Sabbath, Curved Air, Deep Purple, Caravan, Rory Gallagher, Groundhogs, Steeleye Span, Mott the Hoople, King Crimson, Soft Machine, Fairport Convention and T-Rex again. The next year Pink Floyd playing *Dark Side of the Moon*, Lou Reed again, T-Rex once more, Roxy Music and David Bowie again – the last four especially giving me important, detailed information about how you could invent for yourself your own presence and role in life.

The world and my mind were getting bigger, pushed and pulled by the alien complexity, variety, volume and energy of these charged, confident characters, challenging, mirroring, destroying, reinventing a whole host of musical traditions and ideals. Another venue opened a couple of hundred yards along the Hyde Road from Belle Vue, on Birch Street between Gorton and Ardwick – the Stoneground, formerly the Corona Cinema and then the Southern Sporting Club, where the Beatles had played in 1963. The superstars did not come here. This was not as grand as the Free Trade Hall, more a dimly lit large undistinguished bar with a small low-lying stage, and a few seats and tables around the edges of a bumpy, tacky floor. You walked through the door, past the dubious hot-dog stall lurking outside under the still-existing Corona sign, into what was probably in daylight a wreck but which at night seemed curiously enticing. It was close enough to the Belle Vue complex, by the entrance to the speedway, that when I needed to queue for a ticket to a big concert at the King's Hall – by the likes of the

Rolling Stones or the Who – I would go to a gig at the Stoneground, and about 2 a.m. join the line for tickets so that I'd be near the front when the box office opened at nine.

The Who played two nights at the King's Hall, on 2 and 3 November 1973, the week their mod song-cycle double album *Quadrophenia* was released. Showbusiness, an entertainment loaded with conviction, was presented with theatrical even violent force. The Rolling Stones played a couple of months earlier on 11 and 12 September during their European tour, a couple of weeks after the release of *Goats Head Soup*, the follow-up to *Exile on Main Street*, 'the end of their golden age', the last tour featuring Mick Taylor. They started with 'Brown Sugar' and 'Gimme Shelter' and ended with 'Jumpin' Jack Flash' and 'Street Fighting Man'. Jagger was in a chest-baring jewel-encrusted skin-tight jumpsuit, wore full eye make-up, and looked as though he might have escaped from the nearby reptile house, or maybe from the wrestling ring. I watched both performances, feeling crusading showmanship cut open the moment, exciting but offering few clues about the future, never thinking that forty years later there would be such a thing as the Rolling Stones and the Who, still in action in a manner of speaking, demanding attention, made up of a past I had become a tiny part of.

At the Stoneground, set in a bombed-out wind-gutted wasteland where little would grow but bristly weed, hearing music mostly from what was then a vaguely defined underground, I extended my accelerating knowledge of this new world, which was itself continually changing shape. Exploring the world further, which separated me so satisfyingly from school and the cracking-up of my remote, failing dad, giving me a new sort of knowledge and therefore power. By the end of 1971 I was reading the *New Musical Express*, *Melody Maker* and *Sounds*. Music journalists became a new set of teachers, in new subjects that didn't have names but settled around the ideas of thinking for yourself, relishing new directions and being ready for anything. This writing, about music, but also about other things, which seemed important to me and where I was, and which seemed connected to other reading I was doing, gave me some ideas about what I could do in my life. One thing I was taught by reading the *NME* was that you could earn a living, or at least get a job, writing about Atomic Rooster and the Edgar Broughton Band. This seemed astonishing, but eminently practical. No one had been helping me work out how to become a writer, but seeing these gigs made me plot my own route. This was me doing my homework, having never done any of the homework my teachers gave me.

I was not allowed to go out very often by my dad, certainly not before I was sixteen or seventeen, however much I pleaded and begged, seeing it as positive and enlightening, whereas he saw it as dubious and mysterious if not downright dangerous. It was not clear to me what he had got up to in Margate as a sixteen- and seventeen-year-old in the early 1950s, but he didn't seem keen on releasing me into the night around Manchester.

I occasionally haggled my way out of the house and went to see Budgie, Amon Düül II, Arthur Brown wearing a phone on his head, Can, Alex Harvey Band, Gong, Gentle Giant, Kevin Coyne wearing a shoe on his head, Magma, Backdoor, Horslips, Hatfield and the North, Vinegar Joe and Leo Sayer – who had a hit single at the time, so that the Stoneground was full, people crammed into the often-half-empty hall, falling over each other and spilling out through the front doors. He dressed as a clown, the sort of clown dying across the road at Belle Vue, but which could temporarily come alive on *Top of the Pops* and the tiny taped-together Stoneground stage.

Another venue opened as if solely for me, and everyone else who felt the same way, was the Hard Rock and Village Discotheque, a former bowling alley in Greatstone Road, Stretford with a claustrophobic space-age feel, which could hold 3,000. It was close to the Lancashire cricket ground and symbolised how my allegiances had completely shifted, after initial reluctance, from cricket to pop music. The low-ceilinged chrome-trimmed venue could be turned into either a disco or a rock venue with upstairs seating and cheaper downstairs standing. The opening nights were 2 and 3 September 1972, and on both nights, at more or less the exact moment he was becoming self-defined living legend – the architect of his own fame – David Bowie performed, beginning his shows with 'Let's Spend The Night Together', 'Hang on to Yourself' and 'Ziggy Stardust', and ending them with 'Suffragette City' and 'Rock 'n' roll Suicide' a few months after he had played a less-than-half-full Free Trade Hall, which I also went to. Seeing Bowie, leading his Spiders from Mars, turning the spur of the moment into mesmeric, lacerating entertainment, was like being able to get inside, and live there for a while, an enigmatic, hallucinatory story by the science-fiction writers I had started reading, Michael Moorcock, J. G. Ballard, Philip K. Dick, Norman Spinrad, or even the books I'd struggled to interpret by Orwell, Huxley, Borges, Pynchon, Nabokov, Burroughs, Burgess and Kafka.

I went to both nights, although I now don't understand how I got permission from my suspicious, anxious dad, other than the two shows were on a Saturday and Sunday, or how I could afford the one-pound entry. Morrissey lived around the corner, so you would think, even though he was only thirteen, he was there – or some spectral representative on his behalf. Maybe he hung around outside in the car park in a sad teenage sort of way, feeling rejected enough to fuel an entire lifetime of expressions of disappointment and exclusion.

Morrissey's first gig (in the audience) was in fact also T-Rex, his at the Belle Vue King's Hall on 16 June 1972. Marc Bolan and T-Rex had fuelled twelve months of unprecedented teenage hysteria, and Morrissey and I were among the only fifty or so boys in an audience of 5,000 frantically screaming girls. Over their sparking heads, in about the tenth row, in the midst of their tumultuous collective orgasms, on my own like Morrissey, as much worked up inside my own head, I caught vivid sight of the now-famous Marc Bolan adoring being adored, transferring the chaotic, urgent energy into ravishing enchantment. 'It was messianic and complete chaos,' Morrissey recalled. 'My father dropped me off outside. I was wearing a purple satin jacket. I think he thought I'd be killed and he waved me off like it was the last time he'd ever see me alive. It must have been like losing your child to a deadly cult.' What kind of kids liked T-Rex? he once asked. 'School-hating anarchists.' (Oddly enough, fans at my school of the apparently more dark and devious Sabbath, Purple, ELP and Zep tended to be more obedient; fans of the apparently teenybop Bolan and the tarted-up, surely fraudulent Bowie were more untamed.)

A few months after his September Hard Rock shows, at the end of December, Bowie returns, for two nights, the tickets twenty-five pence extra, supported by Stealers Wheel, and I am there again on my own under fluorescent lights amid a stunning smell of incense that seems to lift you an inch or two off the floor. I get myself to the very front, right under the intensely present Bowie, and touch his red shiny space-age boots, just to see if I receive an electric shock. In a way, I do. Another abstract shock had hit the city.

Seeing Bowie five times in 1972, with more to come in 1973, including a visit to the Free Trade Hall the night before my maths O level under the cover of revising at a friend's house, Bowie entering like a returning emperor checking his conquered empire, dressed as Aladdin Sane, yet another electrifying version of himself, leaping off the planet and back on, seemingly at will, he made it seem like what he was doing was calculating exactly how amazing the future could be, a future that was always on the verge of happening but always out of reach. He proposed an alternative reality, a number of alternative realities, getting to the very essence of what we want from our pop stars, who should, essentially, be at the dazzling forefront of the militant young using art as a cover for more direct action.

What makes you great, he was suggesting, is not necessarily your individual works, but your very existence and your personality. Borrowing from other visionaries and master illusionists, from Syd Barrett and Marc Bolan, from John Heartfield and the Velvet Underground, from Dada and Elvis, Cocteau and Cage, Modigliani and Ballard, from Burroughs and Houdini, but ahead of his time, as sampler, collagist and appropriating technological prophet, the one-time junior paste-up artist at an advertising agency took bits and fragments from the past, the rubble of art, entertainment, philosophy, music and film, and turned them into new ways of seeing the world. Intent on smashing the boundaries that separated art, he sewed together scattered fragments from wildly different traditions and scattered himself into one ready-made whole.

I came to the conclusion in my own teenage way that he was thinking the most astounding things, sometimes very calmly, sometimes in a deep frenzy, about what it was to think at all, how comic, deeply tragic and astounding it was to move from thought to thought and use these thoughts to make yourself up, to invent who you were going to be from

The Granada Television studios

moment to moment. As a soft-centred lonely teenage someone who noticed that David Bowie really seemed to know things, and was so clever he could make an entirely original creation out of his mind and memory, I watched him closely during those fantastic and yet-to-be-fully fathomed 1970s. I wanted to know things too. I wanted to be that clever. I wanted to be that beautiful. I wanted to do something that no one else could do, like him, whatever it took. Bowie changing all the time suited how I was changing as an adolescent – his move from image to image, concept to concept, name to name was something I recog-nised as I went through all the planned and unplanned changes you go through as a teenager. Like a roving soul in search of a body, he entered another person whenever he wished and made them seem exciting and glamorous – one day your hair is orange and spiky, then it is white and cropped, then it is blonde and floppy . . . one day your clothes are space-age Edwardian, then they are Victorian surreal, then they are undeniably dubious . . . suddenly you are taller, hairier, stranger, with deeper, darker lusts, a deeper, darker voice . . . people around you are boring, and you are not, because of all this change, which no one can keep up with, bar Bowie and the other pop stars that ripped through reality with their speed of thought and their clear aversion to cliché and obviousness . . . and as you change, if people don't like you, or ignore you, then you become someone else, another person, with another appearance, and another set of characteristics.

At the Hard Rock I saw Stephen Stills, Focus, Michael Chapman, Jeff Beck, went regularly to the 'heavy night' on Thursdays, but remember well not managing to get to see Led Zeppelin. I was there in 1975 for the last Hard Rock show on 19 October by Tangerine Dream, still a pound to get in if you stood downstairs; in many ways I am still at that concert, which is going on for ever, and everything else is a hallucination induced by the ecstatic pulses emerging from the machines on stage which three men with much hair and straight faces are operating, abstractly connecting with the atom-locating atom-splitting computer-pioneering history of Manchester and the questing, conspiring, analytical German curiosity of Marx and Engels.

93

1641

The first mention of the soft and beautiful substance forming the covering or envelope of the seeds of the cotton plant (genus *Gossypium*) in manufacturing appears in a small treatise entitled the 'Treasure of Traffic', written in 1641 by Sir Lewes Roberts (author of the noted book *The Merchants Mappe of Commerce*), in which he states that 'the town of Manchester buys the linen yarn of the Irish in great quantity, and, weaving it, returns the same again to Ireland to sell; neither doth her industry rest here, for they buy cotton wool in London that comes first from Cyprus and Smyrna, and work the same into fustians, vermilions, dimities, and other such stuffs; which they return to London, where they are sold; and thence, not seldom, are sent into foreign parts, which have means on far easier terms to provide themselves of the first materials.'

Jeremiah Horrocks died on 3 January 1641 in Toxteth, Liverpool, aged twenty-two. A memorial plaque in Westminster Abbey in London, erected in 1874, after two centuries of neglect, eloquently records his achievements.

IN MEMORY OF JEREMIAH HORROCKS

CURATE OF HOOLE IN LANCASHIRE

WHO DIED ON THE 3RD OF JANUARY 1641 IN OR NEAR

HIS 22ND YEAR

HAVING IN SO SHORT A LIFE

DETECTED THE LONG INEQUALITY IN THE MEAN MOTION

OF JUPITER AND SATURN

DISCOVERED THE ORBIT OF THE MOON TO BE AN ELLIPSE

DETERMINED THE MOTION OF THE LUNAR APSE

SUGGESTED THE PHYSICAL CAUSE OF ITS REVOLUTION

AND PREDICTED FROM HIS OWN OBSERVATIONS THE

TRANSIT OF VENUS

WHICH WAS SEEN BY HIMSELF AND HIS FRIEND

WILLIAM CRABTREE

ON SUNDAY THE 24TH OF NOVEMBER 1639.

1639

On 24 November 1639, in the tiny Lancashire village of Much Hoole, Jeremiah Horrocks made the first observation of a transit of Venus. He was one of the first Englishmen to appreciate the astronomical revolution going on in Europe following the works of Tycho, Galileo and Kepler. It was Horrocks who first proved that the orbit of the moon is an ellipse, and Newton made good use of Horrocks' discovery. Had he lived, would Jeremiah Horrocks have eclipsed Newton, who followed two generations later? That question obviously touched Horrocks' nineteenth-century biographer A. B. Whatton, who left his own florid lines of Victorian verse:

That meteor-life, soon lost to vision here,
Now shines unclouded in a glorious sphere;
Yet here its light his bright example gives,
And here in fame undying Horrox lives.

1620

England was an importer rather than an exporter of linen, and the Lancashire product was probably intended mainly for the home market. The 'home-made cloth' of the county was coarse and cheap, as may be seen from the prices paid for the 'Lancashire cloth' bought by King's College, Cambridge from 1563, and the 'Preston cloth' bought by King's and Eton College from 1600. In 1620 a Manchester draper was selling in London 'Lynen clothe commmonlie called Stopport [Stockport] cloth'.

1619

Jeremiah Horrocks was born in Toxteth. His father was a watchmaker and the family were deeply religious Puritans. Jeremiah was a brilliant scholar and won a place at Cambridge University at the age of fourteen. By then he was already well versed in Greek, Latin and the Scriptures. He moved to Much Hoole, where he was a curate at St Michael's, the local church.

1606

On Friday 31 January 1606 Guy Fawkes, Thomas Wintour, Ambrose Rookwood and Robert Keyes were taken to the Old Palace Yard at Westminster and hanged, drawn and quartered 'in the very place which they had planned to demolish in order to hammer home the message of their wickedness'. The last of the four to suffer his appointed fate was Fawkes, the 'romantic caped figure of such evil villainy'. A spectator of the scene later wrote, 'Last of all came the great devil of all, Guy Fawkes, alias Johnson, who should have put fire to the powder. His body being weak with the torture and sickness, he was scarce able to go up the ladder, yet with much ado, by the help of the hangman, went high enough to break his neck by the fall. He made no speech, but with his crosses and idle ceremonies made his end upon the gallows and the block, to the great joy of all the beholders that the land was ended of so wicked a villainy. His remains were sent to the four corners of the Kingdom as a warning to other plotters.'

Between October 1605 and August 1606 the plague comes to Stockport. Starting with a woman affectionately known as Mad Mary, fifty-one people die in the borough. But Stockport gets off lightly compared to Manchester, where a quarter of the town's population dies.

On 5 November 1605 a York man, Guy Fawkes, was discovered about to ignite thirty-six barrels of gunpowder underneath the Houses of Parliament and assassinated the protestant James I. His aim was to spark a Catholic revolution. Fawkes, described by those who knew him well as a courteous, gallant and pious man, was known to have been a brave and resolute soldier with special knowledge of the use of gunpowder. A relatively minor player in the Gunpowder Plot, being caught in the act, about to light the fuse, made him the principal character and ensured his notoriety.

1603

The traditional gateway to the north was at Doncaster in north-east England on the River Don. The north began at the point of no return for someone travelling on horseback from London along what had become the main road to Edinburgh, the Great North Road – designated the A1 in 1921. With determined riding you could cover the 170 miles from London to Doncaster in one day. Sir Robert Carey did just this on 24 March 1603, when he rode to take news of Queen Elizabeth's death to James of Scotland. Once a traveller went beyond Doncaster there was no returning until the following day, and the north had begun.

Doncaster has long been significant. The Romans set up a forward base there after driving a road north. Later in history many important meetings between north and south took place at Doncaster. This is where northern nobles assembled in 1399 to proclaim Bolingbroke, son of John of Gaunt and Blanche of Lancaster, as King Henry IV. During the 1536 rebellion known as the Pilgrimage of Grace north once again met south on the bridge over the Don. The Don, like the Danube, takes its name from Danu, the oldest Celtic mother goddess, the power in the land that will never be overcome by mortals. It rises in the Pennines and flows seventy miles east through the Don Valley via Penistone on the northern edge of central Sheffield – where it was once known for entering as a sparkling stream and leaving as a black gurgling mass of pollution – Rotherham, Mexborough, Conisborough, Doncaster and Stainworth before joining the Ouse at Goole in the West Riding of Yorkshire.

1602

Entries in the Bispham parish baptismal register mention 'de Poole' and 'de blackpool', at that time a collection of cobble and clay huts spread along the coast near the Pool. By the end of the century a number of the landed gentry, led by the Tyldesleys of Foxhall, had settled in the area.

1588

William Shakespeare roams as far as Newcastle and Carlisle, possibly as a member of the Queen's Players.

1586

William Camden's *Britannia* is published. It records, 'Cheshire Cheese is more agreeable and better relished than those of other parts of the kingdom.' The 1637 edition refers to cheese making in Cheshire: '. . . the grasse and fodder there is of that goodness and vertue that the cheeses bee made heere in great number of a most pleasing and delicate taste, such as all England againe affordeth not the like, no, though the best dairy women otherwise and skilfullest in cheesemaking be had from hence'. It was said to have been the favourite cheese of Queen Elizabeth I. Even the French, not normally known for their enthusiasm for English food, respect Cheshire cheese, and have a rhyme about it: *Dans le chester sec et rose, a longues dents de l'anglais mordent* (Into the Cheshire cheese, dry and pink, the long teeth of the English sink).

1580

In Northumberland the forests were felled to make pit props for the coal industry and to build docks and wharves, barges, lighters and sea-going ships for the coal trade to London, and firewood became scarce. In Bamburgh 'great woods hath beene, but now utterly decayed and no wood at all remaineth hereon'. William Harrison grimly noted in the 1580s, 'Of coal mines we have such plenties as may suffice for all the realm of England. And so they must do hereafter indeed, if wood be not better cherished than it is at present.'

Merchant and philanthropist Sir Humphrey Chetham was born in Crumpsall in 1580, the son of a successful Manchester merchant who lived in Crumpsall Hall. He was educated at Manchester Grammar School and made his fortune in the cloth trade, mainly dealing in fustian, a strong fabric made of linen and cotton, to the London market. (From Shakespeare's time, fustian, also known as bombast, was also used to refer to pompous or pretentious writing, as it was often used as padding.) It was noted that Chetham's 'strict integrity, his piety, and works of charity secured him the respect and esteem of those around him'. Chetham's wealth made him a public figure, although he was a reluctant official, and in 1631 he was fined for refusing a knighthood, not wanting to share his increasing wealth with the crown. Later, he accepted the title. In 1634 he was appointed high sheriff of the County of Lancashire, but refused a second term on the grounds of infirmity and old age. When the Civil War started, he sided with the Parliamentarians. He was responsible for the creation of Chetham's Hospital (now Chetham's School of Music) and Chetham's Library. Founded in 1653 and intended to rival the college libraries of Oxbridge, this is the oldest public library in the English-speaking world. Together with the school, it is located in the centre of Manchester, north of the cathedral. The library was another way of ensuring that the King did not inherit his fortune. With its large numbers of valuable sources, including works by older pioneering English economists, it became a meeting place for Marx and Engels nearly 200 years later. They would study together, analyse Manchester's particular problems, what Engels called its 'social war', and discuss politics at the table next to the bay window in the alcove of the reading room overlooking the pink sandstone school. The stained-glass window, noted Engels, ensured that the weather was always fine there. These meetings and deliberations resulted in their history of human development based on dialectical materialism and a manifesto for international proletarian revolution. Humphrey Chetham died unmarried on 20 September 1653 at the age of seventy-two, and was buried with much pomp and ceremony at the Collegiate Church of Manchester.

1578

Guy Fawkes attended St Peter's School in York in 1578, where he was exposed to Roman Catholicism. St Peter's previous headmaster, John Fletcher, had been imprisoned for twenty years as a Catholic recusant, and Guy's headmaster, John Pulleyn, outwardly conforming, seems to have influenced the boys greatly in two ways – drama and Catholicism. He was a brave and powerful character, tall, with auburn beard, brown hair and pale blue-grey eyes. Father Greenway described him as 'a man of great piety, of exemplary temperance, mild and cheerful demeanour, enemy of disputes, a faithful friend'.

1571

Harrogate's mineral springs were discovered by William Slingsby in 1571. He was a well travelled man and noticed that the water from Trewit (a local name for lapwing) Well tasted like water he had drunk in continental spas. Tradition has it that Slingsby only stopped and tasted the water because his horse stumbled on some marshy ground. Slingsby arranged for the area to be paved and walled, and in about 1596 it was formally called a spa after the town of Spa in Belgium. About eighty further springs were found, and people visited to take the waters. Before Slingsby's time, Harrogate was merely a village near the historic town of Knaresborough. It was in the early nineteenth century that Harrogate significantly developed as a spa town.

1570

The earliest known reference to cotton in the Manchester area relates to Bury in 1570, and by 1630 cotton was being worked in Bolton, Blackburn and Oldham. It was initially a cottage industry based on the spinning wheel and hand loom, and most workers were also part-time agriculturalists. These people lived in small settlements, generally called folds, which appear to have been fairly stable and therefore were able to develop a sense of cohesion and tradition.

94

I was working hard, gaining the sort of education that would prove more practical and galvanising than the one being distributed around, above and beyond me at school. In 1973, living in Offerton, now shaving, hair hanging over my shoulders, with my own glam-inspired satin jacket with yellow stitching and trousers as wide at the bottom as the Mersey under the streets of Stockport, I left school with no ceremony, simply a dull final day walking away from the scene of the disaster, chucking away the ragged ink-stained yellow and black cap I had never replaced since I was eleven. The years of chalk dust and stupor were over. I remained friendly with one or two of the boys in my class for a couple of years, and then that was that. I had made it through school, retaining approximately seven or eight pieces of hard information, without having a girlfriend, without going to a pub, without smoking a cigarette, and certainly without venturing down the stairs of those inscrutable smoke-marinated venues lurking around the edges of Mersey Square that promised a level of intoxication and abandonment I still didn't understand how to access, even as I was making contact with Marc Bolan and David Bowie.

My dad was a combination of speechless and furious that I had failed so comprehensively at school, perhaps blaming the late-night concerts I had been going to for my decline. It was no use trying to explain that Bowie, Bolan and Roxy Music, *Top of the Pops*, the *New Musical Express* and John Peel were preparing me for the future, devoured as though they were an absolute right.

Hearing my ambition to become a journalist, I was recommended by a weary careers official in a pokey office in Edgeley to use my four hard-won low-graded O levels to get on an Ordinary National Diploma in business studies course at Stockport College along Wellington Road South. He had asked me to fill in a questionnaire to give him an idea of the type of job I was interested in. I completed this, hoping to make it clear through my answers that I did not want to work in an office nine to five, in any job to do with numbers, and that I preferred not to have a boss. I was adamant I was going to avoid the trap my dad seemed to have fallen into. I decided my answers made me seem like someone interested in work that was always different and always on the move, work that required no physical strength and no sticking to a routine, work that would all come from my mind. I think that as far as he was concerned I was another lazy aimless teenager imagining I could somehow earn an income by never actually doing any real work.

Shorthand and typing were a part of the course he suggested, although it turned out to be for girls only. I think he thought the sort of journalist I wanted to be was a reporter covering local traffic, sport and carnivals for the *Stockport Express*, but he hid his opinion that this was way beyond my failed grammar school capabilities better than my old headmaster. But I wanted to be a journalist like Orwell, Norman Mailer, Tom Wolfe, Angela Carter and Joan Didion, or the rock writers I loved – Richard Meltzer, Lester Bangs, Nick Kent, Ian MacDonald – and I felt I was compiling the CV I needed to make this happen. I was sure I could do it – that catching the 192 from Stockport Mersey Square to Manchester Piccadilly, then walking to the Free Trade Hall to watch Van der Graaf Generator was going to help me achieve it.

Compared to listening to records by Faust and the New York Dolls, the OND in business studies was a little like being told to wash dishes instead of taking a spaceship to Mars. I skinny-drizzled out of the college after a few months, before I was seventeen, and began working in a bookshop at the bottom of a narrow, steep winding hill under Stockport's ancient market. It was thirty-eight years since Fred Perry had become the last British player to win Wimbledon, eight years since England had won the World Cup – with that Ashton under Lyne hat-trick and commentator Kenneth Wolstenholme, born on 17 July 1920 in Worsley (the cleared place which was settled), Lancashire, in the city of Salford, six miles west of Manchester, at the beginning of the Bridgewater Canal, announcing with timeless timing on the scoring of Geoff Hurst's third goal and England's fourth in the final few seconds, as Hurst, racing up the pitch, oblivious to little Alan Ball on his left, aimed to kick the ball as far as he could into the stands, to waste time, 'There's some people on the pitch . . . They think it's all over,' and as the ball hurtled into the net with the sure force of destiny, 'It is now.'

My therefore thirty-eight-year-old dad thought my life was over now that I was working in a shop stuck at the very cobbled bottom of sunken Stockport. Where could I possibly go from there? But I approached the bookshop as a positive part of my further education, surrounded by books for hours on end, occasionally disturbed by customers but able to continue my reading and earn enough cash to pay for albums, singles and concerts. The shop, owned by my first boss, Christine Crowther, stocked money-making mainstream books and soft-porn magazines, but also a large amount of mind-watering radical underground publications, avant-garde science fiction, occult classics, poetry and obscure philosophical books. At the back of the shop there were hundreds of second-hand books including unexpected classics and hidden gems. It was Reddish library a few stages on; I was piecing together my own reading list, jumping about from Rimbaud to Roland Barthes, Sontag to Hunter S. Thompson, Walter Benjamin to Thomas Pynchon.

A regular customer was a solemnly eerie-looking young man called Paul with eyes cut from coal bracketed by long lank hair parted in the middle, who always wore black; his sickly-pale silent girlfriend floating at his shoulder with a sad red mouth pulled towards the ground always wore all-white, usually in the form of lace and net, possibly stolen from her nan's bottom drawer. He would bring in copies of a sixteen-page magazine for us to sell which he wrote and printed himself called *Penetration*, after a song by Iggy Pop. He was a fan of Hawkwind, Motörhead and of furtive cultural streams that did not yet have a name but would later pour through punk into the ashen subcult of goth. He looked like he'd been alive since the seventeenth century, had once been an undertaker, and still owned the hat he had worn when he escorted the coffins.

I asked if I could write something for his fanzine, and ended up producing a few hundred words about savagely satirical American comedian Lenny Bruce and a review of curt, speedy Essex blues group Dr Feelgood at the Free Trade Hall. Now eighteen, I was a published writer, even if only in a local magazine that sold a few hundred copies in the left-wing bookshops around Manchester. Truth-telling Bruce I was following as a doomed, vital prophet of rip-roaring logic-reforming common sense, hounded to death by a society threatened by such presumptions of rebellion and resistance. He was so funny it hurt, and then so funny it wasn't funny. This was comedy attacking prejudice and ignorance that I didn't have to share with my mum, dad and sisters on a family Saturday night. He died, from what Phil Spector called 'an overdose of the police', at thirty-nine, the year England won the World Cup, with tough-tackling but otherwise toothless Nobby Stiles of dire, dejected Collyhurst, trapped by the Irk a mile to the north-east of Manchester city centre, at number 4.

I wrote about Dr Feelgood because their lethally austere, extravagantly basic, aggressively self-assured English adaptation of the blues was suddenly refreshing after the raging futurist promise of glam rock had stalled around Bowie's stranded genius, and the underground music of the Stoneground seemed less experimental, more routine and at the progressive rock end horribly bloated and redundant. Monochrome, manic Feelgood of Essex in their workman's suits and ties slashing open traditional blues seemed more revolutionary.

Flattered and excited by seeing something I had written in print, even if it was only a Xeroxed series of A4 pages using a combination of type and Letraset unevenly stapled together in pasty Paul's surely cave-like bedroom, I planned my own magazine. I wrote pieces on Marc Bolan and Brian Eno, stole an imaginary interview with Bob Dylan written by Paul Krassner, the Brucian founder of the American underground magazine *The Realist*, and intimately worshipped New York singer Patti Smith, who turned her mind, body, memory, hair and clothes into a mobile history of art, pop, poetry and philosophy that was both a long way from Stockport and also something that made blazing sense to someone working out how to get out.

It took me about a year of nervous, fussy preparation to get the magazine together, into 1976, but the delays it took to organise what I had entitled *Out There*, because that's where I wanted to be, ended up being a positive thing. There was something missing in contemporary popular music at the time, something that was not obviously noticed or diagnosed, because there seemed enough music to find, enjoy, dissect, collect, plenty from the past to discover, the weekly *New Musical Express* was unmissable, and the John Peel show on Radio 1 was mysteriously, pragmatically filled with the endlessly new and the fascinating. What was missing, and what made it just in time just around the edges into *Out There*, started to appear in the pages of the *NME* as a rumour, as a concert or two by bands with names more like ruthless revolutionary slogans, names with clear, determined intent a long way from the floppy, hippy Gentle Giant and Juicy Luicy or the prog pomposity of Genesis and Yes, which seemed closer to an Edwardian style of rock and roll than anything that belonged in the broken mid-1970s, which was in something of a predicament.

What was missing started to travel over from mental unsentimental New York in the choppy bohemian hairstyle and demented symbolist rhymes of Richard Hell, the abstract transcendent guitar of Tom Verlaine and Patti Smith's continuing explorations into the adventures of language and rhythm. What was missing would turn out to be the universal, and the intensely local, spirit of the city, of the spaces inside and beyond the city, of history, and of what lies in the guts and gore of history.

What was missing made it to mundane and magnificent, mainstream and underground, fractured and dismantled Manchester in June 1976, with a carousing carnival flourish related to the deviant, dissipated, once-vibrant-now-broken Belle Vue, the revolutionary, protesting, turbulent history of the city, the continuing fight between competing interests representing those in power and those fighting for power, the riotous flash of glam, the disruptive underground scenes of the late sixties and even the paranoid, perceptive mind of Lenny Bruce. And there I was, where I was, which enables me now – in this report of how I ended up there, and where I am now, looking back on it like it never happened but certainly did – to say, strangely, I was there, ultimately so that I could add a paragraph or two of facts and romance to history, which was swirling all around me, because that was my destiny all along, it was where my footsteps had taken me, one after the other, to the end of one journey, which becomes the beginning of another.

95

Guy Fawkes was born in York in 1570, probably at a house in Stonegate. He was baptised in St Michael le Belfry church on 16 April, three days after his birth. His father, Edward, a prominent Protestant in the city, died when Guy was only eight. His mother remarried, to a recusant Catholic, and they moved to the village of Scotton near Knaresborough. Fawkes' father was descended from the Fawkeses of Farnley and was either a notary or proctor of the ecclesiastic courts and an advocate in the consistory court of the Archbishop of York. His mother was a Harrington, eminent merchants and aldermen of the city.

1569

The division of England into north and south can be traced back to the Romans. In the early third century AD Britannia was divided in two, with the north of England being granted the status of a separate province, Britannia Inferior, with its capital at Eboracum (York). The north was less settled, the scene of constant scuffles and disagreements with truculent, restless local tribes, and the border (Hadrian's Wall) was falling into disrepair. As a result there was a strong military presence. The lowlands of the south-east were more prosperous, populated by those who had largely embraced the Roman way of life, and consequently were given more freedom in their own affairs, with a consular government based in Londinium (London). This was Britannia Superior.

Around AD 296 the provinces were restructured again, by the Emperor Diocletian, who split each one in two. Britannia Superior in the south became Britannia Prima in the west, governed from Cirencester, and Maxima Caeseriensis in the east, governed from London. Britannia Inferior in the north became Flavia Caeseriensis, controlled from Lincoln, and, up to Hadrian's Wall, Britannia Secunda.

The relationship between north and south then ran through a remarkably regular cycle of independence and centralisation, fluctuating over periods of roughly 200 years. The last major attempt by the north to impose its will by force occurred with the rising of the northern earls in 1569. These magnates were unhappy with the Protestant Queen Elizabeth on the throne, and wished to replace her with Mary, Queen of Scots. The rebellion was launched at Brancepeth Castle, seat of the Neville family. The Neville fortress at Raby was also involved. It was a disaster for the north. About 400 people were executed, and fines crippled the northern economy, which did not recover for 200 years. The succession of James I in 1603 also had the effect of marginalising the north once again. As James was also King of Scotland, the border ceased to have any significance. The north was no longer a vital frontier zone; it was just the north again, a marginal area.

PART TEN

There must be change

I was led to think that the smallest things may be secret mirrors of the past and that perhaps everything is a lock that might open a door somewhere or somehow.

Thomas De Quincey

96

For those relatively few curious onlookers who turned up to see the Sex Pistols play at the Lesser Free Trade Hall on 4 June 1976 it was not a watershed. It didn't seem to be a momentous time when busted post-war Britain needed something to happen or it might come to a halt and then float away from Europe, into a cold isolated zone closer to Iceland and Greenland than the dominant, controlling centre of the world. None of that was apparent. In the 1970s there was not yet the frenetic information-age level of self-awareness and self-analysis about contemporary political and cultural currents, the propulsive, distorting energy of instant hindsight and the urgent making of connections. It wasn't so easy to save up the past alongside the events of the day, and parade it all for immediate consumption and grading. We were simply where we were, and life was happening around us, happening to us, as absurd and frustrating as it all seemed.

We were all of an age that meant that we came to music after the

1960s, missing out on all the trends, clubs, events, styles, fashions that emerged and developed back then, too young for the Twisted Wheel, vaguely feeling that we needed to find something that belonged to us, and represented where we were in social, political, cultural time and space, which was already something distant from the sixties and the early 1970s. We all read the music magazines, or we would not have turned up; we were looking for action, wherever it happened.

We were all used to going to the Free Trade Hall to see concerts, because it was a fixture on all major tours by the main groups of the time. The gig we went to on 4 June was for most of us where we ourselves entered history, as a series of events, or one event adrift among many others that would be stored and pored over. We found that we were on our own, but we belonged to something in particular. It was definitely for me the first time that I connected with the history of the city, without it becoming apparent for decades. That history was channelled through the visiting Sex Pistols, so that my interests in music and ideas, in local interests and wider desires, collided inside a unique space that had opened up because of what had happened in Manchester over the last few hundred years, and what was happening in culture at a certain moment in turbulent, trapped post-war British society.

The Sex Pistols arrived in this damaged northern realm as an underground rumour, an emerging, possibly demented pop craze, with something of the impact of pioneers who indirectly understood what the nineteenth-century poet and cultural critic Matthew Arnold wrote in his book of essays, *Culture and Anarchy* – that the men of culture are the true apostles of equality. 'The great men of culture are those who have had a passion for diffusing, for making prevail, for carrying from one end of society to the other, the best knowledge, the best ideas of their time; who have laboured to divest knowledge of all that was harsh, uncouth, difficult, abstract, professional, exclusive; to humanise it to make it efficient outside the clique of the cultivated and learned, yet still reaming the best knowledge and thoughts of the time, and a true source, therefore, of sweetness and light.' And here were the Sex Pistols, tearaways in torn trousers that quite possibly had P for pauper, or pervert, or punk, but even philosopher, stamped on the backsides, bringing forth a whole new notion of sweetness and light. From where

I had ended up, they were bringing culture, although at the time to me they were clearly the most exciting thing around if you wanted to know exactly where pop music was and where it was heading, and if you thought that was important.

The original Free Trade Hall was built in 1838 on the corner of St Peter Street and Southmill Street, formerly known as South Street. This first structure took the form of a temporary wooden hall, which was built (reportedly by a hundred men in a hundred days) to hold protest meetings of the Anti-Corn Law League – working people protesting against the 1815 Corn Laws, which kept the cost of the common man's staple food high. This was replaced in 1842 by a sturdier but aesthetically unimpressive brick building which also became the venue for concerts and entertainment. Demand soon grew for a grander building, which led to the opening of a third Free Trade Hall in 1856. The architect was one of Manchester's most prominent, Edward Walters, who won the competition for a public hall to dignify a site associated with the 1846 repeal of the Corn Laws. Walters' way of doing this was to make the hall appear to emerge, with cogent splendour, out of a Mancunian-inspired Victorian fantasy of self-assured Roman glory.

Walters had also designed Harvest House, located at the end of Mosley Street, near Piccadilly, the first of the scaled-up palazzo-style warehouses to be built in the commercial quarter of the city centre. It dates from 1839 and was built as the offices of the charismatic radical liberal thinker, Richard Cobden, the champion of Manchester manufacturers, the prime political representative of the industrial north at a time when such men saw the government in Westminster as still run by the ignorant, semi-rural feudal south.

Cobden was actually born near Midhurst, in west Sussex, in 1804, and spent his early life in poverty. The son of a failed farmer, sent to an uncle in Yorkshire, who treated him badly, he received little schooling and at fourteen became a clerk in the textile industry. His first known visit to Manchester was in 1825 as a commercial traveller. By 1832, a successful calico printer, relishing the fortune that could be made in Lancashire at the time by the skilled and ambitious, Cobden was living in Manchester, on Quay Street. One of the country's best-travelled men, he journeyed all over the world and developed a wide interest in history, economics, literature and foreign affairs. He came to believe that British foreign policy benefited the Establishment but handicapped ordinary working people. Writing as 'a Manchester manufacturer', he wrote two influential foreign policy pamphlets, *England, Ireland and America*, and *Russia*, which contained the essence of his thinking: 'It is labour improvements and discoveries that confer the greatest strength upon a people. By these alone and not by the sword of the conqueror, can nations in modern and all future times hope to rise to power and grandeur.'

In the late 1830s, a fierce opponent of social injustice, Cobden's interests were more local. Writing under another anonymous name, Libra, he published many letters in the *Manchester Times* discussing commercial and economic questions and became a conspicuous figure in Manchester political and intellectual life. He championed the foundation of the Manchester Athenaeum (a society for the 'advancement and diffusion of knowledge') after seeing similar institutions in America, delivered its inaugural address, and was elected to the Manchester Chamber of Commerce. In 1838 he became Alderman Cobden of Manchester in the city's first municipal elections, having played a leading part in the campaign for the incorporation of Britain's principal industrial town, which had previously been governed by the baronial court of Sir Oswald Mosley. His pamphlet 'Incorporate Your Borough' portrayed the struggle as one of democracy versus privilege, the rights of the productive classes against the rapacious aristocracy.

Cobden's attack on what he saw as an example of feudal governance was followed by his assumption of the leadership of Manchester's campaign against the Corn Laws, which he saw as the citadel of aristocratic self-interest within the British state. As one of the seven founding members of the Anti-Corn Law League, he set out not only to rid Britain of the laws, which restricted the importation of grain to shield British farmers from competition, but to shape the identity of Britain's entrepreneurs as a new social and political elite. 'The corn laws,' he wrote, 'take from the poorest of the poor to give to the richest of the rich.' The novelist William Thackeray predicted that Cobden could be a future prime minister. Between 1841 and 1847 he was MP for

Stockport, giving him a national platform, and Robert Peel credited Cobden as the main influence on the repeal of the laws. The idealistic, passionate Cobden had done something that for years had seemed impossible: broken the power of the landowners and opened up the British market for grain to free trade.

Cobden was also a dedicated campaigner for the world abolition of slavery and enjoyed considerable popular support. With the onset of the American Civil War in 1861, he made many inspirational anti-slavery speeches in Parliament and at large public meetings in and around Rochdale. After a period as MP for the West Riding of Yorkshire, he was Rochdale's MP from 1859 until his death on 2 April 1865, one week before the Confederate surrender that signalled the end of the war and only twelve days before Abraham Lincoln was assassinated.

'I see in the free trade principle that which will act on the moral world as the principle of gravitation in the universe – drawing men together, thrusting aside the antagonisms of race, and creeds and language, and uniting us in the bonds of eternal peace . . . I believe the effect will be to change the face of the world, so as to introduce a system of government entirely distinct from that which now prevails. I believe the desire and the motive for large and mighty empires and gigantic armies and great navies . . . will die away . . . when man becomes one family, and freely exchanges the fruits of his labour with his brother man.'

Apart from everything else, he helped provide the land for the building of the Free Trade Hall, one of Manchester's most notable buildings, which became the permanent home of Hallé's industrious orchestra; where in 1872 Benjamin Disraeli defended and praised Conservative principles and denounced radical forces in a landmark speech; where Manchester's first cinema show was held in 1896, a programme of Lumière brothers films presented by the eccentric, multi-skilled mime, magician and tightrope walker, Félicien Trewey; where Churchill in 1904 as MP for Oldham spoke 'in this great hall' for ninety minutes in passionate favour of free trade; where the first suffragette protest was held in 1905, Christabel Pankhurst and a mill worker called Annie Kenney being ejected from the hall for interrupting a Liberal Party rally, then being arrested for obstruction outside, which instigated the

Woman's Social and Political Union campaign for the vote; where
Elgar's First Symphony was premiered in 1908; and where anti-Semitic
Mussolini admirer Oswald Mosley addressed a capacity audience of the
British Union of Fascists in 1933, being heckled by *Coronation Street*
writer Jack Rosenthal's father, who got beaten up for his trouble.

Around 1910 Ludwig Wittgenstein would dress up to visit the Free
Trade Hall and whistle intently through entire symphonies as the
Austro-Hungarian Hans Richter, director of the Hallé Orchestra
between 1899 and 1911, colleague of Richard Wagner, dedicatee of
Elgar's First Symphony, conducted Brahms, Bruckner and Beethoven.
The uniquely attentive Wittgenstein heard, perhaps, even though he
had no words for what he would say, how the music should be played
now that the age of mechanical reproduction was taking over and
changing everything. In the late 1920s the twelve-year-old Anthony
Burgess was taken by his father to the Free Trade Hall to see the Hallé
Orchestra perform Wagner. A few of the musicians were Burgess's
father's drinking pals, and the visit was part of his campaign to seduce,
or perhaps distract, his antsy son with the power of music, which eventually succeeded to such an extent that by his late teens Burgess was
determined to be a composer. The teenager became so curious about
what music looked like, written down as a visual language, that in 1934
he would visit the newly opened Central Library, a Roman-inspired
circular building on St Peter's Square abutting the triangular town hall
a hundred yards from the Free Trade Hall, and sit in its vast light-filled
reading hall poring over scores by Stravinsky and Schoenberg, wondering what made them tick. At the time it was the largest library in the
country provided by a local authority, excitedly visited by Ewan McColl
on its opening day, a favourite spot of *Coronation Street* creator Tony
Warren and *Shabby Tiger* author Howard Spring.

Burgess's first visit to the Free Trade Hall was not a great success, as
Wagner failed to astonish him in the life-changing way hearing
Debussy's modern-minded, erotically alert *Prélude à l'après-midi d'un
faune* did a few years later on a crystal radio set he built himself – silvery
wine flowing in a spaceship. With his dad, hearing Wagner solidly
played by the disciplined Hallé, which he would later come to appreciate for introducing him to a wider classical repertoire, he was a little

bored, and because they were standing at the back of the hall, his legs got tired. Enough stuck, though, to make him understand that serious music could be as memorable as the raucous dance tunes he enjoyed. He later remarked that the 'heating grilles at the back of the Free Trade Hall gave off a strange musty smell which I was to meet again in Fraser and Neave's tonic water in Singapore'.

And then, forty-seven years later, in the Lesser Free Trade Hall, up above the main hall, more of a compact lecture theatre than a hall, a smell of Establishment polish merging with the lingering mustiness sensed by Burgess, playing rock music that was not necessarily revolutionary, but using provocative, restless language and looking as though they knew much more than their soft northern audience about the radical, political and theatrical history of the building and the rebellious air in and around the place, the Sex Pistols, as insurgent outsiders, took their place in Manchester history.

Much has been written and said about who was in the small audience for that first Sex Pistols show, but there was some phantom presence of the writer of *A Clockwork Orange*, a book exploring the importance of moral freedom, who believed that art must be dangerous or it was pointless, curiously sniffing the air, while Wittgenstein's terse note that 'music conveys to us itself' was living some sort of unearthly afterlife, and the ghost of the free-spirited Cobden – a preacher of the values of civilisation, demanding practical achievement and progress, intellectually internationalist but profoundly English, keenly aware of the various sorts of bondage that needed to be broken in a country where education was monopolised by the well off, where political and social tyranny was exercised by the aristocracy, the man who had achieved a revolutionary transformation of the business policy of the greatest commercial country in the world, who negotiated life as a series of engagements and personal reinventions – was perhaps looking on with some approval.

Those of us there were not aware of any ghosts around us, but we were all about to become ghosts, ones that exist in the memory, and sometimes in history, which is silent and full of omissions, a hurricane of energy, another dimension, the history you can find ways to write about yourself, for yourself, as far as you can tell.

97

Google 'Sex Pistols Lesser Free Trade Hall 1976' or simply 'June 4 1976' and you can use the resultant 10,700,000 pieces of information to piece together a crudely helpful history of: (a) post-Hollies and -10cc Manchester music, (b) the birth of indie music and (c) the 'greatest gig of all time' that 'changed music for ever'. The fact that if you Google 'I swear I was there' you come across more details about that Sex Pistols performance emphasises the show's reputation, not least because, and this has become an integral element in the ensuing mythologising of the gig, that not that many people bought the fifty-pence tickets but thousands now claim they did, so that the book written about what happened is called *I Swear I Was There*, with the sub-title *The Gig That Changed the World*.

Those who like to nourish the legend favour an audience of around forty; other less romantic minds suggest a number closer to a hundred. The year on the flimsy paper ticket was misprinted as '1076'. The small wood-panelled lecture theatre contained around 350 seats and had been booked by Howard Trafford and Pete Shelley of Bolton's Buzzcocks, playing the role of visionary impresarios. It cost twenty-five pounds to hire the hall, next door to the larger Free Trade Hall, an entertainment venue named after an economic principle, the first home in 1868 of the new Hallé Orchestra, which grew to national prominence after the Second World War, and a grand symbol of once-mighty Victorian civic pride, where bands like Pink Floyd, Black Sabbath, Wings and Little Feat played.

Howard Trafford, soon to be Devoto, an Iggy, Can and Samuel Beckett fan, student at Bolton Institute of Technology, had read a review that promised 'chaos' not music. Trafford and his college friend Shelley travelled to see the Pistols in High Wycombe. They had already been inspired – by the chaos, which promised a new order within new, unplanned urban and mental spaces – to form a group, which would be from Manchester and sound like it was from Manchester, intelligent, radical and provocative outsiders, and which in its own way invented the very idea of an indie world with the release of its self-financed, self-recorded, self-released four-track debut EP *Spiral Scratch*. These songs were a combination of journalism, philosophy, pop music and mental glamour, were local thinkers organising a new presence of mind and turning it into an object, a seven-inch disc inside a riveting slightly solemn black and white sleeve, and seemed as original, as unrepeatable, as the generosity of Chetham, the mischief of Laycock, the spirit of Oldknow, the invention of Lewis Carroll, the natural philosophy of John Dalton, the meritorious determination of Cobden and Pankhurst, the timing of Frank Randle, the presence of Lowry and Hepworth, the observation of Auden, the romantic organisation of Hallé, the crunching smartness of Turing, the future-forming lines of L. C. Howitt and Edgar Wood, the neighbourhood comedy of *Coronation Street*, the self-promoting brilliance of Burgess, the purpose of Stephenson, the drug-fuelled quest of De Quincey, the cosmic certainty of Lovell, and the brain of Sterne – seeking experience for its own sake, finding new ways to refresh his memory.

I was there, I was a witness, although not enough of one to notice at the time that what was taking place was 'history'. I had no idea I would talk and write about the gig for what is turning out to be the rest of my life, finding new ways to point out from anniversary to anniversary that the evening was something of a revelation because it instantly suggested that: (a) there were other people interested in music that made you feel, think and want to do/ be something radical/individual, (b) you could make music without the usual support systems of London record companies, promoters and showbiz managers and, (c) there was an exciting way to effectively and importantly assassinate Emerson Lake and Palmer, who indifferently perpetuated like cruel eighteenth-century landowners various demoralising forms of alienation, elitism, pomposity and complacency. The slick, remote sincerity of the pompous prog acts could be sensationally sabotaged.

I'd gone on my nineteen-year-old own. I'm not sure what I actually recall or what I filled in using data acquired later as the gig was talked up into legend, each subsequent Manchester moment and scene amplifying its apparent importance. I seem to recall lots of empty seats and the Sex Pistols solemnly trying to copy and/or mock slack rock musician poses with slapdash panache. The audience was mostly male, although the exotic Pistols entourage included some women, costumed in a style that to the long-haired flared-trouser still-fairly-cobbled-barely-Roxy'd northerners of the time was somewhere between Fosse's Cabaret and *Clockwork* Kubrick. Enigmatic but earthy collagist and artist Linder Sterling, then Devoto's girlfriend, future muse and friend of Morrissey, would have been there, but behind the scenes, not stuck out front with the music-paper-reading lads. The Pistols seemed more intuitively aware of Manchester's nineteenth-century status as the world-shaking Shock City than the audience. They were for change. There must be change. There was change, and there should be more change, because, without change, the ones with power remain in control, abusing that power, blocking progression. You didn't get that at the Stoneground.

We, the yokel audience, were scruffy isolated obsessive music fans motivated by John Peel and the weekly music papers to search out new music; tribe-less fans of the Stooges, MC5, maybe Can and Roxy and definitely the garage bands of Jac Holzman and Lenny Kaye's *Nuggets* compilations. Many audience members have since become well known. So well known it appears now that the show was attended by a host of rock celebrities – members of Joy Division, New Order, The Fall, the Smiths, A Certain Ratio, Ludus, Simply Red, Buzzcocks, Magazine, the poet John Cooper Clarke, the producer Martin Hannett. It was in fact attended by unassuming nonentities drawn to the gig from within a twenty-mile radius of Manchester city centre, drizzling in like the sixties mods and dancers had rained down on the Twisted Wheel, having caught the bus and train from Salford, Stockport, Oldham, Bury, Stretford, Wigan, Urmston, Macclesfield, Collyhurst, Leigh, Fallowfield and Wythenshawe. I shyly found a seat among empty seats all around me. I might have sat near Morrissey or Bernard Sumner or Peter Hook or Mark E. Smith, but I wouldn't have recognised them. We were all avant-garde music fans craving something new, noting a message from the south that something was stirring that might be especially for us, tapping into the general youthful impatience with our repressive, perpetual provincial impotence.

We were perhaps frustrated by our stranded nonentity status and seeking new purpose, but not really expecting to find blatant clues about how to break out of that post-war, post-sixties, post-industrial breakdown limbo. The Sex Pistols' deviant pop-art rage and indignation was an immediate clue. They played rock music, but they questioned it, reviewed it, toppled it, tore it up and pieced it back together, dressed it up like artists. Artists not using paint and sculpture, but pop music, media manipulation, surrealist humour and appropriated and adjusted conceptual art.

I seem to recall no one in the audience looked as though they were in a group and ever would be, because of course at the time no one (a) local, (b) regional and (c) provincial, who looked a little ordinary even dull and dressed a little second hand, a little charity shop, formed pop groups. This was to change, quite quickly, because the Sex Pistols themselves did not as such look like a band, not as bands were perceived at the time, whether Genesis, Mott or Free, or even those early hints of a certain form of energising cultural and musical correction about to take place, the Ramones and Dr Feelgood.

Would another group of forty have ended up forming the kind of groups that came into being because there had appeared these perverse educators, these militant cultural critics possibly influenced as much by deviant conceptualist Marcel Duchamp and gladitorial philosopher Guy Debord as the Small Faces and the Who, and sensationally branded by wound-up folk-devil-seeking tabloids as grubby nuisances, bringers of vicious punk rock and associated loutish scandals? Or were they the obvious forty or so who would end up forming those bands – and writing those words/taking those photographs/designing those sleeves/managing those bands/starting those labels – because they attended the gig in the first place and had agitating within them all those songs, ideas, words, images, plans, beliefs, manifestos, and just needed some sort of cabalistic psychic trigger, a dressed-up sign, a fearless look in the eye, as delivered by that haughty and amused intellectual hooligan Johnny Rotten? (And what happened to those of the forty that did not form bands, etc., etc.? The ensuing myth does not allow these gaps to be filled in.)

The support at that first show, when the Buzzcocks, despite being billed to play, weren't ready, were Solstice from Bolton, who were more Allman Brothers/Stoneground hippy than Richard Hell surreal. We sat politely, a little non-plussed, through their guitar-dull, long-haired, deeply non-punk show before, abruptly, the Sex Pistols arrived, looking like they were looking for trouble, playing familiar pop songs by the Who, Small Faces and Monkees but also other songs that seemed weirdly charged with a tantalising even shocking new form of bitterness and resentment with words like anarchy and Antichrist exploding out of the top, songs that seemed closer to something futuristic and fantastically English and Dada than ancient irrelevant American blues. They were dead ordinary, really, as English as treacle pudding and freshly mown lawns, but somehow they seemed as exotically extraordinary as the descendants of Lewis Carroll's Alice, Wyndham Lewis, Peter Cook and the Spiders from Mars, and gorgeousness and gorgeosity was made flesh.

It was the abruptness. I still remember the mean funny look on Johnny

Rotten's face and his short ruffled hair as he strolled on to the small stage, all snot, sneer and leer, with a layer of unstable boyish sweetness and a hint of intellectual raffishness, and looked down on us, most if not all scruffy boys with long hair and suddenly stupid flapping flares, and then dragged us away with him. He dragged us away into the future and a world where books and hundreds of articles have been written, and films made, about what happened that night, as if there was some kind of fiery mass orgy and everyone there lost their virginity all at once, and then set out on a deliberate mission to change everything, to do and be the same roughly transcendent reality-checking culturally significant thing. He dragged us into a future where we'd get to know most of the names of the people who turned up, because Rotten and his crooked cohorts made it clear that the best way to get on, to make things happen, was to do it yourself, and think for yourself, and see for yourself. He didn't want us to agree with him. He wanted us to agree to differ.

We couldn't yet articulate it – those in the way of Rotten's piercing gaze – not in special, novel ways, but we were bored in the city, although not bored with what we could find in the city, by what came into it, and out of it, symbolising how the city itself throughout history had combined the energies of those who had settled there with those who brought their outsiders' energy and talent. The city was done for, so something else must happen. Pessimists can be such bores, and it's lazy to believe the worst. We were searching for new passions, and living in and around this particular city had conditioned us to look for those new passions in a particular way, with a particular point of view embedded in a northern history we knew little about but which had soaked into our beings. Our emotions and behaviour were what they were because we lived in an orbit, in a place of flux, around Manchester, pulsating the other side of the Pennines from Yorkshire, at the other end of the Mersey from Liverpool, in one county or another where Lancashire and Cheshire intertwined or where Lancashire set off further north and Cheshire weaved towards Liverpool. Manchester started to speak to us, and we found that we had something to say connected to what it was saying.

Six weeks later, on 20 July, the Pistols returned, stronger, faster, harder, darker, officially nationally notorious, quickly, accidentally and intentionally discovering an astonishing way to transmit tricky subversive messages to a wider audience than the avant garde typically reached. The Lesser Free Trade Hall was now full of more knowing fans, already with shorter hair and narrower trousers and a tougher edge each paying a pound to see the Pistols, the debut of abrasively smart Buzzcocks and rowdy, not so smart Wythenshawe chancers Slaughter and the Dogs who had the gall to promote the show as though they were sharing the top of the bill.

The two shows caused a little confusion, as many who turned up for the second show would claim to have seen the first. For a while the two gigs were compressed into one memory. There was, relatively speaking, someone famous at the second show – passionate local Cambridge-educated TV personality Tony Wilson, obsessed with Manchester's pioneering and progressive credentials. He claimed he was at the first one, but he definitely wasn't – he would not have been missed – although his eventual Factory Records comrades Martin Hannett, Rob Gretton and Alan Erasmus were, not yet knowing each other, and Richard Boon, Buzzcocks manager, who organised the precursor of Factory, New Hormones, was obviously there. Peter Saville, the fifth Factory Man, was at both, or neither, or the first, or the second. Joy Division's Ian Curtis was at the second show not the first, meeting people he had something in common with and totally ready to let the ordinary but uncanny Rotten inspire him.

Rotten stared at us like he hated us but could grow to love us, although that love would pretty soon grow into disgust, so he might as well hate us, and get it over with – we only had ourselves to blame – but even though he hated us, he was going to entertain us, to show us what a wonderful cage-rattling mind he had, and what great taste in music. The bastard made us believe in the dark, menacing, anti-conformist fairy tale of punk, its ability to exercise our intuitions, explore our sensibilities and sort out the modern world in ways that suited our personal, local interests, and the rest was post-punk history.

Manager Malcolm McLaren, the missing link between Don Arden and Marshall McLuhan, a lover of situationism and stunts, fashion and thinking, words and images, and London punk scene queen Jordan were at the first show, part of an extravagantly clad Pistols London entourage that made us locals seem to be wearing flat caps and clogs. They were calling us – dissatisfied individuals not yet knowing how dissatisfied we were – to the circus, to the zoo, to a freak show, to a political rally, to a fight, to a piece of astonishing theatre, to an art exhibition calculated to make our eyes and ears burn, to one other Manchester night that could have gone nowhere.

Or somewhere. Because, as is obvious once time has passed, one surprising thing leads to another: the first Pistols show led to the second Pistols show led to Wilson's experimental pop TV show *So It Goes*, to the bored, alive and anxious Buzzcocks' *Spiral Scratch* EP on their own independent New Hormones label, to the estranged, endless, side-splitting, crying-out-loud Fall, to the utopian disorganisation of Factory Records, to the Hacienda nightclub, the ideal alchemical combination of structure and event, craving to turn life into sheer play, which was the next stage on in the margins of pleasure, of high spirits, of the fortifying spirit of leisure (from the nineteenth-century Bolton Star and Ohmy!'s Th' Owd Circus, the free and easies, from Gracie's lungs, Formby's teeth, Lowry's fairs, Mancunian Films' horseplay, Savile's Ritz, Manning's Embassy, from Belle Vue, the Golden Garter, Talk of the North in Eccles, Moss Side's rough and ready Nile and Reno touting the riveting, pungent pulse of the exiled and reviled, the pepped-up northern soul of the Twisted Wheel, the dolled-up disco of the erotically multi-roomed Pips behind Manchester Cathedral and its Roxy Room dripping with quiffs, fringes and eyeliner, to the worked-up places where punk went – Rafters, the Ranch, the Electric Circus – to Marr and Morrissey of the Smiths, giving such voice to local desire and universal torment, to Madchester, Manchester roughly transformed into myth-making playground, into temporary perfect place, to the Stone Roses at Spike Island, to Oasis, setting rock rebellion and a fascination with novelty in stone, to a postmodern brand of civic pride, a new faith in progress and, what with one thing and another, to *I'm a Celebrity Get Me Out of Here*.

The momentum caused by the event has now perhaps died down, or paused for thought. Or, ultimately, the momentum has turned into a constant nostalgic commentary on the momentum – what caused it, how we remember it and what happened because of it to Manchester and its regenerated sociocultural history. (When the Free Trade Hall was converted into a Radisson Hotel in 2004 L. C. Howitt's cleverly rendered post-war hall was demolished, but a few architectural remnants of the theatre were retained, scattered around the generically sparkling five-star hotel: the plaque commemorating its reopening after the war in 1951 by Princess Elizabeth soon to be Queen, a framed piece of wall plaster autographed by previous performers, Edward Walter's original decorative outside cladding, and the letters showing you where the stall entrance doors were located. Under pressure from energetic intellectual celebrity and Factory Records impresario Tony Wilson, representing the local concern that such a historical building was to be turned into a bland, luxury chain hotel, inheriting if only in his own mind the moral energy of Anthony Burgess and the populist-historian mantle of A. J. P. Taylor, some of the conference rooms were named after local historical figures, including Cobden, Dalton and Howitt, and suites were named after performers who had appeared at the hall. There are Bassey, Garland, Valentino and Fitzgerald Suites – reflecting the American owners' taste – and one of the penthouse suites, with views over the old Central Station, now the Manchester Central convention complex, was named after Dylan. There is no Judas Suite – for the greatest heckle of the twentieth century – no Sex Pistols Suite despite firm requests from Wilson and, shamefully, no Rotten Suite.)

98

Complete with hurriedly inserted mentions of the Sex Pistols and Buzzcocks, I sent my magazine, *Out There*, professionally typeset and printed for fifty pounds at an Offerton industrial estate printers, which my dad helped me pay for, to the editor of the *NME*, Nick Logan, with a terse note suggesting with what must have been Manchester arrogance, Stockport bluffness or reckless Cheshire cheek, that I could do better than him. He took the challenge well, and because I neglected to put a telephone number on the note, sent a telegram to our new house in Heaton Moor, where we now lived after another move within Stockport.

It was a bigger house, with rough, scrappy hints of something once hoping to be grand, but a step or two down from the soft suburban limbo of Offerton. My dad, now perilously close to being unemployed, finding uncomfortable work as a travelling salesman, chased by indeterminate figures demanding payment, had needed to cash in some of the value of the Offerton house and we moved the other side of the Mersey, technically into Lancashire, although still in Stockport and therefore, more or less, Cheshire. My dad's mood darkened further because he'd slipped across the murky river border and further away from where Cheshire turned semi-rural, pointing through lush trees and gentle roads towards elusive peace and quiet. One more move, and we would be in flat, slack Levenshulme, mysteriously stinking of something biscuit-y, tangled up in that done-in ring of rot and ruin which circled central Manchester like a desiccated doughnut, which only Lowry and Morrissey could turn into any sort of poetry. He didn't even make it there.

Logan asked me to come to London for an interview, suggesting there was a chance I could actually write for my favourite music paper. It was now forty years since the last Briton had won at Wimbledon, and ten years since England had won the World Cup, with Roger Hunt, born near Wigan, six miles north of Warrington, Cheshire in Golborne (stream where marsh marigolds grow), Lancashire, playing at inside left, number 10. Geoff Hurst consistently points out that he was confident his controversial second goal, England's third, definitely crossed the line, despite German appeals, because Hunt, a born striker, two yards away, celebrated a goal rather than ensuring that the ball was in the net. Hunt had no doubt; good enough for Hurst. It was Alan Ball, born in Farnworth, then of Lancashire, three miles south-east of Bolton, five miles south-west of Bury, nine miles north of Manchester, on 12 May 1945, at twenty the youngest member of Sir Alf Ramsay's squad of twenty-two, who had chased down the ball in the 101st minute as part of a memorably tireless two-hour display and crossed it for Hurst to smash against the underside of the crossbar, and then down on, over, around the German goal line.

My dad was falling backwards, the wrong side of the line, as shown by the move back up the A6 towards Manchester, away from Cheshire. The house we now had was big, but old and bleak, beyond any possible better days, with a back garden I don't remember anyone ever visiting, filled perhaps with uncherished remnants of our previous houses and lives, falling apart and rotting into the ground. The sun never seemed to shine; neighbours never visited. For me it was just a functional resting place between gigs and music venues, where my life was increasingly located, and it encouraged me to make plans to get away.

The house in Heaton Moor was my dad's last house, his final place, and the last home of the Morley family. You could say it was hopeless, even when there was hope. Together, at the end, perhaps, of our authentic father–son relationship stretching back to standing on thirties-style terraces to see Manchester City win the First Division in 1968, we saw City win the League Cup at Wembley in 1976, against Newcastle United. Peter Barnes, born in Manchester the same year as me, scored the first goal, and after Newcastle equalised, Dennis Tueart, Newcastle-born and a Newcastle fan as a boy, scored the winner with what he called the greatest goal of his career, an overhead shot with his back to the goal. For thirty-five years I could mark this match as the last one I went to with my father, because it was the last trophy City earned until they won the FA Cup in 2011.

I left Stockport station one morning to travel to London and the *NME*. I caught the train from Manchester which had to stop at Stockport after it had crept across the viaduct with a view of the Merseyway shopping centre – now shifting into yesterday, as old-fashioned as the 1960s at a time when five years passing seemed like a generation and a new generation was needed. In London, high up in an office building overlooking the River Thames designed by the same architect who had created the station approach gracefully curving down its sixties groove from Piccadilly into Manchester, and the busy, sleek Euston station where my train arrived, I was asked by Logan to write some concert reviews from Manchester.

Because of the Sex Pistols getting inside our heads at the Lesser Free Trade Hall, there was now a local scene of groups, labels and personalities to report on. My first review in the paper was about the Buzzcocks' sixth gig in a venue along Deansgate. I thought they were amazing, and I was absolutely right, and they made me want to be amazing.

The series of self-inventions I had achieved since arriving in the north – moving to Reddish, walking around Reddish, joining the library, exploring Stockport, taking in Manchester and venues around the city – now reached its latest stage. My father lived long enough to see me write a few articles for the *NME*, including my first interview, with Marc Bolan, which seemed a dream a bit like a night at Belle Vue in the late 1960s, and even now seems like a memory I have made up to satisfy certain narrative requirements.

I'd seen him a couple more times, and he had invited me to the
Granada TV studios, where he was recording his *Marc* series – his
friend David Bowie was a guest on the show – but I had an appointment interviewing C. P. Lee of Alberto Y Los Trios Paranoias in
Didsbury for the *NME* and failed to turn up to watch the pair of them
messing about and singing a new Bowie song called 'Heroes' in what
turned out to be the last few days of Marc's life. This was the only
chance I ever had of meeting David Bowie, as if he was actually real. I
once played Marc some Buzzcocks music in his Granada dressing room
minutes before he went to have his make-up done in a chair next to
William Roache, the actor who had played Ken Barlow since the very
first episode of *Coronation Street* – and who might yet play him after he
has died. Bolan thought Buzzcocks were cute, which I thought was a
bit like calling Albert Camus cute.

One part of my life now clashed with another, and sent me spinning
through space, pretty much to where I am now, writing this sentence.

A few weeks before Bolan died, in June 1977, my dad, not much of
a traveller, set out in his car from Heaton Moor, heading for what may
or may not have been an unknown destination. Within minutes he
would have crossed the hidden Mersey, ignoring the immortal, watch-
ful viaduct, heading away from Manchester, up the sterling Buxton
Road, through devious, renamed Hazel Grove, south into east Cheshire,
and north Derbyshire, and then beyond, to where the north clearly is
no more, and everything changes. Perhaps he took another route out of
Stockport, driving out to Cheadle to join the A34, driving down
towards Handforth, where his wife had been born, between the airport
and Bramhall, joining the A535 outside Alderley Edge, heading towards
Holmes Chapel, crossing the Crewe–Manchester railway line, making
the gentle climb out of Twemlow, spotting for the last time the always
unlikely Jodrell Bank, where the 1950s stayed put in space and time,
joining the M6 near Sandbach, moving west on to the M5 around West
Bromwich, by which time his destination was clearly going to take him
past Worcester and Tewkesbury, driving beyond Gloucester and
Cheltenham, looking for the end of the world.

He found it, and never returned, deciding, in the way you must if
you decide such a thing, to kill himself in the early hours of what must

have been a particularly tense morning outside Stroud, Gloucester, in the south-west of England, a place I had never visited until I went to his funeral on a day that for many people probably turned out fine.

He died in his car, but not in a car crash, crossing a final one-way border separating him from me, turning blue in the face thinking that having to survive one more stunning day, one more hour, one more minute and, in the end, even one more second was more than he could cope with. A man who had seemed particularly undaring for most of his life, give or take the dramatic move north, executed one monstrous dare right at the end of his life with such commitment it wiped him out. He had driven himself to an early grave. It was forty-one years since Fred Perry was the last British tennis player to win Wimbledon.

If he had lived, what would he have made of the new, confident Manchester that started to develop through the 1980s and nineties, building on the past as a foundation, as a direct and indirect bloody-minded response to the startling connection that the Sex Pistols made with local history, to a bomb planted by the IRA, ripping out the Arndale Centre with almost architectural precision, to the Commonwealth Games held in the city in 2002? Would he have felt at home in a post-bomb, modernised, sweet-talking, boutique Manchester, decorated with uninspired examples of contemporary civic space, lacking a little traditional local personality, lacking signs of Toast Rack verve, shoving the gutted, unmodernised past behind the scenes, but nicely relined with swish retro-future trams, streets now tidily draped around rediscovered even cherished canals mostly released from dismal, manky limbo, as though they introduced a continental flair to local proceedings, set in a wider north that at least in the prime city centres was being splashed with post-slum newness, pop-culture life, international festivals, consumer gear, art galleries, slick restaurants, branded cafés, illuminated corporate logos and post-industrial endeavour? Or was he always destined one way or another to leave?

What would he have made of Manchester City becoming by the time he was in his mid-seventies, after nearly forty years of retreat, disappointment and embarrassing mediocrity, the richest team in the world, richer even than their monstrous local rivals Manchester United of Stretford, who played at a refurbished Old Trafford ground next to

where the BBC had built a new 'media city' in a Salford injected with
dust-obliterating Eurostyled steel and glass, as if the Corporation can
bring to national broadcasting something of the spiky, sparring northern views and differences so boldly displayed by the Granada TV of the
1950s, sixties and seventies?

Manchester City would become once more League champions,
forty-four years after me and my dad had seen them win the League
up in Newcastle, and even though there were those who complained
they had merely bought it, been given it as a gift by distant, calculating Arab owners, those who had been around all of those forty-four
years knew that it had taken more than cash to finally win the title
again. It had taken belief and communal willpower, a northern spirit
rooted in centuries of shared experience and an accumulation of attitude, shared among families, friends and communities, many of them
in the Stockport part of Greater Manchester, where United tended to
stand for privilege and City for self-sufficiency and a moral purity
that outside investment however immense, suspicious or unlimited
could never corrupt.

If my father had still been alive, Manchester City winning the
League, in a twenty-first century resembling but complicatedly, technologically removed from the 1970s he never made it beyond, would it
have been an occasion that made it clear, perhaps with a clarity never
previously achieved, that we were deeply, fantastically father and son,
and he loved me, and I loved him, and we now hugged all the time,
making up for all that time in the sixties and part of the seventies when
we just never did, because we were in our own space, in our own minds,
only connected by a shared surname and a vague feeling never quite
openly articulated that we were in this – whatever this was – together?

Winning the League made me think this and about all those years I
had spent without a father, without really, deeply thinking about not
having a father, because it would have been too much to bear, and
would have made me think about my own possible trips to Gloucester,
on the outskirts of oblivion. When City won the Premier League,
losing a match they had to win with four minutes to go and then
scoring two goals when it seemed like it wasn't going to happen, and
the might of United was after all that horribly eternal, and then, in a

moment, it wasn't, because there was such a thing as a change, and you could see history take shape right in front of you, I cried not just because it was all so unexpected and exciting, but because I thought of my father, and it felt like he was thinking of me. That wasn't about money or cynical outsider manipulation of market forces, a despoiling of once-resonant-now-wilting tradition. It was about something else, the something else that makes you think, about how all change begins with someone having a thought.

If he had lived, would he now be northern enough to wonder if this moneyed, mannered, same but different north, home to much of the BBC in a Salford sealed off by committee decisions and diplomatic niceties from the Salford of 'Dirty Old Town', even as it sentimentally clings on to simply put memories and mementos of Lowry, is still the north he never warmed to, but then fell in love with, or at least just grew used to, to the extent of losing his elongated Kent vowels and getting a mite Stocky curt around his accent, or a facile, vapid new north, turned by market research and fine-tuned opinion polls into another place altogether?

Or would he have left the north, a few weeks after his exploratory drive to Gloucester that ended not with a suicide but, after a period of anguished contemplation, a clumsy divorce from his wife, our mum, and a move back to Kent, leaving us behind, because he had to, because we were in the north, and he never really got it, and he never set out to explore it and make it a real home. If he had moved back to Margate, and lived in whatever circumstances until 2012, surviving in his own way, as separated from me as much as he was separated from his father, because some patterns can simply not be altered, what would he have made of the decline of his hometown?

When he grew up in Cliftonville, in the 1940s and 1950s, and then when we visited on holiday during the sixties and seventies, the place seemed to have survived without being marked down, or maimed, by the war and the staggering post-war disorientation. Cliftonville, the more salubrious district of Margate, seemed when I went there as a young boy to be even more clean and smart than an idealised version of Cheshire, and set by the swaying spraying sea in a way that opened up the world and cleared the mind.

A certain amount of fun lay at the end of every street, which all smelled exotically of the English Channel and a wide, perfect, Famous Five sky. The sand glowed, the deckchairs evoked sun-baked contentment, colourful wooden beach huts were arranged along the beaches and bays with an almost glamorous, cheering neatness. Forty years later, the town seemed in tatters, the sheen worn off, Margate a once-perky seaside resort given bad advice by an anonymous part of an unnamed country until quite recently on the other side of the Iron Curtain. The beach huts had gone, pulled like rotten teeth, latterly used by the homeless as places to doss; the sand had somehow faded; the sea seemed more menacing and half-hearted.

The Dreamland Funfair that I visited every year from the early 1960s until I stopped going to Margate in 1973, feeling too old to go on holiday with my parents, once a distant cousin of Belle Vue, a primitive ancestor of the postmodern theme park, was now derelict, the sorry remains hidden from sight, as though what was left had been placed in an unmarked grave because it too had killed itself. The shops on the front, if they were not boarded up, were mostly filled with stuff that had no relation with being so near the sea. The charming, lively amusement arcades glittering with candyfloss promise now monotonously clicked and churned with something a little surly. The cafés looked broken, the sky embarrassed that such squalor had been allowed to grow at the water's edge.

A new art gallery was boldly perched at the edge of the sea up the hill from the main seafront, made out of the nicely balanced space, white and glass you would expect of such buildings, as if blown from across the Channel, a hopeful sign that the inspiration behind the art that would be displayed there might seep out into the town and impress itself upon the torn, splintered ugliness. Imagination might feed imagination, which one day might then take off and change things for the better. Margate had also been given a little manicure, a single kiss of life, and people were trying to spruce up the place with a little spit, polish and attention, because such towns are on the verge of becoming ghost towns right in front of our eyes.

Margate and Stockport, my dad's main homes, where he started, where he ended up, were two of the twelve towns chosen in spring 2012 by the government and their 'high street tsar' Mary Portas for a pilot scheme committed to the regeneration of depleted, depressed high streets. The plan, inevitably framed around a cosmetic television series, was to liven up derelict shops and wrecked communities and inspire new market areas, hopefully recapturing a declining local sense of spirit, enterprise and place in a Britain where town centres were increasingly the home of pawn, betting, charity and pound shops. The intention was to reintroduce some of the original haphazard but determined enterprise that had invented, designed and fuelled the two towns, turning them into places with their own striking, distinctive spaces, faces, walls, roads and dwellings.

Each town received £100,000, as if it had won a quiz show, alongside the haughty motivational hectoring of Portas. The money was perhaps enough to last a day or two, produce some stirring but simplistic television, and add a temporary frisson of jolly, jollying activity to a tiny area of the two tired towns; it was nowhere near enough to inject the necessary level of inspirational power, planning and vision required to alter the direction in which the towns were drifting.

If my father had returned to Margate – had witnessed its decline, seen it become a run-down reflection of his own mean inner tension, resembling more and more those blighted areas around Reddish, so that Cliftonville, unbelievably, started to look like a close cousin of Gorton, Hyde and Denton, as though it was just the other side of North Reddish Park, hemmed in by the Nico Ditch, stuck in the shadows like those thrown over decades and terraced square miles by the Moors Murderers – would he have somehow felt he was to blame? That he had brought something infectious back with him from those cracked, confounded northern streets, a virus that had spread from his tarnished mind and skin out into the fresh Thanet air, that turned Margate, hopeful and happy by the sea, into an abandoned inner-city district where nothing was due to happen but an evacuation of spirit and a squandering of energy? Was that why, when he headed out of Stockport, off into the great unknown, he headed south-west, to Gloucester, so that he didn't take back to his hometown whatever it was that made him think there was no point and purpose to anything? Did he try to save Margate? But it would take a lot more than his terrible self-sacrifice. It was all destined to happen; it wasn't his fault.

Not long after he died I left the north, at least in body. I moved to London to work full time for the *NME*, not knowing how long I would be there, not knowing that whatever happened, whether I knew it or not, I was northern and always would be. I couldn't feel it banked up behind me, and mostly went out of my way to avoid noticing it, but eventually it became clear that whatever reinventions I might have designed in the south – crossing new sorts of borders and making, or missing, very 1980s deadlines – they would never have as much effect on my voice, accent, attitude, character, sensitivity as the few years I spent becoming myself in Reddish and without even knowing it taking in all that north. Nothing outside Reddish had as much impact on the forming, and deforming, of my personality.

Except for being a music critic. There was no escaping that. Being a rock journalist was the perfect job for someone like me. It needed no official qualifications or experience other than having gone to gigs for a few years and listened to records and John Peel all the time on my own. On my own, in my bedroom, I could make up stories about what I thought about various sorts of music, act like I knew what I was talking about – because it was all being made up as we went along – and invent versions of the legends and myths that first got me excited about this sort of music. After leaving Reddish, and spending a few years unknowingly accumulating the correct idiosyncratic qualifications and finessing the perhaps desperate determination, I moved to the *New Musical Express*. In place of the north but still in its shadow, because it had given me the confidence to think for myself, even as I felt there were those who would never take me seriously because I was northern, there was a history of music to absorb and understand, a new path to follow until I reached some sort of destination all of my own making, which would set me off somewhere else, which might take me back where it, I, all began.

After writing for the *New Musical Express* for a few years, as if it was always meant to be, and experiencing the 1980s as if it was another reality, another set of myths and tall tales to turn into facts that challenged fiction, I wrote a book about my father's suicide. It was set in a remote northern world I was beginning to remember after a couple of decades forgetting while I moved in a direction I hoped was forward, and I called it *Nothing* because T. S. Eliot had sat in a shelter on the promenade overlooking the sea in Margate in 1921 and written as part of Part III of *The Waste Land*, 'On Margate Sands./ I can connect/ Nothing with nothing./ The broken fingernails of dirty hands./ My people humble people who expect/ Nothing.'

I sat next to the novelist Doris Lessing at a book awards dinner in the early 2000s, and she was disgusted when I told her the title of my book. She shook her head and tut-tutted like I had named my child Void or Junk. I felt as though I was being scolded by a Stockport Grammar School teacher but then considered that the fact I had travelled all the way from my box-bedroom capsule in Reddish down the road from shabby Houldsworth Square at the lustreless far edge of the collapsed Industrial Revolution to being sat next to a literature Nobel laureate was the equivalent of becoming lord mayor of London, or a prince in my own mind, which even then I was still making up. Other events that were a sign of having made it, if only in my own mind, included sitting in the back of a Ford Granada on the M4 with J. G. Ballard discussing the spiritual and psychological stature of motorways for a 1990 Channel 4 documentary, Lou Reed sneering to my face at the idea I was any kind of journalist – 'Delmore Schwartz was a journalist!' – and comedian Steve Martin telling his press representative to give fifteen more minutes to 'the funny guy' when I interviewed him for a magazine.

Thirty-odd years after the Sex Pistols in Manchester had led, what with one thing and another, to me leaving the north, having spent three decades in the south going round the houses away from the north, I was encouraged to write this book, and to find the north, where it begins, who decides such things, and what has happened to it.

I had written about northern music, including many of the groups that formed after seeing the Sex Pistols at the Lesser Free Trade Hall, and at the end of that year they played, along with the Clash, the Damned, Talking Heads, the Ramones and Buzzcocks, at a new Manchester venue putting on punk gigs, the Electric Circus in bashed-up Collyhurst along the Oldham Road – my Golden Garter, another stage on from Reddish Library.

Tan Hill on the Pennine Way in North Yorkshire

I had written a book about Joy Division, set in a northern world that was all atmosphere, mental noise and close attention to the detail that could erupt in a world where there was the action and reaction of the city, all those buildings and decisions, triumphs and disasters, and there was the rampant quiet and the stillness of the moors, and somewhere in between there were all sorts of astonishing tension and diminished intensity. There had been films about Factory Records of Manchester and Joy Division that I had appeared in either as myself or as a character. I seemed to belong in the north even though I did not live there and had not been born there. The north was the context inside which my life seemed to make sense. I grew up in a society I did not choose and then worked out for myself how to belong. The story of my life was embedded in the community where I had first derived my identity; to cut myself off from my past was to deform my current relationships, with people, with those I loved, and with reality. I am a part of history, and whether I like it or not, the bearer of a tradition. There was, after all that, no escaping it.

I needed to find out what that meant. I wrote a proposal about a north book, to clarify my own thoughts, and see if anyone was interested.

99

Extracts from a proposal about a book on the north

In some ways, *North* will be the sequel – or prequel – to a memoir I wrote about my father's suicide, *Nothing*. (Perhaps it should be titled *Nowt*, as long as Doris Lessing does not find out.) In *Nothing*, I examined how my father, born and bred in the south, found living in the north a dark and diffi-cult prospect. He moved there in his twenties, in the early 1960s, largely because his wife, my mother, was born in the north – and perhaps in the end what separated them was this difference. It became more and more of a problem, and eventually tore them apart completely. I think the north tore apart my father's whole life.

He 'survived' for about fifteen years. I left the north not long after he died in 1977, looking for my own security and stability away from a place that now lacked a centre because of the loss of my father. The north was shattered for me by my father's ultimate rejection of a place that had become my home. I was driven to find another home. I found it in music, in writing, in books, and then, reluctantly, in London. I raced to the city in order to escape the violence of my father's death, imagining perhaps that I was just passing through, on the way to where I needed to get. But I have never left London, and perhaps only will the day that I am described as a Londoner.

I would take the north with me, but I wouldn't stay inside it, as the north had taught me to crave new experiences, and new discoveries. The north had taught me that once you were northern the north was wherever you were. As Ian Brown, the singer in the Stone Roses, would say – the north is not where you are, it's where you're at. To find the north perhaps means always coming to it. Always moving away from it, so that you can continually come back, and see it as something fresh, something alive, always forming. I am not saying this because I moved away, but I feel that to be a northerner does not mean having to live in the north from the moment you are born to the day you die. The north has become the north because of those that have moved there, or simply visited in spectacular circumstances, adding to the mongrel intensity, the hybrid complexity, the stitching together of myriad forms of otherness.

The north has become the north because of those that moved away, and look back to see it more for what it is than if you stay there.

The book will be a kind of travel book that ventures into a part of the world that seems so close to us but which is as exotic as anywhere. I will set off from London's Euston Station and head Up North, looking for that magic moment as I cross a real and/or an imaginary border from outside to inside and begin my search for the heart of the north.

I will disembark at Stockport, which is where I spent my early years, on the edge of Lancashire, Cheshire and Derbyshire, on the edge of the Pennines, a mixture of green and grey located between the country and the city, between past and future, between motorway and valley; take in the death-less desolation of the moors, the cheap flirty fun of Blackpool, the breathtaking beauty of the Lakes; and when you follow the Mersey which flows through Stockport you soon reach the New York of the north, Liverpool. From Liverpool, I will move up the coast, and explore the eastern coast, the other coast, because there is the other north of Yorkshire, Durham and Northumberland. So from Stockport, I would cross the Pennines to Sheffield, Bradford, Hull, move up to Newcastle, across to Carlisle . . . down past the Lakes through the Lancashire of Lancaster, Bolton, Bury, Rochdale, Burnley, through Manchester, learning about the birth, death and rebirth of the Manchester Ship Canal, back to Stockport, easing gently further and further south of Stockport to learn where the north dissolves, and disappears . . . and as I travel, I create a mental map, extending and expanding the idea of the north into something magnificent and secret, imposing and public.

The book will strive once and for all to answer the fundamental questions raised by the idea of the north. Where is it? What does it mean today? Where does it begin? Where did it begin? Where does it end? Where is it going? What is a northerner? Where do you start to be in the north? Does the south become the north at Watford Gap, whereas the north becomes the south at somewhere above Stoke? Does the north stop south of Scotland? Why? Is it a definite geographical location or a state of mind? Is it something that is being transformed, along with most of reality, and our memories and experi-ence of reality, by the existence, expansion, and ultimately distorting presence of the Internet, turning it into an illusion, or more of an illusion? What will I find if I look for the north on the web – and will the web be where ideas, concepts, histories, places like the north end up, in pieces, waiting to be assembled into a new form of sense and meaning?

The book will look beneath the clichés of what makes a northerner: heart, humour, spite, chippiness, determination, passion, toughness, sentimentality, 'northern soul', stoicism . . . to ask what it really means to be a northerner? What makes the north special?

Is it a unique mix of the philosophy of working-class values, and ideals, coupled with the harsh living conditions, that creates a resilience and hardihood . . . Is the idea of The North rooted in what T. E. Lawrence believed, that 'The harder the life, The better the person?'

The book will of course also contain elements of memoir, journalism, fiction, history, cultural analysis; personal memories of the north, why I lived there, why I left, why I still feel northern, why that will never disappear, if in fact the true way to write about the north is to leave it. And it will ask other questions. Why is it that we take our compass from the idea of the north? Why is it the defining upstroke on navigational devices all around the world? Does it also carry the weight of a deeper integrity; a darker intensity; a moral compass?

As the book progresses, and as I travel, looking at what is around me, and into the past, both my own and the region's, I will begin to build some history.

The book will celebrate the brilliance of the north, claiming it as the home of independent thinking.

There will be a chapter on the seismic effect of what Arnold Toynbee dubbed the Industrial Revolution – which changed the face of the world, and which began in the north-west of England at the end of the eighteenth century. It was here that modern industry was born through enterprise, industry and the development of merchant skills, the admixture of climate, natural resources and geography, the inventiveness of its people, the building of transport infrastructures and a powerful industrial entrepreneurial spirit said to typify the region. It still produces more than half of Britain's manufactured goods and consumables.

Before the Industrial Revolution, Lancashire was a backwater: few visited the place, roads were impassable, and there was nothing to come for anyway. But the strategic importance of the north-west has been evident since the times when the Romans mined lead in the Lake District, iron in the Furness peninsula and copper and salt in Cheshire. It was no accident that Lancashire became the home of cotton, and it was cotton that spearheaded the revolution leading to the changes, for better or worse, that we take for granted today.

Lancashire's lowland plain was mainly arable farmland, while the moors supported farming communities which eked out an existence in the harsh winters by weaving wool. But when cotton began to compete, Lancashire had all the attributes to turn it into the workshop of the world: a moist climate, an experienced, honest workforce, and a collection of imaginative men who created the machines that made the Industrial Revolution gain momentum.

Yet every story has its dark side. And so it was the Industrial Revolution, with its dark satanic mills, that gave Lancashire its reputation as a hell on earth where innocence died and the soulless world of organised labour was born – the routines of the modern lifestyle. Fortunes were made overnight. But on the other side there was misery for millions.

I will move from industrial invention to look at the poetry and cultural distinctiveness of the north, home of the Gothic and the sentimental, the romantic and the gritty, the traditional and the radical.

I will note how the history of the north has been entered into the Internet, by thousands of individuals in their own minds, and rooms, and computers, for commercial, or educational, or obsessive, or nostalgic, or arcane, or scholarly, or speculative, or artistic, or poetic, reasons, or reasons so personal they appear unfathomable, and of course for reasons that are simply to maintain threatened historical narrative. The Internet North is most of the history of the north ever written or thought, ideas about the north, people of the north, directions, ancestors, arguments, schedules, triumphs, disasters, plus hints and whispers of all the missing silences, in-between-ness, gaps in the history and unknown blanks, waiting to be filled in or become even more silent, empty and alone. It is an impression of the north combined with the here and now tangled up with the dead and gone. The north, like everything else, has come this far, and now it is placed somewhere strange and new, dumped, perhaps, as some sort of metaphysical waste, as unwanted details that will drift off into the nowhere, as echoes of everything that happened that might yet fade away. Or it is the beginning of a new kind of north, one that brings with it everything anyone could ever need if they want to understand exactly what the north of England was and is?

This journey through the north, through history, through the book, through memories, will come up to date with the way recent popular culture, social regeneration and cosmetically enhanced city-scapes in the north have symbolised or compromised gumptious northern reality and the idealistic northern dream. It will emerge in the twenty-first century and the much-vaunted and genuinely impressive, or merely perfunctory, Renaissance of the north, where the modernisation of the north and the intended transformation of its image have created some of the most enterprising and fashionable areas in all of Europe.

I won't necessarily write this history to claim that the north is 'better' or more transcendentally 'other' – than what, who knows – bolder, more brilliant and more breathtaking, that inside such a small ugly-shaped slab of wet rolling land on a small set of islands broken up amid a lot of water looking a little isolated off the north-west coast of Europe all of THIS happened either to it or because of it. It's more to say this is what makes the north, always on show, and showing off, and showing the way, sometimes on the quiet, behind closed doors, the other side of lace curtains, down forbidding steps, along cryptic corridors, under the radar, and these, sure, are the highlights, with an undercurrent of lowlights, but history itself is made up of high and low lights, and a lot of action replays.

100

I liked the idea of such a book, but to some extent the proposal was a set of instructions so that anyone interested could write their own book about the north, their north. Perhaps these instructions were all that needed to be written – this is the sort of book that should be written about the north; this is a starting point for how you might do it; now imagine it for yourself. In the end I decided, or it was decided for me, that I would follow these instructions, imagine it for myself and find out where I might end up. I would end up in the north, but what kind of north? A true north, a fantasy north, a shadow north, a historical north, a north made up of ghosts and disappearing places, a north setting like concrete, or the sun, into mounting Internet reality, a north all in my own mind – far removed from the north of other northerners, so sure of their north, where they are more northern than others, inside their own rooms, streets, dreams and memories of childhood, their own back gardens, bus stops and sweet shops.

Would I write about a personal, subjective northern front, a map of the north as it seems to me, based on my selective memories and ideological preferences and the selective memories and ideological preferences of others but based on my choice, one that abandons simplistic notions of continuity and coherence, capturing history by focusing on my own small world and my attempts to survive in it, involving a certain amount of forgetting, in order to fulfil my ambitions? And were my ambitions in the end simply to write such a book, as if all my life, everything I remembered in greater detail the older I got, all the skills I achieved, were solely for the purpose of eventually constructing a north, my north, inside a book? I had been writing my own story as I went along, without knowing it, and I would only begin to understand that story, what it was all for, how everything fitted together, where it was all heading, if I wrote a book.

I began to write the book, even if just to see whether such a book could be written, a book that would perhaps finish with the words:

GETTY IMAGES

The Lighthouse at Berwick-upon-Tweed

(a) Liverpool, trendy renovated docks. Liverpool, city centre regeneration. Liverpool, supposed city centre regeneration. Liverpool, where every acre of space in the inner city must be turned into a source of income, and outside the centre the bricks are fixed, the streets unmoved, the world artificially closer, but farther away, moving elsewhere, on to screens, into phones, behind now, within the present, but on the outside, into another dimension altogether. Liverpool, the glazed buildings and top-class design are meant to evoke a combination of eighteenth-century splendour and twenty-first-century vision. Liverpool, 143 new shops, 360 apartments, non-distinct executive office space and new bars and restaurants buzzing with reality-television-inspired energy. Liverpool has always been about the future, seeing it first, digging it up out of nowhere, grasping its potential, exploiting the results. The future that is now being glossily layered over the city is a cosmetic one, a commercially contrived one, an illusion that does not necessarily represent the essential foreignness of the city, the rampant alien vigour. The awkwardly misaligned staid glass windows, chain stores, coffee shops, waterfront apartments, architectural flourishes, tourist trails, heritage points seem all imported from the bland, paved and lacklustre England that has ignored the city for so long. The modernisation seems processed and gift-wrapped and liable to rub away the urgent, chaotic but ultimately grand and unifying elements that have made Liverpool so different, so aggressively outside, a place that helped make England, and Britain, and Europe, a better, stranger, lovelier and more hopeful place than it might otherwise have been. The refurbishment seems not to have come from the city's people, from its thriving, maddening history, its fundamental commitment to invention and innovation, but to have been merely dropped in place, as ordered by glib, dreamless business, as designed by faceless committee.

This alluring, cheerless invasion of the artificially manufactured is maybe the latest threat to a city that in the end has become what it is because of its ability to somehow survive any direct or indirect attempts to undermine its natural resilience. The regeneration does not represent, except superficially, the radical pioneering nature of the city, the way it has changed with the times sometimes by being the place those changes happened first. The rebuilding and cleaning-up is all second hand and selective, and borrowed from other regions and other redevelopments, but Liverpool's battling, roguish history suggests that its radicalism will not be destroyed. The city, uniquely capable of somehow acting collectively, to represent an inner will, a common appetite, will find other ways to maintain the aura of otherness and togetherness that is the heart of its scandalous, edgy specialness. Liverpool, relax, don't do it. Liverpool, an interview in *Nerve* magazine with Alan Bleasdale, in which he says, 'I have occasionally a serious ear infection, and so I go down to the Royal Hospital, say, three times a week – Monday, Wednesday, Friday – get up first thing in the morning to get my ears sorted, and I have to go through Kensington – which is where I used to live, in the seventies with my wife and children – and in Kensington – you'd find this in a lot of other places around Liverpool – it has declined. As much as there are the bright lights and luxury apartments and the wine bars, in the centre of Liverpool, there is also a decline, in places like Bootle, Old Swan and Kensington and areas outside of the city. What I'm trying to say is, I would hope that – in the year 2008 – if I'm still going to the bloody hospital, that Kensington will look a damn sight better than it does now because its . . . by culture you'd still mean poets, and artists, and musicians, and actors, and singers, these are cultural – it should be for the cultural benefit of everyone in this city. And culture includes your culture – how you live. And it will have failed if there's still areas in Liverpool that have just got worse. And I know when I went to Glasgow after the city of culture you could see the amazing effect it had on so many parts of the city, I think it was a great success. I think the people who are organising this have to be aware it's for all the people of Liverpool.'

1552

In the reign of Edward VI Lancashire was described in a government report as 'wyld savage contry ferre from any habitacon'. Its boggy moors and rock-strewn green hills remained forbidding and remote. The land was inhospitable to large farms: sheep roamed fields divided by stone fences, many of which still stand. Its inhabitants made their living largely by harvesting and converting the local wool into yarn, then cloth. Women spun, men wove.

The right of sanctuary – a criminal's right to gain time for a legal defence or passage to exile by reaching a certain place, a Catholic continuation of an Anglo-Saxon tradition – had been granted to Manchester in 1540 but was taken away twelve years later because of the damage done to the textile trade by criminals coming to Manchester to avoid arrest.

By the 1530s and 1540s Lancashire's overwhelmingly agrarian society was becoming more complex. The rise of the textile industries enabled many yeomen and smaller farmers, especially in the south-east of the county, to augment their family income by joining the manufacturing process, preparing raw material, spinning and weaving, although the finishing of cloth remained in the hands of specialist fullers and dyers.

1538

'Coals to Newcastle', meaning a pointless pursuit, was first recorded as a contextualised saying in 1538. The counties of Northumberland and Durham supported a biannual fair in Newcastle, where peddlers sold their goods. The phrase perhaps arose as advice between peddlers from outlying districts not to try to sell coal at the market.

During the Middle Ages the south-east of England – in particular the triangular area between London, Oxford and Cambridge – became a region of special social and economic influence. Social change always has linguistic consequences. It was inevitable that the English of those south-easterners in routine contact with the worlds of courtly culture, commerce and learning would increase in prestige and come to be regarded as more polished, elegant and altogether more desirable than the varieties available elsewhere. The stage was set for the emergence of a standard language.

1537

Henry VIII's dissolution of the monasteries provoked a rebellion in Lincolnshire and the northern counties in the autumn of 1536 and early 1537. For a short time Henry VIII lost control of the north of England and there was the very real possibility of civil war.

1530

'Though betwixt Cawood and Rotherham be good plenty of wood, yet the people burn much earth coal, because it is plentifully round there, and sold good cheap. A mile from Rotherham be very good pits of coal . . . Hallamshire hath plenty of wood, and yet there is burned much sea coal . . . there be plenty of veins of sea coal in the quarters about Wakefield . . . the easterly parts of Richmondshire burn much sea coals brought out of Durhamshire.' John Leland reporting on his travels through Yorkshire in the 1530s.

1515

Lancashire was one of the least affluent English counties in the early sixteenth century. Indeed it had been for some time, and was to remain so for well over a century. In the tax assessments for the lay subsidy of 1515, Lancashire came last of the thirty-eight counties assessed in terms of pounds levied per thousand acres, although four of the very poorest counties, Cumberland, Westmorland, Northumberland and Durham, were exempted. The north was extremely poor and to some extent it was a border province, with sympathies more likely to be with the previously exiled Celtic people who found their land under pressure in Wales and Scotland. Also, it had very limited parliamentary representation, with only ten seats: two for the county and two each for the townships of Preston, Liverpool, Wigan and Lancaster. By the early sixteenth century the county had not actually sent representatives to Parliament for over 200 years.

(b) I visited Reddish for the first time in over thirty years since the day we moved out in 1970, and walked the same streets between North Reddish Junior School, my house and Houldsworth Square that I had walked as an eight-year-old, almost catching sight of my sixties self setting off looking for freedom towards the flowery nooks, leaf-crowned crannies and insect-shrouded woodland trails of Reddish Vale.

I looked at the house where I lived on Westbourne Grove, up at the small window at the front that had been my bedroom, containing the painted wooden capsule where I learned to think for myself. I wondered whether, in the back garden, the crippled little tree still stood that I once climbed on the way to discovering myself. There is a world where I could still live in this house, having got stuck in a family that got stuck, where I stayed put, because everything I needed was nearby, at one end or another of the Gorton Road. I wondered what would have become of me if I had stayed there, in that house, for all the time that I had not been in that house. If I had stayed where I was . . . I would never have known where I was.

The house now was like a re-enactment of something that might not have taken place, and I stared at it as if for inspiration, as if the meek and mild bricks might whisper something significant about the family that once lived there, and the little boy who learned so much about who and where he was without knowing it for years. The bricks were as quiet as dust as silent as yesterday, and there was no reason for me to linger for long. The little boy might still be inside, surrounded by the enchanting shadows of Alan Garner's mind. Or he might have become the middle-aged man who was now looking on and marvelling how that little boy, stuck in a cupboard in the dark, had imagined a reality that eventually became a book that would tell him a lot about what he needed to know about where and who he actually was.

I stood outside my old school, and because there was no one else around, no one in sight, no sound of anything else, no movement behind the limp Victorian lace curtains that had made it into the twenty-first century, I could be a ghost, of no one in particular, haunting the place where I first became someone for real. I stared through the railings at the playground where I queued up for class in the morning, kicked grubby tennis balls against sturdy, docile brick walls, scuffled with classmates, and poked around in brick-shaped corners to escape the alert but passive gaze of monitoring teachers who once had such high hopes.

The place seemed to have got on nicely without me, forgetting me as soon as I left, busy with the next children, who would dissolve into the next children, and the next, as teachers came and went and every year was the same but different, the same dates and routines, different faces, different dreams. I wondered where the children in my class had ended up – still living around the corner, never moving far from the school, feeling safe where they were; or was this just, as it was for me, an early territory to inhabit that encouraged a desire to keep exploring new territory, to move further away until there was no way back, unless you needed to remind yourself of where you'd been, to retrace your steps for the sake of a book? I had got to know Reddish so well, I would know it for ever, even though I had forgotten all about it for years.

Everything around Reddish did indeed seem smaller and humbler, and less packed with mint-condition mysteries, than it had seemed to an eight-year-old, and so little had changed other than signs of wear, tear and modifications in decoration and new front doors, the erratic appearance of satellite dishes, spruced-up pubs making more of an outdoor show of themselves, and the vehicles on the Gorton Road, speeding with tempting colours never known in the 1960s, that it could be claimed that nothing had changed.

Quiet, tree-trapped Reddish North station with its ghostly ticket office and its modest unadorned platforms still seemed set in ways more suited to steam trains, nestled between at one end the big worked-up local city that sent unassuming two-carriage trains trundling its way and politely welcomed them back, and at the other hills, valleys and bridges unchanged for centuries. Smooth, solid rails still four feet eight inches apart just as George Stephenson decided 180 years ago in the coalfields of Durham and Northumberland and used on the world-changing Liverpool to Manchester line, becoming standard in 1845, used by Sir Bernard Lovell to move his great dish around the edge of the cosmos, looking up to date in the twenty-first century, the most modern-looking structure for miles around, flowed through Reddish North on the way to crossing the backbone of the country, towards other counties, featuring other barely-there districts arranged around modest platforms, ghostly spaces and unvaried routine.

The local accents were a little broader, even a little more self-conscious, mirroring and exaggerating their increased use on television and radio, as if the thickening popularity of agreeably blunt, attractively mischievous northern celebrities, actors and pop stars had encouraged an extrovert looseness of the tongue, sometimes to the point of parody, to the point of competing with Scouse, in the way that ostentatious Scouse had chased the warm Lancashire, the softer, more measured Yorkshire, the unembellished Cheshire out of the mellow, mid-range Manc accent, sharp up into the nose, into the heart of the ego.

(In 2011 another Stockport tennis player, teenager Liam Broady, was causing commotion among those counting the years since Fred Perry last won Wimbledon. He had reached the final of the boys' junior singles tournament, and even though he eventually lost, here was a legitimate young candidate to finally end the long wait for a British champion. Wimbledon champions such as Björn Bjorg, Ivan Lendl and Roger Federer had all previously made the boys' junior singles final. Not only that; Broady was from Heaton Chapel, north of the Mersey but emphatically Stockport, a few miles from where Fred Perry was born and, more personally, a few miles from the last Morley family home in Stockport. The arrival of Broady as a serious candidate for tennis greatness meant that newspaper articles could begin 'Where would English tennis be without Stockport?'

Broady, though, was managed by his father, Simon, purposely outside the rigid tennis establishment, which still seemed as elitist and intolerant as in the 1930s. Simon Broady complained that the All England Club was still as hostile to a Stockport accent as it had been in Perry's era – that flat, sardonic Stockport vowels still marked a player out as difficult to control with too much of an independent agenda. There had been northern prime ministers, northern pop stars, northern sporting superstars, northern scientific, technical, social, cultural geniuses, influential northern philosophers, transcendentally romantic and psychedelically perceptive northern writers, poets, artists and film makers, fashion designers, classical music titans, and northern clothing brand names, and computers taking over the world, or at least its reflection, had first thought their first thoughts in the north, but still, far enough into the twenty-first century to consider that the twentieth century was truly over, prejudices reaching back in time about how a so-called provincial accent represented a blunt, uncouth attitude that was somehow fundamentally unschooled and trouble-making were still entrenched.)

The idle supersized mills had been converted into flats and workshops, following the fashion in Manchester city centre for turning immense Victorian warehouses into loft apartments and art spaces, as part of another project to modernise, remake history, renovate the traditions of enterprise, and keep up with the fame and appearance of other driven, yearning cities – as if tarting up these deadlocked mills might confirm they were distant cousins of those charismatic twenty-first-century edifices drawn out of the ground and propelled onto a stage, celebrities as much as buildings, by Reddish lad done good Norman Foster. No signs in Reddish of new versions of the particularly ambitious buildings there had been at the end of the nineteenth and the beginning of the twentieth century. The industrialised energy that took some time to reach Reddish and covered the ground with streets and houses had long since diminished.

The mill-shocked layout of the streets was exactly the same under the same granite sky, and if you went that way, there was still Denton, still gnawing at the edges of Gorton, and the other way, still, there was Stockport, its mid-nineteenth-century viaduct now split asunder by a late-twentieth-century motorway, both standing up for their respective centuries with undimmed mettle, and, another way, there was Longsight, and then Levenshulme, and then Ardwick, and then Manchester, forever fiddling with its appearance, plucking this, boosting that, expanding the other. Look, over there, at the view, the strapping Pennines, as for ever as ever and ever. Reddish looked as if it had not been built but had simply grown, covering the ground like moss. Would it look this way in 200 years, a little more petrified, but with the same markings, in the same order, or look as different then as it looked now from how it would have been 200 years ago?

It could be claimed that Reddish was a classic example of how the social and cultural patterns destroyed by the Industrial Revolution, which had led to a build-up of housing and people in the years that followed and a rush of happening followed by general stagnation, had created a new set of patterns that seem deeply settled, but so settled they were surely coming to an end. People were getting on with their lives, still moving this way and that from here to there, accumulating possessions, looking after their gardens, filling dustbins, watching TV, raising families, facing problems, fixing roofs, losing their grip, going on holiday, but amid the ashes of the Industrial Revolution, of the British Empire, of events in time and space that had happened a long time ago.

The steadiness, the modesty, the secrecy and passive acceptance of the place was a reflection of the shock of how the Industrial Revolution changed everything, and then there was no plan, or system, or conceptual thinking about what would happen next. There was just an aftershock. It carries on.

There had been a material improvement in people's lives, an invention of new traditions, a creation of relative comfort, but there was also a cost, a kind of imprisonment in a mental and physical landscape that was now feeling old and drained, with the only signs of modernisation emerging from inside the houses, and cars, and buildings, from inside the screens that were being carried around by people.

The Industrial Revolution had built the streets where people lived, that they travelled between, created the systems, services, shops, parks and schools, but post-revolution developments were leading to new forms of community, new social and cultural patterns, technologically distributed forms of gossip imported from American pop culture existing in post-geographical spaces and places beyond these Victorian and Edwardian streets, which were now only one form of reality, a reality that was solid but fading, being replaced by a reality that was liquid, transient and mobile, but intensifying. People still loved gossip, found it the best way for the complexities of existence to be simplified and turned into addictive stories, but this gossip was a long way from a century before, when it was restricted to tiny, self-serving local communities. Gossip was now owned and marketed by corporate companies with their own reasons for controlling their customers, wherever they were.

Reddish was of the past, but a new 'past' was discreetly being produced, one that would not leave the sort of public traces and permanent monuments, the roads, railways, town halls, libraries and canals emphasising and commemorating borders, boundaries and anniversaries that the Victorian world left. The new past, the new public, were being led somewhere else. The new traces, monuments, transport systems and emerging borders – or lack of borders – were a result of the continuing refinement and development of technology, which both made people's lives easier and more comfortable and trapped them inside the plans and strategies of those who claimed the power and control; they were computer chips and social networks and disembodied intelligences, and the systems and routes were now miniaturised and virtual, containing a different sort of communal memory, distributed information and administrative disposition, leading to a new potential for moral anarchy, freer exchange and/or imaginative transcendence.

Reddish was still, as though it was waiting for something, still, as though the gates into time opened up by the smoking Industrial

Revolution had been sealed up, still, with the past, and, still, with the inevitable incredible future, which you could not see coming but couldn't be missed.

(c) The last few miles, the last few minutes, the last few pages. The last mile, the last brick, the last drop of rain. The last place on this journey on the way south from the north – Woodford, at the southern tip of the Metropolitan Borough of Stockport, five miles outside the town centre, the most southerly point of Greater Manchester, eleven miles south-south-east of Manchester, on the River Dean border with Cheshire, or Congleton, twenty-one miles south of Manchester, seven miles east of the M6, overlooking the eastern edge of the Cheshire Plain, on the banks of the River Dane, at the foot of the southern reaches of the Pennines, the last train from Manchester Victoria to Blackpool, 23.23, calling at Salford Central, Salford Crescent, Bolton, Lostock, Horwich Parkway, Blackrod, Adlington, Chorley, Buckshaw Parkway, Leyland, Preston, Kirkham and Wesham, Poulton-le-Fylde, Layton, arriving in Blackpool North eighty-seven minutes later, the last cotton mill built in Lancashire, during the 1926 recession, Elk Mill, on the border of Chadderton and Royton, used until 1974, demolished in 1999, the last mill spinning cotton, in the Hurst area of Ashton under Lyne, Cedar Mill, active into the 1970s, the last issue of the *Manchester Guardian* published in 1959, before the paper moved completely to London in 1964, the last programme ABC broadcast from its studios in Didsbury, *Opportunity Knocks*, in July 1968, the last day of Belle Vue zoo 11 September 1977, the last member of the Morley family to live in the north, Dilys, my mother, tucked up in dull boarded-up Rusholme, in a barren, cramped two up two down my dad would have seen as a coffin, who followed her children through the exit in 1987, the last days of the Golden Garter Club in the 1980s, turned into a bingo hall, destroyed by fire in 1990, the last night of the Hacienda 28 June 1997, the last year that the CIS (Solar) Tower was the tallest building in Manchester, 2006, when it was replaced by the 164-feet-higher 551-foot Beetham Tower, a 47-storey skyscraper home to a Hilton hotel built with big money in what is now a city of swish new hotels, some built into the grand old warehouses, making use of Manchester's boastful

Victorian scale, Waterhouse's monumental Refuge Assurance Building given late-twentieth-century life after decades in the wilderness, some built out-of-the-box new, out of hyped-up glass, steel and space, because the city and its people still want to get ahead, get into the fragmented centre of things and show people a good time (the Hilton jutting up towards a scudding sky emits a wind-induced spaceship hum you can hear in Hulme, and from up top out of the city's clutches it has a view on a clear day of Jodrell Bank, still unbelievable, still close to the stars, Blackpool Tower, Snowdonia, Liverpool Cathedral, the Peak District, the Pennines, like they're Manchester's hanging gardens), the last episode of *Coronation Street*, which will never happen until long after we have died, so the last episode of *Coronation Street* that my mum watched, the last episode that I will watch, a few years before the last episodes that my sisters Carol and Jayne will watch, the last book borrowed from the library, the last words of Laurence Sterne: 'Now it has come,' the last lines of *Wuthering Heights*: 'I lingered round them, under that benign sky; watched the moths fluttering among the heath, and hare-bells; listened to the soft wind breathing through the grass; and wondered how anyone could ever imagine unquiet slumbers for the sleepers in that quiet earth,' the controversial, final, twenty-first chapter, 'Amen. And all that cal,' of Anthony Burgess's *A Clockwork Orange*, in which Alex, bored with violence, begins to mature and grasp adulthood, 'Tomorrow is all like sweet flowers and the turning young earth and the stars', the last thoughts of Sir Bernard Lovell about the secrets of the universe, before he died, three weeks short of his ninety-ninth birthday, still in Cheshire, on the outskirts of Neptune, the last performer at the Manchester Free Trade Hall before it was turned into a hotel in 1996, the Dalai Lama, telling his audience, 'Loving oneself is crucial. If we do not love ourselves, how can we love others?' the same year as the premiere performance of Thomas Adès' *These Premises are Alarmed*, when the Hallé Orchestra moved out of its old home to the Bridgewater Hall, ten years after local heroes the Smiths played at the Free Trade Hall, finishing with 'Big Mouth Strikes Again', the last request, the year that Morrissey admits that 50 per cent of his writing can be blamed on Shelagh Delaney, including the last line of the Smiths' debut single 'Hand in Glove', plucked from *Taste of Honey*, twenty years after the all-mouth-and-rousing Lesser Free Trade Sex Pistols, thirty years after the electric Bob Dylan used the Free Trade Hall to tell nothing but the truth, forty years after Muddy Waters appeared with Chris Barber and his Jazz Band, the last smoke clearing from Manchester after the 1956 Clean Air Act so that you could see the Pennines from the city centre and see the city centre from the Pennines, a certain portion of all that visible darkness removed, eighty years after Charles Dickens' final Manchester appearance reading from his books as part of what he called his farewell tour, the last match played at Manchester City's Maine Road on 11 May 2003 after eighty years, a 0–1 defeat to Southampton, the last song recorded by the Smiths, 'I Keep Mine Hidden', third track on the 'Girlfriend in a Coma' twelve-inch single, where Morrissey feels the past, grumbles a bit, sighs a little, and you realise that he's been preparing his last words all his life, on high alert, the last chance, the last quote, last orders, the last line of Howard Spring's disclaimer to *Shabby Tiger*, 'There is no such city as Manchester,' the last two lines of Alan Garner's *Elidor*, first read as an eleven-year-old, 'The song faded. The children were alone with the broken windows of a slum,' the last lines of 'Another Day' by Roy Harper, 'And at the door/we can't say more/than just another day/and without a sound/I turn around/and walk away,' the last lines of the third stanza of W. H. Auden's 'A Lullaby', from the penultimate year of his life, 1972, 'In boyhood/ you were permitted to meet/ beautiful old contraptions/ soon to be banished from earth, saddle-tank locs, beam-engines/ and over-shot waterwheels./ Yes, love, you have been lucky,' the last wanderings of the giant, yawning City fan L. S. Lowry, a Maine Road man, in an overcoat of clay, occasionally brushed but never cleaned, longing for something, walking to clear his head, taking pleasure in his breathing, the tread of his feet on the pavement, with his own style, noticing the smallest things, with a frugal eye, making history, in his own solemn, familiar way, there's nowhere particular he wants to go, before he comes to rest, on the right track, by a fence, on a brick wall, an umbrella propped against it, near the factory gates, under a slender, alert, smoking chimney, watching a man roll a threadlike cigarette on his doorstep from morning till night, opposite a crooked house leaning to the left due to unstable foundations, resting the baggage of hundreds of years of oppression, having the last laugh, a last scone, a last crumb of comfort, a last drag, a last trip to Huddersfield, a last visit to the local shop, a last look at the view, all that muck and brass, nursing a pint, the last hour, the last dab of paint, in the shape of a tear, smeared red with essence of ashy grey, last but not least, making his escape, released at last, the last resting place, the last trudge along the pier to the little red-topped lighthouse, the last sight of a setting sun, the last meander across deserted sands, the last exit to nowhere, the cancelled flesh, as heavy and as weightless as the Stockport Viaduct, as dead but as visible, a brown blur of buildings, the last money spent, poor once more, the quiet nonchalance, crossing the border, on top of the world, where the river meets the sea, in the cold mid-winter, near some ruins, under hills as lonely as God, at the edge of the horizon, at the foot of the stairs, pausing at the junction to eternity, the bliss of solitude, as silent as light, the last look at home, the last paragraph, the last laugh, the last wave, the last breath, the last thing on your mind, a last look behind you to check where you've been, for proof that you existed, and that things are as you left them, just as you remembered them, the last word, the last footstep, until the next time, heading north.

In a dressing room at Granada Television Studios in Quay Street, Manchester, with Marc Bolan, during the recording in August 1977 of his 'Marc' show, a month before he died.

He was the first famous musician I interviewed for the *New Musical Express* – my favourite pop star ushering me into a new world and showing me the way forward. He gave me his telephone number and asked me to call him when I was next in London.

Acknowledgements

I.

This north was made up out of memory, conversation, a number of journeys that began or ended at Stockport station, or Manchester Piccadilly, and various facts, quotes and dates scattered around the Internet. The combination of recollection, impression, assembly and wandering is not intended to achieve conventional scholarly precision. If there was to be a series of bracketed academic numbers attached to these facts, dates, quotes and traces, the straightforward explanation of their source would be that they were found on the World Wide Web, and then framed, filtered and spun until they fitted into my story of the north. I do not claim objectivity, viewing any such certainty, all things considered, as impossible, so there seems no need to produce any proof, evidence or verification, other than – it's all out there.

This north is a hallucination as much as it is a history, a non-fiction dream of what might have been rather than a documented expression of the definite. None of the facts, deeds and claims were included unless they were repeated so many times almost word for word on various sites that they had turned into fixed, neutral objects. These objects became walls, gates, trees, steps, lanes, faces, valleys, roofs, showers, locks, flagstones, patterns, fixtures and fittings, and, at the other extreme, a series of illusions, a miscellany of emotions, owned by no one, something in the air, available to anyone thinking of producing their own map, model or manifesto, their very own version of events.

2.

Thank you to David Godwin, my agent, who sat me down one day, gave me a cup of tea, and told me in so many words, perhaps to get me out of his office, to take a train to Stockport, wander down the hill into the town centre, look around, and write down whatever occurred to me. When I returned many years later, with bags of material, he sat me down, gave me a cup of tea, and like the gentleman he is ignored the fact I was dressed in rags and mumbling deliriously about bus stops, bridges and Reddish Baths. The Venerable Bede, as well, although eventually the great mind-changing monk of Northumbria and the father of English history never quite made it into the book. Thank you also to Caitlin, Anna and Heather at David Godwin Associates.

3.

Thank you to Mike Jones, who commissioned the book in the days before the phrase 'back in the day' was in common use. Before I had even got to the stage of constructing the canals, roads and railways, while I was still stumbling through the woods, digging a few holes, sniffing the air, he moved elsewhere. I hope this north shows him that when I told him at our first meeting what I was going to do, there really was a plan.

4.

Thank you to Michael Fishwick at Bloomsbury, who took over the book, and firmly but gently ushered me into the era of motorways and colour television. Even though I ended up following a number of paths, and a few waterways, and got carried away counting bricks, he made sure I never lost sight of the original path, and that there was enough of a connection between my feet and the ground.

5.

There is a soundtrack to this book that contains, perhaps, for me, the more obvious and expected northern sounds – Joy Division, Magazine, Roy Harper, the Hollies, the Watersons, Cabaret Voltaire, Vini Reilly, ABC, Frankie Vaughan, Ewan MacColl, Autechre, Billy Fury, the Smiths, the Fall, Buzzcocks, the Stone Roses, the Animals, the Brighouse and Rastrick Brass Band, A Certain Ratio, Echo and the Bunnymen, Neil Tennant, Jilted John, Harrison, Lennon, Starr, the Mekons, the Spinners, the Passage, Pulp, Van der Graaf Generator, Robert Smith, Ladytron, Mick Ronson, Frederick Delius, Elvis Costello, New Order, John Barry, Bryan Ferry, the Blue Orchids, Joe Cocker, Everything But The Girl, Paul Rodgers, the Human League, Godley and Creme, Julian Cope, Be Bop Deluxe, the Undertakers, 808 State, the New Music Manchester group, the Searchers, British Electric Foundation, Deaf School, the Distractions, Badly Drawn Boy, Orchestral Manoeuvres in the Dark, Arctic Monkeys, William Walton, the Scaffold, Electronic, Gang of Four, John Cooper Clarke – and then there is another (even) ghostlier soundtrack, also useful for creating the correct atmospheric weight, and weightlessness, inside, and outside, of the thoughtful, and brawling, north, which includes Derek Bailey, Gavin Bryars, Tony Oxley (and therefore the Joseph Holbrooke trio of Sheffield), Harold Riley of Leeds, Trevor Watts of York, John McLaughlin of Doncaster, Georgie Fame of Leigh, Big in Japan of Liverpool, Fila Brazillia of Hull, Elkie Brooks of Broughton and Vinegar Joe, Robert Palmer of Scarborough and Vinegar Joe, John Taylor of Manchester, Azimuth and the University of York, Ian Anderson of Dunfermline and Blackpool, Clock DVA of Sheffield, Section 25 of Blackpool, Prelude of Gateshead, Graham Collier of Tynemouth, Penetration of Ferryhill, County Durham, Lee Griffiths of Collyhurst, Lita 'How Much is That Doggie in the Window' Roza of Liverpool and the first female singer to top the UK singles chart, Alan Hull of Newcastle upon Tyne and Lindisfarne, Annie Haslam of Bolton and Renaissance, Arthur Brown of Whitby, The EmCee Five of 1960 Newcastle, Kathryn Williams of Liverpool and Newcastle, Iain Matthews of Scunthorpe and almost Bradford Park Avenue FC, Back Door of the Lion Inn, Blakey Ridge, Hood of Leeds, John McCabe of Huyton and the Royal Northern College of Music, Mike Harrison of Carlisle and Spooky Tooth, the Oldham Tinkers, Lonelady, the Unthanks, Marconi Union, Antonymes, Quando Quango, Michael Chapman of Hunslet, Ernest Tomlinson of Rawtenstall, Harry Boardman of Failsworth, Alan Rawsthorne of Halsingden, Leslie 'Thomas Barrett' Stuart of Southport, pitman bard Tommy Armstrong of Shotley Bridge and Tanfield Lea, William Blezard of Padiham, Noël Coward and Playschool (and this is where a new path opens up, looping back to Ronnie Hazlehurst of Dukinfield), Ted Astley of Warrington and the theme tunes to *The Champions*, *The Saint* and *Civilisation*, Wally Stott of Leeds, the Goons and Angela Morley, Arthur Wood of Heckmondwike and the theme tune to *The Archers*, and Barry Mason of Wigan, 'Delilah' and 'The Last Waltz'.

6.

Thank you to those who have had an influence on this/my north whether they knew it or not; David Peace of Ossett and Tokyo, Simon Armitage of Marsden, Anthony H. Wilson of Salford, Marple, Granada & Factory, Alan Erasmus of Palatine Road, Didsbury & Factory and Peter Saville of Hale & Factory, and Gretton and Hannett of elsewhere, Johnny Marr of Ardwick and the major 9th, Ron Atkinson of Didsbury, Simon Stephens of Heaton Moor, Richard Boon of New Hormones and the library, Peter Coyle of Liverpool and the middle of somewhere, Kevin Cummins of Salford and City, Mike Garry of Chorlton-on-Medlock and Fallowfield, Philip Cashian of Warrington and the Royal Academy of Music, Chris Austin of Norwich and Peter Maxwell Davies, and Dave Haslam of Manchester and 'Manchester'.

7.

Thank you to everyone at Bloomsbury for waiting so patiently for me to return, and Anna Simpson for making sure once it was all built that the paint was dry, the windows polished, the timetables followed, the roads correctly numbered and the bridges tested. Thank you to the nerveless copy editor, Hugh Davis, who gave the foundations a damned good going over, and recommended a few time-saving short cuts and time-travelling edits, to David Atkinson for the index, which created a wonderful new order, and to Sarah-Jane Forder, for the final survey.

8.

Thank you to Madeleine Morley, for knowing her Marx, as well as her Alice, and questioning everything; Carol Morley of Reddish and way beyond, for checking, and seeing, things, coupled with Cairo Cannon of the east coast and east London; the travelling Morleys, Jayne, Natasha and Florence; and the Mitchells of north Wales, Aunt Sally, Lizzie, Sian and Andrew.

9.

Thank you to those that I miss, who helped me find my place.

10.

And thank you to Elizabeth Levy, of Derbyshire, Persia and north London, who was there every step of the way, whatever the weather, always knowing which direction I should be heading, and how to keep me going.

'Come grow old with me. The best is yet to come.'

William Wordsworth

Permissions Acknowledgements

Extract from 'London Letter', May 1921 © The Estate of T. S. Eliot and reproduced by permission of Faber and Faber Ltd.

Extract from 'Annus Mirabilis' from *High Windows* (1974) © The Estate of Philip Larkin and reproduced by permission of Faber and Faber Ltd.

Lyrics from 'Cemetery Gates', words & music by Johnny Marr & Steven Morrissey © Copyright 1986 Artemis Muziekuitgeverij B.V/ Marr Songs Limited. Universal Music Publishing Limited/Warner/ Chappell Artemis Music. All Rights Reserved. International Copyright Secured. Used by permission of Music Sales Limited.

Extract from *The Road to Wigan Pier* by George Orwell (copyright © George Orwell, 1937) reprinted by permission of Bill Hamilton as the Literary Executor of the Estate of the Late Sonia Brownell Orwell.

Extracts from the works of J. B. Priestley are reprinted by permission of United Agents on behalf of the Estate of the late J. B. Priestley.

Extract from *The Emigrants* by W. G. Sebald © 1992 W. G. Sebald and reprinted by permission of HarperCollins Publishers Ltd.

Lines from the sketches of Victoria Wood are © Victoria Wood and used by kind permission of Victoria Wood/McIntyre Entertainments.

Index